Pro Oracle SQL

Second Edition

Karen Morton

Kerry Osborne

Robyn Sands

Riyaj Shamsudeen

Jared Still

Pro Oracle SQL

ISBN-13 (pbk): 978-1-4302-6220-6

ISBN-13 (electronic): 978-1-4302-6221-3

President and Publisher: Paul Manning
Lead Editor: Jonathan Hassell
Technical Reviewer: Arup Nanda
Editorial Board: Steve Anglin, Mark Beckner, Ewan Buckingham, Gary Cornell, Louise Corrigan, Morgan Ertel, Jonathan Gennick, Jonathan Hassell, Robert Hutchinson, Michelle Lowman, James Markham, Matthew Moodie, Jeff Olson, Jeffrey Pepper, Douglas Pundick, Ben Renow-Clarke, Dominic Shakeshaft, Gwenan Spearing, Matt Wade, Tom Welsh
Coordinating Editor: Mark Powers
Copy Editor: Catherine Ohala
Compositor: SPi Global
Indexer: SPi Global
Artist: SPi Global
Cover Designer: Anna Ishchenko

Distributed to the book trade worldwide by Springer Science+Business Media New York, 233 Spring Street, 6th Floor, New York, NY 10013. Phone 1-800-SPRINGER, fax (201) 348-4505, e-mail orders-ny@springer-sbm.com, or visit www.springeronline.com. Apress Media, LLC is a California LLC and the sole member (owner) is Springer Science + Business Media Finance Inc (SSBM Finance Inc). SSBM Finance Inc is a Delaware corporation.

For information on translations, please e-mail rights@apress.com, or visit www.apress.com.

Apress and friends of ED books may be purchased in bulk for academic, corporate, or promotional use. eBook versions and licenses are also available for most titles. For more information, reference our Special Bulk Sales–eBook Licensing web page at www.apress.com/bulk-sales.

Any source code or other supplementary material referenced by the author in this text is available to readers at www.apress.com/9781430262206. For detailed information about how to locate your book's source code, go to www.apress.com/source-code/.

Contents at a Glance

Contents

About the Authors

For more than 25 years, **Karen Morton** has worked in information technology starting out as a mainframe programmer, then developer, DBA, data architect, author, researcher, educator, and consultant. Having used Oracle since the early '90s, she began teaching others how to use Oracle over 15 years ago. Today she is focused primarily on Oracle performance optimization, particularly in the areas of SQL tuning and understanding the Oracle optimizer.

Karen's years of experience have meshed well into optimizing applications running on both non-Exadata and Exadata platforms. In her role as Senior Technical Consultant for Enkitec, an Oracle–centric consulting and services company, her deep knowledge of how SQL works and how Exadata features require a change in approach to many optimization efforts allows her to understand what to do and when to do it, regardless of whether the environment is Exadata or non-Exadata.

Karen is the co-author of three books from Apress: *Beginning Oracle SQL*, *Expert Oracle Practices: Database Administration from the Oak Table*, and *Pro Oracle SQL*. She's a frequent speaker at conferences and user groups, a member of the OakTable Network, and an Oracle ACE.

Kerry Osborne began working with Oracle (version 2) in 1982. He has worked as both a developer and a DBA. For the past several years he has been focused on understanding Oracle internals and solving performance problems. He is an OakTable member and an Oracle ACE Director. Kerry is a frequent speaker at Oracle conferences. He is also a co-founder of Enkitec, an Oracle-focused consulting company headquartered in Dallas, Texas. He blogs at kerryosborne.oracle-guy.com.

Robyn Sands is a software engineer on Oracle's Real-World Performance team. She has been working with Oracle since 1996, and has extensive experience in application development, large system implementations, and performance measurement. Robyn began her career in industrial and quality engineering, and has combined her prior education and experience with her love of data by searching for new ways to build database systems with consistent performance and minimal maintenance requirements. She is a member of the OakTable Network and co-author of three books: *Expert Oracle Practices, Expert PL/SQL,* and *Pro Oracle SQL*, all published by Apress.

Riyaj Shamsudeen is an industry-recognized RAC expert, database internals specialist, and performance tuning specialist with 20 years of experience in implementing, using, and tuning RAC and Oracle products. He is an Oracle ACE Director and proud member of the OakTable network. Riyaj has co-authored four books about Oracle Database and performance. He is an active blogger (at http://orainternals.wordpress.com), President of OraInternals, and a frequent international speaker in major conferences such as UKOUG, HOTSOS, OpenWorld, and RMOUG. Social: www.linkedin.com/in/riyajshamsudeen; @riyajshamsudeen.

Jared Still is a senior database administrator at Pythian. Jared has been working with databases since 1988, and with Oracle in particular since 1994, beginning with Oracle version 7.0.13. During that time, he participated in a wide range of database administration tasks, as is the norm at smaller companies. Data modeling, database design, and overcoming Compulsive Tuning Disorder (CTD) have all been part of the job. As part of the CTD recovery process, he began learning how databases—and Oracle in particular—actually work.

The revelation was that well-performing databases and applications do not happen by accident, but by design. And "by design" means that you must understand how databases work, and how to make efficient use of the SQL language to create scalable applications and databases. Jared's goal for this book is to make it easier for developers and database administrators to understand and use advanced SQL syntax. There are many features that have been introduced since Oracle 8i, and yet they seem to be seldom used. This book should help rectify that.

About the Technical Reviewer

Arup Nanda (e-mail: arup@proligence.com; Twitter: @arupnanda; LinkedIn: linkedin.com/in/arupnanda/) has been an Oracle DBA for the last 18 years, spanning all aspects of the job—from modeling to performance tuning. He specializes in RAC, Exadata, and High Availability solutions. He has authored four books on Oracle technology, written 500+ published articles, and presented almost 300 training sessions in 22 countries. He is an Oracle–certified professional, Oracle ACE director, member of the OakTable Network, member of the Board of Directors of Exadata SIG, and member of the Editorial Board for SELECT *Journal* (the IOUG publication). Acknowledging his accomplishments and community involvement, Oracle awarded him DBA of the Year in 2003 and Enterprise Architect of the Year in 2012. He blogs at http://arup.blogspot.com.

Acknowledgments

I want to thank my co-authors, the fantastic folks at Apress, and, most of all, my family for their support and patience. The work to update *Pro Oracle SQL* was much easier thanks to all of you.

—Karen Morton

CHAPTER 1

■ ■ ■

Core SQL

Whether you're relatively new to writing SQL or you've been writing it for years, learning to write "good" SQL is a process that requires a strong knowledge foundation of core syntax and concepts. This chapter provides a review of the core concepts of the SQL language and its capabilities, along with descriptions of the common SQL commands with which you should already be familiar. For those of you who have worked with SQL previously and have a good grasp on the basics, this chapter will be a brief refresher to prepare you for the more detailed treatment of SQL we examine in later chapters. If you're a new SQL user, you may want to read *Beginning Oracle SQL* first to make sure you're comfortable with the basics. Either way, Chapter 1 "level sets" you with a whirlwind tour of the five core SQL statements and provides a quick review of the tool we'll be using to execute SQL: SQL*Plus.

The SQL Language

The SQL language was originally developed during the 1970s by IBM and was called *Structured English Query Language*, or *SEQUEL*. The language was based on the model for relational database management systems (RDBMSs) developed by E. F. Codd in 1969. The acronym was later shortened to SQL as a result of a trademark dispute. In 1986, the American National Standards Institute (ANSI) adopted SQL as a standard, and in 1987, the International Organization for Standardization (otherwise known as the *ISO*) did so as well. A piece of not-so-common knowledge is that the official pronunciation of the language was declared to be "ess queue ell" by ANSI. Most people, including me, still use the "see-qwell" pronunciation just because it flows a bit easier linguistically.

The purpose of SQL is simply to provide an interface to a database—in our case, Oracle. Every SQL statement is a command, or instruction, to the database. SQL differs from other programming languages such as C and Java in that it is intended to process data in sets, not individual rows. The language also doesn't require that you provide instructions on how to navigate to the data; this happens transparently, under the covers. But, as you'll see in the chapters ahead, knowing about your data and how and where they are stored is very important if you want to write efficient SQL in Oracle.

Although there are minor differences in how vendors (such as Oracle, IBM, and Microsoft) implement the core functionality of SQL, the skills you learn in one database transfer to another. Basically, you can use the same SQL statements to query, insert, update, and delete data and create, alter, and drop objects regardless of the database vendor.

Although SQL is the standard for use with various RDBMSs, it is not particularly relational in practice (I expand on this a bit later in the book). I recommend that you read C. J. Date's book *SQL and Relational Theory* (O'Reilly Media, 2011) for a detailed review of how SQL and relational theory intersect. Keep in mind that the SQL language doesn't always follow the relational model precisely; it doesn't implement some elements of the relational model at all, and it implements other elements improperly. The fact remains that because SQL is based on this model, you must understand SQL and the relational model as well as know how to write SQL as correctly and efficiently as possible.

Interfacing to the Database

Numerous ways have been developed throughout the years for transmitting SQL to a database and getting results back. The native interface to the Oracle database is the Oracle Call Interface (OCI). The OCI powers the queries that are sent internally by the Oracle kernel to the database. You use the OCI any time you use one of Oracle's tools, such as SQL*Plus or SQL Developer. Various other Oracle tools, including SQL*Loader, Data Pump, and Real Application Testing (RAT), use OCI as well as language-specific interfaces, such as Oracle JDBC-OCI, ODP.Net, Oracle Precompilers, Oracle ODBC, and the Oracle C++ Call Interface (OCCI) drivers.

When you use programming languages such as COBOL or C, the statements you write are known as *embedded SQL statements* and are preprocessed by a SQL preprocessor before the application program is compiled. Listing 1-1 shows an example of a SQL statement that could be used within a C/C++ block.

Listing 1-1. Embedded SQL Statement Used within a C/C++ Block

```
{
int a;
/* ... */
EXEC SQL SELECT salary INTO :a
    FROM hr.employees
    WHERE employee_id = 108;
/* ... */
printf("The salary is %d\n", a);
/* ... */
}
```

Other tools, such as SQL*Plus and SQL Developer, are interactive tools. You enter and execute commands, and the output is displayed back to you. Interactive tools don't require you to compile your code explicitly before running it; you simply enter the command you wish to execute. Listing 1-2 shows an example of using SQL*Plus to execute a statement.

Listing 1-2. Using SQL*Plus to Execute a SQL Statement

```
SQL> select  salary
  2  from     hr.employees
  3  where    employee_id = 108;

     SALARY
---------------
      12000
```

In this book, we'll use SQL*Plus for our example listings for consistency's sake, but keep in mind that whichever method or tool you use to enter and execute SQL statements, everything ultimately goes through the OCI. The bottom line is that the tool you use doesn't matter; the native interface is the same for all.

Review of SQL*Plus

SQL*Plus is a command-line tool provided with every Oracle installation regardless of platform (Windows, Unix). It is used to enter and execute SQL commands and to display the resulting output in a text-only environment. The tool allows you to enter and edit commands, save and execute commands individually or via script files, and display the output in nicely formatted report form. To start SQL*Plus you simply start sqlplus from your host's command prompt.

Connect to a Database

There are multiple ways to connect to a database from SQL*Plus. Before you can connect, however, you likely need to have entries for the databases to which you need to connect entered in the $ORACLE_HOME/network/admin/tnsnames.ora file. Two common ways to supply your connection information when you start SQL*Plus are shown in Listing 1-3; another is to use the SQL*Plus connect command after SQL*Plus starts, as shown in Listing 1-4.

Listing 1-3. Connecting to SQL*Plus from the Windows Command Prompt

```
$ sqlplus hr@ora12c

SQL*Plus: Release 12.1.0.1.0 Production on Tue May 7 12:32:36 2013

Copyright (c) 1982, 2013, Oracle.  All rights reserved.
Enter password:

Last Successful login time: Tue May 07 2013 12:29:09 -04:00
Connected to:
Oracle Database 12c Enterprise Edition Release 12.1.0.1.0 - 64bit Production
With the Partitioning, OLAP, Advanced Analytics and Real Application Testing options

SQL>
```

Listing 1-4. Connecting to SQL*Plus and Logging in to the Database from the SQL> Prompt

```
$ sqlplus /nolog

SQL*Plus: Release 12.1.0.1.0 Production on Tue May 7 12:34:21 2013

Copyright (c) 1982, 2013, Oracle.  All rights reserved.

SQL> connect hr@ora12c
Enter password:
Connected.
SQL>
```

When starting SQL*Plus using the 12c version, you will notice a new feature that displays your last login time by default. If you don't want this to appear, simply use the option -nologintime.

To start SQL*Plus without being prompted to log in to a database, start SQL*Plus with the /nolog option.

Configuring the SQL*Plus Environment

SQL*Plus has numerous commands that allow you to customize the working environment and display options. The SQL*Plus help data must be installed by the database administrator or it may not be available. There are three help script files found in $ORACLE_HOME/SQLPLUS/ADMIN/HELP/ that drop, create, and populate the SQL*Plus help tables: HLPBLD.SQL, HELPDROP.SQL, and HELPUS.SQL. Listing 1-5 shows the SQL*Plus commands available after entering the SQL*Plus help index command at the SQL> prompt.

Listing 1-5. SQL*Plus Command List

```
SQL> help index

Enter Help [topic] for help.
```

@	COPY	PAUSE	SHUTDOWN
@@	DEFINE	PRINT	SPOOL
/	DEL	PROMPT	SQLPLUS
ACCEPT	DESCRIBE	QUIT	START
APPEND	DISCONNECT	RECOVER	STARTUP
ARCHIVE LOG	EDIT	REMARK	STORE
ATTRIBUTE	EXECUTE	REPFOOTER	TIMING
BREAK	EXIT	REPHEADER	TTITLE
BTITLE	GET	RESERVED WORDS (SQL)	UNDEFINE
CHANGE	HELP	RESERVED WORDS (PL/SQL)	VARIABLE
CLEAR	HOST	RUN	WHENEVER OSERROR
COLUMN	INPUT	SAVE	WHENEVER SQLERROR
COMPUTE	LIST	SET	XQUERY
CONNECT	PASSWORD	SHOW	

The set command is the primary command used for customizing your environment settings. Listing 1-6 shows the help text for the set command.

Listing 1-6. SQL*Plus SET Command

```
SQL> help set

  SET
  ---

  Sets a system variable to alter the SQL*Plus environment settings
  for your current session. For example, to:
        -   set the display width for data
        -   customize HTML formatting
        -   enable or disable printing of column headings
        -   set the number of lines per page

  SET system_variable value
  where system_variable and value represent one of the following clauses:

APPI[NFO]{OFF|ON|text}                   NEWP[AGE] {1|n|NONE}
ARRAY[SIZE] {15|n}                             NULL text
AUTO[COMMIT] {OFF|ON|IMM[EDIATE]|n}      NUMF[ORMAT] format
AUTOP[RINT] {OFF|ON}                     NUM[WIDTH] {10|n}
```

```
AUTORECOVERY {OFF|ON}                    PAGES[IZE] {14|n}
AUTOT[RACE] {OFF|ON|TRACE[ONLY]}              PAU[SE] {OFF|ON|text}
   [EXP[LAIN]] [STAT[ISTICS]]          RECSEP {WR[APPED]|EA[CH]|OFF}
BLO[CKTERMINATOR] {.|c|ON|OFF}                RECSEPCHAR {_|c}
CMDS[EP] {;|c|OFF|ON}                  SERVEROUT[PUT] {ON|OFF}
COLSEP {_|text}                                  [SIZE {n | UNLIMITED}]
CON[CAT] {.|c|ON|OFF}                       [FOR[MAT]  {WRA[PPED] |
COPYC[OMMIT] {0|n}                                 WOR[D_WRAPPED] |
COPYTYPECHECK {ON|OFF}                        TRU[NCATED]}]
DEF[INE] {&|c|ON|OFF}                  SHIFT[INOUT] {VIS[IBLE] |
DESCRIBE [DEPTH {1|n|ALL}]                              INV[ISIBLE]}
   [LINENUM {OFF|ON}] [INDENT {OFF|ON}]  SHOW[MODE] {OFF|ON}
ECHO {OFF|ON}                               SQLBL[ANKLINES] {OFF|ON}
EDITF[ILE] file_name[.ext]             SQLC[ASE] {MIX[ED] |
EMB[EDDED] {OFF|ON}                          LO[WER] | UP[PER]}
ERRORL[OGGING] {ON|OFF}                      SQLCO[NTINUE] {> | text}
   [TABLE [schema.]tablename]          SQLN[UMBER] {ON|OFF}
   [TRUNCATE] [IDENTIFIER identifier]  SQLPLUSCOMPAT[IBILITY]
                                                      {x.y[.z]}
ESC[APE] {\|c|OFF|ON}                   SQLPRE[FIX] {#|c}
ESCCHAR {@|?|%|$|OFF}                   SQLP[ROMPT] {SQL>|text}
EXITC[OMMIT] {ON|OFF}                   SQLT[ERMINATOR] {;|c|ON|OFF}
FEED[BACK] {6|n|ON|OFF}                       SUF[FIX] {SQL|text}
FLAGGER {OFF|ENTRY|INTERMED[IATE]|FULL} TAB {ON|OFF}
FLU[SH] {ON|OFF}                              TERM[OUT] {ON|OFF}
HEA[DING] {ON|OFF}                            TI[ME] {OFF|ON}
HEADS[EP] {||c|ON|OFF}                  TIMI[NG] {OFF|ON}
INSTANCE [instance_path|LOCAL]                TRIM[OUT] {ON|OFF}
LIN[ESIZE] {80|n}                             TRIMS[POOL] {OFF|ON}
LOBOF[FSET] {1|n}                             UND[ERLINE] {-|c|ON|OFF}
LOGSOURCE [pathname]                    VER[IFY] {ON|OFF}
LONG {80|n}                                     WRA[P] {ON|OFF}
LONGC[HUNKSIZE] {80|n}                  XQUERY {BASEURI text|
MARK[UP] HTML [OFF|ON]                         ORDERING{UNORDERED|
   [HEAD text] [BODY text] [TABLE text]        ORDERED|DEFAULT}|
   [ENTMAP {ON|OFF}]                           NODE{BYVALUE|BYREFERENCE|
   [SPOOL {OFF|ON}]                            DEFAULT}|
   [PRE[FORMAT] {OFF|ON}]                      CONTEXT text}
SQL>
```

Given the number of commands available, you can customize your environment easily to suit you best. One thing to keep in mind is that the set commands aren't retained by SQL*Plus when you exit/close the tool. Instead of typing in each of the set commands you want to apply each time you use SQL*Plus, you can create a file named login.sql. There are actually two files that SQL*Plus reads by default each time you start it. The first is glogin.sql and it can be found in the directory $ORACLE_HOME/sqlplus/admin. If this file is found, it is read and the statements it contains are executed. This allows you to store the SQL*Plus commands and SQL statements that customize your experience across SQL*Plus sessions.

After reading glogin.sql, SQL*Plus looks for the login.sql file. This file must exist in either the directory from which SQL*Plus was started or in a directory included in the path to which the environment variable SQLPATH points. Any commands in login.sql will take precedence over those in glogin.sql. Since version 10g, Oracle reads both glogin.sql and login.sql each time you either start SQL*Plus or execute the connect command from within

SQL*Plus. Prior to 10g, the login.sql script was only executed when SQL*Plus started. The contents of a common login.sql file are shown in Listing 1-7.

Listing 1-7. A Common login.sql File

```
SET LINES 3000
--Sets width of display line (default 80 characters)
SET PAGES 1000
-Sets number of lines per page (default 14 lines)
SET TIMING ON
--Sets display of elapsed time (default OFF)
SET NULL <null>
--Sets display of nulls to show <null> (default empty)
SET SQLPROMPT '&_user@&_connect_identifier> '
--Sets the prompt to show connected user and instance
```

Note the use of the variables _user and _connect_identifier in the SET SQLPROMPT command. These are two examples of predefined variables. You may use any of the following predefined variables in your login.sql file or in any other script file you may create:

- _connect_identifier (connection identifier used to make the database connection)

- _date (current date)

- _editor (the editor that is started when you use the EDIT command)

- _o_version (current version of the installed Oracle database)

- _o_release (full release number of the installed Oracle database)

- _privilege (privilege level of the current connection)

- _sqlplus_release (full release number of the installed SQL*Plus component)

- _user (username used to make the connection)

Executing Commands

There are two types of commands that can be executed within SQL*Plus: SQL statements and SQL*Plus commands. The SQL*Plus commands shown in Listings 1-5 and 1-6 are specific to SQL*Plus and can be used for customizing the environment and executing commands that are specific to SQL*Plus, such as DESCRIBE and CONNECT. Executing a SQL*Plus command requires only that you type the command at the prompt and press Enter. The command is executed automatically. On the other hand, to execute SQL statements, you must use a special character to indicate you wish to execute the entered command. You may use either a semicolon or a forward slash to do this. A semicolon may be placed directly at the end of the typed command or on a following blank line. The forward slash must be placed on a blank line to be recognized. Listing 1-8 shows how these two execution characters are used.

Listing 1-8. Execution Character Usage

```
SQL>select empno, deptno from scott.emp where ename = 'SMITH' ;
     EMPNO     DEPTNO
---------- ----------
      7369         20
```

```
SQL>select empno, deptno from scott.emp where ename = 'SMITH'
  2 ;
     EMPNO     DEPTNO
---------- ----------
      7369         20
SQL>select empno, deptno from scott.emp where ename = 'SMITH'
  2 /
     EMPNO     DEPTNO
---------- ----------
      7369         20
SQL>select empno, deptno from scott.emp where ename = 'SMITH'
  2
SQL>/
     EMPNO     DEPTNO
---------- ----------
      7369         20
SQL>select empno, deptno from scott.emp where ename = 'SMITH'/
  2
SQL>l
  1* select empno, deptno from scott.emp where ename = 'SMITH'/
SQL>/
select empno, deptno from scott.emp where ename = 'SMITH'/
                                                         *
ERROR at line 1:
ORA-00936: missing expression
```

Notice the fifth example that puts / at the end of the statement. The cursor moves to a new line instead of executing the command immediately. Then, if you press Enter again, the statement is entered into the SQL*Plus buffer but is not executed. To view the contents of the SQL*Plus buffer, the list command is used (abbreviated to l). If you then attempt to execute the statement in the buffer using /, which is how the / command is intended to be used, you get an error because, originally, you placed / at the end of the SQL statement line. The forward slash is not a valid SQL command and thus causes an error when the statement attempts to execute.

Another way to execute commands is to place them in a file. You can produce these files with the text editor of your choice outside of SQL*Plus or you may invoke an editor directly from SQL*Plus using the EDIT command. The EDIT command either opens a named file or creates a file if it doesn't exist. The file must be in the default directory or you must specify the full path of the file. To set the editor to one of your choice, simply set the predefined _editor variable using the following command: define _editor='/<full path>/myeditor.exe'. Files with the extension .sql will execute without having to include the extension and can be run using either the @ or START command. Listing 1-9 shows the use of both commands.

Listing 1-9. Executing .sql Script Files

```
SQL> @list_depts
    DEPTNO DNAME          LOC
---------- -------------- -------------
        10 ACCOUNTING     NEW YORK
        20 RESEARCH       DALLAS
        30 SALES          CHICAGO
        40 OPERATIONS     BOSTON
SQL>
```

```
SQL> start list_depts
    DEPTNO DNAME          LOC
---------- -------------- -------------
        10 ACCOUNTING     NEW YORK
        20 RESEARCH       DALLAS
        30 SALES          CHICAGO
        40 OPERATIONS     BOSTON
SQL>
SQL>l
  1* select * from scott.dept
SQL>
```

SQL*Plus has many features and options—far too many to cover here. For what we need in this book, the previous overview should suffice. However, the Oracle documentation provides guides for SQL*Plus use and there are numerous books, including *Beginning Oracle SQL* (as mentioned earlier), that go in to more depth if you're interested.

The Five Core SQL Statements

The SQL language contains many different statements. In your professional career you may end up using just a small percentage of what is available to you. But isn't that the case with almost any product you use? I once heard a statistic that most people use 20 percent or less of the functionality available in the software products or programming languages they use regularly. I don't know whether this is actually true, but in my experience, it seems fairly accurate. I have found the same basic SQL statement formats in use within most applications for almost 20 years. Very few people ever use everything SQL has to offer—and they often implement improperly those features they do use frequently. Obviously, we will not be able to cover all the statements and their options found in the SQL language. This book is intended to provide you with deeper insight into the most commonly used statements and to help you understand how to apply them more effectively.

In this book, we will examine five of the most frequently used SQL statements. These statements are SELECT, INSERT, UPDATE, DELETE, and MERGE. Although we'll address each of these core statements in some fashion, our focus is primarily on the SELECT statement. Developing a good command of these five statements will provide a strong foundation for your day-to-day work with the SQL language.

The SELECT Statement

The SELECT statement is used to retrieve data from one or more tables or other database objects. You should already be familiar with the basics of the SELECT statement, so instead of reviewing the statement from the beginner's point of view, I want to review how a SELECT statement processes logically. You should have already learned the basic clauses that form a common SELECT statement, but to build the foundation mind-set you need to write well-formed and efficient SQL consistently, you need to understand how SQL processes.

How a query statement is processed logically may be quite different from its actual physical processing. The Oracle cost-based optimizer (CBO) is responsible for generating the actual execution plan for a query, and we will examine what the optimizer does, and how it does it and why. For now, note that the optimizer determines how to access tables and the order in which to process them, and how to join multiple tables and apply filters. The logical order of query processing occurs in a very specific order. However, the steps the optimizer chooses for the physical execution plan can end up actually processing the query in a very different order. Listing 1-10 shows a query stub that contains the main clauses of a SELECT statement with step numbers assigned to each clause in the order it is processed logically.

Listing 1-10. Logical Query Processing Order

```
5       SELECT  <column list>
1       FROM            <source object list>
1.1     FROM            <left source object> <join type>
                JOIN <right source object> ON <on predicates>
2       WHERE           <where predicates>
3       GROUP BY        <group by expression(s)>
4       HAVING          <having predicates>
6       ORDER BY        <order by list>
```

You should notice right away that SQL differs from other programming languages in that the first written statement (SELECT) is not the first line of code that is processed; the FROM clause is processed first. Note that I show two different FROM clauses in this listing. The one marked 1.1 is provided to show the difference when ANSI syntax is used. It may be helpful to imagine that each step in the processing order creates a temporary dataset. As each step is processed, the dataset is manipulated until a final result is formulated. It is this final result set of data that the query returns to the caller.

To walk through each part of the SELECT statement in more detail, you need to use the query in Listing 1-11 that returns a result set that contains a list of female customers that have placed more than four orders.

Listing 1-11. Female Customers Who Have Placed More Than Four Orders

```
SQL> select c.customer_id, count(o.order_id) as orders_ct
  2  from oe.customers c
  3  join oe.orders o
  4  on c.customer_id = o.customer_id
  5  where c.gender = 'F'
  6  group by c.customer_id
  7  having count(o.order_id) > 4
  8  order by orders_ct, c.customer_id
  9  /
CUSTOMER_ID  ORDERS_CT
-----------  ----------
        146          5
        147          5
```

The FROM Clause

The FROM clause lists the source objects from which data are selected. This clause can contain tables, views, materialized views, partitions, or subpartitions, or may specify a subquery that identifies objects. If multiple source objects are used, this logical processing phase also applies to each join type and ON predicate. We explore join types in more detail later, but note that, as joins are processed, they occur in the following order:

1. Cross join, also called a *Cartesian product*

2. Inner join

3. Outer join

In the example query in Listing 1-11, the FROM clause lists two tables: customers and orders. They are joined on the customer_id column. So, when this information is processed, the initial dataset that is produced by the FROM clause includes rows in which customer_id matches in both tables. The result set contains 105 rows at this point. To verify this is true, simply execute only the first four lines of the example query, as shown in Listing 1-12.

Listing 1-12. Partial Query Execution through the FROM Clause Only

```
SQL> select c.customer_id cust_id, o.order_id ord_id, c.gender
  2  from oe.customers c
  3  join oe.orders o
  4  on c.customer_id = o.customer_id;
```

CUST_ID	ORD_ID	G	CUST_ID	ORD_ID	G	CUST_ID	ORD_ID	G
147	2450	F	101	2430	M	109	2394	M
147	2425	F	101	2413	M	116	2453	M
147	2385	F	101	2447	M	116	2428	M
147	2366	F	101	2458	M	116	2369	M
147	2396	F	102	2431	M	116	2436	M
148	2451	M	102	2414	M	117	2456	M
148	2426	M	102	2432	M	117	2429	M
148	2386	M	102	2397	M	117	2370	M
148	2367	M	103	2437	F	117	2446	M
148	2406	M	103	2415	F	118	2457	M
149	2452	M	103	2433	F	118	2371	M
149	2427	M	103	2454	F	120	2373	M
149	2387	M	104	2438	F	121	2374	M
149	2368	M	104	2416	F	122	2375	M
149	2434	M	104	2355	F	123	2376	F
150	2388	M	104	2354	F	141	2377	M
151	2389	M	105	2439	F	143	2380	M
152	2390	M	105	2417	F	144	2445	M
153	2391	M	105	2356	F	144	2422	M
154	2392	F	105	2358	F	144	2382	M
155	2393	M	106	2441	M	144	2363	M
156	2395	F	106	2418	M	144	2435	M
157	2398	M	106	2359	M	145	2448	M
158	2399	M	106	2381	M	145	2423	M
159	2400	M	107	2442	F	145	2383	M
160	2401	M	107	2419	F	145	2364	M
161	2402	M	107	2360	F	145	2455	M
162	2403	M	107	2440	F	119	2372	M
163	2404	M	108	2443	M	142	2378	M
164	2405	M	108	2420	M	146	2449	F
165	2407	M	108	2361	M	146	2424	F
166	2408	F	108	2357	M	146	2384	F
167	2409	M	109	2444	M	146	2365	F
169	2411	F	109	2421	M	146	2379	F
170	2412	M	109	2362	M	168	2410	M

```
105 rows selected.
```

■ **Note**   I formatted the result of this output manually to make it fit nicely on the page. The actual output was displayed over 105 separate lines.

The WHERE Clause

The WHERE clause provides a way to limit conditionally the rows emitted to the query's final result set. Each condition, or predicate, is entered as a comparison of two values or expressions. The comparison matches (evaluates to TRUE) or does not match (evaluates to FALSE). If the comparison is FALSE, then the row is not included in the final result set.

I need to digress just a bit to cover an important aspect of SQL related to this step. Actually, the possible values of a logical comparison in SQL are TRUE, FALSE, and UNKNOWN. The UNKNOWN value occurs when a null is involved. Nulls compared with anything or nulls used in expressions evaluate to null, or UNKNOWN. A null represents a missing value and can be confusing because of inconsistencies in how nulls are treated within different elements of the SQL language. I address how nulls affect the execution of SQL statements throughout the book, although I mention the topic only briefly at this point. What I stated previously is still basically true; comparisons return either TRUE or FALSE. What you'll find is that when a null is involved in a filter comparison, it is treated as if it is FALSE.

In our example, there is a single predicate used to limit the result only to females who have placed orders. If you review the intermediate result after the FROM clause was processed (see Listing 1-12), you'll note that only 31 of the 105 rows were placed by female customers (gender = 'F'). Therefore, after the WHERE clause is applied, the intermediate result set is reduced from 105 rows to 31 rows.

After the WHERE clause is applied, the detailed result set is ready. Note that I use the phrase *detailed result set*. What I mean is the rows that satisfy the query requirements are now available. Other clauses may be applied (GROUP BY, HAVING) that aggregate and limit the final result set further that the caller receives, but it is important to note that, at this point, all the data your query needs to compute the final answer are available.

The WHERE clause is intended to restrict, or reduce, the result set. The less restrictions you include, the more data your final result set contains. The more data you need to return, the longer the query takes to execute.

The GROUP BY Clause

The GROUP BY clause aggregates the filtered result set available after processing the FROM and WHERE clauses. The selected rows are grouped by the expression(s) listed in this clause to produce a single row of summary information for each group. You may group by any column of any object listed in the FROM clause, even if you don't intend to display that column in the list of output columns. Conversely, any nonaggregate column in the select list must be included in the GROUP BY expression.

There are two additional operations that can be included in a GROUP BY clause: ROLLUP and CUBE. The ROLLUP operation is used to produce subtotal values. The CUBE operation is used to produce cross-tabulation values. If you use either of these operations, you get more than one row of summary information. Both these operations are discussed in detail in Chapter 7.

In the example query, the requested grouping is customer_id. This means that there is only one row for each distinct customer_id. Of the 31 rows that represent the females who placed orders that made it through the WHERE clause processing, there are 11 distinct customer_id values, as shown in Listing 1-13.

Listing 1-13. Partial Query Execution through the GROUP BY Clause

```
SQL> select c.customer_id, count(o.order_id) as orders_ct
  2  from oe.customers c
  3  join oe.orders o
  4  on c.customer_id = o.customer_id
  5 where gender = 'F'
  6 group by c.customer_id;
```

CUSTOMER_ID	ORDERS_CT
156	1
123	1
166	1
154	1
169	1
105	4
103	4
107	4
104	4
147	5
146	5

```
11 rows selected.
```

Notice that the output from the query, although grouped, is not ordered. The display makes it appear as though the rows are ordered by order_ct, but this is more coincidence and not guaranteed behavior. This is an important item to remember; the GROUP BY clause does not ensure ordering of data. If you want the list to display in a specific order, you have to specify an ORDER BY clause.

The HAVING Clause

The HAVING clause restricts the grouped summary rows to those for which the condition(s) in the clause are TRUE. Unless you include a HAVING clause, all summary rows are returned. The GROUP BY and HAVING clauses are actually interchangeable positionally (it doesn't matter which one comes first). However, it seems to make more sense to code them with the GROUP BY clause first, because GROUP BY is processed logically first. Essentially, the HAVING clause is a second WHERE clause that is evaluated after GROUP BY occurs, and is used to filter on grouped values. Because the WHERE clause is applied before the GROUP BY occurs, you cannot filter grouped results in the WHERE clause; you must use the HAVING clause instead.

In our example query, the HAVING clause, HAVING COUNT(o.order_id) > 4, limits the grouped result data of 11 rows down to two rows. You can confirm this by reviewing the list of rows returned after GROUP BY is applied, as shown in Listing 1-13. Note that only customers 146 and 147 have placed more than four orders. The two rows that make up the final result set are now ready.

The SELECT List

The SELECT list is where the columns included in the final result set from your query are provided. A column can be an actual column from a table, an expression, or even the result of a SELECT statement, as shown in Listing 1-14.

Listing 1-14. Example Query Showing SELECT List Alternatives

```
SQL> select c.customer_id, c.cust_first_name||' '||c.cust_last_name,
  2  (select e.last_name from hr.employees e where e.employee_id = c.account_mgr_id) acct_mgr
  3  from oe.customers c;

   CUSTOMER_ID CUST_NAME                                ACCT_MGR
-------------- ---------------------------------------- --------------
           147 Ishwarya Roberts                         Russell
           148 Gustav Steenburgen                       Russell
...
           931 Buster Edwards                           Cambrault
           981 Daniel Gueney                            Cambrault
319 rows selected.
```

When another SELECT statement is used to produce the value of a column, the query must return only one row and one column value. These types of subqueries are referred to as *scalar subqueries*. Although this can be very useful syntax, keep in mind that the scalar subquery is executed once for each row in the result set. There are optimizations available that may eliminate some duplicate executions of the subquery, but the worst-case scenario is that each row requires this scalar subquery to be executed. Imagine the possible overhead involved if your result set had thousands, or millions, of rows! I review scalar subqueries later in the book and discuss how to use them optimally.

Another option you may need to use in the SELECT list is the DISTINCT clause. The example provided here doesn't use it, but I want to mention it briefly. The DISTINCT clause causes duplicate rows to be removed from the dataset produced after the other clauses have been processed.

After the SELECT list is processed, you now have the final result set for your query. The only thing that remains to be done, if it is included, is to sort the result set into a desired order.

The ORDER BY Clause

The ORDER BY clause is used to order the final set of rows returned by the statement. In this case, the requested sort order was to be by orders_ct and customer_id. The orders_ct column is the value computed using the COUNT aggregate function in the GROUP BY clause. As shown in Listing 1-13, there are two customers that each placed more than four orders. Because each customer placed five orders, the order_ct is the same, so the second ordering column determines the final display order. As shown in Listing 1-15, the final sorted output of the query is a two-row dataset ordered by customer_id.

Listing 1-15. Example Query Final Output

```
SQL> select c.customer_id, count(o.order_id) as orders_ct
  2  from oe.customers c
  3  join oe.orders o
  4  on c.customer_id = o.customer_id
  5  where c.gender = 'F'
  6  group by c.customer_id
  7  having count(o.order_id) > 4
  8  order by orders_ct, c.customer_id
  9  /
CUSTOMER_ID ORDERS_CT
----------- ----------
        146         5
        147         5
```

When ordered output is requested, Oracle must take the final set of data after all other clauses have been processed and sort them as specified. The size of the data that needs to be sorted is important. When I say size, I mean total bytes of data in the result set. To estimate the size of the dataset, multiply the number of rows by the number of bytes per row. The bytes per row are determined by summing the average column lengths of each of the columns in the SELECT list.

The example query requests only the customer_id and orders_ct column values in the SELECT list. Let's use ten as our estimated bytes-per-row value. In Chapter 6, I show you where to find the optimizer's estimate for this value. So, given that we only have two rows in the result set, the sort size is actually quite small, approximately 20 bytes. Remember, this is only an estimate, but the estimate is an important one.

Small sorts should be accomplished entirely in memory whereas large sorts may have to use temporary disk space to complete the sort. As you may likely deduce, a sort that occurs in memory is faster than a sort that must use disk. Therefore, when the optimizer estimates the effect of sorting data, it has to consider how big the sort is to adjust how to accomplish getting the query result in the most efficient way. In general, consider sorts as a fairly expensive overhead to your query processing time, particularly if the size of your result set is large.

The INSERT Statement

The INSERT statement is used to add rows to a table, partition, or view. Rows can be inserted in either a single-table or multitable method. A single-table insert inserts values into one row of one table either by specifying the values explicitly or by retrieving the values using a subquery. The multitable insert inserts rows into one or more tables and computes the row values it inserts by retrieving the values using a subquery.

Single-Table Inserts

The first example in Listing 1-16 illustrates a single-table insert using the VALUES clause. Each column value is entered explicitly. The column list is optional if you include values for each column defined in the table. However, if you only want to provide values for a subset of the columns, you must specify the column names in the column list. A good practice is to include the column list regardless of whether you specify values for all the columns. Doing so acts to self-document the statement and also helps reduce possible errors that might occur in the future should someone add a new column to the table.

Listing 1-16. Single-Table Insert

```
SQL> insert into hr.jobs (job_id, job_title, min_salary, max_salary)
  2  values ('IT_PM', 'Project Manager', 5000, 11000) ;
1 row created.

SQL> insert into scott.bonus (ename, job, sal)
  2  select ename, job, sal * .10
  3  from scott.emp;

14 rows created.
```

The second example in Listing 1-16 illustrates an insert using a subquery, which is a very flexible option for inserting rows. The subquery can be written to return one or more rows. Each row returned is used to supply column values for the new rows to be inserted. The subquery can be as simple or as complex as needed to satisfy your needs. In this example, we use the subquery to compute a 10 percent bonus for each employee based on his or her current salary. The bonus table actually has four columns, but we only populate three of them with this insert. The comm column isn't populated with a value from the subquery and we do not include it in the column list. Because we don't include this column, the value for it is null. Note that if the comm column had a NOT NULL constraint, you would get a constraint error and the statement would fail.

Multitable Inserts

The multitable insert example in Listing 1-17 illustrates how rows returned from a single subquery can be used to insert rows into more than one table. We start with three tables: small_customers, medium_customers, and large_customers. Let's populate these tables with customer data based on the total amount of orders a customer has placed. The subquery sums the order_total column for each customer, and then the insert places a row conditionally in the proper table based on whether the customer is considered to be small (less than $10,000 of total orders), medium (between $10,000 and $99,999.99), or large (greater than or equal to $100,000).

Listing 1-17. Multitable Insert

```
SQL> select * from small_customers ;

no rows selected

SQL> select * from medium_customers ;

no rows selected

SQL> select * from large_customers ;

no rows selected

SQL> insert all
  2   when sum_orders < 10000 then
  3   into small_customers
  4   when sum_orders >= 10000 and sum_orders < 100000 then
  5   into medium_customers
  6   else
  7   into large_customers
  8   select customer_id, sum(order_total) sum_orders
  9   from oe.orders
 10   group by customer_id ;

47 rows created.

SQL> select * from small_customers ;

CUSTOMER_ID SUM_ORDERS
----------- ----------
        120        416
        121       4797
        152     7616.8
        157     7110.3
        160      969.2
        161        600
        162        220
        163        510
        164       1233
        165       2519
        166        309
        167         48

12 rows selected.
```

```
SQL> select * from medium_customers ;
CUSTOMER_ID SUM_ORDERS
----------- ----------
        102    69211.4
        103    20591.4
        105    61376.5
        106    36199.5
        116      32307
        119    16447.2
        123    11006.2
        141    38017.8
        142    25691.3
        143    27132.6
        145    71717.9
        146    88462.6
        151      17620
        153    48070.6
        154      26632
        155    23431.9
        156      68501
        158    25270.3
        159    69286.4
        168      45175
        169    15760.5
        170      66816

22 rows selected.

SQL> select * from large_customers ;

CUSTOMER_ID SUM_ORDERS
----------- ----------
        101   190395.1
        104   146605.5
        107   155613.2
        108   213399.7
        109   265255.6
        117   157808.7
        118   100991.8
        122   103834.4
        144   160284.6
        147   371278.2
        148   185700.5
        149   403119.7
        150   282694.3

13 rows selected.
```

Note the use of the ALL clause after the INSERT keyword. When ALL is specified, the statement performs unconditional multitable inserts, which means that each WHEN clause is evaluated for each row returned by the subquery regardless of the outcome of a previous condition. Therefore, you need to be careful about how you specify each condition. For example, if I had used WHEN sum_orders < 100000 instead of the range I specified, the medium_customers table would have included the rows that were also inserted into small_customers.

Specify the FIRST option to cause each WHEN to be evaluated in the order it appears in the statement and to skip subsequent WHEN clause evaluations for a given subquery row. The key is to remember which option, ALL or FIRST, best meets your needs, then use the one most suitable.

The UPDATE Statement

The UPDATE statement is used to change the column values of existing rows in a table. The syntax for this statement is composed of three parts: UPDATE, SET, and WHERE. The UPDATE clause specifies the table to update. The SET clause specifies which columns are changed and the modified values. The WHERE clause is used to filter conditionally which rows are updated. This clause is optional; if it is omitted, the update operation is applied to all rows of the specified table.

Listing 1-18 demonstrates several different ways an UPDATE statement can be written. First, I create a duplicate of the employees table called employees2, then I execute several different updates that accomplish basically the same task: the employees in department 90 are updated to have a 10 percent salary increase and, in the case of example 5, the commission_pct column is also updated. The following list includes the different approaches taken:

> *Example 1*: Update a single column value using an expression.

> *Example 2*: Update a single column value using a subquery.

> *Example 3*: Update a single column using a subquery in the WHERE clause to determine which rows to update.

> *Example 4*: Update a table using a SELECT statement to define the table and the column values.

> *Example 5*: Update multiple columns using a subquery.

Listing 1-18. UPDATE Statement Examples

```
SQL> -- create a duplicate employees table
SQL> create table employees2 as select * from employees ;
Table created.

SQL> -- add a primary key
SQL> alter table employees2
  1   add constraint emp2_emp_id_pk primary key (employee_id) ;

Table altered.

SQL> -- retrieve list of employees in department 90
SQL> select employee_id, last_name, salary
  2   from employees where department_id = 90 ;

EMPLOYEE_ID LAST_NAME                         SALARY
----------- ------------------------- ---------------
        100 King                               24000
        101 Kochhar                            17000
        102 De Haan                            17000

3 rows selected.
```

```
SQL> -- Example 1: Update a single column value using an expression

SQL> update employees2
  2  set salary = salary * 1.10 -- increase salary by 10%
  3  where department_id = 90 ;

3 rows updated.

SQL> commit ;

Commit complete.

SQL> select employee_id, last_name, salary
  2  from employees2 where department_id = 90 ;

EMPLOYEE_ID LAST_NAME  SALARY
----------- ---------- ------
        100 King        26400 -- previous value 24000
        101 Kochhar     18700 -- previous value 17000
        102 De Haan     18700 -- previous value 17000

3 rows selected.

SQL> -- Example 2: Update a single column value using a subquery

SQL> update employees
  2  set salary = (select employees2.salary
  3                  from employees2
  4                 where employees2.employee_id = employees.employee_id
  5                   and employees.salary != employees2.salary)
  6  where department_id = 90 ;

3 rows updated.

SQL> select employee_id, last_name, salary
  2  from employees where department_id = 90 ;

    EMPLOYEE_ID LAST_NAME                           SALARY
--------------- -------------------------- ----------------
            100 King                                 26400
            101 Kochhar                              18700
            102 De Haan                              18700

3 rows selected.

SQL> rollback ;

Rollback complete.

SQL> -- Example 3: Update single column using subquery in
SQL> -- WHERE clause to determine which rows to update
```

```
SQL> update employees
  2   set salary = salary * 1.10
  3   where department_id in (select department_id
  4                               from departments
  5                               where department_name = 'Executive') ;

3 rows updated.
SQL> select employee_id, last_name, salary
  2   from employees
  3   where department_id in (select department_id
  4                               from departments
  5                               where department_name = 'Executive') ;

    EMPLOYEE_ID LAST_NAME                            SALARY
--------------- ------------------------- ---------------
            100 King                                26400
            101 Kochhar                             18700
            102 De Haan                             18700

3 rows selected.

SQL> rollback ;

Rollback complete.

SQL> -- Example 4: Update a table using a SELECT statement
SQL> -- to define the table and column values

SQL> update (select e1.salary, e2.salary new_sal
  2            from employees e1, employees2 e2
  3            where e1.employee_id = e2.employee_id
  4              and e1.department_id = 90)
  5   set salary = new_sal;

3 rows updated.

SQL> select employee_id, last_name, salary, commission_pct
  2   from employees where department_id = 90 ;

    EMPLOYEE_ID LAST_NAME                            SALARY  COMMISSION_PCT
--------------- ------------------------- --------------- ---------------
            100 King                                26400
            101 Kochhar                             18700
            102 De Haan                             18700

3 rows selected.

SQL> rollback ;

Rollback complete.

SQL> -- Example 5: Update multiple columns using a subquery
```

```
SQL> update employees
  2   set (salary, commission_pct) = (select employees2.salary, .10 comm_pct
  3                     from employees2
  4                    where employees2.employee_id = employees.employee_id
  5                      and employees.salary != employees2.salary)
  6   where department_id = 90 ;

3 rows updated.
SQL> select employee_id, last_name, salary, commission_pct
  2   from employees where department_id = 90 ;

    EMPLOYEE_ID LAST_NAME                             SALARY COMMISSION_PCT
--------------- ------------------------- --------------- ---------------
            100 King                                   26400             .1
            101 Kochhar                                18700             .1
            102 De Haan                                18700             .1

3 rows selected.

SQL> rollback ;

Rollback complete.

SQL>
```

The DELETE Statement

The DELETE statement is used to remove rows from a table. The syntax for this statement is composed of three parts: DELETE, FROM, and WHERE. The DELETE keyword stands alone. Unless you decide to use a hint, which we examine later, there are no other options associated with the DELETE keyword. The FROM clause identifies the table from which rows are to be deleted. As the examples in Listing 1-19 demonstrate, the table can be specified directly or via a subquery. The WHERE clause provides any filter conditions to help determine which rows are deleted. If the WHERE clause is omitted, the DELETE operation deletes all rows in the specified table.

Listing 1-19. DELETE Statement Examples

```
SQL> select employee_id, department_id, last_name, salary
  2   from employees2
  3   where department_id = 90;
    EMPLOYEE_ID   DEPARTMENT_ID LAST_NAME                     SALARY
--------------- --------------- ------------------------- ---------------
            100              90 King                          26400
            101              90 Kochhar                       18700
            102              90 De Haan                       18700

3 rows selected.
SQL> -- Example 1: Delete rows from specified table using
SQL> -- a filter condition in the WHERE clause
SQL> delete from employees2
  2   where department_id = 90;
```

```
3 rows deleted.

SQL> select employee_id, department_id, last_name, salary
  2  from employees2
  3  where department_id = 90;

no rows selected

SQL> rollback;

Rollback complete.

SQL> select employee_id, department_id, last_name, salary
  2  from employees2
  3  where department_id = 90;

    EMPLOYEE_ID   DEPARTMENT_ID LAST_NAME                          SALARY
--------------- --------------- ------------------------- ---------------
            100              90 King                                26400
            101              90 Kochhar                             18700
            102              90 De Haan                             18700

3 rows selected.

SQL> -- Example 2: Delete rows using a subquery in the FROM clause
SQL> delete from (select * from employees2 where department_id = 90);

3 rows deleted.

SQL> select employee_id, department_id, last_name, salary
  2  from employees2
  3  where department_id = 90;

no rows selected

SQL> rollback;

Rollback complete.

SQL> select employee_id, department_id, last_name, salary
  2  from employees2
  3  where department_id = 90;

    EMPLOYEE_ID   DEPARTMENT_ID LAST_NAME                          SALARY
--------------- --------------- ------------------------- ---------------
            100              90 King                                26400
            101              90 Kochhar                             18700
            102              90 De Haan                             18700

3 rows selected.
```

```
SQL> -- Example 3: Delete rows from specified table using
SQL> -- a subquery in the WHERE clause
SQL> delete from employees2
  2  where department_id in (select department_id
  3                            from departments
  4                            where department_name = 'Executive');

3 rows deleted.

SQL> select employee_id, department_id, last_name, salary
  2  from employees2
  3  where department_id = 90;

no rows selected

SQL> rollback;

Rollback complete.

SQL>
```

Listing 1-19 demonstrates several different ways a DELETE statement can be written. Note that I am using the employees2 table created in Listing 1-18 for these examples. The following are the different delete methods that you can use:

Example 1: Delete rows from a specified table using a filter condition in the WHERE clause.

Example 2: Delete rows using a subquery in the FROM clause.

Example 3: Delete rows from a specified table using a subquery in the WHERE clause.

The MERGE Statement

The MERGE statement is a single command that combines the ability to update or insert rows into a table by deriving conditionally the rows to be updated or inserted from one or more sources. It is used most frequently in data warehouses to move large amounts of data, but its use is not limited only to data warehouse environments. The big value-add this statement provides is that you have a convenient way to combine multiple operations into one, which allows you to avoid issuing multiple INSERT, UPDATE, and DELETE statements. And, as you'll see later in the book, if you can avoid doing work you really don't have to do, your response times will likely improve.

The syntax for the MERGE statement is as follows:

```
MERGE <hint>
INTO <table_name>
USING <table_view_or_query>
ON (<condition>)
WHEN MATCHED THEN <update_clause>
DELETE <where_clause>
WHEN NOT MATCHED THEN <insert_clause>
[LOG ERRORS <log_errors_clause> <reject limit <integer | unlimited>];
```

To demonstrate the use of the MERGE statement, Listing 1-20 shows how to create a test table and then insert or update rows appropriately into that table based on the MERGE conditions.

Listing 1-20. MERGE Statement Example

```
SQL> create table dept60_bonuses
  2  (employee_id      number
  3  ,bonus_amt        number);

Table created.

SQL> insert into dept60_bonuses values (103, 0);

1 row created.

SQL> insert into dept60_bonuses values (104, 100);

1 row created.

SQL> insert into dept60_bonuses values (105, 0);

1 row created.

SQL> commit;

Commit complete.

SQL> select employee_id, last_name, salary
  2  from employees
  3  where department_id = 60 ;

    EMPLOYEE_ID LAST_NAME                            SALARY
--------------- ------------------------- ---------------
            103 Hunold                                 9000
            104 Ernst                                  6000
            105 Austin                                 4800
            106 Pataballa                              4800
            107 Lorentz                                4200

5 rows selected.

SQL> select * from dept60_bonuses;

    EMPLOYEE_ID       BONUS_AMT
--------------- ---------------
            103               0
            104             100
            105               0

3 rows selected.

SQL> merge into dept60_bonuses b
  2  using (
  3     select employee_id, salary, department_id
  4     from employees
```

```
  5    where department_id = 60) e
  6  on (b.employee_id = e.employee_id)
  7  when matched then
  8    update set b.bonus_amt = e.salary * 0.2
  9      where b.bonus_amt = 0
 10    delete where (e.salary > 7500)
 11  when not matched then
 12    insert (b.employee_id, b.bonus_amt)
 13    values (e.employee_id, e.salary * 0.1)
 14    where (e.salary < 7500);

4 rows merged.

SQL> select * from dept60_bonuses;

  EMPLOYEE_ID        BONUS_AMT
--------------- ----------------
            104              100
            105              960
            106              480
            107              420

4 rows selected.

SQL> rollback;

Rollback complete.

SQL>
```

The MERGE accomplished the following:

- Two rows were inserted (employee_ids 106 and 107).

- One row was updated (employee_id 105).

- One row was deleted (employee_id 103).

- One row remained unchanged (employee_id 104).

Without the MERGE statement, you would have had to write at least three different statements to complete the same work.

Summary

As you can tell from the examples shown so far, the SQL language offers many alternatives that can produce the same result set. What you may have also noticed is that each of the five core statements can use similar constructs, such as subqueries. The key is to learn which constructs are the most efficient under various circumstances. We look at how to do this later.

If you had any trouble following the examples in this chapter, make sure to take the time to review either *Beginning Oracle SQL* (mentioned earlier) or *The SQL Reference Guide* in the Oracle documentation. The rest of this book assumes you are comfortable with the basic constructs for each of the five core SQL statements: SELECT, INSERT, UPDATE, DELETE, and MERGE.

■ ■ ■

SQL Execution

You likely learned the mechanics of writing basic SQL in a relatively short period of time. Throughout the course of a few weeks or few months, you became comfortable with the general statement structure and syntax, how to filter, how to join tables, and how to group and order data. But, how far beyond that initial level of proficiency have you traveled? Writing complex SQL that executes efficiently is a skill that requires you to move beyond the basics. Just because your SQL gets the job done doesn't mean it does the job well.

In this chapter, I'm going to raise the hood and look at how SQL executes from the inside out. I'll discuss basic Oracle architecture and introduce the cost-based query optimizer. You'll learn how and why the way you formulate your SQL statements affects the optimizer's ability to produce the most efficient execution plan possible. You may already know what to do, but understanding how SQL execution works will help you help Oracle accomplish the results you need in less time and with fewer resources.

Oracle Architecture Basics

The SQL language is seemingly easy enough that you can learn to write simple SQL statements in fairly short order. But, just because you can write SQL statements that are functionally correct (in other words, produce the proper result set) doesn't mean you've accomplished the task in the most effective and efficient way.

Moving beyond basic skills requires deeper understanding. For instance, when I learned to drive, my father taught me the basics. We walked around the car and discussed the parts of the car that he thought were important to be aware of as the driver of the vehicle. We talked about the type of gas I should put in the car, the proper air pressure for the tires, and the importance of getting regular oil changes. Being aware of these things would help make sure the vehicle was in good condition when I wanted to drive it.

He then taught me the mechanics of driving. I learned how to start the engine, shift gears, increase and decrease my speed, use the brake, use turn signals, and so on. But, what he didn't teach me was specifically how the engine worked, how to change the oil myself, or anything else other than what I needed to do to allow me to drive the vehicle safely from place to place. If I needed my car to do anything aside from what I learned, I had to take it to a professional mechanic, which isn't a bad thing. Not everyone needs to have the skills and knowledge of a professional mechanic just to drive a car. However, the analogy applies to anyone who writes SQL. You can learn the basics and be able to get your applications from place to place; but, without extending your knowledge, I don't believe you'll ever be more than an everyday driver. To get the most out of SQL, you need to understand how it does what it does, which means you need to understand the basics of the underlying architecture on which the SQL you write will execute.

Figure 2-1 depicts how most people view the database when they first learn to write SQL. It is simply a black box to which they direct SQL requests and from which they get data back. The "machinery" inside the database is a mystery.

SQL request

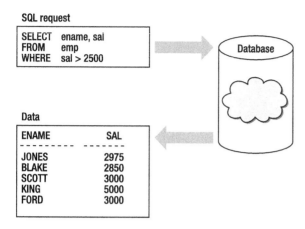

Figure 2-1. *Using SQL and the database*

The term *Oracle database* is typically used to refer to the files, stored on disk, where data reside along with the memory structures used to manage those files. In reality, the term *database* belongs to the data files; the term *instance* belongs to the memory structures and the processes. An instance consists of the system global area (SGA) and a set of background processes. Each user connection to the database is managed via a server process. Each client connection is associated with server processes that are each allocated their own private memory area called the *program*, or *process, global area* (PGA).

The *Oracle Concepts Guide* goes into detail about each of the memory structures and processes. I think it's a great idea for everyone who will use Oracle to read the *Oracle Concepts Guide*. For our purposes, however, I limit my discussion to a few key areas to help you understand how SQL operates. Specifically, I review two areas of the SGA: the shared pool (specifically, the library cache within the shared pool) and the database buffer cache. Later in the book, I discuss some particulars about the PGA, but for now, I'm keeping our review limited to the SGA . Note that these discussions will present a fairly broad picture. As I said, I don't want to overwhelm you, but I do think this is critical information on which to get a grasp before you go any further.

SGA: The Shared Pool

The shared pool is one of the most critical memory components, particularly when it comes to how SQL executes. The way you write SQL affects more than the individual SQL statement itself. The combination of all SQL that executes against the database has a tremendous effect on overall performance and scalability resulting from how it affects the shared pool.

The shared pool is where Oracle caches program data. Every SQL statement executed has its parsed form stored in the shared pool. The area within the shared pool where statements are stored is called the *library cache*. Even before any statement is parsed, Oracle checks the library cache to determine whether that same statement already exists there. If it does, then Oracle retrieves and uses the cached information instead of going through all the work to parse the same statement again. The same thing goes for any PL/SQL (PL/SQL is Oracle's Procedural Language extension to SQL) code you run. The really nifty part is that, no matter how many users may want to execute the same SQL statement, Oracle typically only parses that statement once and then shares it among all users who want to use it. Now maybe you can understand why the shared pool gets its name.

SQL statements you write aren't the only things stored in the shared pool. The system parameters Oracle uses are stored in the shared pool as well. In an area called the *dictionary cache*, Oracle also stores information about all the database objects. In general, Oracle stores pretty much everything you can think of in the shared pool. As you can imagine, this makes the shared pool a very busy and important memory component.

Because the memory area allocated to the shared pool is finite, statements that get loaded originally may not stay there for very long as new statements are executed. A least recently used (LRU) algorithm regulates how objects in the shared pool are managed. To borrow an accounting term, it's similar to a FIFO (first in; first out) system. The basic idea is that statements that are used most frequently and most currently are retained. Unlike a straight FIFO method, however, how frequently the same statements are used affects how long they remain in the shared pool. If you execute a SELECT statement at 8 AM and then execute the same statement again at 4 PM, the parsed version that was stored in the shared pool at 8 AM may not still be there. Depending on the overall size of the shared pool and how much activity it has seen between 8 AM and 4 PM—Oracle needs space to store the latest information throughout the day—it simply reuses older areas and overlays newer information into them. But, if you execute a statement every few seconds throughout the day, the frequent reuse causes Oracle to retain that information over something else that may have been originally stored later than your statement but hasn't been executed frequently, or at all, since it was loaded.

One of the things you need to keep in mind as you write SQL is that, to use the shared pool most efficiently, statements need to be shareable. If every statement you write is unique, you basically defeat the purpose of the shared pool. The less shareable it is, the more effect you'll see on overall response times. I show you exactly how expensive parsing can be in the next section.

The Library Cache

The first thing that must happen to every SQL statement you execute is that it must be parsed and loaded into the library cache. The library cache, as mentioned earlier, is the area within the shared pool that holds previously parsed statements. Parsing involves verifying the statement syntax, validating objects being referred to, and confirming user privileges on the objects. If these checks are passed, the next step is for Oracle to determine whether that same statement has been executed previously. If it has, then Oracle grabs the stored information from the previous parse and reuses it. This type of parse is called a *soft parse*. If the statement hasn't been executed previously, then Oracle does all the work to develop the execution plan for the current statement and then stores it in the cache for later reuse. This type of parse is called a *hard parse*.

Hard parses require Oracle to do a lot more work than soft parses. Every time a hard parse occurs, Oracle must gather all the information it needs before it can actually execute the statement. To get the information it needs, Oracle executes a bunch of queries against the data dictionary. The easiest way to see what Oracle does during a hard parse is to turn on extended SQL tracing, execute a statement, and then review the trace data. Extended SQL tracing captures every action that occurs, so not only do you see the statement you execute, but also you see every statement that Oracle must execute as well. Because I haven't covered the details of how tracing works and how to read a trace file, I'm not going to show the detailed trace data. Instead, Table 2-1 provides the list of system tables that were queried during a hard parse of select * from employees where department_id = 60.

Table 2-1. *System Objects Queried during Hard Parse*

Tables	No. of Queries	Purpose
aud_object_opt$	1	Object audit data
ccol$	1	Constraint column-specific data
cdef$	4	Constraint-specific definition data
col$	1	Table column-specific data
hist_head$	1	Histogram header data
histgrm$	1	Histogram specifications
icol$	1	Index columns
ind$	1	Indexes

(continued)

Table 2-1. (*continued*)

Tables	No. of Queries	Purpose
ind_stats$	1	Index statistics
obj$	3	Objects
objauth$	2	Table authorizations
opt_directive_own$	1	SQL plan directives
seg$	1	Mapping of all database segments
tab$	2	Tables
tab_stats$	1	Table statistics
user$	2	User definitions

In total, there were 19 queries against system objects executed during the hard parse. This number, from version 12c, is less than the version 11g total of 59 for the same query. The soft parse of the same statement did not execute any queries against the system objects because all that work was done during the initial hard parse. The elapsed time for the hard parse was 0.030641 second whereas the elapsed time for the soft parse was 0.000025 second. As you can see, soft parsing is a much more desirable alternative to hard parsing. Don't ever fool yourself into thinking parsing doesn't matter. It does!

Identical Statements

For Oracle to determine whether a statement has been executed previously, it checks the library cache for the identical statement. You can see which statements are currently stored in the library cache by querying the v$sql view. This view lists statistics on the shared SQL area and contains one row for each "child" of the original SQL text entered. Listing 2-1 shows three different executions of a query against the employees table followed by a query against v$sql showing information about the three queries that have been stored in the library cache.

Listing 2-1. Queries against Employees and v$sql Contents

```
SQL> select * from employees where department_id = 60;

    EMPLOYEE_ID FIRST_NAME           LAST_NAME                  EMAIL
--------------- -------------------- -------------------------- -----------
            103 Alexander            Hunold                     AHUNOLD
            104 Bruce                Ernst                      BERNST
            105 David                Austin                     DAUSTIN
            106 Valli                Pataballa                  VPATABAL
            107 Diana                Lorentz                    DLORENTZ

SQL> SELECT * FROM EMPLOYEES WHERE DEPARTMENT_ID = 60;

    EMPLOYEE_ID FIRST_NAME           LAST_NAME                  EMAIL
--------------- -------------------- -------------------------- -----------
            103 Alexander            Hunold                     AHUNOLD
            104 Bruce                Ernst                      BERNST
            105 David                Austin                     DAUSTIN
            106 Valli                Pataballa                  VPATABAL
            107 Diana                Lorentz                    DLORENTZ
```

```
SQL> select /* a_comment */ * from employees where department_id = 60;
```

EMPLOYEE_ID	FIRST_NAME	LAST_NAME	EMAIL
103	Alexander	Hunold	AHUNOLD
104	Bruce	Ernst	BERNST
105	David	Austin	DAUSTIN
106	Valli	Pataballa	VPATABAL
107	Diana	Lorentz	DLORENTZ

```
SQL> select sql_text, sql_id, child_number, hash_value, executions
  2  from v$sql where upper(sql_text) like '%EMPLOYEES%';
```

SQL_TEXT	SQL_ID	CHILD_NUMBER	HASH_VALUE	EXECUTIONS
select * from employees where department_id = 60	0svc967bxf4yu	0	3621196762	1
SELECT * FROM EMPLOYEES WHERE DEPARTMENT_ID = 60	cq7t1xq95bpm8	0	2455098984	1
select /* a_comment */ * from employees where department_id = 60	2dkt13j0cyjzq	0	1087326198	1

Although all three statements return the exact same result, Oracle considers them to be different. This is because, when a statement is executed, Oracle first converts the string to a hash value. That hash value is used as the key for that statement when it is stored in the library cache. As other statements are executed, their hash values are compared with the existing hash values to find a match.

So, why would these three statements produce different hash values, even though they return the same result? Because the statements are not identical. Lowercase text is different from uppercase text. Adding a comment into the statement makes it different from the statements that don't have a comment. Any differences cause a different hash value to be created for the statement, and cause Oracle to hard parse the statement.

The execution of statements that differ only by their literals can cause significant parsing overhead, which is why it is important to use bind variables instead of literals in your SQL statements. When you use a bind variable, Oracle is able to share the statement even as you change the values of the bind variables, as shown in Listing 2-2.

Listing 2-2. The Effect of Using Bind Variables on Parsing

```
SQL> variable v_dept number
SQL> exec :v_dept := 10
SQL> select * from employees where department_id = :v_dept;
```

EMPLOYEE_ID	FIRST_NAME	LAST_NAME	EMAIL
200	Jennifer	Whalen	JWHALEN

```
1 row selected.

SQL> exec :v_dept := 20

PL/SQL procedure successfully completed.
```

```
SQL> select * from employees where department_id = :v_dept;

    EMPLOYEE_ID FIRST_NAME           LAST_NAME                  EMAIL
--------------- -------------------- -------------------------- -----------
            201 Michael              Hartstein                  MHARTSTE
            202 Pat                  Fay                        PFAY

2 rows selected.

SQL> exec :v_dept := 30

PL/SQL procedure successfully completed.

SQL> select * from employees where department_id = :v_dept;

    EMPLOYEE_ID FIRST_NAME           LAST_NAME                  EMAIL
--------------- -------------------- -------------------------- -----------
            114 Den                  Raphaely                   DRAPHEAL
            115 Alexander            Khoo                       AKHOO
            116 Shelli               Baida                      SBAIDA
            117 Sigal                Tobias                     STOBIAS
            118 Guy                  Himuro                     GHIMURO
            119 Karen                Colmenares                 KCOLMENA

6 rows selected.

SQL> select sql_text, sql_id, child_number, executions
  2    from v$sql where sql_text like '%v_dept';

SQL_TEXT                         SQL_ID          CHILD_NUMBER EXECUTIONS
-------------------------------- --------------- ------------ ----------
select * from employees          72k66s55jqk1j              0          3
  where department_id = :v_dept

1 row selected.
```

Notice how there is only one statement with three executions stored in the library cache. If I had executed the queries using the literal values (10, 20, 30), there would have been three different statements. Always keep this in mind and try to write SQL that takes advantage of bind variables and uses exactly the same SQL. The less hard parsing that is required means your applications perform better and are more scalable.

There are two final mechanisms that are important to understand. The first is something called a *latch*. A latch is a type of lock that Oracle must acquire to read information stored in the library cache as well as other memory structures. Latches protect the library cache from becoming corrupted by concurrent modifications by two sessions, or by one session trying to read information that is being modified by another one. Before reading any information from the library cache, Oracle acquires a latch that then causes all other sessions to wait until that latch is released before they can acquire the latch and do the work they need to complete.

This is a good place to mention the second mechanism: the *mutex*. A mutex (mutual exclusion lock) is similar to a latch in that it is a serialization device used to prevent multiple threads from accessing shared structures simultaneously. The biggest advantage of mutexes over latches is that mutexes require less memory and are faster to acquire and release. Also, mutexes are used to avoid the need to get the library cache latch for a previously opened cursor (in the session cursor cache) by modifying the cursor's mutex reference count directly. A mutex is a better performing and more scalable mechanism than a latch. Note that library cache latching is still needed for parsing, however.

Latches, unlike typical locks, are not queued. In other words, if Oracle attempts to acquire a latch on the library cache to determine whether the statement you are executing already exists, it checks whether the latch is available. If the latch is available, it acquires the latch, does the work it needs to do, then releases the latch. However, if the latch is already in use, Oracle does something called *spinning*. Think of spinning as repetitive—like a kid in the backseat of a car asking, "Are we there yet?" over and over and over. Oracle basically iterates in a loop, and continues to determine whether the latch is available. During this time, Oracle is actively using the central processing unit (CPU) to do these checks, but your query is actually "on hold" and not really doing anything until the latch is acquired.

If the latch is not acquired after spinning for a while (Oracle spins up to the number of times indicated by the _spin_count hidden parameter, which is set to 2000 by default), then the request is halted temporarily and your session has to get in line behind other sessions that need to use the CPU. It must wait its turn to use the CPU again to determine whether the latch is available. This iterative process continues until the latch can be acquired. You don't just get in line and wait on the latch to become available; it's entirely possible that another session acquires the latch while your session is waiting in line to get back on the CPU to check the latch again. As you can imagine, this can be quite time-consuming if many sessions all need to acquire the latch concurrently.

The main thing to remember is that latches and mutexes are serialization devices. The more frequently Oracle needs to acquire one, the more likely it is that contention will occur, and the longer you'll have to wait. The effects on performance and scalability can be dramatic. So, writing your code so that it requires fewer mutexes and latches (in other words, less hard parsing) is critical.

SGA: The Buffer Cache

The buffer cache is one of the largest components of the SGA. It stores database blocks after they have been read from disk or before they are written to disk. A block is the smallest unit with which Oracle works. Blocks contain rows of table data or index entries, and some blocks contain temporary data for sorts. The key thing to remember is that Oracle must read blocks to get to the rows of data needed to satisfy a SQL statement. Blocks are typically either 4KB, 8KB, or 16KB, although the only restricting factor to the size of a block depends on your operating system.

Each block has a certain structure. Within the block there are a few areas of block overhead that contain information about the block itself that Oracle uses to manage the block. There is information that indicates the type of block it is (table, index, and so forth), a bit of information about transactions against the block, the address where the block resides physically on the disk, information about the tables that store data in the block, and information about the row data contained in the block. The rest of the block contains either the actual data or free space where new data can be stored. There's more detail about how the buffer cache can be divided into multiple pools and how it has varying block sizes, but I'll keep this discussion simple and just consider one big default buffer pool with a single block size.

At any given time, the blocks in the buffer cache will either be *dirty*, which means they have been modified and need to be written into a physical location on the disk, or *not dirty*. During the earlier discussion of the shared pool, I mentioned the LRU algorithm used by Oracle to manage the information there. The buffer cache also uses an LRU list to help Oracle know which blocks are used most recently to determine how to make room for new blocks as needed. Besides the LRU list, Oracle maintains a *touch count* for each block in the buffer cache. This count indicates how frequently a block is used; blocks with higher touch counts remain in the cache longer than those with lower touch counts.

Also similar to the shared pool, latches must be acquired to verify whether blocks are in the buffer cache, and to update the LRU information and touch counts. One of the ways you can help Oracle use less latches is to write your SQL in such a way that it accesses the fewest blocks possible when trying to retrieve the rows needed to satisfy your query. I discuss how you can do this throughout the rest of the book, but for now, keep in mind that, if all you think about when writing a SQL statement is getting the functionally correct answer, you may write your SQL in such a way that it accesses blocks inefficiently and therefore uses more latches than needed. The more latches required, the more chance for contention, and the more likely your application will be less responsive and less scalable than others that are better written.

Executing a query with blocks that are not in the buffer cache requires Oracle to make a call to the operating system to retrieve those blocks and then place them in the buffer cache before returning the result set to you. In general, any block that contains rows needed to satisfy a query must be present in the buffer cache. When Oracle determines that a block already exists in the buffer cache, such access is referred to as a *logical read*. If the block must be retrieved from disk, it is referred to as a *physical read*. As you can imagine, because the block is already in memory, response times to complete a logical read are faster than physical reads. Listing 2-3 shows the differences between executing the same statement multiple times under three scenarios. First, the statement is executed after clearing both the shared pool and the buffer cache. This means that the statement will be hard parsed, and the blocks that contain the data to satisfy the query (and all the queries from the system objects to handle the hard parse) have to be read physically from disk. The second example shows what happens if only the buffer cache is cleared. The third example shows what happens if both the shared pool and buffer cache are populated.

Listing 2-3. Hard Parsing and Physical Reads Versus Soft Parsing and Logical Reads

```
SQL> alter system flush buffer_cache;

System altered.

SQL> alter system flush shared_pool;

System altered.

SQL> set autotrace traceonly statistics
SQL>
SQL> select * from employees where department_id = 60;

5 rows selected.

Statistics
----------------------------------------------------------
        951  recursive calls
          0  db block gets
        237  consistent gets
         27  physical reads
          0  redo size
       1386  bytes sent via SQL*Net to client
        381  bytes received via SQL*Net from client
          2  SQL*Net roundtrips to/from client
          9  sorts (memory)
          0  sorts (disk)
          5  rows processed

SQL> set autotrace off
SQL>
SQL> alter system flush buffer_cache;

System altered.
```

```
SQL> set autotrace traceonly statistics
SQL>
SQL> select * from employees where department_id = 60;

5 rows selected.

Statistics
----------------------------------------------------------
          0  recursive calls
          0  db block gets
          4  consistent gets
          2  physical reads
          0  redo size
       1386  bytes sent via SQL*Net to client
        381  bytes received via SQL*Net from client
          2  SQL*Net roundtrips to/from client
          0  sorts (memory)
          0  sorts (disk)
          5  rows processed

SQL> select * from employees where department_id = 60;

5 rows selected.

Statistics
----------------------------------------------------------
          0  recursive calls
          0  db block gets
          4  consistent gets
          0  physical reads
          0  redo size
       1386  bytes sent via SQL*Net to client
        381  bytes received via SQL*Net from client
          2  SQL*Net roundtrips to/from client
          0  sorts (memory)
          0  sorts (disk)
          5  rows processed

SQL> set autotrace off
```

You can see from the statistics that when a query is executed and does only a soft parse and finds the blocks in the buffer cache, the work done is minimal. Your goal should be to develop code that promotes reusability in both the shared pool and the buffer cache.

Query Transformation

Before the development of the execution plan, a step called *query transformation* occurs. This step happens just after a query is checked for syntax and permissions, and just before the optimizer computes cost estimates for the various plan operations it considers when determining the final execution plan. In other words, transformation and optimization are two different tasks.

After your query passes the syntactical and permissions checks, the query enters the transformation phase in a set of query blocks. A query block is defined by the keyword SELECT. For example, select * from employees where department_id = 60 has a single query block. However, select * from employees where department_id in (select department_id from departments) has two query blocks. Each query block is either nested within another or interrelated in some way. The way the query is written determines the relationships between query blocks. It is the query transformer's main objective to determine whether changing the way the query is written provides a better query plan.

Make sure you caught that last sentence. The query transformer can—and will—rewrite your query. This is something you may have never realized. What you write may not end up being the exact statement for which the execution plan is developed. Many times this is a good thing. The query transformer knows how the optimizer deals with certain syntax and does everything it can to render your SQL in a way that helps the optimizer come up with the best, most efficient execution plan. However, the fact that what you write can be changed may mean that a behavior you expected—particularly the order in which certain parts of the statement occur—doesn't happen the way you intended. Therefore, you must understand how query transformation works so that you can make sure to write your SQL properly to get the behaviors you intend.

The query transformer may change the way you originally formulated your query as long as the change does not affect the result set. Any change that might cause the result set to differ from the original query syntax is not considered. The change that is most often made is to transform separate query blocks into straight joins. For example, the statement

```
select * from employees where department_id in (select department_id from departments)
```

will likely be transformed to

```
select e.* from employees e, departments d where e.department_id = d.department_id
```

The result set doesn't change, but the execution plan choices for the transformed version are better from the optimizer's point of view. The transformed version of the query can open up additional operations that might allow for better performance and resource utilization than was possible with the original SQL.

Query Blocks

As mentioned earlier, the way the query can be transformed depends on how each query block is formed. Each query block is named either by Oracle with a system-generated name or by you using the QB_NAME hint. Listing 2-4 shows the execution plans for this query with system-generated query block names and with assigned query block names using the QB_NAME hint.

Listing 2-4. Query Block Naming

```
-- System-generated query block names
```

```
-----------------------------------------------------------------
| Id  | Operation             | Name      | Starts | E-Rows | A-Rows |
-----------------------------------------------------------------
|   0 | SELECT STATEMENT      |           |      1 |        |    106 |
|*  1 |  FILTER               |           |      1 |        |    106 |
|   2 |   TABLE ACCESS FULL   | EMPLOYEES |      1 |    107 |    107 |
|*  3 |   INDEX UNIQUE SCAN   | DEPT_ID_PK|     12 |      1 |     11 |
-----------------------------------------------------------------
```

```
Query Block Name / Object Alias (identified by operation id):
------------------------------------------------------------

   1 - SEL$1
   2 - SEL$1 / EMPLOYEES@SEL$1
   3 - SEL$2 / DEPARTMENTS@SEL$2

Predicate Information (identified by operation id):
--------------------------------------------------

   1 - filter( IS NOT NULL)
   3 - access("DEPARTMENT_ID"=:B1)

-- User-defined query block names

select /*+ qb_name(outer_employees) */ *
from employees where department_id in
(select /*+ qb_name(inner_departments) */ department_id from departments)
```

Id	Operation	Name	Starts	E-Rows	A-Rows
0	SELECT STATEMENT		1		106
* 1	FILTER		1		106
2	TABLE ACCESS FULL	EMPLOYEES	1	107	107
* 3	INDEX UNIQUE SCAN	DEPT_ID_PK	12	1	11

```
Query Block Name / Object Alias (identified by operation id):
------------------------------------------------------------

   1 - OUTER_EMPLOYEES
   2 - OUTER_EMPLOYEES   / EMPLOYEES@OUTER_EMPLOYEES
   3 - INNER_DEPARTMENTS / DEPARTMENTS@INNER_DEPARTMENTS

Predicate Information (identified by operation id):
--------------------------------------------------

   1 - filter( IS NOT NULL)
   3 - access("DEPARTMENT_ID"=:B1)
```

Note the system-generated query block names are numbered sequentially as SEL$1 and SEL$2. In Chapter 6, we cover the DBMS_XPLAN package, which is used here to display the execution plan along with the Query Block Name section. Just note for now that the +ALIAS option was added to the format parameter to produce this section of the output. When the QB_NAME hint is used, the blocks use the specified names OUTER_EMPLOYEES and INNER_DEPARTMENTS. When you name a query block, it allows you to qualify where other hints are applied that you may want to use in the SQL. For instance, you could apply a full table scan hint to the DEPARTMENTS table by specifying a hint as follows:

```
select /*+ full(@inner_departments departments) */ *
from employees where department_id in
(select /*+ qb_name(inner_departments) */ department_id from departments)
```

This hinted SQL would produce the following execution plan:

```
-------------------------------------------------------------------
| Id | Operation          | Name        | Starts | E-Rows | A-Rows |
-------------------------------------------------------------------
|  0 | SELECT STATEMENT   |             |    1   |        |   106  |
|* 1 |  FILTER            |             |    1   |        |   106  |
|  2 |   TABLE ACCESS FULL| EMPLOYEES   |    1   |   107  |   107  |
|* 3 |   TABLE ACCESS FULL| DEPARTMENTS |   12   |     1  |    11  |
-------------------------------------------------------------------
```

Another benefit to using the QB_NAME hint is that you can use the name you specify to locate the query in the shared pool. The V$SQL_PLAN view has a QBLOCK_NAME column that contains the query block name you used so that you can query from that view using a predicate like WHERE QBLOCK_NAME = 'INNER_DEPARTMENTS' to find a SQL statement you executed previously. This strategy can come in handy when you want to locate previously executed SQL statements for analysis or troubleshooting.

When you learn what to look for, you can usually tell by looking at the execution plan if a transformation occurred. You can also execute your query using the NO_QUERY_TRANSFORMATION hint and compare the execution plan from this query with the plan from the query without the hint. I actually used the NO_QUERY_TRANSFORMATION hint when demonstrating the previous QB_NAME hint use. If the two plans are not the same, the differences can be attributed to query transformation. When using the hint, all query transformations, with the exception of predicate pushing (which I review shortly), are prohibited.

There are numerous transformations that can be applied to a given query. I review several of the more common ones to give you a feel for how the optimizer refactors your query text in an attempt to produce better execution plans. In the next sections, we examine the following:

- View merging

- Subquery unnesting

- Join elimination

- ORDER BY elimination

- Predicate pushing

- Query rewrite with materialized views

View Merging

As the name implies, view merging is a transformation that expands views, either inline views or stored views, into separate query blocks that can either be analyzed separately or merged with the rest of the query to form a single overall execution plan. Basically, the statement is rewritten without the view. A statement like select * from my_view would be rewritten as if you had simply typed in the view source. View merging usually occurs when the outer query block's predicate contains the following:

- A column that can be used in an index within another query block

- A column that can be used for partition pruning within another query block

- A condition that limits the rows returned from one of the tables in a joined view

Most people believe that a view is always treated as a separate query block, and that it always has its own subplan and is executed prior to joining to other query blocks. This is not true because of the actions of the query transformer. The truth is that, sometimes, views are analyzed separately and have their own subplan, but more often than not, merging views with the rest of the query provides a greater performance benefit. For example, the following query might use resources quite differently depending on whether the view is merged:

```
select *
from   orders o,
       (select sales_rep_id
              from orders
       ) o_view
where  o.sales_rep_id = o_view.sales_rep_id(+)
and    o.order_total > 100000;
```

Listing 2-5 shows the execution plans for this query when view merging occurs and when it doesn't. Notice the plan operations chosen and the A-Rows count (actual rows retrieved during that step of the plan) in each step.

Listing 2-5. View Merging Plan Comparison

```
-- View merging occurs
```

Id	Operation	Name	Starts	E-Rows	A-Rows
0	SELECT STATEMENT		1		31
1	NESTED LOOPS OUTER		1	384	31
* 2	TABLE ACCESS FULL	ORDERS	1	70	7
* 3	INDEX RANGE SCAN	ORD_SALES_REP_IX	7	5	26

```
Predicate Information (identified by operation id):
-------------------------------------------------

   2 - filter("O"."ORDER_TOTAL">100000)
   3 - access("O"."SALES_REP_ID"="SALES_REP_ID")
       filter("SALES_REP_ID" IS NOT NULL)
```

```
-- View merging does not occur
```

Id	Operation	Name	Starts	E-Rows	A-Rows
0	SELECT STATEMENT		1		31
* 1	HASH JOIN OUTER		1	384	31
* 2	TABLE ACCESS FULL	ORDERS	1	70	7
3	VIEW		1	105	105
4	TABLE ACCESS FULL	ORDERS	1	105	105

```
Predicate Information (identified by operation id):
-------------------------------------------------

   1 - access("O"."SALES_REP_ID"="O_VIEW"."SALES_REP_ID")
   2 - filter("O"."ORDER_TOTAL">100000)
```

Did you notice how in the second, nonmerged plan the view is handled separately? The plan even indicates the view was kept "as is" by showing the VIEW keyword in line 3 of the plan. By treating the view separately, a full scan of the orders table occurs before it is joined with the outer orders table. But, in the merged version, the plan operations are merged into a single plan instead of keeping the inline view separate. This results in a more efficient index access operation being chosen and requires fewer rows to be processed (26 vs. 105). This example uses small tables, so imagine how much work would occur if you had really large tables involved in the query. The transformation to merge the view makes the plan perform more optimally overall.

The misconception that an inline or normal view is considered first and separately from the rest of the query often comes from our education about execution order in mathematics. Let's consider the following examples:

$$6 + 4 \div 2 = 8 \qquad\qquad (6 + 4) \div 2 = 5$$

The parentheses in the right-hand example cause the addition to happen first, whereas in the left-hand example, the division would happen first based on the rules of precedence order. We are trained to know that when we use parentheses, that action happens first; however, the SQL language doesn't follow the same rules that mathematical expressions do. Using parentheses to set a query block apart from another does not in any way guarantee that that block will be executed separately or first. If you have written your statement to include an inline view because you intend for that view to be considered separately, you may need to add the NO_MERGE hint to that query block to prevent it from being rewritten. As a matter of fact, using the NO_MERGE hint is how I was able to produce the nonmerged plan in Listing 2-5. With this hint, I was able to tell the query transformer that I wanted the o_view query block to be considered independently from the outer query block. The query using the hint actually looked like this:

```
select *
from    orders o,
        (select /*+ NO_MERGE */ sales_rep_id
                from orders
        ) o_view
where   o.sales_rep_id = o_view.sales_rep_id(+)
and     o.order_total > 100000;
```

There are some conditions that, if present, also prevent view merging from occurring. If a query block contains analytic or aggregate functions, set operations (such as UNION, INTERSECT, MINUS), or an ORDER BY clause, or uses ROWNUM, view merging is prohibited or limited. Even if some of these conditions are present, you can force view merging to take place by using the MERGE hint. If you force view merging to occur by using the hint, you must make sure that the query result set is still correct after the merge. If view merging does not occur, it is likely a result of the fact that the merge might cause the query result to be different. By using the hint, you are indicating the merge does affect the answer. Listing 2-6 shows a statement with an aggregate function that does not view merge, and exemplifies how the use of a MERGE hint can force view merging to occur.

Listing 2-6. The MERGE Hint

```
-- No hint used

SQL> SELECT e1.last_name, e1.salary, v.avg_salary
  2      FROM employees e1,
  3        (SELECT department_id, avg(salary) avg_salary
  4            FROM employees e2
  5            GROUP BY department_id) v
  6      WHERE e1.department_id = v.department_id AND e1.salary > v.avg_salary;
```

```
-------------------------------------------------------------------
| Id | Operation            | Name        | Starts | E-Rows | A-Rows |
-------------------------------------------------------------------
|   0 | SELECT STATEMENT     |             |    1 |        |     38 |
|*  1 |  HASH JOIN           |             |    1 |     17 |     38 |
|   2 |   VIEW               |             |    1 |     11 |     12 |
|   3 |    HASH GROUP BY     |             |    1 |     11 |     12 |
|   4 |     TABLE ACCESS FULL| EMPLOYEES   |    1 |    107 |    107 |
|   5 |   TABLE ACCESS FULL  | EMPLOYEES   |    1 |    107 |    107 |
-------------------------------------------------------------------
```

Predicate Information (identified by operation id):

```
  1 - access("E1"."DEPARTMENT_ID"="V"."DEPARTMENT_ID")
      filter("E1"."SALARY">"V"."AVG_SALARY")

SQL> SELECT /*+ MERGE(v) */ e1.last_name, e1.salary, v.avg_salary
  2    FROM employees e1,
  3      (SELECT department_id, avg(salary) avg_salary
  4         FROM employees e2
  5         GROUP BY department_id) v
  6    WHERE e1.department_id = v.department_id AND e1.salary > v.avg_salary;
```

-- MERGE hint used

```
-------------------------------------------------------------------
| Id | Operation            | Name        | Starts | E-Rows | A-Rows |
-------------------------------------------------------------------
|   0 | SELECT STATEMENT     |             |    1 |        |     38 |
|*  1 |  FILTER              |             |    1 |        |     38 |
|   2 |   HASH GROUP BY      |             |    1 |    165 |    106 |
|*  3 |    HASH JOIN         |             |    1 |   3298 |   3298 |
|   4 |     TABLE ACCESS FULL| EMPLOYEES   |    1 |    107 |    107 |
|   5 |     TABLE ACCESS FULL| EMPLOYEES   |    1 |    107 |    107 |
-------------------------------------------------------------------
```

Predicate Information (identified by operation id):

```
  1 - filter("E1"."SALARY">SUM("SALARY")/COUNT("SALARY"))
  3 - access("E1"."DEPARTMENT_ID"="DEPARTMENT_ID")
```

-- When _complex_view_merging is turned off

```
SQL> alter session set "_complex_view_merging" = FALSE ;
SQL>
SQL> explain plan for
SELECT /*+ merge (v) */ e1.last_name, e1.salary, v.avg_salary
  FROM employees e1,
  4        (SELECT department_id, avg(salary) avg_salary
  5            FROM employees e2
```

```
  6           GROUP BY department_id) v
  7     WHERE e1.department_id = v.department_id
  8       AND e1.salary > v.avg_salary;

SQL> select * from table(dbms_xplan.display) ;

PLAN_TABLE_OUTPUT
--------------------------------------------------------------------------------------
Plan hash value: 2695105989


------------------------------------------------------------------------------
| Id  | Operation            | Name      | Rows  | Bytes | Cost (%CPU)| Time     |
------------------------------------------------------------------------------
|   0 | SELECT STATEMENT     |           |    17 |   697 |     6  (0)| 00:00:01 |
|*  1 |  HASH JOIN           |           |    17 |   697 |     6  (0)| 00:00:01 |
|   2 |   VIEW               |           |    11 |   286 |     3  (0)| 00:00:01 |
|   3 |    HASH GROUP BY     |           |    11 |    77 |     3  (0)| 00:00:01 |
|   4 |     TABLE ACCESS FULL| EMPLOYEES |   107 |   749 |     3  (0)| 00:00:01 |
|   5 |   TABLE ACCESS FULL  | EMPLOYEES |   107 |  1605 |     3  (0)| 00:00:01 |
------------------------------------------------------------------------------


Predicate Information (identified by operation id):
---------------------------------------------------

   1 - access("E1"."DEPARTMENT_ID"="V"."DEPARTMENT_ID")
       filter("E1"."SALARY">"V"."AVG_SALARY")
```

The examples in Listings 2-5 and 2-6 demonstrate two different types of view merging: simple and complex, respectively. Simple view merging, which occurs automatically for most Select–Project–Join (SPJ)-type queries, is demonstrated in Listing 2-5. SPJ queries containing user-defined views or inline views are transformed into a single query block when possible. For our example query, when it is merged, you can think of it as being transformed as follows:

```
SELECT *
FROM    orders o, orders o2
WHERE   o.sales_rep_id = o2.sales_rep_id(+)
AND     o.order_total > 100000;
```

Complex view merging, as shown in Listing 2-6, is used when the query contains aggregation using GROUP BY, DISTINCT, or outer joins. With complex view merging, the idea is to eliminate the view that contains the aggregation in the hope that fewer resources are needed to produce the result set. In this case, our example query, when it is merged, would likely be transformed as follows:

```
SELECT e1.last_name, e1.salary, avg(e2.salary) avg_salary
FROM    employees e1, employees e2
WHERE   e1.department_id = e2.department_id
GROUP BY e2.department_id, e1.rowid, e1.salary,e1.last_name
HAVING e1.salary > avg(e2.salary);
```

Complex view-merging behavior is controlled by the hidden parameter _complex_view_merging that defaults to TRUE in version 9 and higher. Starting in version 10, transformed queries are reviewed by the optimizer, then the costs of both the merged and nonmerged plans are evaluated. The optimizer then chooses the plan that is the least costly. As shown at the end of Listing 2-6, when _complex_view_merging is set to FALSE, the optimizer does not merge the view even if directed to do so with the MERGE hint.

Subquery Unnesting

Subquery unnesting is similar to view merging in that, just like a view, a subquery is represented by a separate query block. The main difference between "mergeable" views and subqueries that can be unnested is location; subqueries located within the WHERE clause are reviewed for unnesting by the transformer. The most typical transformation is to convert the subquery into a join. The join is a statistically preferable choice because the original syntax may be suboptimal; for example, it may require multiple, redundant reevaluations of the subquery. Unnesting is actually a combination of actions that first converts the subquery into an inline view connected using a join, then merging occurs with the outer query. There is a wide variety of operators that are unnested if possible: IN, NOT IN, EXISTS, NOT EXISTS, correlated or uncorrelated, and others. If a subquery isn't unnested, a separate subplan is generated for it and is executed in an order within the overall plan that allows for optimal execution speed.

When the subquery is not correlated, the transformed query is very straightforward, as shown in Listing 2-7.

Listing 2-7. Unnesting Transformation of an Uncorrelated Subquery

```
SQL> select * from employees
  2  where employee_id in
  3  (select manager_id from departments);
```

Id	Operation	Name	Starts	E-Rows	A-Rows
0	SELECT STATEMENT		1		11
* 1	HASH JOIN RIGHT SEMI		1	11	11
* 2	TABLE ACCESS FULL	DEPARTMENTS	1	11	11
3	TABLE ACCESS FULL	EMPLOYEES	1	107	107

```
Predicate Information (identified by operation id):
---------------------------------------------------

   1 - access("EMPLOYEE_ID"="MANAGER_ID")
   2 - filter("MANAGER_ID" IS NOT NULL)
```

The subquery in this case is simply merged into the main query block and converted to a table join. Notice that the join operation is a HASH JOIN RIGHT SEMI, which is an indication that the transformation resulted in a semijoin operation being selected. We examine both semijoins and antijoins extensively in Chapter 11, and look at more details about this specific type of operation then. The query plan is derived as if the statement was written as follows:

```
select e.*
from    employees e, departments d
where   e.department_id S= d.department_id
```

Using the NO_UNNEST hint, I could have forced the query to be optimized as written, which would mean that a separate subplan would be created for the subquery (as shown in Listing 2-8).

Listing 2-8. Using the NO_UNNEST Hint

```
SQL> select *
  2  from    employees
  3  where   employee_id in
  4              (select /*+ NO_UNNEST */ manager_id
  5               from departments);
```

```
--------------------------------------------------------------------
| Id  | Operation             | Name        | Starts | E-Rows | A-Rows |
--------------------------------------------------------------------
|   0 | SELECT STATEMENT      |             |      1 |        |     11 |
|*  1 |   FILTER              |             |      1 |        |     11 |
|   2 |    TABLE ACCESS FULL| EMPLOYEES   |      1 |    107 |    107 |
|*  3 |    TABLE ACCESS FULL| DEPARTMENTS |    107 |      2 |     11 |
--------------------------------------------------------------------
```

```
Predicate Information (identified by operation id):
---------------------------------------------------

   1 - filter( IS NOT NULL)
   3 - filter("MANAGER_ID"=:B1)
```

The main difference between the plans is that, without query transformation, a FILTER operation is chosen instead of a HASH JOIN join. I discuss both of these operations in detail in Chapters 3 and 6, but for now, just note that the FILTER operation typically represents a less efficient way of accomplishing a match—or join—between two tables. You can see that the subquery remains intact if you look at the Predicate Information for step 3. What happens with this as-is version is that, for each row in the employees table, the subquery must execute using the employees table employee_id column as a bind variable for comparison with the list of manager_ids returned from the execution of the subquery. Because there are 107 rows in the employees table, the subquery executes once for each row. This is not precisely what happens, because of a nice optimization feature Oracle uses called *subquery caching*, but hopefully you can see that executing the query for each row isn't as efficient as joining the two tables. I discuss in the chapters ahead the details of these operations and review why the choice of HASH JOIN is more efficient than the FILTER operation.

The subquery unnesting transformation is a bit more complicated when a correlated subquery is involved. In this case, the correlated subquery is typically transformed into a view, unnested, and then joined to the table in the main query block. Listing 2-9 shows an example of subquery unnesting of a correlated subquery.

Listing 2-9. Unnesting Transformation of a Correlated Subquery

```
SQL> select outer.employee_id, outer.last_name,
  2         outer.salary, outer.department_id
  3  from employees outer
  4  where outer.salary >
  5     (select avg(inner.salary)
  6         from employees inner
  7         where inner.department_id = outer.department_id)
  8  ;
```

```
-----------------------------------------------------------------------
| Id  | Operation            | Name      | Starts | E-Rows | A-Rows |
-----------------------------------------------------------------------
|   0 | SELECT STATEMENT     |           |     1  |        |    38  |
|*  1 |  HASH JOIN           |           |     1  |    17  |    38  |
|   2 |   VIEW               | VW_SQ_1   |     1  |    11  |    12  |
|   3 |    HASH GROUP BY     |           |     1  |    11  |    12  |
|   4 |     TABLE ACCESS FULL| EMPLOYEES |     1  |   107  |   107  |
|   5 |   TABLE ACCESS FULL  | EMPLOYEES |     1  |   107  |   107  |
-----------------------------------------------------------------------

Predicate Information (identified by operation id):
---------------------------------------------------

   1 - access("ITEM_1"="OUTER"."DEPARTMENT_ID")
       filter("OUTER"."SALARY">"AVG(INNER.SALARY)")
```

Notice in this example how the subquery is transformed into an inline view, then merged with the outer query and joined. The correlated column becomes the join condition and the rest of the subquery is used to formulate an inline view. The rewritten version of the query would look something like this:

```
select outer.employee_id, outer.last_name, outer.salary, outer.department_id
   from employees outer,
        (select department_id, avg(salary) avg_sal
            from employees
           group by department_id) inner
  where outer.department_id = inner.department_id
```

Subquery unnesting behavior is controlled by the hidden parameter _unnest_subquery, which defaults to TRUE in version 9 and higher. This parameter is described specifically as controlling unnesting behavior for correlated subqueries. Just like with view merging, starting in version 10, transformed queries are reviewed by the optimizer, and the costs are evaluated to determine whether an unnested version would be the least costly.

Join Elimination

The transformation for table elimination (alternately called *join elimination*) was introduced in Oracle version 10gR2 and is used to remove redundant tables from a query. A redundant table is defined as a table that has only columns present in the join predicate, and a table in which the joins are guaranteed not to affect the resulting rows by filtering rows out or by adding rows.

The first case when Oracle eliminates a redundant table is when there is a primary key-foreign key constraint. Listing 2-10 shows a very simple query between the employees and departments tables in which the join columns are the primary key and foreign key columns in the two tables.

Listing 2-10. Primary Key–Foreign Key Table Elimination

```
SQL> select e.* from employees e, departments d where
  2  e.department_id = d.department_id;


------------------------------------------------------------------
| Id  | Operation          | Name      | Starts | E-Rows | A-Rows |
------------------------------------------------------------------
|   0 | SELECT STATEMENT   |           |   1    |        |   106  |
|*  1 |   TABLE ACCESS FULL| EMPLOYEES |   1    |  106   |   106  |
------------------------------------------------------------------

Predicate Information (identified by operation id):
-------------------------------------------------------

   1 - filter("E"."DEPARTMENT_ID" IS NOT NULL)
```

Notice how the join to departments is eliminated completely. The elimination can occur because no columns from departments are referenced in the column list and the primary key–foreign key constraint guarantees there is, at most, one match in departments for each row in employees, which is why you see filter ("E"."DEPARTMENT_ID" IS NOT NULL) in the Predicate Information section. This filter must be present to guarantee an equivalent set of resulting rows from the transformed query. The only case when eliminating the table wouldn't be valid would be if the employees table department_id column was null. As we see later, nulls cannot be compared with other values using an equality check. Therefore, to guarantee that the predicate e.department_id = d.department_id is satisfied properly, all nulls have to be removed from consideration. This filter would have been unnecessary if the department_id column had a NOT NULL constraint; but, because it didn't, the filter had to be added to the plan.

The second case when Oracle eliminates a redundant table is in the case of outer joins. Even without any primary key–foreign key constraints, an outer join to a table that does not have any columns present in the column list can be eliminated if the join column in the table to be eliminated has a unique constraint. The example in Listing 2-11 demonstrates this type of table elimination.

Listing 2-11. Outer Join Table Elimination

```
SQL> select e.first_name, e.last_name, e.job_id
  2  from employees e, jobs j
  3  where e.job_id = j.job_id(+) ;


------------------------------------------------------------------
| Id  | Operation          | Name      | Starts | E-Rows | A-Rows |
------------------------------------------------------------------
|   0 | SELECT STATEMENT   |           |   1    |        |   107  |
|   1 |   TABLE ACCESS FULL| EMPLOYEES |   1    |  107   |   107  |
------------------------------------------------------------------
```

The outer join guarantees that every row in employees appears at least once in the result set. There is a unique constraint on jobs.job_id that guarantees that every row in employees matches, at most, one row in jobs. These two properties guarantee that every row in employees appears in the result exactly once.

The two examples here are quite simplistic, and you might be wondering why this transformation is useful because most people would just write the queries without the joins present to begin with. Take a minute to imagine a more complex query, particularly queries that have joins to views that include joins in their source. The way a query uses a view may require only a subset of the columns present in the view. In that case, the joined tables that aren't requested could be eliminated. Just keep in mind that if a table doesn't show up in the execution plan, you are seeing the results of the join elimination transformation. Although you wouldn't have to do so, the original query could be changed to remove the unneeded table for the sake of clarity.

There are a few limitations for this transformation:

- If the join key is referred to elsewhere in the query, join elimination is prevented.

- If the primary key-foreign key constraints have multiple columns, join elimination is not supported.

ORDER BY Elimination

Similar to join elimination, ORDER BY elimination removes unnecessary operations. In this case, the unnecessary operation is a sort. If you include an ORDER BY clause in your SQL statement, the SORT ORDER BY operation is in the execution plan. But, what if the optimizer can deduce that the sorting is unnecessary? How could it do this? Listing 2-12 shows an example in which an ORDER BY clause is unnecessary.

Listing 2-12. ORDER BY Elimination

```
SQL> select count(*) from
  2  (
  3  select d.department_name
  4  from    departments d
  5  where   d.manager_id = 201
  6  order by d.department_name
  7  ) ;
```

```
----------------------------------------------------
| Id  | Operation           | Name        | Rows |
----------------------------------------------------
|   0 | SELECT STATEMENT    |             |      |
|   1 |  SORT AGGREGATE     |             |    1 |
|*  2 |   TABLE ACCESS FULL | DEPARTMENTS |    1 |
----------------------------------------------------

Predicate Information (identified by operation id):
----------------------------------------------------

   2 - filter("D"."MANAGER_ID"=201)
```

```
SQL> select /*+ no_query_transformation */ count(*) from
  2  (
  3  select d.department_name
  4  from    departments d
  5  where   d.manager_id = 201
  6  order by d.department_name
  7  ) ;
```

```
--------------------------------------------------------
| Id  | Operation            | Name        |   Rows |
--------------------------------------------------------
|   0 | SELECT STATEMENT     |             |        |
|   1 |  SORT AGGREGATE      |             |      1 |
|   2 |   VIEW               |             |      1 |
|   3 |    SORT ORDER BY     |             |      1 |
|*  4 |     TABLE ACCESS FULL| DEPARTMENTS |      1 |
--------------------------------------------------------

Predicate Information (identified by operation id):
--------------------------------------------------------

   4 - filter("D"."MANAGER_ID"=201)
```

In the second part of the example, I used the NO_QUERY_TRANSFORMATION hint to stop the optimizer from transforming the query to remove the sort. In this case, you see the SORT ORDER BY operation in the plan whereas in the transformed version there is no sort operation present. The final output of this query is the answer to a COUNT aggregate function. It, by definition, returns just a single row value. There actually is nothing to sort in this case. The optimizer understands this and simply eliminates the ORDER BY to save doing something that doesn't really need to be done.

There are other cases when this type of transformation occurs. The most common one is when the optimizer chooses to use an index on the column in the ORDER BY. Because the index is stored in sorted order, the rows are read in order as they are retrieved and there is no need for a separate sort.

In the end, the reason for this transformation is to simplify the plan to remove unnecessary or redundant work. In doing so, the plan is more efficient and performs better.

Predicate Pushing

Predicate pushing is used to apply the predicates from a containing query block into a nonmergeable query block. The goal is to allow an index to be used or to allow for other filtering of the dataset earlier in the query plan rather than later. In general, it is always a good idea to filter out rows that aren't needed as soon as possible. Always think: Filter early.

A real-life example in which the downside of filtering late is readily apparent when you consider moving to another city. Let's say you are moving from Portland, Oregon, to Jacksonville, Florida. If you hire a moving company to pack and move you—and they charge by the pound—it wouldn't be a very good idea to realize that you really didn't need or want 80% of the stuff that was moved. If you'd just taken the time to check out everything before the movers packed you up in Portland, you could have saved yourself a lot of money!

That's the idea with predicate pushing. If a predicate can be applied earlier by pushing it into a nonmergeable query block, there is less data to carry through the rest of the plan. Less data means less work. Less work means less time. Listing 2-13 shows the difference between when predicate pushing happens and when it doesn't.

Listing 2-13. Predicate Pushing

```
SQL> SELECT e1.last_name, e1.salary, v.avg_salary
  2     FROM employees e1,
  3          (SELECT department_id, avg(salary) avg_salary
  4             FROM employees e2
  5            GROUP BY department_id) v
  6    WHERE e1.department_id = v.department_id
  7      AND e1.salary > v.avg_salary
  8      AND e1.department_id = 60;
```

```
----------------------------------------------------------------------
| Id  | Operation                               | Name            | Rows  |
----------------------------------------------------------------------
|   0 | SELECT STATEMENT                        |                 |       |
|   1 |  NESTED LOOPS                           |                 |       |
|   2 |   NESTED LOOPS                          |                 |     1 |
|   3 |    VIEW                                 |                 |     1 |
|   4 |     HASH GROUP BY                       |                 |     1 |
|   5 |      TABLE ACCESS BY INDEX ROWID BATCHED| EMPLOYEES       |     5 |
|*  6 |       INDEX RANGE SCAN                  | EMP_DEPT_ID_IDX |     5 |
|*  7 |    INDEX RANGE SCAN                     | EMP_DEPT_ID_IDX |     5 |
|*  8 |   TABLE ACCESS BY INDEX ROWID           | EMPLOYEES       |     1 |
----------------------------------------------------------------------
```

Predicate Information (identified by operation id):

```
   6 - access("DEPARTMENT_ID"=60)
   7 - access("E1"."DEPARTMENT_ID"=60)
   8 - filter("E1"."SALARY">"V"."AVG_SALARY")
```

```
SQL> SELECT e1.last_name, e1.salary, v.avg_salary
  2    FROM employees e1,
  3      (SELECT department_id, avg(salary) avg_salary
  4         FROM employees e2
  5        WHERE rownum > 1   -- rownum prohibits predicate pushing!
  6        GROUP BY department_id) v
  7   WHERE e1.department_id = v.department_id
  8     AND e1.salary > v.avg_salary
  9     AND e1.department_id = 60;
```

```
----------------------------------------------------------------------
| Id  | Operation                               | Name            | Rows  |
----------------------------------------------------------------------
|   0 | SELECT STATEMENT                        |                 |       |
|*  1 |  HASH JOIN                              |                 |     3 |
|   2 |   JOIN FILTER CREATE                    | :BF0000         |     5 |
|   3 |    TABLE ACCESS BY INDEX ROWID BATCHED| EMPLOYEES       |     5 |
|*  4 |     INDEX RANGE SCAN                    | EMP_DEPT_ID_IDX |     5 |
|*  5 |   VIEW                                  |                 |    11 |
|   6 |    HASH GROUP BY                        |                 |    11 |
|   7 |     JOIN FILTER USE                     | :BF0000         |   107 |
|   8 |      COUNT                              |                 |       |
|*  9 |       FILTER                            |                 |       |
|  10 |        TABLE ACCESS FULL                | EMPLOYEES       |   107 |
----------------------------------------------------------------------
```

```
Predicate Information (identified by operation id):
---------------------------------------------------

   1 - access("E1"."DEPARTMENT_ID"="V"."DEPARTMENT_ID")
       filter("E1"."SALARY">"V"."AVG_SALARY")
   4 - access("E1"."DEPARTMENT_ID"=60)
   5 - filter("V"."DEPARTMENT_ID"=60)
   9 - filter(ROWNUM>1)
```

Notice step 6 of the first plan. The `WHERE department_id = 60` predicate was pushed into the view, allowing the average salary to be determined for one department only. When the predicate is not pushed, as shown in the second plan, the average salary must be computed for every department. Then, when the outer query block and inner query blocks are joined, all the rows that are not `department_id` 60 get thrown away. You can tell from the Rows estimates of the second plan that the optimizer realizes that having to wait to apply the predicate requires more work and therefore is a more expensive and time-consuming operation.

I used a little trick to stop predicate pushing in this example that I want to point out. The use of the `rownum` pseudocolumn in the second query (I added the predicate `WHERE rownum > 1`) acted to prohibit predicate pushing. As a matter of fact, `rownum` not only prohibits predicate pushing, but also it prohibits view merging as well. Using `rownum` is like adding the `NO_MERGE` and `NO_PUSH_PRED` hints to the query. In this case, it allowed me to point out the ill effects that occur when predicate pushing doesn't happen, but I also want to make sure you realize that using `rownum` affects the choices the optimizer has available when determining the execution plan. Be careful when you use `rownum`; it makes any query block in which it appears both nonmergeable and unable to have predicates pushed into it.

Other than through the use of `rownum` or a `NO_PUSH_PRED` hint, predicate pushing happens without any special action on your part—and that's just what you want! Although there may be a few corner cases when predicate pushing might be less advantageous, these cases are few and far between. So, make sure to check execution plans to ensure predicate pushing happens as expected.

Query Rewrite with Materialized Views

Query rewrite is a transformation that occurs when a query, or a portion of a query, has been saved as a materialized view and the transformer can rewrite the query to use the precomputed materialized view data instead of executing the current query. A materialized view is like a normal view except that the query has been executed and its result set has been stored in a table. What this does is to precompute the result of the query and make it available whenever the specific query is executed. This means that all the work to determine the plan, execute it, and gather all the data has already been done. So, when the same query is executed again, there is no need to go through all that effort again.

The query transformer matches a query with available materialized views and then rewrites the query simply to select from the materialized result set. Listing 2-14 walks you through creating a materialized view and shows how the transformer rewrites the query to use the materialized view result set.

Listing 2-14. Query Rewrite with Materialized Views

```
SQL> SELECT p.prod_id, p.prod_name, t.time_id, t.week_ending_day,
  2          s.channel_id, s.promo_id, s.cust_id, s.amount_sold
  3   FROM   sales s, products p, times t
  4   WHERE  s.time_id=t.time_id  AND s.prod_id = p.prod_id;
```

```
-------------------------------------------------------------
| Id  | Operation             | Name     | Rows  | Pstart| Pstop |
-------------------------------------------------------------
|   0 | SELECT STATEMENT      |          |  918K |       |       |
|*  1 |  HASH JOIN            |          |  918K |       |       |
|   2 |   TABLE ACCESS FULL   | TIMES    |  1826 |       |       |
|*  3 |   HASH JOIN           |          |  918K |       |       |
|   4 |    TABLE ACCESS FULL  | PRODUCTS |    72 |       |       |
|   5 |    PARTITION RANGE ALL|          |  918K |     1 |    28 |
|   6 |     TABLE ACCESS FULL | SALES    |  918K |     1 |    28 |
-------------------------------------------------------------

Predicate Information (identified by operation id):
---------------------------------------------------

   1 - access("S"."TIME_ID"="T"."TIME_ID")
   3 - access("S"."PROD_ID"="P"."PROD_ID")

SQL>
SQL> CREATE MATERIALIZED VIEW sales_time_product_mv
  2  ENABLE QUERY REWRITE AS
  3  SELECT p.prod_id, p.prod_name, t.time_id, t.week_ending_day,
  4         s.channel_id, s.promo_id, s.cust_id, s.amount_sold
  5  FROM   sales s, products p, times t
  6  WHERE  s.time_id=t.time_id  AND s.prod_id = p.prod_id;
SQL>
SQL> SELECT p.prod_id, p.prod_name, t.time_id, t.week_ending_day,
  2         s.channel_id, s.promo_id, s.cust_id, s.amount_sold
  3  FROM   sales s, products p, times t
  4  WHERE  s.time_id=t.time_id  AND s.prod_id = p.prod_id;
```

```
-------------------------------------------------------------
| Id  | Operation             | Name     | Rows  | Pstart| Pstop |
-------------------------------------------------------------
|   0 | SELECT STATEMENT      |          |  918K |       |       |
|*  1 |  HASH JOIN            |          |  918K |       |       |
|   2 |   TABLE ACCESS FULL   | TIMES    |  1826 |       |       |
|*  3 |   HASH JOIN           |          |  918K |       |       |
|   4 |    TABLE ACCESS FULL  | PRODUCTS |    72 |       |       |
|   5 |    PARTITION RANGE ALL|          |  918K |     1 |    28 |
|   6 |     TABLE ACCESS FULL | SALES    |  918K |     1 |    28 |
-------------------------------------------------------------

Predicate Information (identified by operation id):
---------------------------------------------------

   1 - access("S"."TIME_ID"="T"."TIME_ID")
   3 - access("S"."PROD_ID"="P"."PROD_ID")
```

```
SQL>
SQL> SELECT /*+ rewrite(sales_time_product_mv) */
  2        p.prod_id, p.prod_name, t.time_id, t.week_ending_day,
  3          s.channel_id, s.promo_id, s.cust_id, s.amount_sold
  4  FROM   sales s, products p, times t
  5  WHERE  s.time_id=t.time_id  AND s.prod_id = p.prod_id;
```

```
---------------------------------------------------------------------
| Id | Operation                  | Name                 | Rows  |
---------------------------------------------------------------------
|  0 | SELECT STATEMENT           |                      | 909K|
|  1 |  MAT_VIEW REWRITE ACCESS FULL| SALES_TIME_PRODUCT_MV |  909K|
---------------------------------------------------------------------
```

To keep the example simple, I used a REWRITE hint to turn on the query rewrite transformation. You can enable query rewrite to happen automatically, and, actually, it is enabled by default using the query_rewrite_enabled parameter. But as you notice in the example, when the rewrite does occur, the plan simply shows a full access on the materialized view instead of the entire set of operations required to produce the result set originally. As you can imagine, the time savings can be substantial for complicated queries with large results sets, particularly if the query contains aggregations. For more information on query rewrite and materialized views, refer to the *Oracle Data Warehousing Guide, (http://www.oracle.com/technetwork/indexes/documentation/index.html)* in which you'll find an entire chapter on advanced query rewrite.

Determining the Execution Plan

When a hard parse occurs, Oracle determines which execution plan is best for the query. An execution plan is simply the set of steps that Oracle takes to access the objects used by your query, and it returns the data that satisfy your query's question. To determine the plan, Oracle gathers and uses a lot of information, as you've already seen. One of the key pieces of information that Oracle uses to determine the plan is statistics. Statistics can be gathered on objects, such as tables and indexes; system statistics can be gathered as well. System statistics provide Oracle data about average speeds for block reads and much more. All this information is used to help Oracle review different scenarios for how a query could execute, and to determine which of these scenarios is likely to result in the best performance.

Understanding how Oracle determines execution plans not only helps you write better SQL, but also helps you to understand how and why performance is affected by certain execution plan choices. After Oracle verifies the syntax and permissions for a SQL statement, it uses the statistics information it collects from the data dictionary to compute a *cost* for each operation and combination of operations that could be used to get the result set your query needs. Cost is an internal value Oracle uses to compare different plan operations for the same query with each other, with the lowest cost option considered to be the best. For example, a statement could be executed using a full table scan or an index. Using the statistics, parameters, and other information, Oracle determines which method results in the fastest execution time.

Because Oracle's main goal in determining an execution plan is to choose a set of operations that results in the fastest response time possible for the SQL statement being parsed, the more accurate the statistics, the more likely Oracle is to compute the best execution plan. In the chapters ahead, I provide details about the various access methods and join methods available, and how to review execution plans in detail. For now, I want to make sure you understand what statistics are, why they're important, and how to review them for yourself.

The optimizer is the code path within the Oracle kernel that is responsible for determining the optimal execution plan for a query. So, when I talk about statistics, I'm talking about how the optimizer uses statistics. I use the script named st-all.sql to display statistics for the employees table, as shown in Listing 2-15. I refer to this information to discuss how statistics are used by the optimizer.

Listing 2-15. Statistics for the employees Table

```
SQL> @st-all
Enter the owner name: hr
Enter the table name: employees
=========================================================================
  TABLE STATISTICS
=========================================================================
Owner         : hr
Table name    : employees
Tablespace    : example
Partitioned   : no
Last analyzed : 05/26/2013 14:12:28
Degree        : 1
# Rows        : 107
# Blocks      : 5
Empty Blocks  : 0
Avg Space     : 0
Avg Row Length: 68
Monitoring?   : yes
Status        : valid


=========================================================================
  COLUMN STATISTICS
=========================================================================
Name             Null?  NDV  # Nulls  # Bkts  AvLn  Lo-Hi Values
=========================================================================
commission_pct   Y      7    72       1       2     .1 | .4
department_id    Y      11   1        11      3     10 | 110
email            N      107  0        1       8     ABANDA | WTAYLOR
employee_id      N      107  0        1       4     100 | 206
first_name       Y      91   0        1       7     Adam | Winston
hire_date        N      98   0        1       8     06/17/1987 | 04/21/2000
job_id           N      19   0        19      9     AC_ACCOUNT | ST_MAN
last_name        N      102  0        1       8     Abel | Zlotkey
manager_id       Y      18   1        18      4     100 | 205
phone_number     Y      107  0        1       15    214.343.3292 |650.509.4876
salary           Y      57   0        1       4     2100 | 24000


=========================================================================
  INDEX INFORMATION
=========================================================================

Index Name        BLevel Lf Blks #Rows Dist Keys LB/Key DB/Key ClstFctr Uniq?
----------------- ------ ------- ----- --------- ------ ------ -------- -----
EMP_DEPARTMENT_IX   0      1     106       11       1      1        7 NO
EMP_EMAIL_UK        0      1     107      107       1      1       19 YES
EMP_EMP_ID_PK       0      1     107      107       1      1        2 YES
EMP_JOB_IX          0      1     107       19       1      1        8 NO
EMP_MANAGER_IX      0      1     106       18       1      1        7 NO
EMP_NAME_IX         0      1     107      107       1      1       15 NO
```

Index Name	Pos#	Order	Column Name
emp_department_ix	1	ASC	department_id
emp_email_uk	1	ASC	email
emp_emp_id_pk	1	ASC	employee_id
emp_job_ix	1	ASC	job_id
emp_manager_ix	1	ASC	manager_id
emp_name_ix	1	ASC	last_name

The first set of statistics shown in Listing 2-15 is table statistics. These values can be queried from the all_tables view (or dba_tables or user_tables as well). The next section lists column statistics and can be queried from the all_tab_cols view. The final section lists index statistics and can be queried from the all_indexes and all_ind_columns views.

Just like statistics in baseball, the statistics the optimizer uses are intended to be predictive. For example, if a baseball player has a batting average of .333, you'd expect that he'd get a hit about one out of every three times. This won't always be true, but it is an indicator on which most people rely. Likewise, the optimizer relies on the num_distinct column statistic to compute how frequently values within a column occur. By default, the assumption is that any value occurs in the same proportion as any other value. If you look at the num_distinct statistic for a column named color and it is set to 10, it means that the optimizer is going to expect there to be 10 possible colors and that each color would be present in one tenth of the total rows of the table.

So, let's say that the optimizer was parsing the following query:

```
select * from widgets where color = 'BLUE'
```

The optimizer could choose to read the entire table (TABLE ACCESS FULL operation) or it could choose to use an index (TABLE ACCESS BY INDEX ROWID). But how does it decide which one is best? It uses statistics. I'm just going to use two statistics for this example. I'll use the statistic that indicates the number of rows in the widgets table (num_rows = 1000) and the statistic that indicates how many distinct values are in the color column (num_distinct = 10). The math is quite simple in this case:

```
Number of rows query should return =  (1 / num_distinct) x num_rows
    = (1 / 10) x 1000
    = 100
```

If you think about it for a second, it makes perfect sense. If there are 1000 rows in the table and there are 10 distinct colors present in the table, then if your query only wants rows in which the color is blue, you'll be asking for only one tenth of the data, or 100 rows. This computed value is called *selectivity*. By dividing the number of distinct values into one, you determine how selective any single value is. Easy, right?

Well, as you can imagine, the computations do get more complex, but I hope this simple example helps you see how the optimizer is doing nothing more than some fairly straightforward calculations. No rocket science—really! But, as you can see, even something so simple can be dramatically affected if the values used aren't accurate.

What if, at the time the optimizer parsed this query, the statistics were out of date or missing? For example, let's say that instead of indicating there were 1000 rows and 10 colors, the statistics showed 100 rows in the table and one color. Using these values, the number of rows the query should return would be computed to be 100 (1 / 1 x 100). The number of rows is the same as our original computation, but is it really the same? No, it's very different. In the case of the first calculation, the optimizer would have assumed 10 percent of 1000 rows were returned whereas, in the second case, the 100 rows returned represent all the rows in the table (at least according to the statistics). Can you see how this would influence the optimizer's decision about which operation to choose to retrieve the data?

Understanding the importance of statistics helps you know how to identify performance problems that are not necessarily related to the way you wrote the SQL, but instead are rooted in issues with the statistics. You could have done everything right, but if the statistics are wrong or inaccurate enough that they don't reflect the reality of your data, you need to be able to pinpoint that quickly and not spend hours or days trying to fix a code problem that isn't really a code problem.

However, just to keep you from getting too happy that you've now got a way to point the finger of blame away from yourself, let me show you an example of how you can write SQL in such a way that the optimizer can't use the statistics properly. In this case, you write a very simple query as follows:

```
select * from car_purchases where manufacturer = 'Ford' and make = 'Focus'
```

The query uses a table containing information about car purchases for all American-model cars. For the sake of this example, let's assert that each make of car is produced only by one manufacturer, which means that only Ford has a Focus. So, what's the problem with the way this query is written? It certainly returns the correct result set, but that's not the only question that needs to be answered. You also need to determine whether the optimizer is able to understand the data accurately given this query formulation. So, let's look at the statistics:

```
num_rows (car_purchases):  1,000,000
num_distinct (manufacturer): 4
num_distinct (make):   1000
```

Because there are two different conditions (or predicates) to apply, you first need to figure out the selectivities of each one by itself. The selectivity of manufacturer would be 1/4 or .25. The selectivity of make would be 1/1000 or .001. Because the predicates are combined with AND, the two selectivities are multiplied together to get the correct overall selectivity for both combined. So, the final selectivity is .00025 (.25 × .001), which means the optimizer determines that the query returns 250 rows (.00025 × 1,000,000).

Remember that I began this example by asserting that only one manufacturer would produce a certain make of car. This means that, because none of the other three manufacturers could have possibly produced a Focus, the calculation that includes the selectivity for manufacturer is flawed. The truth is that we know all Focus-model vehicles have to be manufactured by Ford. Including the condition where manufacturer = 'Ford' reduces the overall selectivity by 25 percent. In this case, the true selectivity should have been only the selectivity for the model column alone. If just that predicate had been written, then the selectivity would have been 1/1000 or .001, and the optimizer would have computed that 1000 rows would be returned by the query instead of 250. This means the answer the optimizer comes up with is "off" by a factor of four. You may look at the difference between 250 and 1000 and think, "So what's the big deal? That's not that far off, is it?" Let's go back to the baseball example and apply this same logic to see if it stands out more to you. If a player normally has a .333 average and you were to tack on another meaningless condition that would require you to multiply his average by .25 as well, what happens? All of a sudden, the high-paid professional athlete looks like a sandlot wanna-be with an average of .083 (.333 × .25)!

Numbers can change everything—and not just in baseball. The calculations the optimizer makes affects drastically the choice of execution plan operations. These choices can make the difference between response times of a few seconds to response times of several hours. In this particular example, you get to see what happens when the optimizer doesn't know something that you do. All the optimizer can do is to plug in the statistics and come up with an answer. If you know something about your data that the optimizer can't know, make sure you code your SQL accordingly and don't lead the optimizer astray.

Executing the Plan and Fetching Rows

After the optimizer determines the plan and stores it in the library cache for later reuse, the next step is actually to execute the plan and fetch the rows of data that satisfy your query. I'm going to cover much more on plan operations and how to read and understand execution plan output in the chapters ahead, but for now, let's talk about what happens after the plan is chosen.

An execution plan is just a set of instructions that tell Oracle which access method to use for each table object, and which order and join method to use to join multiple table objects together. Each step in the plan produces a row source that is then joined with another row source until all objects have been accessed and joined. As rows are retrieved that satisfy the query, they must be returned from the database to the application. For result sets of any size, the rows that need to be returned are very likely not all passed to the application in a single round-trip. Packets of data are transmitted from the database and across the network until all rows ultimately arrive back to the user/requestor.

When you execute a query, what appears to you to be a single response consisting of the rows that satisfy your query is really a series of calls executed independently. Your query completes PARSE, BIND, EXEC, and FETCH steps. One or more FETCH calls occurs for a query that each return a portion of the rows that satisfy the query. Figure 2-2 shows the steps that actually occur "under the covers" when a SELECT statement is executed.

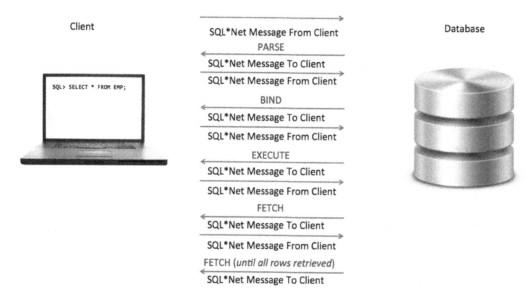

Figure 2-2. *"Under the covers" of a SELECT statement execution*

The network round-trip between the client and the database for each call contributes to the overall response time of the statement. There is only one of each type of database call except for FETCH. As mentioned previously, Oracle needs to execute as many FETCH calls as necessary to retrieve and return all the rows required to satisfy your query.

A single FETCH call accesses one or more blocks of data from the buffer cache. Each time a block is accessed, Oracle takes rows from the block and returns them to the client in one round-trip. The number of rows that are returned is a configurable setting called arraysize. The arraysize is the number of rows to be transmitted in a single network round-trip, if possible. If the size of the rows is too large to fit in a single packet, Oracle breaks up the rows into multiple packets, but even then, only a single FETCH call is needed to provide the specified number of rows.

The arraysize setting is set programmatically; how it is accomplished depends on which calling application environment you use. In SQL*Plus, in which the default arraysize is 15, you change the arraysize setting using the command SET ARRAYSIZE n. The JDBC default is ten and may be changed using ((OracleConnection)conn).setDefaultRowPrefetch (n). Make sure to discover your application's arraysize setting and increase it as necessary. The benefit to having a larger arraysize is twofold: reduction of FETCH calls and reduction of network round-trips. It may not seem like much, but the impact can be quite stunning. Listing 2-16 demonstrates how logical reads for the same query are reduced simply by changing arraysize. Note that logical reads are labeled as *buffers* in the autotrace output.

Listing 2-16. How the arraysize Setting Affects Logical Reads

```
SQL> set arraysize 15
SQL>
SQL> set autotrace traceonly statistics
SQL>
SQL> select * from order_items ;
Statistics
----------------------------------------------------------
          0  recursive calls
          0  db block gets
         52  consistent gets
          0  physical reads
          0  redo size
      18815  bytes sent via SQL*Net to client
        865  bytes received via SQL*Net from client
         46  SQL*Net roundtrips to/from client
          0  sorts (memory)
          0  sorts (disk)
        664  rows processed

SQL>
SQL> set arraysize 45
SQL> /

Statistics
----------------------------------------------------------
          0  recursive calls
          0  db block gets
         22  consistent gets
          0  physical reads
          0  redo size
      15026  bytes sent via SQL*Net to client
        535  bytes received via SQL*Net from client
         16  SQL*Net roundtrips to/from client
          0  sorts (memory)
          0  sorts (disk)
        664  rows processed
```

Even for this small result set of 664 rows, the difference that increasing the arraysize setting produces is clearly visible. I increased the setting from 15 to 45, reduced the logical reads from 52 to 22, and reduced the number of network round-trips from 46 to 16! This change had nothing to do with the SQL statement and everything to do with how Oracle was able to access and return the rows. This is just one more example of how understanding how things work can help you to help Oracle use less resources and time to do what you ask of it.

SQL Execution: Putting It All Together

Now that I've covered the details, I'm ready to put together the whole picture of how a SQL statement executes. Figure 2-3 shows the steps that are involved when a SQL statement executes.

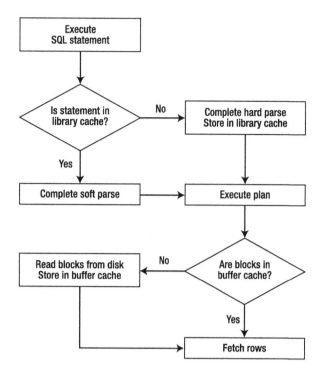

Figure 2-3. *Overview of steps that occur when a SQL statement is executed*

This is a simplified view, but it encapsulates the view of the process. From a big-picture perspective, every query must complete PARSE, EXECUTE, and FETCH steps. Data Manipulation Language (DML) statements (INSERT, UPDATE, DELETE) only need to parse and execute. In addition to these steps, statements that use bind variables also include a step to read the bind values as part of the parse component.

Summary

Understanding how SQL executes enables you to write it more effectively. The optimizer is at the heart of every SQL statement you write; writing SQL with the optimizer in mind helps you more than you can imagine. On this point, I'll ask you to trust me for now. I can assure you that understanding the optimizer has been one of the most beneficial pieces of knowledge I've gained, so don't get frustrated if you're just itching to start looking at syntax and specific SQL code. What you end up with by the end of this journey is well worth it.

At this point, I hope you feel more comfortable with at least some of the key parts of Oracle's architecture that are involved in the execution of the SQL you send to the database. You should also have a flavor for the power of statistics and how they are used by the optimizer. It is outside the scope of this book to go into more detail about this topic, but I highly recommend picking up Jonathan Lewis's *Cost-Based Oracle Fundamentals* (Apress 2006) if you really want to take a deep dive into this subject matter. The more you know, the better equipped you'll be to write SQL that works with the optimizer and not against it.

In the next chapter, I cover the access and join methods the optimizer can choose, and review numerous examples of how and why the optimizer does what it does. What I've covered so far has built the foundation for what I cover next, and each chapter continues to add to this foundation. The goal is to shed some light on the black box into which you've been throwing SQL and to help you develop an enriched perspective on the importance of what's under the covers of Oracle—in particular, the optimizer—and how to interact properly with it.

CHAPTER 3

■ ■ ■

Access and Join Methods

The optimizer must determine how to access the data your SQL statements require. You formulate your statement and the optimizer, during a hard parse, figures out which operations should provide the data in the most effective way possible. Using statistics as the primary guide, the optimizer computes the cost of the possible alternatives first to access data and then to join multiple tables to get the final result set. The more you understand the different access and join methods the optimizer considers, the more likely you are to formulate your SQL to help the optimizer make the best choices. And, when the operation chosen by the optimizer doesn't provide the performance you need, you can determine more accurately which operations would be more suited to produce the response times you want.

After your SQL statement's expressions and conditions are evaluated and any query transformation that might help it develop the execution plan more clearly are complete, the next step in developing the execution plan is for the optimizer to determine which method of accessing the data is best. In general, there are only two basic ways to access data: either via a full scan or an index scan. During a full scan (which, by the way, can be a full table scan or a fast full index scan), multiple blocks are read in a single input/output (IO) operation. Index scans first scan index leaf blocks to retrieve specific rowids and then hand those rowids to the parent table access step to retrieve the actual row data. These accesses are performed via single-block reads. If there are additional filters that need to be applied to the data after the table access step, the rows pass through that filter before being included in the final result set from that step.

The access method that is chosen for a table is used to determine the join methods and join orders that are used in the final plan. So, if the access method chosen for a table is suboptimal, the likelihood that the whole plan is faulty is high. As discussed in Chapter 2, statistics play a vital role in how accurate the optimizer is in determining the best method. Along with representative statistics, the optimizer uses your query to figure out how much data you are requesting and which access method provides that data as quickly as possible. Each table in the query is first evaluated independently from the others to determine its optimal access path. In the next sections, I review each of the access methods in detail.

Full Scan Access Methods

When full scanning an object, all the blocks associated with that object must be retrieved and processed to determine whether rows in a block match your query's needs. Remember that Oracle must read an entire block into memory to get to the row data stored in that block. So, when a full scan occurs, there are actually two things the optimizer—and you—need to consider: How many blocks must be read and how much data in each block is to be thrown away? The idea I want you to grab on to at this point is that the decision regarding whether a full scan is the right choice isn't based simply on how many rows your query returns. There have been many rules of thumb published that state things like: If your query retrieves more than *x* percent of rows from the table, then a full scan should be chosen. There's more to the decision than just that ROT (rule of thumb = ROT), and I don't want you to get stuck on a rule that limits the consideration that should be given to the choice.

I'm not saying the theory behind the rule of thumb doesn't make logical sense; I'm just saying that it isn't everything that must be considered. In a case when the query returns a very high percentage of rows, the likelihood that a full scan should be used is certainly high, but the trouble with a generalized rule is that the percentage of rows chosen is somewhat arbitrary. Throughout the years, I've seen this rule published in various books, articles, and forums with percentages varying from 20 percent to 70 percent. Why should it change?

How Full Scan Operations Are Chosen

At this point, now that I've briefly discussed the problem with generalizing how full table scans are chosen, I can continue with the rest of the story. It's not just about rows; it's also about blocks and about throwaway. The combination of all these pieces of information may lead to a conclusion that it makes sense to do a full scan even when the percentage of rows is quite small. On the other hand, a full scan may not be chosen even when a large percentage of the rows is returned. Let's walk through an example in Listing 3-1 that shows how even when a small percentage of rows satisfies the query, the optimizer may choose a full table scan plan. First, two tables are created that contain the exact same 10,000 rows. Next, the execution plans for the same query against each table are shown. Notice how even though the query returns 100 rows (only 1 percent of the total data), a full scan plan can be chosen.

Listing 3-1. Creating Two Test Tables

```
SQL> create table t1 as
  2  select  trunc((rownum-1)/100) id,
  3          rpad(rownum,100) t_pad
  4  from    dba_source
  5  where   rownum <= 10000;

Table created.

SQL> create index t1_idx1 on t1(id);

Index created.

SQL> exec dbms_stats.gather_table_stats(user,'t1',method_opt=>'FOR ALL COLUMNS SIZE
1',cascade=>TRUE);

PL/SQL procedure successfully completed.

SQL> create table t2 as
  2  select  mod(rownum,100) id,
  3          rpad(rownum,100) t_pad
  4  from    dba_source
  5  where   rownum <= 10000;

Table created.

SQL> create index t2_idx1 on t2(id);

Index created.

SQL> exec dbms_stats.gather_table_stats(user,'t2',method_opt=>'FOR ALL COLUMNS SIZE
1',cascade=>TRUE);

PL/SQL procedure successfully completed.
```

Both tables have 10,000 rows. The id columns in both tables have 100 rows for each value between zero and 99. So, in terms of the data content, the tables are identical. However, notice that for t1, the id column is populated using the expression trunc((rownum-1)/100), whereas for t2, the id column is populated using mod(rownum,100). Figure 3-1 shows how the rows might be stored physically in the table's data blocks.

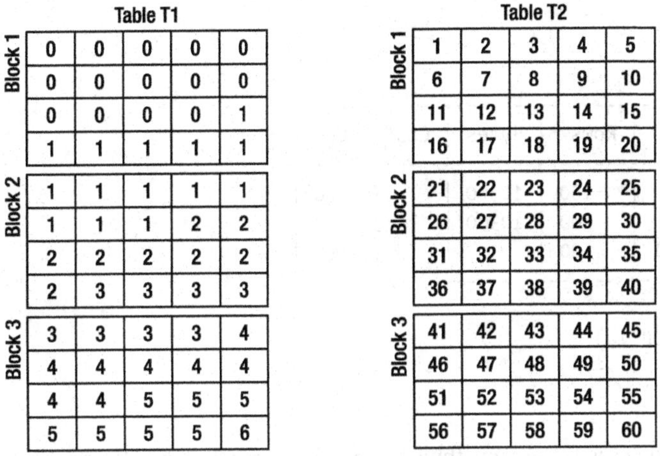

Table T1

Block 1				
0	0	0	0	0
0	0	0	0	0
0	0	0	0	1
1	1	1	1	1

Block 2				
1	1	1	1	1
1	1	1	2	2
2	2	2	2	2
2	3	3	3	3

Block 3				
3	3	3	3	4
4	4	4	4	4
4	4	5	5	5
5	5	5	5	6

Table T2

Block 1				
1	2	3	4	5
6	7	8	9	10
11	12	13	14	15
16	17	18	19	20

Block 2				
21	22	23	24	25
26	27	28	29	30
31	32	33	34	35
36	37	38	39	40

Block 3				
41	42	43	44	45
46	47	48	49	50
51	52	53	54	55
56	57	58	59	60

Figure 3-1. *Diagram of random vs. sequentially stored row values*

Given what we just inserted, we expect to get a result set of 100 rows if we execute a query for any single value of either table. We know how many rows we should get because we just created the tables. But, how can we get an idea of what the tables contain and how those rows are stored otherwise? One way is to run a query and use the COUNT aggregate function, as shown in Listing 3-2.

Listing 3-2. count(*) Queries against Tables t1 and t2

```
SQL> select count(*) ct from t1 where id = 1 ;

            CT
---------------
           100

1 row selected.

SQL> select count(*) ct from t2 where id = 1 ;

            CT
---------------
           100

1 row selected.
```

Notice that, as expected, we get 100 rows from both tables. If it is reasonable to query actual data to determine the result set sizes, this is a great way to know what to expect from your query. For each table involved in the query you write, you can execute individual queries that apply the predicates for that table and that count the number of rows returned, which helps you estimate which access method is best suited for your final query. But, knowing row counts is only part of the information you need. Now you need to go back to how the data are stored.

Of 10,000 total rows in each table, if you query for a single value (where id = 1), you know you'll get back 100 rows. That's just 1 percent of the total rows. Given that small percentage, you'd also then likely expect the optimizer to choose to use the index on id to access those rows, right? This certainly seems like a logical conclusion, but here is where knowing how your data are stored comes in. If your data are stored sequentially, with most of the rows where id = 1 stored physically in just a few blocks, as is the case with table t1, this conclusion is correct, as shown in the explain plan in Listing 3-3.

Listing 3-3. Explain Plan for Query against t1

```
-------------------------------------------------------------------------
| Id  | Operation                   | Name    | Rows  | Bytes | Cost (%CPU)|
-------------------------------------------------------------------------
|   0 | SELECT STATEMENT            |         |   100 | 10300 |     3   (0)|
|   1 |  TABLE ACCESS BY INDEX ROWID| T1      |   100 | 10300 |     3   (0)|
|*  2 |   INDEX RANGE SCAN          | T1_IDX1 |   100 |       |     1   (0)|
-------------------------------------------------------------------------

Predicate Information (identified by operation id):
---------------------------------------------------

   2 - access("ID"=1)
```

So, wouldn't you expect the query against t2 to do exactly the same thing because it returns the same 100 rows? As you can see from the explain plan shown in Listing 3-4, this is not the case at all.

Listing 3-4. Explain Plan for Query against t2

```
----------------------------------------------------------------
| Id  | Operation          | Name | Rows  | Bytes | Cost (%CPU)|
----------------------------------------------------------------
|   0 | SELECT STATEMENT   |      |   100 | 10300 |    39   (3)|
|*  1 |  TABLE ACCESS FULL | T2   |   100 | 10300 |    39   (3)|
----------------------------------------------------------------

Predicate Information (identified by operation id):
---------------------------------------------------

   1 - filter("ID"=1)
```

Why didn't the optimizer make the same plan choice for both queries? It's because of *how* the data are stored in each table. The query against table t1 requires that Oracle access only a few blocks to get the 100 rows needed to satisfy the query. Therefore, the index scan costs out to be the most attractive option. But, the query against table t2 ends up having to read practically every block in the table to get the same 100 rows because the rows are scattered physically throughout all the table blocks. The optimizer calculates that the time to read every block in the table using an index is likely more than just reading all the blocks in the table using a full table scan and simply throwing away rows that aren't needed from each block. Retrieving the rows from an index requires approximately 200 block accesses. I discuss why it's 200 in the next section, when I cover index scans. So, the query against t2 uses a TABLE ACCESS FULL operation instead of an index.

This demonstration shows you that there can be differences in the optimizer's plan choices based on how the data are stored. Although knowing this may not necessarily make a difference in how you end up writing a query, it can make a difference in how you determine whether the performance of the query meets your Service Level Agreements (SLA). If you keep seeing a full table scan plan operation, you may think you need to change or add a hint to your query to force the use of the index; however, doing so might make performance worse in the long term. If you don't understand how the data are stored, you may make poor decisions about what should happen when your query executes.

■ **Note** The demonstration in this section of how a full table scan is chosen is based on behavior exhibited by Oracle version 11gR2 and earlier. Improvements to the optimizer in Oracle version 12c allow both plans to use the index.

Full Scans and Throwaway

Always remember that whether a full scan is an effective choice depends on the number of blocks that need to be read as much as on how many rows end up in the final result set. Again, how the data are stored plays an important role in the decision, as demonstrated in the earlier example. However, the other key factor in whether a full scan is an effective choice is *throwaway*. Throwaway rows are those rows that are checked against a filter predicate and don't match the filter, and thus are rejected from the final result set.

In the previous example, the full table scan operation would have to check all 10,000 rows in the table and throw away 9900 of them to end up with the final result set of 100 rows. The check on each row is simply the filter predicate on id = 1 (seen in Listing 3-4 in the Predicate Information section for step 1). To execute this filter, the CPU is used for each check, which means that, although the number of blocks accessed is limited, there are quite a bit of CPU resources used to complete the filter checks for each row. The use of the CPU is factored into the cost of the full scan.

As the number of blocks accessed and the amount of throwaway increases, the more costly the full scan becomes. Listing 3-5 is a simple query to show the number of rows and number of blocks for table t2 in our example. Based on the number of blocks shown, the full table scan accesses approximately 164 blocks.

Listing 3-5. Rows and Blocks Statistics for Tables t1 and t2

```
SQL> select table_name, num_rows, blocks from user_tables where table_name = 'T2' ;

TABLE_NAME                                   NUM_ROWS         BLOCKS
-----------------------------   ---------------   ---------------
T2                                              10000            164

1 rows selected.
```

Over time, as rows are added to the table and the table grows larger, the cost of throwing away so many rows increases enough to cause the optimizer to switch to an index scan operation instead. The point when the optimizer decides to switch over may not necessarily be the point where you achieve optimal performance. You can use hints to force the optimizer to use an index, and to test to determine at what point it might make more sense to use an index. If the optimizer doesn't choose that path, you can consider using hints or SQL profiles to help. Chapters 16 and 17 covers using hints and profiles so you are prepared to use them if you ever need to do so.

Full Scans and Multiblock Reads

Another thing you need to know about full scans is how blocks are read. A full scan operation makes multiblock reads, which means that a single IO call requests several blocks instead of just one. The number of blocks requested varies and can actually range anywhere from one to the number of blocks specified in the db_file_multiblock_read_count parameter. For example, if the parameter is set to 16 and there are 160 blocks in the table, there could be only 10 calls made to get all the blocks.

I say that only 10 calls *could* be made because of the following limitations on multiblock read calls. Oracle reads db_file_multiblock_read_count blocks unless reading the full number of blocks

- causes Oracle to have to read blocks that cross an extent boundary. In this case, Oracle reads the blocks up to the extent boundary in one call, then issues another call to read the remainder.

- means a block already in the buffer cache would be read again as part of the multiblock read. Oracle simply reads the blocks up to those not already in memory, then issues another read call that skips those blocks to read the rest. This could mean that a multiblock read might be truncated to a single-block read because of the blocks that are already in the buffer cache. For example, let's say the multiblock read count is 16 and the range of blocks to be read is between block numbers 1 and 16. If the even-numbered blocks are already placed in the buffer cache, individual single-block reads are done for each odd-numbered block in that range. In this case, eight read calls are made—one for each block in the range not already in the buffer cache.

- would exceed an operating system limit for multiblock read sizes. The size of a multiblock read depends on your operating system, so it can vary.

Full Scans and the High-Water Mark

A final point of note regarding full table scans is that, as the multiblock read calls for the scan are made, Oracle reads blocks up to the high-water mark in the table. The high-water mark is the last block in the table that has ever had data written to it. To be technically correct, it is actually called the *low high-water mark*. For our purposes, the low high-water mark is what I discuss, and I refer to it generically as the high-water mark. For a more detailed discussion, please see the Oracle documentation.

When rows are inserted into a table, blocks are allocated and the rows are placed in the blocks. Figure 3-2 shows how a table might look after a large insert to populate the table.

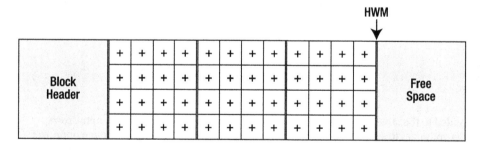

Figure 3-2. *Blocks allocated to a table with rows indicated with a +. HWM, high-water mark*

Throughout the course of normal operations, rows are deleted from the blocks. Figure 3-3 shows how the table might look after a large number of rows have been deleted from the table.

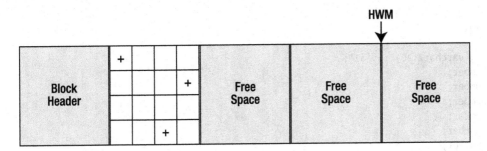

Figure 3-3. *The blocks after rows have been deleted. The high-water mark (HWM) remains unchanged*

Even though almost all the rows have been deleted and some blocks have actually become completely unused, the high-water mark remains the same. When a full scan operation occurs, all blocks up to the high-water mark are read in and scanned, even if they are empty, which means that many blocks that don't need to be read because they are empty are still read. Listing 3-6 shows an example of how the high-water mark doesn't change, even if all the rows in the table are deleted.

Listing 3-6. High-water Mark

```
SQL> -- List number of allocated blocks (table has 800,000 rows)
SQL> -- The highwater mark is the last block containing data.
SQL> -- While this query doesn't specifically show the HWM, it gives you an idea.
SQL>
SQL> select blocks from user_segments where segment_name = 'T2';

      BLOCKS
---------------
       12288

1 row selected.

SQL> -- List how many blocks contain data
SQL>
SQL> select count(distinct (dbms_rowid.rowid_block_number(rowid))) block_ct from t2 ;

     BLOCK_CT
---------------
       12122

1 row selected.

SQL> -- List the lowest and highest block numbers for this table
SQL>
SQL> select min(dbms_rowid.rowid_block_number(rowid)) min_blk, max(dbms_rowid.rowid_block_
number(rowid)) max_blk from t2 ;

     MIN_BLK         MAX_BLK
--------------- ---------------
     1302492         1386248

1 row selected.
```

```
SQL> -- Check the space usage in the table
SQL> get space_usage.sql
  1  declare
  2      l_tabname           varchar2(30) := '&1';
  3      l_fs1_bytes number;
  4      l_fs2_bytes number;
  5      l_fs3_bytes number;
  6      l_fs4_bytes number;
  7      l_fs1_blocks number;
  8      l_fs2_blocks number;
  9      l_fs3_blocks number;
 10      l_fs4_blocks number;
 11      l_full_bytes number;
 12      l_full_blocks number;
 13      l_unformatted_bytes number;
 14      l_unformatted_blocks number;
 15  begin
 16      dbms_space.space_usage(
 17          segment_owner       => user,
 18          segment_name        => l_tabname,
 19          segment_type        => 'TABLE',
 20          fs1_bytes           => l_fs1_bytes,
 21          fs1_blocks          => l_fs1_blocks,
 22          fs2_bytes           => l_fs2_bytes,
 23          fs2_blocks          => l_fs2_blocks,
 24          fs3_bytes           => l_fs3_bytes,
 25          fs3_blocks          => l_fs3_blocks,
 26          fs4_bytes           => l_fs4_bytes,
 27          fs4_blocks          => l_fs4_blocks,
 28          full_bytes          => l_full_bytes,
 29          full_blocks         => l_full_blocks,
 30          unformatted_blocks => l_unformatted_blocks,
 31          unformatted_bytes  => l_unformatted_bytes
 32      );
 33      dbms_output.put_line('0-25% Free   = '||l_fs1_blocks||' Bytes = '||l_fs1_bytes);
 34      dbms_output.put_line('25-50% Free  = '||l_fs2_blocks||' Bytes = '||l_fs2_bytes);
 35      dbms_output.put_line('50-75% Free  = '||l_fs3_blocks||' Bytes = '||l_fs3_bytes);
 36      dbms_output.put_line('75-100% Free = '||l_fs4_blocks||' Bytes = '||l_fs4_bytes);
 37      dbms_output.put_line('Full Blocks  = '||l_full_blocks||' Bytes = '||l_full_bytes);
 38* end;
SQL>
SQL> @space_usage T2
0-25% Free   = 0 Bytes = 0
25-50% Free  = 0 Bytes = 0
50-75% Free  = 0 Bytes = 0
75-100% Free = 16 Bytes = 131072
Full Blocks  = 12121 Bytes = 99295232

PL/SQL procedure successfully completed.
```

```
SQL> -- Note that most blocks are full
SQL> -- A full table scan would have to read all the blocks (12137 total)
SQL>
SQL> -- Delete all the rows from the table
SQL> delete from t2 ;

800000 rows deleted.

SQL>
SQL> commit ;

Commit complete.

SQL> -- Check the space usage after all rows are deleted
SQL> @space_usage T2
0-25% Free   = 0 Bytes = 0
25-50% Free  = 0 Bytes = 0
50-75% Free  = 0 Bytes = 0
75-100% Free = 12137 Bytes = 99426304
Full Blocks  = 0 Bytes = 0
PL/SQL procedure successfully completed.
SQL> -- Note that blocks are now free but the same space is still consumed
SQL> -- A full table scan would still read 12137 blocks
SQL> -- List number of blocks (table has 0 rows)
SQL> select blocks from user_segments where segment_name = 'T2';

        BLOCKS
---------------
         12288

1 row selected.

SQL> -- List how many blocks contain data
SQL> select count(distinct (dbms_rowid.rowid_block_number(rowid))) block_ct from t2 ;

      BLOCK_CT
---------------
             0

1 row selected.

SQL> -- Execute a full table scan and note the consistent gets (logical block reads)
SQL>
SQL> set autotrace traceonly
SQL> select * from t2 ;
no rows selected
Execution Plan
----------------------------------------------------------
Plan hash value: 1513984157
```

```
--------------------------------------------------------------------------
| Id  | Operation          | Name | Rows  | Bytes | Cost (%CPU)| Time      |
--------------------------------------------------------------------------
|   0 | SELECT STATEMENT   |      |     1 |    65 |  2674   (1)| 00:00:33 |
|   1 |  TABLE ACCESS FULL | T2   |     1 |    65 |  2674   (1)| 00:00:33 |
--------------------------------------------------------------------------
Statistics
---------------------------------------------------------
          0  recursive calls
          0  db block gets
      12148  consistent gets
      11310  physical reads
          0  redo size
        332  bytes sent via SQL*Net to client
        370  bytes received via SQL*Net from client
          1  SQL*Net roundtrips to/from client
          0  sorts (memory)
          0  sorts (disk)
          0  rows processed

SQL> set autotrace off
SQL>

SQL> -- Truncate the table to deallocate the space and reset the HWM
SQL> truncate table t2 ;

Table truncated.

SQL> -- Check the space usage after table is truncated
SQL> @space_usage T2
0-25% Free    = 0 Bytes = 0
25-50% Free   = 0 Bytes = 0
50-75% Free   = 0 Bytes = 0
75-100% Free  = 0 Bytes = 0
Full Blocks   = 0 Bytes = 0

PL/SQL procedure successfully completed.

SQL> -- Note that the space has been deallocated
SQL>
SQL> -- List number of blocks (table has 0 rows and all space recovered)
SQL> select blocks from user_segments where segment_name = 'T2';

        BLOCKS
    ---------------
             8

1 row selected.
```

```
SQL> set autotrace traceonly
SQL> select * from t2 ;

no rows selected

Execution Plan
----------------------------------------------------------
Plan hash value: 1513984157

---------------------------------------------------------------------------
| Id  | Operation          | Name | Rows  | Bytes | Cost (%CPU)| Time     |
---------------------------------------------------------------------------
|   0 | SELECT STATEMENT   |      |     1 |    65 |  2674   (1)| 00:00:33 |
|   1 |  TABLE ACCESS FULL | T2   |     1 |    65 |  2674   (1)| 00:00:33 |
---------------------------------------------------------------------------


Statistics
----------------------------------------------------------
          0  recursive calls
          0  db block gets
          3  consistent gets
          0  physical reads
          0  redo size
        332  bytes sent via SQL*Net to client
        370  bytes received via SQL*Net from client
          1  SQL*Net roundtrips to/from client
          0  sorts (memory)
          0  sorts (disk)
          0  rows processed

SQL> set autotrace off
```

I hope this example illustrates that even when a full table scan is the "right" plan operation choice, the overhead of reading additional empty blocks can mean performance takes a significant hit. For tables that are loaded and unloaded frequently (using DELETE instead of TRUNCATE), you may discover that response time suffers. This occurs often with tables that are used for ETL or any form of load/process/unload activity. Now that you know how full scan behavior can be affected, you can diagnose and correct related performance problems more easily.

Index Scan Access Methods

If you have a book about U.S. presidents and want to find information on Jimmy Carter, you could start on the first page and visually scan each page until you come to the section of the book about Carter. However, it would take a lot of time to do this scan, so you might find it more expedient to look up Carter in the book's index. After you determine the page number for the Carter text, you can go directly to that location. An index scan operation is conceptually similar to using an index in a book.

The default index type is a B-tree index and is the only type I discuss in this chapter. Indexes are created on one or more table columns or column expressions, and they store the column values along with a rowid. There are other pieces of information stored in the index entry, but for our purposes, we concern ourselves only with the column value and the rowid. rowid is a pseudocolumn that uniquely identifies a row within a table. It is the internal address of a physical table row and it consists of an address that points to the data file that contains the table block that contains the row and the address of the row within the block that leads directly to the row itself. Listing 3-7 shows how to decode rowid into a readable form.

Listing 3-7. Decoding rowid

```
SQL> column filen format a50 head 'File Name'
SQL>
SQL> select   e.rowid ,
  2              (select file_name
  3                 from dba_data_files
  4                where file_id = dbms_rowid.rowid_to_absolute_fno(e.rowid, user, 'EMPLOYEES')) filen,
  5              dbms_rowid.rowid_block_number(e.rowid) block_no,
  6              dbms_rowid.rowid_row_number(e.rowid) row_no
  7      from   employees e
  8     where   e.email = 'SKING' ;

ROWID               File Name                          BLOCK_NO   ROW_NO
------------------  --------------------------------   ---------- ---------
AABMTiAAGAAEgWdAAA  /u02/oradata/ORA12C/users01.dbf     1181085         1

1 row selected.
```

As you can see, rowid points to the exact location of a particular row. Therefore, when an index is used to access a row, all that happens is that a match is made on the access criteria provided in the predicate, then rowid is used to access the specific file/block/row of data. Block accesses made via an index scan are usually made using single-block reads (there are cases when multiblock reads occur, but discussing them here would be getting a bit ahead of ourselves). This makes sense when you consider how rowid is used. When the index entry is read, only the single block of data identified by that rowid is retrieved. After it is retrieved, only the row specified by the rowid is accessed.

What this means is that for each row retrieved via an index scan, at least two block accesses are required: at least one index block and one data block. If your final result set contains 100 rows and those 100 rows are retrieved using an index scan, there would be at least 200 block accesses required. I keep saying "at least" because, depending on the size of the index, Oracle may have to access several index blocks initially to get to the first matching column value needed.

Index Structure

An index is structured logically, as shown in Figure 3-4. Indexes are comprised of one or more levels of branch blocks and a single level of leaf blocks. Branch blocks hold information about the range of values contained in the next level of branch blocks, and they are used to search the index structure to find the needed leaf blocks. The *height* of an index is the number of branch levels between the initial branch block (referred to as the *root block*) and the leaf blocks. The leaf blocks contain the indexed values and the rowid for each in sorted order, as mentioned previously.

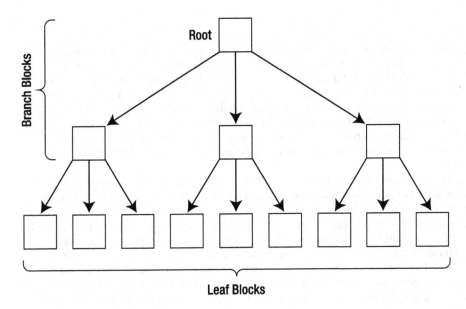

Figure 3-4. *Logical view of an index structure*

If you start with a newly created, empty table and create an index on that table, the index consists of one empty block. In this case, the single block acts as both a root block and a leaf block. The height of the index is one. There is another statistic called *blevel* that represents the number of branch levels present in an index. In this case, the blevel would be zero.

As new rows are added to the table, new index entries are added to the block, and it fills to the point where additional entries won't fit. At this point, Oracle allocates two new index blocks and places all the index entries into these two new leaf blocks. The previously filled single root block is now replaced with pointers to the two new blocks. The pointers are made up of the relative block address (RBA) to the new index blocks and a value indicating the lowest indexed value (in other words, lowest in sorted order) found in the referenced leaf block. With this information in the root block, Oracle can now search the index to find specific leaf blocks that hold a requested value. At this point, the index now has a height of two and a blevel of one.

Over time, as more rows are inserted into the table, index entries are added into the two leaf blocks that were just created. As these leaf blocks fill up, Oracle adds one leaf block and allocates the index entries between the full and new leaf blocks. Every time a leaf block fills up and splits, a new pointer for this new leaf block is added to the root block. Eventually, the root block fills up and the process repeats, with the root being split into two new branch blocks. When this split occurs, the height of the index increases to three and the blevel to two.

At this point, as new index entries are made, the leaf blocks fill and split, but instead of a new pointer being added to the root block, the pointer is added to the corresponding branch block. Eventually, the branch blocks fill and split. It is at this point that a new entry gets added to the root block. As this process continues, eventually the root block fills up and splits, increasing the height of the index once again. Just remember that the only time the height of an index increases is when the root block splits. For this reason, all leaf blocks are always the same distance from the root block, which is why you'll hear the term *balanced* used in regard to Oracle B-tree indexes. Indexes are guaranteed to remain height balanced.

Why go through all this detail? Understanding how an index structure is created and maintained will help you understand how the various types of index scans work. Now that you have an understanding of how indexes are structured, you're ready to discover how the different index scans traverse the structure to retrieve the row data your query needs.

Index Scan Types

There are several different types of index scans, but each shares some common ground in how they must traverse the index structure to access the leaf block entries that match the values being searched. First, the root block of the index is accessed with a single-block read. The next step is to read a branch block. Depending on the height of the index, one or more branch blocks may need to be read. Each read is for a separate single block. Last, the first index leaf block that contains the start of the index entries needed is read. If the height of an index is four, to get to the leaf block needed, four single-block reads are performed. At this point, the row ID for the first matching index value in the leaf block is read and used to make a single-block read call to retrieve the table block where the entire row resides. Therefore, in this example, to retrieve a single row from a table using an index, Oracle has to read five blocks: four index blocks and one table block.

The various index scan types we examine are index range scan, index unique scan, index full scan, index skip scan, and index fast full scan. An index fast full scan is actually more like a full table scan, but because the scans are against an index structure, I cover them in this section.

Before I review the different scan types, I want to point out a very important index statistic called *clustering factor*. The clustering factor statistic of an index helps the optimizer generate the cost of using the index, and it is a measure of how well ordered the table data are related to the indexed values. Recall that index entries are stored in sorted order whereas table data are stored in random order. Unless an effort has been made to load data specifically into a table in a specific order, you are not guaranteed where individual rows of data end up. For example, rows from the orders table that share the same order_date may not all reside in the same blocks. They are likely to be scattered randomly across the blocks in the table.

The clustering factor of an index indicates to the optimizer whether data rows containing the same indexed values are located in the same or a small set of contiguous blocks, or whether rows are scattered across numerous table blocks. Figure 3-5 shows how the rows might be stored physically in the table's data blocks.

Table T1

0	0	0	0	0
0	0	0	0	0
0	0	0	0	1
1	1	1	1	1
1	1	1	1	1
1	1	1	2	2
2	2	2	2	2
2	3	3	3	3
3	3	3	3	4
4	4	4	4	4
4	4	5	5	5
5	5	5	5	6

(Block 1: rows 1–4, Block 2: rows 5–8, Block 3: rows 9–12)

Table T2

1	2	3	4	5
6	7	8	9	10
11	12	13	14	15
16	17	18	19	20
21	22	23	24	25
26	27	28	29	30
31	32	33	34	35
36	37	38	39	40
41	42	43	44	45
46	47	48	49	50
51	52	53	54	55
56	57	58	59	60

(Block 1: rows 1–4, Block 2: rows 5–8, Block 3: rows 9–12)

Figure 3-5. *Diagram of random vs. sequentially loaded row values*

In the diagram showing table T1, you see how rows containing the value 2 are loaded into the same block. But, in table T2, rows with a value of 2 are not loaded in contiguous blocks. In this example, an index on this column for table T1 would have a lower clustering factor. Lower numbers that are closer to the number of table blocks are used to indicate highly ordered, or clustered, rows of data based on the indexed value. The clustering factor for this column in table T2, however, is higher and typically closer to the number of rows in the table. Listing 3-8 shows the clustering factor statistic for each of these two tables.

Listing 3-8. Index clustering_factor

```
SQL> select t.table_name||'.'||i.index_name idx_name,
  2          i.clustering_factor, t.blocks, t.num_rows
  3     from user_indexes i, user_tables t
  4    where i.table_name = t.table_name
  5      and t.table_name in ('T1','T2')
  6    order by t.table_name, i.index_name;
```

IDX_NAME	CLUSTERING_FACTOR	BLOCKS	NUM_ROWS
T1.T1_IDX1	152	164	10000
T2.T2_IDX1	10000	164	10000

```
2 rows selected.
```

As demonstrated earlier in this chapter (see Listings 3-3 and 3-4), the optimizer in Oracle version 11gR2 and earlier chooses an index scan when querying table T1, but opts for a full table scan when querying table T2. The clustering_factor was the key piece of information that helped the optimizer make that decision. In version 12c, the clustering_factor is still used, but it does not have the extreme effect on the plan operation choice as it had in earlier versions.

So, although clustering_factor is a statistic associated with an index, it is computed by looking at the blocks of data in the table. When computing clustering_factor, Oracle version 11gR2 and earlier does something similar to what is shown in Listing 3-9.

Listing 3-9. Computing Index clustering_factor

```
SQL> select t.table_name||'.'||i.index_name idx_name,
  2          i.clustering_factor, t.blocks, t.num_rows
  3     from all_indexes i, all_tables t
  4    where i.table_name = t.table_name
  5      and t.table_name = 'EMPLOYEES'
  6      and t.owner = 'HR'
  7      and i.index_name = 'EMP_DEPARTMENT_IX'
  8    order by t.table_name, i.index_name;
```

IDX_NAME	CLUSTERING_FACTOR	BLOCKS	NUM_ROWS
EMPLOYEES.EMP_DEPARTMENT_IX	7	5	107

```
1 row selected.
SQL> select department_id, last_name, blk_no,
  2          lag (blk_no,1,blk_no) over (order by department_id) prev_blk_no,
  3          case when blk_no != lag (blk_no,1,blk_no) over
  4           (order by department_id)  or rownum = 1
```

```
 5                then '*** +1'
 6                else null
 7          end cluf_ct
 8  from (
 9  select department_id, last_name,
10         dbms_rowid.rowid_block_number(rowid) blk_no
11    from hr.employees
12   where department_id is not null
13   order by department_id
14  );
```

DEPARTMENT_ID	LAST_NAME	BLK_NO	PREV_BLK_NO	CLUF_CT
10	Whalen	84	84	*** +1
20	Hartstein	84	84	
20	Fay	84	84	
30	Raphaely	88	84	*** +1
30	Colmenares	88	88	
...				
30	Himuro	88	88	
40	Mavris	84	88	*** +1
50	OConnell	84	84	
50	Grant	84	84	
50	Weiss	88	84	*** +1
50	Fripp	88	88	
50	Kaufling	88	88	
...				
70	Baer	84	88	*** +1
80	Bates	88	84	*** +1
80	Smith	88	88	
100	Sciarra	88	88	
110	Gietz	84	88	*** +1
110	Higgins	84	84	

```
106 rows selected.
```

As I mentioned, this isn't precisely how the clustering factor is computed, but this query can help you see how it is done in general terms. Note that I deleted some of the output rows for brevity, but left enough of the output so you can see where the block number for the row changed from the previous row's block number. Clustering factor is computed by adding one to a counter each time the block number for the current row is different from the previous row. In this example, this happens seven times. What this number is supposed to represent is seven *different* table blocks that hold data for this table. As you can see from the output, there are really only two blocks that contain data (block numbers 84 and 88). In reality, the clustering factor isn't exactly accurate. In this case, it is off by a factor of 3.5.

■ **Note**   Bug 13262857 Enh: provide some control over DBMS_STATS index clustering factor computation INDEX was addressed in Oracle version 12c. Patches are also available for 11.1.07, 11.2.0.2, and 11.2.0.3 (patch ID 15830250 "Index Clustering Factor Computation Is Pessimistic").

In Oracle version 12c, a new statistics collection preference, called TABLE_CACHED_BLOCKS, can be defined to correct the issue just described. By setting the preference to a value greater than one (in other words, as performed currently), but less than or equal to 255, the collection does not increment the clustering factor if the table block being referenced by the current index entry has already been referenced by any of the prior *n* index entries (where *n* is a number between one and 255). This preference can be set using the DBMS_STATS.SET_TABLE_PREFS (it can also be set using DBMS_STATS.SET_SCHEMA_PREFS or DBMS_STATS.SET_DATABASE_PREFS) procedure as follows:

```
dbms_stats.set_table_prefs (
  ownname=>'HR',
  tabname=>'EMPLOYEES',
  pname=>'TABLE_CACHED_BLOCKS',
  pvalue=>50
)
```

Recall from Listing 3-8, the original clustering factors for tables T1 and T2 were as follows:

IDX_NAME	CLUSTERING_FACTOR	BLOCKS	NUM_ROWS
T1.T1_IDX1	152	164	10000
T2.T2_IDX1	10000	164	10000

In Listing 3-10, note how the clustering factor for T2 changes when the statistics collection is altered using the TABLE_CACHE_BLOCKS parameter setting.

Listing 3-10. Using the TABLE_CACHED_BLOCKS Parameter to Alter Clustering Factor Statistic Collection

```
SQL> exec dbms_stats.set_table_prefs(user, 'T2', pname=>'TABLE_CACHED_BLOCKS', pvalue=>255);

PL/SQL procedure successfully completed.

SQL> exec dbms_stats.gather_table_stats(user,'T2') ;

PL/SQL procedure successfully completed.

SQL> select t.table_name||'.'||i.index_name idx_name,
  2          i.clustering_factor, t.blocks, t.num_rows
  3     from user_indexes i, user_tables t
  4    where i.table_name = t.table_name
  5      and t.table_name in ('T1','T2')
  6    order by t.table_name, i.index_name;
```

IDX_NAME	CLUSTERING_FACTOR	BLOCKS	NUM_ROWS
T1.T1_IDX1	152	164	10000
T2.T2_IDX1	**152**	**164**	**10000**

```
2 rows selected.
```

The clustering factor improved from 10,000 to 152. This change helps the optimizer compute a lower cost to use the T2_IDX1 index and choose it, if appropriate, for the plan. This addition of the TABLE_CACHED_BLOCKS setting to 12c allows a less pessimistic clustering_factor value to be computed and can help lead to a more informed and accurate decision by the optimizer.

Even prior to 12c, the inaccuracy in the way clustering_factor is computed won't make a significant difference to cause the optimizer to overcost the index so it will not be utilized. If the optimizer doesn't choose the index you expect, it may choose another index that can satisfy the predicate that contains similar columns. In this situation, you may need to do a careful analysis of the indexes you created to determine whether there is a way to consolidate several indexes into a single compound index. Do not make the mistake of rebuilding the index, thinking it will help "fix" the clustering_factor. As I have demonstrated here, the clustering_factor is related to the table data, not the index. So, rebuilding the index won't have any effect on it.

On the other hand, if you start to consider rebuilding the table to improve the clustering_factor, proceed with caution. Tables typically have numerous indexes. You can't rebuild the table to make the order match one index without causing it to be less ordered by other columns. So, a rebuild may help in relation to one index but may hurt others. Also, rebuilding tables is typically a time-consuming and resource-intensive process. Just because you rebuild the table in a particular order today doesn't mean it's going to stay in that order over time as rows are inserted, updated, and deleted. As you proceed through the rest of the book, you'll learn enough to understand when clustering_factor may be part of a problem, and you'll likely be able to find ways to adjust for it if needed.

■ **Note**　In each of the following examples that show explain plan output, the output has been edited. I've removed columns for brevity.

Index Unique Scan

An index unique scan is chosen when a predicate contains a condition using a column defined with a UNIQUE or PRIMARY KEY index. These types of indexes guarantee that only one row is ever returned for a specified value. In this case, the index structure is traversed from root to leaf block to a single entry, the rowid is retrieved, and it is used to access the table data block containing the one row. The TABLE ACCESS BY INDEX ROWID step in the plan indicates the table data block access. The number of block accesses required is always equal to the height of the index plus one, unless there are special circumstances, such as the row is chained or contains a large object (LOB) that is stored elsewhere. Listing 3-11 shows an example query that produces an index unique scan plan.

Listing 3-11. Index Unique Scan

```
SQL> select * from employees where employee_id = 100;


-------------------------------------------------------------------
| Id | Operation                    | Name          | Cost (%CPU)|
-------------------------------------------------------------------
|  0 | SELECT STATEMENT             |               |   1 (100)|
|  1 |  TABLE ACCESS BY INDEX ROWID| EMPLOYEES     |   1   (0)|
|  2 |   INDEX UNIQUE SCAN          | EMP_EMP_ID_PK |   0   (0)|
-------------------------------------------------------------------

Predicate Information (identified by operation id):
---------------------------------------------------

   2 - access("EMPLOYEE_ID"=100)
```

Index Range Scan

An index range scan is chosen when a predicate contains a condition that returns a range of data. The index can be unique or nonunique, because it is the condition that determines whether multiple rows are returned. The conditions specified can use operators such as <, >, LIKE, BETWEEN, and even =. For a range scan to be selected, the range needs to be fairly selective. The larger the range, the more likely a full scan operation is chosen instead. Listing 3-12 shows an example of a query that produces an index range scan plan.

Listing 3-12. Index Range Scan

```
SQL> select * from employees where department_id = 60 ;

---------------------------------------------------------------------
| Id  | Operation                            | Name          | Cost (%CPU)|
---------------------------------------------------------------------
|   0 | SELECT STATEMENT                     |               |   2 (100)|
|   1 |   TABLE ACCESS BY INDEX ROWID BATCHED| EMPLOYEES     |   2   (0)|
|*  2 |     INDEX RANGE SCAN                 | EMP_DEPT_ID_IDX |   1   (0)|
---------------------------------------------------------------------

Predicate Information (identified by operation id):
---------------------------------------------------

   2 - access("DEPARTMENT_ID"=60)
```

A range scan traverses the index structure from the root block to the first leaf block containing an entry matching the specified condition. From that starting point, a rowid is retrieved from the index entry and the table data block is retrieved (TABLE ACCESS BY INDEX ROWID). After the first row is retrieved, the index leaf block is accessed again and the next entry is read to retrieve the next rowid. This back-and-forth between the index leaf blocks and the data blocks continues until all the matching index entries have been read. Therefore, the number of block accesses required includes the number of branch blocks in the index (which can be found using the blevel statistic for the index) plus the number of index entries that match the condition multiplied by two. You have to multiply by two because each retrieval of a single row in the table requires the index leaf block to be accessed to retrieve the rowid, and then the table data block is accessed using that rowid. Therefore, if the example returns five rows and the blevel is three, the total block accesses required is (5 rows × 2) + 3 = 13.

If the range of entries matching the condition is large enough, it is likely that more than one leaf block has to be accessed. When this is the case, the next leaf block needed can be read using a pointer stored in the current leaf block that leads to the next leaf block (there's also a pointer to the previous leaf block). Because these pointers exist, there is no need to go back up to the branch block to determine where to go next.

When an index range scan is chosen, the predicate information in the plan shows the condition used to access the index. In the example, step 2 in the plan has an asterisk beside it, which is an indicator that predicate information for that step is listed below the plan. In that section, you see an entry that shows that the index entry access was determined using the condition DEPARTMENT_ID = 60.

There are cases when predicates that you might think should use index range scans do not. For example, if you use a LIKE operator with a condition that starts with a wildcard such as '%abc', the optimizer does not choose a range scan on an index for that column because the condition is too broad. Basically, leading wildcards need to be compared with the indexed column values in every index block to determine a match, which can result in a significant amount of work. This work may appear significant enough to the optimizer that it prefers to use a different operation, such as a full table scan, instead. Another similar case is when you have a predicate that uses a column that isn't the leading column in a compound index. In this case, as I discuss shortly, it is more likely for an index skip scan to be chosen instead.

One final nuance of an index range scan that I'd like to note is the ability of an ascending ordered index (the default) to return rows in descending sorted order. The optimizer may choose to use an index to access rows via an index even if a full scan might be warranted. This may occur when the query includes an ORDER BY clause on a column that is indexed. Because the index is stored in sorted order, reading rows using the index means the rows are retrieved in sorted order, and the need to do a separate sort step can be avoided. But, what if the ORDER BY clause is requested in descending order? Because the index is stored in ascending order, the index can't be used for a descending order request, can it? Listing 3-13 shows an example of this behavior and the special range scan operation used to handle it.

Listing 3-13. An Index Range Scan Used to Avoid a Sort

```
SQL> select * from employees
  2   where department_id in (90, 100)
  3   order by department_id  desc;


-------------------------------------------------------------------
| Id | Operation                      | Name          | Cost (%CPU)|
-------------------------------------------------------------------
|  0 | SELECT STATEMENT               |               |   2 (100)|
|  1 |  INLIST ITERATOR               |               |          |
|  2 |   TABLE ACCESS BY INDEX ROWID  | EMPLOYEES     |   2   (0)|
|* 3 |    INDEX RANGE SCAN DESCENDING | EMP_DEPT_ID_IDX |  1   (0)|
-------------------------------------------------------------------


Predicate Information (identified by operation id):
---------------------------------------------------

   3 - access(("DEPARTMENT_ID"=90 OR "DEPARTMENT_ID"=100))
```

In this case, the index entries are actually read in reverse order to avoid the need for a separate sort.

Index Full Scan

An index full scan is chosen under several conditions. For example, when there is no predicate but the column list can be satisfied through an index on a column, the predicate contains a condition on a nonleading column in an index, or the data can be retrieved via an index in sorted order and saves the need for a separate sort step. Listing 3-14 shows an example of each of these cases.

Listing 3-14. Index Full Scan Examples

```
SQL> select email from employees ;


------------------------------------------------------
| Id | Operation           | Name         | Cost (%CPU)|
------------------------------------------------------
|  0 | SELECT STATEMENT    |              |   1 (100)|
|  1 |  INDEX FULL SCAN    | EMP_EMAIL_UK |   1   (0)|
------------------------------------------------------


SQL>
SQL> select first_name, last_name from employees
  2   where first_name like 'A%' ;
```

```
--------------------------------------------------------
| Id  | Operation          | Name       | Cost (%CPU)|
--------------------------------------------------------
|   0 | SELECT STATEMENT   |            |    3 (100)|
|*  1 |   TABLE ACCESS FULL| EMPLOYEES  |    3   (0)|
--------------------------------------------------------

Predicate Information (identified by operation id):
---------------------------------------------------

   1 - filter("FIRST_NAME" LIKE 'A%')
```

SQL> select * from employees order by employee_id ;

```
------------------------------------------------------------------
| Id  | Operation                   | Name          | Cost (%CPU)|
------------------------------------------------------------------
|   0 | SELECT STATEMENT            |               |    3 (100)|
|   1 |  TABLE ACCESS BY INDEX ROWID| EMPLOYEES     |    3   (0)|
|   2 |   INDEX FULL SCAN           | EMP_EMP_ID_PK |    1   (0)|
------------------------------------------------------------------
```

SQL> select * from employees order by employee_id desc ;

```
------------------------------------------------------------------
| Id  | Operation                    | Name          | Cost (%CPU)|
------------------------------------------------------------------
|   0 | SELECT STATEMENT             |               |    3 (100)|
|   1 |  TABLE ACCESS BY INDEX ROWID | EMPLOYEES     |    3   (0)|
|   2 |   INDEX FULL SCAN DESCENDING | EMP_EMP_ID_PK |    1   (0)|
------------------------------------------------------------------
```

An index full scan operation scans every leaf block in the index structure, reads the row IDs for each entry, and retrieves the table rows. Every leaf block is accessed. This is often more efficient than doing a full table scan because the index blocks contain more entries than the table blocks; therefore, fewer overall blocks may need to be accessed. In cases when the columns needed to satisfy the column list are all present as part of the index entry, the table access step is avoided as well, which means that choosing an index full scan operation is more efficient than reading all the table blocks.

You may have noticed in the last example that the index full scan operation also has the ability to read in descending order to avoid the need for a separate descending ordered sort request. There is another optimization for index full scans, and it occurs when a query requests the minimum or maximum column value and that column is indexed. Listing 3-15 shows an example of this operation choice.

Listing 3-15. Index Full Scan Min/Max Optimization

SQL> select min(department_id) from employees ;

```
------------------------------------------------------------------
| Id  | Operation                  | Name           | Cost (%CPU)|
------------------------------------------------------------------
|   0 | SELECT STATEMENT           |                |    1 (100)|
|   1 |  SORT AGGREGATE            |                |           |
|   2 |   INDEX FULL SCAN (MIN/MAX)| EMP_DEPT_ID_IDX |    1   (0)|
------------------------------------------------------------------
```

```
SQL> select max(department_id) from employees ;
```

```
--------------------------------------------------------------
| Id | Operation                    | Name          | Cost (%CPU)|
--------------------------------------------------------------
|  0 | SELECT STATEMENT             |               |    1 (100)|
|  1 |  SORT AGGREGATE              |               |           |
|  2 |   INDEX FULL SCAN (MIN/MAX)  | EMP_DEPT_ID_IDX |   1   (0)|
--------------------------------------------------------------
```

```
SQL> select min(department_id), max(department_id) from employees ;
```

```
----------------------------------------------------
| Id | Operation            | Name      | Cost (%CPU)|
----------------------------------------------------
|  0 | SELECT STATEMENT     |           |    3 (100)|
|  1 |  SORT AGGREGATE      |           |           |
|  2 |   TABLE ACCESS FULL  | EMPLOYEES |    3   (0)|
----------------------------------------------------
```

```
SQL> select (select min(department_id) from employees) min_id,
  2          (select max(department_id) from employees) max_id
  3     from dual
  4
```

```
--------------------------------------------------------------
| Id | Operation                    | Name          | Cost (%CPU)|
--------------------------------------------------------------
|  0 | SELECT STATEMENT             |               |    4 (100)|
|  1 |  SORT AGGREGATE              |               |           |
|  2 |   INDEX FULL SCAN (MIN/MAX)  | EMP_DEPT_ID_IDX |   1   (0)|
|  3 |  SORT AGGREGATE              |               |           |
|  4 |   INDEX FULL SCAN (MIN/MAX)  | EMP_DEPT_ID_IDX |   1   (0)|
|  5 |  FAST DUAL                   |               |    2   (0)|
--------------------------------------------------------------
```

As the example shows, when a MIN or MAX aggregate is requested, the optimizer can choose a special optimized version of the index full scan operation. In these special cases, when the index is used to retrieve the minimum value quickly, it is the first entry in the first index leaf block; when it retrieves the maximum value, it is the last entry in the last index leaf block. This makes perfect sense because the index is stored in sorted order so the minimum and maximum values have to be at either end of the first and last leaf blocks. However, the really great part is that, in these special cases, the index full scan isn't really a full scan; it is a scan of only the root block, one or more branch blocks, and the first or last leaf blocks. This means that finding these values is very fast and very low cost in terms of the number of block accesses required. The index full scan operation title may seem a bit confusing because index full scans typically read all the index leaf blocks. However, this optimization is a nice win in terms of performance.

I did include an example of where the query includes both a MIN and a MAX aggregate, and as you may have noticed, the optimizer chose to do a full table scan with a sort instead of the nice optimized index full scan operation. Although I think this is a shortcoming in the way the optimizer handles this situation, there is a fairly easy way to get the same optimized behavior—just code the two queries separately. In this way, you get the benefits of the optimization.

Index Skip Scan

An index skip scan is chosen when the predicate contains a condition on a nonleading column in an index and the leading columns are fairly distinct. In earlier releases of Oracle, if a predicate used a column that wasn't the leading column in an index, the index couldn't be chosen. This behavior changed in Oracle version 9 with the introduction of the *index skip scan*. A skip scan works by splitting a multicolumn index logically into smaller subindexes. The number of logical subindexes is determined by the number of distinct values in the leading columns of the index. Therefore, the more distinct the leading columns, the more logical subindexes need to be created. If too many subindexes are required, the operation isn't as efficient as simply doing a full scan. However, in cases when the number of subindexes needed is smaller, the operation can be many times more efficient than a full scan because scanning a smaller number of index blocks can be more efficient than scanning a larger number of table blocks. Listing 3-16 shows an example of an index skip scan plan. Note that for this example, I use a copy of the hr.employees table, which has more than 28,000 rows.

Listing 3-16. Index Skip Scan Example

```
SQL> create index emp_jobfname_ix on employees2(job_id, first_name, salary);

Index created.

SQL> select * from employees2 where first_name = 'William';
```

```
---------------------------------------------------------------------------
| Id | Operation                    | Name           | A-Rows | Buffers |
---------------------------------------------------------------------------
|  0 | SELECT STATEMENT             |                |    559 |    465  |
|  1 |  TABLE ACCESS BY INDEX ROWID | EMPLOYEES2     |    559 |    465  |
|    |       BATCHED                |                |        |         |
|* 2 |   INDEX SKIP SCAN            | EMP2_JOBFNAME_IX|   559 |     59  |
---------------------------------------------------------------------------

Predicate Information (identified by operation id):
---------------------------------------------------

   2 - access("FIRST_NAME"='William')
       filter("FIRST_NAME"='William')
```

```
SQL> select /*+ full(employees2) */ * from employees2 where first_name = 'William';
```

```
-------------------------------------------------------------
| Id | Operation         | Name       | A-Rows | Buffers |
-------------------------------------------------------------
|  0 | SELECT STATEMENT  |            |    559 |    581  |
|* 1 |  TABLE ACCESS FULL| EMPLOYEES2 |    559 |    581  |
-------------------------------------------------------------

Predicate Information (identified by operation id):
---------------------------------------------------
```

```
    1 - filter("FIRST_NAME"='William')

SQL> -- How many distinct values of job_id?
SQL> select count(distinct job_id) ct from employees ;

            CT
---------------
            19
```

In this example, the leading column of the index, job_id, has 19 distinct values. Using an index skip scan to access the 559 rows that match the condition (first_name = 'William'), there are 465 buffer gets (logical block accesses). However, if a full table scan is used, 581 blocks are accessed. As you can see, the skip scan is more efficient. What happened was that the index was divided logically into 19 subindexes and then each subindex was scanned for a match for first_name = 'William'. For this index scan type, just keep in mind that the fewer distinct values the leading column (or columns) has, the fewer logical subindexes are needed, and therefore the fewer total block accesses are required.

Index Fast Full Scan

An index fast full scan is more like a full table scan than like other index scan types. When an index fast full scan operation is chosen, all the index blocks are read using multiblock reads. This type of scan is chosen as an alternative to a full table scan when all the columns needed to satisfy the query's column list are included in the index and at least one column in the index has the NOT NULL constraint. In this case, the data are accessed from the index instead of having to access table blocks. Unlike other index scan types, the index fast full scan cannot be used to avoid a sort because the blocks are read using unordered multiblock reads. Listing 3-17 shows an example of an index fast full scan plan.

Listing 3-17. Index Fast Full Scan

```
SQL> alter table employees2 modify (email null) ;

Table altered.

SQL> select email from employees2 ;
```

```
---------------------------------------------------------------------
| Id  | Operation          | Name      | A-Rows | Buffers | Reads  |
---------------------------------------------------------------------
|   0 | SELECT STATEMENT   |           |  29784 |   2537  |  565   |
|   1 |  TABLE ACCESS FULL | EMPLOYEES2|  29784 |   2537  |  565   |
---------------------------------------------------------------------
```

```
SQL>
SQL> alter table employees2 modify (email not null) ;

Table altered.

SQL> select email from employees2 ;
```

Id	Operation	Name	A-Rows	Buffers	Reads
0	SELECT STATEMENT		29784	2064	80
1	INDEX FAST FULL SCAN	EMP2_EMAIL_IDX	29784	2064	80

This example demonstrates how the index fast full scan operation relies on the NOT NULL constraint to be chosen. Without the constraint, a full scan operation is chosen instead.

Join Methods

If there are multiple tables in your query, after the optimizer determines the access methods most appropriate for each of the tables, the next step is to determine the way the tables can best be joined together and the proper order in which to join them. Anytime you have multiple tables in the FROM clause, you have a join. Table relationships are defined with a condition in the WHERE clause. If no condition is specified, the join is defined implicitly such that each row in one table is matched with every row in the other table. This is called a *Cartesian join* and I discuss it in detail later in this section.

Joins occur between pairs of tables or row sources. When multiple tables exist in the FROM clause, the optimizer determines which join operation is most efficient for each pair. The join methods are nested loops joins, hash joins, sort–merge joins, and Cartesian joins. Each join method has specific conditions to which it is best suited. For each pair, the optimizer must also determine the order in which the tables are joined. Figure 3-6 shows a diagram of how a query with four tables might be joined.

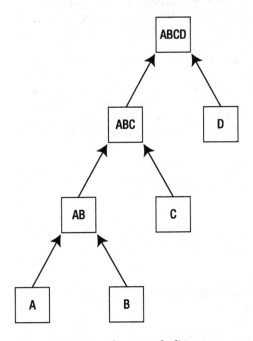

Figure 3-6. *Join order example diagram*

Notice that after the first pair of tables is joined, the next table is joined to the resulting row source from the first join. After that join is made, the next table is joined to that row source. This continues until all tables have been joined.

Each join method has two children. The first table accessed is typically called the *driving table* and the second table is called the *inner* or *driven-to table*. The optimizer determines the driving table by using the statistics and the filter conditions in the WHERE clause to calculate how many rows are returned from each table. The table with the smallest estimated size (in terms of blocks, rows, and bytes) is typically the driving table. This is true particularly if the optimizer can determine that one of the tables returns, at most, one row based on a UNIQUE or PRIMARY KEY constraint. These tables are placed first in the join. Tables with outer join operators (which I discuss later) must come after the table to which it is joined. Other than these two specific cases, the join order of the other tables is evaluated using their computed selectivities based on the optimizer's calculations using available table, column, and index statistics.

■ **Note** I use hints (covered in more detail later in the book) in the sections that follow to produce execution plans for each type of join method. In this way, I demonstrate the differences not only in the plan output, but also in resource consumption—in particular, logical reads—for each.

Nested Loops Joins

Nested loops joins use each row of the query result reached through one access operation to drive into another table. These joins are typically most effective if the result set is limited in size and indexes are present on the columns used for the join. With nested loops, the cost of the operation is based on reading each row of the outer row source and joining it with the matching row of the inner row source.

A nested loops join is, as its name implies, a loop inside a loop. The outer loop is basically a query against the driving table that uses only the conditions from the WHERE clause that pertain to that table. As rows pass the outer conditional check and are confirmed to match the request, they are passed into the second inner loop one at a time. Each row is then checked to determine whether it matches the joined-to table based on the join column. If the row matches this second check, it is then passed on to the next step in the plan or is included in the final result set if no further steps are present.

These kinds of joins are quite robust in that they use very little memory. Because row sets are built one row at a time, there is little overhead required. For this reason, they are actually good for huge result sets, except for the fact that building a huge result set one row at a time can take quite a long time. This is why I mentioned earlier that nested loops are typically best when result sets are smaller. The primary measurement for nested loops is the number of block accesses required to prepare the final result set.

Let's take a simple query and break it down into how the nested loop join is processed.

```
select empno, ename, dname, loc
from emp, dept
where emp.deptno = dept.deptno
```

This query is processed as if it is written like the following pseudocode:

```
for each row in (select empno, ename, deptno from emp) loop
for (select dname, loc from dept where deptno =        outer.deptno) loop
            If match then pass the row on to the next step
            If inner join and no match then discard the row
            If outer join and no match set inner column values to null
                  and pass the row on to the next step
      end loop
end loop
```

Listing 3-18 shows the plan for this query.

Listing 3-18. Nested Loops

```
SQL> select /*+ leading (emp, dept) use_nl (emp) */ empno, ename, dname, loc
  2  from emp, dept
  3  where emp.deptno = dept.deptno;
```

```
-----------------------------------------------------------------------------
| Id  | Operation                     | Name    | A-Rows | Buffers | Reads |
-----------------------------------------------------------------------------
|   0 | SELECT STATEMENT              |         |     14 |     26  |     8 |
|   1 |  NESTED LOOPS                 |         |     14 |     26  |     8 |
|   2 |   NESTED LOOPS                |         |     14 |     12  |     7 |
|   3 |    TABLE ACCESS FULL          | EMP     |     14 |      8  |     6 |
|*  4 |    INDEX UNIQUE SCAN          | PK_DEPT |     14 |      4  |     1 |
|   5 |   TABLE ACCESS BY INDEX ROWID | DEPT    |     14 |     14  |     1 |
-----------------------------------------------------------------------------
```

```
Predicate Information (identified by operation id):
---------------------------------------------------

   4 - access("EMP"."DEPTNO"="DEPT"."DEPTNO")
```

The plan shows the nested loops method with the emp table as the driving table and the dept table as the inner (or driven-to) table. With a nested loops plan, the first table listed after the NESTED LOOPS operation is the driving table. That table is accessed via the method chosen for it. In this case, it is a full table scan on emp, which means that all the blocks in the emp table are read using multiblock reads, then each row is accessed one at a time, and the deptno (the join column) is passed to the inner loop query against the dept table. For an inner join, for each row in which there is a match on the dept table's deptno column, the row is returned. For an outer join, each row from emp is returned and null values are used to populate the columns from dept.

Think about having the emp table as the driving table for this query. The query is asking for all rows in which there is a match between the two tables on deptno. In my test, the emp table did not have an index on deptno, so the only way it could be accessed was with a full table scan. Because the way a nested loops join works is to process the inner join for each row of the outer table, if the dept table had been the driving table, for every row in dept a full table scan on emp would have occurred. On the other hand, driving the join with the emp table means that only one full table scan is needed, and because there is an index on deptno in the dept table (it's the primary key), the inner loop can access the row it needs directly from dept. Listing 3-19 shows the comparison of the plan with the dept table as the driving table (note the increase in buffer gets from 26 to 37).

Listing 3-19. Nested Loops Join Order Comparison

```
SQL> select /*+ leading (dept, emp) use_nl (dept) */ empno, ename, dname, loc
  2  from scott.emp, scott.dept
  3  where emp.deptno = dept.deptno;
```

```
-------------------------------------------------------------------
| Id  | Operation              | Name | A-Rows | Buffers | Reads |
-------------------------------------------------------------------
|   0 | SELECT STATEMENT       |      |     14 |     37  |     5 |
|   1 |  NESTED LOOPS          |      |     14 |     37  |     5 |
|   2 |   TABLE ACCESS FULL    | DEPT |      4 |      8  |     5 |
|*  3 |   TABLE ACCESS FULL    | EMP  |     14 |     29  |     0 |
-------------------------------------------------------------------
```

```
Predicate Information (identified by operation id):
---------------------------------------------------

   3 - filter("EMP"."DEPTNO"="DEPT"."DEPTNO")
```

Notice that when the join is driven by dept, the logical reads (Buffers) are higher than when the join is driven by the emp table. One of the keys to optimizing performance is to make sure that only work that needs to happen is done. The extra work (in other words, extra logical reads) that would have occurred if the dept table had been the driving table is avoided with the emp-to-dept join order choice.

Sort–Merge Joins

Sort-merge joins read the two tables to be joined independently, sort the rows from each table (but only those rows that meet the conditions for the table in the WHERE clause) in order by the join key, and then merge the sorted row sets. The sort operations are the expensive part of this join method. For large row sources that won't fit into memory, the sorts end up using temporary disk space to complete, which can be quite memory and time-consuming. However, when the row sets are sorted, the merge happens quickly. To merge, the database alternates down the two lists, compares the top rows, discards rows that are earlier in the sort order than the top of the other list, and only returns matching rows.

Let's use the same query used earlier and break it down into how the sort-merge join is processed.

```
select empno, ename, dname, loc
from emp, dept
where emp.deptno = dept.deptno
```

This query is processed as if it is written like the following pseudocode:

```
select empno, ename, deptno from emp order by deptno

select dname, loc, deptno from dept order by deptno

compare the rowsets and return rows where deptno in both lists match

for an outer join, compare the rowsets and return all rows from
the first list

setting column values for the other table to null
```

Listing 3-20 shows the plan for this query.

Listing 3-20. Sort-Merge Join

```
SQL> select /*+ ordered */ empno, ename, dname, loc
  2  from    dept,emp
  3  where   emp.deptno = dept.deptno;
```

```
-------------------------------------------------------------------------
| Id  | Operation                     | Name    | A-Rows | Buffers | Reads |
-------------------------------------------------------------------------
|   0 | SELECT STATEMENT              |         |     14 |      11 |     8 |
|   1 |  MERGE JOIN                   |         |     14 |      11 |     8 |
|   2 |   TABLE ACCESS BY INDEX ROWID | DEPT    |      4 |       4 |     2 |
|   3 |    INDEX FULL SCAN            | PK_DEPT |      4 |       2 |     1 |
|*  4 |   SORT JOIN                   |         |     14 |       7 |     6 |
|   5 |    TABLE ACCESS FULL          | EMP     |     14 |       7 |     6 |
-------------------------------------------------------------------------
```

Predicate Information (identified by operation id):

```
   4 - access("EMP"."DEPTNO"="DEPT"."DEPTNO")
       filter("EMP"."DEPTNO"="DEPT"."DEPTNO")
```

I used the same query as before but forced the plan with an ordered hint. Notice how the plan operations show a MERGE JOIN operation followed by an index access on the dept table and a SORT JOIN operation of a full table scan on the emp table. The first thing to note is the use of the index scan on dept. In this case, the optimizer chose to read the table data from the index because the index returns the data in sorted order. This means a separate sort step is avoided. The emp table was full scanned and required a separate sort step because there was no index on deptno that could be used. After both row sets were ready and in sorted order, they were merged together.

A sort–merge join accesses the blocks needed and then does the work to sort and merge them in memory (or by using temporary disk space if there isn't enough memory). So, when you do a comparison of logical reads for a sort–merge join with a nested loops join, particularly for a query against a larger row source, you likely find that there are more block accesses required for the nested loops join. Does this mean that the sort–merge is a better choice? It depends. You have to take into account all the work required to complete the sort and merge steps, and realize that work may end up taking much more time than doing more block accesses might.

Sort–merge joins are typically best suited to queries that have limited data filtering and return lots of rows. They are also often a better choice if there are no suitable indexes that can be used to access the data more directly. Last, a sort–merge is often the best choice when the join is an inequality. For example, a join condition of WHERE table1.column1 between table2.column1 and table2.column2 is a candidate for a sort–merge. As we see in the next section, a hash join is not possible for such a join; if the row sources are large, the sort–merge is likely the only viable choice.

Hash Joins

Hash joins, like sort–merge joins, first read the two tables to be joined independently and then apply the criteria in the WHERE clause. When considering a two-table join, based on table and index statistics, the table that is determined to return the fewest rows is hashed in its entirety (in other words, the selected columns and the columns that are joined to other the other table) into memory. This hash table includes all the row data for that table and they are loaded into hash buckets based on a randomizing function that converts the join key to a hash value. As long as there is enough memory available, this hash table resides in memory. However, if there is not enough memory available, the hash table may be written to temporary disk space.

The next step is for the other larger table to be read, and the hash function is applied to the join key column. That hash value is then used to probe the smaller in-memory hash table for the matching hash bucket where the row data for the first table resides. Each bucket has a list (represented by a bitmap) of the rows in that bucket. The list is checked for matches with the probing row. If a match is made, the row is returned; otherwise, it is discarded. The larger table is read only once and each row is checked for a match. This is different from the nested loops join in which the inner table is read multiple times. So really, in this case, the larger table is the driving table because it is read only once and the smaller hashed table is probed many times. Unlike a nested loops join plan, however, the tables are listed in the plan output with the smaller hashed table first and the larger probe table second.

Let's use the same query used earlier and break it down into how the hash join is processed.

```
select empno, ename, dname, loc
from emp, dept
where emp.deptno = dept.deptno
```

This query is processed as if it is written like the following pseudocode:

```
determine the smaller row set, or in the case of an outer join,
        use the outer joined table
select dname, loc, deptno from dept
hash the deptno column and build a hash table
select empno, ename, deptno from emp
hash the deptno column and probe the hash table
if match made, check bitmap to confirm row match
if no match made, discard the row
```

Listing 3-21 shows the plan for this query.

Listing 3-21. Hash Join

```
SQL> select /*+ use_hash(dept,emp) */ empno, ename, dname, loc
  2  from    dept,emp
  3  where   emp.deptno = dept.deptno;
```

```
-----------------------------------------------------------------
| Id | Operation          | Name | A-Rows | Buffers | Reads |
-----------------------------------------------------------------
|  0 | SELECT STATEMENT   |      |   14 |      15 |    12 |
|* 1 |  HASH JOIN         |      |   14 |      15 |    12 |
|  2 |   TABLE ACCESS FULL| DEPT |    4 |       7 |     6 |
|  3 |   TABLE ACCESS FULL| EMP  |   14 |       8 |     6 |
-----------------------------------------------------------------
```

```
Predicate Information (identified by operation id):
---------------------------------------------------

   1 - access("EMP"."DEPTNO"="DEPT"."DEPTNO")
```

In the hash join plan, the smaller hash table is listed first and the probe table is listed second. Keep in mind that the decision regarding which table is the smallest depends not just on the number of rows, but also on the size of those rows as well, because the entire row must be stored in the hash table.

Hash joins are considered more preferable when the row sources are larger and the result set is larger as well. Also, if one of the tables in the join is determined always to return the same row source, a hash join is preferable because it accesses that table only once. If a nested loops join is chosen in this case, the row source is accessed over and over again, requiring more work than a single, independent access. Last, if the smaller table can fit in memory, a hash join may be favored.

Blocks are accessed for hash joins similar to how they are accessed for a sort–merge join. The blocks needed to build the hash table are read and then the rest of the work is done against the hashed data stored in memory (from temporary disk space if there isn't enough memory). So, when you do a comparison of logical reads for a hash join with a sort-merge join, the block accesses are approximately identical. However, the number of logical reads compared with a nested loops join are less because the blocks are read once and are placed into memory (for the hash table), where they are then accessed, or they are only read once (for the probe table).

Hash joins are only possible if the join is an equijoin. As mentioned previously, a sort-merge join can be used to handle joins specified with an inequality condition. The reason why hash joins can't be chosen unless the join is an equijoin is that the matches are made on hashed values and it doesn't make sense to consider hashed values in a range. Listing 3-22 demonstrates how a computed hash value doesn't necessarily correspond to the key value being hashed (in terms of its numeric value, in this case).

Listing 3-22. Hash Values

```
SQL> select distinct deptno,
  2            ora_hash(deptno,1000) hv
  3    from emp
  4    order by deptno;

        DEPTNO               HV
--------------- ----------------
            10              547
            20              486
            30              613

SQL>
SQL> select deptno
  2      from
  3    (
  4    select distinct deptno,
  5            ora_hash(deptno,1000) hv
  6      from emp
  7    order by deptno
  8    )
  9    where hv between 100 and 500;

        DEPTNO
---------------
            20

SQL>
SQL> select distinct deptno,
  2            ora_hash(deptno,1000,50) hv
  3      from emp
  4    order by deptno;

        DEPTNO               HV
--------------- ----------------
            10              839
            20              850
            30              290

SQL>
SQL> select deptno
  2      from
  3    (
  4    select distinct deptno,
  5            ora_hash(deptno,1000,50) hv
```

```
6     from emp
7    order by deptno
8  )
9    where hv between 100 and 500;

        DEPTNO
- - - - - - - - - - - - - - -
           30
```

I used the ora_hash function to demonstrate how a hash value might be generated. The ora_hash function takes up to three parameters: an input value of any base type, the maximum hash bucket value (the minimum value is zero), and a seed value (which also defaults to zero). So, for example, ora_hash(10,1000) returns an integer value between zero and 1000.

In the two examples, I use the default seed in the first and a seed value of 50 for the second. Notice how the hash values for each deptno are quite different in each query. So when I try to query a range of hash values for each, I get a different result. However, in both cases, if I was simply querying a range of the column values, I could easily formulate what I wanted and be assured of always getting the right answer. This example is a bit forced, but I want to give you a visual on hash value comparisons so you can understand more completely why they don't work with inequality joins.

Cartesian Joins

Cartesian joins occur when all the rows from one table are joined to all the rows of another table. Therefore, the total number of rows resulting from the join equals the number of rows from one table (A) multiplied by the number of rows in the other table (B) such that A × B = total rows in the result set. Cartesian joins often occur when a join condition is overlooked or left out, such that there isn't a specified join column, so the only operation possible is simply to join everything from one row source to everything from the other.

Let's use the same query used earlier, but leave off the WHERE clause, and break it down into how the Cartesian join is processed.

```
select empno, ename, dname, loc
from emp, dept
```

This query is processed as if it is written like the following pseudocode:

```
determine the smaller table

select dname, loc from dept

select empno, ename from emp

for each row in dept match it to every row in emp retaining all rows
```

Listing 3-23 shows the plan for this query.

Listing 3-23. Cartesian Join

```
SQL> select empno, ename, dname, loc
  2  from   dept, emp ;
```

Id	Operation	Name	A-Rows	Buffers	Reads
0	SELECT STATEMENT		56	17	12
1	MERGE JOIN CARTESIAN		56	17	12
2	TABLE ACCESS FULL	DEPT	4	10	6
3	BUFFER SORT		56	7	6
4	TABLE ACCESS FULL	EMP	14	7	6

Notice the actual rows (A-Rows) in the plan and how the final row estimate is the product of the rows from the two tables ($4 \times 14 = 56$). What you end up with in this case is likely a result set that has a whole lot more rows than you want or intended to have. When plans aren't checked properly while developing SQL, Cartesian joins may end up causing the result set to appear to have numerous duplicate rows. And, unfortunately, the first thing many people do is add a distinct operator to the SQL. This has the effect of getting rid of the duplicates so that the result set is correct, but at a significant cost. The duplicates shouldn't have been there in the first place, but because they're there, adding distinct causes a sort to occur and then all the duplicates are eliminated. This is a lot of wasted work. So, always make sure to verify the plan for Cartesian joins if you end up with unexpected duplicate rows in your result set before you simply add distinct out of hand.

One thing you'll notice about the Cartesian join plan is the presence of the BUFFER SORT operation. This isn't really a sort, but because Oracle is joining every row to every row, using the sort buffer mechanism to copy the blocks from the second row source out of the buffer cache and into private memory has the benefit of not requiring the same blocks in the buffer cache to be revisited over and over again. These revisits require a lot more logical reads and also create more opportunity for contention on these blocks in the buffer cache. So, buffering the blocks into a private memory area can be a much more efficient way to accomplish the repeated join.

Outer Joins

An outer join returns all rows from one table and only those rows from the joined table where the join condition is met. Oracle uses the + character to indicate an outer join. The + is placed in parentheses on the side of the join condition with the table where only rows that match is located. As I've indicated in each of the join method overviews, outer joins require that the outer joined table be the driving table. This can mean that join orders that might be more optimal are not used. So, use outer joins properly and with care because their use has implications related to performance of the overall plan.

Listing 3-24 shows an example of how outer joins work. In the example, you are asked to produce a count of how many customers have placed between $0 and $5000 in orders.

Listing 3-24. Outer Join

```
SQL> -- Query to show customers with total orders between $0 and $5000
SQL> select c.cust_last_name, nvl(sum(o.order_total),0) tot_orders
  2    from customers c, orders o
  3   where c.customer_id = o.customer_id
  4   group by c.cust_last_name
  5  having nvl(sum(o.order_total),0) between 0 and 5000
  6   order by c.cust_last_name ;
```

```
CUST_LAST_NAME             TOT_ORDERS
--------------------    ----------------
Alexander                        309
Chandar                          510
George                           220
Hershey                           48
Higgins                          416
Kazan                           1233
Sen                             4797
Stern                          969.2
Weaver                           600

9 rows selected.

SQL> -- To produce just a count, modify the query slightly
SQL> select count(*) ct
  2      from
  3   (
  4   select c.cust_last_name, nvl(sum(o.order_total),0) tot_orders
  5     from customers c, orders o
  6    where c.customer_id = o.customer_id
  7    group by c.cust_last_name
  8   having nvl(sum(o.order_total),0) between 0 and 5000
  9    order by c.cust_last_name
 10   );

          CT
---------------
           9
1 row selected.
SQL> -- What about customers who haven't placed orders (they would have $0 order amount)?
SQL> -- Change the query to an outer join to include customers without orders
SQL> select count(*) ct
  2      from
  3   (
  4   select c.cust_last_name, nvl(sum(o.order_total),0) tot_orders
  5     from customers c, orders o
  6    where c.customer_id = o.customer_id(+)
  7    group by c.cust_last_name
  8   having nvl(sum(o.order_total),0) between 0 and 5000
  9    order by c.cust_last_name
 10   );

          CT
---------------
         140
1 row selected.
```

```
-------------------------------------------------------------------------------
| Id  | Operation                             | Name            | A-Rows |
-------------------------------------------------------------------------------
|   0 | SELECT STATEMENT                      |                 |   140  |
|*  1 |  FILTER                               |                 |   140  |
|   2 |   SORT GROUP BY                       |                 |   176  |
|*  3 |    HASH JOIN OUTER                    |                 |   377  |
|   4 |     VIEW                              | index$_join$_001|   319  |
|*  5 |      HASH JOIN                        |                 |   319  |
|   6 |       INDEX FAST FULL SCAN            | CUSTOMERS_PK    |   319  |
|   7 |       INDEX FAST FULL SCAN            | CUST_LNAME_IX   |   319  |
|   8 |     TABLE ACCESS BY INDEX ROWID BATCHED| ORDERS         |   105  |
|*  9 |      INDEX RANGE SCAN                 | ORD_CUSTOMER_IX |   105  |
-------------------------------------------------------------------------------

Predicate Information (identified by operation id):
---------------------------------------------------

   1 - filter((NVL(SUM("O"."ORDER_TOTAL"),0)>=0 AND NVL(SUM("O"."ORDER_TOTAL"),0)<=5000))
   3 - access("C"."CUSTOMER_ID"="O"."CUSTOMER_ID")
   5 - access(ROWID=ROWID)
   9 - access("O"."CUSTOMER_ID">0)
```

The example shows how the original answer wasn't exactly correct without using an outer join. Because customers who haven't yet placed orders would not have rows in the order table, they are not included in the query result set. Changing the query to be an outer join causes those customers to be included. Also notice the plan operation on line 5 that specifies the HASH JOIN OUTER. Outer joins can be used with any join method (nested loops, hash, sort–merge) and are denoted with the word OUTER at the end of the normal operation name.

As mentioned earlier, the use of the (+) operator to denote an outer join is Oracle–specific syntax. The same thing can be accomplished using ANSI join syntax as well, as shown in Listing 3-25.

Listing 3-25. Outer Join Using ANSI Join Syntax

```
SQL> select count(*) ct
  2    from
  3    (
  4    select c.cust_last_name, nvl(sum(o.order_total),0) tot_orders
  5      from customers c
  6         left outer join
  7         orders o
  8         on (c.customer_id = o.customer_id)
  9     group by c.cust_last_name
 10    having nvl(sum(o.order_total),0) between 0 and 5000
 11     order by c.cust_last_name
 12    );

         CT
---------------
        140

1 row selected.
```

With ANSI syntax, you simply use the keywords LEFT OUTER JOIN, which indicates that the table on the left (the first table listed) is the one you want to have all rows included, even if a match on the join condition isn't found. You could use RIGHT OUTER JOIN if you wanted to have all rows from orders included even if there was no match in customers.

Prior to version 12c, when you use the Oracle (+) operator, you have some limitations that do not exist if you use ANSI syntax. Oracle throws an error if you attempt to outer-join the same table to more than one other table. The error message you get is "ORA-01417: a table may be outer joined to at most one other table." Beginning with 12c, as with ANSI syntax, there is no limit on the number of tables to which a single table can be outer-joined.

Another limitation of Oracle's outer join syntax still present in version 12c is that it doesn't support full outer joins. A full outer join joins two tables from left to right and from right to left. Records that join in both directions are output once to avoid duplication. To demonstrate a full outer join, Listing 3-26 shows the creation of two tables that contain a small subset of common data but have some data that are present only in the single table. The full outer join returns all the rows from both tables that match plus the rows that are unique to each table.

Listing 3-26. Full Outer Join Using ANSI Join Syntax

```
SQL> create table e1 as select * from emp where deptno in (10,20);

Table created.

SQL> create table e2 as select * from emp where deptno in (20,30);

Table created.

SQL> select e1.ename, e1.deptno, e1.job
  2        ,e2.ename, e2.deptno, e2.job
  3  from   e1
  4         full outer join
  5         e2
  6         on (e1.empno = e2.empno);

ENAME        DEPTNO JOB        ENAME        DEPTNO JOB
---------- ---------- --------- ---------- ---------- ---------
SMITH            20 CLERK      SMITH            20 CLERK
                              ALLEN            30 SALESMAN
                              WARD             30 SALESMAN
JONES            20 MANAGER    JONES            20 MANAGER
                              MARTIN           30 SALESMAN
                              BLAKE            30 MANAGER
SCOTT            20 ANALYST    SCOTT            20 ANALYST
                              TURNER           30 SALESMAN
ADAMS            20 CLERK      ADAMS            20 CLERK
                              JAMES            30 CLERK
FORD             20 ANALYST    FORD             20 ANALYST
KING             10 PRESIDENT
CLARK            10 MANAGER
MILLER           10 CLERK

14 rows selected.
```

```
-------------------------------------------------------
| Id  | Operation             | Name      | A-Rows |
-------------------------------------------------------
|   0 | SELECT STATEMENT      |           |     14 |
|   1 |  VIEW                 | VW_FOJ_0  |     14 |
|*  2 |   HASH JOIN FULL OUTER|           |     14 |
|   3 |    TABLE ACCESS FULL  | E1        |      8 |
|   4 |    TABLE ACCESS FULL  | E2        |     11 |
-------------------------------------------------------

Predicate Information (identified by operation id):
---------------------------------------------------

   2 - access("E1"."EMPNO"="E2"."EMPNO")
```

Note that rows from both tables appear in the output, even if they do not have a match in the opposite table. This is what a full outer join does and it can be useful when partial datasets need to be joined. As you can see from the plan, the full outer join is executed as part of a transformed view named VW_FOJ_0. In previous Oracle versions, and when using the Oracle-specific syntax (shown in Listing 3-27), the plan actually executes two separate query blocks and appends the results with UNION ALL. The result set is the same, but the transformation for the ANSI version provides a cleaner and clearer set of execution operations.

Using the plan from the ANSI full outer join example, you can write an equivalent statement using Oracle's syntax that results in the same final result set. Listing 3-27 shows how the statement is coded.

Listing 3-27. Oracle-Equivalent Syntax for Full Outer Join Functionality

```
SQL> select e1.ename, e1.deptno, e1.job,
  2          e2.ename, e2.deptno, e2.job
  3  from    e1,
  4          e2
  5  where   e1.empno (+) = e2.empno
  6  union all
  7  select e1.ename, e1.deptno, e1.job,
  8          e2.ename, e2.deptno, e2.job
  9  from    e1, e2
 10  where   e1.empno = e2.empno (+)
 11  and     e2.rowid is null;
```

ENAME	DEPTNO	JOB	ENAME	DEPTNO	JOB
ADAMS	20	CLERK	ADAMS	20	CLERK
CLARK	10	MANAGER			
FORD	20	ANALYST	FORD	20	ANALYST
JONES	20	MANAGER	JONES	20	MANAGER
KING	10	PRESIDENT			
MILLER	10	CLERK			
SCOTT	20	ANALYST	SCOTT	20	ANALYST
SMITH	20	CLERK	SMITH	20	CLERK
			ALLEN	30	SALESMAN
			BLAKE	30	MANAGER
			JAMES	30	CLERK

MARTIN		30	SALESMAN
TURNER		30	SALESMAN
WARD		30	SALESMAN

14 rows selected.

```
-------------------------------------------------
| Id  | Operation           | Name | A-Rows |
-------------------------------------------------
|   0 | SELECT STATEMENT     |      |     14 |
|   1 |  UNION-ALL           |      |     14 |
|*  2 |   HASH JOIN OUTER     |      |     11 |
|   3 |    TABLE ACCESS FULL  | E2   |     11 |
|   4 |    TABLE ACCESS FULL  | E1   |      8 |
|*  5 |   FILTER             |      |      3 |
|*  6 |    HASH JOIN OUTER    |      |      8 |
|   7 |     TABLE ACCESS FULL | E1   |      8 |
|   8 |     TABLE ACCESS FULL | E2   |     11 |
-------------------------------------------------
```

Predicate Information (identified by operation id):

```
   2 - access("E1"."EMPNO"="E2"."EMPNO")
   5 - filter("E2".ROWID IS NULL)
   6 - access("E1"."EMPNO"="E2"."EMPNO")
```

You may have noticed that the Oracle–equivalent plan is different from the ANSI plan. This is why Oracle uses two outer joins, one in each direction, which is exactly what you asked it to do. So you could use Oracle syntax to accomplish a full outer join, but the ANSI syntax is certainly more straightforward. Also, keep in mind that full outer joins can be quite costly in terms of the amount of resources required to execute. Always be sure to understand the implications of coding such queries and note the performance implications.

Summary

The optimizer must make a few key choices when determining the execution plan for any SQL statement. First, the best way to access each table used in the statement has to be determined. There are basically two choices: an index scan or a full table scan. Each access method works differently to access the blocks containing the row data your SQL statement needs. After the optimizer chooses the access methods, the join methods have to be selected. Tables are joined together in pairs, with the row source from one join result being used to join to another table until all the tables are joined to produce the final result set.

Understanding how each access and join method works can help you write your SQL so that the optimizer makes the most efficient choices. Being able to review the execution plans, understand the operations chosen, and know how these operations work also helps you notice areas where performance problems might occur. Once again, knowing what is "under the hood" helps you write better, faster SQL.

CHAPTER 4

■ ■ ■

SQL Is about Sets

One of the most difficult transitions to make to become highly proficient at writing SQL well is to shift from thinking procedurally to thinking declaratively (or in sets). It is often hardest to learn to think in sets if you've spent time working with virtually any programming language. If this is the case for you, you are likely very comfortable with constructs such as IF-THEN-ELSE, WHILE-DO, LOOP-END LOOP, and BEGIN-END. These constructs support working with logic and data in a very procedural, step-by-step, top-down–type approach. The SQL language is not intended to be implemented from a procedural point of view, but from a set-oriented one. The longer it takes you to shift to a set-oriented point of view, the longer it takes for you to become truly proficient at writing SQL that is functionally correct and also highly optimized to perform well.

In this chapter, we explore common areas where you may need to shift your procedural way of thinking to nonprocedural ways, which allows you to start to understand how to work with sets of data elements vs. sequential steps. We also look at several specific set operations (UNION, INTERSECT, MINUS) and how nulls affect set-thinking.

Thinking in Sets

Using a real-world example as a way to help you start thinking in sets, consider a deck of playing cards. A standard card deck consists of 52 cards, but the deck can be broken into multiple sets as well. How many sets can you make from the main set of standard playing cards? Your answer depends, in part, on any rules that might be applied to how a set is defined. So, for our purposes, let's say there is only one rule for making a set: All cards in a set must have something in common. With that rule in place, let's count the sets. There are a total of 22 sets:

- Four sets—one for each suit (diamonds, clubs, spades, hearts)

- Two sets—one for each color (red, black)

- Thirteen sets—one for each individual card (Ace, 2 through 10, Jack, Queen, King)

- One set—face cards only (Jack, Queen, King)

- One set—nonface cards only (Ace, 2 through 10)

You might be able to think up some other sets in addition to the 22 I've defined, but you get the idea, right? The idea is that if you think of this example in terms of SQL, there is a table, named DECK, with 52 rows in it. The table could have several indexes on columns by which we intend to filter regularly. For instance, we could create indexes on the suit column (diamonds, clubs, spades, hearts), the color column (red, black), the card_name column (Ace, 2 through 10, Jack, Queen, King), and the card_type column (face card/nonface card). We could write some PL/SQL code to read the table row by row in a looping construct and to ask for different cards (rows) to be returned or we could write a single query that returns the specific rows we want. Which method do you think is more efficient?

Consider the PL/SQL code method. You can open a cursor containing all the rows in the DECK table and then read the rows in a loop. For each row, you check the criteria you want, such as all cards from the suit of hearts. This method requires the execution of 52 fetch calls, one for each row in the table. Then, each row is examined to check the value of the suit column to determine whether it is hearts. If it is hearts, the row is included in the final result; otherwise, it is rejected. This means that out of 52 rows fetched and checked, only 13 are a match. In the end, 75 percent of the rows are rejected. This translates to doing 75 percent more work than absolutely necessary.

However, if you think in sets, you can write a single query, SELECT * FROM DECK WHERE SUIT = 'HEARTS', to solve the problem. Because there is an index on the suit column, the execution of the query uses the index to return only the 13 cards in the suit of hearts. In this case, the query is executed once and there is nothing rejected. Only the rows wanted are accessed and returned.

The point of this example is to help you to think in sets. With something you can actually visualize, like a deck of cards, it seems quite obvious that you should think in sets. It just seems natural. But, if you find it hard to make a set with a deck of cards, I bet you find it harder to think in sets when writing SQL. Writing SQL works under the same premise (set-thinking is a must!); it's just a different game. Now that you're warmed up to think in sets, let's look at several ways to switch procedural thinking to set-thinking.

Moving from Procedural to Set-Based Thinking

The first thing you need to do is to stop thinking about process steps that handle data one row at a time. If you're thinking one row at a time, your thinking uses phrases such as "for each row, do x" or "while value is y, do x." Try to shift this thinking to use phrases such as "for all." A simple example of this is adding numbers. When you think procedurally, you think of adding the number value from one row to the number value from another row until you've added all the rows together. Thinking of summing all rows is different. This is a very simple example, but the same shift in thinking applies to situations that aren't as obvious.

For example, if I asked you to produce a list of all employees who spent the same number of years in each job they held within the company during their employment, how would you do it? If you think procedurally, you look at each job position, compute the number of years that position was held, and compare it with the number of years any other positions were held. If the number of years don't match, you reject the employee from the list. This approach might lead to a query that uses a self-join, such as the following:

```
select distinct employee_id
  from job_history j1
 where not exists
       (select null
          from job_history j2
         where j2.employee_id = j1.employee_id
           and round(months_between(j2.start_date,j2.end_date)/12,0) <>
               round(months_between(j1.start_date,j1.end_date)/12,0) )
```

On the other hand, if you look at the problem from a set-based point of view, you might write the query by accessing the table only once, grouping rows by employee, and filtering the result to retain only those employees whose minimum years in a single position match their maximum years in a single position, like this:

```
select employee_id
  from job_history
 group by employee_id
having min(round(months_between(start_date,end_date)/12,0)) =
max(round(months_between(start_date,end_date)/12,0))
```

Listing 4-1 shows the execution of each of these alternatives. You can see that the set-based approach uses fewer logical reads and has a more concise plan that accesses the job_history table only once instead of twice.

Listing 4-1. Procedural vs. Set-Based Approach

```
SQL> select distinct employee_id
  2     from job_history j1
  3    where not exists
  4          (select null
  5             from job_history j2
  6            where j2.employee_id = j1.employee_id
  7              and round(months_between(j2.start_date,j2.end_date)/12,0) <>
  8                  round(months_between(j1.start_date,j1.end_date)/12,0) );

    EMPLOYEE_ID
---------------
            102
            201
            114
            176
            122
```

Id	Operation	Name	A-Rows	Buffers
0	SELECT STATEMENT		5	14
1	HASH UNIQUE		5	14
* 2	HASH JOIN ANTI		6	14
3	TABLE ACCESS FULL	JOB_HISTORY	10	7
4	TABLE ACCESS FULL	JOB_HISTORY	10	7

```
Predicate Information (identified by operation id):
---------------------------------------------------

   2 - access("J2"."EMPLOYEE_ID"="J1"."EMPLOYEE_ID")
       filter(ROUND(MONTHS_BETWEEN(INTERNAL_FUNCTION("J2"."START_DATE"),
       INTERNAL_FUNCTION("J2"."END_DATE"))/12,0)<>
       ROUND(MONTHS_BETWEEN(INTERNAL_FUNCTION("J1"."START_DATE"),
       INTERNAL_FUNCTION("J1"."END_DATE"))/12,0))

SQL> select employee_id
  2     from job_history
  3    group by employee_id
  4   having min(round(months_between(start_date,end_date)/12,0)) =
  5          max(round(months_between(start_date,end_date)/12,0));

    EMPLOYEE_ID
---------------
            102
            114
            122
            176
            201
```

```
-----------------------------------------------------------------
| Id  | Operation                     | Name         | A-Rows | Buffers |
-----------------------------------------------------------------
|   0 | SELECT STATEMENT              |              |    5   |    4    |
|*  1 |  FILTER                       |              |    5   |    4    |
|   2 |   SORT GROUP BY NOSORT        |              |    7   |    4    |
|   3 |    TABLE ACCESS BY INDEX ROWID| JOB_HISTORY  |   10   |    4    |
|   4 |     INDEX FULL SCAN           | JHIST_PK     |   10   |    2    |
-----------------------------------------------------------------
```

```
Predicate Information (identified by operation id):
-------------------------------------------------

   1 - filter(MIN(ROUND(MONTHS_BETWEEN(INTERNAL_FUNCTION("START_DATE"),
         INTERNAL_FUNCTION("END_DATE"))/12,0))=MAX(ROUND(MONTHS_BETWEEN(
         INTERNAL_FUNCTION("START_DATE"),INTERNAL_FUNCTION("END_DATE"))
         /12,0)))
```

The key is to start thinking in terms of completed results, not process steps. Look for group characteristics and not individual steps or actions. In set-based thinking, everything exists in a state defined by the filters or constraints applied to the set. You don't think in terms of process flow but in terms of the state of the set. Figure 4-1 shows a comparison between a process flow diagram and a nested sets diagram to illustrate my point.

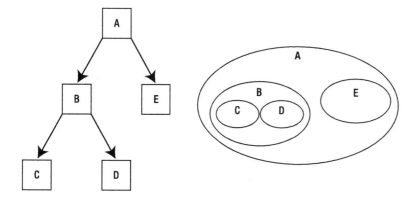

Figure 4-1. *A process flow diagram vs. a nested set diagram*

The process flow diagram implies the result set (A) is achieved through a series of steps that build on one another to produce the final answer. B is built by traversing C and D, and then A is built by traversing B and E. However, the nested sets diagram views A as a result of a combination of sets.

Another common but erroneous way of thinking is to consider tables to be ordered sets of rows. Just think of how you typically see table contents listed. They're shown in a grid or spreadsheet-type view. However, a table represents a set, and a set has no order. Showing tables in a way that implies a certain order can be confusing. Remember from Chapter 2 that the ORDER BY clause is applied last when a SQL statement is executed. SQL is based on set theory, and because sets have no predetermined order to their rows, order has to be applied separately after the rows that satisfy the query result have been extracted from the set. Figure 4-2 shows a more correct way to depict the content of tables that doesn't imply order.

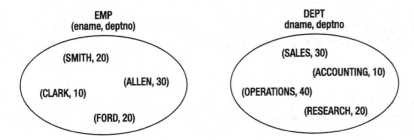

Figure 4-2. *The EMP and DEPT sets*

It may not seem important to make these seemingly small distinctions in how you think, but these small shifts are fundamental to understanding SQL correctly. Let's look at an example of writing a SQL statement taking both a procedural thinking approach and a set-based approach to help clarify the distinctions between the two.

Procedural vs. Set-Based Thinking: An Example

In this example, the task is to compute an average number of days between orders for a customer. Listing 4-2 shows one way to do this from a procedural thinking approach. To keep the example output shorter, I work with one customer only, but I could convert this easily to handle all customers.

Listing 4-2. Procedural Thinking Approach

```
SQL> -- Show the list of order dates for customer 102
SQL> select customer_id, order_date
  2  from orders
  3  where customer_id = 102 ;

   CUSTOMER_ID ORDER_DATE
-------------- ------------------------------
           102 19-NOV-99 06.41.54.696211 PM
           102 14-SEP-99 11.53.40.223345 AM
           102 29-MAR-99 04.22.40.536996 PM
           102 14-SEP-98 09.03.04.763452 AM
SQL>
SQL> -- Determine the order_date prior to the current row's order_date
SQL> select customer_id, order_date,
  2           lag(order_date,1,order_date)
  3           over (partition by customer_id order by order_date)
  4           as prev_order_date
  5  from orders
  6  where customer_id = 102;

   CUSTOMER_ID ORDER_DATE                      PREV_ORDER_DATE
-------------- ------------------------------- ----------------------------
           102 14-SEP-98 09.03.04.763452 AM    14-SEP-98 09.03.04.763452 AM
           102 29-MAR-99 04.22.40.536996 PM    14-SEP-98 09.03.04.763452 AM
           102 14-SEP-99 11.53.40.223345 AM    29-MAR-99 04.22.40.536996 PM
           102 19-NOV-99 06.41.54.696211 PM    14-SEP-99 11.53.40.223345 AM
```

```
SQL>
SQL> -- Determine the days between each order
SQL> select trunc(order_date) - trunc(prev_order_date)  days_between
  2  from
  3  (
  4  select customer_id, order_date,
  5              lag(order_date,1,order_date)
  6              over (partition by customer_id order by order_date)
  7              as prev_order_date
  8  from orders
  9  where customer_id = 102
 10  );


   DAYS_BETWEEN
---------------
              0
            196
            169
             66
SQL>
SQL> -- Put it together with an AVG function to get the final answer
SQL> select avg(trunc(order_date) - trunc(prev_order_date))  avg_days_between
  2  from
  3  (
  4  select customer_id, order_date,
  5              lag(order_date,1,order_date)
  6              over (partition by customer_id order by order_date)
  7              as prev_order_date
  8  from orders
  9  where customer_id = 102
 10  );

AVG_DAYS_BETWEEN
----------------
          107.75
```

This looks pretty elegant, doesn't it? In this example, I executed several queries one by one to show you how my thinking follows a step-by-step procedural approach to writing the query. Don't worry if you're unfamiliar with the use of the analytic function LAG; analytic functions are covered in Chapter 8. Briefly, what I've done is to read each order row for customer 102 in order by order_date and, using the LAG function, look back at the prior order row to get its order_date. When I have both dates—the date for the current row's order and the date for the previous row's order—it's a simple matter to subtract the two to get the days in between. Last, I use the average aggregate function to get my final answer.

You can tell that this query is built following a very procedural approach. The best giveaway to knowing the approach is the way I can walk through several different queries to show how the final result set is built. I can see the detail as I go along. When you're thinking in sets, you find that you don't really care about each individual element. Listing 4-3 shows the query written using a set-based thinking approach.

Listing 4-3. Set-Based Thinking Approach

```
SQL> select (max(trunc(order_date)) - min(trunc(order_date))) / count(*) as avg_days_between
  2  from orders
  3  where customer_id = 102 ;

AVG_DAYS_BETWEEN
----------------
          107.75
```

How about that? I really didn't need anything fancy to solve the problem. All I needed to compute the average days between orders was the total duration of time between the first and last order, and the number of orders placed. I didn't need to go through all that step-by-step thinking as if I was writing a program that would read the data row by row and compute the answer. I just needed to shift my thinking to consider the problem in terms of the set of data as a whole.

I do not discount the procedural approach completely. There may be times when you have to take that approach to get the job done. However, I encourage you to shift your thinking. Start by searching for a set-based approach and move toward a more procedural approach only when and to the degree needed. By doing this, you likely find that you can come up with simpler, more direct, and often better performing solutions.

Set Operations

Oracle supports four set operators: UNION, UNION ALL, MINUS, and INTERSECT. Set operators combine the results from two or more SELECT statements to form a single result set. This differs from joins in that joins are used to combine columns from each joined table into one row. The set operators compare completed rows between the input queries and return a distinct set of rows. The exception to this is the use of UNION ALL, which returns all rows from both sets, including duplicates. UNION returns a result set from all input queries with no duplicates. MINUS returns distinct rows that appear in the first input query result but not in the subsequent ones. INTERSECT returns the distinct rows that appear in all input queries.

All queries that are used with set operators must conform to the following conditions:

- All input queries must retrieve the same number of columns.

- The data types of each column must match the corresponding column (by order in the column list) for each of the other input queries. It is possible for data types not to match directly, but only if the data types of all input queries can be converted implicitly to the data types of the first input query.

- The ORDER BY clause may not be used in the individual queries and may only be used at the end of the query, where it applies to the entire result of the set operation.

- Column names are derived from the first input query.

Each input query is processed separately and then the set operator is applied. Last, the ORDER BY is applied to the total result set if one is specified. When using UNION and INTERSECT, the operators are commutative (in other words, the order of the queries doesn't matter). However, when using MINUS, the order is important because this set operation uses the first input query result as the base for comparison with other results. All set operations except for UNION ALL require that the result set go through a sort/distinct process that means additional overhead to process the query. If you know that no duplicates ever exist, or you don't care whether duplicates are present, make sure to use UNION ALL.

UNION and UNION ALL

UNION and UNION ALL are used when the results of two or more separate queries need to be combined to provide a single, final result set. Figure 4-3 uses Venn diagrams to show how the result set for each type can be visualized.

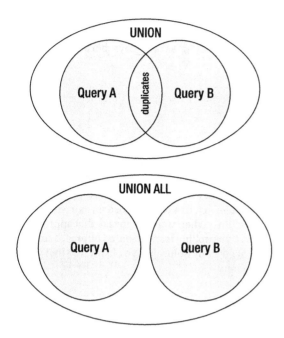

Figure 4-3. Venn diagram for UNION and UNION ALL result sets

The UNION set operation returns the results of both queries but removes duplicates whereas the UNION ALL returns all rows including duplicates. As mentioned previously, in cases when you need to eliminate duplicates, use UNION. But, when either you don't care if duplicates exist or you don't expect duplicates to occur, choose UNION ALL. Using UNION ALL has a less resource-intensive footprint than using UNION because UNION ALL does not have to do any processing to remove duplicates. This processing can be quite expensive in terms of both resources and response time to complete. Prior to Oracle version 10, a sort operation was used to remove duplicates. Beginning with version 10, an option to use a HASH UNIQUE operation to remove duplicates is available. The HASH UNIQUE doesn't sort, but uses hash value comparisons instead. I mention this to make sure you realize that even if the result set appears to be in sorted order, the result set is not guaranteed to be sorted unless you explicitly include an ORDER BY clause. UNION ALL avoids this "distincting" operation entirely, so it is best to use it whenever possible. Listing 4-4 shows examples of using UNION and UNION ALL.

Listing 4-4. UNION and UNION ALL Examples

```
SQL> CREATE TABLE table1 (
  2     id_pk INTEGER NOT NULL PRIMARY KEY,
  3     color VARCHAR(10) NOT NULL);
SQL> CREATE TABLE table2 (
  2     id_pk INTEGER NOT NULL PRIMARY KEY,
  3     color VARCHAR(10) NOT NULL);
SQL> CREATE TABLE table3 (
  2     color VARCHAR(10) NOT NULL);
SQL> INSERT INTO table1 VALUES (1, 'RED');
SQL> INSERT INTO table1 VALUES (2, 'RED');
SQL> INSERT INTO table1 VALUES (3, 'ORANGE');
SQL> INSERT INTO table1 VALUES (4, 'ORANGE');
SQL> INSERT INTO table1 VALUES (5, 'ORANGE');
SQL> INSERT INTO table1 VALUES (6, 'YELLOW');
```

```
SQL> INSERT INTO table1 VALUES (7, 'GREEN');
SQL> INSERT INTO table1 VALUES (8, 'BLUE');
SQL> INSERT INTO table1 VALUES (9, 'BLUE');
SQL> INSERT INTO table1 VALUES (10, 'VIOLET');
SQL> INSERT INTO table2 VALUES (1, 'RED');
SQL> INSERT INTO table2 VALUES (2, 'RED');
SQL> INSERT INTO table2 VALUES (3, 'BLUE');
SQL> INSERT INTO table2 VALUES (4, 'BLUE');
SQL> INSERT INTO table2 VALUES (5, 'BLUE');
SQL> INSERT INTO table2 VALUES (6, 'GREEN');
SQL> COMMIT;
SQL>
SQL> select color from table1
  2  union
  3  select color from table2;

COLOR
----------
BLUE
GREEN
ORANGE
RED
VIOLET
YELLOW

6 rows selected.

SQL> select color from table1
  2  union all
  3  select color from table2;

COLOR
----------
RED
RED
ORANGE
ORANGE
ORANGE
YELLOW
GREEN
BLUE
BLUE
VIOLET
RED
RED
BLUE
BLUE
BLUE
GREEN

16 rows selected.
```

```
SQL> select color from table1;

COLOR
----------
RED
RED
ORANGE
ORANGE
ORANGE
YELLOW
GREEN
BLUE
BLUE
VIOLET

10 rows selected.

SQL> select color from table3;

no rows selected

SQL> select color from table1
  2  union
  3  select color from table3;

COLOR
----------
BLUE
GREEN
ORANGE
RED
VIOLET
YELLOW

6 rows selected.

SQL> -- The first query will return a differen number of columns than the second
SQL> select * from table1
  2  union
  3  select color from table2;
select * from table1
*
ERROR at line 1:
ORA-01789: query block has incorrect number of result columns
```

These examples demonstrate the UNION of two queries. Keep in mind that you can have multiple queries that are "unioned" together.

MINUS

MINUS is used when the results of the first input query are used as the base set from which the other input query result sets are subtracted to end up with the final result set. The use of MINUS has often been used instead of using NOT EXISTS (antijoin) queries. The problem being solved is something like, "I need to return the set of rows that exists in row source A but not in row source B." Figure 4-4 uses a Venn diagram to show how the result set for this operation can be visualized.

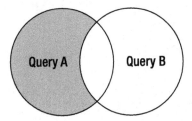

Figure 4-4. *Venn diagram for MINUS result sets*

Listing 4-5 shows examples of using MINUS.

Listing 4-5. MINUS Examples

```
SQL> select color from table1
  2  minus
  3  select color from table2;

COLOR
----------
ORANGE
VIOLET
YELLOW

3 rows selected.

SQL> -- MINUS queries are equivalent to NOT EXISTS queries
SQL> select distinct color from table1
  2  where not exists (select null from table2 where table2.color = table1.color) ;

COLOR
----------
ORANGE
VIOLET
YELLOW

3 rows selected.

SQL>
SQL> select color from table2
  2  minus
  3  select color from table1;
```

```
no rows selected

SQL> -- MINUS using an empty table
SQL> select color from table1
  2  minus
  3  select color from table3;

COLOR
----------
BLUE
GREEN
ORANGE
RED
VIOLET
YELLOW

6 rows selected.
```

INTERSECT

INTERSECT is used to return a distinct set of rows that appear in all input queries. The use of INTERSECT has often been used instead of using EXISTS (semijoin) queries. The problem being solved is something like, "I need to return the set of rows from row source A only if a match exists in row source B." Figure 4-5 uses a Venn diagram to show how the result set for this operation can be visualized.

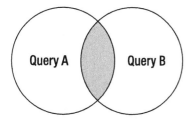

Figure 4-5. *Venn diagram for INTERSECT result sets*

Listing 4-6 shows examples of using INTERSECT.

Listing 4-6. INTERSECT Examples

```
SQL> select color from table1
  2  intersect
  3  select color from table2;

COLOR
----------
BLUE
GREEN
RED

3 rows selected.
```

```
SQL> select color from table1
  2  intersect
  3  select color from table3;
```

no rows selected

Sets and Nulls

You often hear the term *null value*, but in truth, a null isn't a value at all. A null is, at best, a marker. I always think of null as meaning "I don't know." The SQL language handles nulls in unintuitive ways—at least from my point of view; results from their use are often not what I expect in terms of real-world functionality.

IS THE TERM *NULL VALUE* WRONG?

Strictly speaking, a null is not a value, but rather is the absence of a value. However, the term *null value* is in wide use. Work in SQL long enough and you surely encounter someone who pontificates on how wrong it is to use the term *null value*.

But is it really wrong to use the term *null value?*

If you find yourself on the receiving end of such a lecture, feel free to argue right back. The term *null value* is widely used in both the ANSI and ISO editions of the SQL standard. *Null value* is an official part of the description of the SQL language and thus is fair game for use when discussing the language.

Keep in mind, though, that there is a distinction to be drawn between the SQL language and relational theory. A really picky person can argue for the use of "null value" when speaking of SQL, and yet argue against that very same term when speaking of relational theory, on which SQL is loosely based.

NULLs and Unintuitive Results

Listing 4-7 shows a simple query for which I expect a certain result set but end up with something different than my expectations. I expect that if I query for the absence of a specific value and no matches are found, including when the column contains a null, Oracle should return that row in the result set.

Listing 4-7. Examples Using NULL

```
SQL> -- select all rows from emp table
SQL> select * from scott.emp ;
```

EMPNO	ENAME	JOB	MGR	HIREDATE	SAL	COMM	DEPTNO
7369	SMITH	CLERK	7902	17-DEC-80	800		20
7499	ALLEN	SALESMAN	7698	20-FEB-81	1600	300	30
7521	WARD	SALESMAN	7698	22-FEB-81	1250	500	30
7566	JONES	MANAGER	7839	02-APR-81	2975		20
7654	MARTIN	SALESMAN	7698	28-SEP-81	1250	1400	30
7698	BLAKE	MANAGER	7839	01-MAY-81	2850		30
7782	CLARK	MANAGER	7839	09-JUN-81	2450		10

7788	SCOTT	ANALYST	7566	19-APR-87	3000		20
7839	KING	PRESIDENT		17-NOV-81	5000		
7844	TURNER	SALESMAN	7698	08-SEP-81	1500	0	30
7876	ADAMS	CLERK	7788	23-MAY-87	1100		20
7900	JAMES	CLERK	7698	03-DEC-81	950		30
7902	FORD	ANALYST	7566	03-DEC-81	3000		20
7934	MILLER	CLERK	7782	23-JAN-82	1300		10

```
14 rows selected.

SQL> -- select only rows with deptno of 10, 20, 30
SQL> select * from scott.emp where deptno in (10, 20, 30) ;
```

EMPNO	ENAME	JOB	MGR	HIREDATE	SAL	COMM	DEPTNO
7369	SMITH	CLERK	7902	17-DEC-80	800		20
7499	ALLEN	SALESMAN	7698	20-FEB-81	1600	300	30
7521	WARD	SALESMAN	7698	22-FEB-81	1250	500	30
7566	JONES	MANAGER	7839	02-APR-81	2975		20
7654	MARTIN	SALESMAN	7698	28-SEP-81	1250	1400	30
7698	BLAKE	MANAGER	7839	01-MAY-81	2850		30
7782	CLARK	MANAGER	7839	09-JUN-81	2450		10
7788	SCOTT	ANALYST	7566	19-APR-87	3000		20
7844	TURNER	SALESMAN	7698	08-SEP-81	1500	0	30
7876	ADAMS	CLERK	7788	23-MAY-87	1100		20
7900	JAMES	CLERK	7698	03-DEC-81	950		30
7902	FORD	ANALYST	7566	03-DEC-81	3000		20
7934	MILLER	CLERK	7782	23-JAN-82	1300		10

```
13 rows selected.

SQL> -- select only rows with deptno not 10, 20, 30
SQL> select * from scott.emp where deptno not in (10, 20, 30) ;

no rows selected

SQL> -- select only rows with deptno not 10, 20, 30 or null
SQL> select * from scott.emp where deptno not in (10, 20, 30)
  2       or deptno is null;
```

EMPNO	ENAME	JOB	MGR	HIREDATE	SAL	COMM	DEPTNO
7839	KING	PRESIDENT		17-NOV-81	5000		

```
1 row selected.
```

This listing demonstrates what is frustrating to me about nulls: They don't get included unless specified explicitly. In my example, 13 of the 14 rows in the table have deptno 10, 20, or 30. Because there are 14 total rows in the table, I expect a query that asks for rows that do not have a deptno of 10, 20, or 30 to then show the remaining one row. But, I'm wrong in expecting this, as you can see from the results of the query. If I include explicitly the condition also to include where deptno is null, I get the full list of employees that I expect.

I realize what I'm doing when I think this way is considering nulls to be "low values." I suppose it's the old COBOL programmer in me that remembers the days when LOW-VALUES and HIGH-VALUES were used. I also suppose that my brain wants to make nulls equate with an empty string. But, no matter what my brain wants to make of them, nulls are nulls. Nulls do not participate in comparisons. Nulls can't be added, subtracted, multiplied, or divided by anything. If they are, the return value is null. Listing 4-8 demonstrates this fact about nulls and how they participate in comparisons and expressions.

Listing 4-8. NULLs in Comparisons and Expressions

```
SQL> select * from scott.emp where deptno is null ;

   EMPNO ENAME      JOB         MGR HIREDATE      SAL   COMM  DEPTNO
 ------- ---------- ---------- ------- ---------- ------ ------ -------
    7839 KING       PRESIDENT           17-NOV-81 5000

1 row selected.

SQL>
SQL> select * from scott.emp where deptno = null ;

no rows selected

SQL> select sal, comm, sal + comm as tot_comp
  2  from scott.emp where deptno = 30;

    SAL   COMM    TOT_COMP
 ------ ------ ---------------
   1600    300         1900
   1250    500         1750
   1250   1400         2650
   2850
   1500      0         1500
    950

6 rows selected.
```

So, when my brain wants rows with a null deptno to be returned in the query from Listing 4-7, I have to remind myself that when a comparison is made with a null, the answer is always "I don't know." It's the same as you asking me if there is orange juice in *your* refrigerator and me answering, "I don't know." You might have orange juice there or you might not, but I don't know. So, I can't answer in any different way and be truthful.

The relational model is based on two-value logic (TRUE, FALSE), but the SQL language allows three-value logic (TRUE, FALSE, UNKNOWN)—and this is where the problem comes in. With that third value in the mix, your SQL returns the "correct" answer as far as how three-value logic considers the comparison, but the answers may not be correct in terms of what you expect in the real world. In the example in Listing 4-8, the answer of "no rows selected" is correct in that, because one deptno column contains a null, you can't know one way or the other if the column might possibly be something other than 10, 20, or 30. To answer truthfully, the answer has to be UNKNOWN. It's just like me knowing whether you have orange juice in your refrigerator!

So, you have to make sure you keep the special nature of nulls in mind when you write SQL. If you're not vigilant in watching out for nulls, you'll very likely have SQL that returns the wrong answer. At least it is wrong as far as the answer you *expect*.

NULL Behavior in Set Operations

Set operations treat nulls as if they are able to be compared using equality checks. This is an interesting, and perhaps unexpected, behavior given the previous discussion. Listing 4-9 shows how nulls are treated when used in set operations.

Listing 4-9. NULLs and Set Operations

```
SQL> select null from dual
  2  union
  3  select null from dual
  4  ;

N
-

1 row selected.

SQL> select null from dual
  2  union all
  3  select null from dual
  4  ;

N
-

2 rows selected.

SQL> select null from dual
  2  intersect
  3  select null from dual;

N
-

1 row selected.

SQL> select null from dual
  2  minus
  3  select null from dual;

no rows selected

SQL> select 1 from dual
  2  union
  3  select null from dual;

         1
---------------
         1
2 rows selected.
```

```
SQL> select 1 from dual
  2  union all
  3  select null from dual;

            1
---------------
            1
2 rows selected.

SQL> select 1 from dual
  2  intersect
  3  select null from dual ;

no rows selected

SQL> select 1 from dual
  2  minus
  3  select null from dual ;

            1
---------------
            1

1 row selected.
```

In the first example, when you have two rows with nulls that are "unioned," you end up with only one row, which implies that the two rows are equal to one another and, therefore, when the union is processed, the duplicate row is excluded. As you can see, the same is true for how the other set operations behave, so keep in mind that set operations treat nulls as equals.

NULLs and GROUP BY and ORDER BY

Just as in set operations, the GROUP BY and ORDER BY clauses process nulls as if they are able to be compared using equality checks. Notice that with both grouping and ordering, nulls are always placed together, just like known values. Listing 4-10 shows an example of how nulls are handled in the GROUP BY and ORDER BY clauses.

Listing 4-10. NULLs and GROUP BY and ORDER BY

```
SQL> select comm, count(*) ctr
  2  from scott.emp
  3  group by comm ;

COMM              CTR
------ ---------------
                   10
  1400              1
   500              1
   300              1
     0              1
5 rows selected.
```

111

```
SQL> select comm, count(*) ctr
  2  from scott.emp
  3  group by comm
  4  order by comm ;

  COMM          CTR
------ ---------------
     0            1
   300            1
   500            1
  1400            1
                 10
5 rows selected.
SQL> select comm, count(*) ctr
  2  from scott.emp
  3  group by comm
  4  order by comm
  5  nulls first ;

  COMM          CTR
------ ---------------
                 10
     0            1
   300            1
   500            1
  1400            1
5 rows selected.

SQL> select ename, sal, comm
  2  from scott.emp
  3  order by comm, ename ;

ENAME        SAL   COMM
---------- ------ ------
TURNER      1500      0
ALLEN       1600    300
WARD        1250    500
MARTIN      1250   1400
ADAMS       1100
BLAKE       2850
CLARK       2450
FORD        3000
JAMES        950
JONES       2975
KING        5000
MILLER      1300
SCOTT       3000
SMITH        800

14 rows selected.
```

The first two examples show the behavior of nulls within a GROUP BY clause. Because the first query returns the result in what appears to be descending sorted order by the comm column, I want to issue the second query to make a point that I made earlier in the book: The only way to ensure order is to use an ORDER BY clause. Just because the first query result appears to be in a sorted order doesn't mean it is. When I add the ORDER BY clause in the second query, the null group moves to the bottom. In the last ORDER BY example, note that the nulls are displayed last. This is not because nulls are considered to be "high values"; it is because the default for ordered sorting is to place nulls last. If you want to display nulls first, you simply add the clause NULLS FIRST after your ORDER BY clause, as shown in the third example.

NULLs and Aggregate Functions

This same difference in the treatment of nulls with some operations such as set operations, grouping, and ordering also applies to aggregate functions. When nulls are present in columns that have aggregate functions such as SUM, COUNT, AVG, MIN, or MAX applied to them, they are removed from the set being aggregated. If the set that results is empty, then the aggregate returns a null.

An exception to this rule involves the use of the COUNT aggregate function. The handling of nulls depends on whether the COUNT function is formulated using a column name or a literal (such as * or 1). Listing 4-11 demonstrates how aggregate functions handle nulls.

Listing 4-11. NULLs and Aggregate Functions

```
SQL> select count(*) row_ct, count(comm) comm_ct,
  2         avg(comm) avg_comm, min(comm) min_comm,
  3         max(comm) max_comm, sum(comm) sum_comm
  4  from scott.emp ;

  ROW_CT  COMM_CT AVG_COMM MIN_COMM MAX_COMM SUM_COMM
-------- -------- -------- -------- -------- --------
      14        4      550        0     1400     2200

1 row selected.
```

Notice the difference in the value for COUNT(*) and COUNT(comm). Using * produces the answer of 14, which is the total of all rows, whereas using comm produces the answer of 4, which is only the number of nonnull comm values. You can also verify easily that nulls are removed prior to the computation of AVG, MIN, MAX, and SUM because all the functions produce an answer. If nulls aren't removed, the answers are all null.

Summary

Thinking in sets is a key skill to master to write SQL that is easier to understand and that typically performs better than SQL written from a procedural approach. When you think procedurally, you attempt to force the SQL language, which is nonprocedural, to function in ways it shouldn't need to function. In this chapter, we examined these two approaches and discussed how to begin to shift your thinking from procedural to set based. As you proceed through the rest of the book, work to keep a set-based approach in mind. If you find yourself thinking row by row in a procedural fashion, stop and check yourself. The more you practice, the easier it becomes.

CHAPTER 5

■ ■ ■

It's about the Question

"It's not about the query; it's about the question." This is one of my favorite sayings when it comes to writing SQL. Regardless of your level of proficiency, writing SQL well is as much about questions as it is about queries.

There are many ways that questions play an important role when writing SQL. First, understanding the question behind the query is often more important than the query syntax itself. If you start with the question the SQL is intended to answer, you are more likely to think through and understand how best to formulate the query to get the desired result. Second, it is critical to be able to ask good questions to clarify what the SQL is intended to do, and to gather all the pertinent information you need to write SQL that is not only functionally correct, but also efficient. Last, you must be able to create well-formed logical expressions that help answer the questions behind the SQL.

In this chapter, I cover how to go about ferreting out all the information you need to write the query in the best way possible. The way you do this is by asking good questions. Regardless of whether you are writing a new SQL statement or modifying an existing one, questions are the heart of the process.

Asking Good Questions

Asking good questions is an intellectual habit, and habits don't form overnight. Long ago, I read that it takes between 21 days and 28 days to form a new habit. However, a 2009 research study published in the *European Journal of Social Psychology*[1] suggests that forming new habits actually takes an average of 66 days; however, the more complex the behavior, the longer it takes for that behavior to become a habit. So, if you're not already in the habit of asking good questions, it's important to understand that learning to do so takes specific effort on your part to gain proficiency.

You may be wondering what any of this has to do with writing SQL. I believe knowing how to ask good questions and, even more specifically, knowing how to ask questions that allow you to determine the correct question your SQL statement is intended to answer, is a crucial habit you need to form if you really want to elevate your SQL skills to the next level.

To write any SQL statement, begin with a question you need to answer. The answer is a result set comprised from one or more rows of data from the tables in your database. As a starting point, you may be given the answer being sought in the form of a sample report or screen display. At other times, you may be given a more complete specification for what the query needs to deliver. You shouldn't be surprised when I tell you that you get weak query specifications more often than you get strong, detailed ones. No matter how much information you are given about the queries you need to write, you need to make sure to ask good questions that ensure you have everything you need to write SQL that does what it is supposed to—and does it quickly and efficiently.

---

[1]See www3.interscience.wiley.com/journal/122513384/abstract?CRETRY=1&SRETRY=0, www.telegraph.co.uk/health/healthnews/5857845/It-takes-66-days-to-form-a-habit.html, and www.spring.org.uk/2009/09/how-long-to-form-a-habit.php.

The Purpose of Questions

Questions help you clarify the request and help you probe assumptions that either you or the requestor may hold. Questions also help you to gather evidence and work out the implications or consequences of implementing code in certain ways. Questions are gold. Well, I suppose you could say that the answers are the gold, but questions are the tools you need to mine the gold.

To ask questions that get you the information you need to write functionally correct and optimally performing SQL, you must be able to formulate your questions properly. Regardless of how much you know, or think you know, about what you've been asked to code, it can be helpful to start with a blank slate and ask questions as if you know nothing. By doing so, you are more likely to reach greater levels of detail and avoid making assumptions.

Many people think that asking questions makes them appear ignorant. I believe questions are a magic tool. Asking intelligent, well-crafted questions cause people to think. And when someone thinks, the door is open for new ideas, new answers, and new possibilities to emerge. When you ask people a question, particularly those who want something from you, you are letting them know you care about what they want and you want to service their request in the best way possible. Keeping silent out of a fear of looking dumb has more potential to backfire. If you don't ask questions and then deliver something that doesn't satisfy the request effectively, you call more negative attention to yourself than asking questions ever could.

I want to point out that you should ask questions even if you ask them only to yourself. As odd as this may sound, if you happen to be in a situation in which there is no good resource at your disposal, you still need to ask questions and get answers. The answers have to come from research you do, but if you start by preparing a good list of questions, you can direct your research more clearly.

Categories of Questions

There are many categorizations of questions. Typically, questions are categorized primarily as open or closed. The category you choose depends on whether you want a longer, detailed answer or a short, limited answer.

Open questions are intended to open a dialogue and help you engage in a conversation. Answers to open questions usually provide more detail and can't be answered with a simple yes or no. Questions that begin with *What*, *How*, *Who*, *When*, and *Why* are open questions. Just be careful when asking Why questions because they may come across as confrontational. Remember that your questions should be intended to help you get all the detail you need, but not put anyone on the defensive. For example, asking, "Why would anyone ever choose to do it that way?" has a very different feeling than "What rationale prompted that choice?" Even if you discover something questionable, or just plain wrong, you can provide feedback directly and may not need to use Why questions very often.

Most of the time, your questions should be aimed at digging out facts. Objective, open questions ask for specific information and tend to be answered with facts. However, you must take care to make sure you are getting facts and not opinions. Formulating a question subjectively by asking someone what they think about something elicits a response that is more subjective. The difference can be a critical one.

Some open questions are intended to get responses to help you get ideas—in particular, ideas about actions you should take. These are problem-solving questions. These types of questions are great to aid in brainstorming different approaches to take. Your colleagues are great people sources for the answers to these types of questions. After you have the detail you need, don't hesitate to bounce things off other developers. They often offer solutions you never would have thought of.

The two most common types of questions you should ask when developing SQL are objective and problem-solving questions. Here are a few examples:

- What is the data model and is a data dictionary or entity relationship diagram (ERD) available?

- How have other related queries, if any, been written?

- Who is the subject matter expert for this application?

- What are the response time requirements for this query?

- How would you implement the request?

- What steps should I take next?

- What resources do you suggest I review?

If you need a yes or no response or just a short answer, closed questions suit that purpose best. Questions that begin with *Are, Can, Did,* or *Do* elicit short, direct responses. These types of questions should not be ambiguous. You want to make sure you ask the question so that you don't end up getting a long response if all you really want is a yes or no. These kinds of questions are intended to prevent or inhibit long discussions.

Closed questions can be separated into three types: identification, selection, and yes/no. When you use an identification-type question, you want to know a specific answer but don't provide choices. A selection-type question provides a list of two or more choices. The yes/no type asks for a simple yes or no response only.

To demonstrate the differences between these three types, I ask the same question in three different ways:

- *Identification*: What kind of table is employees?

- *Selection*: Is the employees table a heap table or an Index-Organized Table (IOT)?

- *Yes/no*: Is the employees table a heap table?

Of these types, the selection type is the one you need to formulate most carefully. In this example, I provided only two selections: heap and IOT. But what if the table is a clustered table type? If you don't include that option in the selection list, you could end up getting a yes/no answer to the original question. The person answering the question might (rudely) answer with a simple "No," and then you have to follow up with an identification question to get the answer you need.

Selecting the right type of question is almost as important as the question itself. You want to get the details needed as expeditiously as possible. So, remember to use closed questions if you want to keep answers short, and to use open questions if you want to open up a discussion and get more detail. The most common mistake is asking a closed question when you really want more detail. For example, "Will you tell me about the project?" is technically a closed question that should return a yes or no answer. Most people have learned to provide a polite response (with detail) even when asked the wrong type of question. But, it is truly your responsibility to ask the correct type and style of question to make it easier for the responder to provide you with the appropriate answer.

Questions about the Question

Developing new queries is usually easier than trying to modify a query that someone else has already written. This is because when you write a brand new query, you don't have to worry about interpreting the meaning of someone else's code. But, what you do have to worry about is the query specification. Regardless of whether it's detailed, it's your job to make sure you code the SQL to deliver the answer to the question you've been handed.

Let's walk through an example of how this process might work. I'll play the role of business user and you play the role of application developer. My request is for you to write a query that provides a list of employees who have held more than one job in the company. I'd like the output to display only the employee_id and a count of how many total jobs each employee has held. Listing 5-1 shows the query you create to satisfy my request.

Listing 5-1. List of Employees Who Have Held Multiple Jobs

```
SQL> desc job_history
 Name                                      Null?    Type
 ----------------------------------------- -------- --------------------
 EMPLOYEE_ID                               NOT NULL NUMBER(6)
 START_DATE                                NOT NULL DATE
 END_DATE                                  NOT NULL DATE
 JOB_ID                                    NOT NULL VARCHAR2(10)
 DEPARTMENT_ID                                      NUMBER(4)
```

```
SQL> select employee_id, count(*) job_ct
  2  from job_history
  3  group by employee_id
  4  having count(*) > 1;

    EMPLOYEE_ID            JOB_CT
--------------- ---------------
            101                 2
            176                 2
            200                 2

3 rows selected.
```

Note that we are making an assumption that the job_history table contains the history of all jobs, including the current ones. Even though this isn't accurate for this dataset, for purposes of this example, we're going to pretend that it is. So, that was pretty simple, right? You complete your testing and deliver this code. However, I come back to you and say it's wrong. The list is missing some employees who have held more than one job. I produced this list manually before I came to seek your help, and I know that the following list of employees should be displayed: 101, 102, 114, 122, 176, 200, and 201.

What went wrong? This seems like a fairly simple query, doesn't it? It went wrong because the solution was developed without any questions being asked. By not asking questions, you made some assumptions (regardless of whether you realized it). The assumptions you made caused you to write the query as you did. The way you wrote the query didn't provide the result I expected. Admittedly, I could have helped you out more by giving you a more detailed specification or by providing you with the expected result set initially. Regardless of the quality of the query specification you have, never forget that it is your job to ferret out the details and make sure you develop code that answers specifically the real question being asked.

Let's start over. The query specification I provided asked you to write a query that provides a list of employees who have held more than one job in the company, displaying the employee_id and a count of how many total jobs they've held. Although at first glance the query request seems straightforward, the apparent simplicity hides several nuances that you can't be aware of unless you ask some questions. The following list includes a few questions you could ask to help clarify the request:

- Should the query consider the employee's current job as part of the count or only jobs held other than the current position?

- Where are the data that satisfy the request stored (in other words, in one table or several)?

- What is the data model and can I get a copy of the data dictionary or an ERD if one exists?

- Is there an expected typical size of the result set?

- How are the data stored? In particular, are they stored in some sorted order or not?

- Must this query meet any response time SLA?

- How frequently will the query execute?

If you receive a request from a business user, it might not be feasible to ask him or her all these questions. Asking a business user about which tables contain the data he or she wants or whether you can get a copy of the ERD might be answered with blank stares, because these things aren't typically in the domain of the business user's knowledge. It is important to note whether the request for the query is coming from an application user or an application technical architect. Many of these questions can be answered only by someone with an understanding of the application from the technical perspective. Therefore, learn who the "go-to" people are when you need to get detailed technical information. This may be the database administrator (DBA), the data architect, or perhaps a developer who worked initially on other code in this particular application. Over time, you build the knowledge you need to determine many of these answers for yourself, but it's always good to know who the subject matter experts are for any application you support.

Getting answers to the first three questions in the previous list are the most important, initially. You must know more than just a description of what the query needs to ask for. Being as familiar as possible with the data model is the starting point. When writing the original query, an assumption was made that the only table containing information needed to satisfy the query was the job_history table. If you had asked the first three questions, you'd have found out that the job_history table is truly a history table; it only contains historical data, not current data. The employees table contains a job_id column that holds the employees' current position information. Therefore, to determine how many positions an employee has held, you need to get their current job from the employees table and their previous jobs from the job_history table. With this information, you might rewrite the query as shown in Listing 5-2.

Listing 5-2. The Rewritten Employee Jobs Query

```
SQL> select employee_id, count(*) job_ct
  2  from
  3  (
  4  select e.employee_id, e.job_id
  5  from employees e
  6  union all
  7  select j.employee_id, j.job_id
  8  from job_history j
  9  )
 10  group by employee_id
 11  having count(*) > 1;
```

EMPLOYEE_ID	JOB_CT
102	2
201	2
101	3
114	2
200	2
176	2
122	2

```
7 rows selected.
```

It looks like the answer is correct now. It's at this point that the answers to the next questions come in to play. Knowing what to ask for is certainly important, and the first three questions helped me describe the data the query needed to return. Most people would stop here. However, knowing *how* to get the data I'm after is just as important. This is contrary to what most of us are taught about relational databases in general. In one of my college courses on RDBMSs, I was taught that SQL is used to access data. There is no requirement that I need to know anything about where or how the data are stored or how the RDBMS processes a SQL statement to access that data. In other words, SQL is used to describe what is done, not how it is done.

The reality is that knowing how your data are stored and accessed is just as important as describing the data your query retrieves. Let's say you need to book a trip from Washington, DC, to Los Angeles, California. You call your travel agent to handle the booking for you. If the only information you provide to the agent is your departure and arrival cities and that you want the least expensive fare possible, what could happen? Well, it's possible that the least expensive fare involves leaving at 5:30 AM from Washington, DC, then making stopovers in Atlanta, Chicago, and Dallas before finally connecting into Los Angeles at midnight (Los Angeles time, which means it would be 3 AM in DC time). Would that be OK with you? Probably not. Personally, I'd be willing to pay extra to get a direct flight from DC to Los Angeles. Think about it. If you could get a direct flight leaving from DC at 8 AM and arriving into Los Angeles at 10 AM, wouldn't it be worth quite a bit to you vs. making multiple stopovers and spending nearly a full day to complete the trip? And what if the direct flight cost only 10 percent more than the nightmare flight? Your original request to book the least expensive fare didn't include any conditions under which you'd be willing to pay more, so your request was satisfied but you probably won't be happy with the outcome.

Knowing how the data are stored and how they *should* be accessed ensures your query not only returns the correct answer, but also does so as quickly and efficiently as possible. That's why questions like, "How big is the typical expected result set?" and "How are the data stored?" and "How fast and how frequently do they need to execute?" must be asked. Without the answers to these questions, your query may get the correct answer but still be a failure because of poor performance. Simply getting the right result isn't enough. To be successful, your query must be *right* and it must be *fast.*

Questions about Data

I hope at this point you agree that you do need to concern yourself with how data are stored and how they should be accessed. Where do you find this information? The database can give you most of the answers you need when you execute a few simple queries. After you have this information, you then need to determine how data should be accessed, which comes from understanding how the various access and join methods work and when it is appropriate to use each. I've already covered access and join methods, so you've got the information you need to help you there, but how do you discover how the data are stored? Let's walk through the questions you need to ask and queries you can execute to get the answers.

As a first step, try to think like the optimizer. The optimizer needs statistics and instance parameter values to be able to compute a plan. Therefore, it's a good idea for you to put yourself in the optimizer's place and gather the information to help formulate the execution plan. Always seek out the answers to the following questions about the data:

- Which tables are needed to gather all the data required?

- Are any of the tables partitioned and, if so, how are the partitions defined?

- What columns are in each table?

- What indexes are available in each table?

- What are the statistics for each table, column, and index?

- Are there histograms on any of the columns?

Statistics help the optimizer paint a picture of how the various ways of accessing and joining data perform. You can know what the optimizer knows. All you need to be able to do is query the information from the data dictionary. One thing to keep in mind when you're reviewing statistics is that statistics may or may not represent your data accurately. If the statistics are stale, missing, or poorly collected, it's possible they may paint the wrong picture. The optimizer can only know what the statistics tell it. You, on the other hand, have the ability to determine whether the statistics make sense. For example, if a date column in one of your tables has a high value of six months ago, you can see this quickly and know that rows exist with current date values. This visual inspection can help you determine whether statistics need to be updated, but you can't know these kinds of things unless you look. A key question you must always ask is whether the statistics represent your data accurately. Listing 5-3 uses a single script named st-all.sql (previously used in Chapter 2) to answer each of the questions listed previously in one simple script. The script gives you a single source to review to verify how representative the available statistics really are.

Listing 5-3. Getting All the Statistics Information You Need

```
SQL> @st-all
Enter the owner name: sh
Enter the table name: sales
================================================================================
  TABLE STATISTICS
================================================================================
Owner        : sh
Table name   : sales
Tablespace   : EXAMPLE
Partitioned  : yes
Last analyzed : 05/31/2013 20:17:03
Sample size  : 918843
Degree       : 1
# Rows       : 918843
# Blocks     : 1769
Empty Blocks : 0

Avg Space    : 0
Avg Row Length: 29
Monitoring?  : yes
================================================================================
  PARTITION INFORMATION
================================================================================
 Part# Partition Name     Sample Size        # Rows         # Blocks
 ----- ---------------    ---------------    ---------------  ---------------
     1 SALES_1995          .                       0                0
     2 SALES_1996          .                       0                0
     3 SALES_H1_1997       .                       0                0
     4 SALES_H2_1997       .                       0                0
     5 SALES_Q1_1998         43687               43687              90
...
    28 SALES_Q4_2003       .                       0                0

 Part# Partition Name  Partition Bound
 ----- ---------------  ----------------------------------------------------------
     1 SALES_1995       TO_DATE(' 1996-01-01 00:00:00', 'SYYYY-MM-DD HH24:MI:SS', ...
     2 SALES_1996       TO_DATE(' 1997-01-01 00:00:00', 'SYYYY-MM-DD HH24:MI:SS', ...
     3 SALES_H1_1997    TO_DATE(' 1997-07-01 00:00:00', 'SYYYY-MM-DD HH24:MI:SS', ...
     4 SALES_H2_1997    TO_DATE(' 1998-01-01 00:00:00', 'SYYYY-MM-DD HH24:MI:SS', ...
     5 SALES_Q1_1998    TO_DATE(' 1998-04-01 00:00:00', 'SYYYY-MM-DD HH24:MI:SS', ...
...
    28 SALES_Q4_2003    TO_DATE(' 2004-01-01 00:00:00', 'SYYYY-MM-DD HH24:MI:SS', ...
================================================================================
  COLUMN STATISTICS
================================================================================
 Name          Null? NDV    Density # Nulls  # Bkts  AvgLen  Lo-Hi Values
================================================================================
 amount_sold   N     3586   .000279  0         1       5      6.4 | 1782.72
 channel_id    N     4      .250000  0         1       3      2 | 9
 cust_id       N     7059   .000142  0         1       5      2 | 101000
```

```
prod_id           N      72     .000001  0        72      4      13 | 148
promo_id          N      4      .000001  0        4       4      33 | 999
quantity_sold     N      1     1.000000  0        1       3      1 | 1
time_id           N      1460   .000685  0        1       8      01/01/1998 00:00:00 |
                                                                 12/31/2001 00:00:00
```

```
===============================================================================
  HISTOGRAM STATISTICS     Note: Only columns with buckets containing > 5% are shown.
===============================================================================
```

```
PROMO_ID (4 buckets)
1 97%
```

```
===============================================================================
  INDEX INFORMATION
===============================================================================
```

Index Name	BLevel	Lf Blks	# Rows	Dstnct Keys	Lf/Blks /Key	Dt/Blks /Key	Cluf	Unq?	Type	Part?
SALES_CHANNEL_BIX	1	47	92	4	11	23	92	NO	BITM	YES
SALES_CUST_BIX	1	475	35808	7059	1	5	35808	NO	BITM	YES
SALES_PROD_BIX	1	32	1074	72	1	14	1074	NO	BITM	YES
SALES_PROMO_BIX	1	30	54	4	7	13	54	NO	BITM	YES
SALES_TIME_BIX	1	59	1460	1460	1	1	1460	NO	BITM	YES

Index Name	Pos#	Order	Column Name
sales_channel_bix	1	ASC	channel_id
sales_cust_bix	1	ASC	cust_id
sales_prod_bix	1	ASC	prod_id
sales_promo_bix	1	ASC	promo_id
sales_time_bix	1	ASC	time_id

```
===============================================================================
  PARTITIONED INDEX INFORMATION
===============================================================================
```

Index: SALES_CHANNEL_BIX

Part#	Partition Name	BLevel	LfBlks	# Rows	Dst Keys	LfBlk /Key	DtBlk /Key	CluF	Partition Bound
1	SALES_1995	0	0	0	0	0	0	0	TO_DATE('1996-01-01...
2	SALES_1996	0	0	0	0	0	0	0	TO_DATE('1997-01-01...
3	SALES_H1_1997	0	0	0	0	0	0	0	TO_DATE('1997-07-01...
4	SALES_H2_1997	0	0	0	0	0	0	0	TO_DATE('1998-01-01...
5	SALES_Q1_1998	1	2	5	4	1	1	5	TO_DATE('1998-04-01...

...

28 SALES_Q4_2003	0	0	0	0	0	0	0	TO_DATE('2004-01-01...

Index: SALES_CUST_BIX

1 SALES_1995	0	0	0	0	0	0	0	TO_DATE('1996-01-01...
2 SALES_1996	0	0	0	0	0	0	0	TO_DATE('1997-01-01...
3 SALES_H1_1997	0	0	0	0	0	0	0	TO_DATE('1997-07-01...
4 SALES_H2_1997	0	0	0	0	0	0	0	TO_DATE('1998-01-01...
5 SALES_Q1_1998	1	28	3203	3203	1	1	3203	TO_DATE('1998-04-01...
...								
28 SALES_Q4_2003	0	0	0	0	0	0	0	TO_DATE('2004-01-01...

Index: SALES_PROD_BIX

1 SALES_1995	0	0	0	0	0	0	0	TO_DATE('1996-01-01...
2 SALES_1996	0	0	0	0	0	0	0	TO_DATE('1997-01-01...
3 SALES_H1_1997	0	0	0	0	0	0	0	TO_DATE('1997-07-01...
4 SALES_H2_1997	0	0	0	0	0	0	0	TO_DATE('1998-01-01...
5 SALES_Q1_1998	1	2	60	60	1	1	60	TO_DATE('1998-04-01...
...								
28 SALES_Q4_2003	0	0	0	0	0	0	0	TO_DATE('2004-01-01...

Index: SALES_PROMO_BIX

1 SALES_1995	0	0	0	0	0	0	0	TO_DATE('1996-01-01...
2 SALES_1996	0	0	0	0	0	0	0	TO_DATE('1997-01-01...
3 SALES_H1_1997	0	0	0	0	0	0	0	TO_DATE('1997-07-01...
4 SALES_H2_1997	0	0	0	0	0	0	0	TO_DATE('1998-01-01...
5 SALES_Q1_1998	0	1	3	2	1	1	3	TO_DATE('1998-04-01...
...								
28 SALES_Q4_2003	0	0	0	0	0	0	0	TO_DATE('2004-01-01...

Index: SALES_TIME_BIX

1 SALES_1995	0	0	0	0	0	0	0	TO_DATE('1996-01-01...
2 SALES_1996	0	0	0	0	0	0	0	TO_DATE('1997-01-01...
3 SALES_H1_1997	0	0	0	0	0	0	0	TO_DATE('1997-07-01...
4 SALES_H2_1997	0	0	0	0	0	0	0	TO_DATE('1998-01-01...
5 SALES_Q1_1998	1	3	90	90	1	1	90	TO_DATE('1998-04-01...
...								
27 SALES_Q3_2003	0	0	0	0	0	0	0	TO_DATE('2003-10-01...
28 SALES_Q4_2003	0	0	0	0	0	0	0	TO_DATE('2004-01-01...

With this information, you can answer almost any question about the data. It is best if these statistics are from your production database, where the SQL you are writing is executed. If your development database doesn't have a copy of the production statistics, it's a good idea to request that the production stats be imported into the development database so that the optimizer is formulating plans based on information that is as close to production as possible. Even if the data don't match, remember that it's the statistics that the optimizer uses to determine the plan.

Now that you've obtained the statistics, you can use the information to ask, and answer, questions about what you expect the optimizer to do with your SQL. For example, if you were writing a query that needed to return all sales data for a specified customer (cust_id), you might want to know how many rows the optimizer estimates the query to return. With the statistics information you have queried, you could compute the number of rows estimated to be returned by the query to be 130 (918,843 total rows × 1/7059 distinct values). You can see there is an index on cust_id, so the proper access operation to use to satisfy the query should be the SALES_CUST_BIX index. When you execute the query, you can verify this operation is selected by checking the execution plan.

In Chapter 3, I discussed the index statistic called *clustering factor*. This statistic helps the optimizer compute how many blocks of data are accessed. Basically, the closer the clustering factor is to the number of blocks in the table, the fewer the estimated number of blocks to be accessed when using the index. The closer the clustering factor is to the number of rows in the table, the greater the estimated number of blocks. The fewer blocks to be accessed, the lower the cost of using that index and the more likely it is that the optimizer chooses that index for the plan. Therefore, you can check this statistic to determine how favorable the index will appear. Listing 5-4 shows the clustering factor statistics for the SALES table.

Listing 5-4. Index clustering_factor

```
SQL> select t.table_name||'.'||i.index_name idx_name,
  2           i.clustering_factor, t.blocks, t.num_rows
  3      from user_indexes i, user_tables t
  4     where i.table_name = t.table_name
  5       and t.table_name = 'SALES'
  6     order by t.table_name, i.index_name;
```

IDX_NAME	Clustering Factor	# Blocks	# Rows
SALES.SALES_CHANNEL_BIX	92	1769	918843
SALES.SALES_CUST_BIX	35808	1769	918843
SALES.SALES_PROD_BIX	1074	1769	918843
SALES.SALES_PROMO_BIX	54	1769	918843
SALES.SALES_TIME_BIX	1460	1769	918843

5 rows selected.

In this case, the clustering factors for all the indexes for the SALES table have a low value (in other words, closer to the number of blocks in the table). This is a good indication that when the optimizer computes the cost of using these indexes, they are not weighted too heavily based on the estimated number of blocks they return if used.

In addition to using statistics, you can execute actual queries against the tables to get an idea of the data and number of rows to be accessed or returned from a single table. Regardless of how complex a statement is, you can do just what the optimizer does and break down the statement into single table accesses. For each table involved, simply execute one or more queries to count and review the data to be returned using the filter conditions your SQL uses. Always think "divide and conquer." Breaking down a statement into small increments helps you understand how best to put it together in the most efficient way to arrive at the final result.

Building Logical Expressions

When you understand the question that the statement you are writing needs to answer, you have to be able to build the SQL to provide the answer. There are often many possible ways to express the same predicate logic. Being able to formulate the conditions in a way that is easy to read and efficient requires you to think in ways you may not be used to. Remember when I discussed the idea of thinking in sets vs. thinking procedurally in Chapter 4? There is a similar thought shift you may need to make to be able to build predicates for your SQL statements most efficiently.

The key is to learn some good Boolean logic techniques so that you don't have to rely on only one way to express conditional logic. You may find that using Boolean logic expressions always produces the most efficient plan operation choices (make sure to test alternatives thoroughly), but it's good to know how to formulate different alternatives so you aren't stuck with a single way to do things.

When I say *conditional logic*, I mean an expression something like, "if X then Y" where X and Y are both conditions. In a WHERE clause, you might want to have a condition like if :GetAll <> 1 then empno = :empno. In other words, if the value of the input bind variable named :GetAll is 1, then you want to return all rows, but if :GetAll is not 1, then only return rows in which empno is equal to the :empno bind variable supplied. A WHERE clause to express this logic might be coded like this:

```
WHERE empno = CASE WHEN :GetAll <> 1 THEN :empno ELSE empno END
```

This logic works, but it's a bit counterintuitive to me. Why would you even want to check empno = empno? There are other problems with this kind of formulation as well. If you need to check multiple columns, then you need multiple CASE statements. Plus, if empno is null, this check is going to fail, or at the very least give you a result you don't expect.

The key is to change this expression to use a regular Boolean expression that uses only AND, OR, and NOT so that your "if X then Y" condition is translated to "(Not X) or Y," which becomes the following:

```
WHERE (:GetAll = 1) OR (empno = :empno)
```

What you are covering with this expression is that if :GetAll = 1, then you don't even want to bother with checking any more of the expression. Always remember that when using an OR condition, if one condition evaluates to TRUE, then the whole expression is TRUE. There is no need to check the remaining expression. This "short-circuit" mechanism can save time by not requiring some of the code path to be evaluated, which means you won't burn as many CPU cycles overall. Only if the first condition that the optimizer chooses to test evaluates to FALSE would the other expression need to be evaluated. Regardless of the method you choose, each of the options just discussed results in the optimizer using a full table scan and filtering the data based on your condition.

Although you're not looking at expressions involving ANDed conditions in these examples, you can apply similar thinking to the use of ANDed predicates. When using an AND condition, if the first condition evaluates to FALSE, then the whole expression is FALSE. There is no need to evaluate the second expression because both conditions must evaluate to TRUE for the whole condition to be TRUE. So, when you're using AND conditions, it's a good idea to write the condition so the expression that is most likely to evaluate to FALSE is placed first. Doing so allows the second expression evaluation to be short-circuited with similar savings as noted when placing a TRUE expression first in an OR condition. In reality, the cost-based optimizer evaluates and determines the order in which the conditions are evaluated. When you write the conditions in a certain order, you are simply helping yourself define your expectations of what *should* happen.

A similar way of approaching this type of conditional expression is to use a single bind variable instead of two. In this case, you would say "if X is not null then Y = X." This becomes as follows:

```
WHERE empno = NVL(:empno, empno)
```

This is basically the same as writing the CASE expression from the earlier example and can be converted to the following:

```
WHERE (:empno is null) OR (empno = :empno)
```

In both these cases, the optimizer may have a bit of a dilemma with determining the optimal plan. The reason is that if the binds you use cause the comparison to end up returning all rows, then the plan operation best suited for that would likely be a full table scan. However, if you specify binds that end up limiting the result set, an index scan might be best. Because you're using bind variables, each time you execute the query, the input bind values could change. So, the optimizer has to choose a plan that covers both situations. Most likely, you end up with a full table scan. Listings 5-5 and 5-6 demonstrate one scenario for each of the similar alternatives I covered and show the execution plan output for each.

Listing 5-5. Using Two Bind Variables to Create a Conditional WHERE Clause

```
SQL> variable empno number
SQL> variable getall number
SQL>
SQL> exec :empno := 7369;

PL/SQL procedure successfully completed.

SQL>
SQL> exec :getall := 1;

PL/SQL procedure successfully completed.

SQL>
SQL> select /* opt1 */ empno, ename from emp
  2  where empno = CASE WHEN :GetAll <> 1 THEN :empno ELSE empno END;

     EMPNO ENAME
---------------- ----------
      7369 SMITH
      7499 ALLEN
      7521 WARD
      7566 JONES
      7654 MARTIN
      7698 BLAKE
      7782 CLARK
      7788 SCOTT
      7839 KING
      7844 TURNER
      7876 ADAMS
      7900 JAMES
      7902 FORD
      7934 MILLER

14 rows selected.

SQL>
SQL> @pln opt1

PLAN_TABLE_OUTPUT
--------------------------------------------------------------------------------
SQL_ID  gwcmrzfqf8cu2, child number 0
-------------------------------------
select /* opt1 */ empno, ename from emp where empno = CASE WHEN :GetAll
<> 1 THEN :empno ELSE empno END

Plan hash value: 3956160932
```

```
---------------------------------------------------------------
| Id  | Operation         | Name | Starts | E-Rows | A-Rows | Buffers |
---------------------------------------------------------------
|   0 | SELECT STATEMENT  |      |    1   |        |   14   |    8    |
|*  1 |  TABLE ACCESS FULL| EMP  |    1   |    1   |   14   |    8    |
---------------------------------------------------------------

Predicate Information (identified by operation id):
---------------------------------------------------

   1 - filter("EMPNO"=CASE  WHEN (:GETALL<>1) THEN :EMPNO ELSE "EMPNO" END )

19 rows selected.
```

Listing 5-6. Using One Bind Variable to Create a Conditional WHERE Clause

```
SQL> exec :getall := 0;

PL/SQL procedure successfully completed.

SQL>
SQL> select /* opt5 */ empno, ename from emp
  2  where empno = NVL(:empno, empno);

      EMPNO ENAME
--------------- ----------
       7369 SMITH

1 row selected.

SQL>
SQL> @pln opt5

PLAN_TABLE_OUTPUT
---------------------------------------------------------------------------------------
SQL_ID  605p3gyjbw82b, child number 0
-------------------------------------
select /* opt5 */ empno, ename from emp where empno = NVL(:empno, empno)

Plan hash value: 1977813858

---------------------------------------------------------------------------
| Id  | Operation                     | Name   | Starts | E-Rows | A-Rows | Buffers |
---------------------------------------------------------------------------
|   0 | SELECT STATEMENT              |        |    1   |        |    1   |    2    |
|   1 |  CONCATENATION                |        |    1   |        |    1   |    2    |
|*  2 |   FILTER                      |        |    1   |        |    0   |    0    |
|   3 |    TABLE ACCESS BY INDEX ROWID| EMP    |    0   |   14   |    0   |    0    |
|*  4 |     INDEX FULL SCAN           | PK_EMP |    0   |   14   |    0   |    0    |
```

```
|*  5 |    FILTER                   |        |    1 |       |    1 |     2 |
|   6 |     TABLE ACCESS BY INDEX ROWID| EMP  |    1 |    1 |    1 |     2 |
|*  7 |      INDEX UNIQUE SCAN      | PK_EMP |    1 |    1 |    1 |     1 |
-----------------------------------------------------------------------------
```

Predicate Information (identified by operation id):

```
   2 - filter(:EMPNO IS NULL)
   4 - filter("EMPNO" IS NOT NULL)
   5 - filter(:EMPNO IS NOT NULL)
   7 - access("EMPNO"=:EMPNO)
```

27 rows selected.

```
SQL>
SQL> select /* opt6 */ empno, ename from emp
  2  where (:empno is null) OR (:empno = empno);

        EMPNO ENAME
--------------- ----------
         7369 SMITH
```

1 row selected.

```
SQL>
SQL> @pln opt6

PLAN_TABLE_OUTPUT
------------------------------------------------------------------------------------
SQL_ID  gng6x7nrrrhy9, child number 0
-------------------------------------
select /* opt6 */ empno, ename from emp where (:empno is null) OR
(:empno = empno)

Plan hash value: 3956160932


-------------------------------------------------------------------------
| Id  | Operation         | Name | Starts | E-Rows | A-Rows | Buffers |
-------------------------------------------------------------------------
|   0 | SELECT STATEMENT  |      |    1 |        |    1 |     8 |
|*  1 |  TABLE ACCESS FULL| EMP  |    1 |    2 |    1 |     8 |
-------------------------------------------------------------------------
```

Predicate Information (identified by operation id):

```
   1 - filter((:EMPNO IS NULL OR "EMPNO"=:EMPNO))
```

Note that if you used the format WHERE (:GetAll = 1) OR (empno = :empno) instead, you get the same plan shown in Listing 5-5. There is no real difference between the two.

In this example, note that there is a difference between the plan when you use the first technique of WHERE empno = NVL(:empno, empno) vs. using WHERE (:empno is null) OR (:empno = empno). For the first example in Listing 5-5, in which there are two bind variables, notice that the optimizer chooses a full table scan operation. But, notice what happens when you use only a single variable in Listing 5-6 for the second set of examples. In the second case, the optimizer uses a CONCATENATION plan for the NVL predicate and full table scan for the Boolean expression. The CONCATENATION plan is the best in this case because it works such that when the bind variable is null, the plan executes the INDEX FULL SCAN operation to get all the rows; when the bind variable is not null, the plan executes the INDEX UNIQUE SCAN operation to get just the one row that is needed. In this way, both options use an optimal execution path.

In this case, the Boolean logic didn't give you the best plan, so it's good to know several alternative ways to formulate the predicate so you can work to achieve the best possible plan. With this in mind, you actually could have written the query as shown in Listing 5-7.

Listing 5-7. Using UNION ALL to Handle Conditional Logic

```
SQL> select /* opt9 */ empno, ename from emp
  2  where :empno is null
  3  union all
  4  select empno, ename from emp
  5  where :empno = empno;

       EMPNO ENAME
--------------- ----------
        7369 SMITH

1 row selected.

SQL>
SQL> @pln opt9

PLAN_TABLE_OUTPUT
--------------------------------------------------------------------------------
SQL_ID  ab0juatnpc5ug, child number 0
-------------------------------------
select /* opt9 */ empno, ename from emp where :empno is null union all
select empno, ename from emp where :empno = empno

Plan hash value: 2001993376
```

Id	Operation	Name	Starts	E-Rows	A-Rows	Buffers
0	SELECT STATEMENT		1		1	2
1	UNION-ALL		1		1	2
* 2	FILTER		1		0	0
3	TABLE ACCESS FULL	EMP	0	14	0	0
4	TABLE ACCESS BY INDEX ROWID	EMP	1	1	1	2
* 5	INDEX UNIQUE SCAN	PK_EMP	1	1	1	1

```
Predicate Information (identified by operation id):
---------------------------------------------------

   2 - filter(:EMPNO IS NULL)
   5 - access("EMPNO"=:EMPNO)
```

Similar to the CONCATENATION plan, in this case you get a plan in which two separate subplans are "unioned" together to get the result. If the bind variable is null, you get a full scan operation and get all rows returned. When the bind variable is not null, you get the unique index scan and return only the one row needed. The FILTER operation acts to determine whether the first subplan should be executed. Notice the Predicate Information section in which step 2 shows filter(:EMPNO IS NULL), indicating that only if the bind is null does the operation actually happen.

In general, you'll find that the optimizer is able to make better plan operation choices when AND conditions are used. As mentioned earlier, this is because an OR condition means there could be two different possible operations that could be used based on how the expression evaluates. With an AND condition, it is more likely that only a single choice, or at least choices that are not opposite in nature, are considered. So, if you can figure out a way to formulate your predicates to use ANDed conditions only, you may find that the SQL produces more efficient plans and is even easier to maintain.

Also, if you are writing SQL statements inside a larger code body, such as in a PL/SQL procedure, use conditional constructs in the language and don't put that logic in the SQL. The simpler you can make your SQL, and the fewer conditions that have to be handled in the statement directly, the less complexity the optimizer needs to sort through to determine an optimal plan.

Summary

Questions are an important part of the process of writing good SQL. You begin by understanding the question the SQL needs to answer, then you follow up by asking questions about the data to formulate a SQL statement that is functionally correct as well as optimized for performance. The ability to ask good questions is an intellectual habit that must be developed over time. The more you work to ask questions that clarify and enhance your understanding of what you need to do, the greater your skills as a writer of high-quality, high-performing SQL become.

CHAPTER 6

SQL Execution Plans

You've seen quite a few execution plans in the first chapters of this book, but in this chapter I go into detail about how to produce and read plans correctly. I've built the foundation of knowledge you need to understand the most common operations you'll see used in execution plans, but now you need to put this knowledge into practice.

By the end of this chapter, I want you to feel confident that you can break down even the most complex execution plan and understand how any SQL statement you write is being executed. With the prevalence of development tools such as SQL Developer, SQL Navigator, and TOAD (just to name a few), which can produce explain plan output (which is simply the estimated execution plan), it is fairly easy to generate explain plan output. What isn't as easy is to get execution plan output. You may be wondering what the difference is between an explain plan and an execution plan. As you'll see in this chapter, there can be a significant difference. I'll walk through the differences between explain plan output and actual execution plan information. You'll learn how to compare the estimated plans with the actual plans, and how to interpret any differences that are present. This is "where the rubber meets the road," as race car drivers would say.

Explain Plan

The EXPLAIN PLAN statement is used to display the plan operations chosen by the optimizer for a SQL statement. The first thing I want to clarify is that when you have EXPLAIN PLAN output, you have the estimated execution plan that *should be* used when the SQL statement is actually executed. You do not have the actual execution plan and its associated row-source execution statistics. You have estimates only—not the real thing. Throughout this chapter, I make the distinction between actual and estimated plan output by referring to estimated information as *explain plan output* and calling actual information as *execution plan output*.

Using Explain Plan

When using EXPLAIN PLAN to produce the estimated execution plan for a query, the output shows the following:

- Each of the tables referred to in the SQL statement

- The access method used for each table

- The join methods for each pair of joined row sources

- An ordered list of all operations to be completed

- A list of predicate information related to steps in the plan

- For each operation, the estimates for number of rows and bytes manipulated by that step

- For each operation, the computed cost value

- If applicable, information about partitions accessed

- If applicable, information about parallel execution

Listing 6-1 shows how to create and display the explain plan output for a query that joins five tables.

Listing 6-1. EXPLAIN PLAN Example

```
SQL> explain plan for
  2   select e.last_name || ', ' || e.first_name as full_name,
  3          e.phone_number, e.email, e.department_id,
  4          d.department_name, c.country_name, l.city, l.state_province,
  5          r.region_name
  6    from hr.employees e, hr.departments d, hr.countries c,
  7          hr.locations l, hr.regions r
  8   where e.department_id = d.department_id
  9     and d.location_id = l.location_id
 10     and l.country_id = c.country_id
 11     and c.region_id = r.region_id;

Explained.

SQL>select * from table(dbms_xplan.display(format=>'BASIC +COST +PREDICATE'));

PLAN_TABLE_OUTPUT
-------------------------------------------------------------------------
Plan hash value: 2352397467
```

```
-------------------------------------------------------------------------
| Id  | Operation                          | Name            | Cost (%CPU)|
-------------------------------------------------------------------------
|   0 | SELECT STATEMENT                   |                 |   3    (0)|
|   1 |  NESTED LOOPS                      |                 |           |
|   2 |   NESTED LOOPS                     |                 |   3    (0)|
|   3 |    NESTED LOOPS                    |                 |   3    (0)|
|   4 |     NESTED LOOPS                   |                 |   3    (0)|
|   5 |      NESTED LOOPS                  |                 |   3    (0)|
|   6 |       TABLE ACCESS FULL            | EMPLOYEES       |   3    (0)|
|   7 |       TABLE ACCESS BY INDEX ROWID| DEPARTMENTS     |   0    (0)|
|*  8 |        INDEX UNIQUE SCAN           | DEPT_ID_PK      |   0    (0)|
|   9 |      TABLE ACCESS BY INDEX ROWID  | LOCATIONS       |   0    (0)|
|* 10 |       INDEX UNIQUE SCAN            | LOC_ID_PK       |   0    (0)|
|* 11 |     INDEX UNIQUE SCAN              | COUNTRY_C_ID_PK |   0    (0)|
|* 12 |    INDEX UNIQUE SCAN               | REG_ID_PK       |   0    (0)|
|  13 |   TABLE ACCESS BY INDEX ROWID      | REGIONS         |   0    (0)|
-------------------------------------------------------------------------

Predicate Information (identified by operation id):
---------------------------------------------------

   8 - access("E"."DEPARTMENT_ID"="D"."DEPARTMENT_ID")
  10 - access("D"."LOCATION_ID"="L"."LOCATION_ID")
  11 - access("L"."COUNTRY_ID"="C"."COUNTRY_ID")
  12 - access("C"."REGION_ID"="R"."REGION_ID")
```

For this example, I used the EXPLAIN PLAN command to generate the explain plan content. I could have used AUTOTRACE instead to automate the steps to generate a plan so that all you have to do is turn on AUTOTRACE (using the TRACEONLY EXPLAIN option) and execute a query. The plan is generated and the output is displayed all in one step. In this example, I use the dbms_xplan.display function to display the output instead (I discuss dbms_xplan in more detail shortly). When using either method to generate a plan, neither the EXPLAIN PLAN command nor the SET AUTOTRACE TRACEONLY EXPLAIN option actually executes the query. It only generates the plan that is estimated to be executed. The development tool you use (SQL Developer, TOAD, and so forth) should also have an option to generate explain plans. I may be a bit old-fashioned, but I find the text output often easier to read than the semigraphical trees some of these common development tools use. I don't particularly need or care to see any little graphical symbols, so I'm very happy with text output without any of the extra icons and such. But, don't feel you have to generate explain plans using these methods if you prefer to use your tool.

The Plan Table

The information you see in explain plan output is generated by the EXPLAIN PLAN command and is stored in a table named PLAN_TABLE by default. The AUTOTRACE command calls the display function from the supplied package named dbms_xplan to format the output automatically. I executed the query manually using dbms_xplan when using EXPLAIN PLAN without turning on AUTOTRACE. For reference, Listing 6-2 shows the table description for the Oracle version 12c PLAN_TABLE.

Listing 6-2. PLAN_TABLE

```
SQL> desc plan_table
 Name                            Null?    Type
 ------------------------------- -------- -------------------
 STATEMENT_ID                             VARCHAR2(30)
 PLAN_ID                                  NUMBER
 TIMESTAMP                                DATE
 REMARKS                                  VARCHAR2(4000)
 OPERATION                                VARCHAR2(30)
 OPTIONS                                  VARCHAR2(255)
 OBJECT_NODE                              VARCHAR2(128)
 OBJECT_OWNER                             VARCHAR2(30)
 OBJECT_NAME                              VARCHAR2(30)
 OBJECT_ALIAS                             VARCHAR2(65)
 OBJECT_INSTANCE                          NUMBER(38)
 OBJECT_TYPE                              VARCHAR2(30)
 OPTIMIZER                                VARCHAR2(255)
 SEARCH_COLUMNS                           NUMBER
 ID                                       NUMBER(38)
 PARENT_ID                                NUMBER(38)
 DEPTH                                    NUMBER(38)
 POSITION                                 NUMBER(38)
 COST                                     NUMBER(38)
 CARDINALITY                              NUMBER(38)
 BYTES                                    NUMBER(38)
 OTHER_TAG                                VARCHAR2(255)
 PARTITION_START                          VARCHAR2(255)
 PARTITION_STOP                           VARCHAR2(255)
 PARTITION_ID                             NUMBER(38)
 OTHER                                    LONG
```

```
OTHER_XML                        CLOB
DISTRIBUTION                     VARCHAR2(30)
CPU_COST                         NUMBER(38)
IO_COST                          NUMBER(38)
TEMP_SPACE                       NUMBER(38)
ACCESS_PREDICATES                VARCHAR2(4000)
FILTER_PREDICATES                VARCHAR2(4000)
PROJECTION                       VARCHAR2(4000)
TIME                             NUMBER(38)
QBLOCK_NAME                      VARCHAR2(30)
```

I'm not going to review every column listed, but I wanted to provide a table description from which you can do further study if you desire. You can find more information in the Oracle documentation.

The columns from PLAN_TABLE shown in the explain plan output in Listing 6-1 are only a few of the columns from the table. One of the nice things about the dbms_xplan.display function is that it has intelligence built in so that it displays the appropriate columns based on the specific plan generated for each SQL statement. For example, if the plan used partition operations, the PARTITION_START, PARTITION_STOP, and PARTITION_ID columns would appear in the display. The ability of dbms_xplan.display to determine automatically the columns that should be shown is a super feature that beats using the old do-it-yourself query against the PLAN_TABLE hands down.

The columns shown in the display for the example query plan are ID, OPERATION, OPTIONS, OBJECT_NAME, COST, ACCESS_PREDICATES, and FILTER_PREDICATES. These are the columns displayed based on the use of the format parameter of 'BASIC +COST +PREDICATE'. Table 6-1 provides a brief definition of each of these common columns.

Table 6-1. *Most Commonly Used PLAN_TABLE Columns*

Column	Description
ID	Unique number assigned to each step
OPERATION	Internal operation performed by the step
OPTIONS	Additional specification for the operation column (appended to OPERATION)
OBJECT_NAME	Name of the table or index
COST	Weighted cost value for the operation as determined by the optimizer
ACCESS_PREDICATES	Conditions used to locate rows in an access structure (typically an index)
FILTER_PREDICATES	Conditions used to filter rows after they have been accessed

One of the columns from the PLAN_TABLE that is not displayed in the plan display output when using the dbms_xplan.display function is the PARENT_ID column. Instead of displaying this column value, the output is indented to provide a visual cue for the parent–child relationships within the plan. I think it is helpful to include the PARENT_ID column value as well, for clarity, but you have to write your own query against the PLAN_TABLE to produce the output to include that column if you want it. I use a script from Randolf Geist's blog (http://oracle-randolf. blogspot.com/2011/12/extended-displaycursor-with-rowsource.html) that adds the PARENT_ID column to the dbms_xplan.display output. Another column, Ord, has also been added to indicate the execution order of the operations. The script provides lots of other additional output that you can use as well. I recommend reading Geist's full blog post and downloading the script for your own use. Although I have elided some of the output available, Listing 6-3 shows using this script for our previous query executed for Listing 6-1. Note that I had to execute the query (not just use EXPLAIN PLAN) and capture SQL_ID to supply the correct input parameters to the script (again, see Geist's blog for usage details).

Listing 6-3. Displaying the PARENT_ID and Ord columns using the xpext.sql script

```
SQL>@xpext cqbz6zv6tu5g3 0 "BASIC +PREDICATE"
EXPLAINED SQL STATEMENT:
------------------------
select e.last_name | ', ' || e.first_name as full_name,
    e.phone_number, e.email, e.department_id,
d.department_name, c.country_name, l.city, l.state_province,
r.region_name   from hr.employees e, hr.departments d, hr.countries c,
     hr.locations l, hr.regions r  where e.department_id =
d.department_id    and d.location_id = l.location_id    and
l.country_id = c.country_id    and c.region_id = r.region_id


Plan hash value: 2352397467
```

```
-------------------------------------------------------------------------------
| Id  | Pid | Ord | Operation                    | Name            |E-Rows*Sta|
-------------------------------------------------------------------------------
|   0 |     |  14 | SELECT STATEMENT             |                 |          |
|   1 |   0 |  13 |  NESTED LOOPS                |                 |          |
|   2 |   1 |  11 |   NESTED LOOPS               |                 |   106    |
|   3 |   2 |   9 |    NESTED LOOPS              |                 |   106    |
|   4 |   3 |   7 |     NESTED LOOPS             |                 |   106    |
|   5 |   4 |   4 |      NESTED LOOPS            |                 |   106    |
|   6 |   5 |   1 |       TABLE ACCESS FULL      | EMPLOYEES       |   107    |
|   7 |   5 |   3 |       TABLE ACCESS BY INDEX ROWID| DEPARTMENTS |   107    |
|*  8 |   7 |   2 |        INDEX UNIQUE SCAN     | DEPT_ID_PK      |   107    |
|   9 |   4 |   6 |      TABLE ACCESS BY INDEX ROWID | LOCATIONS   |   106    |
|* 10 |   9 |   5 |       INDEX UNIQUE SCAN      | LOC_ID_PK       |   106    |
|* 11 |   3 |   8 |     INDEX UNIQUE SCAN        | COUNTRY_C_ID_PK |   106    |
|* 12 |   2 |  10 |    INDEX UNIQUE SCAN         | REG_ID_PK       |   106    |
|  13 |   1 |  12 |   TABLE ACCESS BY INDEX ROWID| REGIONS         |   106    |
-------------------------------------------------------------------------------
```

```
Predicate Information (identified by operation id):
---------------------------------------------------
   8 - access("E"."DEPARTMENT_ID"="D"."DEPARTMENT_ID")
  10 - access("D"."LOCATION_ID"="L"."LOCATION_ID")
  11 - access("L"."COUNTRY_ID"="C"."COUNTRY_ID")
  12 - access("C"."REGION_ID"="R"."REGION_ID")
```

PARENT_ID (shown in the Pid column in Listing 6-3) is helpful because operations in a plan are easiest to read if you keep in mind the parent–child relationships involved in the plan. Each step in the plan has from zero to two children. If you break down the plan into smaller chunks of parent–child groupings, it makes it easier to read and understand.

Breaking Down the Plan

When learning how to read plan output, it is important to start with an understanding of how the plan is organized. In this section, I help you understand the relationships between various elements of a plan and how to break the plan into smaller groups of related operations. Reading a plan with understanding can be more difficult than it may seem, particularly if the plan is long. But, by breaking the plan apart, it's often easier to put it back together in a way that makes more sense to you.

Let's start by considering the relationships between various plan operations. In the example plan, you have operations with zero, one, and two children. A full table scan operation, for example, doesn't have any children. See the line for ID=5 in Listing 6-3. Another example of an operation with zero children is line 3. If you glance down the Pid column, you can see that neither step 3 nor step 5 show up, which means these operations do not depend on any other operation to complete. Both operations are children of other operations, however, and they pass the data they access to their parent step. When an operation has no children, the Rows (CARDINALITY column in the PLAN_TABLE) estimate represents the number of rows that a single iteration of that operation acquires. This can be a bit confusing when the operation is providing rows to an iterative parent, but the estimate for the operation doesn't indicate the total number of rows accessed in that step. The total is determined by the parent operation. I delve into this in more detail shortly.

The parent steps for steps 3 and 5—steps 2 and 4—are examples of single-child operations. In general, operations with only one child can be divided into three categories:

- *Working operations,* which receive a row set from the child operation and manipulate it further before passing it on to its parent.

- *Pass-thru operations*, which act simply as a pass-thru and don't alter or manipulate the data from the child in any way. They basically serve to identify an operation characteristic. The VIEW operation is a good example of a pass-thru operation.

- *Iterative operations*, which indicate there are multiple executions of the child operation. You typically see the word ITERATOR, INLIST, or ALL in these types of operation names.

Both step 2 and step 4 are working operations. They take the row sets from their children (steps 3 and 5) and do some additional work. In step 2, the rowids returned from the index full scan are used to retrieve the DEPARTMENT table data blocks. In step 4, the rows returned from the full scan of the EMPLOYEES table are sorted in order by the join column.

Last, operations that have two children operate either iteratively or in succession. When the parent type is iterative, the child row sources are accessed such that for each row in row source A, B is accessed. For a parent operation that works on the children in succession, the first child row source is accessed followed by an access of the second row source. Join types such as NESTED LOOPS and MERGE JOIN are iterative, as is the FILTER operation. All other operations with two children work in succession on their child row sources.

The reason for this review is to highlight the importance of learning to take a divide-and-conquer approach to reading and understanding plan output. The larger and more complicated a plan looks, the harder it often is to find the key problem areas. If you learn to look for parent–child relationships in the plan output, and narrow your focus to smaller chunks of the plan, you'll find it much easier to work with what you see.

Understanding How EXPLAIN PLAN Can Miss the Mark

One of the most frustrating things about EXPLAIN PLAN output is that it may not always match the plan that is used when the statement is actually executed, even when no objects referenced in the query change structurally in between. There are four things to keep in mind about using EXPLAIN PLAN that make it susceptible to producing plan output that doesn't match the actual execution plan:

1. EXPLAIN PLAN produces plans based on the environment at the moment you use it.

2. EXPLAIN PLAN doesn't consider the datatype of bind variables (all binds are VARCHAR2).

3. EXPLAIN PLAN doesn't "peek" at bind variable values.

4. EXPLAIN PLAN only shows the original plan and not the final plan (this references a 12c feature called *adaptive query optimization,* which is covered in a later chapter).

For these reasons, as mentioned, it is very possible that EXPLAIN PLAN produces a plan that doesn't match the plan that is produced when the statement is actually executed. Listing 6-4 demonstrates the second point about bind variable datatypes causing EXPLAIN PLAN not to match the actual execution plan.

Listing 6-4. EXPLAIN PLAN and Bind Variable Datatypes

```
SQL>-- Create a test table where primary key column is a string datatype
SQL> create table regions2
  2  (region_id  varchar2(10) primary key,
  3   region_name varchar2(25));

Table created.

SQL>
SQL>-- Insert rows into the test table
SQL> insert into regions2
  2  select * from regions;

4 rows created.

SQL>
SQL>-- Create a variable and set its value
SQL> variable regid number
SQL> exec :regid := 1

PL/SQL procedure successfully completed.

SQL>
SQL>-- Get explain plan for the query
SQL> explain plan for select /* DataTypeTest */ *
  2  from regions2
  3  where region_id = :regid;

Explained.
SQL> select * from table(dbms_xplan.display(format=>'BASIC +COST +PREDICATE'));

Plan hash value: 2358393386

-------------------------------------------------------------
| Id  | Operation                    | Name       | Cost (%CPU)|
-------------------------------------------------------------
|   0 | SELECT STATEMENT             |            |     1   (0)|
|   1 |  TABLE ACCESS BY INDEX ROWID | REGIONS2   |     1   (0)|
|*  2 |   INDEX UNIQUE SCAN          | SYS_C009951|     1   (0)|
-------------------------------------------------------------

Predicate Information (identified by operation id):
---------------------------------------------------

   2 - access("REGION_ID"=:REGID)

SQL>
SQL>-- Execute the query
SQL> select /* DataTypeTest */ *
  2  from regions2
  3  where region_id = :regid;
```

```
REGION_ID  REGION_NAME
---------- ------------------------
1          Europe

SQL>
SQL>-- Review the actual execution plan
SQL> select * from table(dbms_xplan.display_cursor(null,null,format=>'BASIC +COST +PREDICATE'));

EXPLAINED SQL STATEMENT:
------------------------
select /* DataTypeTest */ * from regions2 where region_id = :regid

Plan hash value: 670750275

----------------------------------------------------
| Id | Operation         | Name     | Cost (%CPU)|
----------------------------------------------------
|  0 | SELECT STATEMENT  |          |     3 (100)|
|* 1 |   TABLE ACCESS FULL| REGIONS2 |     3   (0)|
----------------------------------------------------

Predicate Information (identified by operation id):
----------------------------------------------------
   1 - filter(TO_NUMBER("REGION_ID")=:REGID)
```

Did you notice how the explain plan output indicated that the primary key index would be used but the actual plan really used a full table scan? The reason why is clearly shown in the Predicate Information section. In the explain plan output, the predicate is "REGION_ID"=:REGID, but in the actual plan, the predicate shows TO_NUMBER("REGION_ID")=:REGID. This demonstrates how EXPLAIN PLAN doesn't consider the datatype of a bind variable and assumes all bind variables are string types. For EXPLAIN PLAN, the datatypes were considered to be the same (both strings). However, the datatypes were considered when the plan was prepared for the actual execution of the statement, and Oracle implicitly converted the string datatype for the REGION_ID column to a number to match the bind variable datatype (NUMBER). This is expected behavior in that, when datatypes being compared don't match, Oracle always attempts to convert the string datatype to match the nonstring datatype. By doing so in this example, the TO_NUMBER function caused the use of the index to be disallowed. This is another expected behavior to keep in mind: The predicate must match the index definition exactly or else the index is not used.

If you are testing this statement in your development environment and use the explain plan output to confirm that the index is being used, you are wrong. From the explain plan output, it appears that the plan is using the index, as you would expect, but when the statement is actually executed, performance is likely to be unsatisfactory because of the full table scan that really occurs.

Another issue with using explain plan output as your sole source for testing is that you never get a true picture of how the statement uses resources. Estimates are just that—estimates. To confirm the behavior of the SQL and to make intelligent choices about whether the statement will provide optimal performance, you need to look at actual execution statistics. I cover the details of how to capture and interpret actual execution statistics shortly.

Reading the Plan

Before I dive further into capturing actual execution plan data, I want to make sure you are comfortable with reading a plan. I've already discussed the importance of the PARENT_ID column in making it easier for you to break down a long, complex plan into smaller, more manageable sections. Breaking down a plan into smaller chunks helps you read it, but you need to know how to approach reading a whole plan from start to finish.

There are three ways that help you read and understand any plan: (1) learn to identify and separate parent–child groupings (I discussed this earlier in the "Breaking Down the Plan" section), (2) learn the order in which the plan operations execute, and (3) learn to read the plan in narrative form. I learned to do these three things so that when I look at a plan, my eyes move through the plan easily and I notice possible problem areas quickly. The process can be frustrating and you may be a bit slow at first, but given time and practice, this activity becomes second nature.

Let's start with execution order. The plan is displayed in order by the sequential ID of operations. However, the order in which each operation executes isn't accomplished in a precise top-down fashion. To be precise, the first operation executed in an execution plan is actually the first operation from the top of the execution plan that has no child operations. In most cases, using the visual cues of the indentation of the operations, you can scan a plan quickly and look for the operations that are the most indented. The operation that is most indented is usually the first operation that is executed. If there are multiple operations at that same level, the operations are executed in a top-down order. But, in some cases, the visual cue to look for the first most-indented operation won't work and you have to remember simply to find the first operation from the top of the execution plan that has no child operations.

For reference, I relist the example plan here in Listing 6-5 so that you don't have to flip back a few pages to the original example in Listing 6-1.

Listing 6-5. EXPLAIN PLAN Example (Repeated)

```
--------------------------------------------------------------------
| Id  | Operation                       | Name            | Cost (%CPU)|
--------------------------------------------------------------------
|   0 | SELECT STATEMENT                |                 |    3   (0)|
|   1 |  NESTED LOOPS                   |                 |           |
|   2 |   NESTED LOOPS                  |                 |    3   (0)|
|   3 |    NESTED LOOPS                 |                 |    3   (0)|
|   4 |     NESTED LOOPS                |                 |    3   (0)|
|   5 |      NESTED LOOPS               |                 |    3   (0)|
|   6 |       TABLE ACCESS FULL         | EMPLOYEES       |    3   (0)|
|   7 |       TABLE ACCESS BY INDEX ROWID| DEPARTMENTS    |    0   (0)|
|*  8 |        INDEX UNIQUE SCAN        | DEPT_ID_PK      |    0   (0)|
|   9 |      TABLE ACCESS BY INDEX ROWID | LOCATIONS      |    0   (0)|
|* 10 |       INDEX UNIQUE SCAN         | LOC_ID_PK       |    0   (0)|
|* 11 |     INDEX UNIQUE SCAN           | COUNTRY_C_ID_PK |    0   (0)|
|* 12 |    INDEX UNIQUE SCAN            | REG_ID_PK       |    0   (0)|
|  13 |   TABLE ACCESS BY INDEX ROWID   | REGIONS         |    0   (0)|
--------------------------------------------------------------------

Predicate Information (identified by operation id):
---------------------------------------------------
   8 - access("E"."DEPARTMENT_ID"="D"."DEPARTMENT_ID")
  10 - access("D"."LOCATION_ID"="L"."LOCATION_ID")
  11 - access("L"."COUNTRY_ID"="C"."COUNTRY_ID")
  12 - access("C"."REGION_ID"="R"."REGION_ID")
```

At a glance, you can see that lines 6 and 8 are the most deeply indented. Line 6 executes first, then line 8 executes next and passes the rowids from the index unique scan to its parent (line 7). Steps continue to execute from the most indented to the least indented, with each step passing row-source data to its parent until all steps complete. To help see the execution order more clearly, Listing 6-6 repeats a portion of the output from Listing 6-3 for the xpext.sql script, which shows the operations in execution order.

Listing 6-6. Plan Operations Displayed in Execution Order (from `xpext.sql` in Listing 6-3)

```
---------------------------------------------------------------------
| Id | Pid | Ord | Operation                     | Name            |
---------------------------------------------------------------------
|  6 |  5  |  1  |      TABLE ACCESS FULL         | EMPLOYEES       |
|  8 |  7  |  2  |        INDEX UNIQUE SCAN       | DEPT_ID_PK      |
|  7 |  5  |  3  |      TABLE ACCESS BY INDEX ROWID| DEPARTMENTS     |
|  5 |  4  |  4  |      NESTED LOOPS              |                 |
| 10 |  9  |  5  |        INDEX UNIQUE SCAN       | LOC_ID_PK       |
|  9 |  4  |  6  |      TABLE ACCESS BY INDEX ROWID | LOCATIONS       |
|  4 |  3  |  7  |      NESTED LOOPS             |                 |
| 11 |  3  |  8  |      INDEX UNIQUE SCAN         | COUNTRY_C_ID_PK |
|  3 |  2  |  9  |    NESTED LOOPS               |                 |
| 12 |  2  | 10  |    INDEX UNIQUE SCAN          | REG_ID_PK       |
|  2 |  1  | 11  |  NESTED LOOPS                 |                 |
| 13 |  1  | 12  |  TABLE ACCESS BY INDEX ROWID | REGIONS         |
|  1 |  0  | 13  | NESTED LOOPS                 |                 |
|  0 |     | 14  | SELECT STATEMENT             |                 |
---------------------------------------------------------------------
```

I often use an analogy between parent-child relationships in a plan and real life parent-child relationships. A real child doesn't just spontaneously combust into being; a parent is required to "instantiate" the child into being. But, as most any parent will tell you, one of the greatest things about kids is that (sometimes) you can get them to do work for you. This applies to parent-child operations in a plan. The child takes direction from its parent and goes to do a piece of work. When the child completes that work, it reports back to the parent with the result. So, even though an index operation occurs before its parent (for example, step 6 executes before its parent in step 5), the child doesn't have meaning or existence without its parent. This is why it's important always to keep parent-child relationships in mind, because they help make sense of the execution order.

Access and Filter Predicates

One of the most helpful sections of the explained output is the section named Predicate Information. In this section, the ACCESS_PREDICATES and FILTER_PREDICATES columns are displayed. These columns are associated with a line (denoted by the ID column) in the list of plan operations. Notice that for each plan operation that has an access or filter predicate associated with it, there is an asterisk (*)next to the ID. When you see the asterisk, you know to look for that ID number in the Predicate Information section to see which predicate (condition in the WHERE clause) is related to that operation. Using this information, you can confirm that columns are used correctly (or not) for index access and also you can determine where a condition was filtered.

An access predicate is either going to be an index operation or a join operation. An access predicate is simply a more direct way to access the data by retrieving only the rows in the table that match a condition in the WHERE clause or when matching the columns that join two tables. Filter predicates are a less exact way to retrieve the data in that, when a filter predicate is applied, all rows in the current row source must be checked to determine whether they pass the filter. On the other hand, an access predicate only places rows into a resulting row source when there is an exact match. Thus, access predicates are often thought of as more efficient because they typically only gather rows that match the condition vs. hitting all the rows and throwing away what doesn't match.

Filtering late is a common performance inhibitor. For example, if you want to move a pile of 100 rocks from the front yard to your backyard but only need rocks that weigh 5 to 10 pounds, would you move all 100 rocks and then remove the ones you need? Or would you simply move those that are the correct weight? In general, you want to take only the rocks you need, right?

Using the filter predicate information can help you verify that unneeded rows are filtered out of your result set as early as possible in the plan. Just like it doesn't make much sense to carry a whole bunch of extra rocks to the backyard, it doesn't make much sense to carry rows through a whole set of plan operations that ultimately are not included in the final result set. Use the filter information to verify that each condition is applied as early in the plan as possible. If a filter is applied too late, you can adjust your SQL or take other steps (such as verifying that statistics are up to date) to ensure your plan isn't working harder than it needs to.

Reading the Plan as a Narrative

Last, learning to read the plan as if it is a narrative can be extremely helpful. For many people, converting the set of plan operations into a paragraph of text facilitates understanding how the plan executes better than any other method. Let's convert the example plan into a narrative and see whether it makes it easier for you to read and understand. The following paragraph is a sample narrative for the example plan.

To produce the result set for this SELECT statement, rows from the DEPARTMENTS table are accessed using a full scan of the index on the DEPARTMENTS.LOCATION_ID column. Using a full scan of the LOCATIONS table, rows are retrieved and sorted by LOCATION_ID and then merged with the rows from DEPARTMENTS to produce a joined result set of matching rows containing both DEPARTMENTS and LOCATIONS data. This row set, which we call DEPT_LOC, is joined to the COUNTRIES table and matches iteratively one row from DEPT_LOC using COUNTRY_ID to find a matching row in COUNTRIES. This result set, which we call DEPT_LOC_CTRY, now contains data from DEPARTMENTS, LOCATIONS, and COUNTRIES, and is hashed into memory and matched with the REGIONS table data using REGION_ID. This result set, DEPT_LOC_CTRY_REG, is hashed into memory and matched with the EMPLOYEES table using DEPARTMENT_ID to produce the final result set of rows.

To produce this narrative, I simply walk through the steps of the plan in execution order and write out the description of the steps and how they link (join) to each other. I progress through each set of parent-child operations until all the steps are complete. You may find that creating a narrative helps you grasp the overall plan with a bit more clarity. For more complex plans, you may find that breaking out just a few key portions of the whole plan and writing them out in narrative form will help you understand the flow of operations more completely. The key is to use the narrative to help make better sense of the plan. If you find it harder to do this, then just stick with the plan as it is. But, taking time to learn to convert a plan into a narrative form is a good skill to learn, because it can help you describe what your query is doing in a way that doesn't require anyone even looking at plan output. It's similar to giving verbal directions on how to get to the nearest shopping mall. You don't necessarily have to have the map to be able to get from point A to point B.

Execution Plans

The actual execution plan for a SQL statement is produced when a statement is executed. After the statement is hard parsed, the plan that is chosen is stored in the library cache for later reuse. The plan operations can be viewed by querying V$SQL_PLAN, which has basically the same definition as PLAN_TABLE, except that it has several columns that contain the information on how to identify and find the statement in the library cache. These additional columns are ADDRESS, HASH_VALUE, SQL_ID, PLAN_HASH_VALUE, CHILD_ADDRESS, and CHILD_NUMBER. You can find any SQL statement using one or more of these values.

Viewing Recently Generated SQL

Listing 6-7 shows a query against V$SQL for recently executed SQL for the SCOTT user and the identifying values for each column.

Listing 6-7. V$SQL Query to Get Recently Executed SQL

```
SQL>select /* recentsql */ sql_id, child_number,
  2           hash_value, address, executions, sql_text
  3     from v$sql
  4    where parsing_user_id = (select user_id
  5                               from all_users
  6                              where username = 'SCOTT')
  7      and command_type in (2,3,6,7,189)
  8      and UPPER(sql_text) not like UPPER('%recentsql%');
```

SQL_ID	CHILD_NUMBER	HASH_VALUE	ADDRESS	EXECUTIONS	SQL_TEXT
g5wp7pwtq4kwp	0	862079893	3829AE54	1	select * from emp
1gg46m60z7k2p	0	2180237397	38280AD0	1	select * from bonus
4g0qfgmtb7z70	0	4071881952	38281D68	1	select * from dept

```
3 rows selected.
```

After connecting as user SCOTT, you execute the three queries shown. Then, when you run the query against V$SQL, you can see they are now loaded into the library cache and each has identifiers associated with it. The SQL_ID and CHILD_NUMBER columns contain the identifying information that you'll use most often to retrieve a statement's plan and execution statistics.

Viewing the Associated Execution Plan

There are several ways to view the execution plan for any SQL statement that has been previously executed and still remains in the library cache. The easiest way is to use the dbms_xplan.display_cursor function. Listing 6-8 shows how to use dbms_xplan.display_cursor to show the execution plan for the most recently executed SQL statement (note that some output columns have been elided for brevity).

Listing 6-8. Using dbms_xplan.display_cursor

```
SQL>select /*+ gather_plan_statistics */ empno, ename from scott.emp where ename = 'KING' ;

    EMPNO ENAME
---------- ----------
     7839 KING
SQL>
SQL>set serveroutput off
SQL>select * from table(dbms_xplan.display_cursor(null,null,'ALLSTATS LAST'));

PLAN_TABLE_OUTPUT
--------------------------------------------------------------------------
SQL_ID  2dzsuync8upv0, child number 0
-------------------------------------
select empno, ename from scott.emp where ename = 'KING'

Plan hash value: 3956160932
```

```
-------------------------------------------------------------------------
| Id | Operation         | Name | Starts | E-Rows | A-Rows | Buffers |
-------------------------------------------------------------------------
|  0 | SELECT STATEMENT  |      |    1   |        |    1   |    8    |
|* 1 |  TABLE ACCESS FULL| EMP  |    1   |    1   |    1   |    8    |
-------------------------------------------------------------------------

Predicate Information (identified by operation id):
---------------------------------------------------

   1 - filter("ENAME"='KING')
```

First, note the use of the gather_plan_statistics hint in the query. To capture row-source execution statistics for the plan, you must tell Oracle to gather this information as the statement executes. The row-source execution statistics include the number of rows, number of consistent reads, number of physical reads, number of physical writes, and the elapsed time for each operation on a row. This information can be gathered using this hint on a statement-by-statement basis, or you can set the STATISTICS_LEVEL instance parameter to ALL. Capturing these statistics does add some overhead to the execution of a statement, and so you may not want to have it "always on." The hint allows you to use it when you need to—and only for the individual statements you choose. The presence of this hint collects the information and shows it in the Starts, A-Rows, and Buffers columns. Listing 6-9 shows how the plan output appears if you don't use the hint (or set the parameter value to ALL).

Listing 6-9. Using dbms_xplan.display_cursor without the gather_plan_statistics hint

```
SQL>select ename from scott.emp where ename = 'KING' ;

ENAME
----------
KING

SQL>select * from table(dbms_xplan.display_cursor(null,null,'ALLSTATS LAST'));

PLAN_TABLE_OUTPUT
-------------------------------------------------------------------------
SQL_ID 32rvc78ypwhn8, child number 0
-------------------------------------
select ename from scott.emp where ename = 'KING'

Plan hash value: 3956160932

-------------------------------------------------
| Id | Operation         | Name | E-Rows |
-------------------------------------------------
|  0 | SELECT STATEMENT  |      |        |
|* 1 |  TABLE ACCESS FULL| EMP  |    1   |
-------------------------------------------------

Predicate Information (identified by operation id):
---------------------------------------------------

   1 - filter("ENAME"='KING')
```

Note

    - Warning: basic plan statistics not available. These are only collected when:
    * hint 'gather_plan_statistics' is used for the statement or
    * parameter 'statistics_level' is set to 'ALL', at session or system level

As you can see, a note is displayed that indicates the plan statistics aren't available and it tells you what to do to collect them.

Collecting the Plan Statistics

The plan operations shown when no plan statistics are available is essentially the same as the output from EXPLAIN PLAN. To get to the heart of how well the plan worked, you need the plan's row-source execution statistics. These values tell you what actually happened for each operation in the plan. These data are pulled from the V$SQL_PLAN_STATISTICS view, which links each operation row for a plan to a row of statistics data. A composite view named V$SQL_PLAN_STATISTICS_ALL contains all the columns from V$SQL_PLAN plus the columns from V$SQL_PLAN_STATISTICS as well as a few additional columns containing information about memory usage. Listing 6-10 describes the V$SQL_PLAN_STATISTICS_ALL view columns.

Listing 6-10. The V$SQL_PLAN_STATISTICS_ALL View Description

```
SQL> desc v$sql_plan_statistics_all
 Name                                 Null?    Type
 ----------------------------------- -------- ------------------------
 ADDRESS                                       RAW(8)
 HASH_VALUE                                    NUMBER
 SQL_ID                                        VARCHAR2(13)
 PLAN_HASH_VALUE                               NUMBER
 FULL_PLAN_HASH_VALUE                          NUMBER
 CHILD_ADDRESS                                 RAW(8)
 CHILD_NUMBER                                  NUMBER
 TIMESTAMP                                     DATE
 OPERATION                                     VARCHAR2(30)
 OPTIONS                                       VARCHAR2(30)
 OBJECT_NODE                                   VARCHAR2(40)
 OBJECT#                                       NUMBER
 OBJECT_OWNER                                  VARCHAR2(30)
 OBJECT_NAME                                   VARCHAR2(30)
 OBJECT_ALIAS                                  VARCHAR2(65)
 OBJECT_TYPE                                   VARCHAR2(20)
 OPTIMIZER                                     VARCHAR2(20)
 ID                                            NUMBER
 PARENT_ID                                     NUMBER
 DEPTH                                         NUMBER
 POSITION                                      NUMBER
 SEARCH_COLUMNS                                NUMBER
 COST                                          NUMBER
 CARDINALITY                                   NUMBER
 BYTES                                         NUMBER
 OTHER_TAG                                     VARCHAR2(35)
 PARTITION_START                               VARCHAR2(64)
```

PARTITION_STOP	VARCHAR2(64)
PARTITION_ID	NUMBER
OTHER	VARCHAR2(4000)
DISTRIBUTION	VARCHAR2(20)
CPU_COST	NUMBER
IO_COST	NUMBER
TEMP_SPACE	NUMBER
ACCESS_PREDICATES	VARCHAR2(4000)
FILTER_PREDICATES	VARCHAR2(4000)
PROJECTION	VARCHAR2(4000)
TIME	NUMBER
QBLOCK_NAME	VARCHAR2(30)
REMARKS	VARCHAR2(4000)
OTHER_XML	CLOB
EXECUTIONS	NUMBER
LAST_STARTS	NUMBER
STARTS	NUMBER
LAST_OUTPUT_ROWS	NUMBER
OUTPUT_ROWS	NUMBER
LAST_CR_BUFFER_GETS	NUMBER
CR_BUFFER_GETS	NUMBER
LAST_CU_BUFFER_GETS	NUMBER
CU_BUFFER_GETS	NUMBER
LAST_DISK_READS	NUMBER
DISK_READS	NUMBER
LAST_DISK_WRITES	NUMBER
DISK_WRITES	NUMBER
LAST_ELAPSED_TIME	NUMBER
ELAPSED_TIME	NUMBER
POLICY	VARCHAR2(10)
ESTIMATED_OPTIMAL_SIZE	NUMBER
ESTIMATED_ONEPASS_SIZE	NUMBER
LAST_MEMORY_USED	NUMBER
LAST_EXECUTION	VARCHAR2(10)
LAST_DEGREE	NUMBER
TOTAL_EXECUTIONS	NUMBER
OPTIMAL_EXECUTIONS	NUMBER
ONEPASS_EXECUTIONS	NUMBER
MULTIPASSES_EXECUTIONS	NUMBER
ACTIVE_TIME	NUMBER
MAX_TEMPSEG_SIZE	NUMBER
LAST_TEMPSEG_SIZE	NUMBER
CON_ID	NUMBER
CON_DBID	NUMBER

The columns containing the pertinent statistics information that relates to the output from dbms_xplan. display_cursor all begin with the prefix LAST_. When you use the format option of ALLSTATS LAST, the plan shows these column values for each row in the plan. So, for each operation, you know exactly how many rows it returns (LAST_OUTPUT_ROWS is shown in the A-Rows column), how many consistent reads occur (LAST_CR_BUFFER_GETS is shown in the Buffers column), how many physical reads occur (LAST_DISK_READS is shown in the Reads column), and the number of times a step is executed (LAST_STARTS is shown in the Starts column). There are several other columns that display, depending on the operations that take place, but these are the most common.

The dbms_xplan.display_cursor call signature is as follows:

```
FUNCTION DISPLAY_CURSOR RETURNS DBMS_XPLAN_TYPE_TABLE
Argument Name                    Type                    In/Out Default?
------------------------------   ----------------------  ------ --------
SQL_ID                           VARCHAR2                 IN     DEFAULT
CURSOR_CHILD_NO                  NUMBER(38)               IN     DEFAULT
FORMAT                           VARCHAR2                 IN     DEFAULT
```

In the example from Listing 6-8, the three parameters used were SQL_ID => null, CURSOR_CHILD_NO => null, and FORMAT => ALLSTATS LAST. The use of nulls for the SQL_ID and CURSOR_CHILD_NO parameters indicates that the plan for the last executed statement should be retrieved. Therefore, you should be able to execute a statement, then execute the following:

```
select * from table(dbms_xplan.display_cursor(null,null,'ALLSTATS LAST'));
```

This gives you the plan output as shown in Listing 6-8.

■ **Caution** You may have noticed that I executed the SQL*Plus command SET SERVEROUTPUT OFF before executing the call to dbms_xplan.display_cursor. This is a slight oddity that might catch you off-guard if you don't know about it. Whenever you execute a statement and SERVEROUTPUT is ON, a call to dbms_output is executed implicitly. If you don't use SERVEROUTPUT OFF, then the last statement executed is this dbms_output call. Using nulls for the first two parameters does not give you the SQL statement you executed, but instead attempts to give you the plan for the dbms_output call. Simply turning this setting to OFF stops the implicit call and ensures you get the plan for your most recently executed statement.

Identifying SQL Statements for Later Plan Retrieval

If you want to retrieve a statement that was executed in the past, you can retrieve the SQL_ID and CHILD_NUMBER from V$SQL as demonstrated in Listing 6-7. To simplify finding the correct statement identifiers, especially when I'm testing, I add a unique comment that identifies each statement I execute. Then, whenever I want to grab that plan from the library cache, all I have to do is query V$SQL to locate the statement text that includes the comment I used. Listing 6-11 shows an example of this and the query I use to subsequently find the statement I want.

Listing 6-11. Using a Comment to Identify a SQL Statement Uniquely

```
SQL>select /* KM-EMPTEST1 */ empno, ename
  2    from emp
  3   where job = 'MANAGER' ;

    EMPNO ENAME
---------- ----------
     7566 JONES
     7698 BLAKE
     7782 CLARK
```

```
SQL>select sql_id, child_number, sql_text
  2  from v$sql
  3  where sql_text like '%KM-EMPTEST1%';

SQL_ID          CHILD_NUMBER SQL_TEXT
-------------   ------------ ---------------------------------------------------
9qu1dvthfcqsp             0 select /* KM-EMPTEST1 */      empno, ename
                             from emp where job = 'MANAGER'
a7nzwn3t522mt             0 select sql_id, child_number, sql_text from
                             v$sql where sql_text like '%KM-EMPTEST1%'

SQL>select * from table(dbms_xplan.display_cursor('9qu1dvthfcqsp',0,'ALLSTATS LAST'));

PLAN_TABLE_OUTPUT
-----------------------------------------------------------------------------
SQL_ID  9qu1dvthfcqsp, child number 0
-------------------------------------
select /* KM-EMPTEST1 */ empno, ename  from emp where job = 'MANAGER'

Plan hash value: 3956160932

----------------------------------------------------------------------------
| Id  | Operation          | Name | Starts | E-Rows | A-Rows | Buffers |
----------------------------------------------------------------------------
|   0 | SELECT STATEMENT   |      |    1   |        |    3   |     8   |
|*  1 |  TABLE ACCESS FULL | EMP  |    1   |    3   |    3   |     8   |
----------------------------------------------------------------------------

Predicate Information (identified by operation id):
---------------------------------------------------

   1 - filter("JOB"='MANAGER')
```

Notice that when I query V$SQL, two statements show up. One is the SELECT statement I executed to find the entry in V$SQL and one is the query I executed. Although this series of steps gets the job done, I find it easier to automate the whole process into a single script. In this script, I find the statement I want in V$SQL by weeding out the query I'm running to find it and also by ensuring that I find the most recently executed statement that uses my identifying comment. Listing 6-12 shows the script I use in action.

Listing 6-12. Automating Retrieval of an Execution Plan for Any SQL Statement

```
SQL>select /* KM-EMPTEST2 */
  2         empno, ename
  3    from emp
  4   where job = 'CLERK' ;

    EMPNO ENAME
---------- ----------
     7369 SMITH
     7876 ADAMS
     7900 JAMES
     7934 MILLER
```

```
SQL>
SQL>get pln.sql
   1   SELECT xplan.*
   2   FROM
   3   (
   4   select max(sql_id) keep
   5        (dense_rank last order by last_active_time) sql_id
   6        , max(child_number) keep
   7        (dense_rank last order by last_active_time) child_number
   8   from v$sql
   9   where upper(sql_text) like '%&1%'
  10   and upper(sql_text) not like '%FROM V$SQL WHERE UPPER(SQL_TEXT) LIKE %'
  11   ) sqlinfo,
  12   table(DBMS_XPLAN.DISPLAY_CURSOR(sqlinfo.sql_id, sqlinfo.child_number, 'ALLSTATS LAST')) xplan ;

SQL>@pln KM-EMPTEST2

PLAN_TABLE_OUTPUT
-----------------------------------------------------------------------------
SQL_ID  bn37qcafkwkt0, child number 0
-------------------------------------
select /* KM-EMPTEST2 */ empno, ename from emp where job = 'CLERK'

Plan hash value: 3956160932

-------------------------------------------------------------------------
| Id  | Operation          | Name | Starts | E-Rows | A-Rows | Buffers |
-------------------------------------------------------------------------
|   0 | SELECT STATEMENT   |      |      1 |        |      4 |       8 |
|*  1 |  TABLE ACCESS FULL | EMP  |      1 |      3 |      4 |       8 |
-------------------------------------------------------------------------

Predicate Information (identified by operation id):
---------------------------------------------------

   1 - filter("JOB"='CLERK')
```

This script returns the execution plan associated with the most recently executed SQL statement that matches the pattern you enter. As I mentioned, it is easier to find a statement if you make an effort to use a comment to identify it, but it works to find any string of matching text you enter. However, if there are multiple statements with matching text, this script only displays the most recently executed statement matching the pattern. If you want a different statement, you have to issue a query against V$SQL such as the one in Listing 6-11 and then feed the correct SQL_ID and CHILD_NUMBER to the dbms_xplan.display_cursor call.

Understanding DBMS_XPLAN in Detail

The DBMS_XPLAN package is supplied by Oracle and can be used to simplify the retrieval and display of plan output, as I have demonstrated. To use all the procedures and functions in this package fully, you need to have privileges to certain fixed views. A single grant on SELECT_CATALOG_ROLE ensures you have access to everything you need; but, at a minimum, you should have select privileges for VSQL, VSQL_PLAN, V$SESSION, and V$SQL_PLAN_STATISTICS_ALL to execute just the display and display_cursor functions properly. In this section, I cover a few more details about the use of this package and, in particular, the format options for the display and display_cursor functions.

The dbms_xplan package has grown since it first appeared in Oracle version 9. At that time, it contained only the display function. In Oracle version 12c, the package includes 26 functions, although only eight of them are included in the documentation. These functions can be used to display not only explain plan output, but plans for statements stored in the Automatic Workload Repository (AWR), SQL tuning sets, cached SQL cursors, and SQL plan baselines. The main table functions used to display plans from each of these areas are as follows:

- DISPLAY
- DISPLAY_CURSOR
- DISPLAY_AWR
- DISPLAY_SQLSET
- DISPLAY_SQL_PATCH_PLAN
- DISPLAY_SQL_PROFILE_PLAN
- DISPLAY_SQL_PLAN_BASELINE

These table functions all return the DBMS_XPLAN_TYPE_TABLE type, which is made up of 300-byte strings. This type accommodates the variable formatting needs of each table function to display the plan table columns dynamically as needed. The fact that these are table functions means that, to call them, you must use the table function to cast the return type properly when used in a SELECT statement. A table function is simply a stored PL/SQL function that behaves like a regular query to a table. The benefit is that you can write code in the function that performs transformations to data before it is returned in the result set. In the case of queries against the PLAN_TABLE or V$SQL_PLAN, the use of a table function makes it possible to do all the dynamic formatting needed to output only the columns pertinent for a given SQL statement instead of having to try and create multiple queries to handle different needs.

Each of the table functions accepts a FORMAT parameter as input. The FORMAT parameter controls the information included in the display output. The following is a list of documented values for this parameter:

- BASIC displays only the operation name and its option.
- TYPICAL displays the relevant information and variably display options such as partition and parallel usage only when applicable. This is the default.
- SERIAL is the same as TYPICAL, but it always excludes parallel information.
- ALL displays the maximum amount of information in the display.

In addition to the basic format parameter values, there are several additional more granular options that can be used to customize the default behavior of the base values. You can specify multiple keywords separated by a comma or a space and use the prefix of a plus sign (+)to indication inclusion or a minus sign/hyphen (-)to indicate exclusion of that particular display element. All these options display the information only if relevant. The following is a list of optional keywords:

- ADVANCED shows the same as ALL plus the Outline section and the Peeked Binds section.
- ALIAS shows the Query Block Name/Object Alias section.
- ALL shows the Query Block Name/Object Alias section, the Predicate section, and the Column Projection section.
- ALLSTATS* is equivalent to IOSTATS LAST.
- BYTES shows the estimated number of bytes.
- COST is the cost information computed by the optimizer.

- IOSTATS* shows IO statistics for executions of the cursor.

- LAST* shows only the plan statistics for the last execution of the cursor (the default is ALL and is cumulative).

- MEMSTATS* shows the memory management statistics for memory-intensive operations such as hash joins, sorts, or some bitmap operators.

- NOTE shows the Note section.

- OUTLINE shows the Outline section (set of hints that reproduce the plan).

- PARALLEL shows parallel execution information.

- PARTITION shows partition pruning information.

- PEEKED_BINDS shows bind variable values.

- PREDICATE shows the Predicate section.

- PROJECTION shows the Column Projection section (which columns have been passed to their parent by each line, and the size of those columns).

- REMOTE shows distributed query information.

The keywords followed by an asterisk are not available for use with the DISPLAY function because they use information from V$SQL_PLAN_STATISTICS_ALL, which exists only after a statement has been executed. Listing 6-13 shows several examples of the various options in use (note that the Time column has been elided for brevity from each of the examples).

Listing 6-13. Display Options Using Format Parameters

This example shows the output when using the ALL format parameter:
```
SQL> explain plan for
  2  select * from emp e, dept d
  3  where e.deptno = d.deptno
  4  and e.ename = 'JONES' ;

Explained.
```

SQL> select * from table(dbms_xplan.display(format=>'ALL'));

```
PLAN_TABLE_OUTPUT
--------------------------------------------------------------------------------
Plan hash value: 3625962092
```

Id	Operation	Name	Rows	Bytes	Cost (%CPU)
0	SELECT STATEMENT		1	59	4 (0)
1	NESTED LOOPS				
2	NESTED LOOPS		1	59	4 (0)
* 3	TABLE ACCESS FULL	EMP	1	39	3 (0)
* 4	INDEX UNIQUE SCAN	PK_DEPT	1		0 (0)
5	TABLE ACCESS BY INDEX ROWID	DEPT	1	20	1 (0)

```
Query Block Name / Object Alias (identified by operation id):
-------------------------------------------------------------

   1 - SEL$1
   3 - SEL$1 / E@SEL$1
   4 - SEL$1 / D@SEL$1
   5 - SEL$1 / D@SEL$1
Predicate Information (identified by operation id):
---------------------------------------------------

   3 - filter("E"."ENAME"='JONES')
   4 - access("E"."DEPTNO"="D"."DEPTNO")

Column Projection Information (identified by operation id):
-----------------------------------------------------------

   1 - (#keys=0) "E"."EMPNO"[NUMBER,22], "E"."ENAME"[VARCHAR2,10],
       "E"."JOB"[VARCHAR2,9], "E"."MGR"[NUMBER,22], "E"."HIREDATE"[DATE,7],
       "E"."SAL"[NUMBER,22], "E"."COMM"[NUMBER,22], "E"."DEPTNO"[NUMBER,22],
       "D"."DEPTNO"[NUMBER,22], "D"."DNAME"[VARCHAR2,14], "D"."LOC"[VARCHAR2,13]
   2 - (#keys=0) "E"."EMPNO"[NUMBER,22], "E"."ENAME"[VARCHAR2,10],
       "E"."JOB"[VARCHAR2,9], "E"."MGR"[NUMBER,22], "E"."HIREDATE"[DATE,7],
       "E"."SAL"[NUMBER,22], "E"."COMM"[NUMBER,22], "E"."DEPTNO"[NUMBER,22],
       "D".ROWID[ROWID,10], "D"."DEPTNO"[NUMBER,22]
   3 - "E"."EMPNO"[NUMBER,22], "E"."ENAME"[VARCHAR2,10], "E"."JOB"[VARCHAR2,9],
       "E"."MGR"[NUMBER,22], "E"."HIREDATE"[DATE,7], "E"."SAL"[NUMBER,22],
       "E"."COMM"[NUMBER,22], "E"."DEPTNO"[NUMBER,22]
   4 - "D".ROWID[ROWID,10], "D"."DEPTNO"[NUMBER,22]
   5 - "D"."DNAME"[VARCHAR2,14], "D"."LOC"[VARCHAR2,13]
```

This example shows the output when using the ALLSTATS LAST -COST -BYTES format parameter:

```
SQL> select empno, ename from emp e, dept d
  2  where e.deptno = d.deptno
  3  and e.ename = 'JONES' ;

    EMPNO ENAME
---------- ----------
     7566 JONES

1 row selected.
SQL> select * from table(dbms_xplan.display_cursor(null,null,format=>'ALLSTATS LAST -COST -BYTES'));

PLAN_TABLE_OUTPUT
-----------------------------------------------------------------------------

SQL_ID  3mypf7d6npa97, child number 0
-------------------------------------
select empno, ename from emp e, dept d where e.deptno = d.deptno and
e.ename = 'JONES'
```

Plan hash value: 3956160932

```
---------------------------------------------------------------------
| Id  | Operation         | Name | Starts | E-Rows | A-Rows | Buffers | Reads|
---------------------------------------------------------------------
|   0 | SELECT STATEMENT  |      |    1 |        |      1 |      8 |     6|
|*  1 |  TABLE ACCESS FULL| EMP  |    1 |      1 |      1 |      8 |     6|
---------------------------------------------------------------------
```

Predicate Information (identified by operation id):
----

   1 - filter(("E"."ENAME"='JONES' AND "E"."DEPTNO" IS NOT NULL))

    This example shows the output when using the +PEEKED_BINDS format parameter to show the values of the bind variables:

```
SQL> variable v_empno number
SQL> exec :v_empno := 7566 ;

PL/SQL procedure successfully completed.

SQL> select empno, ename, job, mgr, sal, deptno from emp where empno = :v_empno ;

EMPNO ENAME       JOB        MGR     SAL  DEPTNO
------ ---------- --------- ------- -------- --------
 7566 JONES      MANAGER    7839  3272.5      20

1 row selected.
```

SQL> select * from table(dbms_xplan.display_cursor(null,null,format=>'+PEEKED_BINDS'));

```
PLAN_TABLE_OUTPUT
-----------------------------------------------------------------------------

SQL_ID  9q17w9umt58m7, child number 0
-------------------------------------
select * from emp where empno = :v_empno

Plan hash value: 2949544139
```

```
-----------------------------------------------------------------
| Id  | Operation                    | Name   | Rows  | Bytes | Cost (%CPU)|
-----------------------------------------------------------------
|   0 | SELECT STATEMENT             |        |       |       |   1 (100)|
|   1 |  TABLE ACCESS BY INDEX ROWID| EMP    |     1 |    39 |   1   (0)|
|*  2 |   INDEX UNIQUE SCAN          | PK_EMP |     1 |       |   0   (0)|
-----------------------------------------------------------------
```

```
Peeked Binds (identified by position):
--------------------------------------

   1 - :V_EMPNO (NUMBER): 7566

Predicate Information (identified by operation id):
---------------------------------------------------

   2 - access("EMPNO"=:V_EMPNO)
```

This example shows the output when using the BASIC +PARALLEL +PREDICATE format parameters to display parallel-query execution plan details:

```
SQL> select /*+ parallel(d, 4) parallel (e, 4) */
  2  d.dname, avg(e.sal), max(e.sal)
  3  from dept d, emp e
  4  where d.deptno = e.deptno
  5  group by d.dname
  6  order by max(e.sal), avg(e.sal) desc;

DNAME              AVG(E.SAL)      MAX(E.SAL)
--------------     --------------- ---------------
SALES              1723.3333333333           3135
RESEARCH                   2392.5             3300
ACCOUNTING         3208.3333333333           5500
```

SQL> select * from table(dbms_xplan.display_cursor(null,null,'BASIC +PARALLEL +PREDICATE'));

```
PLAN_TABLE_OUTPUT
-------------------------------------------------------------------------------

SQL_ID  gahr597f78j0d, child number 0
-------------------------------------
select /*+ parallel(d, 4) parallel (e, 4) */ d.dname, avg(e.sal),
max(e.sal) from dept d, emp e where d.deptno = e.deptno group by
d.dname order by max(e.sal), avg(e.sal) desc

Plan hash value: 3078011448
```

```
---------------------------------------------------------------------------
| Id  | Operation                      | Name     |   TQ  |IN-OUT| PQ Distrib |
---------------------------------------------------------------------------
|   0 | SELECT STATEMENT               |          |       |      |            |
|   1 |  PX COORDINATOR                |          |       |      |            |
|   2 |   PX SEND QC (ORDER)           | :TQ10004 | Q1,04 | P->S | QC (ORDER) |
|   3 |    SORT ORDER BY               |          | Q1,04 | PCWP |            |
|   4 |     PX RECEIVE                 |          | Q1,04 | PCWP |            |
|   5 |      PX SEND RANGE             | :TQ10003 | Q1,03 | P->P | RANGE      |
|   6 |       HASH GROUP BY            |          | Q1,03 | PCWP |            |
|   7 |        PX RECEIVE             |          | Q1,03 | PCWP |            |
|   8 |         PX SEND HASH          | :TQ10002 | Q1,02 | P->P | HASH       |
|   9 |          HASH GROUP BY        |          | Q1,02 | PCWP |            |
|  10 |           HASH JOIN          |          | Q1,02 | PCWP |            |
|  11 |            PX RECEIVE        |          | Q1,02 | PCWP |            |
|  12 |             PX SEND HYBRID HASH | :TQ10000 | Q1,00 | P->P | HYBRID HASH|
|  13 |              STATISTICS COLLECTOR |        | Q1,00 | PCWC |            |
|  14 |               PX BLOCK ITERATOR |        | Q1,00 | PCWC |            |
|  15 |                TABLE ACCESS FULL | DEPT   | Q1,00 | PCWP |            |
|  16 |            PX RECEIVE        |          | Q1,02 | PCWP |            |
|  17 |             PX SEND HYBRID HASH (SKEW)| :TQ10001 | Q1,01 | P->P | HYBRID HASH|
|  18 |              PX BLOCK ITERATOR |         | Q1,01 | PCWC |            |
|  19 |               TABLE ACCESS FULL | EMP    | Q1,01 | PCWP |            |
---------------------------------------------------------------------------
```

Predicate Information (identified by operation id):

```
  10 - access("D"."DEPTNO"="E"."DEPTNO")
  15 - access(:Z>=:Z AND :Z<=:Z)
  19 - access(:Z>=:Z AND :Z<=:Z)
```

Using SQL Monitor Reports

Since its inclusion in Oracle 11g, SQL Monitor Reports provide another way for you to review execution plan row-source execution statistics to determine how time and resources are used for a given SQL statement. Although it is similar to using the DBMS_XPLAN.DISPLAY_CURSOR function that we already reviewed in detail, it offers several unique features. One key thing to note about the availability of SQL Monitor Reports is that they are on by default, even when the STATISTICS_LEVEL parameter is set to TYPICAL (the default). Furthermore, any statement that consumes more than five seconds of CPU or IO time, as well as any statement using parallel execution, is monitored automatically.

There are two hints—MONITOR and NO_MONITOR—that can be used to override the default behavior. When using the DBMS_XPLAN.DISPLAY_CURSOR function to display row-source execution statistics, you are required to use either a GATHER_PLAN_STATISTICS hint or to set the STATISTICS_LEVEL parameter equal to ALL. The fact that monitoring of statements can happen without either of these settings eliminates some of the overhead. However, if you want to make sure to capture information for SQL statements that may execute for less than five seconds, you need to specify the MONITOR hint in the SQL.

One of the nicest features of SQL Monitor Reports is the ability to request the report in real time. This means that the DBA or performance analyst can monitor a SQL statement while it is executing. Everything from CPU and IO times to number of output rows and memory or temp space used are updated in almost real time while the statement is executing. The V$SQL_MONITOR and V$SQL_PLAN_MONITOR views expose these statistics, and the real-time SQL Monitoring Report is produced using the DBMS_SQLTUNE.REPORT_SQL_MONITOR function, which accesses the data in these views. The output can be formatted as TEXT (the default), HTML, XML, or ACTIVE.

The dbms_sqltune.report_sql_monitor call signature is as follows:

```
FUNCTION REPORT_SQL_MONITOR RETURNS CLOB
 Argument Name                  Type                     In/Out Default?
 ------------------------------ ------------------------ ------ --------
 SQL_ID                         VARCHAR2                 IN     DEFAULT
 SESSION_ID                     NUMBER                   IN     DEFAULT
 SESSION_SERIAL                 NUMBER                   IN     DEFAULT
 SQL_EXEC_START                 DATE                     IN     DEFAULT
 SQL_EXEC_ID                    NUMBER                   IN     DEFAULT
 INST_ID                        NUMBER                   IN     DEFAULT
 START_TIME_FILTER              DATE                     IN     DEFAULT
 END_TIME_FILTER                DATE                     IN     DEFAULT
 INSTANCE_ID_FILTER             NUMBER                   IN     DEFAULT
 PARALLEL_FILTER                VARCHAR2                 IN     DEFAULT
 PLAN_LINE_FILTER               NUMBER                   IN     DEFAULT
 EVENT_DETAIL                   VARCHAR2                 IN     DEFAULT
 BUCKET_MAX_COUNT               NUMBER                   IN     DEFAULT
 BUCKET_INTERVAL                NUMBER                   IN     DEFAULT
 BASE_PATH                      VARCHAR2                 IN     DEFAULT
 LAST_REFRESH_TIME              DATE                     IN     DEFAULT
 REPORT_LEVEL                   VARCHAR2                 IN     DEFAULT
 TYPE                           VARCHAR2                 IN     DEFAULT
 SQL_PLAN_HASH_VALUE            NUMBER                   IN     DEFAULT
 CON_NAME                       VARCHAR2                 IN     DEFAULT
 REPORT_ID                      NUMBER                   IN     DEFAULT
 DBOP_NAME                      VARCHAR2                 IN     DEFAULT
 DBOP_EXEC_ID                   NUMBER                   IN     DEFAULT
```

As you can see, there are numerous parameters that can be used to produce the report. However, if you simply want to report on the last statement monitored by Oracle, you can just execute the function using all defaults, as shown in Listing 6-14.

Listing 6-14. Displaying a SQL Monitor Report

```
SQL> select /*+ monitor */ * from employees2 where email like 'S%';
... 3625 lines of output omitted

SQL> select dbms_sqltune.report_sql_monitor() from dual;

SQL Monitoring Report

SQL Text
------------------------------
select /*+ monitor */ * from employees2 where email like 'S%'
```

```
Global Information
------------------------------
  Status                :  DONE (ALL ROWS)
  Instance ID           :  1
  Session               :  HR (91:44619)
  SQL ID                :  4mxtbapapgfj7
  SQL Execution ID      :  16777216
  Execution Started     :  05/30/2013 21:41:02
  First Refresh Time    :  05/30/2013 21:41:02
  Last Refresh Time     :  05/30/2013 21:41:07
  Duration              :  5s
  Module/Action         :  SQL*Plus/-
  Service               :  SYS$USERS
  Program               :  sqlplus@ora12c (TNS V1-V3)
  Fetch Calls           :  243
```

Global Stats

| Elapsed | Cpu | IO | Other | Fetch | Buffer | Read | Read |
Time(s)	Time(s)	Waits(s)	Waits(s)	Calls	Gets	Reqs	Bytes
0.04	0.02	0.01	0.01	243	807	27	4MB

SQL Plan Monitoring Details (Plan Hash Value=2513133951)

Id	Operation	Name	Rows (Estim)	Cost	Time Active(s)	Start Active
0	SELECT STATEMENT				6	+0
1	TABLE ACCESS FULL	EMPLOYEES2	1628	171	6	+0

SQL Plan Monitoring Details (Plan Hash Value=2513133951)

Id	Execs	Rows (Actual)	Read Reqs	Read Bytes	Activity (%)	Activity Detail (# samples)
0	1	3625				
1	1	3625	1	8192		

I split the SQL Plan Monitoring Details section into two sections to get it to fit on the page properly and repeated the Id column to help identify the rows. As you can see, the information captured is similar to what you get when using dbms_xplan.display_cursor. The main differences are that you don't get buffer gets per operation and you get some additional columns for Active Session History (ASH) data (the Activity and Activity Detail columns). Just as with the dbms_xplan.display_cursor, various columns are visible depending on the type of plan executed (for example, a parallel execution plan). One of the key pieces of information you need when using execution plan data for problem diagnosis is the comparison of estimated rows with actual rows, and you can see both are provided in the SQL Monitor Report (Figure 6-1) just as in the dbms_xplan output.

SQL Monitoring Report

SQL Text

select * from (select i_item_desc ,i_category ,sum(ss_ext_sales_price) as itemrevenue ,sum(ss_ext_sales_price)*100/sum(sum(ss_ext_sales_price)) over (partition by i_class) as revenueratio from store_sales ,item ,date_dim where ss_item_sk = i_item_sk and ss_sold_date_sk = d_date_sk and d_date between to_date('1999-01-01','YYYY-MM-DD') and to_date('2000-01-01','YYYY-MM-DD') group by i_item_id ,i_class ,i_item_desc ,i_category) where rownum <= 1000

Global Information: EXECUTING

Instance ID	: 1
Session ID	: 89
SQL ID	: d3cbkh5wptrt0
SQL Execution ID	: 16777217
Plan Hash Value	: 4268948700
Execution Started	: 01/04/2008 18:48:54
First Refresh Time	: 01/04/2008 18:48:56
Last Refresh Time	: 01/04/2008 18:50:26
Fetch Calls	:

Buffer Gets	IO Count	Database Time	Wait Activity
501K	630K IO	334s	100%

Parallel Execution Details (DOP=8)

PX Processes Drill-Down

Name	Type	Server#	Buffer Gets	IO Count	Database Time	Wait Events
PX Coordinator	QC		2395 (.5%)		0s (,1%)	
p000	Set 1	1	52278 (10%)	51425 IO (8.2%)	26s (7.7%)	15%
p001	Set 1	2	301 (<0.1%)	126 IO (<0.1%)	4s (1.3%)	1.1%
p002	Set 1	3	2901 (.6%)	2618 IO (.4%)	6s (1.9%)	1.1%
p003	Set 1	4	222K (44%)	220K IO (34%)	73s (21%)	34%
p004	Set 1	5	213K (42%)	211K IO (33%)	70s (20%)	38%
p005	Set 1	6	3351 (.7%)	3168 IO (.5%)	12s (3.5%)	2.2%
p006	Set 1	7	832 (.2%)	684 IO (.1%)	11s (3.2%)	
p007	Set 1	8	4541 (.9%)	4289 IO (.7%)	9s (2.7%)	3.2%
p008	Set 2	1	12 (<0.1%)	17112 IO (2.7%)	16s (4.7%)	
p009	Set 2	2	14 (<0.1%)	17112 IO (2.7%)	16s (4.7%)	
p010	Set 2	3	14 (<0.1%)	17205 IO (2.7%)	15s (4.5%)	
p011	Set 2	4	12 (<0.1%)	16864 IO (2.7%)	16s (4.7%)	2.2%
p012	Set 2	5	14 (<0.1%)	17112 IO (2.7%)	16s (4.8%)	1.1%
p013	Set 2	6	12 (<0.1%)	17267 IO (2.7%)	16s (4.7%)	
p014	Set 2	7	12 (<0.1%)	17050 IO (2.7%)	14s (4.3%)	1.1%
p015	Set 2	8	14 (<0.1%)	17330 IO (2.7%)	15s (4.4%)	

SQL Plan Monitoring Details:

Id	Operation	Name	Estimated Rows	Cost	Active Period (93s)	Starts	Actual Rows	Memory	Temp	CPU Activity	Wait Activity	Progress
0	SELECT STATEMENT			342K		1						
1	COUNT STOPKEY					1						
2	PX COORDINATOR					17						
3	PX SEND QC (RANDOM)	:TQ10004	54864K	342K		8						
4	COUNT STOPKEY					8						
5	VIEW		54864K	342K		8						
6	WINDOW BUFFER		54864K	342K		8						
> 7	SORT GROUP BY		54864K	342K		8	0	12376K		20%		
> 8	PX RECEIVE		54864K	13552		8	4225K			5.0%		
> 9	PX SEND HASH	:TQ10003	54864K	13552		8	4321K			3.5%	4.3%	
> 10	HASH JOIN BUFFERED		54864K	13552		8	4321K	63840K	1127M	32%		151s
11	PX RECEIVE		204K	342		8	204K			1.0%		
12	PX SEND HASH	:TQ10001	204K	342		8	204K			.50%		
13	PX BLOCK ITERATOR		204K	342		8	204K					
14	TABLE ACCESS FULL	ITEM	204K	342		111	204K				6.5%	
15	PX RECEIVE		55371K	13017		8	55320K			5.0%		
16	PX SEND HASH	:TQ10002	55371K	13017		8	55320K			8.5%		
17	NESTED LOOPS		55371K	13017		8	55320K					
18	BUFFER SORT					8	2928					
19	PX RECEIVE					8	2928					
20	PX SEND BROADCAST	:TQ10000				8	2928					
21	PX BLOCK ITERATOR		367	32		8	366					
22	TABLE ACCESS FULL	DATE_DIM	367	32		99	366					
23	PX BLOCK ITERATOR		151K	255		2928	55320K			1.0%		
24	TABLE ACCESS FULL	STORE_SALES	151K	255		4006K	55320K			22%		89%

Figure 6-1. *An HTML SQL Monitor Report*

There are a couple limitations you should keep in mind regarding SQL Monitor Reports. Although SQL statement monitoring happens by default, as already mentioned, there are limits to how much monitoring data remain available. The hidden parameter _sqlmon_max_plan controls the size of the memory area dedicated to holding SQL monitoring information. By default, this parameter value is set to 20 times the number of CPUs. Therefore, if there are many different SQL statements being executed in your environment, it is entirely possible that the SQL statement monitoring data you are looking for may have already been pushed out because of newer SQL monitoring data needing space. Of course, you can increase this value if you want to attempt to keep monitoring data available for longer periods of time. But, as with changing any hidden parameter, you should do so with extreme caution and not without input from Oracle Support.

The second parameter that may cause you to not be able to produce a SQL Monitor Report for a given SQL statement is _sqlmon_max_planlines. This parameter defaults to 300 and limits the number of plan lines beyond which a statement is not monitored. In this case, if you have an extremely long execution plan of more than 300 lines, even if it is hinted with the MONITOR hint or if it runs long enough to be monitored normally automatically, it is not. As soon as the number of lines in the plan exceeds the 300 limit, monitoring is disabled.

You can use either a SQL Monitor Report or dbms_xplan.display_cursor output, as you prefer. I've started using SQL Monitor Reports more regularly because they require a bit less overhead to produce (because the STATISTICS_LEVEL parameter doesn't need to be set to ALL to capture the statistics). Also, if you happen to be working on an Exadata platform, the SQL Monitor Report displays a column to include offload percentage, which tells you when full table scan operations use Exadata smart scan technology, and is a key indicator of performance on Exadata machines. This information isn't present when using dbms_xplan.

Using Plan Information for Solving Problems

Now that you know how to access the various bits of information, what do you do with them? The plan information, particularly the plan statistics, helps you confirm how the plan is performing. You can use the information to determine whether there are any trouble spots, so you can then adjust the way the SQL is written, add or modify indexes, or even use the data to support a need to update statistics or adjust instance parameter settings.

Determining Index Deficiencies

If, for example, there is a missing or suboptimal index, you can see this in the plan. The next few listings walk through two examples: one shows how to determine whether an index is suboptimal (Listings 6-15 and 6-16) and the other shows how to determine an index is missing (Listing 6-17).

In each of these examples, there are two keys to look for. I made these example queries short and simple to keep the output easy to view, but regardless of how complex the plan, the way to spot a missing or suboptimal index is to look for (1) a TABLE ACCESS FULL operation with a filter predicate that shows a small A-Rows value (in other words, small in comparison with the total rows in the table) and (2) an index scan operation with a large A-Rows value compared with the parent TABLE ACCESS BY INDEX ROWID A-Rows value.

Listing 6-15. Using Plan Information to Determine Suboptimal Indexes

```
SQL> -- Example 1: sub-optimal index
SQL>
SQL> select /* KM1 */ job_id, department_id, last_name
  2  from employees
  3  where job_id = 'SA_REP'
  4  and department_id is null ;

JOB_ID     DEPARTMENT_ID LAST_NAME
---------- --------------- -------------------------
SA_REP     .               Grant

SQL> @pln KM1
```

PLAN_TABLE_OUTPUT

SQL_ID 0g7fpbvvbgvd2, child number 0

----

select /* KM1 */ job_id, department_id, last_name from hr.employees
where job_id = 'SA_REP' and department_id is null

Plan hash value: 2096651594

Id	Operation	Name	E-Rows	A-Rows	Buffers
0	SELECT STATEMENT			1	4
* 1	TABLE ACCESS BY INDEX ROWID BATCHED	EMPLOYEES	1	1	4
* 2	INDEX RANGE SCAN	EMP_JOB_IX	6	30	2

Predicate Information (identified by operation id):

----

   1 - filter("DEPARTMENT_ID" IS NULL)
   2 - access("JOB_ID"='SA_REP')

So, how do we know the EMP_JOB_IX index is suboptimal? In Listing 6-15, notice the A-Rows statistic for each operation. The INDEX RANGE SCAN uses the job_id predicate to return 30 row IDs from the index leaf blocks that match 'SA_REP'. The parent step, TABLE ACCESS BY INDEX ROWID, retrieves rows by accessing the blocks as specified in the 30 row IDs it received from the child INDEX RANGE SCAN operation. When these 30 rows are retrieved, then the next condition for department_id is null must be checked. In the end, after all 30 rows (requiring four buffer accesses, as shown in the Buffers column) have been checked, only one row is actually a match to be returned in the query result set. This means that 97 percent of the rows that were accessed weren't needed. From a performance perspective, this isn't very effective. In this example, because the table is small (only 107 rows in five blocks), the problem this could cause isn't really noticeable in terms of response time. But, why incur all that unnecessary work? That's where creating a better index comes in. If we simply include both columns in the index definition, the index returns only one row ID, and the parent step does not have to access any data blocks that it has to throw away. Listing 6-16 shows how adding the additional column to the index decreases the total amount of rows accessed.

Listing 6-16. Adding a Column to an Index to Improve a Suboptimal Index

```
SQL> create index emp_job_dept_ix on employees (department_id, job_id) compute statistics ;
SQL>
SQL> select /* KM2 */ job_id, department_id, last_name
  2   from employees
  3   where job_id = 'SA_REP'
  4   and department_id is null ;

JOB_ID      DEPARTMENT_ID LAST_NAME
----------  --------------- -------------------------
SA_REP        .             Grant

SQL> @pln KM2
```

```
PLAN_TABLE_OUTPUT
-------------------------------------------------------------------------------
SQL_ID  a65qqjrawsbfx, child number 0
-------------------------------------
select /* KM2 */ job_id, department_id, last_name from hr.employees
where job_id = 'SA_REP' and department_id is null

Plan hash value: 1551967251

-----------------------------------------------------------------------------
| Id  | Operation                 | Name          | E-Rows | A-Rows | Buffers |
-----------------------------------------------------------------------------
|   0 | SELECT STATEMENT          |               |        |      1 |      2 |
|   1 |  TABLE ACCESS BY INDEX    | EMPLOYEES     |      1 |      1 |      2 |
|     |    ROWID BATCHED          |               |        |        |        |
|*  2 |   INDEX RANGE SCAN        | EMP_JOB_DEPT_IX |    1 |      1 |      1 |
-----------------------------------------------------------------------------

Predicate Information (identified by operation id):
---------------------------------------------------

   2 - access("DEPARTMENT_ID" IS NULL AND "JOB_ID"='SA_REP')
       filter("JOB_ID"='SA_REP')
```

As you can see, by simply adding the department_id column to the index, the amount of work required to retrieve the query result set is minimized. The number of rowids passed from the child INDEX RANGE SCAN to the parent TABLE ACCESS BY INDEX ROWID step drops from 30 to just one, and the total buffer accesses is cut in half from four to two.

What about when no useful index exists? Again, this is a concern for performance. It may even be more of a concern than having a suboptimal index, because without any useful index at all, the only option the optimizer has is to use a full table scan. As the size of data increases, the responses are likely to keep increasing. So, you may "accidentally" miss creating an index in development when you are dealing with small amounts of data, but when data volumes increase in production, you'll likely figure out you need an index pretty quick! Listing 6-17 demonstrates how to identify a missing index.

Listing 6-17. Using Plan Information to Determine Missing Indexes

```
SQL> -- Example 2: missing index
SQL>
SQL> select /* KM3 */ last_name, phone_number
  2  from employees
  3  where phone_number = '650.507.9822';

LAST_NAME                 PHONE_NUMBER
------------------------- --------------------
Feeney                    650.507.9822
SQL>
SQL> @pln KM3
```

```
PLAN_TABLE_OUTPUT
--------------------------------------------------------------------
SQL_ID  26ry1z7z20cat, child number 0
-------------------------------------
select /* KM3 */ last_name, phone_number from hr.employees where
phone_number = '650.507.9822'

Plan hash value: 1445457117


--------------------------------------------------------------------
| Id | Operation          | Name      | E-Rows | A-Rows | Buffers |
--------------------------------------------------------------------
|  0 | SELECT STATEMENT   |           |        |     1  |     7  |
|* 1 |  TABLE ACCESS FULL | EMPLOYEES |     1  |     1  |     7  |
--------------------------------------------------------------------

Predicate Information (identified by operation id):
--------------------------------------------------

   1 - filter("PHONE_NUMBER"='650.507.9822')

SQL> column column_name format a22 heading 'Column Name'
SQL> column index_name heading 'Index Name'
SQL> column column_position format 999999999 heading 'Pos#'
SQL> column descend format a5 heading 'Order'
SQL> column column_expression format a40 heading 'Expression'
SQL>
SQL> break on index_name skip 1
SQL>
SQL> -- Check current indexes
SQL>
SQL> select  lower(b.index_name) index_name, b.column_position,
  2             b.descend, lower(b.column_name) column_name
  3  from       all_ind_columns b
  4  where      b.table_owner = 'HR'
  5  and        b.table_name = 'EMPLOYEES'
  6  order by b.index_name, b.column_position, b.column_name
  7  /
```

Index Name	Pos#	Order	Column Name
emp_department_ix	1	ASC	department_id
emp_email_uk	1	ASC	email
emp_emp_id_pk	1	ASC	employee_id
emp_job_dept_ix	1	ASC	department_id
	2	ASC	job_id
emp_job_ix	1	ASC	job_id

emp_manager_ix	1 ASC	manager_id
emp_name_ix	1 ASC	last_name
	2 ASC	first_name

In this example, the access operation chosen was a full table scan. By querying the ALL_IND_COLUMNS view, we can verify which indexes exist and on which columns. In this case, there is no index on the phone_number column, so the optimizer has no other choice than to use a full table scan and then filter the rows to locate any with a matching number. What is a bit difficult to tell just by looking is how much extra work it is to do the full scan and filter. In this case, the EMPLOYEES table has 107 rows, but the estimated number of rows only reflects how many rows are to be returned, not how many have to be accessed to check the filter condition. Because the query returned only one matching row for the phone number specified, this means 106 (virtually all) rows were rejected. Again, why incur all this work if having an index allows just the data you need to be accessed directly? Listing 6-18 shows what happens when the index is available.

Listing 6-18. Creating a New Index to Improve Performance

```
SQL> -- Create new index on phone_number
SQL>
SQL> create index hr.emp_phone_ix on hr.employees (phone_number) compute statistics ;
SQL>
SQL> select /* KM4 */ last_name, phone_number
  2  from employees
  3  where phone_number = '650.507.9822';

LAST_NAME                 PHONE_NUMBER
------------------------  --------------------
Feeney                    650.507.9822

SQL> @pln KM4

PLAN_TABLE_OUTPUT
----------------------------------------------------------------------------
SQL_ID  cs0bvb2zrsp66, child number 0
-------------------------------------
select /* KM4 */ last_name, phone_number from hr.employees where
phone_number = '650.507.9822'

Plan hash value: 2867517494
```

Id	Operation	Name	E-Rows	A-Rows	Buffers
0	SELECT STATEMENT			1	3
1	TABLE ACCESS BY INDEX ROWID BATCHED	EMPLOYEES	1	1	3
* 2	INDEX RANGE SCAN	EMP_PHONE_IX	1	1	2

```
Predicate Information (identified by operation id):
---------------------------------------------------

    2 - access("PHONE_NUMBER"='650.507.9822')
```

With the index in place, the optimizer chooses it to access the rows needed to satisfy the query. Now, instead of having to check all 107 rows in the table, only the one row that matches the requested phone number is accessed via the index. The number of blocks accessed was cut by more than half from seven to three. Imagine if this table was larger!

Index Deficiencies Wrap-up

In both cases (either finding a missing index or determining the need for a new index), the main thing to watch out for is excess throwaway. The more blocks that have to be accessed to check filter conditions on rows that are ultimately not included in the result set, the poorer the performance becomes. You may not even notice it if data volume is low in the beginning, but the larger the tables become, the more effect accessing unneeded blocks has on response time.

Determining Stale Statistics

Another way plan information can help you is by making it easy to spot when statistics might be out of date. Listing 6-19 shows an example of how plan information can point out stale statistics.

Listing 6-19. Using Plan Information to Determine When Statistics May Be out of Date

```
SQL> -- Check current column statistics (collected at 100%)
SQL>
SQL> select column_name, num_distinct, density
  2  from user_tab_cols
  3  where table_name = 'MY_OBJECTS' ;
```

Column Name	NUM_DISTINCT	DENSITY
OWNER	29	.03448275862069
OBJECT_NAME	44245	.00002260142389
SUBOBJECT_NAME	161	.00621118012422
OBJECT_ID	72588	.00001377638177
DATA_OBJECT_ID	7748	.00012906556531
OBJECT_TYPE	44	.02272727272727
CREATED	1418	.00070521861777
LAST_DDL_TIME	1480	.00067567567568
TIMESTAMP	1552	.00064432989691
STATUS	1	1
TEMPORARY	2	.5
GENERATED	2	.5
SECONDARY	2	.5
NAMESPACE	21	.04761904761905
EDITION_NAME	0	0

```
SQL> -- Execute query for object_type = 'TABLE'
SQL>
SQL> select /* KM7 */ object_id, object_name
  2  from my_objects
  3* where object_type = 'TABLE';
...
365056 rows selected.

SQL> @pln KM7

PLAN_TABLE_OUTPUT
--------------------------------------------------------------------------------
SQL_ID  7xphu2p2m9hdr, child number 0
-------------------------------------
select /* KM7 */ object_id, object_name from my_objects where
object_type = 'TABLE'

Plan hash value: 2785906523

--------------------------------------------------------------------------------
| Id  | Operation             | Name           | E-Rows | A-Rows | Buffers |
--------------------------------------------------------------------------------
|   0 | SELECT STATEMENT      |                |        |  365K  |  55697  |
|   1 |  TABLE ACCESS BY INDEX | MY_OBJECTS    |  1650  |  365K  |  55697  |
|     |   ROWID BATCHED       |                |        |        |         |
|*  2 |   INDEX RANGE SCAN    | OBJECT_TYPE_IX |  1650  |  365K  |  26588  |
--------------------------------------------------------------------------------

Predicate Information (identified by operation id):
---------------------------------------------------

   2 - access("OBJECT_TYPE"='TABLE')
```

In this example, the optimizer computed that only 1650 rows would be returned by the query for OBJECT_TYPE = 'TABLE' when, in reality, the query returned more than 365,000 rows. Because I built the data for this table, I can tell you that this was because the statistics had been gathered prior to the addition of a few hundred thousand rows. When the plan was chosen, the optimizer didn't have the updated information and it selected a plan using an index scan on the object_type index based on the old statistics. However, in reality, there were more than 474,000 total rows in the table and more than 365,000 of them matched the filter criteria. So, how do we correct the problem? Listing 6-20 shows one way you can identify the difference between the actual number of rows and the statistics value.

Listing 6-20. Identifying Difference Between Actual Rows and Statistics Rows Value

```
SQL> -- Compare statistic to actual
SQL>
SQL> select num_rows
  2  from dba_tables
  3  where table_name = 'MY_OBJECTS';
```

```
       NUM_ROWS
---------------
          72588

1 row selected.

SQL> select count(*)
  2  from my_objects ;

       COUNT(*)
---------------
         434792

1 row selected.
```

SQL> -- Update statistics
```
SQL>
SQL> exec dbms_stats.gather_table_stats(user,'MY_OBJECTS',estimate_percent=>100,
cascade=>true,method_opt=>'FOR ALL COLUMNS SIZE 1');

PL/SQL procedure successfully completed.
SQL> select /* KM8 */ object_id, object_name
  2  from my_objects
  3* where object_type = 'TABLE';
...
365056 rows selected.

SQL> @pln KM8

PLAN_TABLE_OUTPUT
-------------------------------------------------------------------------------
SQL_ID  2qq7ram92zc85, child number 0
-------------------------------------
select /* KM8 */ object_id, object_name from my_objects where
object_type = 'TABLE'

Plan hash value: 2785906523
```

Id	Operation	Name	E-Rows	A-Rows	Buffers
0	SELECT STATEMENT			365K	54553
1	TABLE ACCESS BY INDEX ROWID BATCHED	MY_OBJECTS	9882	365K	54553
* 2	INDEX RANGE SCAN	OBJECT_TYPE_IX	9882	365K	25444

```
Predicate Information (identified by operation id):
---------------------------------------------------

   2 - access("OBJECT_TYPE"='TABLE')
```

As this listing shows, when you determine that the actual number of rows in the table is significantly different than the number of rows captured by the statistics, a new collection is made and the query is executed again. This time, the estimate goes up to 9882 rows, but this is still an incorrect estimate compared with the actual rows returned. What happened? You collected fresh statistics and even used a 100 percent estimate, so everything should be correct, right? Well, the problem was that you didn't collect histogram statistics, which tell the optimizer about the heavy skew in the distribution of values of the object_type column. You need to use a method_opt parameter that collects histograms. Actually, you need to use just the default method_opt parameter, which is FOR ALL COLUMNS SIZE AUTO. This value collects histograms on columns automatically. Listing 6-21 shows what happens after collecting histogram statistics and executing the query again.

Listing 6-21. Collecting Histogram Statistics

```
SQL> -- Collect histogram statistics
SQL>
SQL> exec dbms_stats.gather_table_stats(user,'MY_OBJECTS',estimate_percent=>100,
cascade=>true,method_opt=>'FOR ALL COLUMNS SIZE AUTO');

PL/SQL procedure successfully completed.

SQL> select /* KM9 */ object_id, object_name
  2  from my_objects
  3* where object_type = 'TABLE';
...
365056 rows selected.

SQL> @pln KM9

PLAN_TABLE_OUTPUT
-----------------------------------------------------------------------------------------
SQL_ID  dbvrtvutuyp6z, child number 0
-------------------------------------
select /* KM9 */ object_id, object_name from my_objects where
object_type = 'TABLE'

Plan hash value: 880823944


-------------------------------------------------------------------
| Id  | Operation          | Name       | E-Rows | A-Rows | Buffers |
-------------------------------------------------------------------
|   0 | SELECT STATEMENT   |            |        |   365K |  30000 |
|*  1 |  TABLE ACCESS FULL | MY_OBJECTS |   365K |   365K |  30000 |
-------------------------------------------------------------------

Predicate Information (identified by operation id):
---------------------------------------------------

   1 - filter("OBJECT_TYPE"='TABLE')
```

So, you did the collection again and this time used method_opt=>'FOR ALL COLUMNS SIZE AUTO'. This setting allows Oracle to collect a histogram properly on the object_type column. Now when you execute the query, the estimate is right on target and you get a full table scan plan instead. In this case, the full scan operation is the best choice because the query returns nearly 80 percent of all the rows in the table and a full scan accesses fewer blocks than an index scan plan would. We examine histograms and how statistics are used by the optimizer in a later chapter.

By the way, you could also check the STALE_STATS column value for the table in the DBA_TAB_STATISTICS view to determine whether statistics are out of date. This column shows a value of YES if there have been enough changes to the table to exceed a ten-percent threshold.

Summary

There is a wealth of information contained in plan output for every SQL statement. In this chapter, you saw how plan output can be obtained using EXPLAIN PLAN to get only estimated information, or how plan output can be obtained after executing the statement and extracting the plan information from the library cache using DBMS_XPLAN. In addition, plan information can be displayed using a SQL Monitor Report. At times, you may only be able to use EXPLAIN PLAN output, particularly if a query is very long-running and it is not easy or possible to wait to execute the query and get its actual execution data. However, to have the best information possible from which to make decisions about indexing, query syntax changes, or the need to update statistics or parameter settings, the use of actual plan execution statistics is the way to go. And, by using the active SQL Monitoring Report, you can even see the plan data while the statement is still executing, so you don't have to wait until it completes to determine where the most time and resources are being consumed.

I covered some of the ways you can use plan information to help diagnose and solve performance problems for a SQL statement. By carefully reviewing plan output, you can uncover suboptimal or missing indexes and determine whether statistics are stale and need to be updated. Using the knowledge you've gained about the various plan operations for accessing and joining data, and understanding how to read and use plan information effectively, you are equipped not only to solve problems quickly and efficiently when they arise, but also to verify the characteristics and performance footprint of any SQL statement so that you can write well-behaved SQL from the start.

CHAPTER 7

■ ■ ■

Advanced Grouping

The GROUP BY clause is a venerable member of the SQL statement family. After learning basic SELECT statements, it is one of first specialized parts of SQL that many practitioners cut their teeth on when learning to create aggregations from raw data and transforming that data into useful information.

At times in this chapter, you may think the examples seem trivial. These examples are constructed with the purpose of demonstrating the results of different facets of the GROUP BY clause, without any requirement to focus needlessly on the values in the output. Although there are many excellent examples based on financial data throughout the Oracle documentation, those examples are sometimes difficult to follow because too much attention is focused on the output values rather than how they were obtained. The goal in this chapter is to help you see the tremendous possibilities for how grouping techniques can assist you in summarizing data easily and effectively.

Basic GROUP BY Usage

If you needed to know the number of employees in each department of your company, you might use SQL such as that in Listing 7-1, because it produces one row of output for each row in the DEPT table plus a count of the employees from each department. The output includes the OPERATIONS department, which does not have any employees. This row would not appear in the output from a standard JOIN, so the LEFT OUTER JOIN statement was used to include rows from the DEPT table that do not have any matching rows in the EMP table.

Listing 7-1. Basic GROUP BY

```
SQL> select d.dname, count(empno) empcount
  2  from scott.dept d
  3  left outer join scott.emp e on d.deptno = e.deptno
  4  group by d.dname
  5  order by d.dname;

DNAME           EMPCOUNT
-------------- ----------
ACCOUNTING             3
OPERATIONS             0
RESEARCH               5
SALES                  6
```

The columns used in the GROUP BY must match the set of columns in the SELECT statement on which no aggregation functions are used. In Listing 7-1, for example, there are two columns in the SELECT list, deptno and empno. The COUNT() function is used to perform aggregation on the EMPNO column so that the total number of employees in each department can be determined. The only other column in the SELECT list, deptno, must then be included in the GROUP BY clause. Failure to include the correct columns results in an error condition, as seen in Listing 7-2.

Listing 7-2. GROUP BY Columns Requirement

```
SQL>select d.dname, d.loc, count(empno) empcount
  2    from scott.emp e
  3    join scott.dept d on d.deptno = e.deptno
  4    group by d.dname;
select d.dname, d.loc, count(empno) empcount
                *
ERROR at line 1:
ORA-00979: not a GROUP BY expression
```

There is a very important point you need to understand about GROUP BY: Although the output of a SELECT statement that includes a GROUP BY clause may always appear to be sorted, you cannot expect GROUP BY always to return your data in sorted order. If the output must be sorted, you must use an ORDER BY clause. This has always been the case with Oracle, and this behavior has been documented since at least Oracle 7.0.

Although the sorting behavior of GROUP BY is not mentioned specifically in the Oracle 7 documentation, there was little room for doubt when the 9i documentation was published, which specifically states that GROUP BY does not guarantee the order of the result set.

Listing 7-3 provides a good example of GROUP BY not returning results in sorted order. Notice that the data are not sorted. The only way to guarantee sorted data is by including the ORDER BY clause, which must follow the GROUP BY clause.

Listing 7-3. GROUP BY Not Sorted

```
SQL> select deptno, count(*)
  2  from emp
  3  group by deptno;

   DEPTNO    COUNT(*)
---------- ----------
       30          6
       20          5
       10          3
```

The GROUP BY clause may just be one of the most underappreciated workhorses of all the SELECT clauses. It is quite easy to take it for granted, because after you understand how to include it in a SELECT statement, it is quite easy to use. Perhaps a better appreciation for just how much work it does (and how much work it saves you from doing) can be gained by trying to write the SELECT statement in Listing 7-1 without using the GROUP BY clause. There are likely many different methods by which this can be done.

Think for just a moment about how you might write that SELECT statement. One such attempt was made by me, your intrepid author, and this attempt is in Listing 7-4. This is not SQL that most people would care to maintain. As you can see, it does create nearly the same output as that found in Listing 7-1. In addition to being somewhat convoluted, you must ask yourself: What happens when a new department is added to the DEPT table? Just so there's no mistake, when I say this example is convoluted, I actually should say, "Don't do this!" Although this query may provide the correct result set, it is a very poor way to get the job done; it is more of an example of how *not* to write a query.

The answer to the question "What happens when a new department is added to the DEPT table?," of course, is that you then need to modify the SQL statement in Listing 7-4 to accommodate the change in the data. Although it is possible to use dynamic SQL to duplicate the functionality of the SQL to cope with changes to the DEPT table data, doing so creates a piece of SQL that is even more difficult to follow and even harder to maintain.

Listing 7-4. Convoluted SQL

```
SQL> select /* lst7-4 */
  2  distinct dname, decode(
  3     d.deptno,
  4     10, (select count(*) from emp where deptno= 10),
  5     20, (select count(*) from emp where deptno= 20),
  6     30, (select count(*) from emp where deptno= 30),
  7     (select count(*) from emp where deptno not in (10,20,30))
  8  ) dept_count
  9  from (select distinct deptno from emp) d
 10  join dept d2 on d2.deptno = d.deptno;

DNAME           DEPT_COUNT
--------------  ----------
SALES                    6
ACCOUNTING               3
RESEARCH                 5

SQL> @pln lst7-4
```

```
-------------------------------------------------------------------------
| Id  | Operation                    | Name    | Starts | E-Rows | A-Rows |
-------------------------------------------------------------------------
|   0 | SELECT STATEMENT             |         |   1    |        |   3    |
|   1 |  SORT AGGREGATE              |         |   1    |   1    |   1    |
|*  2 |   TABLE ACCESS FULL          | EMP     |   1    |   3    |   3    |
|   3 |  SORT AGGREGATE              |         |   1    |   1    |   1    |
|*  4 |   TABLE ACCESS FULL          | EMP     |   1    |   5    |   5    |
|   5 |  SORT AGGREGATE              |         |   1    |   1    |   1    |
|*  6 |   TABLE ACCESS FULL          | EMP     |   1    |   6    |   6    |
|   7 |  SORT AGGREGATE              |         |   0    |   1    |   0    |
|*  8 |   TABLE ACCESS FULL          | EMP     |   0    |   4    |   0    |
|   9 |  HASH UNIQUE                 |         |   1    |   3    |   3    |
|  10 |   MERGE JOIN SEMI            |         |   1    |   3    |   3    |
|  11 |    TABLE ACCESS BY INDEX ROWID| DEPT   |   1    |   4    |   4    |
|  12 |     INDEX FULL SCAN          | PK_DEPT |   1    |   4    |   4    |
|* 13 |    SORT UNIQUE               |         |   4    |  14    |   3    |
|  14 |     TABLE ACCESS FULL        | EMP     |   1    |  14    |  14    |
-------------------------------------------------------------------------

Predicate Information (identified by operation id):
---------------------------------------------------

   2 - filter("DEPTNO"=10)
   4 - filter("DEPTNO"=20)
   6 - filter("DEPTNO"=30)
   8 - filter(("DEPTNO"<>30 AND "DEPTNO"<>20 AND "DEPTNO"<>10))
  13 - access("D2"."DEPTNO"="DEPTNO")
       filter("D2"."DEPTNO"="DEPTNO")
```

In addition to simplifying immensely the SQL that must be written, the GROUP BY clause eliminates unnecessary IO in the database. Take another look at Listing 7-4. Notice that a full table scan was performed on the EMP table five times. If you think this seems rather excessive, you are on the right track. Listing 7-5 shows the same SQL as executed in Listing 7-1. There is still a full table scan taking place against the EMP table, but it takes place only once—not five times, as in the convoluted SQL in Listing 7-4.

Listing 7-5. GROUP BY Execution Plan

```
SQL> select /* lst7-5 */
  2       d.dname
  3     , count(empno) empcount
  4  from scott.emp e
  5  join scott.dept d on d.deptno = e.deptno
  6  group by d.dname
  7  order by d.dname;
DNAME              EMPCOUNT
-------------- ----------
ACCOUNTING            3
RESEARCH              5
SALES                 6


SQL> @pln lst7-5
```

```
---------------------------------------------------------------------------
| Id  | Operation                      | Name    | Starts | E-Rows | A-Rows |
---------------------------------------------------------------------------
|   0 | SELECT STATEMENT               |         |      1 |        |      3 |
|   1 |  SORT GROUP BY                 |         |      1 |      4 |      3 |
|   2 |   MERGE JOIN                   |         |      1 |     14 |     14 |
|   3 |    TABLE ACCESS BY INDEX ROWID | DEPT    |      1 |      4 |      4 |
|   4 |     INDEX FULL SCAN            | PK_DEPT |      1 |      4 |      4 |
|*  5 |    SORT JOIN                   |         |      4 |     14 |     14 |
|   6 |     TABLE ACCESS FULL          | EMP     |      1 |     14 |     14 |
---------------------------------------------------------------------------

Predicate Information (identified by operation id):
---------------------------------------------------

   5 - access("D"."DEPTNO"="E"."DEPTNO")
       filter("D"."DEPTNO"="E"."DEPTNO")
```

Don't underestimate the power of the GROUP BY clause! As seen in this section, the GROUP BY clause does the following:

- Makes the SQL more readable.

- Is easier to write than using many correlated subqueries.

- Eliminates the need to access the same objects repeatedly (which leads to better performance).

HAVING Clause

Results generated by GROUP BY may be restricted by the criteria found in the HAVING clause. The HAVING clause is quite versatile, resembling the WHERE clause in the conditions that may be used. Functions, operators, and subqueries may all be used in the HAVING clause. Listing 7-6 shows a query that returns all departments that have hired at least five employees since the beginning of the first full year after hiring began.

It's important to note that the HAVING clause applies to the data after they are grouped. On the other hand, the WHERE clause acts on the rows as they are fetched, before they are grouped. That the HAVING operation is executed after all data have been fetched can be seen as FILTER in step 1 of the execution plan shown in Listing 7-6. Notice that an operator, a function, and subqueries have all been used in the HAVING clause.

Listing 7-6. *HAVING Clause*

```
SQL> select /* lst7-6 */
  2     d.dname
  3   , trunc(e.hiredate,'YYYY') hiredate
  4   , count(empno) empcount
  5  from scott.emp e
  6  join scott.dept d on d.deptno = e.deptno
  7  group by d.dname, trunc(e.hiredate,'YYYY')
  8  having
  9     count(empno) >= 5
 10     and trunc(e.hiredate,'YYYY') between
 11      (select min(hiredate) from scott.emp)
 12      and
 13      (select max(hiredate) from scott.emp)
 14  order by d.dname;

DNAME           HIREDATE               EMPCOUNT
--------------- -------------------- ----------
SALES           01/01/1981 00:00:00           6

SQL> @pln lst7-6
```

```
----------------------------------------------------------------------------
| Id  | Operation                      | Name    | Starts | E-Rows | A-Rows |
----------------------------------------------------------------------------
|   0 | SELECT STATEMENT               |         |    1   |        |    1   |
|*  1 |  FILTER                        |         |    1   |        |    1   |
|   2 |   SORT GROUP BY                |         |    1   |    1   |    6   |
|   3 |    MERGE JOIN                  |         |    1   |   14   |   14   |
|   4 |     TABLE ACCESS BY INDEX ROWID| DEPT    |    1   |    4   |    4   |
|   5 |      INDEX FULL SCAN           | PK_DEPT |    1   |    4   |    4   |
|*  6 |     SORT JOIN                  |         |    4   |   14   |   14   |
|   7 |      TABLE ACCESS FULL         | EMP     |    1   |   14   |   14   |
|   8 |   SORT AGGREGATE               |         |    1   |    1   |    1   |
|   9 |    TABLE ACCESS FULL           | EMP     |    1   |   14   |   14   |
|  10 |   SORT AGGREGATE               |         |    1   |    1   |    1   |
|  11 |    TABLE ACCESS FULL           | EMP     |    1   |   14   |   14   |
----------------------------------------------------------------------------
```

```
Predicate Information (identified by operation id):
---------------------------------------------------

   1 - filter((COUNT(*)>=5 AND TRUNC(INTERNAL_FUNCTION("E"."HIREDATE"),
       'fmyyyy')>= AND TRUNC(INTERNAL_FUNCTION("E"."HIREDATE"),'fmyyyy')<=))
   6 - access("D"."DEPTNO"="E"."DEPTNO")
       filter("D"."DEPTNO"="E"."DEPTNO")
```

"New" GROUP BY Functionality

At times, it's necessary to write SQL that appears as unruly as the convoluted example in Listing 7-4 so that the desired output can be obtained. The need for writing such unwieldy SQL has become much less frequent because of the advanced functionality Oracle has included in SQL during the past few years. Much of what is covered in this chapter is not actually new; it has been available for quite some time.

You can start exploring some of the advanced grouping functionality in Oracle Database by experimenting with the CUBE and ROLLUP extensions to GROUP BY, and the GROUPING function. It takes a little effort to get started, because the benefits of newer functionality are not always clear until you spend some time learning to use them.

CUBE Extension to GROUP BY

The CUBE extension is not exactly a newcomer to Oracle. It was first introduced in Oracle 8i in 1999. When used with a GROUP BY clause, it causes all possible combinations of the elements included in the arguments to CUBE to be considered for each row. This operation generates more rows than actually exist in the table.[1]

Let's look at an example that generates all possible combinations of FIRST_NAME and LAST_NAME for each row in the HR.EMPLOYEES table. The CUBE function was intended for use in generating cross-tab reports with lots of numbers and dollar signs. When trying to understand new functionality, I find it helps to dumb down the SQL a bit so I can see what's going on without getting distracted with subtotals.

Examine Listing 7-7 to see the results of using CUBE as described with the HR.EMPLOYEES table. Notice there are three rows returned for most employees. In other words, there are 301 rows returned, even though there are only 107 rows in the table. The first query in the listing shows the basic GROUP BY, and resulting data, for comparison.

Listing 7-7. CUBE Operation on HR.EMPLOYEES

```
SQL>select last_name
       , first_name
   3       from hr.employees
   4       group by first_name,last_name;

LAST_NAME                 FIRST_NAME
------------------------- --------------------
Abel                      Ellen
Ande                      Sundar
Atkinson                  Mozhe
Austin                    David
Baer                      Hermann
Baida                     Shelli
Banda                     Amit
```

---

[1] If there are no rows in the table, GROUP BY CUBE() returns zero rows.

Bates	Elizabeth
Bell	Sarah
Bernstein	David
Bissot	Laura
Bloom	Harrison
Bull	Alexis
Cabrio	Anthony
Cambrault	Gerald
Cambrault	Nanette
Chen	John
Chung	Kelly
Colmenares	Karen
Davies	Curtis
De Haan	Lex
Dellinger	Julia
Dilly	Jennifer
Doran	Louise
Ernst	Bruce
Errazuriz	Alberto
Everett	Britney
Faviet	Daniel
Fay	Pat
Feeney	Kevin
Fleaur	Jean
Fox	Tayler
Fripp	Adam
Gates	Timothy
Gee	Ki
Geoni	Girard
Gietz	William
Grant	Douglas
Grant	Kimberely
Greenberg	Nancy
Greene	Danielle
Hall	Peter
Hartstein	Michael
Higgins	Shelley
Himuro	Guy
Hunold	Alexander
Hutton	Alyssa
Johnson	Charles
Jones	Vance
Kaufling	Payam
Khoo	Alexander
King	Janette
King	Steven
Kochhar	Neena
Kumar	Sundita
Ladwig	Renske
Landry	James
Lee	David

Livingston	Jack
Lorentz	Diana
Mallin	Jason
Markle	Steven
Marlow	James
Marvins	Mattea
Matos	Randall
Mavris	Susan
McCain	Samuel
McEwen	Allan
Mikkilineni	Irene
Mourgos	Kevin
Nayer	Julia
OConnell	Donald
Olsen	Christopher
Olson	TJ
Ozer	Lisa
Partners	Karen
Pataballa	Valli
Patel	Joshua
Perkins	Randall
Philtanker	Hazel
Popp	Luis
Rajs	Trenna
Raphaely	Den
Rogers	Michael
Russell	John
Sarchand	Nandita
Sciarra	Ismael
Seo	John
Sewall	Sarath
Smith	Lindsey
Smith	William
Stiles	Stephen
Sullivan	Martha
Sully	Patrick
Taylor	Jonathon
Taylor	Winston
Tobias	Sigal
Tucker	Peter
Tuvault	Oliver
Urman	Jose Manuel
Vargas	Peter
Vishney	Clara
Vollman	Shanta
Walsh	Alana
Weiss	Matthew
Whalen	Jennifer
Zlotkey	Eleni

107 rows selected.

```
SQL> set autotrace on statistics

SQL> with emps as (
  2  select /* lst7-7 */
  3         last_name
  4       , first_name
  5    from hr.employees
  6    group by cube(first_name,last_name)
  7  )
  8  select rownum
  9       , last_name
 10       , first_name
 11  from emps;

    ROWNUM LAST_NAME                       FIRST_NAME
---------- ------------------------------  --------------------
         1
         2                                 Ki
         3                                 TJ
         4                                 Den
         5                                 Guy
         6                                 Lex
         7                                 Pat
...
       231 Vargas
       232 Vargas                          Peter
       233 Whalen
       234 Whalen                          Jennifer
       235 De Haan
       236 De Haan                         Lex
       237 Everett
       238 Everett                         Britney
...
301 rows selected.

Statistics
---------------------------------------------------
        759  recursive calls
          0  db block gets
        188  consistent gets
          9  physical reads
          0  redo size
       5990  bytes sent via SQL*Net to client
        557  bytes received via SQL*Net from client
          5  SQL*Net roundtrips to/from client
          7  sorts (memory)
          0  sorts (disk)
        301  rows processed
```

PLAN_TABLE_OUTPUT

```
--------------------------------------------------------------------
| Id  | Operation             | Name        | Starts | E-Rows | A-Rows |
--------------------------------------------------------------------
|   0 | SELECT STATEMENT      |             |    1 |        |    301 |
|   1 |  COUNT                |             |    1 |        |    301 |
|   2 |   VIEW                |             |    1 |    107 |    301 |
|   3 |    SORT GROUP BY      |             |    1 |    107 |    301 |
|   4 |     GENERATE CUBE     |             |    1 |    107 |    428 |
|   5 |      SORT GROUP BY NOSORT|          |    1 |    107 |    107 |
|   6 |       INDEX FULL SCAN | EMP_NAME_IX |    1 |    107 |    107 |
--------------------------------------------------------------------
```

Table 7-1 shows why there are three rows returned for each name pair. For each LAST_NAME, FIRST_NAME pair, CUBE substitutes NULL for each element in turn. The rows generated by CUBE are referred to in the Oracle documentation as *superaggregate rows*, which are recognizable by the NULL values placed in the columns being operated in. The results described in Table 7-1 appear in the output in Listing 7-7 as a result of the GROUP BY CUBE(FIRST_NAME,LAST_NAME) operation.

Table 7-1. CUBE *Operation*

First Name	Last Name
Vance	Jones
Vance	NULL
NULL	Jones

Did you notice that the first row returned in Listing 7-7 contains NULL for both LAST_NAME and FIRST_NAME? When considering all possible combinations of a pair of arguments to CUBE, as seen in Listing 7-7, there is a combination of (NULL, NULL) that is returned for each row in the GENERATE CUBE operation. These 428 rows are then processed by the SORT GROUP BY operation, which removes all but one of the NULL pair of columns to produce the final 301 rows to satisfy the query.

Knowing how CUBE operates, you can predict how many rows should be created when using GROUP BY CUBE. Listing 7-8 shows that the number of rows returned can be predicted by adding the count for three different, distinct combinations of names, and adding one to that to account for the null pair.

Listing 7-8. Predicting CUBE Return Rows

```
SQL> with counts as (
  2      select
  3              count(distinct first_name) first_name_count
  4              , count(distinct last_name) last_name_count
  5              , count(distinct(first_name||last_name)) full_name_count
  6      from hr.employees
  7  )
  8  select first_name_count
  9         ,last_name_count
 10         ,full_name_count
 11         ,first_name_count + last_name_count
 12          + full_name_count + 1 total_count
 13  from counts;
```

```
FIRST_NAME_COUNT LAST_NAME_COUNT FULL_NAME_COUNT TOTAL_COUNT
---------------- --------------- --------------- -----------
             91             102             107         301
```

You can simulate the operation of CUBE by using SQL to reproduce the steps taken by the database, both to see how the operation works and to see just how much work the database is saving you by using GROUP BY CUBE.

By examining the execution plan shown in Listing 7-7, you can see that the SORT GROUP BY NOSORT operation (step 5) returns 107 rows to the GENERATE CUBE operation (step 4), which in turn generates 428 rows. Why are 428 rows generated? Listing 7-9 shows that 428 is the expected number of rows if all combinations of LAST_NAME and FIRST_NAME are generated. The GROUP BY then reduces the output to 301 rows, just as the CUBE extension did, but with an important difference: The manual method of UNION ALL and GROUP BY used in Listing 7-9 required three full scans of the EMP_NAME_IX index and one full scan of the EMP_EMAIL_UK index. Contrast this with the single full scan of the EMP_NAME_IX index in Listing 7-7 as performed by the GROUP BY extension.

The CUBE extension didn't merely reduce the SQL required to generate the same data as the UNION ALL and GROUP BY combination, it also reduced the number of full index scans from four to one. The optimizer chose to use index EMP_EMAIL_UK rather than the EMP_NAME_IX index, resulting in ten physical reads rather than the nine seen in Listing 7-7. Using the small dataset in the Oracle demo schemas does not cause a large difference in execution time for the example queries. With large datasets, however, the effect of using four INDEX FULL SCAN operations rather than just one is quite obvious.

Listing 7-9. Generate CUBE Rows with UNION ALL

```
SQL> with emps as (
  2      select last_name, first_name from hr.employees
  3  ),
  4  mycube as (
  5    select last_name, first_name from emps
  6    union all
  7    select last_name, null first_name from emps
  8    union all
  9    select null last_name, first_name from emps
 10    union all
 11    select null last_name, null first_name from emps
 12  )
 13  select /*+ gather_plan_statistics */ *
 14  from mycube
 15  group by last_name, first_name;

LAST_NAME                 FIRST_NAME
------------------------- --------------------
Atkinson                  Mozhe
Bissot                    Laura
Grant                     Kimberely
...
301 rows selected.
```

Statistics
----
        759   recursive calls
          0   db block gets
        191   consistent gets
         10   physical reads
          0   redo size
       5477   bytes sent via SQL*Net to client
        557   bytes received via SQL*Net from client
          5   SQL*Net roundtrips to/from client
          6   sorts (memory)
          0   sorts (disk)
        301   rows processed

PLAN_TABLE_OUTPUT

| Id | Operation | Name | Starts | E-Rows | A-Rows |

0	SELECT STATEMENT		1		301
1	HASH GROUP BY		1	428	301
2	VIEW		1	428	428
3	UNION-ALL		1		428
4	INDEX FULL SCAN	EMP_NAME_IX	1	107	107
5	INDEX FULL SCAN	EMP_NAME_IX	1	107	107
6	INDEX FULL SCAN	EMP_NAME_IX	1	107	107
7	INDEX FULL SCAN	EMP_EMAIL_UK	1	107	107

Putting CUBE to Work

When teaching us a new word in fourth grade English class, Mrs. Draper would say, "Now use it in a sentence." Much like that, you now need to put the CUBE extension to practical use. It was fun to see what it is doing and just how much work it saves you, but now you need to see its practical use.

When using the GROUP BY clause to perform aggregations, you probably write several similar SQL statements—just so you can see the aggregations based on different sets of columns, much like what is included in Listing 7-9. You already know that the CUBE extension can eliminate a lot of work in the database, so now let's put it to "real-world" practice, using the test demo test data created earlier.

The SALES_HISTORY schema contains sales data for the years 1998 to 2001. You need to provide a report to satisfy the following request: *Please show me all sales data for the year 2001. I would like to see sales summarized by product category, with aggregates based on ten-year customer age ranges, income levels, as well as summaries broken out by income level regardless of age group, and by age group regardless of income levels.*

Your task probably seems daunting at first, but you know all the data are available. You need to build a query using the COSTS, CUSTOMERS, PRODUCTS, SALES, and TIMES tables. (Now would be a good time to put this book down and try your hand at building such a query.) Perhaps you create a query like the one in Listing 7-10, because it is a common type of solution for such a request. Prior to the introduction of the CUBE extension, Listing 7-10 is the style of query that would most often be used to satisfy the request.

Listing 7-10. UNION ALL Query of Sales Data

```sql
SQL> with tsales as (
  2    select /* lst7-10 */
  3         s.quantity_sold
  4       , s.amount_sold
  5       , to_char(mod(cust_year_of_birth,10) * 10 ) || '-' ||
  6         to_char((mod(cust_year_of_birth,10) * 10 ) + 10) age_range
  7       , nvl(c.cust_income_level,'A: Below 30,000') cust_income_level
  8       , p.prod_name
  9       , p.prod_desc
 10       , p.prod_category
 11       , (pf.unit_cost * s.quantity_sold)  total_cost
 12       , s.amount_sold - (pf.unit_cost * s.quantity_sold)  profit
 13    from sh.sales s
 14    join sh.customers c on c.cust_id = s.cust_id
 15    join sh.products p on p.prod_id = s.prod_id
 16    join sh.times t on t.time_id = s.time_id
 17    join sh.costs pf on
 18      pf.channel_id = s.channel_id
 19      and pf.prod_id = s.prod_id
 20      and pf.promo_id = s.promo_id
 21      and pf.time_id = s.time_id
 22    where  (t.fiscal_year = 2001)
 23  )
 24  , gb as (
 25    select -- Q1 - all categories by cust income and age range
 26      'Q1' query_tag
 27       , prod_category
 28       , cust_income_level
 29       , age_range
 30       , sum(profit) profit
 31    from tsales
 32    group by prod_category, cust_income_level, age_range
 33    union all
 34    select -- Q2 - all categories by cust age range
 35      'Q2' query_tag
 36       , prod_category
 37       , 'ALL INCOME' cust_income_level
 38       , age_range
 39       , sum(profit) profit
 40    from tsales
 41    group by prod_category, 'ALL INCOME', age_range
 42    union all
 43    select -- Q3 - all categories by cust income
 44      'Q3' query_tag
 45       , prod_category
 46       , cust_income_level
 47       , 'ALL AGE' age_range
 48       , sum(profit) profit
 49    from tsales
 50    group by prod_category, cust_income_level, 'ALL AGE'
```

```
51    union all
52    select -- Q4 - all categories
53      'Q4' query_tag
54      , prod_category
55      , 'ALL INCOME' cust_income_level
56      , 'ALL AGE' age_range
57      , sum(profit) profit
58    from tsales
59    group by prod_category, 'ALL INCOME', 'ALL AGE'
60  )
61  select *
62  from gb
63  order by prod_category, profit;
```

QUERY TAG	PRODUCT CATEGORY	INCOME LEVEL	AGE RANGE	PROFIT
...				
Q2	Hardware	K: 250,000 - 299,999	ALL AGE	$26,678.00
Q2	Hardware	L: 300,000 and above	ALL AGE	$28,974.28
Q1	Hardware	F: 110,000 - 129,999	70-80	$30,477.16
Q2	Hardware	J: 190,000 - 249,999	ALL AGE	$43,761.47
Q2	Hardware	B: 30,000 - 49,999	ALL AGE	$53,612.04
Q2	Hardware	A: Below 30,000	ALL AGE	$55,167.88
Q2	Hardware	I: 170,000 - 189,999	ALL AGE	$57,089.05
Q2	Hardware	C: 50,000 - 69,999	ALL AGE	$76,612.64
Q3	Hardware	ALL INCOME	60-70	$85,314.04
Q3	Hardware	ALL INCOME	10-20	$90,849.87
Q3	Hardware	ALL INCOME	0-10	$92,207.47
Q3	Hardware	ALL INCOME	50-60	$93,811.96
Q3	Hardware	ALL INCOME	80-90	$95,391.82
Q2	Hardware	H: 150,000 - 169,999	ALL AGE	$95,437.74
Q3	Hardware	ALL INCOME	40-50	$97,492.51
Q3	Hardware	ALL INCOME	20-30	$101,140.69
Q2	Hardware	D: 70,000 - 89,999	ALL AGE	$102,940.44
Q3	Hardware	ALL INCOME	30-40	$102,946.85
Q3	Hardware	ALL INCOME	90-100	$110,310.69
Q2	Hardware	G: 130,000 - 149,999	ALL AGE	$112,688.64
Q3	Hardware	ALL INCOME	70-80	$117,920.88
Q2	Hardware	E: 90,000 - 109,999	ALL AGE	$135,154.59
Q2	Hardware	F: 110,000 - 129,999	ALL AGE	$199,270.01
Q4	Hardware	ALL INCOME	ALL AGE	$987,386.78
...				

```
714 rows selected.
Elapsed: 00:00:14.53
```

Statistics

```
    18464  recursive calls
     4253  db block gets
    22759  consistent gets
    10521  physical reads
     4216  redo size
    25086  bytes sent via SQL*Net to client
      601  bytes received via SQL*Net from client
        9  SQL*Net roundtrips to/from client
      174  sorts (memory)
        0  sorts (disk)
      714  rows processed
```

PLAN_TABLE_OUTPUT

Id	Operation	Name	Starts	E-Rows	A-Rows
0	SELECT STATEMENT		1		714
1	TEMP TABLE TRANSFORMATION		1		714
2	LOAD AS SELECT		1		0
* 3	HASH JOIN		1	17116	258K
4	TABLE ACCESS FULL	PRODUCTS	1	72	72
* 5	HASH JOIN		1	17116	258K
* 6	HASH JOIN		1	17116	258K
* 7	TABLE ACCESS FULL	TIMES	1	304	364
8	PARTITION RANGE AND		1	82112	259K
* 9	HASH JOIN		4	82112	259K
10	TABLE ACCESS FULL	COSTS	4	82112	29766
11	TABLE ACCESS FULL	SALES	4	918K	259K
12	TABLE ACCESS FULL	CUSTOMERS	1	55500	55500
13	SORT ORDER BY		1	16	714
14	VIEW		1	16	714
15	UNION-ALL		1		714
16	HASH GROUP BY		1	3	599
17	VIEW		1	17116	258K
18	TABLE ACCESS FULL	SYS_TEMP_0FD9D6620	1	17116	258K
19	HASH GROUP BY		1	4	60
20	VIEW		1	17116	258K
21	TABLE ACCESS FULL	SYS_TEMP_0FD9D6620	1	17116	258K
22	HASH GROUP BY		1	4	50
23	VIEW		1	17116	258K
24	TABLE ACCESS FULL	SYS_TEMP_0FD9D6620	1	17116	258K
25	HASH GROUP BY		1	5	5
26	VIEW		1	17116	258K
27	TABLE ACCESS FULL	SYS_TEMP_0FD9D6620	1	17116	258K

Looking at Listing 7-10, notice four separate queries joined by the UNION ALL operator. These queries are labeled Q1 through Q4. The output from the query includes a QUERY_TAG column so that the results from each separate query can be identified clearly in the output. The customer is happy; the output is exactly the output asked for. The query can also be changed easily to report data for any year.

The operations folks that run the data center, however, are not so happy with this new report. When you take a look at the query statistics for the SQL, you can understand why they may not hold this report in high regard. Maybe it's the 10,521 physical reads that concerns them. If the query was run only once, this would not be problem, but the marketing folks are running this query multiple times daily to report on different years, trying to discover sales trends, and it is causing all sorts of havoc as IO rates and response times increase for other users of the database.

Notice there are four table scans taking place in the execution plan. The factored subquery tsales allows the optimizer to create a temporary table that can then be used by all the queries in the gb subquery, but the use of UNION ALL makes it necessary to do four full table scans on that table, resulting in a lot of database IO.

Thinking back on your earlier experiment with CUBE, you know that multiple queries, each doing a GROUP BY and joined by UNION ALL, can be replaced with one query using GROUP BY with the CUBE extension. This is because of the requirement to create summaries based on all possible combinations of the CUST_INCOME_LEVEL and AGE_RANGE columns output from the tsales subquery. The CUBE extension can accomplish the same result, but with less code and less database IO.

Although the difference in IO rate and timing in our earlier experiment was not very significant, notice now, that when used with larger datasets, the difference can be substantial. Listing 7-11 shows the query after it has been modified to use the CUBE extension to GROUP BY.

Listing 7-11. Replace UNION ALL with CUBE

```
SQL> with tsales as (
  2  select /*+ gather_plan_statistics */
  3         s.quantity_sold
  4       , s.amount_sold
  5       , to_char(mod(cust_year_of_birth,10) * 10 ) || '-' ||
  6         to_char((mod(cust_year_of_birth,10) * 10 ) + 10) age_range
  7       , nvl(c.cust_income_level,'A: Below 30,000') cust_income_level
  8       , p.prod_name
  9       , p.prod_desc
 10       , p.prod_category
 11       , (pf.unit_cost * s.quantity_sold)  total_cost
 12       , s.amount_sold - (pf.unit_cost * s.quantity_sold)  profit
 13    from sh.sales s
 14    join sh.customers c on c.cust_id = s.cust_id
 15    join sh.products p on p.prod_id = s.prod_id
 16    join sh.times t on t.time_id = s.time_id
 17    join sh.costs pf on
 18      pf.channel_id = s.channel_id
 19      and pf.prod_id = s.prod_id
 20      and pf.promo_id = s.promo_id
 21      and pf.time_id = s.time_id
 22    where  (t.fiscal_year = 2001)
 23  )
 24  select
 25    'Q' || decode(cust_income_level,
 26       null,decode(age_range,null,4,3),
 27       decode(age_range,null,2,1)
 28     ) query_tag
 29  , prod_category
 30  , cust_income_level
 31  , age_range
 32  , sum(profit) profit
```

```
33  from tsales
34  group by prod_category, cube(cust_income_level,age_range)
35  order by prod_category, profit;
```

QUERY TAG	PRODUCT CATEGORY	INCOME LEVEL	AGE RANGE	PROFIT
...				
Q2	Hardware	K: 250,000 - 299,999		$26,678.00
Q2	Hardware	L: 300,000 and above		$28,974.28
Q1	Hardware	F: 110,000 - 129,999	70-80	$30,477.16
Q2	Hardware	J: 190,000 - 249,999		$43,761.47
Q2	Hardware	B: 30,000 - 49,999		$53,612.04
Q2	Hardware	A: Below 30,000		$55,167.88
Q2	Hardware	I: 170,000 - 189,999		$57,089.05
Q2	Hardware	C: 50,000 - 69,999		$76,612.64
Q3	Hardware		60-70	$85,314.04
Q3	Hardware		10-20	$90,849.87
Q3	Hardware		0-10	$92,207.47
Q3	Hardware		50-60	$93,811.96
Q3	Hardware		80-90	$95,391.82
Q2	Hardware	H: 150,000 - 169,999		$95,437.74
Q3	Hardware		40-50	$97,492.51
Q3	Hardware		20-30	$101,140.69
Q2	Hardware	D: 70,000 - 89,999		$102,940.44
Q3	Hardware		30-40	$102,946.85
Q3	Hardware		90-100	$110,310.69
Q2	Hardware	G: 130,000 - 149,999		$112,688.64
Q3	Hardware		70-80	$117,920.88
Q2	Hardware	E: 90,000 - 109,999		$135,154.59
Q2	Hardware	F: 110,000 - 129,999		$199,270.01
Q4	Hardware			$987,386.78
...				

```
714 rows selected.
Elapsed: 00:00:08.98


Statistics
----------------------------------------------------------
      17901  recursive calls
          0  db block gets
       5935  consistent gets
       2169  physical reads
        260  redo size
      24694  bytes sent via SQL*Net to client
        601  bytes received via SQL*Net from client
          9  SQL*Net roundtrips to/from client
        174  sorts (memory)
          0  sorts (disk)
        714  rows processed
```

PLAN_TABLE_OUTPUT

Id	Operation	Name	Sts	E-Rows	A-Rows
0	SELECT STATEMENT		1		714
1	SORT ORDER BY		1	2251	714
2	SORT GROUP BY		1	2251	714
3	GENERATE CUBE		1	2251	2396
4	SORT GROUP BY		1	2251	599
* 5	HASH JOIN		1	17116	258K
6	VIEW	index$_join$_004	1	72	72
* 7	HASH JOIN		1		72
8	INDEX FAST FULL SCAN	PRODUCTS_PK	1	72	72
9	INDEX FAST FULL SCAN	PRODUCTS_PCAT_IX	1	72	72
* 10	HASH JOIN		1	17116	258K
* 11	HASH JOIN		1	17116	258K
* 12	TABLE ACCESS FULL	TIMES	1	304	364
13	PARTITION RANGE AND		1	82112	259K
* 14	HASH JOIN		4	82112	259K
15	TABLE ACCESS FULL	COSTS	4	82112	29766
16	TABLE ACCESS FULL	SALES	4	918K	259K
17	TABLE ACCESS FULL	CUSTOMERS	1	55500	55500

After running the new query, the first thing to look at are the statistics and the execution plan. Removing the entire gb subquery and using GROUP BY CUBE on the output from the tsales subquery reduced logical IO (consistent gets) from 22,759 to 5935 (by nearly a factor of four) and reduced physical IO from 10,521 physical reads to 2169 (by nearly a factor of five). Generally speaking, comparing logical IO is the relevant comparison for SQL. If your SQL is written so that it requests fewer blocks, both the logical and physical reads should be reduced. But, for the most part, when comparing performance of different SQL statements, the prime metric is logical IO (consistent gets). The reduction in physical reads alone is enough to recommend the use of CUBE; the fact that it results in much less SQL to write is a bonus.

Eliminate NULLs with the GROUPING() Function

There seems to be a problem with the output from the new query seen in Listing 7-11. Although the numbers match the earlier query that used the UNION ALL operator, some of the rows have NULL values for the CUST_INCOME_LEVEL and AGE_RANGE rows, and one row has a NULL in both of these columns. You saw this type of result earlier in Table 7-1 as an expected part of the operation of CUBE. When generating the combinations of all columns included in the arguments to CUBE, a NULL value is generated $n - 1$ times for each column, where n is the number of columns in the list. In the example query, there are two columns, so you can expect to see a NULL value for CUST_INCOME_LEVEL generated once for each distinct value of AGE_RANGE. The same rule applies to the AGE_RANGE column.

These NULL values[2] can be a problem if there are rows in the data that have NULL values for either of these columns. How do you discern between NULLs in the data and NULLs inserted by the CUBE extension? The GROUPING() function was introduced in Oracle 8i, and it can be used to identify these superaggregate rows. The expression used as an argument to the GROUPING() function must match an expression that appears in the GROUP BY clause. For example, write decode(grouping(age_range),1,'ALL AGE',age_range) age_range to detect whether age_range is null as a result of a row generated by CUBE, or whether it is null as a result of a row in the database. The value returned is 1 if the current row is a superaggregate row generated by CUBE; the value is 0 for all other cases.

---

[2]The NVL() function is used to provide a default value for sh.customers.cust_income_level so that output of examples may be easier to compare.

When used in combination with a CASE expression or the DECODE() function, the NULL values in superaggregate rows can be replaced with values that are useful in a report. In this case, DECODE() appears to be a better choice because of its simplicity and the fact that there are only two possible return values for the GROUPING() function. Listing 7-12 shows how GROUPING() was used to modify the SQL found in Listing 7-11. The relevant before-and-after parts of the SQL are shown, along with the output. Now the report is easier to read, and superaggregate NULLs are discernible from NULLs occurring in the data.

Listing 7-12. GROUPING() Function

Without GROUPING():

```
27      , cust_income_level
28      , age_range
```

With GROUPING():

```
27      -- either CASE or DECODE() works here. I prefer DECODE() for this
28      , case grouping(cust_income_level)
29          when 1 then 'ALL INCOME'
30          else cust_income_level
31        end cust_income_level
32      , decode(grouping(age_range),1,'ALL AGE',age_range) age_range
```

QUERY TAG	PRODUCT CATEGORY	INCOME LEVEL	AGE RANGE	PROFIT
...				
Q2	Hardware	K: 250,000 - 299,999	ALL AGE	$26,678.00
Q2	Hardware	L: 300,000 and above	ALL AGE	$28,974.28
Q1	Hardware	F: 110,000 - 129,999	70-80	$30,477.16
Q2	Hardware	J: 190,000 - 249,999	ALL AGE	$43,761.47
Q2	Hardware	B: 30,000 - 49,999	ALL AGE	$53,612.04
Q2	Hardware	A: Below 30,000	ALL AGE	$55,167.88
Q2	Hardware	I: 170,000 - 189,999	ALL AGE	$57,089.05
Q2	Hardware	C: 50,000 - 69,999	ALL AGE	$76,612.64
Q3	Hardware	ALL INCOME	60-70	$85,314.04
Q3	Hardware	ALL INCOME	10-20	$90,849.87
Q3	Hardware	ALL INCOME	0-10	$92,207.47
Q3	Hardware	ALL INCOME	50-60	$93,811.96
Q3	Hardware	ALL INCOME	80-90	$95,391.82
Q2	Hardware	H: 150,000 - 169,999	ALL AGE	$95,437.74
Q3	Hardware	ALL INCOME	40-50	$97,492.51
Q3	Hardware	ALL INCOME	20-30	$101,140.69
Q2	Hardware	D: 70,000 - 89,999	ALL AGE	$102,940.44
Q3	Hardware	ALL INCOME	30-40	$102,946.85
Q3	Hardware	ALL INCOME	90-100	$110,310.69
Q2	Hardware	G: 130,000 - 149,999	ALL AGE	$112,688.64
Q3	Hardware	ALL INCOME	70-80	$117,920.88
Q2	Hardware	E: 90,000 - 109,999	ALL AGE	$135,154.59
Q2	Hardware	F: 110,000 - 129,999	ALL AGE	$199,270.01
Q4	Hardware	ALL INCOME	ALL AGE	$987,386.78

Extending Reports with GROUPING()

Another use of GROUPING() is in the HAVING clause, where it can be used to control which aggregation levels appear in the output. The report seen in previous examples creates about five pages of output, which may be more than the customer cares to see. By using the GROUPING() function, these aggregations can be condensed to roll up the totals for either or all the columns used in the CUBE extension. Several variations of GROUPING() have been used to modify the previous SQL. The modifications and resulting output are shown in Listing 7-13.

Examining the data in Listing 7-13, notice that applying GROUPING() to the CUST_INCOME_LEVEL column creates aggregates from all AGE_RANGE values to be accumulated across all income levels. Doing so for the AGE_RANGE column has similar effects, with totals aggregated for all values of INCOME_LEVEL without regard for the value of AGE_RANGE. Including all the columns from the CUBE extension as arguments to the GROUPING() function causes the aggregations to be condensed to a single row, similar to what could be done with SUM(PROFIT) and a simple GROUP BY PROD_CATEGORY. Using the CUBE extension, however, allows simple changes to the HAVING clause to create several different reports.

Listing 7-13. GROUPING() in the HAVING Clause

CUST_INCOME_LEVEL

```
35  group by prod_category, cube(cust_income_level,age_range)
36    having grouping(cust_income_level)=1
```

QUERY TAG	PRODUCT CATEGORY	INCOME LEVEL	AGE RANGE	PROFIT
Q3	Hardware	ALL INCOME	60-70	$85,314.04
Q3	Hardware	ALL INCOME	10-20	$90,849.87
Q3	Hardware	ALL INCOME	0-10	$92,207.47
...				
Q4	Hardware	ALL INCOME	ALL AGE	$987,386.78

AGE_RANGE

```
35  group by prod_category, cube(cust_income_level,age_range)
36    having grouping(age_range)=1
```

QUERY TAG	PRODUCT CATEGORY	INCOME LEVEL	AGE RANGE	PROFIT
Q2	Hardware	K: 250,000 - 299,999	ALL AGE	$26,678.00
Q2	Hardware	L: 300,000 and above	ALL AGE	$28,974.28
Q2	Hardware	J: 190,000 - 249,999	ALL AGE	$43,761.47
...				
Q4	Hardware	ALL INCOME	ALL AGE	$987,386.78

CUST_INCOME_LEVEL, AGE_RANGE

```
35  group by prod_category, cube(cust_income_level,age_range)
36    having grouping(cust_income_level)=1 and grouping(age_range)=1
```

```
QUERY                                              AGE
TAG     PRODUCT CATEGORY             INCOME LEVEL  RANGE          PROFIT
------  ---------------------------  ------------  --------  -------------
Q4      Electronics                  ALL INCOME    ALL AGE     $838,994.19
Q4      Hardware                     ALL INCOME    ALL AGE     $987,386.78
Q4      Peripherals and Accessories  ALL INCOME    ALL AGE   $1,751,079.16
Q4      Photo                        ALL INCOME    ALL AGE   $1,570,866.04
Q4      Software/Other               ALL INCOME    ALL AGE     $873,603.25
```

Extending Reports with GROUPING_ID()

The GROUPING_ID() is relatively new compared with the GROUPING() function, having been introduced in Oracle 9i, and is somewhat similar to the GROUPING() function. Although GROUPING() evaluates the expression and returns a value of 0 or 1, the GROUPING_ID() function evaluates an expression, determines which, if any, of the columns in its arguments are being used to generate a superaggregate row, creates a bit vector, and returns that value as an integer.

Perhaps it is simpler to see how GROUPING_ID() works with an example. The SQL in Listing 7-14 first creates a single row consisting of two columns, BIT_1 and BIT_0, with values of 1 and 0, respectively. The subquery cubed uses GROUP BY CUBE to generate four rows from the single row of input. The GROUPING_ID() function returns to the current row the decimal value of the bit vector that represents the actions of CUBE. The first two uses of the GROUPING() function then create a 1 or 0 based on the actions of CUBE on the row, and they are used to create a bit vector in the final output. The next two GROUPING() functions then create values displayed in the final output that indicate on which column CUBE is currently working. The final output displays the decimal bit vector as well as a binary representation of the vector. As expected with two binary digits, there are four rows of output.

Listing 7-14. GROUPING_ID() Bit Vector

```
SQL> with rowgen as (
  2     select 1 bit_1, 0 bit_0
  3     from dual
  4  ),
  5  cubed as (
  6     select
  7       grouping_id(bit_1,bit_0) gid
  8       , to_char(grouping(bit_1)) bv_1
  9       , to_char(grouping(bit_0)) bv_0
 10       , decode(grouping(bit_1),1,'GRP BIT 1') gb_1
 11       , decode(grouping(bit_0),1,'GRP BIT 0') gb_0
 12     from rowgen
 13     group by cube(bit_1,bit_0)
 14  )
 15  select
 16     gid
 17     , bv_1 || bv_0 bit_vector
 18     , gb_1
 19     , gb_0
 20  from cubed
 21  order by gid;
```

GID	BIT VECTOR	GROUPING BIT 1	GROUPING BIT 0
0	00		
1	01		GRP BIT 0
2	10	GRP BIT 1	
3	11	GRP BIT 1	GRP BIT 0

So, what good is this? You already know how to use GROUPING() to control output via the HAVING clause, why learn another way? These are fair questions when you consider that the examples in Listing 7-13 can already create the output needed.

In the interest of database efficiency, a single GROUPING_ID() call can be used to replace all the different HAVING GROUPING() clauses from Listing 7-13. The GROUPING() function is limited in its ability to discriminate rows; it can return only a 0 or a 1. Because the GROUPING_ID() function returns a decimal value based on a bit vector, it can be used easily to make many different comparisons without any changes to the SQL.

Why should you care about changing comparisons without changing the SQL? If you are building an application based on the sales history examples, the user may be given four choices of output, and any one or more of them may be chosen. The user choices can be used as inputs to a single SQL statement that uses HAVING GROUPING_ID(), rather than multiple SQL statements based on different combinations of HAVING GROUPING(), so it requires less parsing of SQL by the database. It also results in fewer SQL statements to execute, less IO, and less memory usage.

Just as using CUBE eliminates multiple SQL statements joined by UNION ALL, GROUPING_ID() can eliminate multiple SQL statements in your application. The choices given to the user are as follows:

> *All data*: Display all income level and age range aggregations.

> *All age*: Aggregate all age ranges together.

> *All income*: Aggregate all income levels together.

> *Summary*: Display a summary only.

The application, a SQL*Plus script in this case, assigns to variables values corresponding to the user's choices. The SQL statement, in turn, evaluates those variables via HAVING GROUPING_ID() to output the requested rows. Listing 7-15 simulates the choices a user might make and demonstrates how to use these inputs in the SQL. In the example, the only rows to be output are those that are aggregates of all income levels regardless of age group (ALL_AGE) and the summary columns for each product category (ALL_AGE and ALL_INCOME_LEVEL). This is accomplished by setting N_AGE_RANGE and N_SUMMARY to 2 and 4, respectively. These values correspond to the bit vector generated by the GROUPING_ID() function found in the HAVING clause.

As used in the HAVING clause, one is added to the value generated by GROUPING_ID(), which enables some consistency in setting the values of the variables that control the output. Without adding one to the value, the N_ALL_DATA variable would be set to 0 to enable output, and some other value, such as –1, to disable it. Increasing this comparison value by one makes it possible to use 0 consistently as a value to disable output.

Listing 7-15. GROUPING_ID() to Control Report Output

```
SQL> variable N_ALL_DATA number
SQL> variable N_AGE_RANGE number
SQL> variable N_INCOME_LEVEL number
SQL> variable N_SUMMARY number
SQL>
SQL> begin
  2      -- set values to 0 to disable
  3      :N_ALL_DATA      := 0; -- 1 to enable
  4      :N_AGE_RANGE     := 2; -- 2 to enable
  5      :N_INCOME_LEVEL  := 0; -- 3 to enable
```

```
  6     :N_SUMMARY       := 4; -- 4 to enable
  7  end;
  8  /

SQL> with tsales as (
  2  select /* lst7-15 */
  3       s.quantity_sold
  4     , s.amount_sold
  5     , to_char(mod(cust_year_of_birth,10) * 10 ) || '-' ||
  6       to_char((mod(cust_year_of_birth,10) * 10 ) + 10) age_range
  7     , nvl(c.cust_income_level,'A: Below 30,000') cust_income_level
  8     , p.prod_name
  9     , p.prod_desc
 10     , p.prod_category
 11     , (pf.unit_cost * s.quantity_sold)  total_cost
 12     , s.amount_sold - (pf.unit_cost * s.quantity_sold)  profit
 13    from sh.sales s
 14    join sh.customers c on c.cust_id = s.cust_id
 15    join sh.products p on p.prod_id = s.prod_id
 16    join sh.times t on t.time_id = s.time_id
 17    join sh.costs pf on
 18      pf.channel_id = s.channel_id
 19      and pf.prod_id = s.prod_id
 20      and pf.promo_id = s.promo_id
 21      and pf.time_id = s.time_id
 22    where  (t.fiscal_year = 2001)
 23  )
 24  select
 25    'Q' || to_char(grouping_id(cust_income_level,age_range)+1) query_tag
 26    , prod_category , decode(grouping(cust_income_level),1,
 27    'ALL INCOME',cust_income_level) cust_income_level
 28    , decode(grouping(age_range),1,'ALL AGE',age_range) age_range
 29    , sum(profit) profit
 30  from tsales
 31  group by prod_category, cube(cust_income_level,age_range)
 32    having grouping_id(cust_income_level,age_range)+1
 33      in(:N_ALL_DATA,:N_AGE_RANGE,:N_INCOME_LEVEL,:N_SUMMARY)
 34  order by prod_category, profit;
```

QUERY TAG	PRODUCT CATEGORY	INCOME LEVEL	AGE RANGE	PROFIT
...				
Q2	Hardware	K: 250,000 - 299,999	ALL AGE	$26,678.00
Q2	Hardware	L: 300,000 and above	ALL AGE	$28,974.28
Q2	Hardware	J: 190,000 - 249,999	ALL AGE	$43,761.47
...				
Q2	Hardware	E: 90,000 - 109,999	ALL AGE	$135,154.59
Q2	Hardware	F: 110,000 - 129,999	ALL AGE	$199,270.01
Q4	Hardware	ALL INCOME	ALL AGE	$987,386.78
...				

```
65 rows selected.
```

To be fair, it is possible to achieve the same results using the GROUPING() function, but it requires several tests to be placed in the HAVING clause. The queries of sample sales history data include only two columns in the CUBE arguments. The total number of tests required in the HAVING clause is four, because the GROUPING() clause returns either a 1 or a 0, so there are two possible values for each of your columns, resulting in four tests. This doesn't seem too bad, but consider what happens when there are three columns; the number of tests goes up to nine. The number of tests required is 2^n, where n is the number of columns or expressions in arguments to CUBE.

Listing 7-16 shows the HAVING clause as it might appear using GROUPING() rather than GROUPING_ID(). This approach soon becomes unwieldy if there are many arguments required for the CUBE extension. The four separate tests shown should not be too much trouble to maintain. However, if the number of columns in the CUBE arguments increases from two to three, there are then nine tests. This is not code that lends itself well to maintenance.

Listing 7-16. Using GROUPING() instead of GROUPING_ID()

```
32 having  -- bin_to_num() requires 9i+
33  ( bin_to_num(grouping(cust_income_level), grouping(age_range))+1 = :N_ALL_DATA)
34  or ( bin_to_num(grouping(cust_income_level), grouping(age_range))+1 = :N_AGE_RANGE)
35  or ( bin_to_num(grouping(cust_income_level), grouping(age_range))+1 = :N_INCOME_LEVEL)
36  or ( bin_to_num(grouping(cust_income_level), grouping(age_range))+1 = :N_SUMMARY)
```

EXPERIMENT WITH GROUPING() AND GROUPING_ID()

As an exercise, modify the code from Listing 7-15 so that it adds another column to the arguments to CUBE. Then, modify the call to GROUPING_ID() in the HAVING clause to work with the new column. This requires a new variable as well in the PL/SQL block.

After you have that working, replace the GROUPING_ID() call with all the tests needed to accomplish the same output control with GROUPING(). Do you like the results? Is this code you would like to maintain?

GROUPING SETS () and ROLLUP()

There is yet another method that may be used to obtain the results seen in the previous two examples. The GROUPING SETS() extension to GROUP BY made its debut with Oracle 9i. The entire GROUP BY . . . HAVING clause of the previous example can be replaced with GROUP BY GROUPING SETS(). However, just because you can do something doesn't mean you should. Let's look at an example to understand just why you may not want to use GROUPING SETS(). Lines 31 through 33 in Listing 7-15 can be replaced with lines 31 through 36 in Listing 7-17.

Listing 7-17. GROUPING SETS()

```
SQL> with tsales as (
  2   select /* lst7-17 */
  3        s.quantity_sold
  4      , s.amount_sold
  5      , to_char(mod(cust_year_of_birth,10) * 10 ) || '-' ||
  6        to_char((mod(cust_year_of_birth,10) * 10 ) + 10) age_range
  7      , nvl(c.cust_income_level,'A: Below 30,000') cust_income_level
  8      , p.prod_name
  9      , p.prod_desc
 10      , p.prod_category
 11      , (pf.unit_cost * s.quantity_sold)  total_cost
```

```
12       , s.amount_sold - (pf.unit_cost * s.quantity_sold)  profit
13     from sh.sales s
14     join sh.customers c on c.cust_id = s.cust_id
15     join sh.products p on p.prod_id = s.prod_id
16     join sh.times t on t.time_id = s.time_id
17     join sh.costs pf on
18       pf.channel_id = s.channel_id
19       and pf.prod_id = s.prod_id
20       and pf.promo_id = s.promo_id
21       and pf.time_id = s.time_id
22     where  (t.fiscal_year = 2001)
23   )
24   select
25     'Q' || to_char(grouping_id(cust_income_level,age_range)+1) query_tag
26     , prod_category, decode(grouping(cust_income_level),1,
27     'ALL INCOME',cust_income_level) cust_income_level
28     , decode(grouping(age_range),1,'ALL AGE',age_range) age_range
29     , sum(profit) profit
30   from tsales
31   group by prod_category, grouping sets(
32     rollup(prod_category), -- sub total by product category
33     (cust_income_level),   -- agg by category and income levels only
34     (age_range),           -- agg by category and age only
35     (cust_income_level,age_range) -- agg by category, all age and income
36   )
37   --having group_id() < 1
38   order by prod_category, profit;
```

```
QUERY                                    AGE
TAG    PRODUCT CATEGORY   INCOME LEVEL   RANGE         PROFIT
------ ----------------- -------------------- -------- ---------------
...
Q2     Software/Other    E: 90,000 - 109,999  ALL AGE   $124,416.04
Q2     Software/Other    F: 110,000 - 129,999 ALL AGE   $169,482.11
Q4     Software/Other    ALL INCOME           ALL AGE   $873,603.25
Q4     Software/Other    ALL INCOME           ALL AGE   $873,603.25
```

756 rows selected.

The output shown in Listing 7-17 is similar to that seen when the SQL from Listing 7-15 is executed with all the output categories enabled. This is a major difference between using GROUP BY CUBE HAVING GROUPING_ID() and GROUP BY GROUPING SETS. The former may be used to modify the output easily simply by setting variables to the correct values, whereas output from the latter cannot be modified except by modifying or generating the SQL dynamically. Modifying the SQL means there is more code to maintain and more resources consumed in the database. Generating the SQL dynamically is, well, usually just not a good idea if it can be avoided; it consumes more database resources and it is much harder to troubleshoot when problems arise.

As mentioned previously, the output in Listing 7-17 is similar to that in Listing 7-15, but it is not the same. The last two lines of the output shown in Listing 7-17 are duplicates. Sometimes, the GROUPING_SETS() extension can cause duplicates to appear in the output. In this case, the duplicates are caused by the ROLLUP(PROD_CATEGORY) line. You can prove this to yourself by removing ROLLUP() from the code in Listing 7-17 and rerunning it. The duplicate lines no longer appear. However, the totals for each product category no longer appear either. The solution is to use the GROUP_ID() function to identify the duplicate rows, and insert it into a HAVING clause.

The HAVING clause can be seen commented out in Listing 7-17. If you "uncomment" it and then rerun the script, the output appears as expected, without the duplicate rows. Interestingly, if the ROLLUP(PROD_CATEGORY) line is replaced with (NULL), the HAVING clause can be removed and the output appears as expected.

The ROLLUP() extension to GROUP BY can also be used by itself to create running subtotals that otherwise require multiple queries joined by UNION ALL. Suppose that someone from the sales department asks you to create a report showing totals of all purchases by customers whose last name begins with Sul. In addition, there need to be subtotals for each year by customer, each product category by customer, and a grand total of all sales. This kind of task is handled easily by ROLLUP(). Listing 7-18 shows one way to write a query to satisfy this request.

Notice that the DECODE()and GROUPING()functions are again used to indicate subtotal rows. Also, the grand total is forced to appear at the end of the report by the use of GROUPING(M.CUST_NAME). Because the only time this value is greater than 0 is when the total for all customers is calculated, the grand total appears at the end of the report, as expected.

Listing 7-18. ROLLUP() Subtotals

```
SQL> with mysales as (
  2    select
  3      c.cust_last_name ||',' || c.cust_first_name cust_name
  4      , p.prod_category
  5      , to_char(trunc(time_id,'YYYY'),'YYYY') sale_year
  6      , p.prod_name
  7      , s.amount_sold
  8    from sh.sales s
  9    join sh.products p on p.prod_id = s.prod_id
 10    join sh.customers c on c.cust_id = s.cust_id
 11    where c.cust_last_name like 'Sul%'
 12    --where s.time_id = to_date('01/01/2001','mm/dd/yyyy')
 13  )
 14  select
 15    decode(grouping(m.cust_name),1,'GRAND TOTAL',m.cust_name) cust_name
 16    ,decode(grouping(m.sale_year),1,'TOTAL BY YEAR',m.sale_year) sale_year
 17    ,decode(grouping(m.prod_category),1,'TOTAL BY CATEGORY',
 18    m.prod_category) prod_category, sum(m.amount_sold) amount_sold
 19  from mysales m
 20  group by rollup(m.cust_name, m.prod_category, m.sale_year)
 21  order by grouping(m.cust_name), 1,2,3;
```

CUSTOMER	SALE_YEAR	PRODUCT CATEGORY	AMT SOLD
...			
Sullivan,Rue	1998	Peripherals and Accessories	$259.90
Sullivan,Rue	1998	Software/Other	$19.59
Sullivan,Rue	2000	Electronics	$2,213.30
Sullivan,Rue	2000	Hardware	$1,359.06
Sullivan,Rue	2000	Peripherals and Accessories	$1,169.94
Sullivan,Rue	2000	Photo	$331.33
Sullivan,Rue	2000	Software/Other	$933.87
Sullivan,Rue	TOTAL BY YEAR	Electronics	$2,213.30
Sullivan,Rue	TOTAL BY YEAR	Hardware	$1,359.06
Sullivan,Rue	TOTAL BY YEAR	Peripherals and Accessories	$1,429.84
Sullivan,Rue	TOTAL BY YEAR	Photo	$331.33

Sullivan,Rue	TOTAL BY YEAR Software/Other	$953.46
Sullivan,Rue	TOTAL BY YEAR TOTAL BY CATEGORY	$6,286.99
GRAND TOTAL	TOTAL BY YEAR TOTAL BY CATEGORY	$86,994.89

68 rows selected.

GROUP BY Restrictions

Our study of GROUP BY is incomplete without considering what it cannot do. The list of restrictions placed on GROUP BY is not very long. The restrictions are listed in the Oracle 12c SQL Language Reference (http://www.oracle.com/technetwork/indexes/documentation/index.html) for Oracle 12.1. For example, note the following:

- LOB columns, nested tables, or arrays may not be used as part of a GROUP BY expression.

- Scalar subquery expressions are not allowed.

- Queries cannot be "parallelized" if the GROUP BY clause references any object type columns.

SQL queries were constructed to demonstrate the first two restrictions, as shown in Listings 7-19 and 7-20. The error messages clearly show that LOB columns and scalar subqueries cannot be used as part of the GROUP BY clause.

Listing 7-19. GROUP BY Restrictions: LOB Not Allowed

```
SQL> with lobtest as (
  2      select to_clob(d.dname ) dname
  3      from scott.emp e
  4      join scott.dept d on d.deptno = e.deptno
  5  )
  6  select l.dname
  7  from lobtest l
  8* group by l.dname
group by l.dname;
               *
ERROR at line 8:
ORA-00932: inconsistent datatypes: expected - got CLOB
```

Listing 7-20. GROUP BY Restrictions: Scalar Subquery Not Allowed

```
SQL> select d.dname, count(empno) empcount
  2  from scott.emp e
  3  join scott.dept d on d.deptno = e.deptno
  4  group by (select dname from scott.dept d2 where d2.dname = d.dname)
  5  order by d.dname;
group by (select dname from scott.dept d2 where d2.dname = d.dname);
          *
ERROR at line 4:
ORA-22818: subquery expressions not allowed here
```

The final restriction listed earlier appears to be a documentation error. Evidence for this can be seen in Listing 7-21, where the GROUP BY on an OBJECT datatype is being executed in parallel, contrary to what the documentation states. The member function match in the dept_location type body is used to compare the value for city, and this in turn is used by GROUP BY to group employees by CITY. Should you need to create aggregations based on data in an OBJECT column, you can certainly do so as of Oracle 11.1.0.7. Testing has shown that the GROUP BY of Listing 7-21 is not executed in parallel in Oracle 11.1.0.6.

Listing 7-21. GROUP BY on Object Column in Parallel

```
SQL> create type dept_location_type
  2  as object
  3    (
  4        street_address      VARCHAR2(40)
  5      , postal_code         VARCHAR2(10)
  6      , city                VARCHAR2(30)
  7      , state_province      VARCHAR2(10)
  8      , country_id          CHAR(2)
  9      , order member function match (e dept_location_type) return integer
 10    );
 11  /

Type created.

SQL>
SQL> create or replace type body dept_location_type
  2  as order member function match (e dept_location_type) return integer
  3  is
  4    begin
  5      if city < e.city then
  6        return -1;
  7      elsif city > e.city then
  8        return 1;
  9      else
 10        return 0;
 11      end if;
 12    end;
 13  end;
 14  /

Type body created.

SQL>
SQL> create table deptobj
  2  as
  3  select d.deptno,d.dname
  4  from scott.dept d;
Table created.
SQL> alter table deptobj add (dept_location dept_location_type);
Table altered.
SQL> update deptobj set dept_location =
  2    dept_location_type('1234 Money St', '97401','Eugene', 'OR', 'US')
  3  where deptno=20;
1 row updated.
SQL> update deptobj set dept_location =
  2    dept_location_type('459 Durella Street', '97463','Oakridge', 'OR', 'US')
  3  where deptno=40;
1 row updated.
```

```
SQL> update deptobj set dept_location =
  2      dept_location_type('12642 Rex Rd', '97006','Beavertown', 'OR', 'US')
  3  where deptno=10;
1 row updated.
SQL> update deptobj set dept_location =
  2      dept_location_type('9298 Hamilton Rd', '97140','George', 'WA', 'US')
  3  where deptno=30;
1 row updated.

1 commit;
Commit complete.
PL/SQL procedure successfully completed.

SQL> select /*+ gather_plan_statistics parallel(e 2)*/
  2      d.dept_location, count(e.ename) ecount
  3  from scott.emp e, deptobj d
  4  where e.deptno = d.deptno
  5  group by dept_location
  6  order by dept_location;

DEPT_LOCATION(STREET_ADDRESS, POSTAL_CODE, CITY, STATE_PROVI        ECOUNT
------------------------------------------------------------       ------
DEPT_LOCATION_TYPE('1234 Money St', '97401', 'Eugene', 'OR', 'US')       5
DEPT_LOCATION_TYPE('12642 Rex Rd', '97006', 'Beavertown','OR','US')      3
DEPT_LOCATION_TYPE('9298 Hamilton Rd', '97140', 'George','WA','US')      6

3 rows selected.

PLAN_TABLE_OUTPUT
--------------------------------------------------------------------------
```

Id	Operation	Name	Starts	E-Rows	A-Rows
0	SELECT STATEMENT		1		3
1	PX COORDINATOR		1		3
2	PX SEND QC (ORDER)	:TQ10002	0	14	0
3	SORT GROUP BY		0	14	0
4	PX RECEIVE		0	14	0
5	PX SEND RANGE	:TQ10001	0	14	0
6	HASH GROUP BY		0	14	0
* 7	HASH JOIN		0	14	0
8	BUFFER SORT		0		0
9	PX RECEIVE		0	4	0
10	PX SEND BROADCAST	:TQ10000	0	4	0
11	TABLE ACCESS FULL	DEPTOBJ	1	4	4
12	PX BLOCK ITERATOR		0	14	0
* 13	TABLE ACCESS FULL	EMP	0	14	0

```
--------------------------------------------------------------------------
```

Summary

Oracle has provided some excellent tools for the SQL practitioner in the form of extensions to the GROUP BY clause. Not only do they reduce code, they improve database efficiency. They do, however, take some dedication and practice to learn how best to use them. The introduction here to the advanced grouping features is by no means comprehensive. Most of these features can be combined for many different effects—far more than is practical to include in a book. Please endeavor to make use of these features in your own applications and continue to experiment with them based on what you have learned in this chapter.

CHAPTER 8

■ ■ ■

Analytic Functions

The use of analytic functions, also known as *windowing functions*, is often overlooked even though they've been around since Oracle 8i. Perhaps because the primary documentation for these functions is found in the *Oracle Database Data Warehousing Guide (http://www.oracle.com/technetwork/indexes/documentation/index.html)*, they are often thought useful only in data warehousing SQL. In the previous chapter, we examined how advanced grouping techniques can be used to accomplish so much that you may be wondering why you need to bother with analytic functions. Well, just like really good carpenters have numerous tools in their toolbox, so should we make sure our developer toolbox is filled with many different tools to help us write good SQL. If we limit ourselves to only a couple tools, we're bound to use constructs every now and then that are less performance friendly than others.

If you follow Tom Kyte (if you don't, you should—at asktom.oracle.com—and you should read his blog at tkyte.blogspot.com), you're probably aware of his "Analytics Rock . . . Analytics Roll!" mantra. In this chapter, we take a look at how analytic functions work. I provide descriptions and examples of many commonly used analytics, and discuss the performance benefits that analytics provide. As with any construct, analytics have their good points and their not-so-good points, so you should always make sure to test carefully to make sure choosing an analytic function is the best option compared with others like advanced grouping (Chapter 7) and subfactored queries (Chapter 10).

Overview

Queries using analytic functions compute aggregates based on groups of rows. Although similar to grouping totals provided by common aggregate functions, the main difference is that analytic functions return more than one row for each group. Instead of just getting a single row per group, you can get all the detail data rows as well. One way to differentiate analytic functions from their aggregate function cousins is to refer to the term *window* when referring to a group of rows used in an analytic function.

Windows are defined by an analytic clause and each row is identified within a sliding window. These sliding windows determine the range of rows used to perform calculations for the current row. Each window can vary in size based on either a physical number of rows or a logical interval such as time. These functions do so much more than common aggregates in that they can reference values across rows, produce multilevel aggregations, and allow subsets of data to be sorted with more granular control.

Although conventional SQL statements can be used to implement online analytic processing (OLAP) queries, these statements are usually more complex and perform poorly in comparison. With analytic functions, repeated access to the same objects can be avoided, saving time and resources. Because both detail data and grouped values can be returned, analytics can be used to provide cumulative, moving, centered, and reporting totals easily.

Analytic functions are the last operations performed in a query except for the final ORDER BY clause. All other clauses are completed, including the WHERE, GROUP BY, and HAVING clauses, before the analytic functions are processed. For this reason, analytic functions can be used only in the select list or ORDER BY clause.

As mentioned, the use of analytic functions is often assumed to be pertinent only in data warehousing or large reporting applications. However, when you see the power and flexibility of what they can do, you'll likely find uses for them everywhere.

Example Data

To begin our investigation of the analytic SQL functions, let's start by creating a denormalized fact table using the script in Listing 8-1. All the tables in this chapter refer to the objects in SH schema supplied by Oracle Corporation example scripts.

Listing 8-1. Denormalized sales_fact Table

```
drop table sales_fact;

CREATE table sales_fact AS
SELECT country_name country,country_subRegion region, prod_name product,
calendar_year year, calendar_week_number week,
SUM(amount_sold) sale,
sum(amount_sold*
( case
 when mod(rownum, 10)=0 then 1.4
 when mod(rownum, 5)=0 then 0.6
 when mod(rownum, 2)=0 then 0.9
 when mod(rownum,2)=1 then 1.2
 else 1
    end )) receipts
FROM sales, times, customers, countries, products
WHERE sales.time_id = times.time_id AND
sales.prod_id = products.prod_id AND
sales.cust_id = customers.cust_id AND
customers.country_id = countries.country_id
GROUP BY
country_name,country_subRegion, prod_name, calendar_year, calendar_week_number;
```

Anatomy of Analytic Functions

Analytic functions have three basic components: partition-by-clause, order-by-clause, and the windowing-clause. The basic syntax of an analytic function is as follows:

```
function1 (argument1, argument2,..argumentN)
over ([partition-by-clause] [order-by-clause] [windowing-clause])
```

function1 is the analytic function you wish to call that accepts zero or more arguments. The partition-by-clause groups the rows by partitioning column values. All rows with the same value for the partitioning column are grouped as a data partition.

Operationally, rows are sorted by the partitioning columns and are separated into data partitions. For example, the SQL clause partition by product, country partitions the data using the product and country columns. Rows are sorted by both columns and are grouped into one partition for each combination of product and country.

The order-by-clause sorts the rows in a data partition by a column or expression. In an analytic SQL statement, the position of a row in the data partition is important and it is controlled by the order-by-clause. Rows are sorted by the sort columns within a data partition. Because the partition-by-clause sorts the rows by the partitioning columns, you actually end up with one sort that includes columns specified in the partition-by-clause and order-by-clause.

Sort order, just like with the SQL statement's ORDER BY, can be specified as ascending or descending order. Nulls can be specified to sort to the top or bottom in a data partition using the clause NULLS FIRST or NULLS LAST.

The windowing-clause specifies the subset of rows on which the analytic function operates. This window can be dynamic and is aptly termed *sliding window*. You can specify the top and bottom boundary condition of the sliding window using the window specification clause. Syntax for the window specification clause is as follows:

```
[ROWS | RANGE] BETWEEN <Start expr> AND <End expr>
```

```
Whereas
<Start expr> is [UNBOUNDED PRECEDING | CURRENT ROW | n PRECEDING | n FOLLOWING]
<End expr> is [UNBOUNDED FOLLOWING | CURRENT ROW | n PRECEDING | n FOLLOWING]
```

The keyword PRECEDING specifies the top boundary condition, and the clause FOLLOWING or CURRENT ROW specifies the bottom boundary condition for the window. A sliding window provides the ability to compute complex metrics with ease. For example, you can compute the running sum of the sale column using the clause rows between unbounded preceding and current row. In this example, the top row in the window is the first row in the current partition and the bottom row in the window is the current row.

■ **Note** The windowing-clause is not supported by all analytic functions.

Analytic functions may not be nested, but a nesting effect can be achieved by placing the encompassing SQL statement in an inline view and then by applying analytic functions outside the view. Analytic functions can be used in deeply nested inline views, too.

List of Functions

Table 8-1 contains the analytic functions for easy reference.

Table 8-1. *Analytic Functions*

Function	Description
lag	To access prior row in a partition or result set.
lead	To access later row in a partition or result set
first_value	To access first row in a partition or result set.
last_value	To access last row in a partition or result set.
nth_value	To access any arbitrary row in a partition or result set.
rank	To rank the rows in a sort order. Ranks are skipped in the case of ties.
dense_rank	To rank the rows in a sort order. Ranks are not skipped in the case of ties.
row_number	To sort the rows and add a unique number to each row. This is a nondeterministic function.
ratio_to_report	To compute the ratio of value to the report.
percent_rank	To compute the rank of value normalized to a value between 0 and 1.

(continued)

Table 8-1. (*continued*)

Function	Description
percentile_cont	To retrieve the value matching with the specified percent_rank. Reverse of percent_rank function.
percentile_dist	To retrieve the value matching with the specified percent_rank. Assumes discreet distribution model.
ntile	To group rows into units.
listagg	To convert column values from different rows into a list format.

Aggregation Functions

Aggregation functions can operate in analytic mode or conventional nonanalytic mode. Aggregation functions in nonanalytic mode reduce the result set to fewer rows. However, in analytic mode, aggregation functions do not reduce the result set but can fetch both aggregated and nonaggregated columns in the same row. Aggregation functions in analytic mode provide the ability to aggregate data at different levels without any need for a self-join.

Analytic functions are useful in writing complex report queries that aggregate data at different levels. Consider a demographic market analysis report for a product, a favorite among advertising executives, that requires sales data to be aggregated at myriad levels such as age, gender, store, district, region, and country. Aggregation functions in the analytic mode can be used effectively to implement this market analysis report with ease. Analytic functions improve the clarity and performance of the SQL statements markedly compared with its nonanalytic counterparts.

Let's review the example in Listing 8-2. The SQL statement calculates the sum of the sale column from the beginning of the year for a product, country, region, and year combination. The clause partition by product, country, region, year specifies the partition columns. Within the data partition, rows are sorted by the week column using the clause order by week.

As mentioned, in Listing 8-2, the SQL calculates the sum of sale column, so the analytic function must operate on a window of rows from the beginning of the year to the current week. This goal is achieved by the windowing clause rows between unbounded preceding and current row. The sum(sale) function calculates the sum of the sale column values over this window of rows. Because the rows are sorted by the week column, the sum function is operating over a set of rows from the beginning of the year until the current week.

Listing 8-2. Running Sum of the sale Column

```
SQL> select  year, week,sale,
2      sum (sale) over(
3            partition by product, country, region, year
4            order by week
5            rows between unbounded preceding and current row
6               ) running_sum_ytd
7      from sales_fact
8      where country in ('Australia')  and product ='Xtend Memory'
9*    order by product, country,year, week ;
```

```
YEAR WEEK      SALE  RUNNING_SUM_YTD
----- ----  -------- ----------------
...
2000   49      42.8          3450.85
2000   50     21.19          3472.04
2000   52     67.45          3539.49
2001    1     92.26            92.26
2001    2    118.38           210.64
2001    3     47.24           257.88
2001    4    256.70           514.58
...
```

Notice in the output of Listing 8-2, column running_sum_ytd is the output of the sum function in the analytic mode. The column value resets at the onset of the new year 2001 because year is also a partitioning column, so a new partition starts with each new year.

When a new year begins, the window slides to the next data partition and the sum function begins aggregating from week 1. Implementing this functionality with a conventional SQL statement requires multiple self-joins and/or costly column-level subqueries.

Aggregate Function over an Entire Partition

In some cases, analytic functions might need to be applied over all rows in a given data partition. For example, computing the maximum value of the sale column for the entire year requires a window encompassing every row in the data partition. In Listing 8-3, I use the SQL clause rows between unbounded preceding and unbounded following to specify that the MAX function applies to all rows in a data partition. The key difference between Listing 8-2 and Listing 8-3 is that the clause unbounded following specifies the window size to include all rows in a data partition.

Listing 8-3. Maximum of sale Column

```
SQL> select  year, week,sale,
2       max (sale) over(
3            partition by product, country, region ,year
4            order by week
5            rows between unbounded preceding and unbounded following
6             ) Max_sale
7      from sales_fact
8      where country in ('Australia')  and product ='Xtend Memory'
9*     order by product, country,year, week ;

YEAR WEEK      SALE     MAX_SALE
----- ----  ---------- ----------------
...
2000   44    135.24          246.74
2000   45     67.62          246.74
2000   46    246.74          246.74
...
2000   50     21.19          246.74
2000   52     67.45          246.74
2001    1     92.26          278.44
2001    2    118.38          278.44
...
```

Granular Window Specifications

Window specifications can be more granular, too. Let's say that we want to calculate the maximum of the `sale` column for a five-week window encompassing two weeks prior to the current week, the current week, and the two weeks following the current week. We do this by using the clause `rows between 2 preceding and 2 following`.

In Listing 8-4, for week 36, the maximum value for the `sale` column during the five-week window is 178.52. For week 37, the maximum value for the `sale` column during the five-week window is 118.41. You can see these values in the `MAX_WEEKS_5` column of the output.

Listing 8-4. Maximum of `sale` Column for a Five-Week Window

```
SQL> select  year, week,sale,
2       max (sale) over(
3              partition by product, country, region ,year
4              order by week
5              rows between 2 preceding and 2 following
6              ) max_weeks_5
7     from sales_fact
8     where country in ('Australia')  and product ='Xtend Memory'
9*    order by product, country,year, week ;

YEAR WEEK       SALE MAX_WEEKS_5
---- ---- ---------- -----------
...
2000   34     178.52      178.52
2000   35      78.82      178.52
2000   36     118.41      178.52
2000   37     117.96      118.41
2000   38      79.36      118.41
...
```

Default Window Specification

The default windowing clause is `rows between unbounded preceding and current row`. If you do not specify a window explicitly, you get the default window. It is a good approach to specify this clause explicitly to avoid ambiguities.

lead and lag

`lag` and `lead` functions provide interrow referencing ability. `lag` provides the ability to access a prior row in the result set. The `lead` function allows access to a later row in the result set.

In the retail industry, *same-store sales* is a metric calculated to measure an outlet's performance, usually sales data compared with the same quarter in the past year. With a normalized data model, this metric calculation could not be computed from a single row; it requires accessing another row because the `sale` column values for current and prior years are stored in different rows. Using the powerful interrow referencing ability of `lead` and `lag` functions, this metric can be calculated with ease.

Another example is percentage increase or decrease calculations requiring access to the prior or following row. This calculation can be written optimally using `lead` and `lag` functions, too.

Syntax and Ordering

As discussed earlier, data in analytic SQL is partitioned on a partitioning column. Fetching a prior row is a position-dependent operation, and the order of the rows in a data partition is important in maintaining logical consistency. Within a data partition, rows are sorted with an order-by-clause to control the position of a row in the result set. Syntax for the lag function is as follows:

```
lag (expression, offset, default ) over (partition-clause order-by-clause)
```

lead and lag do not support the windowing clause. Only the partition by and order by clauses are supported with these two functions.

Example 1: Returning a Value from a Prior Row

Let's say that you need to fetch the sales quantity for the current week and the prior week in the same row. Your requirement indicates an interrow reference, and this in turn necessitates a need for a self-join, or perhaps a column-list subquery, in a nonanalytic SQL statement. However, the lag function provides this interrow reference without requiring that access step.

Listing 8-5 uses lag(sale,1,sale) to retrieve the sale column value from one row prior in the result set. The clause order by year, week specifies the column sort order in each data partition. Because the rows are ordered by the columns year and week, the function lag(sale,1,sale) retrieves the sale column value from the prior row, which is the sale column value from the prior week (assuming no gaps in the week column). For example, refer to the row where year is equal to 1998 and week is equal to 3. For that row, the lag function is retrieving the sale column value from the prior row where year is equal to 1998 and week is equal to 2. Notice that the analytic function does not specify the partitioning column in the clause lag(sale,1,sale). It is referring implicitly to the current partition.

Listing 8-5. lag Function

```
col product format A30
col country format A10
col region format A10
col year format 9999
col week format 99
col sale format 999999.99
col receipts format 999999.99
set lines 120 pages 100

SQL> select  year, week,sale,
2    lag(sale, 1,sale) over(
3          partition by product, country, region
4          order by year, week
5     ) prior_wk_sales
6  from sales_fact
7  where country in ('Australia')  and product ='Xtend Memory'
8  order by product, country,year, week ;
```

YEAR	WEEK	SALE	PRIOR_WK_SALES
1998	1	58.15	58.15
1998	2	29.39	58.15
1998	3	29.49	29.39
...			
1998	52	86.38	58.32
1999	1	53.52	86.38
1999	3	94.60	53.52

The third argument in the lag function specifies a default value and it is optional. If the analytic function refers to a nonexistent row, then a null is returned. This is the default behavior, but you can modify it by specifying some other return value in the third argument. For example, consider the row with year equal to 1998 and week equal to 1. This is the first row in its data partition. In this row's case, the lag function accesses a nonexistent prior row. Because the third argument to lag is sale, the lag function returns the current row's sale value when the referenced row does not exist.

Understanding That Offset Is in Rows

It is possible to access any row within a data partition by specifying a different offset. In Listing 8-6, the lag function is using an offset of ten to access the tenth prior row. Output shows that at the row with year equal to 2001 and week equal to 52, the lag function is accessing the tenth prior row in the result set, which is for week equal to 40. Notice that lag (sale,10,sale) is not accessing week equal to 42 by subtracting ten from the current week column value of 52; rather, this clause is accessing the tenth prior row in the partition. In this case, the tenth prior row is the row with a week column value equal to 40.

Listing 8-6. lag Function with Offset of Ten

```
SQL> select  year, week,sale,
2    lag(sale, 10,sale) over(
3          partition by product, country, region
4          order by year, week
5    ) prior_wk_sales_10
6  from sales_fact
7  where country in ('Australia')  and product ='Xtend Memory'
8  order by product, country,year, week ;
```

YEAR	WEEK	SALE	PRIOR_WK_SALES_10
2001	38	139.00	139.28
2001	39	115.57	94.48
2001	40	45.18	116.85
2001	41	67.19	162.91
...			
2001	49	45.26	93.16
2001	50	23.14	139
2001	51	114.82	115.57
2001	52	23.14	45.18

This issue is tricky, because usually data gaps are not detected in the development environment; but, in the production environment, this problem manifests itself as a bug. If there are gaps in the data, as in this example, you have a few options: populate dummy values for the missing rows or use the MODEL clause discussed in Chapter 9.

Example 2: Returning a Value from an Upcoming Row

The lead function is similar to the lag function except that the lead function accesses later rows in the ordered result set. For example, in Listing 8-7, the clause lead(sale, 1,sale) accesses a later row in the ordered result set.

Listing 8-7. lead Function

```
SQL> select  year, week,sale,
  2      lead(sale, 1,sale) over(
  3            partition by product, country, region
  4            order by year, week
  5       ) prior_wk_sales
  6    from sales_fact
  7    where country in ('Australia')  and product ='Xtend Memory'
  8*   order by product, country,year, week ;

YEAR WEEK      SALE PRIOR_WK_SALES
---- ----  -------- --------------
2000   31     44.78         134.11
2000   33    134.11         178.52
2000   34    178.52          78.82
2000   35     78.82         118.41
...
```

The partition by clause can be used to specify different partition boundaries and the order by clause can be used to alter the sorting order within a partition. With an effective choice of partitioning and order by columns, any row in a result set can be accessed.

first_value and last_value

The first_value and last_value functions are useful in calculating the maximum and minimum values in an ordered result set. The first_value function retrieves the column value from the first row in a window of rows; the last_value function retrieves the column value from the last row in that window. Queries generating reports such as Top Store by Sales for a product and market segment are classic use cases for these analytic functions. Usually, store details and sales amounts are shown in the report together for the store, with the maximum value in the sale column. With the proper partition clause specification, the first_value function can be used to retrieve these values in an optimal manner. Essentially, any report calculating maximum and minimum values can use the first_value and last_value functions.

The power of first_value and last_value functions emanates from the support for partitioning and windowing clauses. Multilevel aggregation can be implemented using the partitioning clause concisely. For example, if the goal is to fetch the rows with maximum or minimum column values aggregated at different levels such as country, product, or region from the sales table, then implementing the multilevel aggregation is akin to deciding the columns to include in the partitioning clause.

Using the windowing clause, you can define a sliding dynamic window for these functions to operate. This window can be defined to include just a few prior and/or later rows or every row in a data partition. Specifically, queries computing metrics such as "maximum sales so far" can be implemented using these functions. Because the window can be defined to be a sliding window, these two functions can be used to answer questions such as "Which store had maximum sales in the past three weeks?" "Which product had maximum returns in the last two weeks?" And so on.

Syntax for the first_value function is as follows:

```
first_value(expression) over (partition-clause order-by-clause windowing-clause)
```

In Listing 8-8, the clause partition by product, country, region, year partitions the rows using the specified partitioning columns. The rows are sorted in a descending order on the sale column values by the clause order by sale desc.

The top and bottom boundary condition of the window is specified by the clause rows between unbounded preceding and unbounded following. In this example, we retrieve the top sales value at a level of product, country, region, and year columns, and hence the window includes all rows in a data partition.

Operationally, data are sorted by the product, country, region, year, and sale columns. Sorting order for the sale column is in descending order, though. The first row in every data partition has the highest value for the sale column because of the descending sort order specification of the sale column. So, the first_value(sale) clause fetches the maximum sale column value in the data partition.

In addition to fetching the maximum column value, you might want to fetch other columns from that top row. For example, you might want to fetch the year and week column values in which the maximum sale occurred. In a conventional SQL statement, implementing this results in a join and subquery. But, with analytic functions, it is simpler to fetch other attributes from that top row, too. Hence, the first_value(week) clause, with other parts of the analytic function kept the same as first_value(sale), fetches the week column value associated with that top row.

Example: first_value to Calculate Maximum

In the output of Listing 8-8, the top_sale_year column is an aggregated column that calculates the maximum value of the sale column. The sale column is a nonaggregated column. Both aggregated and nonaggregated column values are fetched in the same row without a self-join.

Listing 8-8. first_value Function

```
SQL> select  year, week,sale,
  2      first_value (sale) over(
  3              partition by product, country, region ,year
  4              order by sale desc
  5              rows between unbounded preceding and unbounded following
  6          ) top_sale_value,
  7      first_value (week) over(
  8              partition by product, country, region ,year
  9              order by sale desc
 10              rows between unbounded preceding and unbounded following
 11          ) top_sale_week
 12      from sales_fact
 13      where country in ('Australia')  and product ='Xtend Memory'
 14*     order by product, country,year, week;
```

YEAR	WEEK	SALE	TOP_SALE_VALUE	TOP_SALE_WEEK
2000	49	42.38	246.74	46
2000	50	21.19	246.74	46
2000	52	67.45	246.74	46
2001	1	92.26	278.44	16
2001	2	118.38	278.44	16
2001	3	47.24	278.44	16
2001	4	256.70	278.44	16

Aggregation can be performed at a different level with a different partitioning clause. For example, to compute the maximum value at the product, country, and region levels, the partitioning clause is partition by product, country, region.

Example: last_value to Calculate Minimum

Similarly, you can use the last_value function to calculate minimum or maximum values. The last_value function fetches the column values from the last row in a window of rows. For example, if you want to calculate the minimum sale column value, use the combination of the clause last_value(sale) and the clause order by sale desc sorting order. The clause order by sale desc sorts the rows by sale column values in a descending order, and the clause last_value(sale) fetches the sale column value from the last row. Listing 8-9 provides an example for last_value function usage.

Listing 8-9. last_value Function

```
SQL> select  year, week,sale,
  2      last_value (sale) over(
  3              partition by product, country, region ,year
  4              order by sale desc
  5              rows between unbounded preceding and unbounded following
  6          ) low_sale
  7      from sales_fact
  8      where country in ('Australia')  and product ='Xtend Memory'
  9*  order by product, country,year, week ;

YEAR WEEK       SALE   LOW_SALE
----- ---- ---------- ------------
...
2000   49      42.38      19.84
2000   50      21.19      19.84
2000   52      67.45      19.84
2001    1      92.26      22.37
2001    2     118.38      22.37
2001    3      47.24      22.37
...
```

Granular control of window specification can be used effectively to produce complex reports. For example, the clause rows between 10 preceding and 10 following specifies a window of 21 rows to calculate a maximum or minimum value.

Null values are handled by the clause [RESPECT NULLS|IGNORE NULLS]. The clause RESPECT NULLS is the default, and the first_value function returns the null value if the column value in the first row is null. If the clause IGNORE NULLS is specified, then the first_value function returns the first nonnull column value in a window of rows.

Other Analytic Functions

Oracle Database implements a great many other analytic functions. Some of those used more often are described in the following subsections. The functions that follow are the ones that should be on your short list of good functions to know.

nth_value

Although the first_value and last_value functions provide the ability to fetch the first or last row, respectively, in an ordered result set, it is not quite straightforward to fetch any arbitrary row with these functions. In fact, fetching the second row using either the first_value or last_value function is a complex task.

Oracle Database version 11gR2 introduced another analytic function—nth_value—which is a generalization of first_value and last_value functions. Using the nth_value function, you can fetch any row in the ordered result set, not just first or last values. The first_value function can be written as nth_value (column_name, 1).

In statistics analysis, outliers can occur in the head or tail of the result set. In some cases, it might be important to ignore first_value or last_value in an ordered result set, and to fetch the value from the next row. The second value in a result set can be fetched using the nth_value function passing 2 as the offset to the function.

The nth_value function also supports windowing clauses. As discussed earlier, a windowing clause provides the ability to implement a sliding dynamic window. This, in turn, allows you to write simple queries to answer complex questions such as "Which store had the second highest sales for a product in a span of 12 weeks?"

Syntax for the nth_value function is as follows:

```
NTH_VALUE (measure,  n )  [ FROM FIRST| FROM LAST] [RESPECT NULLS|IGNORE NULLS]
OVER (partitioning-clause order-by-clause windowing-clause)
```

The first argument to the nth_value function is the column name; the second argument is the offset in a window. For example, the clause nth_value(sale, 2) accesses the second row in a window. In Listing 8-10, the SQL statement is fetching the week column value with the second highest sale column value at product, country, region, and year levels. The second row in this result set is the row with the second highest value for the sale column because the rows are sorted by sale column in descending order. The clause partition by product, country, region, year specifies the partitioning columns.

Listing 8-10. nth_value

```
SQL> select year, week, sale,
  2      nth_value ( sale, 2) over (
  3        partition by product,country, region, year
  4        order by sale desc
  5        rows between unbounded preceding and unbounded following
  6      ) sale_2nd_top
  7  from sales_fact
  8  where country in ('Australia') and product='Xtend Memory'
  9* order by product, country , year, week ;
```

YEAR	WEEK	SALE	SALE_2ND_TOP
...			
2000	49	42.38	187.48
2000	50	21.19	187.48
2000	52	67.45	187.48
2001	1	92.26	256.7
2001	2	118.38	256.7
2001	3	47.24	256.7
...			

For the nth_value function, clauses FROM FIRST and RESPECT NULLS are the defaults. If the clause FROM FIRST is specified, then the nth_value function finds the offset row from the beginning of the window. The clause RESPECT NULLS returns null values if the column contains null values in the offset row.

With an ability to specify a windowing clause, the nth_value function is quite powerful in accessing an arbitrary row in the result set or in a partition.

rank

The rank function returns the position of a row, as a number, in an ordered set of rows. If the rows are sorted by columns, then the position of a row in a window reflects the rank of the value in that window of rows. In the case of a tie, rows with equal value have the same rank and the ranks are skipped, leaving gaps in the rank values. This means that two rows can have the same rank, and the ranks are not necessarily consecutive.

The rank function is useful to compute the top or bottom *n* rows. For example, a query to find the top ten weeks by sales quantity is a typical retail industry data warehouse query. Such a query greatly benefits from the use of rank. If you need to write any query that computes top or bottom *n* elements of a result set, use the rank function or dense_rank function.

The rank function is also useful in finding inner *n* rows. For example, if the goal is to fetch rows from 21 through 40 sorted by sales, then you can use the rank function in a subquery with a predicate between 21 and 40 to filter 20 inner rows.

Syntax for the rank function is as follows:

```
rank() over (partition-clause order-by-clause)
```

In Listing 8-11, you calculate the top ten rows by sale for product, country, region, and year column values. The clause partition by product, country, region, week specifies the partitioning columns, and the rows are sorted by sale column descending order in that data partition using the order by sale desc clause. The rank function calculates the rank of the row in that data partition. This SQL is wrapped inside an inline view, and then a predicate of sales_rank <=10 is applied to fetch the top ten weeks by sale column. Also, notice that the windowing clause is not applicable in the rank functions, and the rank function is applied over all the rows in a data partition.

Listing 8-11. Use of rank Function: Top Ten Sales Weeks

```
SQL> select * from (
  2    select  year, week,sale,
  3      rank() over(
  4              partition by product, country, region ,year
  5              order by sale desc
  6                ) sales_rank
  7    from sales_fact
  8    where country in ('Australia')  and product ='Xtend Memory'
  9    order by product, country,year, week
 10  ) where sales_rank<=10
 11* order by 1,4 ;

YEAR WEEK       SALE SALES_RANK
---- ---- ---------- ----------
...
2001   16     278.44          1
2001    4     256.70          2
2001   21     233.70          3
2001   48     182.96          4
2001   30     162.91          5
2001   14     162.91          5
2001   22     141.78          7
2001   43     139.58          8
...
```

The rank function assigns the same rank in case of ties. In the output of Listing 8-11, notice that there are two rows with a sales rank of 5, because the sale column value is 162.91 for these two rows. Also, notice that the next rank is 7, not 6. In a nutshell, the rank function skips the ranks if there are ties. Number of rank values skipped equals number of rows with tied values. If there are ties for three rows, then the next rank is 8.

dense_rank

dense_rank is a variant of the rank function. The difference between the rank and dense_rank functions is that the dense_rank function does not skip the ranks in the case of ties. As discussed earlier, the dense_rank function is useful in finding top, bottom, or inner *n* rows in a result set. In Listing 8-12, the dense_rank function is used instead of the rank function. Note that the rank for week equal to 22 is 6 in Listing 8-12 and 7 in Listing 8-11.

Listing 8-12. dense_rank Function

```
SQL> select * from (
  2    select  year, week,sale,
  3      dense_rank() over(
  4            partition by product, country, region ,year
  5            order by sale desc
  6              ) sales_rank
  7    from sales_fact
  8    where country in ('Australia')  and product ='Xtend Memory'
  9    order by product, country,year, week
 10  ) where sales_rank<=10
 11* order by 1,4 ;
```

YEAR	WEEK	SALE	SALES_RANK
2001	16	278.44	1
2001	4	256.70	2
2001	21	233.70	3
2001	48	182.96	4
2001	14	162.91	5
2001	30	162.91	5
2001	22	141.78	6

The dense_rank function is useful in queries in which the ranks need to be consecutive. For example, ranks may not be skipped in a query to compute the top ten students in a class roster. On the other hand, the rank function is useful when ranks need not be consecutive.

Sort order for nulls can be controlled by the NULLS FIRST or NULLS LAST clause in the dense_rank function. NULLS LAST is the default for ascending sort order; NULLS FIRST is the default for the descending sort order. In Listing 8-12, descending sort order is used and the default NULLS FIRST clause is in effect. Rows with null values have a rank of 1 in this case.

Another useful way to use dense_rank is with the FIRST or LAST functions. These functions operate as both aggregate and analytic functions on a set of values from a set of rows that rank as the FIRST or LAST with respect to a given sorting specification. So, when you need a value from the first of last row of an ordered group, but the needed value is not the sort key, the FIRST and LAST functions eliminate the need to join the table back to itself to determine the correct value. The syntax is as follows:

```
Aggregate syntax:
aggregate function KEEP
(dense_rank [FIRST | LAST] ORDER BY expression [DESC | ASC] NULLS [FIRST | LAST])
```

Analytic syntax:
```
aggregate function KEEP
(dense_rank [FIRST | LAST] ORDER BY expression [DESC | ASC] NULLS [FIRST | LAST])
OVER (partition-clause)
```

Note how the dense_rank function basically acts as a modifier to the specified aggregate function (MIN, MAX, SUM, AVG, COUNT, VARIANCE, or STDDEV). The KEEP keyword is for clarity and qualifies the aggregate function, indicating that only the first or last values of the aggregate function will be returned. When used in this scenario, dense_rank indicates that Oracle aggregates over only those rows with the minimum (FIRST) or the maximum (LAST) dense_rank. Listing 8-13 provides a good example of how to use this function as demonstrated in the pln.sql script used earlier in the book.

Listing 8-13. dense_rank Function Used within the FIRST|LAST KEEP function

```
SQL>get pln.sql
  1  select xplan.*
  2  from
  3  (
  4  select max(sql_id) keep
  5         (dense_rank last order by last_active_time) sql_id
  6       , max(child_number) keep
  7         (dense_rank last order by last_active_time) child_number
  8  from v$sql
  9  where upper(sql_text) like '%&1%'
 10  and upper(sql_text) not like '%FROM V$SQL WHERE UPPER(SQL_TEXT) LIKE %'
 11  ) sqlinfo,
 12  table(DBMS_XPLAN.DISPLAY_CURSOR(sqlinfo.sql_id, sqlinfo.child_number,'ALLSTATS LAST')) xplan ;
```

In this SQL, the desired result is to return SQL_ID and CHILD_NUMBER from V$SQL for the most recently executed SQL statement matching the specified SQL_TEXT input string (&1). The dense_rank function ensures the last statement executed based on LAST_ACTIVE_TIME is returned. Without this function, we have to use a LAST_VALUE function in an inline view and execute a MAX aggregate on the return set of that view by grouping by SQL_ID and CHILD_NUMBER. In other words, we have to add an extra step. This method is actually a shorter and more efficient way of getting the answer we want.

row_number

The row_number function assigns a unique number for each row in the ordered result set. If the partitioning clause is specified, then each row is assigned a number unique within a data partition, based on its position in the sort order in that partition. If the partitioning clause is not specified, then each row in the result set is assigned a unique number.

The row_number function is also useful to fetch top, bottom, or inner n queries, similar to the rank and dense_rank functions. Even though the rank, dense_rank, and row_number functions have similar functionality, there are subtle differences among them. One is that the row_number function does not allow windowing clauses.

Syntax for the row_number function is as follows:

```
row_number() over (partition-clause order-by-clause)
```

The row_number function is a nondeterministic function. The value of the row_number function is undetermined if two rows have the same value in a data partition. For example, in Listing 8-14, rows with column values of 19, 8, 12, and 4 have the same value of 46.54 in the sale column. The row_number function returns values of 31, 32, 34, and 33, respectively, for these rows in the example output. But, the result could just as easily be 34, 31, 32, 33 or 32, 34, 31, 33. In fact, you might get different results with execution of the query. On the contrary, rank and dense_rank functions are deterministic and always return consistent values if a query is reexecuted.

Listing 8-14. row_number Function

```
SQL> select  year, week,sale,
  2     row_number() over(
  3             partition by product, country, region ,year
  4             order by sale desc
  5             ) sales_rn,
  6     rank() over(
  7             partition by product, country, region ,year
  8             order by sale desc
  9             ) sales_rank
 10     from sales_fact
 11     where country in ('Australia')  and product ='Xtend Memory'
 12*    order by product, country,year,sales_rank ;

YEAR WEEK        SALE   SALES_RN SALES_RANK
----- ---- ---------- ---------- ----------
...
2000   19      46.54         31         31
2000    8      46.54         32         31
2000   12      46.54         34         31
2000    4      46.54         33         31
...
```

ratio_to_report

The analytic function ratio_to_report calculates the ratio of a value to the sum of values in the data partition. If the partitioning clause is not specified, this function calculates the ratio of a value to the sum values in the whole result set. This analytic function is very useful in calculating ratios at various levels without a need for self-joins.

ratio_to_report is useful in computing the percentage of a value compared with the total value in a report. For example, consider a sales report of a product in a retail chain. Each outlet in the retail chain contributes to the total sum of sales computed for that product, and knowing which percentage of sales is generated from an outlet is quite useful for market trend analysis. ratio_to_report allows you to compute the percentage easily. Furthermore, this ratio can be calculated at various levels such as district, region, and country. Essentially, data can be sliced and diced in various ways for market trend analysis.

In Listing 8-15, the SQL statement computes two ratios: sales_ratio_yr is computed at product, country, region, and year levels, and the ratio sales_ratio_prod is computed at product, country, and region levels. The ratio_to_report function returns a ratio and it is multiplied by 100 to compute a percentage.

Listing 8-15. ratio_to_report Function

```
SQL> select  year, week,sale,
  2  trunc(100*
  3          ratio_to_report(sale) over(partition by product, country, region ,year)
  4          ,2) sales_yr,
  5  trunc(100*
  6          ratio_to_report(sale) over(partition by product, country, region)
  7          ,2) sales_prod
  8  from sales_fact
  9  where country in ('Australia')  and product ='Xtend Memory'
 10  order by product, country,year, week ;
```

YEAR	WEEK	SALE	SALES_YR	SALES_PROD
1998	1	58.15	2.26	.43
1998	2	29.39	1.14	.21
1998	3	29.49	1.15	.22
1998	4	29.49	1.15	.22
1998	5	29.8	1.16	.22
...				
2001	48	182.96	3.96	1.36
2001	49	45.26	.98	.33
2001	50	23.14	.5	.17
2001	51	114.82	2.48	.85
2001	52	23.14	.5	.17

159 rows selected.

The ratio_to_report(sale) over(partition by product, country, region, year) clause calculates the ratio of the sale column value to the sum of sale column values in a data partition, partitioned by the columns product, country, region, and year. The next clause ratio_to_report(sale) over(partition by product, country, region) is different because the year column is not included in the partitioning columns. So, the ratio is calculated for all years.

The ratio_to_report function returns a null value if the expression or column specified in the function returns null values. However, other null values in the data partition are handled as either 0 values or empty strings, similar to aggregation functions.

percent_rank

The percent_rank function returns the rank of a value in a data partition, expressed as a fraction between 0 and 1. percent_rank is calculated as $(rank - 1)/(n - 1)$, where n is the number of elements in the data partition if the partitioning clause is specified, or the total number of rows in the result set if the partitioning clause is not specified. The percent_rank function is useful to compute the relative standing of a value in a result set as a percentile.

This rank can be calculated relative to a partition or the whole result set. For example, computing the sales percentile of a retail outlet in a district or region helps find the top-performing outlets or the worst-performing outlets.

In Listing 8-16, I calculate the top 50 sale percentile by year using the percent_rank function. The clause percent_rank() over(partition by product, country, region , year order by sale desc) calculates the percent rank of the sale column in a data partition defined by the partitioning columns product, country, region, and year. Rows are ordered by the sale column in descending order. Function output is multiplied by 100 to compute a percentage.

Listing 8-16. percent_rank Function

```
SQL> select * from (
  2  select  year, week,sale,
  3      100 * percent_rank() over(
  4              partition by product, country, region , year
  5              order by sale desc
  6              ) pr
  7     from sales_fact
  8     where country in ('Australia')  and product ='Xtend Memory'
  9  ) where pr <50
 10* order by year, sale desc ;
```

YEAR	WEEK	SALE	PR
2001	16	278.44	.00
2001	4	256.70	2.27
2001	21	233.70	4.55
2001	48	182.96	6.82
...			

percentile_cont

The percentile_cont function is useful to compute the interpolated values, such as the median household income per region or city. The percentile_cont function takes a probability value between 0 and 1 and returns an interpolated percentile value that equals the percent_rank value with respect to the sort specification. In fact, the percentile_cont function performs the inverse of the percent_rank function, and it is easier to understand the percentile_cont function in conjunction with the output of the percent_rank function.

The percentile_cont function retrieves the column value matching (or interpolated from) the percent_rank of the argument. For example, the clause percentile_cont(0.25) retrieves the value that has percent_rank 0.25, assuming matching sort order for these two functions. Another example is computing the median household income in a city or region. The median value has percent_rank 0.5 by the definition of *median value*. The clause percentile_cont(0.5) returns the median value because the percentile_cont function is calculating the value with percent_rank 0.5. In fact, median function is a specific case of the percentile_cont function and has a default value of 0.5.

Nulls are ignored by the function. This function does not support windowing clauses either.

Syntax for the percentile_cont function is as follows:

```
Percentile_cont(expr) within group (sort-clause) over (partition-clause order-by-clause)
```

The syntax for the percentile_cont function is slightly different from the analytic functions discussed so far. A new clause within group (order by sale desc) replaces the order by clause, and it is functionally the same as specifying an order by clause. In Listing 8-17, the clause percentile_cont (0.5) within group (order by sale desc) over(partition by product, country, region , year) calls the percentile_cont function and passes a probability value of 0.5. Sort order is defined by the clause within group (order by sale desc). The partition by clause over(partition by product, country, region , year) specifies the partitioning columns.

Listing 8-17 shows the output of percent_rank in a side-by-side comparison with that from percentile_cont, with a similar partition by clause and order by clause. Notice that for the column values year equal to 2001 and week equal to 5, the sale column value is 93.44 and the percent_rank of that value is 0.5. Essentially, a value of 93.44 occurs with a percent_rank of 0.5 in the descending order of the sale column values in that data partition. In a nutshell, the value of 93.44 is a median value and thus percent_rank is 0.5. Hence, the percent_rank function with an argument of 0.5 returns a value of 93.44.

Listing 8-17. The percentile_cont Function

```
SQL> select  year, week,sale,
  2      percentile_cont (0.5)  within group
  3        (order by sale desc)
  4        over( partition by product, country, region , year ) pc,
  5      percent_rank () over (
  6              partition by product, country, region , year
  7              order by sale desc ) pr
  8      from sales_fact
  9*   where country in ('Australia')  and product ='Xtend Memory' ;
```

YEAR	WEEK	SALE	PC	PR
...				
2000	28	88.96	79.09	.461538462
2000	38	79.36	79.09	.487179487
2000	35	78.82	79.09	.512820513
...				
2001	46	93.58	93.44	.477272727
2001	5	93.44	93.44	.5
2001	37	93.16	93.44	.522727273
...				
2001	52	23.14	93.44	.909090909
2001	50	23.14	93.44	.909090909
2001	6	22.44	93.44	.954545455
2001	23	22.38	93.44	.977272727
2001	18	22.37	93.44	1

```
159 rows selected.
```

In addition, note the output row for the column values with year equal to 2000. There is no sale column value with percent_rank matching 0.5 exactly in the data partition. If there is no value matching exactly, then the percentile_cont function computes an interpolated value using the nearest values. Note there is a row in that data partition with a percent_rank of 0.48 for the sale column value of 79.36, and the next row in that sort order has a percent_rank of 0.51 for the sale column value of 78.82. Because the specified percent_rank of 0.5 is between 0.48 and 0.51, the percentile_cont function interpolated these two corresponding sale column values (79.36 and 78.82) and calculated percentile_cont (0.5) as 79.09, an average of the two sale column values. Values are averaged because this function assumes continuous distribution.

Notice that output rows are not sorted in Listing 8-17. The reason for this is that, even though there is an order by clause specified in the analytic function specification (line 3 and line 7), there is no order by clause in the main body of the query. Should you need rows to be sorted, you need to specify sorting order explicitly in the main body of the query as well.

percentile_disc

The percentile_disc function is functionally similar to percentile_cont except that the percentile_cont function uses a continuous distribution model and the percentile_disc function assumes a discrete distribution model. As discussed earlier, when there is no value matching exactly with the specified percent_rank, then percentile_cont (0.5) computes an average of the two nearest values. In contrast, the percentile_disc function retrieves the value with a percent_rank just greater than the passed argument, in the case of ascending order. In the case of descending order, the percentile_cont function retrieves the value that has a percent_rank just smaller than the passed argument.

In Listing 8-18, the percentile_cont function is replaced by two calls to the percentile_disc function. The first call to the function starting in line 2 specifies descending sort order, and the next call in line 4 specifies no sort order, so it defaults to ascending sort order. In both calls to the percentile_disc function, an argument of 0.5 is passed. Because there is no row with a percent_rank of 0.5, the percentile_disc function with the descending sort order specification returns a value of 79.36 (for the rows from the year 2000, weeks 38 and 35), because this value has a percent_rank of 0.48—just below the specified argument of 0.5. For the ascending order, this function returns a value of 78.82, because this value has a percent_rank of 0.51—just above 0.5.

Listing 8-18. The percentile_disc Function

```
SQL> select  year, week,sale,
  2     percentile_disc (0.5)  within group (order by sale desc)
  3        over( partition by product, country, region , year ) pd_desc,
  4     percentile_disc (0.5)  within group (order by sale )
  5        over( partition by product, country, region , year ) pd_asc,
  6     percent_rank () over (
  7             partition by product, country, region , year
  8             order by sale desc ) pr
  9     from sales_fact
 10*   where country in ('Australia')  and product ='Xtend Memory' ;
```

YEAR	WEEK	SALE	PD_DESC	PD_ASC	PR
1998	48	172.56	58.78	58.32	0
1998	10	117.76	58.78	58.32	.028571429
1998	18	117.56	58.78	58.32	.057142857
1998	23	117.56	58.78	58.32	.057142857
1998	26	117.56	58.78	58.32	.057142857
...					
2000	28	88.96	79.36	78.82	.461538462
2000	38	79.36	79.36	78.82	.487179487
2000	35	78.82	79.36	78.82	.512820513
2000	7	70.8	79.36	78.82	.538461538
...					
2001	52	23.14	93.44	93.44	.909090909
2001	50	23.14	93.44	93.44	.909090909
2001	6	22.44	93.44	93.44	.954545455
2001	23	22.38	93.44	93.44	.977272727
2001	18	22.37	93.44	93.44	1

159 rows selected.

NTILE

The NTILE function divides an ordered set of rows in a data partition, groups them into buckets, and assigns a unique group number to each group. This function is useful in statistical analysis. For example, if you want to remove the outliers (values that are outside the norm), you can group them in the top or bottom buckets and eliminate those values from the statistical analysis. Oracle Database statistics collection packages also use NTILE functions to calculate histogram boundaries. In statistical terminology, the NTILE function creates equiwidth histograms.

The number of buckets is passed as the argument to this analytic function. For example, NTILE(100) groups the rows into 100 buckets, assigning a unique number for each bucket. This function does not support windowing clauses, however.

In Listing 8-19, the data partition is split into ten buckets using the clause NTILE (10). Rows are sorted by the sale column in descending order. The NTILE function groups rows into buckets, with each bucket containing an equal number of rows. Because the rows are sorted by the sale column values in descending order, rows with lower group numbers have higher sale column values. Outliers in the data can be removed easily with this technique.

Listing 8-19. NTILE Function

```
1  select  year, week,sale,
2    ntile (10) over(
3           partition by product, country, region , year
4           order by sale desc
5           ) group#
6    from sales_fact
7*   where country in ('Australia')  and product ='Xtend Memory' ;
```

YEAR	WEEK	SALE	GROUP#
...			
2001	16	278.44	1
2001	4	256.7	1
2001	21	233.7	1
2001	48	182.96	1
2001	14	162.91	1
2001	30	162.91	2
2001	22	141.78	2
2001	43	139.58	2
2001	25	139.28	2
2001	38	139	2
2001	42	136.98	3
2001	24	136.92	3
2001	2	118.38	3
2001	20	118.03	3
2001	29	116.85	3
2001	12	116.81	4
2001	13	116.81	4
2001	39	115.57	4
2001	33	115.52	4
2001	51	114.82	4
2001	27	94.48	5
2001	46	93.58	5
2001	5	93.44	5
2001	37	93.16	5
2001	9	92.67	5
2001	1	92.26	6
2001	31	92.21	6
2001	15	91.98	6
2001	36	91.12	6
2001	11	71.57	7
2001	7	69.96	7
2001	10	69.05	7
2001	34	68.9	7
2001	32	68.9	8
2001	41	67.19	8
2001	3	47.24	8
2001	8	46.06	8

2001	49	45.26	9
2001	40	45.18	9
2001	44	23.29	9
2001	52	23.14	9
2001	50	23.14	10
2001	6	22.44	10
2001	23	22.38	10
2001	18	22.37	10

```
159 rows selected.
```

There may be a row count difference of at most one between the buckets if the rows cannot be divided equally. In this example, rows for year equal to 2001 are divided into ten buckets, with each of the first five buckets having five rows, but the last five buckets have only 4 rows.

The NTILE function is useful in real-world applications such as dividing total work among *n* parallel processes. Let's say you have ten parallel processes. You can divide the total work into ten buckets and assign each bucket to a process.

stddev

The stddev function can be used to calculate standard deviation among a set of rows in a data partition, or in the result set if no partitioning clause is specified. This function calculates the standard deviation, defined as the square root of variance, for a data partition specified using a partitioning clause. If a partitioning clause is not specified, this function calculates stddev for all rows in the result set.

In Listing 8-20, the clause stddev (sale) calculates the standard deviation on the sale column among the rows in a data partition. The partitioning clause partition by product, country, region, year specifies the partitioning columns. The windowing clause rows between unbounded preceding and unbounded following specifies the window as all rows in that data partition. Essentially, this SQL calculates the standard deviation on the sale column among all rows in a data partition.

Listing 8-20. stddev Function

```
SQL> select  year, week,sale,
2      stddev (sale) over(
3            partition by product, country, region , year
4            order by Sale desc
5            rows between unbounded preceding and unbounded following
6            ) stddv
7    from sales_fact
8    where country in ('Australia')  and product ='Xtend Memory'
9* order by year, week ;

      YEAR       WEEK       SALE       STDDV
---------- ---------- ---------- ----------
      1998          1      58.15 33.5281435
      1998          2      29.39 33.5281435
      1998          3      29.49 33.5281435
      1998          4      29.49 33.5281435
      1998          5       29.8 33.5281435
  ...
```

2001	48	182.96	59.1063592
2001	49	45.26	59.1063592
2001	50	23.14	59.1063592
2001	51	114.82	59.1063592
2001	52	23.14	59.1063592

159 rows selected.

Standard deviation can be calculated at a coarser or a granular level by specifying an appropriate partition by clause and windowing clause.

There are various other statistics functions that can be used to calculate statistical metrics; for example, stddev_samp calculates the cumulative sample standard deviation, stddev_pop calculates the population standard deviation, and so forth. Detailed discussion about various statistics functions is out of the scope of this book, however.

listagg

Oracle Database version 11gR2 introduced another analytic function, the listagg function, which is very useful in string manipulation. This analytic function provides the ability to convert column values from multiple rows into groups in a list format based on one or more expressions in the partition-by-clause. For example, if you want to concatenate all the employee names in a department, you can use this function to concatenate all names into a list.

Syntax for this function is of the following format:

```
Listagg (string, separator ) within group (order-by-clause) Over (partition-by-clause )
```

Syntax for the listagg function uses the clause within group (order-by-clause) to specify sorting order. This clause is similar to the order by clause in other analytic functions. The first argument to this function is the string or column name to concatenate. The second argument is the separator for the values. In Listing 8-21, the partitioning clause is not specified and rows are ordered by the country column in descending order. The output shows that country names are converted to a list separated by commas.

Note that the listagg function does not support windowing clauses.

Listing 8-21. listagg Function

```
1  select listagg (country, ',')
2    within group (order by country desc)
3  from (
4    select distinct country from sales_fact
5    order by country
6* ) ;

LISTAGG(COUNTRY,',')WITHINGROUP(ORDERBYCOUNTRYDESC)
-----------------------------------------------------------------
United States of America,United Kingdom,Turkey,Spain,Singapore,
Saudi Arabia,Poland,New Zealand, Japan,Italy,Germany,France, Denmark,China,Canada,Brazil,Australia,
Argentina
```

One restriction of the listagg function is that the results of listagg are constrained to the maximum size of a VARCHAR2 datatype. Beginning in 12c, the maximum size of a VARCHAR2 datatype was increased from 4000 to 32,767 bytes. However, it appears that this increase did not affect the maximum size of the result string for listagg, as shown in Listing 8-22.

Listing 8-22. Size Restriction on `listagg` Result String

```
SQL>select length(acol) from (
  2  SELECT LISTAGG(object_name) WITHIN GROUP (ORDER BY NULL) acol
  3    FROM all_objects where rownum < 359);

LENGTH(ACOL)
------------
        3975

SQL>select length(acol) from (
  2  SELECT LISTAGG(object_name) WITHIN GROUP (ORDER BY NULL) acol
  3    FROM all_objects where rownum < 360);
  FROM all_objects where rownum < 360)
      *
ERROR at line 3:
ORA-01489: result of string concatenation is too long
```

Note that when enough rows are returned to make the length of the string exceed 4000 bytes (the pre-12c limit for a VARCHAR2), an ORA-014889 error is raised. I was fully expecting the listagg function to use the new, higher limit, but it appears to have the old 4000-byte limit hard coded. It's likely an oversight that should be corrected because this datatype size increase would make it much easier to use listagg for larger string combinations. However, if your resulting string size exceeds the limit, you need to use an alternative means of producing the final string (such as a collection or a user-defined PL/SQL function).

Performance Tuning

Analytic functions are very useful in tuning complex SQL statements. Interrow referencing, aggregation at multiple levels, and *n*th-row access are a few of the important features analytic functions provide. For example, a typical query fetching both aggregated and nonaggregated rows must perform a self-join. In a data warehouse environments, because of the sheer size of the tables involved, these self-joins can be cost prohibitive.

The efficiency that analytics bring to the table often makes them useful tools in rewriting queries that do not perform well. In turn, however, you can sometimes face the need to tune an analytic function. To this end, there are some useful things to know about analytic functions and execution plans, analytics and predicates, and strategies for indexing.

Execution Plans

Analytic function introduces a few new operations into the SQL execution plan. The presence of the keywords WINDOW SORT indicates that the SQL statement uses an analytic function. In this section, I review the mechanics of analytic function execution.

Listing 8-23 shows a typical explain plan of a SQL statement. Execution of this plan starts at step 4 and works its way outward to step 1:

1. Table sales_fact is accessed using a full table scan access path.

2. Filter predicates on the product, country, region, and year columns are applied to filter-required rows.

3. Analytic functions are applied over the filtered rows from step 3.

4. The predicate on the week column is applied after the execution of these analytic functions.

Listing 8-23. Explain Plan

```
-----------------------------------------------------------------
| Id | Operation          | Name          | Rows | Bytes | Cost (%CPU)|
-----------------------------------------------------------------
|  0 | SELECT STATEMENT   |               |   5  |  290  | 581   (3)|
|* 1 |  VIEW              | MAX_5_WEEKS_VW |   5  |  290  | 581   (3)|
|  2 |   WINDOW SORT      |               |   5  |  330  | 581   (3)|
|* 3 |    TABLE ACCESS FULL| SALES_FACT    |   5  |  330  | 580   (3)|
-----------------------------------------------------------------

Predicate Information (identified by operation id):
---------------------------------------------------

   1 - filter("WEEK"<14)
   3 - filter("PRODUCT"='Xtend Memory' AND "COUNTRY"='Australia' AND
            "REGION"='Australia' AND "YEAR"=2000)
```

■ **Note** The cost-based optimizer does not assign or calculate a cost for analytic functions (as of 11gR2, and it is still true in 12c). The cost of the SQL statement is calculated without considering the cost of analytic functions.

Predicates

Predicates must be applied to the tables as early as possible to reduce the result set for better performance. Rows must be filtered earlier so that analytic functions are applied to relatively fewer rows. Predicate safety is an important consideration when executing analytic functions because not all predicates can be applied beforehand.

In Listing 8-24, a view called max_5_weeks_vw is defined and a SQL statement accesses the view with the predicates on the county, product, region, year, and week columns. The execution plan shows that the following filter predicates are applied in step 3:

```
filter(("PRODUCT"='Xtend Memory' AND "COUNTRY"='Australia' AND "REGION"='Australia' AND "YEAR"=2000))
```

Listing 8-24. Predicates

```
create or replace view max_5_weeks_vw as
   select  country , product, region, year, week,sale,
   max (sale) over(
          partition by product, country, region ,year
          order by year, week
          rows between 2 preceding and 2 following
          ) max_weeks_5
  from sales_fact ;
```

```
SQL> select year, week, sale, max_weeks_5 from  max_5_weeks_vw
2    where country in ('Australia')  and product ='Xtend Memory' and
3    region='Australia' and year= 2000 and week <14
4*   order by year, week ;
```

```
----------------------------------------------------------
| Id | Operation            | Name           | E-Rows |
----------------------------------------------------------
|  0 | SELECT STATEMENT     |                |        |
|* 1 |  VIEW                | MAX_5_WEEKS_VW |      5 |
|  2 |   WINDOW SORT        |                |      5 |
|* 3 |    TABLE ACCESS FULL | SALES_FACT     |      5 |
----------------------------------------------------------
```

```
Predicate Information (identified by operation id):
---------------------------------------------------
   1 - filter("WEEK"<14)
   3 - filter(("PRODUCT"='Xtend Memory' AND "COUNTRY"='Australia' AND
              "REGION"='Australia' AND "YEAR"=2000))
```

However, the predicate "WEEK"<14 is not applied in step 3, and is only applied in step 1, indicating that the predicate is applied after executing the analytic functions in step 2's WINDOW SORT step. All supplied predicates except that on the week column were pushed into the view. Filtering of these predicates then took place before executing the analytic functions.

Predicates on partitioning columns are applied before executing analytic functions because, generally speaking, predicates on the partitioning column can be pushed safely into the view. But, columns in the order-by-clause of the analytic function syntax can't be pushed safely because the interrow references need access to other rows in the same partitions, even if those rows are not returned in the final result set.

Indexes

A good strategy for index selection is to match the predicates applied on the table access step. As discussed earlier, predicates on partitioning columns are pushed into the view, and these predicate are applied before executing the analytic functions. So, it's probably a better approach to index the partitioning columns if the SQL statements are using those predicates.

In Listing 8-25, a new index is added on the columns country and product. Step 4 in the execution plan shows that index-based access is used. The Predicate Information section shows that predicates on all four partitioning columns are applied at step 4 and step 3 before executing the analytic function. However, the predicate on the week column was applied much later in the execution plan, at step 1. So, in this case, adding the week column to the index is not useful because the predicates are not applied until after the analytic function execution completes.

Listing 8-25. Predicates and Indexes

```
create index sales_fact_i1 on  sales_fact( country, product);

SQL> select year, week, sale, max_weeks_5 from  max_5_weeks_vw
2    where country in ('Australia')  and product ='Xtend Memory' and
3    region='Australia' and year= 2000 and week <14
4*   order by year, week ;
```

```
-----------------------------------------------------------------
| Id  | Operation                      | Name          | E-Rows |
-----------------------------------------------------------------
|   0 | SELECT STATEMENT               |               |        |
|*  1 |  VIEW                          | MAX_5_WEEKS_VW |    5  |
|   2 |   WINDOW SORT                  |               |     5  |
|*  3 |    TABLE ACCESS BY INDEX ROWID | SALES_FACT    |     5  |
|*  4 |     INDEX RANGE SCAN           | SALES_FACT_I1 |   147  |
-----------------------------------------------------------------

Predicate Information (identified by operation id):
---------------------------------------------------

   1 - filter("WEEK"<14)
   3 - filter(("REGION"='Australia' AND "YEAR"=2000))
   4 - access("COUNTRY"='Australia' AND "PRODUCT"='Xtend Memory') fs
```

Advanced Topics

A few advanced topics about the analytic functions raise points that are worthy of discussion. In this section I briefly discuss dynamic analytic statements, nesting of analytic functions, parallelism, and PGA size.

Dynamic SQL

A common question about the analytic SQL statement is "Can a bind variable can be used in place of partitioning or sorting columns?" The answer is no. If you want the flexibility to modify the partitioning or sorting columns dynamically, you need to use dynamic SQL statements. Static analytic SQL statements cannot change the partitioning or sorting columns.

If your goal is to modify the partitioning columns dynamically, then consider creating a packaged procedure to capture the logic in the procedure. In Listing 8-26, the procedure analytic_dynamic_prc accepts a string to be used as partitioning columns. A SQL statement is constructed using the arguments passed and is executed dynamically using execute immediate syntax. The result of the analytic statement is fetched into an array and is printed using a call to the dbms_output package.

Listing 8-26. Dynamic SQL Statement

```
create or replace procedure
  analytic_dynamic_prc ( part_col_string varchar2, v_country varchar2, v_product varchar2)
is
  type numtab is table of number(18,2) index by binary_integer;
  l_year numtab;
  l_week numtab;
  l_sale numtab;
  l_rank numtab;
  l_sql_string  varchar2(512) ;
begin
 l_sql_string :=
 'select * from (
   select  year, week,sale,
```

```
      rank() over(
            partition by ' ||part_col_string ||'
            order by sale desc
             ) sales_rank
    from sales_fact
    where country in (' ||chr(39) || v_country || chr(39) || ' )  and
            product =' || chr(39) || v_product || chr(39) ||
          ' order by product, country, year, week
    ) where sales_rank<=10
    order by 1,4';
 execute immediate l_sql_string bulk collect into  l_year, l_week, l_sale, l_rank;
 for  i  in 1 .. l_year.count
  loop
        dbms_output.put_line ( l_year(i) ||' |' || l_week (i) ||
                             '|'|| l_sale(i) || '|' || l_rank(i) );
  end loop;
 end;
/

exec analytic_dynamic_prc ( 'product, country, region','Australia','Xtend Memory');
...
1998 |48|172.56|9
2000 |46|246.74|3
2000 |21|187.48|5
2000 |43|179.12|7
2000 |34|178.52|8
2001 |16|278.44|1
2001 |4|256.7|2

exec analytic_dynamic_prc ( 'product, country,region, year','Australia','Xtend Memory');

1998 |48|172.56|1
1998 |10|117.76|2
1998 |18|117.56|3
1998 |23|117.56|3
1998 |26|117.56|3
1998 |38|115.84|6
1998 |42|115.84|6
...
```

In the first call, analytic_dynamic_prc passes the string product, country, region as the first argument and the columns in this list are used as the partitioning columns. The second call to the procedure uses the string product, country, region, year to use a different list of columns for the partitioning clause.

Note that this procedure is given as an example and as such may not be construed as production-ready code.

Nesting Analytic Functions

Analytic functions cannot be nested, but a nesting effect can be achieved with the use of subqueries. For example, the clause lag(first_value(column,1),1) is syntactically incorrect. Subqueries can be used to create a nesting effect, as explored next.

Suppose your goal is to fetch the maximum sale column value for the year and the prior year in the same row. If so, then the analytic functions lag and first_value can be used in the subqueries to write a SQL statement. In Listing 8-27, an inner subquery fetches the year and week sale column value in which the maximum sale occurred, in addition to fetching the maximum sale column value for that year. The lag function in the outer query retrieves the prior year maximum sale column value.

Listing 8-27. Nesting Analytic Functions

```
select  year, week, top_sale_year,
   lag( top_sale_year) over ( order by year desc) prev_top_sale_yer
from (
 select distinct
    first_value ( year) over (
          partition by product, country, region ,year
          order by sale desc
          rows between unbounded preceding and unbounded following
     ) year,
    first_value ( week) over (
          partition by product, country, region ,year
          order by sale desc
          rows between unbounded preceding and unbounded following
     ) week,
    first_value (sale) over(
          partition by product, country, region ,year
          order by sale desc
          rows between unbounded preceding and unbounded following
     ) top_sale_year
  from sales_fact
  where country in ('Australia')  and product ='Xtend Memory'
)
   order by year, week ;
```

```
    YEAR     WEEK TOP_SALE_YEAR PREV_TOP_SALE_YER
---------- ---------- ------------- -----------------
    1998      48       172.56          148.12
    1999      17       148.12          246.74
    2000      46       246.74          278.44
    2001      16       278.44
```

Notice that the partitioning clause is different between the lag and first_value functions. The analytic function first_value computes the top sale row in a partition specified by the partitioning columns product, country, region, year whereas lag fetches the first row from the prior year specifying only the sorting clause: order by year desc. With multilevel nesting of analytic functions, complex goals can be implemented concisely using the analytic functions.

Parallelism

By specifying a parallel hint in the SQL statement or by setting parallelism at the object level, analytic functions can be "parallelized." If you have huge amount of data that needs to be processed using analytic functions, parallelism is a good choice. A SQL statement using multilevel nesting also can benefit from parallelism.

Listing 8-28 shows the execution plan for the query in Listing 8-27 using parallelism. In the execution plan, there are two WINDOW operations because the SQL statement has nested the lag and first_value analytic functions.

Listing 8-28. Parallelism

```
---------------------------------------------------
 Id  | Operation                  | Name
---------------------------------------------------
   0 | SELECT STATEMENT           |
   1 |  SORT ORDER BY             |
   2 |   WINDOW BUFFER            |
   3 |    PX COORDINATOR          |
   4 |     PX SEND QC (ORDER)     | :TQ10003
   5 |      SORT ORDER BY         |
   6 |       PX RECEIVE           |
   7 |        PX SEND RANGE       | :TQ10002
   8 |         VIEW               |
   9 |          HASH UNIQUE       |
  10 |           PX RECEIVE       |
  11 |            PX SEND HASH    | :TQ10001
  12 |             WINDOW SORT    |
  13 |              PX RECEIVE    |
  14 |               PX SEND HASH | :TQ10000
  15 |                PX BLOCK ITERATOR |
 * 16 |                 TABLE ACCESS FULL| SALES_FACT
```

Optimal distribution of rows between the parallel query (PQ) slaves is critical to maintain functional correctness, and it is handled automatically by Oracle Database.

PGA Size

Most operations associated with the analytic functions are performed in the PGA of the process. Recall that the PGA is a private memory area that contains the data and control information for a server process. Oracle reads and writes information in the PGA on behalf of the server process. So, for optimal performance, it is important to have a big enough memory area so that programs can execute analytic functions without spilling to the disk. This is very analogous to a sort operation. If the sort operation spills to the disk as a result of a lower value of the memory size, then the performance of the sort operation is not optimal. Similarly, the execution performance of analytic functions suffer if the operation spills to the disk.

Database initialization parameter PGA_AGGREGATE_TARGET (PGAT) is a target for the cumulative maximum size of the PGA. By default, a serial process can allocate a PGA up to the maximum size of 5 percent of the PGAT value. For parallel processes, the limit is up to 30 percent of PGAT. The PGA_AGGREGATE_LIMIT (PGAL) parameter enables you to set a hard limit on PGA memory usage. If the PGAL value is exceeded, Oracle aborts or terminates the sessions or processes that are consuming the most PGA memory. The default for this parameter is set to the greater of 2GB, 200 percent of PGAT, or 3MB multiplied by the value of the PROCESSES parameter. Regardless, it never exceeds 120 percent of the physical memory size less the total SGA size.

Excessive PGA usage can lead to high rates of swapping (to TEMP), causing the system to become unresponsive and unstable. It is essential to keep PGAT to a high enough value to improve the performance of analytic functions.

Organizational Behavior

The hardest thing about analytic functions is the organizational resistance to change. Developers and DBAs are comfortable writing SQL statements using conventional syntax. Using analytic syntax does not come easy. However, these developers and DBAs need to embrace the change. Another plus: Use of analytic functions forces one to think in terms of sets.

Oracle releases new features in every major release of Oracle Database. We need to harness the new features to write more efficient and concise SQL statements. Proper training for these new features is also essential and, hopefully, this chapter provided an insight into analytic functions. When you start writing SQL statements using analytic functions, start with a simpler SQL statement, then add more complexity to meet the goal.

Summary

Complex SQL statements can be written concisely using analytic functions. Understanding analytic functions provides with you a whole new way of thinking, analytically speaking. The ability to reference another row, combined with the partitioning and windowing clauses, allows you to simplify complex SQL statements. Many performance issues can be resolved by rewriting SQL statements using analytic functions. You may find resistance from developers and DBAs alike when it comes to using analytic functions, but the resistance can be overcome easily by demonstrating the performance improvements that using them provides.

■ ■ ■

The MODEL Clause

The MODEL clause introduced in Oracle Database version 10g provides an elegant method to replace the spreadsheet. With the MODEL clause, it is possible to use powerful features such as aggregation, parallelism, and multidimensional, multivariate analysis in SQL statements. If you enjoy working with Excel spreadsheets to calculate formulas, you will enjoy working with the MODEL clause, too.

With the MODEL clause, you build matrixes (or a model) of data with a variable number of dimensions. The model uses a subset of the available columns from the tables in your FROM clause and has to contain at least one dimension, at least one measure, and, optionally, one or more partitions. You can think of a model as a spreadsheet file containing separate worksheets for each calculated value (measures). A worksheet has an x- and a y-axis (two dimensions), and you can imagine having your worksheets split up in several identical areas, each for a different attribute (partition).

When your model is defined, you create rules that modify your measure values. These rules are the keys of the MODEL clause. With just a few rules, you can perform complex calculations on your data and even create new rows as well. The measure columns are now arrays that are indexed by the dimension columns, in which the rules are applied to all partitions of this array. After all rules are applied, the model is converted back to traditional rows.

In situations when the amount of data to be processed is small, the interrow referencing and calculating power of the spreadsheet is sufficient to accomplish the task at hand. However, scalability of such a spreadsheet as a data warehouse application is limited and cumbersome. For example, spreadsheets are generally limited to two or three dimensions, and creating spreadsheets with more dimensions is a manually intensive task. Also, as the amount of data increases, the execution of formulas slows down in a spreadsheet. Furthermore, there is an upper limit on the number of rows in a spreadsheet workbook.

Because the MODEL clause is an extension to the SQL language application, it is highly scalable, akin to Oracle Database's scalability. Multidimensional, multivariate calculations over millions of rows, if not billions of rows, can be implemented easily with the Model clause, unlike with spreadsheets. Also, many database features such as object partitioning and parallel execution can be used effectively with the MODEL clause, thereby improving scalability even further.

Aggregation of the data is performed inside the RDBMS engine, avoiding costly round-trip calls, as in the case of the third-party data warehouse tools. Scalability is enhanced further by out-of-the-box parallel processing capabilities and query rewrite facilities.

The key difference between a conventional SQL statement and the MODEL clause is that the MODEL clause supports interrow references, multicell references, and cell aggregation. It is easier to understand the MODEL clause with examples, so I introduce the MODEL clause with examples, then conclude my discussion by reviewing some of the advanced features in the MODEL clause.

Spreadsheets

Let's consider the spreadsheet in Listing 9-1. In this spreadsheet, the inventory for a region and week is calculated using a formula: Current inventory is the sum of last week's inventory and the quantity received in this week less the quantity sold in this week. This formula is shown in the example using Excel spreadsheet notation. For example, the formula for week 2's inventory is =B5+C4-C3, where B5 is the prior week's inventory, C4 is the current week's receipt_qty, and C3 is the current week's sales_qty. Essentially, this formula uses an interrow reference to calculate the inventory.

Listing 9-1. Spreadsheet Formula to Calculate Inventory

Product = Xtend Memory, Country ='Australia'

	A	B	C	D	E	F	G ...
Year=2001	Week➤						
	1	2	3	4	5	6
Sale	92.26	118.38	47.24	256.70	93.44	43.17
Receipts	96.89	149.17	49.60	259.10	98.66	20.20
Inventory	4.63	35.42	37.78	40.18	45.41	22.44
		=B5+C4-C3					

Although it's easy to calculate this formula for a few dimensions using a spreadsheet, it's much more difficult to perform these calculations with more dimensions. Performance suffers as the amount of data increases in the spreadsheet. These issues can be remedied by using the Model clause that Oracle Database provides. Not only does the MODEL clause provide for efficient formula calculations, but the writing of multidimensional, multivariate analysis also becomes much more practical.

Interrow Referencing Via the MODEL Clause

In a conventional SQL statement, emulating the spreadsheet described in Listing 9-1 is achieved by a multitude of self-joins. With the advent of the MODEL clause, you can implement the spreadsheet without self-joins because the MODEL clause provides interrow referencing ability.

Example Data

To begin our investigation of the MODEL clause, let's create a denormalized fact table using the script in Listing 9-2. All the tables referred to in this chapter refer to the objects in SH schema supplied by the Oracle Corporation example scripts.

Listing 9-2. Denormalized sales_fact Table

```
drop table sales_fact;
CREATE table sales_fact AS
SELECT country_name country,country_subRegion region, prod_name product,
calendar_year year, calendar_week_number week,
SUM(amount_sold) sale,
sum(amount_sold*
  ( case
        when mod(rownum, 10)=0 then 1.4
        when mod(rownum, 5)=0 then 0.6
        when mod(rownum, 2)=0 then 0.9
        when mod(rownum,2)=1 then 1.2
        else 1
  end )) receipts
FROM sales, times, customers, countries, products
WHERE sales.time_id = times.time_id AND
```

```
sales.prod_id = products.prod_id AND
sales.cust_id = customers.cust_id AND
customers.country_id = countries.country_id
GROUP BY
country_name,country_subRegion, prod_name, calendar_year, calendar_week_number;
```

Anatomy of a MODEL Clause

To understand how the MODEL clause works, let's review a SQL statement intended to produce a spreadsheetlike listing that computes an inventory value for each week of each year in our sales_fact table. Listing 9-3 shows a SQL statement using the MODEL clause to emulate the functionality of the spreadsheet discussed earlier. Let's explore this SQL statement in detail. We'll look at the columns declared in the MODEL clause and then we examine rules.

Listing 9-3. Inventory Formula Calculation Using the MODEL Clause

```
col product format A30
col country format A10
col region format A10
col year format 9999
col week format 99
col sale format 999999
set lines 120 pages 100

1    select product, country, year, week, inventory, sale, receipts
2    from sales_fact
3    where country in ('Australia') and product ='Xtend Memory'
4    model return updated rows
5    partition by (product, country)
6    dimension by (year, week)
7    measures ( 0 inventory , sale, receipts)
8    rules automatic order(
9        inventory [year, week ] =
10           nvl(inventory [cv(year), cv(week)-1 ] ,0)
11          - sale[cv(year), cv(week) ] +
12          + receipts [cv(year), cv(week) ]
13    )
14*  order by product, country,year, week
```

PRODUCT	COUNTRY	YEAR	WEEK	INVENTORY	SALE	RECEIPTS
..						
Xtend Memory	Australia	2001	1	4.634	92.26	96.89
Xtend Memory	Australia	2001	2	35.424	118.38	149.17
Xtend Memory	Australia	2001	3	37.786	47.24	49.60
...						
Xtend Memory	Australia	2001	9	77.372	92.67	108.64
Xtend Memory	Australia	2001	10	56.895	69.05	48.57
..						

In Listing 9-3, line 3 declares that this statement is using the MODEL clause with the keywords MODEL RETURN UPDATED ROWS. In a SQL statement using the MODEL clause, there are three groups of columns: partitioning columns, dimension columns, and measures columns. Partitioning columns are analogous to a sheet in the spreadsheet. Dimension columns are analogous to row tags (A, B, C, . . .) and column tags (1, 2, 3, . . .). The measures columns are analogous to cells with formulas.

Line 5 identifies the columns product and country as partitioning columns with the clause partition by (product, country). Line 6 identifies columns year and week as dimension columns with the clause dimension by (year, week). Line 7 identifies columns inventory, sales, and receipts as measures columns with the clause measures (0 inventory, sale, receipts). A rule is similar to a formula, and one such rule is defined in lines 8 through 13.

In a mathematical sense, the MODEL clause is implementing partitioned arrays. Dimension columns are indexes into array elements. Each array element, also called a *cell*, is a measures column.

All rows with the same value for the partitioning column or columns are considered to be in a partition. In this example, all rows with the same value for product and country are in a partition. Within a partition, the dimension columns identify a row uniquely. Rules implement formulas to derive the measures columns and they operate within a partition boundary, so partitions are not mentioned explicitly in a rule.

■ **Note**   It is important to differentiate between partitioning columns in the MODEL clause and the object partitioning feature. Although you can use the keyword partition in the MODEL clause as well, it's different from the object partitioning scheme used to partition large tables.

Rules

Let's revisit the rules section from Listing 9-3. You can see both the rule and the corresponding formula together in Listing 9-4. The formula accesses the prior week's inventory to calculate the current week's inventory, so it requires an interrow reference. Note that there is a great similarity between the formula and the rule.

Listing 9-4. Rule and Formula

```
Formula for inventory:

Inventory for (year, week)  = Inventory (year, prior week)
                            - Quantity sold in this week
                            + Quantity received in this week

Rule from the SQL:

  8          inventory [year, week ] =
  9                      nvl(inventory [cv(year), cv(week)-1 ] ,0)
 10                   - sale[cv(year), cv(week) ] +
 11                   + receipts [cv(year), cv(week) ]
```

The SQL statement in Listing 9-4 introduces a useful function named *CV*. CV stands for *current value* and it can be used to refer to a column value in the right-hand side of the rule from the left-hand side of the rule. For example, cv(year) refers to the value of the year column from the left-hand side of the rule. If you think of a formula when it is being applied to a specific cell in a spreadsheet, the CV function allows you to reference the index values for that cell.

Let's discuss rules with substituted values, as in Listing 9-5. Let's say that a row with (year, week) column values of (2001, 3) is being processed. The left-hand side of the rule has the values of (2001, 3) for the year and column. The cv(year) clause in the right-hand side of the rule refers to the value of the year column from the left-hand side of the rule—that is, 2001. Similarly, the clause cv(week) refers to the value of the week column from the left-hand side of the rule—that is, 3. So, the clause inventory [cv(year), cv(week)-1] returns the value of the inventory measures for the year equal to 2001 and the prior week (in other words, week 2).

Listing 9-5. Rule Example

```
Rule example:
 1  rules (
 2       inventory [2001 , 3] = nvl(inventory [cv(year), cv(week)-1 ] ,0)
 3                                   - sale [cv(year), cv(week) ] +
 4                                   + receipts [cv(year), cv(week) ]
 5  )

   rules (
        inventory [2001 , 3] = nvl(inventory [2001, 3-1 ] ,0)
                                   - sale [2001, 3 ] +
                                   + receipts [2001, 3 ]
                           = 35.42  - 47.24 + 49.60
                           = 37.78
   )
```

Similarly, clauses sale[cv(year), cv(week)] and receipts[cv(year), cv(week)] are referring to the sale and receipts column values for the year equal to 2001 and the week equal to 3 using the cv function.

Notice that the partitioning columns product and country are not specified in these rules. Rules refer implicitly to the column values for the product and country columns in the current partition.

Positional and Symbolic References

As discussed previously, the cv function provides the ability to refer to a single cell. It is also possible to refer to an individual cell or group of cells using positional or symbolic notations. In addition, you can write FOR loops as a way to create or modify many cells in an arraylike fashion.

Positional Notation

Positional notation provides the ability to insert a new cell or update an existing cell in the result set. If the referenced cell exists in the result set, then the cell value is updated; if the cell doesn't exist, then a new cell is added. This concept of "update if exists, insert if not" is called the *UPSERT feature*, a fused version of the update and insert facilities. Positional notation provides UPSERT capability.

Suppose that you need to add new cells to initialize the column values for the year equal to 2002 and the week equal to 1. You could achieve this with a rule defined using positional notation. In Listing 9-6, lines 13 and 14 add new cells for the year equal to 2002 and the week equal to 1 using the positional notation with the clause sale[2002,1]=0. Within the square brackets, the position of the value refers to the column order declared in the dimension clause. In this case, column order is (year, week), hence the clause sale[2002,1] refers to the sale column value for the row satisfying the predicates year=2002 and week=1. There are no rows with a column value of year equal to 2002 and week equal to 1, and a new row was inserted with a 0 value for the sale column for the year equal to 2002 and the week equal to 1. The last row in the output was inserted by this rule.

Listing 9-6. Positional Reference to Initialize for Year 2002: UPSERT

```
1     select product, country, year, week, inventory, sale, receipts
2     from sales_fact
3     where country in ('Australia') and product ='Xtend Memory'
4     model return updated rows
5     partition by (product, country)
6     dimension by (year, week)
7     measures ( 0 inventory , sale, receipts)
8     rules automatic order(
9         inventory [year, week ] =
10                  nvl(inventory [cv(year), cv(week)-1 ] ,0)
11               - sale[cv(year), cv(week) ] +
12               + receipts [cv(year), cv(week) ],
13        sale [2002, 1] = 0,
14        receipts [2002,1] =0
15    )
16*   order by product, country,year, week
...
```

PRODUCT	COUNTRY	YEAR	WEEK	INVENTORY	SALE	RECEIPTS
...						
Xtend Memory	Australia	2001	49	2.519	45.26	47.33
Xtend Memory	Australia	2001	50	11.775	23.14	32.40
Xtend Memory	Australia	2001	51	-20.617	114.82	82.43
Xtend Memory	Australia	2001	52	-22.931	23.14	20.83
Xtend Memory	Australia	2002	1	0	.00	.00
...						

Symbolic Notation

Symbolic notation provides the ability to specify a range of values in the left-hand side of a rule. Let's say you want to update the sale column values to 110 percent of their actual value for the weeks 1, 52, and 53 for the years 2000 and 2001. The SQL in Listing 9-7 does this. The clause year in (2000,2001) in line 9 uses an IN operator to specify a list of values for the year column. Similarly, the clause week in (1,52,53) specifies a list of values for the week column.

Listing 9-7. Symbolic Reference: UPDATE

```
1     select product, country, year, week, sale
2     from sales_fact
3     where country in ('Australia') and product ='Xtend Memory'
4     model return updated rows
5     partition by (product, country)
6     dimension by (year, week)
7     measures ( sale)
8     rules(
9       sale [ year in (2000,2001), week in (1,52,53) ] order by year, week
10            = sale [cv(year), cv(week)] * 1.10
11    )
12*   order by product, country,year, week
```

PRODUCT	COUNTRY	YEAR	WEEK	SALE
Xtend Memory	Australia	2000	1	51.37
Xtend Memory	Australia	2000	52	74.20
Xtend Memory	Australia	2001	1	101.49
Xtend Memory	Australia	2001	52	25.45

Note that the output in Listing 9-7 is not a partial output and that there are no rows for the week equal to 53. Even though you specified 53 in the list of values for the week column in line 9, there are no rows returned for that week. The reason is that symbolic notation can only update the existing cells; it does not allow new cells to be added.

■ **Note**   I discuss a method to insert an array of cells in the upcoming section "FOR Loops."

There are no data with a week column value equal to 53 and no new row was added or updated in the result set for the week equal to 53. The ability to generate rows is a key difference between symbolic notation and positional notation. Symbolic notation provides an UPDATE-only facility and positional notation provides an UPSERT facility.

There are a few subtle differences between the SQL statement in Listing 9-7 and prior SQL statements. For example, the statement in Listing 9-7 is missing automatic order in line 8. I discuss the implication of this in the "Rule Evaluation Order" section later in this chapter.

FOR Loops

FOR loops allow you to specify a list of values in the left-hand side of a rule. FOR loops can be defined in the left-hand side of the rule only to add new cells to the output; they can't be used in the right-hand side of the rule. Syntax for the FOR loop is as follows:

```
FOR dimension FROM <value1> TO <value2>
[INCREMENT | DECREMENT] <value3>
```

For example, let's say you want to add cells for the weeks ranging from 1 to 53 for the year 2002, and initialize those cells with a value of 0. Line 13 in Listing 9-8 inserts new rows for the year 2002 and weeks ranging from 1 to 53 using a FOR loop. Clause Increment 1 increments the week column values to generate weeks from 1 to 53. Similarly, the receipts column is initialized using the clause receipts [2002, for week from 1 to 53 increment 1] =0.

Listing 9-8. Positional Reference, Model, and FOR Loops

```
1    select product, country, year, week, inventory, sale, receipts
2    from sales_fact
3    where country in ('Australia') and product ='Xtend Memory'
4    model return updated rows
5    partition by (product, country)
6    dimension by (year, week)
7    measures ( 0 inventory , sale, receipts)
8    rules automatic order(
9        inventory [year, week ] =
10                        nvl(inventory [cv(year), cv(week)-1 ] ,0)
11                        - sale[cv(year), cv(week) ] +
12                        + receipts [cv(year), cv(week) ],
```

```
13            sale [2002, for week from 1 to 53 increment 1] = 0,
14            receipts [2002,for week from 1 to 53 increment 1] =0
15    )
16*   order by product, country,year, week
```

PRODUCT	COUNTRY	YEAR	WEEK	INVENTORY	SALE	RECEIPTS
-----------	----------	-----	----	----------	----------	----------
...						
Xtend Memory	Australia	2001	52	-22.931	23.14	20.83
Xtend Memory	Australia	2002	1	0	.00	.00
...						
Xtend Memory	Australia	2002	52	0	.00	.00
Xtend Memory	Australia	2002	53	0	.00	.00
...						

Returning Updated Rows

In Listing 9-7, just four rows were returned even though there are rows for other weeks. The clause RETURN UPDATED ROWS controls this behavior and provides the ability to limit the cells returned by the SQL statement. Without this clause, all rows are returned regardless of whether the rules update the cells. The rule in Listing 9-7 updates only four cells and other cells are untouched, and so just four rows are returned.

What happens if you don't specify the clause return updated rows? Listing 9-9 shows the output without the RETURN UPDATED ROWS clause. The output in this listing shows that both updated and nonupdated rows are returned from the SQL statement. The rule updates cells for weeks 1, 52, and 53 only, but the output rows in Listing 9-9 show rows with other column values such as 2, 3, and 4, too.

Listing 9-9. SQL without RETURN UPDATED ROWS

```
1     select product, country, year, week, sale
2     from sales_fact
3     where country in ('Australia') and product ='Xtend Memory'
4     model
5     partition by (product, country)
6     dimension by (year, week)
7     measures ( sale)
8     rules(
9       sale [ year in (2000,2001), week in (1,52,53) ] order by year, week
10          = sale [cv(year), cv(week)] * 1.10
11    )
12*   order by product, country,year, week
```

PRODUCT	COUNTRY	YEAR	WEEK	SALE
-----------	----------	-----	----	----------
...				
Xtend Memory	Australia	2000	50	21.19
Xtend Memory	Australia	2000	52	74.20
Xtend Memory	Australia	2001	1	101.49
Xtend Memory	Australia	2001	2	118.38
Xtend Memory	Australia	2001	3	47.24
Xtend Memory	Australia	2001	4	256.70
...				

The clause RETURN UPDATED ROWS is applicable to statements using positional notation as well. In Listing 9-10, a rule using a positional notation is shown, inserting a row. Note there are more rows in the table matching with the predicate country in ('Australia') and product ='Xtend Memory'. But, just one row is returned because only one cell is inserted by the rule in line 9. Essentially, the RETURN UPDATED ROWS clause is a limiting clause; it only fetches the rows modified by the rule.

Listing 9-10. RETURN UPDATED ROWS and UPSERT

```
1    select product, country, year, week, sale
2    from sales_fact
3    where country in ('Australia') and product ='Xtend Memory'
4    model return updated rows
5    partition by (product, country)
6    dimension by (year, week)
7    measures ( sale)
8    rules(
9            sale [2002, 1] = 0
10   )
11*  order by product, country,year, week
```

```
PRODUCT       COUNTRY     YEAR WEEK      SALE
------------- ----------- ---- ---- ----------
Xtend Memory Australia   2002    1       .00
```

Evaluation Order

Multiple rules can be specified in the rules section, and the rules can be specified with dependencies among them. The rule evaluation sequence can affect the functional behavior of the SQL statement, as you will see in this section. Furthermore, even within a single rule, the evaluation of the rule must adhere to a logical sequence. I discuss intrarule valuation order first, then interrule evaluation.

Row Evaluation Order

Let's look at row evaluation order *within* a rule. Listing 9-11 is copied from Listing 9-3. However, this time, I've commented out the keywords AUTOMATIC ORDER in line 8. By commenting these keywords, I force the default behavior of SEQUENTIAL ORDER.

Listing 9-11. Sequential order with Error ORA-32637

```
1    select product, country, year, week, inventory, sale, receipts
2    from sales_fact
3    where country in ('Australia')
4    model return updated rows
5    partition by (product, country)
6    dimension by (year, week)
7    measures ( 0 inventory , sale, receipts)
8    rules  -- Commented: automatic order
9    (
10         inventory [year, week ] =
```

```
11                          nvl(inventory [cv(year), cv(week)-1 ] ,0)
12                          - sale[cv(year), cv(week) ] +
13                          + receipts [cv(year), cv(week) ]
14     )
15*    order by product, country,year, week
       *
ERROR at line 2:
ORA-32637: Self cyclic rule in sequential order MODEL
```

The rule has an interrow reference with the clause inventory [cv(year), cv(week)-1]. Inventory column values must be calculated in ascending order of the week. For example, the inventory rule for week 40 must be evaluated before evaluating the inventory rule for week 41. With AUTOMATIC ORDER, the database engine identifies the row dependencies and evaluates the rows in strict dependency order. Without the AUTOMATIC ORDER clause, row evaluation order is undetermined, which leads to ORA-32637 errors, as shown in Listing 9-11.

It is a better practice to specify the row evaluation order explicitly to avoid this error. Listing 9-12 provides an example. In the rule section, we can specify the order of row evaluation using an ORDER BY year, week clause. This clause specifies that rules must be evaluated in the ascending order of year, week column values. That is, the inventory rule for the year equal to 2000 and the week equal to 40 must be evaluated before evaluating the inventory rule for the year equal to 2000 and the week equal to 41.

Listing 9-12. Evaluation Order at the Cell Level

```
1      select product, country, year, week, inventory, sale, receipts
2      from sales_fact
3      where country in ('Australia')
4      model return updated rows
5      partition by (product, country)
6      dimension by (year, week)
7      measures ( 0 inventory , sale, receipts)
8      rules (
9          inventory [year, week ] order by year, week =
10                              nvl(inventory [cv(year), cv(week)-1 ] ,0)
11                              - sale[cv(year), cv(week) ] +
12                              + receipts [cv(year), cv(week) ]
13     )
14*    order by product, country,year, week
```

PRODUCT	COUNTRY	YEAR	WEEK	INVENTORY	SALE	RECEIPTS
...						
Xtend Memory	Australia	2001	49	2.519	45.26	47.33
Xtend Memory	Australia	2001	50	11.775	23.14	32.40
...						

Note there is no consistency check performed to determine whether this specification of row evaluation order is consistent logically. It is up to the coder—you!—to understand the implications of evaluation order. For example, the row evaluation order in Listing 9-13 is specified with the DESC keyword. Although the rule is syntactically correct, semantic correctness is only known to the coder. Semantic correctness might well require the specification of ASC for an ascending sort. Only the person writing the SQL statement can know which order meets the business problem being addressed.

Listing 9-13. Evaluation Order using the DESC Keyword

```
1     select product, country, year, week, inventory, sale, receipts
2     from sales_fact
3     where country in ('Australia') and product in ('Xtend Memory')
4     model return updated rows
5     partition by (product, country)
6     dimension by (year, week)
7     measures ( 0 inventory , sale, receipts)
8     rules (
9          inventory [year, week ] order by year, week desc  =
10                    nvl(inventory [cv(year), cv(week)-1 ] ,0)
11                  - sale[cv(year), cv(week) ] +
12                  + receipts [cv(year), cv(week) ]
13         )
14*   order by product, country,year, week
```

PRODUCT	COUNTRY	YEAR	WEEK	INVENTORY	SALE	RECEIPTS
...						
Xtend Memory	Australia	2001	49	2.068	45.26	47.33
Xtend Memory	Australia	2001	50	9.256	23.14	32.40
...						

Notice that inventory column values are different between the Listings 9-12 and 9-13. You need to ensure that the order of row evaluation is consistent with the requirements.

Rule Evaluation Order

In addition to the order in which rows are evaluated, you also have the issue of the order in which the rules are applied. In Listing 9-14, there are two rules with an interdependency between them. The first rule is evaluating the rule, and it refers to the receipts column, which is calculated by the second rule. These two rules can be evaluated in any order, and the results depend on the order of rule evaluation. It is important to understand the order of rule evaluation because the functional behavior of the SQL statement can change with the rule evaluation order.

Listing 9-14. Rule Evaluation Order: Sequential Order

```
1     select * from  (
2     select product, country, year, week, inventory, sale, receipts
3     from sales_fact
4     where country in ('Australia') and product in ('Xtend Memory')
5     model return updated rows
6     partition by (product, country)
7     dimension by (year, week)
8     measures ( 0 inventory , sale, receipts)
9     rules sequential order (
10         inventory [year, week ] order by year, week  =
11                    nvl(inventory [cv(year), cv(week)-1 ] ,0)
12                  - sale[cv(year), cv(week) ] +
13                  + receipts [cv(year), cv(week) ],
14         receipts [ year in (2000,2001), week in (51,52,53) ]
```

```
15                      order by year, week
16                        = receipts [cv(year), cv(week)] * 10
17          )
18      order by product, country,year, week
19*    ) where week >50
```

```
PRODUCT        COUNTRY      YEAR WEEK  INVENTORY      SALE   RECEIPTS
------------   ----------   ----- ---- ----------  ---------- ----------
...
Xtend Memory Australia     2000   52     -6.037      67.45     614.13
Xtend Memory Australia     2001   51    -20.617     114.82     824.28
Xtend Memory Australia     2001   52    -22.931      23.14     208.26
```

To improve clarity, filter on rows with week greater than 50. In Listing 9-14, line 9 specifies sequential order, which means the rules are evaluated in the order in which they are listed. In this example, the rule for the inventory column is evaluated, followed by the rule for the receipts column. Because the receipts rule is evaluated after the inventory rule, the inventory rule uses the unaltered values before the evaluation of the receipts rule. Essentially, changes from the receipts rule for the receipts column calculation are not factored into the inventory calculation.

The situation with rule evaluation is the same as with rows. Only the coder knows which order of evaluation is appropriate for the business problem being solved. Only the coder knows whether the inventory rule should use altered values from execution of the receipts rule, or otherwise.

Another method of evaluating the order used by Oracle Database is automatic order. In Listing 9-15, the evaluation order is changed to automatic order. With automatic order, dependencies among the rules are resolved automatically by Oracle and the order of rule evaluation depends on the dependencies between the rules.

Listing 9-15. Rule Evaluation Order: Automatic Order

```
...
9    rules automatic order (
...
```

```
PRODUCT        COUNTRY      YEAR WEEK  INVENTORY      SALE   RECEIPTS
------------   ----------   ----- ---- ----------  ---------- ----------
...
Xtend Memory Australia     2000   52     546.68      67.45     614.13
Xtend Memory Australia     2001   51    721.235     114.82     824.28
Xtend Memory Australia     2001   52    906.355      23.14     208.26
```

The results from Listing 9-15 and Listing 9-14 do not match. For example, inventory for week 52 is –22.931 in Listing 9-14 and 906.355 in Listing 9-15. By specifying automatic order, you allow the database engine to identify a dependency between the rules. Thus, the engine evaluates the receipts rule first, followed by the inventory rule.

Clearly, the order of rule evaluation can be quite important. If there are complex interdependencies, then you might want to specify sequential order and list the rules in a strict evaluation sequence. In this way, you are in full control and nothing is left to doubt.

Aggregation

Data aggregation is commonly used in data warehouse queries. The Model clause provides the ability to aggregate the data using aggregate functions over the range of dimension columns.

Many different aggregation function calls such as sum, max, avg, stddev, and OLAP function calls can be used to aggregate the data in a rule. It is easier to understand aggregation with an example.

In Listing 9-16, the rule in lines 9 through 12 calculates average inventory by year using the clause avg_inventory[year,ANY] = avg(inventory) [cv(year), week]. In the left-hand side of the rule, avg_inventory is the rule name. The first dimension in this rule is the year column. Because the dimension clause is specifying the week column as the second dimension, specifying ANY in the second position of the rule argument matches with any value of the week column, including nulls. In the right-hand side of the rule, the clause avg(inventory) applies the avg function on the inventory column. The first dimension is cv(year). The second dimension is specified as week. There is no need for the use of cv in the second dimension, because the function must be applied on all weeks in the year as computed by the clause cv(year). Line 13 shows the use of avg; line 14 shows an example of using the max function.

Listing 9-16. Aggregation

```
1     select product, country, year, week, inventory, avg_inventory, max_sale
2         from sales_fact
3         where country in ('Australia') and product ='Xtend Memory'
4         model return updated rows
5         partition by (product, country)
6         dimension by (year, week)
7         measures ( 0 inventory ,0  avg_inventory , 0 max_sale, sale, receipts)
8         rules automatic order(
9             inventory [year, week ] =
10                                    nvl(inventory [cv(year), cv(week)-1 ] ,0)
11                                    - sale[cv(year), cv(week) ] +
12                                    + receipts [cv(year), cv(week) ],
13            avg_inventory [ year,ANY ] = avg (inventory) [ cv(year), week ],
14            max_Sale [ year, ANY ]    = max( sale) [ cv(year), week ]
15         )
16*    order by product, country,year, week
```

```
PRODUCT        COUNTRY     YEAR WEEK  INVENTORY AVG_INVENTORY MAX_SALE
------------   ----------  ----- ---- ---------- ------------- ---------
...
Xtend Memory Australia    2001   42     17.532        28.60     278.44
Xtend Memory Australia    2001   43     24.511        28.60     278.44
Xtend Memory Australia    2001   44     29.169        28.60     278.44
...
Xtend Memory Australia    2001   52    -22.931        28.60     278.44
```

Iteration

Iteration provides another facility to implementing complex business requirements using a concise Model SQL statement. A block of rules can be executed in a loop a certain number of times or while a condition remains TRUE. The syntax for the iteration is as follows:

```
[ITERATE (n) [UNTIL <condition>] ]
( <cell_assignment> = <expression> ... )
```

Use the syntax ITERATE (n) to execute an expression *n* times. Use the expression ITERATE UNTIL <condition> to iterate while the given condition remains TRUE.

An Example

Suppose the goal is to show five weeks of sale column values in a comma-separated list format. This requirement is implemented in Listing 9-17.

Listing 9-17. Iteration

```
1    select year, week,sale, sale_list
2        from sales_fact
3        where country in ('Australia') and product ='Xtend Memory'
4        model return updated rows
5        partition by (product, country)
6        dimension by (year, week)
7        measures ( cast(' ' as varchar2(50) ) sale_list, sale)
8        rules  iterate (5) (
9           sale_list [ year, week ] order by year, week =
10               sale [cv(year), CV(week)-ITERATION_NUMBER +2 ]         ||
11               case when iteration_number=0 then '' else ', '  end  ||
12               sale_list [cv(year) ,cv(week)]
13      )
14*   order by year, week

 YEAR WEEK        SALE SALE_LIST
 ----- ----  ---------- -------------------------------------------------
 2001   20       118.03 22.37, , 118.03, 233.7, 141.78
 2001   21       233.70 , 118.03, 233.7, 141.78, 22.38
 2001   22       141.78 118.03, 233.7, 141.78, 22.38, 136.92
 2001   23        22.38 233.7, 141.78, 22.38, 136.92, 139.28
 2001   24       136.92 141.78, 22.38, 136.92, 139.28,
 2001   25       139.28 22.38, 136.92, 139.28, , 94.48
```

■ **Note**   Conversion of rows to columns is termed *pivoting*. Oracle Database 11g introduced syntax to implement pivoting function natively. In Oracle Database 10g, you could use the MODEL clause to implement pivoting.

Line 8 specifies that the rules block is to be iterated five times for each row. This is done through the clause rules iterate(5). In line 10, you use iteration_number, which is a variable available within the rules section, to access the current iteration count of the loop. iteration_number starts with a value of 0 for the first iteration in the loop and ends at $n-1$, where n is the number of loops as specified in the iterate(n) clause. In this example, the Iteration_number variable value ranges from 0 to 4. With Iteration_number and bit of arithmetic, you can access the prior two weeks and the next two weeks' values using the clause cv(week)-ITERATION_NUMBER +2. The CASE statement adds a comma for each element in the list, except for the first element.

For example, let's assume the current row in the process has a value of year equal to 2001 and week equal to 23. In the first iteration of the loop, iteration_number is 0, and the clause cv(week)-iteration_number +2 accesses the row with week equal to 23 – 0 + 2 = 25. In the next iteration, week 24 is accessed, and so on. The FOR loop is repeated for every row in the model output.

Let's review the output rows in Listing 9-17. For the year 2001, week 23, column sale_list has the following values: 233.7, 141.78, 22.38, 136.92, and 139.28. You can see how these values are centered on the current week. The first two come from the sale column for the immediately preceding weeks, then you have the current week's sales, and then the values from the following two weeks.

PRESENTV and NULLs

If a rule accesses a nonexistent row, the rule returns a null value. Notice that in the output of Listing 9-17, the sale_list column in the first row has two commas consecutively. The reason is that the row for week equal to 19 does not exist in the data, so accessing that nonexistent cell returns a null value. You can correct this double-comma issue using a function to check for cell existence using the PRESENTV function. This function accepts three parameters and the syntax for the function is as follows:

```
PRESENTV (cell_reference, expr1, expr2)
```

If cell_reference references an existing cell, then the PRESENTV function returns expr1. If the cell_reference references a nonexisting cell, then the second argument, expr2, is returned. In Listing 9-18, line 10 performs this existence check on the sale column for the year and week combination using the clause sale [cv(year), CV(week)-iteration_number + 2]. If the cell exists, then the function adds the value of the cell and comma to the returned string (lines 11 to 13). If the cell does not exist, the function returns the sale_list column without altering the string (line 14). This solution eliminates the double comma in the sale_list column value.

Listing 9-18. Iteration and PRESNTV

```
1      select year, week,sale, sale_list
2         from sales_fact
3         where country in ('Australia') and product ='Xtend Memory'
4         model return updated rows
5         partition by (product, country)
6         dimension by (year, week)
7         measures ( cast(' ' as varchar2(120) ) sale_list, sale, 0 tmp)
8         rules  iterate (5) (
9            sale_list [ year, week ] order by year, week =
10                presentv ( sale [cv(year), CV(week)-iteration_number + 2 ],
11                       sale [cv(year), CV(week)-iteration_number +2 ]              ||
12                          case when iteration_number=0 then '' else ', ' end  ||
13                          sale_list [cv(year) ,cv(week)]   ,
14                       sale_list [cv(year) ,cv(week)] ) )
15      )
16*     order by year, week

YEAR WEEK        SALE SALE_LIST
----- ----  ---------- --------------------------------------------------
2001   20     118.03 22.37, 118.03, 233.7, 141.78
2001   21     233.70 118.03, 233.7, 141.78, 22.38
2001   22     141.78 118.03, 233.7, 141.78, 22.38, 136.92
...
2001   29     116.85 94.48, 116.85, 162.91, 92.21
```

The PRESENTNNV function is similar to PRESENTV, but it provides an additional ability to differentiate between references to nonexistent cells and null values in existing cells. The syntax for the function PRESENTNNV is as follows:

```
PRESENTNNV (cell_reference, expr1, expr2)
```

If the first argument cell_reference references an existing cell and if that cell contains a nonnull value, then the first argument, expr1, is returned; otherwise, the second argument, expr2, is returned. In contrast, the PRESENTV function checks for just the existence of a cell, whereas the PRESENTNNV function checks for both the existence of a cell and null values in that cell. Table 9-1 shows the values returned from these two functions in four different cases.

Table 9-1. *PRESENTV and PRESENTNNV Comparison*

Cell exists?	Null?	**PRESENTV**	**PRESENTNNV**
Yes	Not null	expr1	expr1
Yes	Null	expr1	expr2
No	Not null	expr2	expr2
No	Null	expr2	expr2

Lookup Tables

You can define a lookup table and refer to that lookup table in the rules section. Such a lookup table is sometimes termed a *reference table*. Reference tables are defined in the initial section of the SQL statement and are then referred to in the rules section of the SQL statement.

In Listing 9-19, lines 5 through 9 define a lookup table ref_prod using a REFERENCE clause. Line 5 REFERENCE ref_prod is specifying ref_prod as a lookup table. Column prod_name is a dimension column as specified in line 8, and column prod_list_price is a measures column. Note that the reference table must be unique on the dimension column and should retrieve exactly one row per dimension column value.

Listing 9-19. Reference Model

```
1     select year, week,sale, prod_list_price
2        from sales_fact
3        where country in ('Australia') and product ='Xtend Memory'
4        model return updated rows
5        REFERENCE ref_prod on
6          (select prod_name, max(prod_list_price) prod_list_price
7             from products group by prod_name)
8           dimension by (prod_name)
9           measures (prod_list_price)
10       MAIN main_section
11         partition by (product, country)
12         dimension by (year, week)
13         measures ( sale, receipts, 0 prod_list_price )
14         rules   (
15            prod_list_price[year,week] order by year, week =
16                         ref_prod.prod_list_price [ cv(product) ]
17       )
18*   order by year, week;

YEAR WEEK      SALE PROD_LIST_PRICE
----- ---- ---------- ---------------
2000   31     44.78          20.99
2000   33    134.11          20.99
2000   34    178.52          20.99
...
```

Line 10 specifies the main model section starting with the keyword MAIN. This section is named main_section for ease of understanding, although any name can be used. In line 15, a rule for the column prod_list_price is specified and populated from the lookup table ref_prod. Line 16 shows that the reference table that measures columns is accessed using the clause ref_prod.prod_list_price [cv(product)]. The current value of the product column is passed as a lookup key in the lookup table using the clause cv(product).

In summary, you define a lookup table using a REFERENCE clause and then access that lookup table using the syntax look_table_name.measures column. For example, the syntax in this example is ref_prod.prod_list_price [cv(product)]. To access a specific row in the lookup table, you pass the current value of the dimension column from the left-hand side of the rule—in this example, using the cv(product) clause. You might be able to understand better if you imagine ref_prod as a table, cv(product) as the primary key for that table, and prod_list_price as a column to fetch from that lookup table.

More lookup tables can be added if needed. Suppose you also need to retrieve the country_iso_code column values from another table. You achieve this by adding the lookup table ref_country, as shown in Listing 9-20, lines 10 through 13. Column country_name is the dimension column and country_iso_code is a measures column. Lines 22 and 23 refer to the lookup table using a new rule Iso_code. This rule accesses the lookup table ref_country using the cv of the country column as the lookup key.

Listing 9-20. More Lookup Tables

```
1     select year, week,sale,  prod_list_price, iso_code
2        from sales_fact
3        where country in ('Australia') and product ='Xtend Memory'
4        model return updated rows
5        REFERENCE ref_prod on
6          (select prod_name, max(prod_list_price) prod_list_price from
7             products group by prod_name)
8           dimension by (prod_name)
9           measures (prod_list_price)
10       REFERENCE ref_country on
11         (select country_name, country_iso_code from countries)
12          dimension by (country_name )
13          measures (country_iso_code)
14       MAIN main_section
15         partition by (product, country)
16         dimension by (year, week)
17         measures (  sale, receipts, 0 prod_list_price ,
18                            cast(' ' as varchar2(5)) iso_code)
19         rules    (
20             prod_list_price[year,week] order by year, week =
21                            ref_prod.prod_list_price [ cv(product) ],
22             iso_code [year, week] order by year, week =
23                            ref_country.country_iso_code [ cv(country)]
24         )
25*   order by year, week
```

YEAR	WEEK	SALE	PROD_LIST_PRICE	ISO_C
----	----	----------	----------------	-----
2000	31	44.78	20.99	AU
2000	33	134.11	20.99	AU
2000	34	178.52	20.99	AU
2000	35	78.82	20.99	AU
2000	36	118.41	20.99	AU

...

NULLs

In SQL statements using Model SQL, values can be null for two reasons: null values in the existing cells and references to nonexistent cells. I discuss the latter scenario in this section.

By default, the reference to nonexistent cells returns null values. In Listing 9-21, the rule in line 10 accesses the sale column for the year equal to 2002 and the week equal to 1 using the clause sale[2002,1]. There are no data in the sales_fact table for the year 2002, and so sale[2002,1] is accessing a nonexistent cell. Output in this listing is null because of the arithmetic operation with a null value.

Listing 9-21. KEEP NAV Example

```
1    select product, country, year, week,  sale
2    from sales_fact
3    where country in ('Australia') and product ='Xtend Memory'
4    model KEEP NAV return updated rows
5    partition by (product, country)
6    dimension by (year, week)
7    measures ( sale)
8    rules sequential  order(
9      sale[2001,1] order by year, week= sale[2001,1],
10     sale [ 2002, 1] order by year, week = sale[2001,1] + sale[2002,1]
11     )
12*  order by product, country,year, week
```

PRODUCT	COUNTRY	YEAR	WEEK	SALE
Xtend Memory	Australia	2001	1	92.26
Xtend Memory	Australia	2002	1	

In line 4, I added a KEEP NAV clause after the MODEL keyword explicitly even though KEEP NAV is the default value. NAV stands for nonavailable values, and references to a nonexistent cell returns a null value by default.

This default behavior can be modified using the IGNORE NAV clause. Listing 9-22 shows an example. If the nonexistent cells are accessed, then 0 is returned for numeric columns and an empty string is returned for text columns instead of null values. You can see that the output in Listing 9-22 shows that a value of 92.26 is returned for the clause sale[2001,1] + sale[2002,1] and a 0 is retuned for the nonexisting cell sale[2002,1].

Listing 9-22. IGNORE NAV

```
1    select product, country, year, week,  sale
2    from sales_fact
3    where country in ('Australia') and product ='Xtend Memory'
4    model IGNORE NAV return updated rows
5    partition by (product, country)
6    dimension by (year, week)
7    measures ( sale)
8    rules sequential  order(
9      sale[2001,1] order by year, week= sale[2001,1],
10     sale [ 2002, 1] order by year, week = sale[2001,1] + sale[2002,1]
11     )
12*  order by product, country,year, week
```

PRODUCT	COUNTRY	YEAR	WEEK	SALE
Xtend Memory	Australia	2001	1	92.26
Xtend Memory	Australia	2002	1	92.26

The functions PRESENTV and PRESNTNNV are also useful in handling NULL values. Refer to the earlier section "Iteration" for a discussion and examples of these two functions.

Performance Tuning with the MODEL Clause

As with all SQL, sometimes you need to tune statements using the MODEL clause. To this end, it helps to know how to read execution plans involving the clause. It also helps to know about some of the issues you may encounter—such as predicate pushing and partitioning—when working with MODEL clause queries.

Execution Plans

In the MODEL clause, rule evaluation is the critical step. Rule evaluation can use one of five algorithm types: ACYCLIC, ACYCLIC FAST, CYCLIC, ORDERED, and ORDERED FAST. The algorithm chosen depends on the complexity and dependency of the rules themselves. The algorithm chosen also affects the performance of the SQL statement. But, details of these algorithms are not well documented.

ACYCLIC FAST and ORDERED FAST algorithms are more optimized algorithms that allow cells to be evaluated efficiently. However, the algorithm chosen depends on the type of the rules that you specify. For example, if there is a *possibility* of a cycle in the rules, then the algorithm that can handle cyclic rules is chosen.

The algorithms of type ACYCLIC and CYCLIC are used if the SQL statement specifies the rules automatic order clause. An ORDERED type of the rule evaluation algorithm is used if the SQL statement specifies rules sequential order. If a rule accesses individual cells without any aggregation, then either the ACYCIC FAST or ORDERED FAST algorithm is used.

ACYCLIC

In Listing 9-23, a MODEL SQL statement and its execution plan is shown. Step 2 in the execution plan shows that this SQL is using the SQL MODEL ACYCLIC algorithm for rule evaluation. The keyword ACYCLIC indicates there are no possible cyclic dependencies between the rules. In this example, with the order by year, week clause you control the dependency between the rules, avoiding cycle dependencies,

Listing 9-23. Automatic order and ACYCLIC

```
1     select product, country, year, week, inventory, sale, receipts
2     from sales_fact
3     where country in ('Australia') and product='Xtend Memory'
4     model return updated rows
5     partition by (product, country)
6     dimension by (year, week)
7     measures ( 0 inventory , sale, receipts)
8     rules automatic order(
9         inventory [year, week ] order by year, week =
10                  nvl(inventory [cv(year), cv(week)-1 ] ,0)
11               - sale[cv(year), cv(week) ] +
12               + receipts [cv(year), cv(week) ]
13      )
14*   order by product, country,year, week
```

```
----------------------------------------------------
| Id  | Operation           | Name       | E-Rows |
----------------------------------------------------
|   0 | SELECT STATEMENT    |            |        |
|   1 |  SORT ORDER BY      |            |    147 |
|   2 |   SQL MODEL ACYCLIC |            |    147 |
|*  3 |    TABLE ACCESS FULL| SALES_FACT |    147 |
----------------------------------------------------
```

ACYCLIC FAST

If a rule is a simple rule accessing just one cell, the ACYCLIC FAST algorithm can be used. The execution plan in Listing 9-24 shows that the ACYCLIC FAST algorithm is used to evaluate the rule in this example.

Listing 9-24. Automatic Order and ACYCLIC FAST

```
1    select distinct product, country, year,week, sale_first_Week
2    from sales_fact
3    where country in ('Australia') and product='Xtend Memory'
4    model return updated rows
5    partition by (product, country)
6    dimension by (year,week)
7    measures ( 0 sale_first_week     ,sale )
8    rules automatic order(
9       sale_first_week [2000,1] = 0.12*sale [2000, 1]
10    )
11*   order by product, country,year, week
```

```
-----------------------------------------------
| Id  | Operation            | Name       |
-----------------------------------------------
|   0 | SELECT STATEMENT     |            |
|   1 |  SORT ORDER BY       |            |
|   2 |   SQL MODEL ACYCLIC FAST|         |
|*  3 |    TABLE ACCESS FULL  | SALES_FACT |
-----------------------------------------------
```

CYCLIC

The execution plan in Listing 9-25 shows the use of the CYCLIC algorithm to evaluate the rules. The SQL in Listing 9-25 is a copy of Listing 9-23, except that the clause order by year, week is removed from the rule in line 9. Without the order by clause, row evaluation can happen in any order, and so the CYCLIC algorithm is chosen.

Listing 9-25. Automatic Order and CYCLIC

```
1    select product, country, year, week, inventory, sale, receipts
2    from sales_fact
3    where country in ('Australia') and product='Xtend Memory'
4    model return updated rows
5    partition by (product, country)
6    dimension by (year, week)
```

```
 7     measures ( 0 inventory , sale, receipts)
 8     rules automatic order(
 9          inventory [year, week ] =
10                    nvl(inventory [cv(year), cv(week)-1 ] ,0)
11                - sale[cv(year), cv(week) ] +
12                + receipts [cv(year), cv(week) ]
13          )
14*    order by product, country,year, week
```

```
-------------------------------------------
| Id | Operation         | Name       |
-------------------------------------------
|  0 | SELECT STATEMENT  |            |
|  1 |  SORT ORDER BY     |            |
|  2 |   SQL MODEL CYCLIC |            |
|* 3 |    TABLE ACCESS FULL| SALES_FACT |
-------------------------------------------
```

Sequential

If the rule specifies sequential order, then the evaluation algorithm of the rules is shown as ORDERED. Listing 9-26 shows an example.

Listing 9-26. Sequential Order

```
 1     select product, country, year, week, inventory, sale, receipts
 2     from sales_fact
 3     where country in ('Australia') and product='Xtend Memory'
 4     model return updated rows
 5     partition by (product, country)
 6     dimension by (year, week)
 7     measures ( 0 inventory , sale, receipts)
 8     rules sequential order(
 9          inventory [year, week ] order by year, week =
10                    nvl(inventory [cv(year), cv(week)-1 ] ,0)
11                - sale[cv(year), cv(week) ] +
12                + receipts [cv(year), cv(week) ]
13          )
14*    order by product, country,year, week
```

```
-------------------------------------------
| Id | Operation         | Name       |
-------------------------------------------
|  0 | SELECT STATEMENT  |            |
|  1 |  SORT ORDER BY     |            |
|  2 |   SQL MODEL ORDERED |           |
|* 3 |    TABLE ACCESS FULL| SALES_FACT |
-------------------------------------------
```

In a nutshell, the complexity and interdependency of the rules plays a critical role in the algorithm chosen. ACYCLIC FAST and ORDERED FAST algorithms are more scalable. This becomes important as the amount of data increases.

Predicate Pushing

Conceptually, the Model clause is a variant of analytic SQL and is typically implemented in a view or inline view. Predicates are specified outside the view, and these predicates must be pushed into the view for acceptable performance. In fact, predicate pushing is critical to the performance of the Model clause. Unfortunately, not all predicates can be pushed safely into the view because of the unique nature of the Model clause. If predicates are not pushed, then the Model clause executes on the larger set of rows, which can result in poor performance.

In Listing 9-27, an inline view is defined from lines 2 through 14, and then predicates on columns country and product are added. Step 4 in the execution plan shows that both predicates are pushed into the view, rows are filtered applying these two predicates, and then the Model clause executes on the result set. This is good, because the Model clause is operating on a smaller set of rows than it would otherwise—just 147 rows in this case.

Listing 9-27. Predicate Pushing

```
1    select * from (
2    select product, country, year, week, inventory, sale, receipts
3    from sales_fact
4    model return updated rows
5    partition by (product, country)
6    dimension by (year, week)
7    measures ( 0 inventory , sale, receipts)
8    rules automatic order(
9         inventory [year, week ] =
10                  nvl(inventory [cv(year), cv(week)-1 ] ,0)
11               - sale[cv(year), cv(week) ] +
12               + receipts [cv(year), cv(week) ]
13    )
14   ) where country in ('Australia') and product='Xtend Memory'
15*  order by product, country,year, week
...

select * from table (dbms_xplan.display_cursor('','','ALLSTATS LAST'));
```

Id	Operation	Name	E-Rows	OMem	1Mem	Used-Mem
0	SELECT STATEMENT					
1	SORT ORDER BY		147	18432	18432	16384 (0)
2	VIEW		147			
3	SQL MODEL CYCLIC		147	727K	727K	358K (0)
* 4	TABLE ACCESS FULL	SALES_FACT	147			

```
Predicate Information (identified by operation id):
---------------------------------------------------
   4 - filter(("PRODUCT"='Xtend Memory' AND "COUNTRY"='Australia'))
```

Listing 9-28 is an example in which the predicates are not pushed into the view. In this example, predicate year=2000 is specified, but it is not pushed into the inline view. The optimizer estimates show that the MODEL clause needs to operate on some 111,000 rows.

Predicates can be pushed into a view only if it's safe to do so. The SQL in Listing 9-28 uses both the year and week columns as dimension columns. In general, predicates on the partitioning columns can be pushed into a view safely, but not all predicates on the dimension column can be pushed.

Listing 9-28. Predicate Not Pushed

```
1    select * from (
2    select product, country, year, week, inventory, sale, receipts
3    from sales_fact
4    mod el return updated rows
5    partition by (product, country)
6    dimension by (year, week)
7    measures ( 0 inventory , sale, receipts)
8    rules automatic order(
9        inventory [year, week ] =
10                   nvl(inventory [cv(year), cv(week)-1 ] ,0)
11              - sale[cv(year), cv(week) ] +
12              + receipts [cv(year), cv(week) ]
13   )
14   ) where year=2000
15*  order by product, country,year, week
```

```
-------------------------------------------------------------------
| Id | Operation          | Name       | E-Rows| OMem | 1Mem | Used-Mem |
-------------------------------------------------------------------
|  0 | SELECT STATEMENT   |            |       |      |      |          |
|  1 |  SORT ORDER BY     |            | 111K| 2604K|  733K| 2314K (0)|
|* 2 |   VIEW             |            | 111K|      |      |          |
|  3 |    SQL MODEL CYCLIC|            | 111K|  12M| 1886K|  12M (0)|
|  4 |     TABLE ACCESS FULL| SALES_FACT| 111K|      |      |          |
-------------------------------------------------------------------
```

Predicate Information (identified by operation id):
```
---------------------------------------------------
   2 - filter("YEAR"=2000)
```

Materialized Views

Typically, SQL statements using the MODEL clause access very large tables. Oracle's query rewrite feature and materialized views can be combined to improve performance of such statements.

In Listing 9-29, a materialized view mv_model_inventory is created with the enable query rewrite clause. Subsequent SQL in the listing executes the SQL statement accessing the sales_fact table with the MODEL clause. The execution plan for the statement shows that the query rewrite feature rewrites the query, redirecting access to the materialized view instead of the base table. The rewrite improves the performance of the SQL statement because the materialized view has preevaluated the rules and stored the results.

■ **Note**   The fast incremental refresh is not available for materialized views involving the Model clause.

Listing 9-29. Materialized View and Query Rewrite

```
create materialized view mv_model_inventory
enable query rewrite as
  select product, country, year, week, inventory, sale, receipts
  from sales_fact
  model return updated rows
  partition by (product, country)
  dimension by (year, week)
  measures ( 0 inventory , sale, receipts)
  rules sequential order(
      inventory [year, week ] order by year, week =
                nvl(inventory [cv(year), cv(week)-1 ] ,0)
              - sale[cv(year), cv(week) ] +
              + receipts [cv(year), cv(week) ]
  )
/
Materialized view created.

select * from (
 select product, country, year, week, inventory, sale, receipts
  from sales_fact
  model return updated rows
  partition by (product, country)
  dimension by (year, week)
  measures ( 0 inventory , sale, receipts)
  rules sequential order(
      inventory [year, week ] order by year, week =
                nvl(inventory [cv(year), cv(week)-1 ] ,0)
              - sale[cv(year), cv(week) ] +
              + receipts [cv(year), cv(week) ]
  )
 )
where country in ('Australia') and product='Xtend Memory'
order by product, country,year, week
/
```

```
-------------------------------------------------------------
| Id  | Operation                    | Name               |
-------------------------------------------------------------
|   0 | SELECT STATEMENT             |                    |
|   1 |  SORT ORDER BY               |                    |
|*  2 |   MAT_VIEW REWRITE ACCESS FULL | MV_MODEL_INVENTORY |
-------------------------------------------------------------

Predicate Information (identified by operation id):
---------------------------------------------------
  2 - filter(("MV_MODEL_INVENTORY"."COUNTRY"='Australia' AND
            "MV_MODEL_INVENTORY"."PRODUCT"='Xtend Memory'))
```

Parallelism

MODEL -based SQL works seamlessly with Oracle's parallel execution features. Queries against partitioned tables benefit greatly from parallelism and MODEL -based SQL statements.

An important concept with parallel query execution and MODEL SQL is that parallel query execution needs to respect the partition boundaries. Rules defined in the MODEL clause-based SQL statement might access another row. After all, accessing another row is the primary reason to use MODEL SQL statements. So, a parallel query slave must receive all rows from a model data partition so that the rules can be evaluated. This distribution of rows to parallel query slaves is taken care of seamlessly by the database engine. The first set of parallel slaves reads row pieces from the table and distributes the row pieces to a second set of slaves. The distribution is such that one slave receives all rows of a given model partition.

Listing 9-30 shows an example of MODEL and parallel queries. Two sets of parallel slaves are allocated to execute the statement shown. The first set of slaves is read from the table; the second set of slaves evaluates the MODEL rule.

Listing 9-30. Model and Parallel Queries

```
select  /*+ parallel ( sf 4) */
  product, country, year, week, inventory, sale, receipts
  from sales_fact sf
  where country in ('Australia') and product='Xtend Memory'
  model return updated rows
  partition by (product, country)
  dimension by (year, week)
  measures ( 0 inventory , sale, receipts)
  rules automatic order(
      inventory [year, week ] order by year, week =
              nvl(inventory [cv(year), cv(week)-1 ] ,0)
           - sale[cv(year), cv(week) ] +
           + receipts [cv(year), cv(week) ]
  )
/
```

```
-----------------------------------------...-----------------------------
| Id | Operation                | Name       |    TQ |IN-OUT| PQ Distrib |
-----------------------------------------------------------------------
|  0 | SELECT STATEMENT          |            |  ... |      |            |
|  1 |  PX COORDINATOR           |            |       |      |            |
|  2 |   PX SEND QC (RANDOM)      | :TQ10001   | Q1,01 | P->S | QC (RAND)  |
|  3 |    BUFFER SORT             |            | Q1,01 | PCWP |            |
|  4 |     SQL MODEL ACYCLIC      |            | Q1,01 | PCWP |            |
|  5 |      PX RECEIVE            |            | Q1,01 | PCWP |            |
|  6 |       PX SEND HASH         | :TQ10000   | Q1,00 | P->P | HASH       |
|  7 |        PX BLOCK ITERATOR   |            | Q1,00 | PCWC |            |
|* 8 |         TABLE ACCESS FULL| SALES_FACT | Q1,00 | PCWP |            |
-----------------------------------------------------------------------
Predicate Information (identified by operation id):
---------------------------------------------------

   8 - access(:Z>=:Z AND :Z<=:Z)
       filter((("PRODUCT"='Xtend Memory' AND "COUNTRY"='Australia'))
```

Partitioning in MODEL Clause Execution

Table partitioning can be used to improve the performance of MODEL SQL statements. In general, if the partitioning columns in the MODEL SQL matches the partitioning keys of the table, partitions are pruned. Partition pruning is a technique for performance improvement to limit scanning few partitions.

In Listing 9-31, the table sales_fact_part is list partitioned by year using the script Listing_9_31_partition. sql (part of the example download for this book). The partition with partition_id=3 contains rows with the value of 2000 for the year column. Because the MODEL SQL is using year as the partitioning column and because a year=2000 predicate is specified, partition pruning lead to scanning partition 3 alone. The execution plan shows that both the pstart and pstop columns have a value of 3, indicating that the range of partitions to be processed begins and ends with the single partition having an ID equal to 3.

Listing 9-31. Partition Pruning

```
select * from (
  select product, country, year, week, inventory, sale, receipts
  from sales_fact_part sf
  model return updated rows
  partition by (year, country )
  dimension by (product, week)
  measures ( 0 inventory , sale, receipts )
  rules automatic order(
      inventory [product, week ] order by product,  week =
                nvl(inventory [cv(product),  cv(week)-1 ] ,0)
             - sale[cv(product),  cv(week) ] +
             + receipts [cv(product), cv(week) ]
   )
 )   where year=2000 and country='Australia' and product='Xtend Memory'
/
```

```
-------------------------------------------------...----------------
| Id  | Operation              | Name            |... Pstart| Pstop |
-------------------------------------------------...----------------
|   0 | SELECT STATEMENT       |                 |      |       |     |
|   1 |  SQL MODEL ACYCLIC     |                 |      |       |     |
|   2 |   PARTITION LIST SINGLE|                 |  KEY |   KEY |
|*  3 |    TABLE ACCESS FULL   | SALES_FACT_PART |    3 |     3 |
-------------------------------------------------...----------------

Predicate Information (identified by operation id):
---------------------------------------------------

   1 - filter("PRODUCT"='Xtend Memory')
   4 - filter("COUNTRY"='Australia')
```

In Listing 9-32, columns product and county are used as partitioning columns, but the table sales_fact_part has the year column as the partitioning key. Step 1 in the execution plan indicates that predicate year=2000 was not pushed into the view because the rule can access other partitions (because year is a dimension column). Because the partitioning key is not pushed into the view, partition pruning is not allowed and all partitions are scanned. You can see that pstart and pstop are 1 and 5, respectively, in the execution plan.

Listing 9-32. No Partition Pruning

```
select * from (
select product, country, year, week, inventory, sale, receipts
from sales_fact_part sf
model return updated rows
partition by (product, country)
dimension by (year, week)
measures ( 0 inventory , sale, receipts)
rules automatic order(
     inventory [year, week ] order by year,  week =
               nvl(inventory [cv(year),  cv(week)-1 ] ,0)
            - sale[cv(year),  cv(week) ] +
            + receipts [cv(year), cv(week) ]
  )
)   where year=2000 and country='Australia' and product='Xtend Memory'
/
```

```
-----------------------------------------------...------------
| Id  | Operation           | Name            | Pstart| Pstop |
-----------------------------------------------...------------
|   0 | SELECT STATEMENT    |                 |       |       |
|*  1 |  VIEW               |                 |       |       |
|   2 |   SQL MODEL ACYCLIC |                 |       |       |
|   3 |    PARTITION LIST ALL|                |    1  |    5  |
|*  4 |     TABLE ACCESS FULL| SALES_FACT_PART |   1  |    5  |
-----------------------------------------------...------------
Predicate Information (identified by operation id):
---------------------------------------------------

1 - filter("YEAR"=2000)
4 - filter((("PRODUCT"='Xtend Memory' AND "COUNTRY"='Australia'))
```

Indexes

Choosing indexes to improve the performance of SQL statements using a MODEL clause is no different from choosing indexes for any other SQL statements. You use the access and filter predicates to determine the optimal indexing strategy.

As an example, the execution plan in Listing 9-32 shows that the filter predicates "PRODUCT"='Xtend Memory' and "COUNTRY"='Australia' are applied at step 4. Indexing on the two columns product and country is helpful if there are many executions with these column predicates.

In Listing 9-33, I added an index to the columns country and product. The resulting execution plan shows table access via the index, possibly improving performance.

Listing 9-33. Indexing with SQL Access in Mind

```
create index sales_fact_part_i1 on sales_fact_part (country, product) ;
select * from (
select product, country, year, week, inventory, sale, receipts
from sales_fact_part sf
model return updated rows
partition by (product, country)
dimension by (year, week)
measures ( 0 inventory , sale, receipts)
```

```
    rules automatic order(
        inventory [year, week ] order by year,  week =
                    nvl(inventory [cv(year),  cv(week)-1 ] ,0)
                  - sale[cv(year),  cv(week) ] +
                  + receipts [cv(year), cv(week) ]
    )
)   where year=2000 and country='Australia' and product='Xtend Memory'
/
```

```
---------------------------------------------------------------------
|Id |Operation                              |Name              | Pstart| Pstop|
---------------------------------------------------------------------
| 0 |SELECT STATEMENT                       |                  |       |      |
|*1 | VIEW                                  |                  |       |      |
| 2 |  SQL MODEL ACYCLIC                    |                  |       |      |
| 3 |   TABLE ACCESS BY GLOBAL INDEX ROWID|SALES_FACT_PART     | ROWID | ROWID|
|*4 |    INDEX RANGE SCAN                   |SALES_FACT_PART_I1|       |      |
---------------------------------------------------------------------
```

```
Predicate Information (identified by operation id):r
---------------------------------------------------
   1 - filter("YEAR"=2000)
   4 - access("COUNTRY"='Australia' AND "PRODUCT"='Xtend Memory')
```

Subquery Factoring

In a business setting, requirements are complex and multiple levels of aggregation are often needed. When writing complex queries, you can often combine subquery factoring with the MODEL clause to prevent a SQL statement from becoming unmanageably complex.

Listing 9-34 provides one such example. Two MODEL clauses are coded in the same SQL statement. The first MODEL clause is embedded within a view that is the result of a subquery being factored into the WITH clause. The main query uses that view to pivot the value of the sale column from the prior year. The output shows that the prior week's sales are pivoted into the current week's row.

Listing 9-34. More Indexing with SQL Access in Mind

```
with t1 as (
  select  product, country, year, week, inventory, sale, receipts
  from sales_fact sf
  where country in ('Australia') and product='Xtend Memory'
  model return updated rows
  partition by (product, country)
  dimension by (year, week)
  measures ( 0 inventory , sale, receipts)
  rules automatic order(
      inventory [year, week ] order by year, week =
                  nvl(inventory [cv(year), cv(week)-1 ] ,0)
                - sale[cv(year), cv(week) ] +
                + receipts [cv(year), cv(week) ]
  )
)
```

```
select product, country, year, week , inventory,
sale, receipts, prev_sale
from t1
model return updated rows
partition by (product, country)
dimension by (year, week)
measures (inventory, sale, receipts,0 prev_sale)
rules sequential order (
  prev_sale [ year, week ] order by year, week =
              nvl (sale [ cv(year) -1, cv(week)],0 )
)
order by 1,2,3,4
/
```

PRODUCT	COUNTRY	YEAR	WEEK	INVENTORY	SALE	RECEIPTS	PREV_SALE
Xtend Memory	Australia	1998	1	8.88	58.15	67.03	0
...							
Xtend Memory	Australia	1999	1	2.676	53.52	56.196	58.15
...							
Xtend Memory	Australia	2000	1	-11.675	46.7	35.025	53.52
...							
Xtend Memory	Australia	2001	1	4.634	92.26	96.894	46.7

Summary

I can't stress enough the importance of thinking in terms of sets when writing SQL statements. Many SQL statements can be rewritten concisely using the MODEL clause discussed in this chapter. As an added bonus, rewritten queries such as model or analytic functions can perform much better than traditional SQL statements. A combination of subquery factoring, model, and analytic functions features can be used effectively to implement complex requirements.

CHAPTER 10

Subquery Factoring

You may not be familiar with the term *subquery factoring*. Prior to the release of Oracle 11gR2, the official Oracle documentation barely mentions it, providing just a brief synopsis of its use, a couple of restrictions, and a single example. If I instead refer to the WITH clause of the SELECT statement, you probably know immediately what I mean, because these terms are more recognizable. Both terms are used in this chapter.

In Oracle 11gR2 (version 11.2), the WITH clause was enhanced with the ability to recurse; that is, the factored subquery is allowed to call itself within some limitation. The value of this may not be readily apparent. If you have used the CONNECT BY clause to create hierarchical queries, you can appreciate that recursive subqueries allow the same functionality to be implemented in an ANSI standard format.

If the term *subquery factoring* is not known to you, perhaps you have heard of the ANSI standard term *common table expression* (commonly called *CTE*). Common table expressions were first specified in the 1999 ANSI SQL Standard. For some reason, Oracle has chosen to obfuscate this name. Other database vendors refer to common table expressions, so perhaps Oracle chose subquery factoring just to be different.

Standard Usage

One of the most useful features of the WITH clause when it was first introduced was to clean up complex SQL queries. When a large number of tables and columns are involved in a query, it can become difficult to follow the flow of data through the query. Via the use of subquery factoring, a query can be made more understandable by moving some of the complexity away from the main body of the query.

The query in Listing 10-1 generates a cross-tab report using the PIVOT operator. The formatting helps make the SQL somewhat readable, but there is quite a bit going on here. The innermost query is creating a set of aggregates on key sales columns, whereas the next most outer query simply provides column names that are presented to the PIVOT operator, where the final values of sales by channel and quarter for each product are generated.

Listing 10-1. Cross-tab without Subquery Factoring

```
select *
from (
    select /*+ gather_plan_statistics */
        product
        , channel
        , quarter
        , country
        , quantity_sold
```

```
    from
    (
        select
            prod_name product
            , country_name country
            , channel_id channel
            , substr(calendar_quarter_desc, 6,2) quarter
            , sum(amount_sold) amount_sold
            , sum(quantity_sold) quantity_sold
        from
            sh.sales
            join sh.times on times.time_id = sales.time_id
            join sh.customers on customers.cust_id = sales.cust_id
            join sh.countries on countries.country_id = customers.country_id
            join sh.products on products.prod_id = sales.prod_id
        group by
            prod_name
            , country_name
            , channel_id
            , substr(calendar_quarter_desc, 6, 2)
    )
) PIVOT (
    sum(quantity_sold)
    FOR (channel, quarter) IN
    (
        (5, '02') AS CATALOG_Q2,
        (4, '01') AS INTERNET_Q1,
        (4, '04') AS INTERNET_Q4,
        (2, '02') AS PARTNERS_Q2,
        (9, '03') AS TELE_Q3
    )
)
order by product, country;
```

Now let's use the WITH clause to break the query into byte-size chunks that are easier to comprehend. The SQL has been rewritten in Listing 10-2 using the WITH clause to create three subfactored queries: sales_countries, top_sales, and sales_rpt. Notice that both the top_sales and sales_rpt subqueries refer to other subqueries by name, as if they are a table or a view. By choosing names that make the intent of each subquery easy to follow, the readability of the SQL is improved. For instance, the subquery name sales_countries refers to the countries in which the sales took place, top_sales collects the sales data, and the sales_rpt subquery aggregates the data. The results of the sales_rpt subquery are used in the main query, which answers the question "What is the breakdown of sales by product and country per quarter?" If you were not told the intent of the SQL in Listing 10-1, it would take some time to discern its purpose; on the other hand, the structure of the SQL in Listing 10-2 with subfactored queries makes it easier to understand the intent of the code.

In addition, the statements associated directly with the PIVOT operator are in the same section of the SQL statement at the bottom, further enhancing readability.

Listing 10-2. Cross-tab with Subquery Factoring

```
with
sales_countries as (
   select /*+ gather_plan_statistics */
      cu.cust_id
      , co.country_name
   from  sh.countries co, sh.customers cu
   where cu.country_id = co.country_id
),
top_sales as (
   select
      p.prod_name
      , sc.country_name
      , s.channel_id
      , t.calendar_quarter_desc
      , s.amount_sold
      , s.quantity_sold
   from
      sh.sales s
      join sh.times t on t.time_id = s.time_id
      join sh.customers c on c.cust_id = s.cust_id
      join sales_countries sc on sc.cust_id = c.cust_id
      join sh.products p on p.prod_id = s.prod_id
),
sales_rpt as (
   select
      prod_name product
      , country_name country
      , channel_id channel
      , substr(calendar_quarter_desc, 6,2) quarter
      , sum(amount_sold) amount_sold
      , sum(quantity_sold) quantity_sold
   from top_sales
   group by
      prod_name
      , country_name
      , channel_id
      , substr(calendar_quarter_desc, 6, 2)
)
select * from
(
   select product, channel, quarter, country, quantity_sold
   from sales_rpt
) pivot (
   sum(quantity_sold)
   for (channel, quarter) in
   (
      (5, '02') as catalog_q2,
      (4, '01') as internet_q1,
```

```
      (4, '04') as internet_q4,
      (2, '02') as partners_q2,
      (9, '03') as tele_q3
   )
)
order by product, country;
```

Although this is not an extremely complex SQL example, it does serve to illustrate the point of how the WITH clause can be used to make a statement more readable and easier to maintain. Large, complex queries can be made more understandable by using this technique.

WITH Using a PL/SQL Function

Oracle 12c introduced the ability to declare and define PL/SQL functions and procedures using the WITH clause. Once defined, you can reference the PL/SQL functions in the query in which you specify this clause (including any of its subqueries). Listing 10-3 walks through a simple example of how to create and use this new feature.

Listing 10-3. WITH Function Clause

```
SQL>WITH
  2   function calc_markup(p_markup number, p_price number) return number
  3   is
  4   begin
  5       return p_markup*p_price;
  6     end;
  7   select prod_name,
  8   prod_list_price cur_price,
  9   calc_markup(.05,prod_list_price) mup5,
 10   round(prod_list_price + calc_markup(.10,prod_list_price),2) new_price
 11   from sh.products;
 12   /
```

PROD_NAME	CUR_PRICE	MUP5	NEW_PRICE
5MP Telephoto Digital Camera	899.99	44.9995	989.99
17" LCD w/built-in HDTV Tuner	999.99	49.9995	1099.99
Envoy 256MB - 40GB	999.99	49.9995	1099.99
Y Box	299.99	14.9995	329.99
Mini DV Camcorder with 3.5" Swivel LCD	1099.99	54.9995	1209.99
...			
Finding Fido	12.99	.6495	14.29
Adventures with Numbers	11.99	.5995	13.19
Extension Cable	7.99	.3995	8.79
Xtend Memory	20.99	1.0495	23.09

```
72 rows selected.

Elapsed: 00:00:00.02

-- Using a WITH function within an outer query block
```

```
SQL>SELECT prod_name, cur_price, mup5, new_price
  2  FROM (
  3  WITH
  4    function calc_markup(p_markup number, p_price number) return number
  5    is
  6    begin
  7      return p_markup*p_price;
  8    end;
  9  select  prod_name,
 10  prod_list_price cur_price,
 11  calc_markup(.05,prod_list_price) mup5,
 12  round(prod_list_price + calc_markup(.10,prod_list_price),2) new_price
from sh.products
)
WHERE cur_price < 1000
AND   new_price >= 1000 ;
 17  /
WITH
*
ERROR at line 3:
ORA-32034: unsupported use of WITH clause

Elapsed: 00:00:00.01
SQL>
SQL>SELECT /*+ WITH_PLSQL */ prod_name, cur_price, mup5, new_price
  2  FROM (
  3  WITH
  4    function calc_markup(p_markup number, p_price number) return number
  5    is
  6    begin
  7      return p_markup*p_price;
  8    end;
  9  select  prod_name,
 10  prod_list_price cur_price,
 11  calc_markup(.05,prod_list_price) mup5,
 12  round(prod_list_price + calc_markup(.10,prod_list_price),2) new_price
 13  from sh.products
)
 15  WHERE cur_price < 1000
 16  AND   new_price >= 1000 ;
 17  /
```

PROD_NAME	CUR_PRICE	MUP5	NEW_PRICE
17" LCD w/built-in HDTV Tuner	999.99	49.9995	1099.99
Envoy 256MB - 40GB	999.99	49.9995	1099.99

```
2 rows selected.

Elapsed: 00:00:00.02
```

To run the statement, you must use the forward slash (/), which resembles how you would execute an anonymous PL/SQL block. This example shows only a single function declaration, but you may create as many functions and/or procedures as you wish. As also shown, one problem you may face occurs when you wish to place the WITH function inside an outer query block. When the WITH function is not the first declaration before the top-level query, you get an "ORA-32034: unsupported use of WITH clause" error. Fortunately, you can use the WITH_PLSQL hint to correct the problem. The hint, however, enables you to specify only the WITH function as shown; it is not an optimizer hint in that it does not have any bearing on the optimizer's execution plan decisions.

Although this example is quite simple, imagine the possibilities of how you could use the WITH function clause. There are some expressions that are difficult to build without multiple steps, and you may have created user-defined PL/SQL functions that you use in your SQL statements. However, doing so requires that context switches must occur between the SQL and PL/SQL "engines" when your SQL statement is executed. These context switches incur overhead and can cause performance problems if used frequently. But now, with the advent of the WITH function clause in 12c, we have a construct built into the SQL language that can reduce or eliminate the need for user-defined PL/SQL functions and can allow you to do everything you need directly inline in your SQL statement.

Optimizing SQL

When a SQL query is designed or modified to take advantage of subquery factoring, there are some not-so-subtle changes that may take place when the optimizer creates an execution plan for the query. The following quote comes from the Oracle documentation in the *Oracle Database SQL Language Reference* (http://www.oracle.com/technetwork/indexes/documentation/index.html) for SELECT, under the subquery_factoring_clause heading: "The WITH query_name clause lets you assign a name to a subquery block. You can then reference the subquery block multiple places in the query by specifying query_name. Oracle Database optimizes the query by treating the query name as either an inline view or as a temporary table."

Notice that Oracle may treat the factored subquery as a temporary table. In queries in which a table is referenced more than once, this could be a distinct performance advantage, because Oracle can materialize result sets from the query, thereby avoiding performing some expensive database operations more than once. The caveat here is that it "could be" a distinct performance advantage. Keep in mind that materializing the result set requires creating a temporary table and inserting the rows into it. Doing so may be of value if the same result set is referred to many times, or it may be a big performance penalty.

Testing Execution Plans

When examining the execution plans for subfactored queries, it may not be readily apparent whether Oracle is choosing the best execution plan. It may seem that the use of the INLINE or MATERIALIZE[1] hint would result in better performing SQL. In some cases it may, but the use of these hints needs to be tested and considered in the context of overall application performance.

The need to test for optimum query performance can be illustrated by a report that management has requested. The report must show the distribution of customers by country and income level, showing only those countries and income levels that make up 1 percent or more of the entire customer base. A country and income level should also be reported if the number of customers in an income level bracket is greater than or equal to 25 percent of all customers in that income bracket.[2]

---

[1]Although well known in the Oracle community for some time now, the INLINE and MATERIALIZE hints remain undocumented by Oracle.

[2]If you run these examples on different versions of Oracle, the output may appear differently because the test data sometimes change with versions of Oracle.

The query in Listing 10-4 is the end result.[3] The cust factored subquery has been retained from previous queries. New are the subqueries in the HAVING clause; these are used to enforce the rules stipulated for the report.

Listing 10-4. WITH and MATERIALIZE

```
 1  with cust as (
 2   select /*+ materialize gather_plan_statistics */
 3     b.cust_income_level,
 4     a.country_name
 5   from sh.customers b
 6   join sh.countries a on a.country_id = b.country_id
 7  )
 8  select country_name, cust_income_level, count(country_name) country_cust_count
 9  from cust c
10  having count(country_name) >
11   (
12     select count(*) * .01
13     from cust c2
14   )
15   or count(cust_income_level) >=
16   (
17     select median(income_level_count)
18     from (
19       select cust_income_level, count(*) *.25 income_level_count
20       from cust
21       group by cust_income_level
22     )
23   )
24  group by country_name, cust_income_level
25  order by 1,2;
```

COUNTRY	INCOME LEVEL	CUSTOMER COUNT
France	E: 90,000 - 109,999	585
France	F: 110,000 - 129,999	651
...		
United States of America	H: 150,000 - 169,999	1857
United States of America	I: 170,000 - 189,999	1395
...		

35 rows selected.

Elapsed: 00:00:01.37

---

[3]The MATERIALIZE hint was used to ensure that the example works as expected, given that you may be testing on a different version or patch level of Oracle. On the test system I used, this was the default action by Oracle.

Statistics

```
   1854  recursive calls
    307  db block gets
   2791  consistent gets
   1804  physical reads
    672  redo size
   4609  bytes sent via SQL*Net to client
    700  bytes received via SQL*Net from client
     18  SQL*Net roundtrips to/from client
     38  sorts (memory)
      0  sorts (disk)
     35  rows processed
```

Id	Operation	Name	Starts	E-Rows	A-Rows
0	SELECT STATEMENT		1		35
1	TEMP TABLE TRANSFORMATION		1		35
2	LOAD AS SELECT		1		0
* 3	HASH JOIN		1	55500	55500
4	TABLE ACCESS FULL	COUNTRIES	1	23	23
5	TABLE ACCESS FULL	CUSTOMERS	1	55500	55500
* 6	FILTER		1		35
7	SORT GROUP BY		1	18	209
8	VIEW		1	55500	55500
9	TABLE ACCESS FULL	SYS_TEMP_OF	1	55500	55500
10	SORT AGGREGATE		1	1	1
11	VIEW		1	55500	55500
12	TABLE ACCESS FULL	SYS_TEMP_OF	1	55500	55500
13	SORT GROUP BY		1	1	1
14	VIEW		1	11	13
15	SORT GROUP BY		1	11	13
16	VIEW		1	55500	55500
17	TABLE ACCESS FULL	SYS_TEMP_OF	1	55500	55500

When executing[4] the SQL, all appears as you expect, then you check the execution plan and find that the join of the customers and countries tables underwent a TEMP TABLE TRANSFORMATION, and the rest of the query was satisfied by using the temporary table sys_temp_of.[5] At this point, you might rightly wonder if the execution plan chosen was a reasonable one. This can be tested easily, thanks to the MATERIALIZED and INLINE hints.

By using the INLINE hint, Oracle can be instructed to satisfy all portions of the query without using a TEMP TABLE TRANSFORMATION. The results of doing so are shown in Listing 10-5. Only the relevant portion of the SQL that has changed is shown here (the rest is identical to that in Listing 10-4).

---

[4]Initial executions are run after first flushing shared_pool and buffer_cache.
[5]The actual table name was sys_temp_0fd9d66a2_453290, but was shortened in the listing for formatting purposes.

Listing 10-5. WITH and INLINE Hint

```
1  with cust as (
2     select /*+ inline gather_plan_statistics */
3        b.cust_income_level,
4        a.country_name
5     from sh.customers b
6     join sh.countries a on a.country_id = b.country_id
7  )
...
```

COUNTRY	INCOME LEVEL	COUNT
France	E: 90,000 - 109,999	585
France	F: 110,000 - 129,999	651
...		
United States of America	I: 170,000 - 189,999	1395
United States of America	J: 190,000 - 249,999	1390

...

35 rows selected.

Elapsed: 00:00:00.62

Statistics

```
      1501  recursive calls
         0  db block gets
      4758  consistent gets
      1486  physical reads
         0  redo size
      4609  bytes sent via SQL*Net to client
       700  bytes received via SQL*Net from client
        18  SQL*Net roundtrips to/from client
        34  sorts (memory)
         0  sorts (disk)
        35  rows processed
```

Id	Operation	Name	Starts	E-Rows	A-Rows
0	SELECT STATEMENT		1		35
* 1	FILTER		1		35
2	SORT GROUP BY		1	20	236
* 3	HASH JOIN		1	55500	55500
4	TABLE ACCESS FULL	COUNTRIES	1	23	23
5	TABLE ACCESS FULL	CUSTOMERS	1	55500	55500
6	SORT AGGREGATE		1	1	1
* 7	HASH JOIN		1	55500	55500
8	INDEX FULL SCAN	COUNTRIES_PK	1	23	23
9	TABLE ACCESS FULL	CUSTOMERS	1	55500	55500
10	SORT GROUP BY		1	1	1

11	VIEW			1	12	13
12	SORT GROUP BY			1	12	13
* 13	HASH JOIN			1	55500	55500
14	INDEX FULL SCAN	COUNTRIES_PK		1	23	23
15	TABLE ACCESS FULL	CUSTOMERS		1	55500	55500

From the execution plan in Listing 10-5, you can see that three full scans were performed on the customers table and one full scan on the countries table. Two of the executions against the cust subquery required only the information in the COUNTRIES_PK index, so a full scan of the index was performed rather than a full scan of the table, saving time and resources. In this example, the query that used the MATERIALIZE hint had 2791 consistent gets whereas the second had 4758. However, it's also important to note there was another difference: The second query used less resources for redo generation: 0 vs. 672. When deciding which format works best for your environment, you must consider carefully the decreased CPU resulting from lower consistent gets against the higher redo required to materialize the temporary table.

What may be surprising is that the execution using full table scans took 0.75 second, which is about 100 percent faster than when a temporary table is used. Of course, the cache was cold for both queries, because both the buffer cache and the shared pool were flushed prior to running each query. From these simple tests you might feel safe using the INLINE hint

in this bit of code, convinced that it will perform well based on the amount of physical IO required in the first test outweighing the memory usage and the logical IO required for the second test. If you know for sure that the size of the datasets will not grow and that the system load will remain fairly constant, using the INLINE hint in this query is probably a good idea. The problem, however, is that data are rarely static; often, data grow to a larger size than originally intended when developing a query. In this event, retesting these queries is in order to determine whether the use of the INLINE hint is still valid.

Testing the Effects of Query Changes

Even as data do not remain static, SQL is not always static. Sometimes requirements change, so code must be modified. What if the requirements changed for the examples in Listings 10-4 and 10-5? Would minor changes invalidate the use of the hints embedded in the SQL? This is probably something worth investigating, so let's do so.

Previously, we were reporting on income brackets when the count of them for any country was greater than or equal to 25 percent of the total global count for that bracket. Now we are asked to include an income bracket if it is among those income brackets the number of which is greater than the median, based on the number of customers per bracket. This SQL is seen in Listing 10-6. Notice that the INLINE hint has been left in. So now there's an additional full table scan and index scan compared with the execution plan in Listing 10-5. Although the elapsed time has increased, it still seems reasonable.

Listing 10-6. Modified Income Search: INLINE

```
 1  with cust as (
 2   select /*+ inline gather_plan_statistics */
 3     b.cust_income_level,
 4     a.country_name
 5   from sh.customers b
 6   join sh.countries a on a.country_id = b.country_id
 7  ),
 8  median_income_set as (
 9   select /*+ inline */ cust_income_level, count(*) income_level_count
10   from cust
```

```
11    group by cust_income_level
12    having count(cust_income_level) > (
13       select median(income_level_count) income_level_count
14       from (
15          select cust_income_level, count(*) income_level_count
16          from cust
17          group by cust_income_level
18       )
19    )
20  )
21  select country_name, cust_income_level, count(country_name) country_cust_count
22  from cust c
23  having count(country_name) >
24    (
25       select count(*) * .01
26       from cust c2
27    )
28    or cust_income_level in ( select mis.cust_income_level from median_income_set mis)
29  group by country_name, cust_income_level;
```

COUNTRY	INCOME LEVEL	CUSTOMER COUNT
Argentina	D: 70,000 - 89,999	25
Argentina	E: 90,000 - 109,999	39
...		
United States of America	K: 250,000 - 299,999	1062
United States of America	L: 300,000 and above	982

123 rows selected.

Elapsed: 00:00:01.26

Statistics

```
      1524  recursive calls
         0  db block gets
     23362  consistent gets
      1486  physical reads
         0  redo size
     15570  bytes sent via SQL*Net to client
      1195  bytes received via SQL*Net from client
        63  SQL*Net roundtrips to/from client
         3  sorts (memory)
         0  sorts (disk)
       123  rows processed
```

```
-------------------------------------------------------------------
| Id  | Operation                 | Name          |Starts|E-Rows|A-Rows |
-------------------------------------------------------------------
|   0 | SELECT STATEMENT          |               |    1|      |   123 |
|*  1 |  FILTER                   |               |    1|      |   123 |
|   2 |   SORT GROUP BY           |               |    1|   20|   236 |
|*  3 |    HASH JOIN              |               |    1| 55500| 55500 |
|   4 |     TABLE ACCESS FULL     | COUNTRIES     |    1|   23|    23 |
|   5 |     TABLE ACCESS FULL     | CUSTOMERS     |    1| 55500| 55500 |
|   6 |   SORT AGGREGATE          |               |    1|    1|     1 |
|*  7 |    HASH JOIN              |               |    1| 55500| 55500 |
|   8 |     INDEX FULL SCAN       | COUNTRIES_PK  |    1|   23|    23 |
|   9 |     TABLE ACCESS FULL     | CUSTOMERS     |    1| 55500| 55500 |
|* 10 |  FILTER                   |               |   13|      |     6 |
|  11 |   HASH GROUP BY           |               |   13|    1|   133 |
|* 12 |    HASH JOIN              |               |   13| 55500|  721K |
|  13 |     INDEX FULL SCAN       | COUNTRIES_PK  |   13|   23|   299 |
|  14 |     TABLE ACCESS FULL     | CUSTOMERS     |   13| 55500|  721K |
|  15 |   SORT GROUP BY           |               |    1|    1|     1 |
|  16 |    VIEW                   |               |    1|   12|    13 |
|  17 |     SORT GROUP BY         |               |    1|   12|    13 |
|* 18 |      HASH JOIN            |               |    1| 55500| 55500 |
|  19 |       INDEX FULL SCAN     | COUNTRIES_PK  |    1|   23|    23 |
|  20 |       TABLE ACCESS FULL   | CUSTOMERS     |    1| 55500| 55500 |
-------------------------------------------------------------------
```

Now that there's an additional table scan and index scan, how do you think the performance of this query fares if temporary table transformations are allowed to take place? The results can be seen in Listing 10-7.

Listing 10-7. Modified Income Search: MATERIALIZE

```
1  with cust as (
2   select /*+ materialize gather_plan_statistics */
3     b.cust_income_level,
4     a.country_name
5   from sh.customers b
6   join sh.countries a on a.country_id = b.country_id
7  ),
...
```

COUNTRY	INCOME LEVEL	CUSTOMER COUNT
Argentina	D: 70,000 - 89,999	25
Argentina	E: 90,000 - 109,999	39
...		
United States of America	K: 250,000 - 299,999	1062
United States of America	L: 300,000 and above	982

123 rows selected.

Elapsed: 00:00:00.87

```
Statistics
----------------------------------------------------------------
       2001  recursive calls
        324  db block gets
       3221  consistent gets
       1822  physical reads
       1244  redo size
      15570  bytes sent via SQL*Net to client
       1195  bytes received via SQL*Net from client
         63  SQL*Net roundtrips to/from client
         38  sorts (memory)
          0  sorts (disk)
        123  rows processed
```

Id	Operation	Name	Starts	E-Rows	A-Rows
0	SELECT STATEMENT		1		123
1	TEMP TABLE TRANSFORMATION		1		123
2	LOAD AS SELECT		1		0
* 3	HASH JOIN		1	55500	55500
4	TABLE ACCESS FULL	COUNTRIES	1	23	23
5	TABLE ACCESS FULL	CUSTOMERS	1	55500	55500
6	LOAD AS SELECT		1		0
* 7	FILTER		1		6
8	HASH GROUP BY		1	1	13
9	VIEW		1	55500	55500
10	TABLE ACCESS FULL	SYS_TEMP_OF	1	55500	55500
11	SORT GROUP BY		1	1	1
12	VIEW		1	12	13
13	SORT GROUP BY		1	12	13
14	VIEW		1	55500	55500
15	TABLE ACCESS FULL	SYS_TEMP_OF	1	55500	55500
* 16	FILTER		1		123
17	SORT GROUP BY		1	20	236
18	VIEW		1	55500	55500
19	TABLE ACCESS FULL	SYS_TEMP_OF	1	55500	55500
20	SORT AGGREGATE		1	1	1
21	VIEW		1	55500	55500
22	TABLE ACCESS FULL	SYS_TEMP_OF	1	55500	55500
* 23	VIEW		13	1	6
24	TABLE ACCESS FULL	SYS_TEMP_OF	13	1	63

Because there's that additional scan taking place in the modified version of the query, the overhead of logical IO becomes more apparent. It is significantly more efficient with this query to allow Oracle to perform table transformations, writing the results of the hash join to a temporary table on disk, where they can be reused throughout the query.

Seizing Other Optimization Opportunities

There are other opportunities when subquery factoring may be used to your advantage. If you are working on applications that were originally written several years ago, you may find that some of the SQL could use a bit of improvement based on the features offered by Oracle versions 9i and later. The query in Listing 10-8, for example, does exactly what it was asked to do, which is to find the average, minimum, and maximum costs for each product that was produced in the year 2000, with the costs calculated for each of the sale channels in which the product was sold. This SQL is not only difficult to read and hard to modify, but also it is somewhat inefficient.

Listing 10-8. Old SQL to Calculate Costs

```
 1  select /*+ gather_plan_statistics */
 2      substr(prod_name,1,30) prod_name
 3      , channel_desc
 4      , (
 5          select avg(c2.unit_cost)
 6          from sh.costs c2
 7          where c2.prod_id = c.prod_id and c2.channel_id = c.channel_id
 8          and c2.time_id between to_date('01/01/2000','mm/dd/yyyy')
 9           and to_date('12/31/2000')
10          ) avg_cost
11      , (
12          select min(c2.unit_cost)
13          from sh.costs c2
14          where c2.prod_id = c.prod_id and c2.channel_id = c.channel_id
15          and c2.time_id between to_date('01/01/2000','mm/dd/yyyy')
16           and to_date('12/31/2000')
17          ) min_cost
18      , (
19          select max(c2.unit_cost)
20          from sh.costs c2
21          where c2.prod_id = c.prod_id and c2.channel_id = c.channel_id
22          and c2.time_id between to_date('01/01/2000','mm/dd/yyyy')
23           and to_date('12/31/2000')
24          ) max_cost
25  from (
26      select distinct pr.prod_id, pr.prod_name, ch.channel_id, ch.channel_desc
27      from sh.channels ch
28          , sh.products pr
29          , sh.costs co
30      where ch.channel_id = co.channel_id
31          and co.prod_id = pr.prod_id
32          and co.time_id between to_date('01/01/2000','mm/dd/yyyy')
33           and to_date('12/31/2000')
34  ) c
35 order by prod_name, channel_desc;
```

PRODUCT	CHANNEL_DESC	AVG COST	MIN COST	MAX COST
1.44MB External 3.5" Diskette	Direct Sales	8.36	7.43	9.17
1.44MB External 3.5" Diskette	Internet	8.59	7.42	9.55
...				
Y Box	Internet	266.73	245.00	282.30
Y Box	Partners	272.62	242.79	293.68
sum		27,961.39	24,407.85	34,478.10

216 rows selected.
COLD CACHE Elapsed: 00:00:02.30
WARM CACHE Elapsed: 00:00:01.09

```
--------------------------------------------------------------------------------
| Id  | Operation                              |Name           |Starts|E-Rows|A-Rows |
--------------------------------------------------------------------------------
|   0 | SELECT STATEMENT                       |               |    1|      |   216 |
|   1 |  SORT AGGREGATE                        |               |  216|     1|   216 |
|*  2 |   FILTER                               |               |  216|      | 17373 |
|   3 |    PARTITION RANGE ITERATOR            |               |  216|    96| 17373 |
|*  4 |     TABLE ACCESS BY LOCAL INDEX ROWID  |COSTS          |  864|    96| 17373 |
|   5 |      BITMAP CONVERSION TO ROWIDS       |               |  864|      | 52119 |
|   6 |       BITMAP AND                       |               |  864|      |   840 |
|   7 |        BITMAP MERGE                    |               |  864|      |   864 |
|*  8 |         BITMAP INDEX RANGE SCAN        |COSTS_TIME_BIX |  864|      | 79056 |
|*  9 |        BITMAP INDEX SINGLE VALUE       |COSTS_PROD_BIX |  864|      |   840 |
|  10 |  SORT AGGREGATE                        |               |  216|     1|   216 |
|* 11 |   FILTER                               |               |  216|      | 17373 |
|  12 |    PARTITION RANGE ITERATOR            |               |  216|    96| 17373 |
|* 13 |     TABLE ACCESS BY LOCAL INDEX ROWID  |COSTS          |  864|    96| 17373 |
|  14 |      BITMAP CONVERSION TO ROWIDS       |               |  864|      | 52119 |
|  15 |       BITMAP AND                       |               |  864|      |   840 |
|  16 |        BITMAP MERGE                    |               |  864|      |   864 |
|* 17 |         BITMAP INDEX RANGE SCAN        |COSTS_TIME_BIX |  864|      | 79056 |
|* 18 |        BITMAP INDEX SINGLE VALUE       |COSTS_PROD_BIX |  864|      |   840 |
|  19 |  SORT AGGREGATE                        |               |  216|     1|   216 |
|* 20 |   FILTER                               |               |  216|      | 17373 |
|  21 |    PARTITION RANGE ITERATOR            |               |  216|    96| 17373 |
|* 22 |     TABLE ACCESS BY LOCAL INDEX ROWID  |COSTS          |  864|    96| 17373 |
|  23 |      BITMAP CONVERSION TO ROWIDS       |               |  864|      | 52119 |
|  24 |       BITMAP AND                       |               |  864|      |   840 |
|  25 |        BITMAP MERGE                    |               |  864|      |   864 |
|* 26 |         BITMAP INDEX RANGE SCAN        |COSTS_TIME_BIX |  864|      | 79056 |
|* 27 |        BITMAP INDEX SINGLE VALUE       |COSTS_PROD_BIX |  864|      |   840 |
|  28 |  SORT ORDER BY                         |               |    1| 20640|   216 |
|  29 |   VIEW                                 |               |    1| 20640|   216 |
|  30 |    HASH UNIQUE                         |               |    1| 20640|   216 |
|* 31 |     FILTER                             |               |    1|      | 17373 |
|* 32 |      HASH JOIN                         |               |    1| 20640| 17373 |
|  33 |       TABLE ACCESS FULL                |PRODUCTS       |    1|    72|    72 |
|* 34 |       HASH JOIN                        |               |    1| 20640| 17373 |
|  35 |        TABLE ACCESS FULL               |CHANNELS       |    1|     5|     5 |
|  36 |        PARTITION RANGE ITERATOR        |               |    1| 20640| 17373 |
|* 37 |         TABLE ACCESS FULL              |COSTS          |    4| 20640| 17373 |
--------------------------------------------------------------------------------
```

■ **Note** In several of the following listings, you will see an elapsed time for COLD CACHE and WARM CACHE. The COLD CACHE time is the first execution of the statement immediately following a flush of both the buffer cache and the shared pool.

Examining the output of Listing 10-8, note that the elapsed execution time on a cold cache is 2.30 seconds, and 1.09 seconds on a warm cache. These times don't seem all that bad at first; but, when you examine the execution plan, you find that this query can be improved on from a performance perspective as well as a readability perspective.

The starts column is telling. Each execution against the costs table is executed 864 times. This is because there are 216 rows produced by a join between channels, products, and costs. Also, the costs table is queried in four separate places for the same information. By using subquery factoring, not only can this SQL be cleaned up and made easier to read, but also it can be made more efficient.

As seen in Listing 10-9, you can start by putting the begin_date and end_date columns in a separate query bookends, leaving only one place that the values need to be set. The data for products are placed in the prodmaster subquery. Although this bit of the SQL worked fine as a subquery in the FROM clause, the readability of the SQL statement as a whole is greatly improved by moving it to a factored subquery.

Listing 10-9. Old SQL Refactored Using the WITH Clause

```
 1  with bookends as (
 2      select
 3        to_date('01/01/2000','mm/dd/yyyy') begin_date
 4          ,to_date('12/31/2000','mm/dd/yyyy') end_date
 5      from dual
 6  ),
 7  prodmaster as (
 8      select distinct pr.prod_id, pr.prod_name, ch.channel_id, ch.channel_desc
 9      from sh.channels ch
10          , sh.products pr
11          , sh.costs co
12      where ch.channel_id = co.channel_id
13          and co.prod_id = pr.prod_id
14          and co.time_id between (select begin_date from bookends)
15           and (select end_date from bookends)
16  ),
17  cost_compare as (
18          select
19              prod_id
20            , channel_id
21            , avg(c2.unit_cost) avg_cost
22            , min(c2.unit_cost) min_cost
23            , max(c2.unit_cost) max_cost
24          from sh.costs c2
25          where c2.time_id between (select begin_date from bookends)
26           and (select end_date from bookends)
27          group by c2.prod_id, c2.channel_id
28  )
29  select /*+ gather_plan_statistics */
30      substr(pm.prod_name,1,30) prod_name
31    , pm.channel_desc
32    , cc.avg_cost
33    , cc.min_cost
34    , cc.max_cost
35  from prodmaster pm
36  join cost_compare cc on cc.prod_id = pm.prod_id
37      and cc.channel_id = pm.channel_id
38  order by pm.prod_name, pm.channel_desc;
```

```
PRODUCT                        CHANNEL_DESC         AVG COST   MIN COST   MAX COST
-----------------------------  -------------------  ---------  ---------  ---------
1.44MB External 3.5" Diskette  Direct Sales              8.36       7.43       9.17
1.44MB External 3.5" Diskette  Internet                  8.59       7.42       9.55

Y Box                          Internet                266.73     245.00     282.30
Y Box                          Partners                272.62     242.79     293.68
                                                    ---------  ---------  ---------
sum                                                 27,961.39  24,407.85  34,478.10

216 rows selected.

COLD CACHE Elapsed: 00:00:01.48
WARM CACHE Elapsed: 00:00:00.17
```

```
--------------------------------------------------------------------------------
| Id |Operation                               |Name           |Starts|E-Rows|A-Rows|
--------------------------------------------------------------------------------
|   0|SELECT STATEMENT                         |               |    1|       |   216|
|   1| SORT ORDER BY                           |               |    1| 17373|   216|
|*  2|  HASH JOIN                              |               |    1| 17373|   216|
|   3|   VIEW                                  |               |    1|   216|   216|
|   4|    HASH GROUP BY                        |               |    1|   216|   216|
|   5|     PARTITION RANGE ITERATOR            |               |    1| 17373| 17373|
|   6|      TABLE ACCESS BY LOCAL INDEX ROWID  |COSTS          |    4| 17373| 17373|
|   7|       BITMAP CONVERSION TO ROWIDS       |               |    4|       | 17373|
|*  8|        BITMAP INDEX RANGE SCAN          |COSTS_TIME_BIX |    4|       |   366|
|   9|         FAST DUAL                       |               |    1|     1|     1|
|  10|         FAST DUAL                       |               |    1|     1|     1|
|  11|   VIEW                                  |               |    1| 17373|   216|
|  12|    HASH UNIQUE                          |               |    1| 17373|   216|
|* 13|     HASH JOIN                           |               |    1| 17373| 17373|
|  14|      TABLE ACCESS FULL                  |PRODUCTS       |    1|    72|    72|
|  15|      MERGE JOIN                         |               |    1| 17373| 17373|
|  16|       TABLE ACCESS BY INDEX ROWID       |CHANNELS       |    1|     5|     4|
|  17|        INDEX FULL SCAN                  |CHANNELS_PK    |    1|     5|     4|
|* 18|       SORT JOIN                         |               |    4| 17373| 17373|
|  19|        PARTITION RANGE ITERATOR         |               |    1| 17373| 17373|
|  20|         TABLE ACCESS BY LOCAL INDEX RO  |COSTS          |    4| 17373| 17373|
|  21|          BITMAP CONVERSION TO ROWIDS    |               |    4|       | 17373|
|* 22|           BITMAP INDEX RANGE SCAN       |COSTS_TIME_BIX |    4|       |   366|
|  23|            FAST DUAL                    |               |    1|     1|     1|
|  24|            FAST DUAL                    |               |    1|     1|     1|
--------------------------------------------------------------------------------
```

The calculations for the average, minimum, and maximum costs are replaced with a single subquery called cost_compare. Last, the SQL that joins the prodmaster and cost_compare subqueries is added. The structure of the SQL is now much easier on the eyes and the overworked developer's brain. It's also simpler for the DBA to understand. The DBA will be especially happy with the execution statistics.

Where the old SQL queried the costs table and costs_time_bix index several hundred times, the new SQL queries each only eight times. This is quite an improvement, and it shows in the elapsed times. The query time on a cold cache is 1.48 seconds, about 25 percent better than the old SQL. On a warm cache, however, the refactored SQL really shines, running at 0.17 second whereas the old SQL managed only 1.09 seconds.

Applying Subquery Factoring to PL/SQL

We discussed the new 12c WITH PL/SQL function earlier, but there are other ways that PL/SQL can present golden opportunities for optimization using subquery factoring. Something that most of us have done at one time or another is to write a PL/SQL routine when we cannot figure out how to do what we want in a single SQL query. Sometimes it can be very difficult to capture everything in a single statement. It's often just easier to think procedurally rather than in sets of data, and just write some code to do what we need. As you gain experience, you will rely less and less on thinking in terms of "How would I code this in PL/SQL?" and will rely more along the lines of "How do I capture this problem in a single SQL statement?" The more advanced features that Oracle has packed into SQL can help as well.

Here's an example. You've been asked to create a report with the following criteria:

- Only include customers who have purchased products in at least three different years.

- Compute total aggregate sales per customer, broken down by product category.

At first, this doesn't seem too difficult, but you may struggle for a bit when trying to capture this in one SQL statement. So, you decide to use a PL/SQL routine to get the needed data. The results may be similar to those in Listing 10-10. The logic is simple. Find all customers that fit the criteria and store their IDs in a temporary table. Then, loop through the newly saved customer IDs and find all their sales, sum them up, and add them to another temporary table. The results are then joined to the customers and products tables to generate the report.

Listing 10-10. PL/SQL to Generate Customer Report

```
SQL> create global temporary table cust3year ( cust_id number );
Table created.

SQL> create global temporary table sales3year(
  2      cust_id number ,
  3      prod_category varchar2(50),
  4      total_sale number
  5  )
  6  /
Table created.

SQL> begin
  2      execute immediate 'truncate table cust3year';
  3      execute immediate 'truncate table sales3year';
  4
  5      insert into cust3year
  6      select cust_id --, count(cust_years) year_count
  7      from (
  8              select distinct cust_id, trunc(time_id,'YEAR') cust_years
  9              from sh.sales
 10      )
 11      group by cust_id
 12      having count(cust_years) >= 3;
 13
 14      for crec in ( select cust_id from cust3year)
 15      loop
 16              insert into sales3year
 17              select s.cust_id,p.prod_category, sum(co.unit_price * s.quantity_sold)
 18              from sh.sales s
 19              join sh.products p on p.prod_id = s.prod_id
```

```
20              join sh.costs co on co.prod_id = s.prod_id
21                   and co.time_id = s.time_id
22              join sh.customers cu on cu.cust_id = s.cust_id
23              where s.cust_id = crec.cust_id
24              group by s.cust_id, p.prod_category;
25      end loop;
26  end;
27  /
PL/SQL procedure successfully completed.
Elapsed: 00:01:17.48
SQL> break on report
SQL> compute sum of total_sale on report

SQL> select c3.cust_id, c.cust_last_name, c.cust_first_name, s.prod_category, s.total_sale
  2  from cust3year c3
  3  join sales3year s on s.cust_id = c3.cust_id
  4  join sh.customers c on c.cust_id = c3.cust_id
  5  order by 1,4;
```

CUST ID	LAST NAME	FIRST NAME	PRODUCT CATEGORY	TOTAL SALE
6	Charles	Harriett	Electronics	2,838.57
6	Charles	Harriett	Hardware	19,535.38
...				
50833	Gravel	Grover	Photo	15,469.64
50833	Gravel	Grover	Software/Other	9,028.87
sum				167,085,605.71

```
16018 rows selected.
```

The code in Listing 10-10 is fairly succinct and it only takes 1:17 minutes to run. This isn't too bad, is it? Although this is a nice little chunk of PL/SQL, take another look at it and think in terms of subfactored subqueries. The section that determines the correct customer IDs can be captured in a WITH clause fairly easily. Once the customers are identified, it is then a fairly easy job to use the results of the subquery to look up the needed sales, product, and customer information to create the report.

Listing 10-11 has a single SQL statement that captures what is done with the PL/SQL routine from Listing 10-10—without the need to create temporary tables manually or use PL/SQL loops. Should the use of temporary tables make for a more efficient query, Oracle does so automatically, or you can choose how Oracle preserves the subquery results via the INLINE and MATERIALIZE hints. It is more efficient, too, with an elapsed time of 6.13 seconds.

Listing 10-11. Use of the WITH Clause to Generate the Customer Report

```
1  with custyear as (
2    select cust_id, extract(year from time_id) sales_year
3    from sh.sales
4    where extract(year from time_id) between 1998 and 2002
5    group by cust_id,  extract(year from time_id)
6  ),
7  custselect as (
8    select distinct cust_id
9    from (
```

```
10        select cust_id, count(*) over ( partition by cust_id) year_count
11        from custyear
12    )
13    where  year_count >= 3 -- 3 or more years as a customer during period
14    )
15    select cu.cust_id, cu.cust_last_name, cu.cust_first_name, p.prod_category,
sum(co.unit_price * s.quantity_sold) total_sale
16    from custselect cs
17    join sh.sales s on s.cust_id = cs.cust_id
18    join sh.products p on p.prod_id = s.prod_id
19    join sh.costs co on co.prod_id = s.prod_id
20      and co.time_id = s.time_id
21    join sh.customers cu on cu.cust_id = cs.cust_id
22    group by cu.cust_id, cu.cust_last_name, cu.cust_first_name, p.prod_category
23    order by cu.cust_id;
```

CUST ID	LAST NAME	FIRST NAME	PRODUCT CATEGORY	TOTAL SALE
6	Charles	Harriett	Electronics	2,838.57
6	Charles	Harriett	Hardware	19,535.38
...				
50833	Gravel	Grover	Photo	15,469.64
50833	Gravel	Grover	Software/Other	9,028.87
				----------------
sum				167,085,605.71

16018 rows selected.

Elapsed: 00:00:06.13

The WITH clause in Listing 10-11 actually uses two subqueries that can be combined into a single query, but I thought it easier to read when they are broken into two queries. Notice the use of the EXTRACT() function; it simplifies comparing years by extracting the year from a date and converting it to an integer.

The SQL examples in this section of the chapter are not meant to be tuning exercises, but merely demonstrations that show how subquery factoring may be used. When refactoring legacy SQL to take advantage of the WITH clause, be sure to test the results. Subquery factoring can be used to organize some queries better, and in some cases can even be used as an optimization tool. Learning to use it adds another tool to your Oracle toolbox.

EXPERIMENT WITH SUBQUERY FACTORING

Included in this chapter are two scripts in the Exercises folder that you may want to experiment with. These scripts both run against the SH demo schema.

- Exercises/I_10_exercise_1.sql

- Exercises/I_10_exercise_2.sql

Run these scripts with both the MATERIALIZE and INLINE hints to compare performance. In the tsales subquery, a WHERE clause limits the data returned to a single year. Comment out the WHERE clause and run the queries again. How does the efficiency of the two hints compare now? Would you feel comfortable using these hints when the size of the data set is set at runtime by user input?

Recursive Subqueries

Beginning in Oracle 11.2, *recursive subquery factoring* (RSF for the remainder of this chapter) was added. As you can probably guess, the ANSI name for this feature is *recursive common table expression*. Regardless of what you call it, Oracle has had a similar feature for a very long time in the form of the CONNECT BY[6] clause of the SELECT statement. This feature has been enhanced in Oracle 11gR2.

A CONNECT BY Example

Let's begin by looking at a traditional CONNECT BY query such as that in Listing 10-12. The emp inline view is used to join the employee and department tables, and then the single dataset is presented to the SELECT ... CONNECT BY statement. The PRIOR operator is used to match the current EMPLOYEE_ID to rows where this value is in the MANAGER_ID column. Doing so iteratively creates a recursive query.

Listing 10-12 contains a number of extra columns in the output to help explain how the PRIOR operator works. Let's take a look at the output beginning with the row for Lex De Haan. You can see that the employee_id for Lex is 102. The PRIOR operator finds all rows for which the manager_id is 102 and includes them under the hierarchy for Lex De Haan. The only row that meets these criteria is the one for Alexander Hunold, with an employee_id of 103. The process is then repeated for Alexander Hunold: Are there any rows for which the manager_id is 103? There are four rows found with a manager_id of 103—those for employees Valli Pattaballa, Diana Lorentz, Bruce Ernst, and David Austin—so these are included in the output below Alexander Hunold. Because there are no rows for which any of the employee_id values for these four employees appears as a manager_id, Oracle moves back up to a level for which the rows have not yet been processed (in this case, for Alberto Errazuriz) and continues on to the end until all rows have been processed.

Listing 10-12. Basic CONNECT BY

```
1  select lpad(' ', level*2-1,' ') || emp.emp_last_name emp_last_name
2    , emp.emp_first_name
3    , emp.employee_id
4    , emp.mgr_last_name, emp.mgr_first_name
5    , emp.manager_id
6    , department_name
7  from (
8    select /*+ inline gather_plan_statistics */
9      e.last_name emp_last_name, e.first_name emp_first_name
10     , e.employee_id, d.department_id
11     , e.manager_id, d.department_name
12     , es.last_name mgr_last_name, es.first_name mgr_first_name
13   from hr.employees e
14   left outer join hr.departments d on d.department_id = e.department_id
15   left outer join hr.employees es on es.employee_id = e.manager_id
16   ) emp
17   connect by prior emp.employee_id = emp.manager_id
18   start with emp.manager_id is null
19 order siblings by emp.emp_last_name;
```

---

[6]CONNECT BY was first available in Oracle version 2 or, in others words, from the very beginning.

EMP_LAST_NAME	EMP_FIRST_NAME	EMP ID	MGR_LAST_NAME	MGR_FIRST_NAME	MGR ID	DEPARTMENT
King	Steven	100				Executive
Cambrault	Gerald	148	King	Steven	100	Sales
Bates	Elizabeth	172	Cambrault	Gerald	148	Sales
Bloom	Harrison	169	Cambrault	Gerald	148	Sales
Fox	Tayler	170	Cambrault	Gerald	148	Sales
Kumar	Sundita	173	Cambrault	Gerald	148	Sales
Ozer	Lisa	168	Cambrault	Gerald	148	Sales
Smith	William	171	Cambrault	Gerald	148	Sales
De Haan	Lex	102	King	Steven	100	Executive
Hunold	Alexander	103	De Haan	Lex	102	IT
Austin	David	105	Hunold	Alexander	103	IT
Ernst	Bruce	104	Hunold	Alexander	103	IT
Lorentz	Diana	107	Hunold	Alexander	103	IT
Pataballa	Valli	106	Hunold	Alexander	103	IT
Errazuriz	Alberto	147	King	Steven	100	Sales
Ande	Sundar	166	Errazuriz	Alberto	147	Sales
Banda	Amit	167	Errazuriz	Alberto	147	Sales

...

107 rows selected.

The START WITH clause is instructed to begin with a value for which manager_id is null. Because this is an organizational hierarchy with a single person at the top of the hierarchy, this causes the query to start with Stephen King. As the chief executive officer, King does not have a manager, so the manager_id column is set to NULL for his row.

The level pseudocolumn holds the value for the depth of the recursion, allowing for a simple method to indent the output so that the organizational hierarchy is visible.

The Example Using an RSF

The example query on the employees table has been rewritten in Listing 10-13 to use RSF, in which the main subquery is emp_recurse. The anchor member in this case simply selects the topmost row in the hierarchy by selecting the only row where manager_id is null. This is equivalent to start with emp.manager_id is null in Listing 10-12. The recursive member references the defining query emp_recurse by joining it to emp query. This join is used to locate the row corresponding to each employee's manager, which is equivalent to connect by prior emp.employee_id = emp.manager_id in Listing 10-12. The results in Listing 10-13 are identical to those in Listing 10-12.

Listing 10-13. Basic Recursive Subquery Factoring

```
 1  with emp as (
 2    select /*+ inline gather_plan_statistics */
 3       e.last_name, e.first_name, e.employee_id, e.manager_id, d.department_name
 4    from hr.employees e
 5    left outer join hr.departments d on d.department_id = e.department_id
 6  ),
 7  emp_recurse (last_name,first_name,employee_id,manager_id,department_name,lvl) as (
 8    select e.last_name, e.first_name
 9      , e.employee_id, e.manager_id
10      , e.department_name, 1 as lvl
11    from emp e where e.manager_id is null
12    union all
13    select emp.last_name, emp.first_name
```

```
14    , emp.employee_id, emp.manager_id
15    ,emp.department_name, empr.lvl + 1 as lvl
16    from emp
17    join emp_recurse empr on empr.employee_id = emp.manager_id
18  )
19    search depth first by last_name set order1
20  select lpad(' ', lvl*2-1,' ') || er.last_name last_name
21    , er.first_name
22    , er.department_name
23 from emp_recurse er;
```

LAST_NAME	FIRST_NAME	DEPARTMENT
King	Steven	Executive
Cambrault	Gerald	Sales
Bates	Elizabeth	Sales
Bloom	Harrison	Sales
Fox	Tayler	Sales
Kumar	Sundita	Sales
Ozer	Lisa	Sales
Smith	William	Sales
De Haan	Lex	Executive
Hunold	Alexander	IT
Austin	David	IT
Ernst	Bruce	IT
Lorentz	Diana	IT
Pataballa	Valli	IT
Errazuriz	Alberto	Sales
Ande	Sundar	Sales
Banda	Amit	Sales
...		

```
107 rows selected.
```

Although the new RSF method may at first appear verbose, the basis of how it works is simpler to understand than CONNECT BY, and it allows for more complex queries. The recursive WITH clause requires two query blocks: the anchor member and the recursive member. These two query blocks must be combined with the UNION ALL set operator. The anchor member is the query prior to the UNION ALL, whereas the recursive member is the query that follows. The recursive member must reference the defining subquery; in doing so, it is recursive.

Restrictions on RSF

As you might imagine, the use of RSF is quite a bit more flexible than CONNECT BY. There are some restrictions on its use, however. Per the Oracle documentation for the SELECT statement, the following elements cannot be used in the recursive member of an RSF:

- The DISTINCT keyword or a GROUP BY clause

- The MODEL clause

- An aggregate function; however, analytic functions are permitted in the select list

- Subqueries that refer to query_name

- Outer joins that refer to query_name as the right table

Differences from CONNECT BY

There are several differences when using RSF compared with CONNECT BY, and some of them are apparent in Listing 10-13. You may have wondered what happened to the level pseudocolumn because it is missing in this query, replaced by the lvl column. I explain this a little later on. Also, notice that the columns returned by an RSF query must be specified in the query definition, as seen in line 7 of Listing 10-13. One more new feature is SEARCH DEPTH FIRST seen on line 19. The default search is BREADTH FIRST, which is not usually the output you want from a hierarchical query. Listing 10-14 shows the output when the SEARCH clause is not used or it is set to BREADTH FIRST. This search returns rows of all siblings at each level before returning any child rows. Specifying SEARCH DEPTH FIRST returns the rows in hierarchical order. The SET ORDER1 portion of the SEARCH clause sets the value of the order1 pseudocolumn to the value of the order in which the rows are returned, similar to what you might see with ROWNUM, but you get to name the column. This is also used in later examples.

Listing 10-14. Default BREADTH FIRST Search

```
...
      search breadth first by last_name set order1
select lpad(' ', lvl*2-1,' ') || er.last_name last_name
...
```

LAST_NAME	FIRST_NAME	DEPARTMENT_NAME
King	Steven	Executive
Cambrault	Gerald	Sales
De Haan	Lex	Executive
Errazuriz	Alberto	Sales
Fripp	Adam	Shipping
Hartstein	Michael	Marketing
Kaufling	Payam	Shipping
Kochhar	Neena	Executive
Mourgos	Kevin	Shipping
Partners	Karen	Sales
Raphaely	Den	Purchasing
Russell	John	Sales
Vollman	Shanta	Shipping
Weiss	Matthew	Shipping
Zlotkey	Eleni	Sales
Abel	Ellen	Sales
Ande	Sundar	Sales

```
...
```

Notice that the SEARCH clause, as it is used in Listings 10-13 and 10-14, specifies that the search be by last_name. This could also be by first_name, or by a column list, such as last_name,first_name. Doing so controls the order of the rows within each level. The SEARCH clause ends with SET ORDER1, which effectively adds the order1 pseudocolumn to the column list returned by the recursive subquery. You will see it used more in some of the following examples.

Duplicating CONNECT BY Functionality

As Oracle Database has progressed through several versions, the functionality of the CONNECT BY clause has progressed as well. There are a number of hierarchical query operators, pseudocolumns, and one function available to CONNECT BY that are not natively available to RSF. The functionality these provide, however, can be duplicated in RSF. The functionality may not mimic exactly what occurs when CONNECT BY is used, but it can likely be made to do what you need. The trick to getting what you want from RSF sometimes requires stepping away from the keyboard and thinking about the results you want to achieve, rather than thinking about how you are going to code it. It is amazing how the change in perspective helps you achieve the desired output easily from the SQL you write.

The operators and pseudocolumns for CONNECT BY are listed in Table 10-1. I go through each of these as needed, showing example usages for CONNECT BY, and then duplicating that functionality with RSF. Keep in mind that RSF is quite versatile, so TMTOWTDI (There's More Than One Way to Do It) is definitely in force. Feel free to experiment and find other methods to achieve the same results.

Table 10-1. *CONNECT BY Functions, Operators, and Pseudocolumns*

Type	Name	Purpose
Function	SYS_CONNECT_BY_PATH	Returns all ancestors for the current row.
Operator	CONNECT_BY_ROOT	Returns the value from a root row.
Operator	PRIOR	Used to indicate hierarchical query. Not needed in a recursive subquery.
Pseudocolumn	connect_by_iscycle	Detects cycles in the hierarchy.
Parameter	NOCYCLE	Used with CONNECT_BY_ISCYCLE. Parameter for CONNECT BY.
Pseudocolumn	connect_by_isleaf	Identifies leaf rows.
Pseudocolumn	level	Used to indicate level of depth in the hierarchy.

I also cover the SEARCH clause of RSF because it is instrumental in solving some problems.

The level Pseudocolumn

Let's start with the level pseudocolumn, which is used frequently in hierarchical queries to indent the output, creating a visual representation of the hierarchy. Listing 10-15 contains a simple example showing how level is generated. As the hierarchy increases in depth, level is incremented. Likewise, level is decremented when the hierarchy goes back a level.

Listing 10-15. The level Pseudocolumn

```
1  select lpad(' ', level*2-1,' ') || e.last_name last_name, level
2  from hr.employees e
3  connect by prior e.employee_id = e.manager_id
4  start with e.manager_id is null
5  order siblings by e.last_name;
```

```
LAST_NAME                   LEVEL
------------------------- ----------
King                          1
  Cambrault                   2
    Bates                     3
    Bloom                     3
    Fox                       3
    Kumar                     3
    Ozer                      3
    Smith                     3
  De Haan                     2
...

107 rows selected.
```

This can also be accomplished in RSF (see Listing 10-16), although it does require a little effort on your part. It may be somewhat surprising to see that this actually works. The value for lvl is never decremented, only incremented. Recall that the default search method for RSF is BREADTH FIRST. It is apparent that Oracle is processing the rows in sibling order, with the top of the hierarchy (King), followed by the child rows at the next level, continuing until the last row is reached. This behavior allows you to solve some other problems as well.

Listing 10-16. Create a lvl Column

```
1  with emp_recurse(employee_id,manager_id,last_name,lvl) as (
2    select e.employee_id, null, e.last_name, 1 as lvl
3    from hr.employees e
4    where e.manager_id is null
5    union all
6    select e1.employee_id, e1.manager_id, e1.last_name, e2.lvl + 1 as lvl
7    from hr.employees e1
8    join emp_recurse e2 on e2.employee_id= e1.manager_id
9  )
10 search depth first by last_name set last_name_order
11 select lpad(' ', r.lvl*2-1,' ') || r.last_name last_name, r.lvl
12 from emp_recurse r
13 order by last_name_order;
```

```
LAST_NAME                       LVL
------------------------- ----------
King                              1
   Cambrault                      2
     Bates                        3
     Bloom                        3
     Fox                          3
     Kumar                        3
     Ozer                         3
     Smith                        3
   De Haan                        2
...
107 rows selected.
```

The SYS_CONNECT_BY_PATH Function

The SYS_CONNECT_BY_PATH function is used to return the values that comprise the hierarchy up to the current row. It's best explained with an example, such as the one in Listing 10-17, In which the SYS_CONNECT_BY_PATH function is used to build a colon-delimited list of the hierarchy, complete from root to node.

Listing 10-17. SYS_CONNECT_BY_PATH

```
1  select lpad(' ',2*(level-1)) || e.last_name last_name
2    , sys_connect_by_path(last_name,':') path
3  from hr.employees e
4  start with e.manager_id is null
5  connect by prior e.employee_id = e.manager_id
6  order siblings by e.last_name;
```

```
LAST_NAME                   PATH
------------------------    -----------------------
King                        :King
  Cambrault                 :King:Cambrault
    Bates                   :King:Cambrault:Bates
    Bloom                   :King:Cambrault:Bloom
    Fox                     :King:Cambrault:Fox
    Kumar                   :King:Cambrault:Kumar
    Ozer                    :King:Cambrault:Ozer
    Smith                   :King:Cambrault:Smith
  De Haan                   :King:De Haan
...
107 rows selected.
```

Although the SYS_CONNECT_BY_PATH function is not available to RSF queries, this function can be duplicated using much the same method that was used to reproduce the level pseudocolumn. Rather than incrementing a counter, however, you now append to a string value. Listing 10-18 shows how this is done.

Listing 10-18. Build Your Own SYS_CONNECT_BY_PATH

```
 1  with emp_recurse(employee_id,manager_id,last_name,lvl,path) as (
 2   select e.employee_id, null, e.last_name
 3     , 1 as lvl
 4     ,':' || to_char(e.last_name) as path
 5   from hr.employees e
 6   where e.manager_id is null
 7   union all
 8   select e1.employee_id, e1.manager_id, e1.last_name
 9     ,e2.lvl + 1 as lvl
10     ,e2.path || ':' || e1.last_name as path
11   from hr.employees e1
12   join emp_recurse e2 on e2.employee_id= e1.manager_id
13  )
14  search depth first by last_name set last_name_order
15  select lpad(' ', r.lvl*2-1,' ') || r.last_name last_name, r.path
16  from emp_recurse r
17  order by last_name_order;
```

```
LAST_NAME                   PATH
------------------------    -----------------------
King                        :King
  Cambrault                 :King:Cambrault
    Bates                   :King:Cambrault:Bates
    Bloom                   :King:Cambrault:Bloom
    Fox                     :King:Cambrault:Fox
    Kumar                   :King:Cambrault:Kumar
    Ozer                    :King:Cambrault:Ozer
    Smith                   :King:Cambrault:Smith
  De Haan                   :King:De Haan
...
107 rows selected.
```

The output of the SYS_CONNECT_BY_PATH as seen in Listing 10-17 is duplicated by the roll-your-own version using RSF in Listing 10-18. Take another look at this SQL. You may notice that there's something here that SYS_CONNECT_BY_PATH cannot do. Consider, for instance, if you want the hierarchy to be displayed as a comma-delimited list. This is accomplished simply enough by changing ":" to ",". The problem with SYS_CONNECT_BY_PATH is that the first character in the output is always a comma.

Using the RSF method, you can simply remove the delimiter in the anchor member and then change the delimiter in the recursive member to a comma. This is shown in Listing 10-19, along with a sample of the output. Should you feel inclined, the first character of the path could remain a colon, with the values delimited by commas.

Listing 10-19. Comma-Delimited PATH

```
 1  with emp_recurse(employee_id,manager_id,last_name,lvl,path) as (
 2   select e.employee_id, null, e.last_name
 3      , 1 as lvl
 4      ,e.last_name as path
 5   from hr.employees e
 6   where e.manager_id is null
 7   union all
 8   select e1.employee_id, e1.manager_id, e1.last_name
 9      ,e2.lvl + 1 as lvl
10      ,e2.path || ',' || e1.last_name as path
11   from hr.employees e1
12   join emp_recurse e2 on e2.employee_id= e1.manager_id
13  )
14  search depth first by last_name set last_name_order
15  select lpad(' ', r.lvl*2-1,' ') || r.last_name last_name, r.path
16  from emp_recurse r
17  order by last_name_order;
```

```
LAST_NAME                     PATH
--------------------------    ----------------------
King                          King
  Cambrault                   King,Cambrault
    Bates                     King,Cambrault,Bates
    Bloom                     King,Cambrault,Bloom
    Fox                       King,Cambrault,Fox
    Kumar                     King,Cambrault,Kumar
    Ozer                      King,Cambrault,Ozer
    Smith                     King,Cambrault,Smith
  De Haan                     King,De Haan
...
107 rows selected.
```

The CONNECT_BY_ROOT Operator

The CONNECT_BY_ROOT operator enhances the CONNECT BY syntax by returning the root node of the current row. In the example of the hr.employees table, all rows return King as the root. You can change it up a bit, however, by modifying the row temporarily for Neena Kochhar, putting her on the same level as the company president, Steven King. Then, the hierarchy can be shown for Kochhar by using the CONNECT_BY_ROOT operator to restrict the output. The results are shown in Listing 10-20.

Listing 10-20. CONNECT_BY_ROOT

```
1* update hr.employees set manager_id= null where last_name ='Kochhar';
1 row updated.

1  select /*+ inline gather_plan_statistics */
2    level
3    , lpad(' ',2*(level-1)) || last_name last_name
4    , first_name
5    , CONNECT_BY_ROOT last_name as root
6    , sys_connect_by_path(last_name,':') path
7  from hr.employees
8  where connect_by_root last_name = 'Kochhar'
9  connect by prior employee_id = manager_id
10   start with manager_id is null;
```

LEVEL	LAST_NAME	FIRST_NAME	ROOT	PATH
1	Kochhar	Neena	Kochhar	:Kochhar
2	Greenberg	Nancy	Kochhar	:Kochhar:Greenberg
3	Faviet	Daniel	Kochhar	:Kochhar:Greenberg:Faviet
3	Chen	John	Kochhar	:Kochhar:Greenberg:Chen
3	Sciarra	Ismael	Kochhar	:Kochhar:Greenberg:Sciarra
3	Urman	Jose Manuel	Kochhar	:Kochhar:Greenberg:Urman
3	Popp	Luis	Kochhar	:Kochhar:Greenberg:Popp
2	Whalen	Jennifer	Kochhar	:Kochhar:Whalen
2	Mavris	Susan	Kochhar	:Kochhar:Mavris
2	Baer	Hermann	Kochhar	:Kochhar:Baer
2	Higgins	Shelley	Kochhar	:Kochhar:Higgins
3	Gietz	William	Kochhar	:Kochhar:Higgins:Gietz

```
12 rows selected.
1 rollback;
```

This functionality can be duplicated in RSF, but it does require a little more SQL. The code in Listing 10-21 is based on the SYS_CONNECT_BY_PATH example, with some minor changes and additions. The delimiting character is now prepended and appended to the value for PATH in the anchor member. In the recursive member, the delimiter is appended to the PATH, whereas previously it was prepended to the last_name column. Doing so ensures that the root records always have a delimiting character at the end of the value, allowing the SUBSTR() function in the emps subquery to parse the root correctly from the string when the path comes from the anchor member only, such as the rows for King and Kochar. This is probably better explained by examining the output from the query.

Listing 10-21. Duplicate CONNECT_BY_ROOT

```
1 update hr.employees set manager_id= null where last_name ='Kochhar';
1 row updated.

1  with emp_recurse(employee_id,manager_id,last_name,lvl,path) as (
2    select /*+ gather_plan_statistics */
3      e.employee_id
4      , null as manager_id
5      , e.last_name
```

```
 6        , 1 as lvl
 7        , ':' || e.last_name || ':' as path
 8      from hr.employees   e
 9      where e.manager_id is null
10      union all
11      select
12        e.employee_id
13        , e.manager_id
14        , e.last_name
15        , er.lvl + 1 as lvl
16        , er.path || e.last_name   || ':' as path
17      from hr.employees e
18      join emp_recurse er on er.employee_id = e.manager_id
19      join hr.employees e2 on e2.employee_id = e.manager_id
20    )
21    search depth first by last_name set order1 ,
22    emps as (
23      select lvl
24        , last_name
25        , path
26        , substr(path,2,instr(path,':',2)-2) root
27      from emp_recurse
28    )
29    select
30      lvl
31    , lpad(' ',2*(lvl-1)) || last_name last_name
32    , root
33    , path
34    from emps
35    where root = 'Kochhar';
```

```
        LVL LAST_NAME        ROOT              PATH
---------- ---------------  ---------------  ------------------------------
          1 Kochhar          Kochhar          :Kochhar:
          2   Baer           Kochhar          :Kochhar:Baer:
          2   Greenberg      Kochhar          :Kochhar:Greenberg:
          3     Chen         Kochhar          :Kochhar:Greenberg:Chen:
          3     Faviet       Kochhar          :Kochhar:Greenberg:Faviet:
          3     Popp         Kochhar          :Kochhar:Greenberg:Popp:
          3     Sciarra      Kochhar          :Kochhar:Greenberg:Sciarra:
          3     Urman        Kochhar          :Kochhar:Greenberg:Urman:
          2   Higgins        Kochhar          :Kochhar:Higgins:
          3     Gietz        Kochhar          :Kochhar:Higgins:Gietz:
          2   Mavris         Kochhar          :Kochhar:Mavris:
          2   Whalen         Kochhar          :Kochhar:Whalen:

12 rows selected.
1* rollback;
```

This is not a perfect duplication of the CONNECT_BY_ROOT operator. In this case, it does exactly what is needed. The built-in operator, however, does allow some flexibility in specifying the level and returning the root at that level. The example given needs more modification to match this ability; however, you may find that this example works well for most cases.

The connect_by_iscycle Pseudocolumn and NOCYCLE Parameter

The connect_by_iscycle pseudocolumn makes it easy to detect loops in a hierarchy. This is illustrated by the SQL in Listing 10-22. There, an intentional error has been introduced by updating the hr.employees row for the president, assigning Smith as King's manager, which causes an error in the CONNECT BY.

Listing 10-22. Cycle Error in CONNECT BY

```
1 update hr.employees set manager_id = 171 where employee_id = 100;
1 row updated.
Elapsed: 00:00:00.02

  1  select lpad(' ',2*(level-1)) || last_name last_name
  2    ,first_name, employee_id, level
  3  from hr.employees
  4  start with employee_id = 100
  5* connect by prior employee_id = manager_id
```

LAST_NAME	FIRST_NAME	EMPLOYEE_ID	LEVEL
King	Steven	100	1
Kochhar	Neena	101	2
Greenberg	Nancy	108	3
...			
Smith	William	171	3
King	Steven	100	4
...			

```
ERROR:
ORA-01436: CONNECT BY loop in user data

187 rows selected.
  1 rollback;
```

In the output, Smith appears as the manager of King, which you know to be incorrect. But, if you didn't already know what the problem is, how would you find it? This is where the NOCYCLE parameter and CONNECT_BY_ISCYCLE operator come into play. These are used to detect a cycle in the hierarchy. The NOCYCLE parameter prevents the ORA-1436 error from occurring, allowing all rows to be output. The CONNECT_BY_ISCYCLE operator allows you to find the row causing the error easily.

As seen in Listing 10-23, the value of CONNECT_BY_ISCYCLE is 1, indicating that the row for Smith is somehow causing the error. The next query looks up the data for Smith, and all appears normal. Last, you query the table again, this time using Smith's employee ID, to find all employees that he manages. The error becomes apparent—the president of the company does not have a manager—so the solution is to set the manager_id back to NULL for this row.

Listing 10-23. Detect the Cycle with `CONNECT_BY_ISCYCLE`

```
1* update hr.employees set manager_id = 171 where employee_id = 100
1 row updated.

  1  select lpad(' ',2*(level-1)) || last_name last_name
  2   ,first_name, employee_id, level
  3   , connect_by_iscycle
  4  from hr.employees
  5  start with employee_id = 100
  6  connect by nocycle prior employee_id = manager_id;
```

```
LAST_NAME                 FIRST_NAME   EMPLOYEE_ID LEVEL CONNECT_BY_ISCYCLE
------------------------- ------------ ----------- ----- ------------------
King                      Steven               100     1                  0
  Kochhar                 Neena                101     2                  0
...
    Smith                 William              171     3                  1
...
107 rows selected.
```

```
Elapsed: 00:00:00.03
  1  select last_name, first_name, employee_id, manager_id
  2  from hr.employees
  3* where employee_id = 171
```

```
LAST_NAME                 FIRST_NAME   EMPLOYEE_ID MANAGER_ID
------------------------- ------------ ----------- ----------
Smith                     William              171        148
```

```
  1  select last_name, first_name, employee_id, manager_id
  2  from hr.employees
  3* where manager_id = 171
```

```
LAST_NAME                 FIRST_NAME   EMPLOYEE_ID MANAGER_ID
------------------------- ------------ ----------- ----------
King                      Steven               100        171
```

```
  1 rollback;
```

So, how do you do this with RSF? It's really quite simple, because Oracle has provided the built-in CYCLE clause that makes short work of detecting cycles in recursive queries. It is somewhat more robust than the connect_by_iscycle pseudocolumn in that it lets you determine which values are used to indicate a cycle, as well as provides a column name at the same time. Listing 10-24 uses the same data error in Listing 10-23, but this time it uses a recursive subfactored query.

Listing 10-24. Detect Cycles in Recursive Queries

```
1 update hr.employees set manager_id = 171 where employee_id = 100;
1 row updated.
Elapsed: 00:00:00.00

  1  with emp(employee_id,manager_id,last_name,first_name,lvl) as (
  2  select e.employee_id
  3     , null as manager_id
  4     , e.last_name
  5     , e.first_name
  6     , 1 as lvl
  7  from hr.employees  e
  8  where e.employee_id =100
  9  union all
 10  select e.employee_id
 11     , e.manager_id
 12     , e.last_name
 13     , e.first_name
 14     , emp.lvl + 1 as lvl
 15  from hr.employees e
 16  join emp on emp.employee_id = e.manager_id
 17  )
 18  search depth first by last_name set order1
 19  CYCLE employee_id SET is_cycle TO '1' DEFAULT '0'
 20  select lpad(' ',2*(lvl-1)) || last_name last_name
 21     , first_name
 22     , employee_id
 23     , lvl
 24     , is_cycle
 25  from emp
 26  order by order1;
```

```
LAST_NAME                  FIRST_NAME    EMPLOYEE_ID      LVL I
------------------------   ------------  -----------  ---------- -
King                       Steven                100          1 0
  Cambrault                Gerald                148          2 0
    Bates                  Elizabeth             172          3 0
    Bloom                  Harrison              169          3 0
    Fox                    Tayler                170          3 0
    Kumar                  Sundita               173          3 0
    Ozer                   Lisa                  168          3 0
    Smith                  William               171          3 0
      King                 Steven                100          4 1
...

108 rows selected.

Elapsed: 00:00:00.04
```

```
1  select last_name, first_name, employee_id, manager_id
2  from hr.employees
3  where employee_id = 100;
```

```
LAST_NAME                 FIRST_NAME   EMPLOYEE_ID MANAGER_ID
------------------------- ------------ ----------- ----------
King                      Steven               100        171
1 row selected.
```

```
1  rollback;
```

Notice how the CYCLE clause lets you set the two possible values for the is_cycle column to 0 or 1. Only single-value characters are allowed here. The name of the column is also user defined and is set to is_cycle in this example. Examining the output, it appears that the CYCLE clause in RSF does a somewhat better job of identifying the row that causes the data cycle. The row with the error is identified clearly as that of King, so you can query that row and determine the error immediately.

The connect_by_isleaf Pseudocolumn

Last, there is the connect_by_isleaf pseudocolumn, which permits easy identification of leaf[7] nodes in hierarchical data. You can see that leaf nodes are identified in the output of Listing 10-25 when the value of connect_by_isleaf is 1.

Listing 10-25. CONNECT_BY_ISLEAF

```
1  select lpad(' ',2*(level-1)) || e.last_name last_name, connect_by_isleaf
2  from hr.employees e
3  start with e.manager_id is null
4  connect by prior e.employee_id = e.manager_id
5  order siblings by e.last_name;
```

```
LAST_NAME                 CONNECT_BY_ISLEAF
------------------------- -----------------
King                                      0
  Cambrault                               0
    Bates                                 1
    Bloom                                 1
    Fox                                   1
    Kumar                                 1
    Ozer                                  1
    Smith                                 1
  De Haan                                 0
    Hunold                                0
      Austin                              1
      Ernst                               1
      Lorentz                             1
      Pataballa                           1
...

107 rows selected.
```

---

[7]A leaf node is a node in the hierarchical tree that has no children.

```
---------------------------------------------------------------------
| Id  | Operation                                | Name      | E-Rows |
---------------------------------------------------------------------
|  0  | SELECT STATEMENT                         |           |        |
|* 1  |  CONNECT BY NO FILTERING WITH START-WITH |           |        |
|  2  |   TABLE ACCESS FULL                      | EMPLOYEES |   107  |
---------------------------------------------------------------------
```

Duplicating this in RSF is somewhat of a challenge. There are probably many methods that can be used to accomplish this, with some limitations. This is one of those problems that may require a little extra thought to solve, where "solve" means you get the output you desire, but you won't necessarily duplicate the functionality of CONNECT_BY_ISLEAF completely.

In this case, you want to identify the leaf nodes in the employee hierarchy. By definition, none of the leaf nodes can be managers, so one way to accomplish this is to determine which rows are those of managers. All rows that are not those of managers are then leaf nodes.

Listing 10-26 uses this approach to solve the problem. The cost of solving it is two more extra scans of the hr.employees table and three index scans, but if RSF must be used, this is one way to get the desired results. The leaves subquery is used find the leaf nodes. This is then left outer joined to the employees table, and the value (or lack of a value) of the leaves.employee_id column indicates whether the current row is a leaf.

Listing 10-26. Finding Leaf Nodes in a Recursive Query

```
 1   with leaves as (
 2    select employee_id
 3    from hr.employees
 4    where employee_id not in (
 5       select manager_id
 6       from hr.employees
 7       where manager_id is not null
 8    )
 9   ),
10   emp(manager_id,employee_id,last_name,lvl,isleaf) as (
11    select e.manager_id, e.employee_id, e.last_name, 1 as lvl, 0 as isleaf
12    from hr.employees e
13    where e.manager_id is null
14    union all
15    select e.manager_id,nvl(e.employee_id,null) employee_id,e.last_name,emp.lvl + 1 as lvl
16       , decode(l.employee_id,null,0,1) isleaf
17    from hr.employees e
18    join emp on emp.employee_id = e.manager_id
19    left outer join leaves l on l.employee_id = e.employee_id
20   )
21   search depth first by last_name set order1
22   select lpad(' ',2*(lvl-1)) || last_name last_name, isleaf
23   from emp;
```

```
LAST_NAME                      ISLEAF
------------------------- ----------
King                                0
  Cambrault                         0
    Bates                           1
    Bloom                           1
    Fox                             1
    Kumar                           1
    Ozer                            1
    Smith                           1
  De Haan                           0
    Hunold                          0
      Austin                        1
      Ernst                         1
      Lorentz                       1
      Pataballa                     1
...
107 rows selected.
```

```
-------------------------------------------------------------------------
| Id  | Operation                              | Name           | E-Rows |
-------------------------------------------------------------------------
|   0 | SELECT STATEMENT                       |                |        |
|   1 |  VIEW                                  |                |      7 |
|   2 |   UNION ALL (RECURSIVE WITH) DEPTH FIRST|               |        |
|*  3 |    TABLE ACCESS FULL                   | EMPLOYEES      |      1 |
|   4 |    NESTED LOOPS OUTER                   |                |      6 |
|   5 |     NESTED LOOPS                        |                |      6 |
|   6 |      RECURSIVE WITH PUMP                |                |        |
|   7 |      TABLE ACCESS BY INDEX ROWID        | EMPLOYEES      |      6 |
|*  8 |       INDEX RANGE SCAN                  | EMP_MANAGER_IX |      6 |
|   9 |     VIEW PUSHED PREDICATE               |                |      1 |
|  10 |      NESTED LOOPS ANTI                  |                |      1 |
|* 11 |       INDEX UNIQUE SCAN                 | EMP_EMP_ID_PK  |      1 |
|* 12 |       INDEX RANGE SCAN                  | EMP_MANAGER_IX |      6 |
-------------------------------------------------------------------------
```

Another way to accomplish this is presented in Listing 10-27, in which the analytic function LEAD() uses the value of the lvl column to determine whether a row is a leaf node. Although it does avoid two of the index scans that were seen in Listing 10-26, determining correctly whether a row is a leaf node is dependent on the order of the output, as seen in line 16. The LEAD() function depends on the value of the last_name_order column that is set in the SEARCH clause.

Listing 10-27. Using LEAD() to Find Leaf Nodes

```
1  with emp(manager_id,employee_id,last_name,lvl) as (
2  select e.manager_id, e.employee_id, e.last_name, 1 as lvl
3  from hr.employees e
4  where e.manager_id is null
5  union all
6  select e.manager_id, nvl(e.employee_id,null) employee_id
7     , e.last_name, emp.lvl + 1 as lvl
```

```
 8    from hr.employees e
 9    join emp on emp.employee_id = e.manager_id
10  )
11  search depth first by last_name set last_name_order
12  select lpad(' ',2*(lvl-1)) || last_name last_name,
13    lvl,
14    lead(lvl) over (order by last_name_order) leadlvlorder,
15    case
16    when ( lvl - lead(lvl) over (order by last_name_order) ) < 0
17    then 0
18    else 1
19    end isleaf
20  from emp;
```

```
LAST_NAME                            LVL LEADLVLORDER    ISLEAF
------------------------      ---------- -------------  ----------
King                                   1            2          0
  Cambrault                            2            3          0
    Bates                              3            3          1
    Bloom                              3            3          1
    Fox                                3            3          1
    Kumar                              3            3          1
    Ozer                               3            3          1
    Smith                              3            2          1
  De Haan                              2            3          0
    Hunold                             3            4          0
      Austin                           4            4          1
      Ernst                            4            4          1
      Lorentz                          4            4          1
      Pataballa                        4            2          1
...
107 rows selected.
```

```
------------------------------------------------------------------------
| Id  | Operation                                | Name           | E-Rows |
------------------------------------------------------------------------
|   0 | SELECT STATEMENT                         |                |        |
|   1 |  WINDOW BUFFER                           |                |      7 |
|   2 |   VIEW                                   |                |      7 |
|   3 |    UNION ALL (RECURSIVE WITH) DEPTH FIRST|                |        |
|*  4 |     TABLE ACCESS FULL                    | EMPLOYEES      |      1 |
|   5 |     NESTED LOOPS                         |                |        |
|   6 |      NESTED LOOPS                        |                |      6 |
|   7 |       RECURSIVE WITH PUMP                |                |        |
|*  8 |       INDEX RANGE SCAN                   | EMP_MANAGER_IX |      6 |
|   9 |      TABLE ACCESS BY INDEX ROWID         | EMPLOYEES      |      6 |
------------------------------------------------------------------------
```

What might happen if the SEARCH clause is changed from DEPTH FIRST to BREADTH FIRST? The results are shown in Listing 10-28. The use of the LEAD() function appears, at first, to be an elegant solution, but it is somewhat fragile in its dependency on the order of the data. The example in Listing 10-26 works regardless of the SEARCH clause parameters. It is readily apparent that the output in Listing 10-28 is incorrect.

Listing 10-28. LEAD() with BREADTH FIRST

```
 1  with emp(manager_id,employee_id,last_name,lvl) as (
 2   select e.manager_id, e.employee_id, e.last_name, 1 as lvl
 3   from hr.employees e
 4   where e.manager_id is null
 5   union all
 6   select e.manager_id, nvl(e.employee_id,null) employee_id
 7     , e.last_name, emp.lvl + 1 as lvl
 8   from hr.employees e
 9   join emp on emp.employee_id = e.manager_id
10  )
11  search breadth first by last_name set last_name_order
12  select lpad(' ',2*(lvl-1)) || last_name last_name,
13   lvl,
14   lead(lvl) over (order by last_name_order) leadlvlorder,
15   case
16   when ( lvl - lead(lvl) over (order by last_name_order) ) < 0
17   then 0
18   else 1
19   end isleaf
20  from emp;
```

LAST_NAME	LVL	LEADLVLORDER	ISLEAF
King	1	2	0
Cambrault	2	2	1
De Haan	2	2	1
Errazuriz	2	2	1
Fripp	2	2	1
Hartstein	2	2	1
Kaufling	2	2	1

Summary

Although the functionality of CONNECT BY can be duplicated for most practical purposes in recursive subfactored queries, the question is, should you do so? In many cases, the CONNECT BY syntax is simpler to use, although the syntax does take some getting used to. Doing the same things in RSF requires quite a bit more SQL in most cases. In addition, CONNECT BY may produce better execution plans than RSF, especially for relatively simple queries. Keep in mind, however, that RSF is a new feature, and will likely improve in later versions of Oracle.

In addition, there may be good reasons not to use CONNECT BY. Perhaps you need to maintain ANSI compatibility in your application. Or perhaps the ability to write hierarchical queries that work in other databases that support recursive common table expressions simplifies the code for an application that runs on databases from different vendors. In this circumstance, RSF is quite useful. Whatever the need for hierarchical queries, with a little ingenuity you can write suitable queries on hierarchical data using recursive subfactored queries, and they will be capable of doing everything that can be done currently with CONNECT BY.

CHAPTER 11

■ ■ ■

Semijoins and Antijoins

Semijoins and antijoins are two closely related join methods (options of join methods, actually) that the Oracle optimizer can choose to apply when retrieving information. The SQL language is designed to specify the set of data the user wishes to retrieve, but to leave the decisions regarding how to navigate to the data up to the database itself. Therefore, there is no SQL syntax to invoke a particular join method specifically. Of course, Oracle does provide the ability to give the optimizer directives via hints. In this chapter, I explain these two join optimization options, the SQL syntax that can provoke them, requirements for and restrictions on their use, and, last, some guidance on when and how they should be used.

It is important to be aware that Oracle is constantly improving the optimizer code and that not all details of its behavior are documented. All examples in this chapter were created on an Oracle 12c database (12.1.0.1). My version of 12c currently has 3332 parameters, many of which affect the way the optimizer behaves. When appropriate, I mention parameter settings that have a direct bearing on the topics at hand. However, you should verify the behavior on your own system.

Semijoins

A semijoin is a join between two sets of data (tables) in which rows from the first set are returned based on the presence or absence of at least one matching row in the other set. I revisit the "absence" of a matching row later—this is a special case of the semijoin called an *antijoin*. If you think back to your days in grade school math, you should be able to visualize this operation with a typical set theory picture such as the one shown in Figure 11-1.

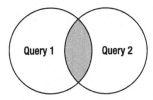

Figure 11-1. *Ilustration of a semijoin*

Figure 11-1 provides a basic idea of what a semijoin is but it's not detailed enough to describe the nuances. Diagrams of this sort are called *Venn diagrams*; this particular Venn diagram is used often to illustrate an inner join, which is essentially an intersection. Unfortunately, there is not a convenient way to describe a semijoin completely with a Venn diagram. The main difference between a normal inner join and a semijoin is that, with a semijoin, each record in the first set (Query 1 in Figure 11-1) is returned only once, regardless of how many matches there are in the second set (Query 2 in Figure 11-1). This definition implies that the actual processing of the query can be optimized by stopping Query 2 as soon as the first match is found. And at its heart, this is what a semijoin is—the optimization that allows processing to stop before the Query 2 part is complete. This join technique is a choice that's available to

Oracle's cost-based optimizer when the query contains a subquery inside an IN or EXISTS clause (or inside the rarely used =ANY clause, which is synonymous with IN). The syntax should look pretty familiar. Listings 11-1 and 11-2 show examples of the two most common forms of semijoin queries using IN and EXISTS.

Listing 11-1. Semijoin IN example

```
SQL>
SQL> select /* using in */ department_name
  2  from hr.departments dept
  3  where department_id IN (select department_id from hr.employees emp);

DEPARTMENT_NAME
------------------
Administration
Marketing
Purchasing
Human Resources
Shipping
IT
Public Relations
Sales
Executive
Finance
Accounting

11 rows selected.
```

Listing 11-2. Semijoin EXISTS example

```
SQL> select /* using exists */ department_name
  2  from hr.departments dept
  3  where EXISTS (select null from hr.employees emp
  4                    where emp.department_id = dept.department_id);

DEPARTMENT_NAME
------------------
Administration
Marketing
Purchasing
Human Resources
Shipping
IT
Public Relations
Sales
Executive
Finance
Accounting

11 rows selected.
```

These two queries are functionally equivalent. That is to say, they always return the same set of data, given the same inputs. There are several other forms that are closely related. Listings 11-3 through 11-6 show several examples of closely related alternatives.

Listing 11-3. Alternatives to EXISTS and IN: Inner Join

```
SQL> select /* inner join */ department_name
  2  from hr.departments dept, hr.employees emp
  3  where dept.department_id = emp.department_id;

DEPARTMENT_NAME
------------------------------
Administration
Marketing
Marketing
Purchasing
Purchasing
Shipping
IT
IT
Public Relations
Sales
Sales
. . .
Executive
Finance
Finance
Accounting

106 rows selected.
```

Obviously the inner join is not functionally equivalent to the semijoin because of the number of rows returned. Note that there are many repeating values. Let's try using DISTINCT to eliminate the duplicates. Look at Listing 11-4.

Listing 11-4. Alternatives to EXISTS and IN: Inner Join with DISTINCT

```
SQL> select /* inner join with distinct */ distinct department_name
  2  from hr.departments dept, hr.employees emp
  3  where dept.department_id = emp.department_id;

DEPARTMENT_NAME
------------------------------
Administration
Accounting
Purchasing
Human Resources
IT
Public Relations
Executive
Shipping
Sales
Finance
Marketing

11 rows selected.
```

The inner join with DISTINCT looks pretty good. In this case, it actually returns the same exact set of records. As previously mentioned, the INTERSECT set operation is very close to a semijoin, so let's try that next in Listing 11-5.

Listing 11-5. Alternatives to EXISTS and IN: Ugly INTERSECT

```
SQL> select /* ugly intersect */ department_name
  2  from hr.departments dept,
  3    (select department_id from hr.departments
  4     intersect
  5     select department_id from hr.employees) b
  6  where b.department_id = dept.department_id;

DEPARTMENT_NAME
------------------------------
Administration
Marketing
Purchasing
Human Resources
Shipping
IT
Public Relations
Sales
Executive
Finance
Accounting

11 rows selected.
```

The INTERSECT also looks pretty good, but the syntax is convoluted. Last, let's try the somewhat obscure =ANY keyword with a subquery in Listing 11-6.

Listing 11-6. Alternatives to EXISTS and IN: =ANY Subquery

```
SQL> select /* ANY subquery */ department_name
  2  from hr.departments dept
  3  where department_id = ANY (select department_id from hr.employees emp);

DEPARTMENT_NAME
------------------------------
Administration
Marketing
Purchasing
Human Resources
Shipping
IT
Public Relations
Sales
Executive
Finance
Accounting

11 rows selected.
```

There isn't much to say about the =ANY version because it is merely an alternate way of writing IN. So, to recap, the query in Listing 11-3 (inner join) doesn't look promising because it obviously doesn't return the same set of data. And because it returns a row for each match, the total number of records returned is 106 instead of 11. Let's skip over the second one using the DISTINCT operator for a moment. Note that the query in Listing 11-5 (an ugly INTERSECT), although it returns the correct set of records, doesn't look promising either because it uses convoluted syntax, even for the simple case I'm illustrating. Of course, the query in Listing 11-6 (using the =ANY syntax) is exactly the same as the IN version because IN and =ANY are the same thing.

The query in Listing 11-4 (inner join with DISTINCT) looks promising, but is it functionally equivalent to the queries in Listings 11-1 and 11-2? The short answer is no; it's not. In many situations the inner join with the DISTINCT query returns the same data as a semijoin (using IN or EXISTS), as it does in this case. But, this is because of a convenient fluke of the data model, and it does not make the query in Listing 11-3 equivalent to the semijoin queries in Listing 11-1 and 11-2. Consider the example in Listing 11-7, which shows a case when the two forms return different results.

Listing 11-7. Semijoin and DISTINCT Are Not the Same

```
SQL> select /* SEMI using IN */ department_id
  2  from hr.employees
  3  where department_id in (select department_id from hr.departments);

DEPARTMENT_ID
-------------
           10
           20
           20
           30
           30
           30
           30
           30
           30
           40
           50
           50
           50
          . . .
           80
          110
          110

106 rows selected.

SQL>
SQL> select /* inner join with distinct */ distinct emp.department_id
  2  from hr.departments dept, hr.employees emp
  3  where dept.department_id = emp.department_id;
```

```
DEPARTMENT_ID
-------------
           10
           20
           30
           40
           50
           60
           70
           80
           90
          100
          110
```

```
11 rows selected.
```

So it's clear from this example that the two constructs are not equivalent. The IN/EXISTS form takes each record in the first set and, if there is at least one match in the second set, returns the record. It does not apply a DISTINCT operator at the end of the processing (in other words, it doesn't sort and throw away duplicates). Therefore, it is possible to get repeating values, assuming that there are duplicates in the records returned by Query 1. The DISTINCT form, on the other hand, retrieves all the rows, sorts them, and then throws away any duplicate values. As you can see from the example, these are clearly not the same. And as you might expect from the description, the DISTINCT version can end up doing significantly more work because it has no chance to bail out of the subquery early. I talk more about this shortly.

There is another common mistake that is made with the EXISTS syntax that should probably be mentioned. If you use EXISTS, you need to make sure you include a subquery that is correlated to the outer query. If the subquery does not reference the outer query, it's meaningless. Listing 11-8 shows an example from a web page that is currently number one on Google for the search term "Oracle EXISTS."

Listing 11-8. Common Mistake with EXISTS: Noncorrelated Subquery

```
select
    book_key
from
    book
where
    exists (select book_key from sales) ;
```

Because the subquery in this example is not related to the outer query, the end result is to return every record in the book table (as long as there is at least one record in the sales table). This is probably not what the author of this statement intended. Listing 11-9 shows a few examples demonstrating the difference between using correlated and noncorrelated subqueries—the first two showing EXISTS with a proper correlated subquery, and the last two showing EXISTS with noncorrelated subqueries.

Listing 11-9. Common Mistake with EXISTS: Correlated vs. Noncorrelated Subquery

```
SQL> select /* correlated */ department_id
  2      from hr.departments dept
  3      where exists (select department_id from hr.employees emp
  4                        where emp.department_id = dept.department_id);
```

```
DEPARTMENT_ID
-------------
           10
           20
           30
           40
           50
           60
           70
           80
           90
          100
          110
```

11 rows selected.

```
SQL>
SQL> select /* not correlated */ department_id
  2     from hr.departments dept
  3     where exists (select department_id from hr.employees emp);
```

```
DEPARTMENT_ID
-------------
           10
           20
           30
           40
           50
           60
           70
           80
           90
          100
          110
          120
          130
          140
          150
          160
          170
          180
          190
          200
          210
          220
          230
          240
          250
          260
          270
```

27 rows selected.

```
SQL>
SQL> select /* not correlated no nulls */ department_id
  2      from hr.departments dept
  3      where exists (select department_id from hr.employees emp
  4                          where department_id is not null);

DEPARTMENT_ID
-------------
           10
           20
           30
           40
           50
           60
           70
           80
           90
          100
          110
          120
          130
          140
          150
          160
          170
          180
          190
          200
          210
          220
          230
          240
          250
          260
          270

27 rows selected.

SQL>
SQL> select /* non-correlated totally unrelated */ department_id
  2      from hr.departments dept
  3      where exists (select null from dual);

DEPARTMENT_ID
-------------
           10
           20
           30
           40
           50
           60
           70
```

```
                 80
                 90
                100
                110
                120
                130
                140
                150
                160
                170
                180
                190
                200
                210
                220
                230
                240
                250
                260
                270

27 rows selected.

SQL>
SQL> select /* non-correlated empty subquery */ department_id
  2      from hr.departments dept
  3      where exists (select 'anything' from dual where 1=2);

no rows selected
```

So the correlated queries get the records we expect (in other words, only the ones that have a match in the second query). Obviously, the noncorrelated subqueries do not work as expected. They return every record from the first table, which is actually what you've asked for if you write a query that way. In fact, as you can see in the next-to-last example (with the noncorrelated query against the dual table), no matter what you select in the subquery, all the records from the first table are returned. The last example shows what happens when no records are returned from the subquery. In this case, no records are returned at all. So, without a correlated subquery, you either get all the records in the outer query or none of the records in the outer query, without regard to what the inner query is actually doing.

Semijoin Plans

I mentioned in the introduction that semijoins are not really a join method on their own, but rather are an option of other join methods. The three most common join methods in Oracle are nested loops, hash joins, and merge joins. Each of these methods can have the semi option applied to it. Remember, also, that it is an optimization that allows processing to stop when the first match is found in the subquery. Let's use a little pseudocode to exemplify the process more fully. The outer query is Q1 and the inner (subquery) is Q2. What you see in Listing 11-10 is the basic processing of a nested loop semijoin.

Listing 11-10. Pseudocode for Nested Loop Semijoin

```
open Q1
while Q1 still has records
   fetch record from Q1
   result = false
   open Q2
   while Q2 still has records
      fetch record from Q2
      if (Q1.record matches Q2.record) then    ⬅= semijoin optimization
         result = true
         exit loop
      end if
   end loop
   close Q2
   if (result = true) return Q1 record
end loop
close Q1
```

The optimization provided by the semi option is the IF statement that lets the code exit the inner loop as soon as it finds a match. Obviously, with large datasets, this technique can result in significant time savings compared with a normal nested loops join that must loop through every record returned by the inner query for every row in the outer query. At this point, you may be thinking that this technique could save a lot of time with a nested loops join vs. the other two, and you'd be right because the other two have to get all the records from the inner query before they start checking for matches. So the nested loops joins in general have the most to gain from this technique. Keep in mind that the optimizer still picks which join method to use based on its costing algorithms, which include the various semi options.

Now let's rerun the queries from Listings 11-1 and 11-2 and look at the plans the optimizer generates (shown in Listing 11-11). Note that some of the plan output has been removed for brevity.

Listing 11-11. Semijoin Execution Plans

```
SQL> -- semi_ex1.sql
SQL>
SQL> select /* in */ department_name
  2      from hr.departments dept
  3      where department_id in (select department_id from hr.employees emp);

DEPARTMENT_NAME
------------------------------
Administration
Marketing
Purchasing
Human Resources
Shipping
IT
Public Relations
Sales
Executive
Finance
Accounting

11 rows selected.
```

```
Execution Plan
--------------------------------------------------------------
Plan hash value: 954076352

--------------------------------------------------------------------
| Id  | Operation                    | Name              | Rows  |
--------------------------------------------------------------------
|   0 | SELECT STATEMENT             |                   |       |
|   1 |  MERGE JOIN SEMI             |                   |    11 |
|   2 |   TABLE ACCESS BY INDEX ROWID| DEPARTMENTS       |    27 |
|   3 |    INDEX FULL SCAN           | DEPT_ID_PK        |    27 |
|   4 |   SORT UNIQUE                |                   |   107 |
|   5 |    INDEX FULL SCAN           | EMP_DEPARTMENT_IX |   107 |
--------------------------------------------------------------------

Predicate Information (identified by operation id):
---------------------------------------------------


   4 - access("DEPARTMENT_ID"="DEPARTMENT_ID")
       filter("DEPARTMENT_ID"="DEPARTMENT_ID")


Statistics
--------------------------------------------------------------
          0  recursive calls
          0  db block gets
          5  consistent gets
          0  physical reads
          0  redo size
        758  bytes sent via SQL*Net to client
        544  bytes received via SQL*Net from client
          2  SQL*Net roundtrips to/from client
          1  sorts (memory)
          0  sorts (disk)
         11  rows processed

SQL>
SQL> select /* exists */ department_name
  2       from hr.departments dept
  3       where exists (select null from hr.employees emp
  4                        where emp.department_id = dept.department_id);

DEPARTMENT_NAME
------------------------------
Administration
Marketing
Purchasing
Human Resources
Shipping
IT
Public Relations
Sales
```

```
Executive
Finance
Accounting

11 rows selected.

Elapsed: 00:00:00.05

Execution Plan
----------------------------------------------------------
Plan hash value: 954076352

----------------------------------------------------------------------
| Id | Operation                    | Name              | Rows  |
----------------------------------------------------------------------
|  0 | SELECT STATEMENT             |                   |       |
|  1 |  MERGE JOIN SEMI             |                   |    11 |
|  2 |   TABLE ACCESS BY INDEX ROWID| DEPARTMENTS       |    27 |
|  3 |    INDEX FULL SCAN           | DEPT_ID_PK        |    27 |
|  4 |   SORT UNIQUE                |                   |   107 |
|  5 |    INDEX FULL SCAN           | EMP_DEPARTMENT_IX |   107 |
----------------------------------------------------------------------

Predicate Information (identified by operation id):
---------------------------------------------------

   4 - access("EMP"."DEPARTMENT_ID"="DEPT"."DEPARTMENT_ID")
       filter("EMP"."DEPARTMENT_ID"="DEPT"."DEPARTMENT_ID")

Statistics
----------------------------------------------------------
          0  recursive calls
          0  db block gets
          5  consistent gets
          0  physical reads
          0  redo size
        758  bytes sent via SQL*Net to client
        544  bytes received via SQL*Net from client
          2  SQL*Net roundtrips to/from client
          1  sorts (memory)
          0  sorts (disk)
         11  rows processed
```

The autotrace statistics are included so that you can see that these statements are indeed processed the same way. The plans are identical and the statistics are identical. I make this point to dispel the long-held belief that queries written with EXIST behave very differently than queries written with IN. This was an issue in the past (version 8i), but it has not been an issue for many years. The truth is that the optimizer can and does transform queries in both forms to the same statement.

Note that there is a way to get a better idea of the decision-making process the optimizer goes through when parsing a statement. You can have the optimizer log its actions in a trace file by issuing the following command:

```
alter session set events '10053 trace name context forever, level 1';
```

Setting this event causes a trace file to be created in the USER_DUMP_DEST directory when a hard parse is performed. I call it *Wolfganging*, because Wolfgang Breitling was the first guy really to analyze the content of these 10053 trace files and publish his findings. For further information, please refer to Wolfgang's paper called "A Look Under the Hood of CBO." (http://www.centrexcc.com/A%20Look%20under%20the%20Hood%20of%20CBO%20-%20the%2010053%20Event.pdf) At any rate, a close look at 10053 trace data for each statement confirms that both statements are transformed into the same statement before the optimizer determines a plan. Listing 11-12 and 11-13 show excerpts of 10053 trace files generated for both the IN and the EXISTS versions.

Listing 11-12. Excerpts from 10053 traces for the IN version

```
***************
QUERY BLOCK TEXT
***************
select /* using in */ department_name
    from hr.departments dept
    where department_id IN (select department_id from hr.employees emp)


****************************
Cost-Based Subquery Unnesting
****************************
SU: Unnesting query blocks in query block SEL$1 (#1) that are valid to unnest.
Subquery removal for query block SEL$2 (#2)
RSW: Not valid for subquery removal SEL$2 (#2)
Subquery unchanged.
Subquery Unnesting on query block SEL$1 (#1)SU: Performing unnesting that does not require costing.
SU: Considering subquery unnest on query block SEL$1 (#1).
SU:    Checking validity of unnesting subquery SEL$2 (#2)
SU:    Passed validity checks.
SU:    Transforming ANY subquery to a join.

Final query after transformations:****** UNPARSED QUERY IS ******
SELECT "DEPT"."DEPARTMENT_NAME" "DEPARTMENT_NAME" FROM "HR"."EMPLOYEES" "EMP","HR"."DEPARTMENTS"
"DEPT" WHERE "DEPT"."DEPARTMENT_ID"="EMP"."DEPARTMENT_ID"
```

Listing 11-13. Excerpts from 10053 traces for the EXISTS version

```
***************
QUERY BLOCK TEXT
***************
select /* using exists */ department_name
    from hr.departments dept
    where EXISTS (select null from hr.employees emp
                      where emp.department_id = dept.department_id)


****************************
Cost-Based Subquery Unnesting
****************************
SU: Unnesting query blocks in query block SEL$1 (#1) that are valid to unnest.
Subquery Unnesting on query block SEL$1 (#1)SU: Performing unnesting that does not require costing.
SU: Considering subquery unnest on query block SEL$1 (#1).
SU:    Checking validity of unnesting subquery SEL$2 (#2)
SU:    Passed validity checks.
SU:    Transforming EXISTS subquery to a join.
```

```
Final query after transformations:******* UNPARSED QUERY IS *******
SELECT "DEPT"."DEPARTMENT_NAME" "DEPARTMENT_NAME" FROM "HR"."EMPLOYEES"
 "EMP","HR"."DEPARTMENTS" "DEPT" WHERE "EMP"."DEPARTMENT_ID"="DEPT"."DEPARTMENT_ID"
```

As you can see in the trace file excerpts, subquery unnesting has occurred on both queries and they have both been transformed into the same statement (in other words, the Final Query after Transformations section is exactly the same for both versions). Oracle Database releases from 10gR2 onward behave the same way, by the way.

Controlling Semijoin Plans

Now let's look at some of the methods to control the execution plan, should the optimizer need a little help. There are two mechanisms at your disposal. One mechanism is a set of hints that you can apply to individual queries. The other is an instance-level parameter that affects all queries.

Controlling Semijoin Plans Using Hints

There are several hints that may be applied to encourage or discourage semijoins. As of 11gR2, the following hints are available:

> SEMIJOIN: Perform a semijoin (the optimizer gets to pick which kind).

> NO_SEMIJOIN: Obviously, don't perform a semijoin.

> NL_SJ: Perform a nested loops semijoin (deprecated as of 10g).

> HASH_SJ: Perform a hash semijoin (deprecated as of 10g).

> MERGE_SJ: Perform a merge semijoin (deprecated as of 10g).

The more specific hints (NL_SJ, HASH_SJ, MERGE_SJ) have been deprecated since 10g. Although they continue to work as in the past, even with 12c, be aware that the documentation says they may be going away at some point. All the semijoin-related hints need to be specified in the subquery, as opposed to in the outer query. Listing 11-14 shows an example using the NO_SEMIJOIN hint.

Listing 11-14. EXISTS with NO_SEMIJOIN Hint

```
SQL> set autotrace trace
SQL> -- semi_ex5a.sql - no_semijoin hint
SQL>
SQL> select /* exists no_semijoin */ department_name
  2     from hr.departments dept
  3     where exists (select /*+ no_semijoin */ null from hr.employees emp
  4                     where emp.department_id = dept.department_id);

DEPARTMENT_NAME
------------------------------
Human Resources
Executive
Marketing
Shipping
Accounting
```

Administration
Purchasing
Public Relations
Sales
Finance
IT

11 rows selected.

Execution Plan

Plan hash value: 3628941896

```
--------------------------------------------------------------------
| Id | Operation                     | Name             | Rows |
--------------------------------------------------------------------
|  0 | SELECT STATEMENT              |                  |      |
|  1 |  VIEW                         | VM_NWVW_2        |  106 |
|  2 |   HASH UNIQUE                 |                  |  106 |
|  3 |    NESTED LOOPS               |                  |      |
|  4 |     NESTED LOOPS              |                  |  106 |
|  5 |      INDEX FULL SCAN          | EMP_DEPARTMENT_IX|  107 |
|  6 |      INDEX UNIQUE SCAN        | DEPT_ID_PK       |    1 |
|  7 |     TABLE ACCESS BY INDEX ROWID| DEPARTMENTS     |    1 |
--------------------------------------------------------------------
```

Predicate Information (identified by operation id):
----

   6 - access("EMP"."DEPARTMENT_ID"="DEPT"."DEPARTMENT_ID")

Statistics
----
          0 recursive calls
          0 db block gets
        111 consistent gets
          0 physical reads
          0 redo size
        758 bytes sent via SQL*Net to client
        544 bytes received via SQL*Net from client
          2 SQL*Net roundtrips to/from client
          0 sorts (memory)
          0 sorts (disk)
         11 rows processed

In this example, I turned off the optimizer's ability to use semijoins via the NO_SEMIJOIN hint. As expected, the query no longer does a semijoin, but instead joins the two row sources and removes duplicates as indicated by the HASH UNIQUE operation. This is actually different behavior than exhibited in Oracle 11g, in which a FILTER operation was used to combine the two row sources. Listing 11-15 shows the Oracle 11g plan output for the same statement.

Listing 11-15. EXISTS with NO_SEMIJOIN Hint (Oracle 11g)

```
Execution Plan
------------------------------------------------------------
Plan hash value: 440241596

-----------------------------------------------------------------------
| Id|Operation             |Name            |Rows|Bytes|Cost (%CPU)|Time     |
-----------------------------------------------------------------------
|  0|SELECT STATEMENT      |                |  1|   16|   17   (0)|00:00:01|
|* 1| FILTER               |                |   |     |           |        |
|  2|  TABLE ACCESS FULL|  DEPARTMENTS      | 27|  432|    3   (0)|00:00:01|
|* 3|  INDEX RANGE SCAN |  EMP_DEPARTMENT_IX|  2|    6|    1   (0)|00:00:01|
-----------------------------------------------------------------------

Predicate Information  (identified by operation id):
---------------------------------------------------

   1 - filter( EXISTS (SELECT 0 FROM "HR"."EMPLOYEES" "EMP" WHERE
             "EMP"."DEPARTMENT_ID"=:B1))
   3 - access("EMP"."DEPARTMENT_ID"=:B1)
```

Note that the Predicate Information section of 11g explain plan output shows the FILTER operation is used to enforce the EXISTS clause. As is often the case, a new version of Oracle changes the plan choices the optimizer makes, so never assume you know what the choice is. Always verify!

Controlling Semijoin Plans at the Instance Level

There is also a hidden parameter that exerts control over the optimizer's semijoin choices; _always_semi_join was a normal parameter originally, but was changed to a hidden parameter in 9i. Listing 11-16 shows a list of the valid values for the parameter.

Listing 11-16. Valid Values for _always_semi_join

```
SYS@LAB112> select NAME_KSPVLD_VALUES name, VALUE_KSPVLD_VALUES value
  2  from X$KSPVLD_VALUES
  3  where NAME_KSPVLD_VALUES like nvl('&name',NAME_KSPVLD_VALUES);
Enter value for name: _always_semi_join

NAME                   VALUE
--------------------   -------------
_always_semi_join      HASH
_always_semi_join      MERGE
_always_semi_join      NESTED_LOOPS
_always_semi_join      CUBE
_always_semi_join      CHOOSE
_always_semi_join      OFF
```

The parameter has a somewhat misleading name because it does not force semijoins at all. The default value is CHOOSE, which allows the optimizer to evaluate all the semi-join methods and to choose the one it thinks is the most efficient. Setting the parameter to HASH, MERGE, or NESTED_LOOPS appears to reduce the optimizer's choices to the specified join method. Setting the parameter to OFF disables semijoins. The parameter can be set at the session level.

Listing 11-17 contains an example showing how the parameter can be used to change the optimizer's choice from a MERGE semi to a NESTED_LOOPS semi.

Listing 11-17. Using _always_semi_join to Change Plan to NESTED_LOOPS Semijoin

```
SQL> @semi_ex1a
SQL> -- semi_ex1a.sql
SQL>
SQL> select /* using in */ department_name
  2      from hr.departments dept
  3      where department_id IN (select department_id from hr.employees emp);

DEPARTMENT_NAME
------------------------------
Administration
Marketing
Purchasing
Human Resources
Shipping
IT
Public Relations
Sales
Executive
Finance
Accounting

11 rows selected.

Execution Plan
----------------------------------------------------------
Plan hash value: 954076352
```

Id	Operation	Name	Rows
0	SELECT STATEMENT		
1	MERGE JOIN SEMI		11
2	TABLE ACCESS BY INDEX ROWID	DEPARTMENTS	27
3	INDEX FULL SCAN	DEPT_ID_PK	27
4	SORT UNIQUE		107
5	INDEX FULL SCAN	EMP_DEPARTMENT_IX	107

```
Predicate Information (identified by operation id):
---------------------------------------------------

   4 - access("DEPARTMENT_ID"="DEPARTMENT_ID")
       filter("DEPARTMENT_ID"="DEPARTMENT_ID")

SQL> alter session set "_always_semi_join"=NESTED_LOOPS;

Session altered.
```

```
SQL> @semi_ex1a
SQL> -- semi_ex1a.sql
SQL>
SQL> select /* using in */ department_name
  2      from hr.departments dept
  3      where department_id IN (select department_id from hr.employees emp);

DEPARTMENT_NAME
------------------
Administration
Marketing
Purchasing
Human Resources
Shipping
IT
Public Relations
Sales
Executive
Finance
Accounting

11 rows selected.

Execution Plan
----------------------------------------------------------
Plan hash value: 1089943216

--------------------------------------------------------------------
| Id  | Operation                     | Name              | Rows  |
--------------------------------------------------------------------
|   0 | SELECT STATEMENT              |                   |       |
|   1 |  NESTED LOOPS                 |                   |       |
|   2 |   NESTED LOOPS                |                   |    11 |
|   3 |    SORT UNIQUE                |                   |   107 |
|   4 |     INDEX FULL SCAN           | EMP_DEPARTMENT_IX |   107 |
|   5 |    INDEX UNIQUE SCAN          | DEPT_ID_PK        |     1 |
|   6 |   TABLE ACCESS BY INDEX ROWID| DEPARTMENTS       |     1 |
--------------------------------------------------------------------

Predicate Information (identified by operation id):
---------------------------------------------------

   5 - access("DEPARTMENT_ID"="DEPARTMENT_ID")
```

Semijoin Restrictions

There is only one major documented restriction controlling when the optimizer can use a semijoin (in 11gR2). The optimizer does not choose a semijoin for any subqueries inside an OR branch. In previous versions of Oracle, the inclusion of the DISTINCT keyword would also disable semijoins, but that restriction no longer exists. Listing 11-18 contains an example showing a semijoin being disabled inside an OR branch.

Listing 11-18. Semijoins disabled inside an OR branch in 11gR2

```
SQL> select /* exists with or */ department_name
  2      from hr.departments dept
  3      where 1=2 or exists (select null from hr.employees emp
  4                      where emp.department_id = dept.department_id);


DEPARTMENT_NAME
------------------
Administration
Marketing
Purchasing
Human Resources
Shipping
IT
Public Relations
Sales
Executive
Finance
Accounting

11 rows selected.

Execution Plan
----------------------------------------------------------
Plan hash value: 1089943216


-----------------------------------------------------------------
| Id  | Operation                      | Name              | Rows  |
-----------------------------------------------------------------
|   0 | SELECT STATEMENT               |                   |   11  |
|   1 |  NESTED LOOPS                  |                   |       |
|   2 |   NESTED LOOPS                 |                   |   11  |
|   3 |    SORT UNIQUE                 |                   |  107  |
|   4 |     INDEX FULL SCAN            | EMP_DEPARTMENT_IX |  107  |
|*  5 |     INDEX UNIQUE SCAN          | DEPT_ID_PK        |    1  |
|   6 |    TABLE ACCESS BY INDEX ROWID | DEPARTMENTS       |    1  |
-----------------------------------------------------------------

Predicate Information (identified by operation id):
---------------------------------------------------

   5 - access("EMP"."DEPARTMENT_ID"="DEPT"."DEPARTMENT_ID")
```

In 12c, however, this restriction seems to have been lifted, as demonstrated in Listing 11-19. As you can see, a semijoin plan is chosen.

Listing 11-19. Semijoin Restriction Lifted in 12c

```
SQL> select /* exists with or */ department_name
  2      from hr.departments dept
  3      where 1=2 or exists (select null from hr.employees emp
  4                      where emp.department_id = dept.department_id);
```

```
DEPARTMENT_NAME
-------------------------------
Administration
Marketing
Purchasing
Human Resources
Shipping
IT
Public Relations
Sales
Executive
Finance
Accounting

11 rows selected.

Execution Plan
------------------------------------------------------------
Plan hash value: 954076352


-------------------------------------------------------------------
| Id | Operation                     | Name              | Rows  |
-------------------------------------------------------------------
|  0 | SELECT STATEMENT              |                   |       |
|  1 |  MERGE JOIN SEMI              |                   |    11 |
|  2 |   TABLE ACCESS BY INDEX ROWID | DEPARTMENTS       |    27 |
|  3 |    INDEX FULL SCAN            | DEPT_ID_PK        |    27 |
|  4 |   SORT UNIQUE                 |                   |   107 |
|  5 |    INDEX FULL SCAN            | EMP_DEPARTMENT_IX |   107 |
-------------------------------------------------------------------


Predicate Information (identified by operation id):
---------------------------------------------------

   4 - access("EMP"."DEPARTMENT_ID"="DEPT"."DEPARTMENT_ID")
       filter("EMP"."DEPARTMENT_ID"="DEPT"."DEPARTMENT_ID")
```

Semijoin Requirements

Semijoins are an optimization that can improve performance of some queries dramatically. They are not used that often, however. Here, briefly, are the requirements for Oracle's cost-based optimizer to decide to use a semijoin:

- The statement must use either the keyword IN (= ANY) or the keyword EXISTS.

- The statement must have a subquery in the IN or EXISTS clause.

- If the statement uses the EXISTS syntax, it must use a correlated subquery (to get the expected results).

- The IN or EXISTS clause may not be contained inside an OR branch.

Many systems have queries with massive numbers of literals (thousands sometimes) inside IN clauses. These are often generated statements that get populated by doing a query to find the list in the first place. These statements can occasionally benefit from being rewritten to let the optimizer take advantage of a semijoin—that is, taking the query that populated the literals in the IN clause and combining it with the original, instead of running them as two separate queries.

One of the reasons that developers avoid this approach is fear of the unknown. The IN and EXISTS syntax was at one time processed very differently, leading to situations in which performance could vary considerably depending on the method chosen. The good news is that the optimizer is smart enough now to transform either form into a semijoin, or not, depending on the optimizer costing algorithms. The question of whether to implement a correlated subquery with EXISTS or the more simple IN construct is now pretty much a moot point from a performance standpoint. And with that being the case, there seems to be little reason to use the more complicated EXISTS format. No piece of software is perfect, though; occasionally, the optimizer makes incorrect choices. Fortunately, when the optimizer does make a mistake, there are tools available to "encourage" it to do the right thing.

Antijoins

Antijoins are basically the same as semijoins in that they are an optimization option that can be applied to nested loop, hash, and merge joins. However, they are the opposite of semijoins in terms of the data they return. Those mathematician types familiar with relational algebra would say that antijoins can be defined as the complement of semijoins.

Figure 11-2 shows a Venn diagram that is often used to illustrate a MINUS operation (all the records from table A, MINUS the records from table B). The diagram in Figure 11-2 is a reasonable representation of an antijoin as well. The *Oracle Database SQL Language Reference, 11g Release 2,()* describes the antijoin this way: "An antijoin returns rows from the left side of the predicate for which there are no corresponding rows on the right side of the predicate. It returns rows that fail to match (NOT IN) the subquery on the right side" (http://docs.oracle.com/cd/E11882_01/server.112/e41084/queries006.htm#sthref2260).

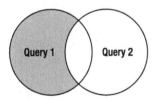

Figure 11-2. Illustration of an antijoin

The Oracle manual also provides this example of an antijoin (http://docs.oracle.com/cd/E11882_01/server.112/e41084/statements_10002.htm#i2182875):

```
SELECT * FROM employees
   WHERE department_id NOT IN
   (SELECT department_id FROM departments
      WHERE location_id = 1700)
   ORDER BY last_name;
```

As with semijoins, there is no specific SQL syntax that invokes an anti-join. Antijoins are one of several choices that the optimizer may use when the SQL statement contains the keywords NOT IN or NOT EXISTS. By the way, NOT IN is much, much more common than NOT EXISTS, probably because it is easier to understand.

So let's take a look at our standard queries, now altered to anti form (in other words, using NOT IN and NOT EXISTS instead of IN and EXISTS) in Listing 11-20.

Listing 11-20. Standard NOT IN and NOT EXISTS Examples

```
SQL> -- anti_ex1.sql
SQL>
SQL> select /* NOT IN */ department_name
  2      from hr.departments dept
  3      where department_id NOT IN
  4      (select department_id from hr.employees emp);

no rows selected

SQL>
SQL> select /* NOT EXISTS */ department_name
  2      from hr.departments dept
  3      where NOT EXISTS (select null from hr.employees emp
  4                         where emp.department_id = dept.department_id);

DEPARTMENT_NAME
------------------------------
Treasury
Corporate Tax
Control And Credit
Shareholder Services
Benefits
Manufacturing
Construction
Contracting
Operations
IT Support
NOC
IT Helpdesk
Government Sales
Retail Sales
Recruiting
Payroll

16 rows selected.
```

Clearly NOT IN and NOT EXISTS do not return the same data in this example, and are therefore not functionally equivalent. The reason for this behavior has to do with how the queries deal with null values being returned by the subquery. If a null value is returned to a NOT IN operator, then no records are returned by the overall query, which seems counterintuitive. But, if you think about it for a minute, it should make a little more sense. In the first place, the NOT IN operator is just another way of saying !=ANY. So you can think of it as a loop comparing values. If it finds a match, the record is discarded. If it doesn't, the record gets returned to the user. But what if it doesn't know whether the records match? Remember that a null is not equal to anything, not even another null. In this case, Oracle has chosen to return a value of FALSE, even though the theoretical answer is unknown. C. J. Date[1] would probably argue that this is a shortcoming of Oracle's implementation of relational theory, because it should provide for all three potential answers. At any rate, this is the way it works in Oracle.

---

[1]C.J. Date is most well known for his work, while working for IBM in the late 1960's, with Ted Codd on the development of the relational model for database management.

Assuming that your requirements are to return records even in the case of nulls being returned by the subquery, you have the following options:

- Apply an NVL function to the column or columns returned by the subquery.

- Add an IS NOT NULL predicate to the subquery.

- Implement a NOT NULL constraint or constraints

- Don't use NOT IN; use the NOT EXISTS form, which doesn't care about nulls.

In many cases a NOT NULL constraint is the best option, but there are situations when there are valid arguments against them. Listing 11-21 shows two examples of dealing with the null issue.

Listing 11-21. Avoiding Nulls with NOT IN

```
SQL> select /* IN with NVL */ department_name
  2      from hr.departments dept
  3      where department_id NOT IN
  4      (select nvl(department_id,-10) from hr.employees emp);

DEPARTMENT_NAME
------------------------------
Treasury
Corporate Tax
Control And Credit
Shareholder Services
Benefits
Manufacturing
Construction
Contracting
Operations
IT Support
NOC
IT Helpdesk
Government Sales
Retail Sales
Recruiting
Payroll

16 rows selected.

SQL>
SQL> select /* IN with NOT NULL */ department_name
  2      from hr.departments dept
  3      where department_id NOT IN (select department_id
  4      from hr.employees emp where department_id is not null);

DEPARTMENT_NAME
------------------------------
Treasury
Corporate Tax
Control And Credit
Shareholder Services
```

Benefits
Manufacturing
Construction
Contracting
Operations
IT Support
NOC
IT Helpdesk
Government Sales
Retail Sales
Recruiting
Payroll

16 rows selected.

As you can see, although an unconstrained NOT IN statement is not the same as a NOT EXISTS, applying an NVL function or adding an IS NOT NULL clause to the subquery predicate solves the issue.

Although NOT IN and NOT EXISTS are the most commonly chosen syntax options for producing an antijoin, there are at least two other options that can return the same data. The MINUS operator can obviously be used for this purpose. A clever trick with an outer join can also be used. Listing 11-22 shows examples of both techniques.

Listing 11-22. Alternative Syntax to NOT IN and NOT EXISTS

```
SQL> select /* MINUS */ department_name
  2      from hr.departments
  3      where department_id in
  4        (select department_id from hr.departments
  5         minus
  6         select department_id from hr.employees);

DEPARTMENT_NAME
-------------------------------
Treasury
Corporate Tax
Control And Credit
Shareholder Services
Benefits
Manufacturing
Construction
Contracting
Operations
IT Support
NOC
IT Helpdesk
Government Sales
Retail Sales
Recruiting
Payroll

16 rows selected.
```

```
SQL> select /* LEFT OUTER */ department_name
  2       from hr.departments dept left outer join
  3            hr.employees emp on dept.department_id = emp.department_id
  4       where emp.department_id is null;

DEPARTMENT_NAME
------------------------------
Treasury
Corporate Tax
Control And Credit
Shareholder Services
Benefits
Manufacturing
Construction
Contracting
Operations
IT Support
NOC
IT Helpdesk
Government Sales
Retail Sales
Recruiting
Payroll

16 rows selected.

SQL> select /* LEFT OUTER OLD (+) */ department_name
  2       from hr.departments dept, hr.employees emp
  3       where dept.department_id = emp.department_id(+)
  4       and emp.department_id is null;

DEPARTMENT_NAME
------------------------------
Treasury
Corporate Tax
Control And Credit
Shareholder Services
Benefits
Manufacturing
Construction
Contracting
Operations
IT Support
NOC
IT Helpdesk
Government Sales
Retail Sales
Recruiting
Payroll

16 rows selected.
```

So the MINUS is slightly convoluted but it returns the right data and is functionally equivalent to the NOT EXISTS form and the null constrained NOT IN form. The LEFT OUTER statement probably needs a little discussion. It makes use of the fact that an outer join creates a dummy record on the right side for each record on the left that doesn't have an actual match. Because all the columns in the dummy record are null, we can get the records without matches by adding the EMP.DEPARTMENT_ID IS NULL clause to the outer join. This statement is also functionally equivalent to the NOT EXISTS statement and the null constrained NOT IN form. There is a myth that this form performs better than NOT EXISTS, and maybe this was true at some point, but it is not the case now. Therefore, there appears to be little reason to use it because it is considerably less clear in its intent.

Antijoin Plans

As with semijoins, antijoins are an optimization option that may be applied to nested loop joins, hash joins, or merge joins. Also remember that it is an optimization that allows processing to stop when the first match is found in the subquery. Listing 11-23 shows the pseudocode that should help to describe the process more fully. Note that the outer query is Q1 and the inner (subquery) is Q2.

Listing 11-23. Pseudocode for Nested Loop Antijoin

```
open Q1
while Q1 still has records
   fetch record from Q1
   result = true
   open Q2
   while Q2 still has records
      fetch record from Q2
      if (Q1.record matches Q2.record) then    ←= antijoin optimization
         result = false                        ←= difference from semijoin
         exit loop
      end if
   end loop
   close Q2
   if (result = true) return Q1 record
end loop
close Q1
```

This example is basically a nested loop antijoin. The optimization provided by the anti option is the IF statement that lets the code bail out of the inner loop as soon as it finds a match. Obviously, with large datasets, this technique can result in significant time savings compared with a normal nested loops join that must loop through every record returned by the inner query.

Now let's rerun our first two antijoin examples (the standard NOT IN and NOT EXISTS queries) in Listing 11-24 and look at the plans the optimizer generates.

Listing 11-24. Antijoin Execution Plans

```
SQL> select /* NOT IN */ department_name
  2      from hr.departments dept
  3      where department_id NOT IN (select department_id from hr.employees emp);

no rows selected
```

Execution Plan

Plan hash value: 4208823763

```
-----------------------------------------------------------------------
| Id  | Operation                            | Name        | Rows  |
-----------------------------------------------------------------------
|   0 | SELECT STATEMENT                     |             |       |
|   1 |  MERGE JOIN ANTI NA                  |             |    17 |
|   2 |   SORT JOIN                          |             |    27 |
|   3 |    TABLE ACCESS BY INDEX ROWID BATCHED| DEPARTMENTS |    27 |
|   4 |     INDEX FULL SCAN                  | DEPT_ID_PK  |    27 |
|   5 |   SORT UNIQUE                        |             |   107 |
|   6 |    TABLE ACCESS FULL                 | EMPLOYEES   |   107 |
-----------------------------------------------------------------------
```

Predicate Information (identified by operation id):

```
   5 - access("DEPARTMENT_ID"="DEPARTMENT_ID")
       filter("DEPARTMENT_ID"="DEPARTMENT_ID")
```

```
SQL>
SQL> select /* NOT EXISTS */ department_name
  2      from hr.departments dept
  3      where NOT EXISTS (select null from hr.employees emp
  4                    where emp.department_id = dept.department_id);
```

```
DEPARTMENT_NAME
------------------------------
Treasury
Corporate Tax
Control And Credit
Shareholder Services
Benefits
Manufacturing
Construction
Contracting
Operations
IT Support
NOC
IT Helpdesk
Government Sales
Retail Sales
Recruiting
Payroll

16 rows selected.
```

```
Execution Plan
-----------------------------------------------------------
Plan hash value: 1314441467

---------------------------------------------------------------
| Id  | Operation                    | Name              | Rows  |
---------------------------------------------------------------
|   0 | SELECT STATEMENT             |                   |       |
|   1 |  MERGE JOIN ANTI             |                   |    17 |
|   2 |   TABLE ACCESS BY INDEX ROWID| DEPARTMENTS       |    27 |
|   3 |    INDEX FULL SCAN           | DEPT_ID_PK        |    27 |
|   4 |   SORT UNIQUE                |                   |   107 |
|   5 |    INDEX FULL SCAN           | EMP_DEPARTMENT_IX |   107 |
---------------------------------------------------------------

Predicate Information (identified by operation id):
---------------------------------------------------

   4 - access("EMP"."DEPARTMENT_ID"="DEPT"."DEPARTMENT_ID")
       filter("EMP"."DEPARTMENT_ID"="DEPT"."DEPARTMENT_ID")
```

Notice that the NOT EXISTS statement generated a MERGE JOIN ANTI plan whereas the NOT IN statement generated a MERGE JOIN ANTI NA plan. The MERGE JOIN ANTI is the standard antijoin that has been available since version 7 or thereabouts. The ANTI NA that was applied to the MERGE JOIN, however, is a new optimization that was introduced in 11g. (NA stands for *null aware*.) This new optimization allows the optimizer to deal with NOT IN queries when the optimizer doesn't know if nulls can be returned by the subquery. Prior to 11g, antijoins could not be performed on NOT IN queries unless the optimizer was sure the nulls would not be returned. Note that this optimization technique has nothing at all to do with the "unintuitive" behavior of NOT IN clauses with respect to nulls that was mentioned previously. The query still returns no records if a null is returned by the subquery, but it does it a lot faster with the ANTI NA option. Listing 11-25 provides another example that shows how the various ways of handling nulls in the subquery affect the optimizer's choices. (Note that the fsp.sql script shows some execution statistics from v$sql along with the operation and options from v$sql_plan if a semi- or antijoin is used.)

Listing 11-25. Antijoin Execution Plans

```
SQL > set echo on
SQL > @flush_pool
SQL > alter system flush shared_pool;

System altered.

SQL > @anti_ex2
SQL > set echo on
SQL > -- anti_ex2.sql
SQL >
SQL > select /* IN */ department_name
  2      from hr.departments dept
  3      where department_id not in
  4      (select department_id from hr.employees emp);
```

```
no rows selected
SQL >
SQL > select /* IN with NVL */ department_name
  2       from hr.departments dept
  3       where department_id not in
  4       (select nvl(department_id,-10) from hr.employees emp);

DEPARTMENT_NAME
------------------------------
Treasury
Corporate Tax
Control And Credit
Shareholder Services
Benefits
Manufacturing
Construction
Contracting
Operations
IT Support
NOC
IT Helpdesk
Government Sales
Retail Sales
Recruiting
Payroll

16 rows selected.

SQL >
SQL > select /* IN with NOT NULL */ department_name
  2       from hr.departments dept
  3       where department_id not in (select department_id
  4       from hr.employees emp where department_id is not null);

DEPARTMENT_NAME
------------------------------
Treasury
Corporate Tax
Control And Credit
Shareholder Services
Benefits
Manufacturing
Construction
Contracting
Operations
IT Support
NOC
IT Helpdesk
Government Sales
Retail Sales
Recruiting
Payroll

16 rows selected.
```

```
SQL>
SQL > select /* EXISTS */ department_name
  2      from hr.departments dept
  3      where not exists (select null from hr.employees emp
  4                          where emp.department_id = dept.department_id);

DEPARTMENT_NAME
------------------------------
Treasury
Corporate Tax
Control And Credit
Shareholder Services
Benefits
Manufacturing
Construction
Contracting
Operations
IT Support
NOC
IT Helpdesk
Government Sales
Retail Sales
Recruiting
Payroll

16 rows selected.

SQL >
SQL > set echo off
SQL > set echo on
SQL > @fsp
SQL > select distinct s.sql_id,
  2  -- s.child_number,
  3  s.plan_hash_value plan_hash,
  4    sql_text,
  5  -- decode(options,'SEMI',operation||' '||options,null) join
  6    case when options like '%SEMI%' or options like '%ANTI%' then
  7    operation||' '||options end join
  8    from v$sql s, v$sql_plan p
  9    where s.sql_id = p.sql_id
 10    and s.child_number = p.child_number
 11    and upper(sql_text) like upper(nvl('&sql_text','%department%'))
 12    and sql_text not like '%from v$sql where sql_text like nvl(%'
 13    and s.sql_id like nvl('&sql_id',s.sql_id)
 14    order by 1, 2, 3
 15    /
Enter value for sql_text:
Enter value for sql_id:
```

SQL_ID	PLAN_HASH	SQL_TEXT	JOIN
0pcrmdk1tw0tf	4201340344	select /* IN */ department_name from hr.departments dept where department_id not in (select department_id from hr.employees emp)	MERGE JOIN ANTI NA
56d82nhza8ftu	3082375452	select /* IN with NOT NULL */ department_name from hr.departments dept where department_id not in (select department_id from hr.employees emp where department_id is not null)	MERGE JOIN ANTI
5c77dgzy60ubx	3082375452	select /* EXISTS */ department_name from hr.departments dept where not exists (select null from hr.employees emp where emp.department_id = dept.department_id)	MERGE JOIN ANTI
a71yzhpc0n2uj	3822487693	select /* IN with NVL */ department_name from hr.departments dept where department_id not in (select nvl(department_id,-10) from hr.employees emp)	MERGE JOIN ANTI

As you can see, the EXISTS, NOT IN with NOT NULL, and NOT IN with NVL all use the normal antijoin, whereas the NOT IN that ignores the handling of nulls must use the new null-aware antijoin (ANTI NA). Now let's rerun our examples of LEFT OUTER and MINUS and see what plans they come up with. Listing 11-26 shows the results of the optimizer for several alternative syntax variations.

Listing 11-26. Alternate Antijoin Syntax Execution Plans

```
SQL> set echo on
SQL> @flush_pool
SQL> alter system flush shared_pool;

System altered.

SQL > @anti_ex3
SQL > set echo on
SQL > -- anti_ex3.sql
SQL >
SQL > select /* NOT EXISTS */ department_name
  2       from hr.departments dept
  3       where not exists (select null from hr.employees emp
  4                    where emp.department_id = dept.department_id);

DEPARTMENT_NAME
------------------------------
Treasury
Corporate Tax
Control And Credit
Shareholder Services
Benefits
Manufacturing
Construction
```

```
Contracting
Operations
IT Support
NOC
IT Helpdesk
Government Sales
Retail Sales
Recruiting
Payroll

16 rows selected.

SQL >
SQL > select /* NOT IN NOT NULL */ department_name
  2      from hr.departments dept
  3      where department_id not in (select department_id
  4          from hr.employees emp where department_id is not null);

DEPARTMENT_NAME
-------------------------------
Treasury
Corporate Tax
Control And Credit
Shareholder Services
Benefits
Manufacturing
Construction
Contracting
Operations
IT Support
NOC
IT Helpdesk
Government Sales
Retail Sales
Recruiting
Payroll

16 rows selected.

SQL >
SQL > select /* LEFT OUTER */ department_name
  2      from hr.departments dept left outer join
  3          hr.employees emp on dept.department_id = emp.department_id
  4      where emp.department_id is null;

DEPARTMENT_NAME
-------------------------------
Treasury
Corporate Tax
Control And Credit
Shareholder Services
Benefits
```

```
Manufacturing
Construction
Contracting
Operations
IT Support
NOC
IT Helpdesk
Government Sales
Retail Sales
Recruiting
Payroll

16 rows selected.

SQL >
SQL > select /* LEFT OUTER OLD (+) */ department_name
  2      from hr.departments dept, hr.employees emp
  3      where dept.department_id = emp.department_id(+)
  4      and emp.department_id is null;

DEPARTMENT_NAME
-------------------------------
Treasury
Corporate Tax
Control And Credit
Shareholder Services
Benefits
Manufacturing
Construction
Contracting
Operations
IT Support
NOC
IT Helpdesk
Government Sales
Retail Sales
Recruiting
Payroll

16 rows selected.

SQL >
SQL > select /* MINUS */ department_name
  2      from hr.departments
  3      where department_id in
  4        (select department_id from hr.departments
  5         minus
  6         select department_id from hr.employees);

DEPARTMENT_NAME
-------------------------------
Treasury
Corporate Tax
Control And Credit
Shareholder Services
```

```
Benefits
Manufacturing
Construction
Contracting
Operations
IT Support
NOC
IT Helpdesk
Government Sales
Retail Sales
Recruiting
Payroll
16 rows selected.
SQL >
SQL > set echo off
SQL > @fsp
Enter value for sql_text:
Enter value for sql_id:


SQL_ID          PLAN_HASH  SQL_TEXT                                               JOIN
-------------   ---------- -----------------------------------------------------  ----------------
6ttOzwazv6my9  3082375452  select /* NOT EXISTS */ department_name                 MERGE JOIN ANTI
                           from hr.departments dept where not exists
                           (select null from hr.employees emp where
                           emp.department_id = dept.department_id)

as34zpj5n5dfd  3082375452  select /* LEFT OUTER */ department_name                 MERGE JOIN ANTI
                           from hr.departments dept left outer join
                           hr.employees emp on dept.department_id =
                           emp.department_id where emp.department_id is null

czsqu5txh5tyn  3082375452  select /* NOT IN NOT NULL */ department_name            MERGE JOIN ANTI
                           from hr.departments dept where department_id
                           not in (select department_id from hr.employees
                           emp where department_id is not null)

dcxOkqhwbuv6r  3082375452  select /* LEFT OUTER OLD (+) */ department_name         MERGE JOIN ANTI
                           from hr.departments dept, hr.employees emp where
                           dept.department_id = emp.department_id(+) and
                           emp.department_id is null

gvdsm57xf24jv  2972564128  select /* MINUS */ department_name from
                           hr.departments where department_id in
                           (select department_id from hr.departments
                           minus select department_id from hr.employees)
```

Although all these statements return the same data, the MINUS does not use the antijoin optimization. If you look closely, you can see that all the other statements have the same plan hash value—meaning, they have exactly the same plan.

Controlling Antijoin Plans

Not surprisingly, the mechanisms for controlling antijoin plans are similar to those available for controlling semijoins. As before, you have both hints and parameters to work with.

Controlling Antijoin Plans Using Hints

There are several hints:

ANTIJOIN: Perform an antijoin (the optimizer gets to pick which kind).

USE_ANTI: Perform an antijoin (this is an older version of the ANTIJOIN hint).

NL_AJ: Perform a nested loops antijoin (deprecated as of 10g).

HASH_AJ: Perform a hash antijoin (deprecated as of 10g).

MERGE_AJ: Perform a merge antijoin (deprecated as of 10g).

As with the hints controlling semijoins, several of the antijoin hints (NL_AJ, HASH_AJ, MERGE_AJ) have been documented as being deprecated. Nevertheless, they continue to work in 12c. However, it should be noted that these specific hints do not work in situations when the optimizer must use the new null-aware version of antijoin (more on that in a moment). All the antijoin hints should be specified in the subquery, as opposed to in the outer query. Also note that there is not a NO_ANTIJOIN hint, which is a bit unusual. Listing 11-27 shows an example of using the NL_AJ hint.

Listing 11-27. Controlling Antijoin Execution Plans with Hints

```
SQL> set autotrace traceonly exp
SQL> @anti_ex4
SQL> -- anti_ex4.sql
SQL>
SQL> select /* IN */ department_name
  2      from hr.departments dept
  3      where department_id not in (select /*+ nl_aj */ department_id
  4                                  from hr.employees emp);

Execution Plan
----------------------------------------------------------
Plan hash value: 4208823763

---------------------------------------------------------------------------
| Id  | Operation                             | Name         | Rows |
---------------------------------------------------------------------------
|   0 | SELECT STATEMENT                      |              |      |
|   1 |  MERGE JOIN ANTI NA                   |              |   17 |
|   2 |   SORT JOIN                           |              |   27 |
|   3 |    TABLE ACCESS BY INDEX ROWID BATCHED| DEPARTMENTS  |   27 |
|   4 |     INDEX FULL SCAN                   | DEPT_ID_PK   |   27 |
|   5 |   SORT UNIQUE                         |              |  107 |
|   6 |    TABLE ACCESS FULL                  | EMPLOYEES    |  107 |
---------------------------------------------------------------------------
```

```
Predicate Information (identified by operation id):
--------------------------------------------------

   5 - access("DEPARTMENT_ID"="DEPARTMENT_ID")
       filter("DEPARTMENT_ID"="DEPARTMENT_ID")

SQL>
SQL> select /* EXISTS */ department_name
  2      from hr.departments dept
  3      where not exists (select /*+ nl_aj */ null from hr.employees emp
  4                        where emp.department_id = dept.department_id);

Execution Plan
----------------------------------------------------------
Plan hash value: 3082375452
```

```
--------------------------------------------------------
| Id | Operation           | Name             | Rows |
--------------------------------------------------------
|  0 | SELECT STATEMENT    |                  |      |
|  1 |  NESTED LOOPS ANTI  |                  |   17 |
|  2 |   TABLE ACCESS FULL | DEPARTMENTS      |   27 |
|  3 |   INDEX RANGE SCAN  | EMP_DEPARTMENT_IX|   41 |
--------------------------------------------------------
```

```
Predicate Information (identified by operation id):
--------------------------------------------------

   3 - access("EMP"."DEPARTMENT_ID"="DEPT"."DEPARTMENT_ID")
```

Controlling Antijoin Plans at the Instance Level

There are also a number of parameters (all hidden) that affect the optimizer's behavior with respect to antijoins:

- _always_anti_join

- _gs_anti_semi_join_allowed

- _optimizer_null_aware_antijoin

- _optimizer_outer_to_anti_enabled

The main parameter to be concerned about is _always_anti_join, which is equivalent to _always_semi_join in its behavior (it has the same valid values, and the options do the same things). Note that it's been documented as being obsolete for some time. Nevertheless, as with _always_semi_join, it still appears to work in 12c. Listing 11-28 shows an example of using a hint and turning off antijoins altogether with the _optimizer_null_aware_antijoin parameter.

Listing 11-28. Controlling Antijoin Execution Plans with Parameters

```
SQL> -- anti_ex5.sql
SQL>
SQL> select /* EXISTS */ department_name
  2      from hr.departments dept
  3      where not exists (select null from hr.employees emp
  4                        where emp.department_id = dept.department_id);
```

```
DEPARTMENT_NAME
------------------------------
Treasury
Corporate Tax
Control And Credit
Shareholder Services
Benefits
Manufacturing
Construction
Contracting
Operations
IT Support
NOC
IT Helpdesk
Government Sales
Retail Sales
Recruiting
Payroll

16 rows selected.

SQL>
SQL> select /* EXISTS with hint */ department_name
  2      from hr.departments dept
  3      where not exists (select /*+ hash_aj */ null from hr.employees emp
  4                        where emp.department_id = dept.department_id);

DEPARTMENT_NAME
------------------------------
NOC
Manufacturing
Government Sales
IT Support
Benefits
Shareholder Services
Retail Sales
Control And Credit
Recruiting
Operations
Treasury
Payroll
Corporate Tax
Construction
Contracting
IT Helpdesk

16 rows selected.
```

```
SQL>
SQL> select /* IN */ department_name
  2      from hr.departments dept
  3      where department_id not in
  4      (select department_id from hr.employees emp);

no rows selected

SQL>
SQL> alter session set "_optimizer_null_aware_antijoin"=false;

Session altered.

SQL>
SQL> select /* IN with AAJ=OFF*/ department_name
  2      from hr.departments dept
  3      where department_id not in
  4      (select department_id from hr.employees emp);

no rows selected

SQL>
SQL> alter session set "_optimizer_null_aware_antijoin"=true;

Session altered.

SQL>
SQL> set echo off
SQL> @fsp
Enter value for sql_text:
Enter value for sql_id:

SQL_ID        PLAN_HASH SQL_TEXT                                            JOIN
------------- --------- --------------------------------------------------- --------------------
0kvb76bzacc7b 3587451639 select /* EXISTS with hint */ department_name        HASH JOIN ANTI
                         from hr.departments dept where not exists
                         (select /*+ hash_aj */ null from hr.employees
                         emp where emp.department_id = dept.department_id)

0pcrmdk1tw0tf 4201340344 select /* IN */ department_name from               MERGE JOIN ANTI NA
                         hr.departments dept where department_id not in
                         (select department_id from hr.employees emp)

5c77dgzy6Oubx 3082375452 select /* EXISTS */ department_name from           NESTED LOOPS ANTI
                         hr.departments dept where not exists
                         (select null from hr.employees emp where
                         emp.department_id = dept.department_id)

67u11c3rv1aag 3416340233 select /* IN with AAJ=OFF*/ department_name from
                         hr.departments dept where department_id not in
                         (select department_id from hr.employees emp)
```

Antijoin Restrictions

As with semijoins, antijoin transformations cannot be performed if the subquery is on an OR branch of a WHERE clause. I trust you will take my word for this one, because the behavior has already been demonstrated with semijoins in the previous sections.

As of 12c, there are no major restrictions on the use of antijoins. The major restriction in 10g was that any subquery that could return a null was not a candidate for antijoin optimization. The new ANTI NA (and ANTI SNA) provide the optimizer with the capability to apply the antijoin optimization even in those cases when a null may be returned by a subquery. Note that this does not change the somewhat confusing behavior causing no records to be returned from a subquery contained in a NOT IN clause if a null value is returned by the subquery.

Because 10g is still in wide use, a brief discussion of the restriction that has been removed in 11g and above by the null-aware antijoin is warranted. When a NOT IN clause is specified in 10g, the optimizer checks to see if the column or columns being returned are guaranteed not to contain nulls. This is done by checking for NOT NULL constraints, IS NOT NULL predicates, or a function that translates null into a value (typically NVL). If all three of these checks fail, the 10g optimizer does not choose an antijoin. Furthermore, it transforms the statement by applying an internal function (LNNVL) that has the possible side effect of disabling potential index access paths. Listing 11-29 shows an example from a 10.2.0.4 database.

Listing 11-29. 10g NOT NULL Antijoin Behavior

```
> !sql
sqlplus "/ as sysdba"

SQL*Plus: Release 10.2.0.4.0 - Production on Tue Jun 29 14:50:25 2010

Copyright (c) 1982, 2007, Oracle.  All Rights Reserved.

Connected to:
Oracle Database 10g Enterprise Edition Release 10.2.0.4.0 - Production
With the Partitioning, OLAP, Data Mining and Real Application Testing options

SQL> @anti_ex6
SQL> -- anti_ex6.sql
SQL>
SQL> set autotrace trace exp
SQL>
SQL> select /* NOT IN */ department_name
  2     from hr.departments dept
  3     where department_id not in (select department_id from hr.employees emp);

Execution Plan
----------------------------------------------------------
Plan hash value: 3416340233

----------------------------------------------------------------------------
|Id|Operation              |Name        |Rows|Bytes|Cost (%CPU)|Time     |
----------------------------------------------------------------------------
| 0|SELECT STATEMENT       |            |  26|  416|   29   (0)|00:00:01|
|*1| FILTER                |            |    |     |           |         |
| 2|  TABLE ACCESS FULL    |DEPARTMENTS |  27|  432|    2   (0)|00:00:01|
|*3|  TABLE ACCESS FULL    |EMPLOYEES   |   2|    6|    2   (0)|00:00:01|
----------------------------------------------------------------------------
```

Predicate Information (identified by operation id):

```
   1 - filter( NOT EXISTS (SELECT /*+ */ 0 FROM "HR"."EMPLOYEES" "EMP"
               WHERE LNNVL("DEPARTMENT_ID"<>:B1)))
   3 - filter(LNNVL("DEPARTMENT_ID"<>:B1))
```

```
SQL> select /* NOT NULL */ department_name
  2      from hr.departments dept
  3      where department_id not in (select department_id
  4          from hr.employees emp where department_id is not null);
```

Execution Plan

Plan hash value: 3082375452

```
-------------------------------------------------------------------------
|Id|Operation           |Name            |Rows|Bytes|Cost (%CPU)|Time    |
-------------------------------------------------------------------------
| 0|SELECT STATEMENT    |                |  17|  323|   2   (0)|00:00:01 |
| 1| NESTED LOOPS ANTI  |                |  17|  323|   2   (0)|00:00:01 |
| 2|  TABLE ACCESS FULL |DEPARTMENTS     |  27|  432|   2   (0)|00:00:01 |
|*3|  INDEX RANGE SCAN  |EMP_DEPARTMENT_IX|  41| 123|   0   (0)|00:00:01 |
-------------------------------------------------------------------------
```

Predicate Information (identified by operation id):

```
   3 - access("DEPARTMENT_ID"="DEPARTMENT_ID")
       filter("DEPARTMENT_ID" IS NOT NULL)
```

```
SQL>
SQL> select /* NVL */ department_name
  2      from hr.departments dept
  3      where department_id not in (select nvl(department_id,'-10')
  4                                  from hr.employees emp);
```

Execution Plan

Plan hash value: 2918349777

```
-----------------------------------------------------------------
|Id|Operation           |Name          |Rows|Bytes|Cost (%CPU)|Time    |
-----------------------------------------------------------------
| 0|SELECT STATEMENT    |              |  17|  323|   5  (20)|00:00:01|
|*1| HASH JOIN ANTI     |              |  17|  323|   5  (20)|00:00:01|
| 2|  TABLE ACCESS FULL |DEPARTMENTS   |  27|  432|   2   (0)|00:00:01|
| 3|  TABLE ACCESS FULL |EMPLOYEES     | 107|  321|   2   (0)|00:00:01|
-----------------------------------------------------------------
```

Predicate Information (identified by operation id):

```
   1 - access("DEPARTMENT_ID"=NVL("DEPARTMENT_ID",(-10)))
```

The first statement in this example is the same old NOT IN query that we've run several times already in 12c. Note that in 10g, instead of doing an ANTI NA, it doesn't apply the anti optimization at all. This is because of the restriction guaranteeing that nulls are not returned from the subquery in 10g. The second statement (NOT NULL) applies the NOT NULL predicate to the WHERE clause in the subquery, which enables the optimizer to pick a standard antijoin. The third statement uses the NVL function to ensure that no nulls are returned by the subquery. Notice that it also is able to apply the antijoin. Last, notice the Predicate Information section below the plan for the first statement (NOT IN). Note that the optimizer has transformed the statement by adding the LNNVL function, which can have the unpleasant side effect of disabling index access paths. The other plans do not have this transformation applied. Listing 11-30 shows the same NOT IN statement run in 12c.

Listing 11-30. 12c NOT NULL Antijoin Behavior

```
SQL> -- anti_ex6.sql
SQL>
SQL> set autotrace trace exp
SQL>
SQL> select /* NOT IN */ department_name
  2     from hr.departments dept
  3     where department_id not in (select department_id from hr.employees emp);

Execution Plan
----------------------------------------------------------
Plan hash value: 4208823763

--------------------------------------------------------------------------
| Id  | Operation                            | Name        | Rows  |
--------------------------------------------------------------------------
|   0 | SELECT STATEMENT                     |             |       |
|   1 |  MERGE JOIN ANTI NA                  |             |    17 |
|   2 |   SORT JOIN                          |             |    27 |
|   3 |    TABLE ACCESS BY INDEX ROWID BATCHED| DEPARTMENTS |    27 |
|   4 |     INDEX FULL SCAN                  | DEPT_ID_PK  |    27 |
|   5 |   SORT UNIQUE                        |             |   107 |
|   6 |    TABLE ACCESS FULL                 | EMPLOYEES   |   107 |
--------------------------------------------------------------------------

Predicate Information (identified by operation id):
-----------------------------------------------------

   5 - access("DEPARTMENT_ID"="DEPARTMENT_ID")
       filter("DEPARTMENT_ID"="DEPARTMENT_ID")
```

Notice that in 12c the optimizer generates the new null-aware ANTI join (ANTI NA). Also note that the internally applied LNNVL function that is used in 10g is no longer necessary.

Antijoin Requirements

Requirements is such a strong word. Oracle's optimizer is a very complex piece of software. Producing an exhaustive list of every possible way to get a specified result is a difficult task at best. With respect to antijoins, Oracle has recently implemented some clever ways of making use of this join option that you would not normally expect. So please take these "requirements" as a list of the most probable ways to cause Oracle to produce an anti-join, as opposed to an exhaustive list:

- The statement should use either the NOT IN (!= ALL) or NOT EXISTS phrases.

- The statement should have a subquery in the NOT IN or NOT EXISTS clause.

- The NOT IN or NOT EXISTS clause should not be contained inside an OR branch.

- Subqueries in NOT EXISTS clauses should be correlated to the outer query.

■ **Note** 10g requires NOT IN subqueries to be coded to not return nulls (11g and higher doesn't).

Antijoins are a powerful optimization option that can be applied by the optimizer. They can provide impressive performance improvements, particularly when large data volumes are involved. Although the NOT IN syntax is more intuitive, it also has some counterintuitive behavior when it comes to dealing with nulls. The NOT EXISTS syntax is better suited to handling subqueries that may return nulls, but is, in general, a little harder to read and—probably for that reason—is not used as often. The outer join trick is even less intuitive than the NOT EXISTS syntax and, in general, provides no advantage over it. The MINUS operator does not appear to offer any advantages over the other forms and does not currently use the antijoin optimization. It is apparent that Oracle's intent is to allow the optimizer to use the antijoin option whenever possible because of the dramatic performance enhancement potential that it provides.

Summary

Antijoins and sSemijoins are options that the optimizer can apply to many of the common join methods. The basic idea of these optimization options is to cut short the processing of the normal hash, merge, or nested loop joins. In some cases, antijoins and semijoins can provide dramatic performance improvements. There are multiple ways to construct SQL statements that result in the optimizer using these options. The most common are the IN and EXISTS keywords. When these optimizations were first released, the processing of the statements varied significantly, depending on whether you used IN or EXISTS. Over the years, the optimizer has been enhanced to allow many statement transformations; the result is that, in 11g and higher, there is little difference between using one form or the other. In many cases, the statements get transformed into the same form anyway. In this chapter you've seen how this optimization technique works, when it can be used, and how to verify whether it is being used. You've also seen some mechanisms for controlling the optimizer's use of this feature.

CHAPTER 12

■ ■ ■

Indexes

Indexes are critical structures needed for efficient retrieval of rows, for uniqueness enforcement, and for the efficient implementation of referential constraints. Oracle Database provides many index types suited for different needs of application access methods. Effective choice of index type and critical choice of columns to index are of paramount importance for optimal performance. Inadequate or incorrect indexing strategy can lead to performance issues. In this chapter, I discuss basic implementation of indexes, various index types, their use cases, and strategy to choose optimal index type. Indexes available in Oracle Database as of version 12c can be classified broadly into one of three categories based on the algorithm they use: B-tree indexes, bitmap indexes, and index-organized tables, or IOTs.

Implementation of bitmap indexes is suitable for columns with infrequent update, insert, and delete activity. Bitmap indexes are better suited for static columns with lower distinct values—a typical case in data warehouse applications. A gender column in a table holding population data is a good example, because as there are only a few distinct values for this column. I discuss this in more detail later in this chapter.

■ **Note** All tables mentioned in this chapter refer to the objects in SH schema supplied by Oracle Corporation example scripts.

B-tree indexes are commonly used in all applications. There are many index types such as partitioned indexes, compressed indexes, and function-based indexes implemented as B-tree indexes. Special index types such as IOTs and secondary indexes on IOTs are also implemented as B-tree indexes.

THE IMPORTANCE OF CHOOSING CORRECTLY

I have a story to share about the importance of indexing choice. During an application upgrade, an application designer chose bitmap indexes on a few key tables that were modified heavily. After the application upgrade, the application response time was not acceptable. Because this application was a warehouse management application, performance issues were affecting the shipping and order fulfillment process of this U.S. retail giant.

We were called in to troubleshoot the issue. We reviewed the database performance metrics and quickly realized that the poor choice of index type was the root cause of the performance issue. Database metrics were showing that the application was suffering from locking contention, too. These bitmap indexes used to grow from about 100MB in the morning to around 4 to 5GB by midafternoon. The designer even introduced a job to rebuild the index at regular intervals. We resolved the issue by converting the bitmap indexes to B-tree indexes. This story demonstrates you the importance of choosing an optimal indexing strategy.

Understanding Indexes

Is a full table scan access path always bad? Not necessarily. Efficiency of an access path is very specific to the construction of the SQL statement, application data, distribution of data, and the environment. No one access path is suitable for all execution plans. In some cases, a full table scan access path is better than an index-based access path. Next, I discuss choice of index usage, considerations for choosing columns to index, and special considerations for null clauses.

When to Use Indexes

In general, index-based access paths perform better if the predicates specified in the SQL statement are selective—meaning, that few rows are fetched applying the specified predicates. A typical index-based access path usually involves following three steps:

1. Traversing the index tree and collecting the rowids from the leaf block after applying the SQL predicates on indexed columns

2. Fetching the rows from the table blocks using the rowids

3. Applying the remainder of the predicates on the rows fetched to derive a final result set

The second step of accessing the table block is costlier if numerous rowids are returned during step 1. For every rowid from the index leaf blocks, table blocks need to be accessed, and this might result in multiple physical IOs, leading to performance issues. Furthermore, table blocks are accessed one block at a time physically and can magnify performance issues. For example, consider the SQL statement in Listing 12-1 accessing the sales table with just one predicate, country='Spain'; the number of rows returned from step 5 is estimated to be 7985. So, 7985 rowids estimated to be retrieved from that execution step and table blocks must be accessed at least 7985 times to retrieve the row pieces. Some of these table block accesses might result in physical IO if the block is not in the buffer cache already. So, the index-based access path might perform worse for this specific case.

Listing 12-1. Index Access Path

```
create index sales_fact_c2 on sales_fact ( country);

select /*+ index (s sales_fact_c2) */ count(distinct(region))
from sales_fact s where country='Spain';
```

```
-------------------------------------------------------------------------
| Id  | Operation                   | Name          | E-Rows | Cost (%CPU)|
-------------------------------------------------------------------------
|   0 | SELECT STATEMENT            |               |        |   930 (100)|
|   1 |  SORT AGGREGATE             |               |      1 |            |
|   2 |   VIEW                      | VW_DAG_0      |      7 |   930   (0)|
|   3 |    HASH GROUP BY            |               |      7 |   930   (0)|
|   4 |     TABLE ACCESS BY INDEX   | SALES_FACT    |   7985 |   930   (0)|
|     |         ROWID BATCHED       |               |        |            |
|*  5 |      INDEX RANGE SCAN       | SALES_FACT_C2 |   7985 |    26   (0)|
-------------------------------------------------------------------------
```

```
select count(distinct(region)) from sales_fact s where country='Spain';
```

```
--------------------------------------------------------------
| Id | Operation            | Name        | E-Rows | Cost (%CPU)|
--------------------------------------------------------------
|  0 | SELECT STATEMENT     |             |        |  309 (100)|
|  1 |  SORT AGGREGATE      |             |      1 |           |
|  2 |   VIEW               | VW_DAG_0    |      7 |  309   (1)|
|  3 |    HASH GROUP BY     |             |      7 |  309   (1)|
|* 4 |     TABLE ACCESS FULL| SALES_FACT  |   7985 |  309   (1)|
--------------------------------------------------------------
```

In Listing 12-1, in the first SELECT statement, I force an index-based access path using the hint index (s sales_fact_c2), and the optimizer estimates the cost of the index-based access plan as 930. The execution plan for the next SELECT statement without the hint shows that the optimizer estimates the cost of the full table scan access path as 309. Evidently, the full table scan access path is estimated to be cheaper and more suited for this SQL statement.

■ **Note** In Listing 12-1 and the other listings in this chapter, the statements have been run and their execution plans displayed. However, for brevity, much of the output has been elided.

Let's consider another SELECT statement. In Listing 12-2, all three columns are specified in the predicate of the SQL statement. Because the predicates are more selective, the optimizer estimates that eight rows will be retrieved from this SELECT statement, and the cost of the execution plan is 3. I force the full table scan execution plan in the subsequent SELECT statement execution, and then the cost of this execution plan is 309. Index-based access is more optimal for this SQL statement.

Listing 12-2. Index Access Path 2

```
select product, year, week from sales_fact
where product='Xtend Memory' and  year=1998 and week=1;
```

```
-------------------------------------------------------------
| Id | Operation          | Name         | E-Rows | Cost (%CPU)|
-------------------------------------------------------------
|  0 | SELECT STATEMENT   |              |        |   3 (100)|
|* 1 |  INDEX RANGE SCAN  | SALES_FACT_C1 |     8 |   3   (0)|
-------------------------------------------------------------
```

```
select /*+ full(sales_fact) */ product, year, week from sales_fact where product='Xtend Memory'and
year=1998 and week=1;
```

```
-------------------------------------------------------------
| Id | Operation          | Name        | E-Rows | Cost (%CPU)|
-------------------------------------------------------------
|  0 | SELECT STATEMENT   |             |        | 309 (100)|
|* 1 |  TABLE ACCESS FULL | SALES_FACT  |     8 | 309   (1)|
-------------------------------------------------------------
```

Evidently, no single execution plan is better for all SQL statements. Even for the same statement, depending on the data distribution and the underlying hardware, execution plans can behave differently. If the data distribution changes, the execution plans can have different costs. This is precisely why you need to collect statistics that reflect the distribution of data so the optimizer can choose the optimal plan.

Furthermore, full table scans and fast full scans perform multiblock read calls whereas index range scans or index unique scans do single-block reads. Multiblock reads are much more efficient than single-block reads on a block-by-block basis. Optimizer calculations factor this difference and choose an index-based access path or full table access path as appropriate. In general, an Online Transaction Processing (OLTP) application uses index-based access paths predominantly, and the data warehouse application uses full table access paths predominantly.

A final consideration is parallelism. Queries can be tuned to execute faster using parallelism when the predicates are not selective enough. The cost of an execution plan using a parallel full table scan can be cheaper than the cost of a serial index range scan, leading to an optimizer choice of a parallel execution plan.

Choice of Columns

Choosing optimal columns for indexing is essential to improve SQL access performance. The choice of columns to index should match the predicates used by the SQL statements. The following are considerations for choosing an optimal indexing column:

- If the application code uses the equality or range predicates on a column while accessing a table, it's a good strategy to consider indexing that column. For multicolumn indexes, the leading column should be the column used in most predicates. For example, if you have a choice to index the columns c1 and c2, then the leading column should be the column used in most predicates.

- It is also important to consider the cardinality of the predicates and the selectivity of the columns. For example, if a column has just two distinct values with a uniform distribution, then that column is probably not a good candidate for B-tree indexes because 50 percent of the rows will be fetched by equality predicates on the column value. On the other hand, if the column has two distinct values with skewed distribution—in other words, one value occurs in a few rows *and* the application accesses that table with the infrequently occurring column value—it is preferable to index that column.

- An example is a processed column in a work-in-progress table with three distinct values (P, N, and E). The application accesses that table with the processed='N' predicate. Only a few unprocessed rows are left with a status of 'N' in processed_column, so access through the index is optimal. However, queries with the predicate Processed='Y' should not use the index because nearly all rows are fetched by this predicate. Histograms can be used so that the optimizer can choose the optimal execution plan, depending on the literal or bind variables.

▪ **Note** Cardinality is defined as the number of rows expected to be fetched by a predicate or execution step. Consider a simple equality predicate on the column assuming uniform distribution in the column values. Cardinality is calculated as the number of rows in the table divided by the number of distinct values in the column. For example, in the sales table, there are 918,000 rows in the table, and the prod_id column has 72 distinct values, so the cardinality of the equality predicate on the prod_id column is 918,000 ÷ 72 = 12,750. So, in other words, the predicate prod_id=:b1 expects to fetch 12,750 rows. Columns with lower cardinality are better candidates for indexing because the index selectivity is better. For unique columns, cardinality of an equality predicate is one. Selectivity is a measure ranging between zero and one, simplistically defined as 1 ÷ NDV, where NDV stands for number of distinct values. So, the cardinality of a predicate can be defined as the selectivity multiplied by the number of rows in the table.

- Think about column ordering, and arrange the column order in the index to suit the application access patterns. For example, in the sales table, the selectivity of the prod_id column is $1 \div 72$ and the selectivity of the cust_id column is $1 \div 7059$. It might appear that column cust_id is a better candidate for indexes because the selectivity of that column is lower. However, if the application specifies equality predicates on the prod_id column and does not specify cust_id column in the predicate, then the cust_id column need not be indexed even though the cust_id column has better selectivity. If the application uses the predicates on both the prod_id and cust_id columns, then it is preferable to index both columns, with the cust_id column as the leading column. Consideration should be given to the column usage in the predicates instead of relying on the selectivity of the columns.

- You should also consider the cost of an index. Inserts, deletes, and updates (updating the indexed columns) maintain the indexes—meaning, if a row is inserted into the sales table, then a new value pair is added to the index matching the new value. This index maintenance is costlier if the columns are updated heavily, because the indexed column update results in a delete and insert at the index level internally, which could introduce additional contention points, too.

- Consider the length of the column. If the indexed column is long, then the index is big. The cost of that index may be higher than the overall gain from the index. A bigger index also increases undo size and redo size.

- In a multicolumn index, if the leading column has only a few distinct values, consider creating that index as a compressed index. The size of these indexes are then smaller, because repeating values are not stored in a compressed index. I discuss compressed indexes later in this chapter.

- If the predicates use functions on indexed columns, the index on that column may not be chosen. For example, the predicate to_char(prod_id) =:B1 applies a to_char function on the prod_id column. A conventional index on the prod_id column might not be chosen for this predicate, and a function-based index needs to be created on the to_char(prod_id) column.

- Do not create bitmap indexes on columns modified aggressively. Internal implementation of a bitmap index is more suitable for read-only columns with few distinct values. The size of the bitmap index grows rapidly if the indexed columns are updated. Excessive modification to a bitmap index can lead to enormous locking contention, too. Bitmap indexes are more prevalent in data warehouse applications.

The Null Issue

It is common practice for a SQL statement to specify the IS NULL predicate. Null values are not stored in single-column indexes, so the predicate IS NULL does not use a single-column index. But, null values *are* stored in a multicolumn index. By creating a multicolumn index with a dummy second column, you can enable the use of an index for the IS NULL clause

In Listing 12-3, a single-column index T1_N1 is created on column n1. The optimizer does not choose the index access path for the SELECT statement with the predicate n1 is null. Another index, t1_n10, is created on the expression (n1,0), and the optimizer chooses the access path using the index because the null values are stored in this multicolumn index. The size of the index is kept smaller by adding a dummy value of 0 to the index.

Listing 12-3. NULL Handling

```
drop table t1;
create table  t1 (n1 number, n2 varchar2(100) );
insert into t1 select object_id, object_name from dba_objects where rownum<101;
commit;
create index t1_n1 on t1(n1);
select * from t1 where n1 is null;
```

```
-------------------------------------------------------
| Id  | Operation       | Name | E-Rows | Cost (%CPU)|
-------------------------------------------------------
|   0 | SELECT STATEMENT |     |        |   3 (100)|
|*  1 |  TABLE ACCESS FULL| T1  |      1 |   3   (0)|
-------------------------------------------------------
```

```
create index t1_n10 on t1(n1,0);
select * from t1 where n1 is null;
```

```
-------------------------------------------------------------------
| Id  | Operation                        | Name    | E-Rows | Cost (%CPU)|
-------------------------------------------------------------------
|   0 | SELECT STATEMENT                 |         |        |   2 (100)|
|   1 |  TABLE ACCESS BY INDEX ROWID BATCHED| T1   |      1 |   2   (0)|
|*  2 |   INDEX RANGE SCAN               | T1_N10  |      5 |   1   (0)|
-------------------------------------------------------------------
```

Index Structural Types

Oracle Database provides various types of indexes to suit application access paths. These index types can be classified loosely into three broad categories based on the structure of an index: B-tree indexes, bitmap indexes, and IOTs.

B-tree indexes

B-tree indexes implement a structure similar to an inverted tree with a root node, branch nodes, and leaf nodes, and they use tree traversal algorithms to search for a column value. The leaf node holds the (value, rowid) pair for that index key column, and the rowid refers to the physical location of a row in the table block. The branch block holds the directory of leaf blocks and the value ranges stored in those leaf blocks. The root block holds the directory of branch blocks and the value ranges addressed in those branch blocks.

Figure 12-1 shows the B-tree index structure for a column with a number datatype. This figure is a generalization of the index structure to help you improve your understanding; the actual index structures are far more complex. The root block of the index holds branch block addresses and the range of values addressed in the branch blocks. The branch blocks hold the leaf block addresses and the range of values stored in the leaf blocks.

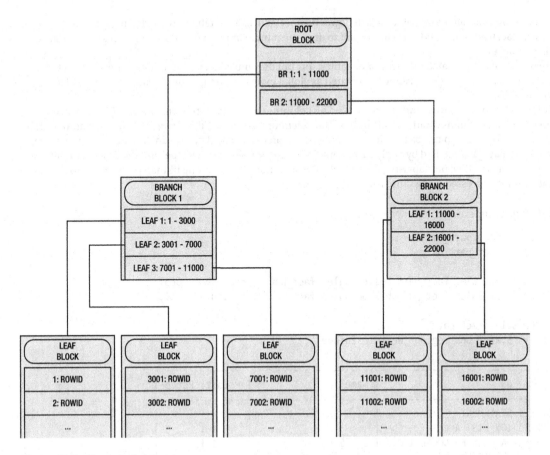

Figure 12-1. *B-tree index structure*

A search for a column value using an index usually results in an index range scan or an index unique scan. Such a search starts at the root block of the index tree, traverses to the branch block, and then traverses to the leaf block. Rowids are fetched from the leaf blocks from the (column value, rowid) pairs, and each row piece is fetched from the table block using the rowid. Without the indexes, searching for a key inevitably results in a full table scan of the table.

In Figure 12-1, if the SQL statement is searching for a column value of 12,000 with a predicate n1=12000, the index range scan starts at the root block, traverses to the second branch block because the second branch block holds the range of values from 11,001 to 22,000, and then traverses to the fourth leaf block because that leaf block holds the column value range from 11,001 to 16,000. As the index stores the sorted column values, the range scan quickly accesses the column value matching n1=12000 from the leaf block entries, reads the rowids associated with that column value, and accesses the rows from the table using those rowids. Rowids are pointers to the physical location of a row in the table block.

B-tree indexes are suitable for columns with lower selectivity. If the columns are not selective enough, the index range scan is slower. Furthermore, less selective columns retrieve numerous rowids from the leaf blocks, leading to excessive single-block access to the table.

Bitmap Indexes

Bitmap indexes are organized and implemented differently than B-tree indexes. Bitmaps are used to associate the rowids with the column value. Bitmap indexes are not suitable for columns with a higher number of updates or for tables with heavy Data Manipulation Language (DML) activity. Bitmap indexes are suitable for data warehouse tables with mostly read-only operations on columns with lower distinct values. If the tables are loaded regularly, as in the case of a typical data warehouse table, it is important to drop the bitmap index before the load, then load the data and recreate the bitmap index.

Bitmap indexes can be created on partitioned tables, too, but they must be created as local indexes. As of Oracle Database release 12c, bitmap indexes cannot be created as global indexes. Bitmap indexes cannot be created as unique indexes either.

In Listing 12-4, two new bitmap indexes are added on columns country and region. The SELECT statement specifies predicates on columns country and region. The execution plan shows three major operations: bitmaps from the bitmap index sales_fact_part_bm1 fetched by applying the predicate country='Spain', bitmaps from the bitmap index sales_fact_part_bm2 fetched by applying the predicate region='Western Europe', and then those two bitmaps are ANDed to calculate the final bitmap using the BITMAP AND operation. The resulting bitmap is converted to rowids, and the table rows are accessed using those rowids.

Listing 12-4. Bitmap Indexes

```
drop index sales_fact_part_bm1;
drop index sales_fact_part_bm2;

create bitmap index sales_fact_part_bm1 on sales_fact_part ( country ) Local;
create bitmap index sales_fact_part_bm2 on sales_fact_part ( region ) Local;

select * from sales_fact_part
where country='Spain' and region='Western Europe' ;
```

```
-------------------------------------------------------------------------------
| Id  | Operation                     | Name                | Pstart| Pstop |
-------------------------------------------------------------------------------
|   0 | SELECT STATEMENT              |                     |       |       |
|   1 |  PARTITION LIST ALL           |                     |     1 |     5 |
|   2 |   TABLE ACCESS BY LOCAL INDEX | SALES_FACT_PART     |     1 |     5 |
|     |       ROWID BATCHED           |                     |       |       |
|   3 |    BITMAP CONVERSION TO ROWIDS|                     |       |       |
|   4 |     BITMAP AND                |                     |       |       |
|*  5 |      BITMAP INDEX SINGLE VALUE| SALES_FACT_PART_BM1 |     1 |     5 |
|*  6 |      BITMAP INDEX SINGLE VALUE| SALES_FACT_PART_BM2 |     1 |     5 |
-------------------------------------------------------------------------------
```

Bitmap indexes can introduce severe locking issues if the index is created on columns modified heavily by DML activity. Updates to a column with a bitmap index must update a bitmap, and the bitmaps usually cover a set of rows. So, an update to one row can lock a set of rows in that bitmap. Bitmap indexes are used predominantly in data warehouse applications; they are of limited use in OLTP applications.

Index-Organized Tables

Conventional tables are organized as heap tables because the table rows can be stored in any table block. Fetching a row from a conventional table using a primary key involves primary key index traversal, followed by a table block access using the rowid. In IOTs, the table itself is organized as an index, all columns are stored in the index tree itself, and the access to a row using a primary key involves index access only. This access using IOTs is better because all columns can be fetched by accessing the index structure, thereby avoiding the table access. This is an efficient access pattern because the number of accesses is minimized.

With conventional tables, every row has a rowid. When rows are created in a conventional table, they do not move (row chaining and row migration are possible, but the headpiece of the row does not move). However, IOT rows are stored in the index structure itself, so rows can be migrated to different leaf blocks as a result of DML operations, resulting in index leaf block splitting and merging. In a nutshell, rows in the IOTs do not have physical rowids whereas rows in the heap tables always have fixed rowids.

IOTs are appropriate for tables with the following properties:

- *Tables with shorter row length*: Tables with fewer short columns are appropriate for IOTs. If the row length is longer, the size of the index structure can be unduly large, leading to more resource usage than the heap tables.

- *Tables accessed mostly through primary key columns*: Although secondary indexes can be created on IOTs, secondary indexes can be resource intensive if the primary key is longer. I cover secondary indexes later in this section.

In Listing 12-5, an IOT sales_iot is created by specifying the keywords organization index. Note that the SELECT statement specifies only a few columns in the primary key, and the execution plan shows that columns are retrieved by an index range scan, thereby avoiding a table access. Had this been a conventional heap table, you would see an index unique scan access path followed by rowid-based table access.

Listing 12-5. Index Organized Tables

```
drop table sales_iot;
create table sales_iot
  ( prod_id number not null,
    cust_id number not null,
    time_id date not null,
    channel_id number not null,
    promo_id number not null,
    quantity_sold number (10,2) not null,
    amount_sold number(10,2) not null,
    primary key ( prod_id, cust_id, time_id, channel_id, promo_id)
 )
organization index ;
insert into sales_iot select * from sales;
commit;

@analyze_table

select quantity_sold, amount_sold from sales_iot where
prod_id=13 and cust_id=2 and channel_id=3 and promo_id=999;
```

```
-----------------------------------------------------------------
| Id  | Operation       | Name             | E-Rows | Cost (%CPU)|
-----------------------------------------------------------------
|   0 | SELECT STATEMENT |                 |        |    3 (100)|
|*  1 |   INDEX RANGE SCAN| SYS_IOT_TOP_94835 |    1 |    3   (0)|
-----------------------------------------------------------------
```

A secondary index can be created on an IOT, too. Conventional indexes store the (column value, rowid) pair. But, in IOTs, rows do not have a physical rowid; instead, a (column value, logical rowid) pair is stored in the secondary index. This logical rowid is essentially a primary key column with the values of the row stored efficiently. Access through the secondary index fetches the logical rowid using the secondary index, then uses the logical rowid to access the row piece using the primary key IOT structure.

In Listing 12-6, a secondary index `sales_iot_sec` is created on an IOT `sales_iot`. The SELECT statement specifies the predicates on secondary index columns. The execution plan shows an all index access, where logical rowids are fetched from the secondary index `sales_iot_sec` with an index range scan access method, and then rows are fetched from the IOT primary key using the logical rowids fetched with an index unique scan access method. Also, note that the size of the secondary index is nearly one half the size of the primary index, and secondary indexes can be resource intensive if the primary key is longer.

Listing 12-6. Secondary Indexes on an IOT

```
drop index sales_iot_sec ;
create index sales_iot_sec on
 sales_iot (channel_id, time_id, promo_id, cust_id) ;

select quantity_sold, amount_sold from sales_iot where
channel_id=3 and promo_id=999 and cust_id=12345 and time_id='30-JAN-00';
```

```
-----------------------------------------------------------------------
| Id  | Operation          | Name             | E-Rows | Cost (%CPU)|
-----------------------------------------------------------------------
|   0 | SELECT STATEMENT   |                  |        |   7 (100)|
|*  1 |  INDEX UNIQUE SCAN| SYS_IOT_TOP_94835 |     4 |   7   (0)|
|*  2 |   INDEX RANGE SCAN| SALES_IOT_SEC     |     4 |   3   (0)|
-----------------------------------------------------------------------
```

```
select segment_name, sum( bytes/1024/1024) sz from dba_segments
where segment_name in ('SYS_IOT_TOP_94835','SALES_IOT_SEC')
group by segment_name ;
```

```
SEGMENT_NAME                         SZ
----------------------------- ----------
SALES_IOT_SEC                        36
SYS_IOT_TOP_94835                    72
```

IOTs are special structures that are useful to eliminate additional indexes on tables with short rows that undergo heavy DML and SELECT activity. However, adding secondary indexes on IOTs can cause an increase in index size, redo size, and undo size if the primary key is longer.

Partitioned Indexes

Indexes can be partitioned similar to a table partitioning scheme. There is a variety of ways to partition the indexes. Indexes can be created on partitioned tables as local or global indexes, too. Furthermore, there are various partitioning schemes available, such as range partitioning, hash partitioning, list partitioning, and composite partitioning. From Oracle Database version 10g onward, partitioned indexes also can be created on nonpartitioned tables.

Local Indexes

Locally partitioned indexes are created with the LOCAL keyword and have the same partition boundaries as the table. In a nutshell, there is an index partition associated with each table partition. Availability of the table is better because the maintenance operations can be performed at the individual partition level. Maintenance operations on the index partitions lock only the corresponding table partitions, not the whole table. Figure 12-2 shows how a local index corresponds to a table partition.

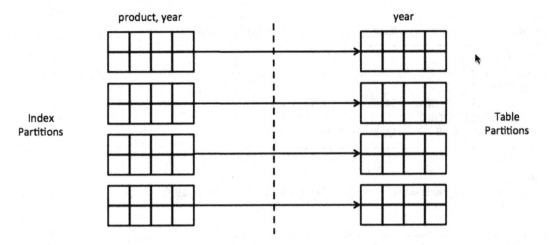

Figure 12-2. *Local partitioned index*

If the local index includes the partitioning key columns *and* if the SQL statement specifies predicates on the partitioning key columns, the execution plan needs to access just one or a few index partitions. This concept is known as *partition elimination*. Performance improves if the execution plan searches in a minimal number of partitions. In Listing 12-6, a partitioned table sales_fact_part is created with a partitioning key on the year column. A local index sales_fact_part_n1 is created on the product and year columns. First, the SELECT statement specifies the predicates on just the product column without specifying any predicate on the partitioning key column. In this case, all five index partitions must be accessed using the predicate product = 'Xtend Memory'. Columns Pstart and Pstop in the execution plan indicate that all partitions are accessed to execute this SQL statement.

Next, the SELECT statement in Listing 12-7 specifies the predicates on columns product and year. Using the predicate year=1998, the optimizer determines that only the second partition is to be accessed, eliminating access to all other partitions, because only the second partition stores the year column 1998 as indicated by the Pstart and Pstop columns in the execution plan. Also, the keywords in the execution plan TABLE ACCESS BY LOCAL INDEX ROWID BATCHED indicate that the row is accessed using a local index.

Listing 12-7. Local Indexes

```
drop table sales_fact_part;
CREATE table sales_fact_part
partition by range ( year )
( partition p_1997 values less than ( 1998) ,
  partition p_1998 values less than ( 1999),
  partition p_1999 values less than (2000),
  partition p_2000 values less than (2001),
  partition p_max values less than (maxvalue)
)
AS SELECT * from sales_fact;

create index sales_fact_part_n1 on sales_fact_part( product, year) local;

select * from  (
 select * from sales_fact_part where product = 'Xtend Memory'
) where rownum <21 ;
```

```
---------------------------------------------------------------------
| Id  | Operation                     | Name               | Pstart| Pstop |
---------------------------------------------------------------------
|   0 | SELECT STATEMENT              |                    |       |       |
|*  1 |  COUNT STOPKEY                |                    |       |       |
|   2 |   PARTITION LIST ALL          |                    |    1  |    5  |
|   3 |    TABLE ACCESS BY LOCAL      | SALES_FACT_PART    |    1  |    5  |
|     |    INDEX ROWID BATCHED        |                    |       |       |
|*  4 |     INDEX RANGE SCAN          | SALES_FACT_PART_N1 |    1  |    5  |
---------------------------------------------------------------------
```

```
select * from  (
 select * from sales_fact_part where product = 'Xtend Memory' and year=1998
) where rownum <21 ;
```

```
---------------------------------------------------------------------
| Id  | Operation                     | Name               | Pstart| Pstop |
---------------------------------------------------------------------
|   0 | SELECT STATEMENT              |                    |       |       |
|*  1 |  COUNT STOPKEY                |                    |       |       |
|   2 |   PARTITION LIST SINGLE       |                    |  KEY  |  KEY  |
|   3 |    TABLE ACCESS BY LOCAL      | SALES_FACT_PART    |    1  |    1  |
|     |    INDEX ROWID BATCHED        |                    |       |       |
|*  4 |     INDEX RANGE SCAN          | SALES_FACT_PART_N1 |    1  |    1  |
---------------------------------------------------------------------
```

Although the application availability is important, consider another point: If the predicate does not specify the partitioning key column, then all index partitions must be accessed to identify the candidate rows in the case of local indexes. This could lead to a performance issue if the partition count is very high, in the order of thousands. Even then, you want to measure the impact of creating the index as a local instead of a global index.

Creating local indexes improves the concurrency, too. I discuss this concept while discussing hash partitioning schemes.

Global Indexes

Global indexes are created with the keyword GLOBAL. In global indexes, partition boundaries of the index and the table do not need to match, and the partition keys can be different between the table and the index. Figure 12-3 shows how a global index bound does not have to match a table partition.

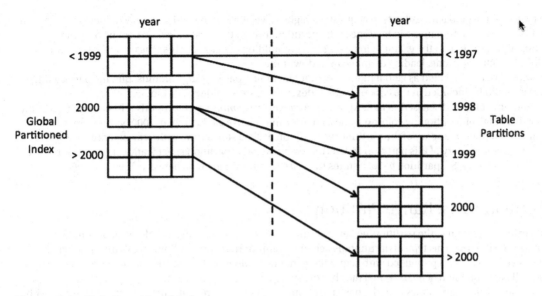

Figure 12-3. *Global partitioned index*

In Listing 12-8, a global index sales_fact_part_n1 is created on the year column. The partition boundaries are different between the table and the index, even though the partitioning column is the same. The subsequent SELECT statement specifies the predicate year=1998 to access the table, and the execution plan shows that partition 1 of the index and partition 2 of the table are accessed. Partition pruning was performed both at the table and index levels.

Listing 12-8. Global Indexes

```
create index sales_fact_part_n1 on sales_fact_part (year)
global partition by range ( year)
  (partition p_1998 values less than (1999),
   partition p_2000 values less than (2001),
   partition p_max values less than  (maxvalue)
);

select * from  (
 select * from sales_fact_part where product = 'Xtend Memory' and year=1998
) where rownum <21 ;
```

```
---------------------------------------------------------------------
| Id  | Operation                 | Name               | Pstart| Pstop |
---------------------------------------------------------------------
|   0 | SELECT STATEMENT          |                    |       |       |
|*  1 |  COUNT STOPKEY            |                    |       |       |
|   2 |   PARTITION LIST SINGLE   |                    |     1 |     1 |
|   3 |    TABLE ACCESS BY LOCAL  | SALES_FACT_PART    |     1 |     1 |
|     |    INDEX ROWID BATCHED    |                    |       |       |
|*  4 |     INDEX RANGE SCAN      | SALES_FACT_PART_N1 |     1 |     1 |
---------------------------------------------------------------------
```

Maintenance on the global index leads to acquiring a higher level lock on the table, thereby reducing application availability. In contrast, maintenance can be done at the partition level in the local indexes, affecting only the corresponding table partition. In the example in Listing 12-8, rebuilding the index Sales_fact_part_n1 acquires a table-level lock in exclusive mode, leading to application downtime.

Unique indexes can be created as global indexes without including partitioning columns. But, the partitioning key of the table should be included in the case of local indexes to create a unique local index.

The partitioning scheme discussed so far is known as a *range partitioning scheme*. In this scheme, each partition stores rows with a range of partitioning column values. For example, clause partition p_2000 values less than (2001) specifies the upper boundary of the partition, so partition p_2000 stores rows with year column values less than 2001. The lower boundary of this partition is determined by the prior partition specification partition p_1998 values less than (1999). So, partition p_2000 stores the year column value range between 1999 and 2000.

Hash Partitioning vs. Range Partitioning

In the hash partitioning scheme, the partitioning key column values are hashed using a hashing algorithm to identify the partition to store the row. This type of partitioning scheme is appropriate for partitioning columns populated with artificial keys, such as rows populated with sequence-generated values. If the distribution of the column value is uniform, then all partitions store a nearly equal number of rows.

There are a few added advantages with the hash partitioning scheme. There is an administration overhead with the range partitioning scheme because new partitions need to be added regularly to accommodate future rows. For example, if the partitioning key is order date_column, then the new partitions must be added (or the partition with maxvalue specified must be split) to accommodate rows with future date values. With the hash partitioning scheme, the overhead is avoided because the rows are distributed equally among the partitions using a hashing algorithm. All partitions have nearly equal numbers of rows if the distribution of the column value is uniform and there is no reason to add more partitions regularly.

■ **Note** Because of the nature of hashing algorithms, it is better to use a partition count of binary powers (in other words, 2, 4, 8, and so on). If you are splitting the partitions, it's better to double the number of partitions to keep near equal-size partitions. If you do not do this, the partitions all have different numbers of rows, which defeats the purpose of partitioning.

Hash partitioned tables and indexes are effective in combating concurrency-related performance associated with unique and primary key indexes. It is typical of primary key columns to be populated using a sequence of generated values. Because the indexes store the column values in a sorted order, the column values for new rows go into the rightmost leaf block of the index. After that leaf block is full, subsequently inserted rows go into the new rightmost leaf block, with the contention point moving from one leaf block to another leaf block. As the concurrency of the insert into the table increases, sessions modify the rightmost leaf block of the index aggressively. Essentially, the current rightmost leaf block of that index is a major contention point. Sessions wait for block contention wait events such as buffer busy waits. In Real Application Clusters(RAC), this problem is magnified as a result of global cache communication overhead, and the event gc buffer busy becomes the top wait event. This type of index that grows rapidly on the right-hand side is called a *right-hand growth index*.

Concurrency issues associated with right-hand growth indexes can be eliminated by hash partitioning the index with many partitions. For example, if the index is partitioned by a hash with 32 partitions, then inserts are spread effectively among the 32 rightmost leaf blocks because there are 32 index trees (an index tree for an index partition). Partitioning the table using a hash partitioning scheme and then creating a local index on that partitioned table also has the same effect.

In Listing 12-9, a hash partitioned table sales_fact_part is created and the primary key id column is populated from the sequence sfseq. There are 32 partitions in this table with 32 matching index partitions for the sales_fact_part_n1 index, because the index is defined as a local index. The subsequent SELECT statement accesses the table with the predicate id=1000. The Pstart and Pstop columns in the execution plan show that partition pruning has taken place and only partition 25 is being accessed. The optimizer identifies partition 25 by applying a hash function on the column value 1000.

Listing 12-9. Hash Partitioning Scheme

```
drop sequence sfseq;
create sequence sfseq cache 200;

drop table sales_fact_part;
CREATE table sales_fact_part
partition by hash ( id )
partitions 32
AS SELECT sfseq.nextval id , f.* from sales_fact f;

create unique index sales_fact_part_n1 on sales_fact_part( id ) local;

select * from sales_fact_part where id =1000;
```

```
-------------------------------------------------------------------------
| Id  | Operation                 | Name               | Pstart| Pstop |
-------------------------------------------------------------------------
|   0 | SELECT STATEMENT          |                    |       |       |
|   1 |  PARTITION HASH SINGLE    |                    |    25 |    25 |
|   2 |   TABLE ACCESS BY LOCAL   | SALES_FACT_PART    |    25 |    25 |
|     |          INDEX ROWID      |                    |       |       |
|*  3 |    INDEX UNIQUE SCAN      | SALES_FACT_PART_N1 |    25 |    25 |
-------------------------------------------------------------------------
```

If the data distribution is uniform in the partitioning key, as in the case of values generated from a sequence, then the rows are distributed uniformly to all partitions. You can use the dbms_rowid package to measure the data distribution in a hash partitioned table. In Listing 12-10, I use the dbms_rowid.rowid_object call to derive the object_id of the partition. Because every partition has its own object_id, you can aggregate the rows by object_id to measure the distribution of rows among the partitions. The output shows that all partitions have a nearly equal number of rows.

Listing 12-10. Hash Partitioning Distribution

```
select dbms_rowid.rowid_object(rowid) obj_id, count(*) from sales_fact_part
group by dbms_rowid.rowid_object(rowid);

OBJ_ID   COUNT(*)
-------  ----------
  94855       3480
  94866       3320
  94873       3544
...
  94869       3495
  94876       3402
  94881       3555

32 rows selected.
```

Rows are distributed uniformly among partitions using the hashing algorithm. In a few cases, you might need to precalculate the partition where a row is to be stored. This knowledge is useful to improve massive loading of data into a hash partitioned table. As of Oracle Database version 12c, the ora_hash function can be used to derive the partition ID if supplied with a partition key value. For example, for a table with 32 partitions, ora_hash(column_name, 31, 0) returns the partition ID. The second argument to the ora_hash function is the partition count less one. In Listing 12-11, I use both ora_hash and dbms_rowid.rowid_object to show the mapping between object_id and the hashing algorithm output. A word of caution, though: In future releases of Oracle Database, you need to test this before relying on this strategy because the internal implementation of hash partitioned tables may change.

Listing 12-11. Hash Partitioning Algorithm

```
select dbms_rowid.rowid_object(rowid) obj_id, ora_hash ( id, 31, 0) part_id ,count(*)
from sales_fact_part
group by dbms_rowid.rowid_object(rowid), ora_hash(id,31,0)
order by 1;

OBJ_ID  PART_ID  COUNT(*)
-------  -------- ---------
  94851        0      3505
  94852        1      3492
  94853        2      3572
...
  94880       29      3470
  94881       30      3555
  94882       31      3527

32 rows selected.
```

In essence, concurrency can be increased by partitioning the table and creating the right-hand growth indexes as local indexes. If the table cannot be partitioned, then that index alone can be partitioned to hash partitioning schema to resolve the performance issue.

Solutions to Match Application Characteristics

Oracle Database also provides indexing facilities to match the application characteristics. For example, some applications might be using function calls heavily, and SQL statements from those applications can be tuned using function-based indexes. I now discuss a few special indexing options available in Oracle Database.

Compressed Indexes

Compressed indexes are a variation of the conventional B-tree indexes. This type of index is more suitable for columns with repeating values in the leading columns. Compression is achieved by storing the repeating values in the leading columns once in the index leaf block. Pointers from the row area point to these prefix rows, avoiding explicit storage of these repeating values in the row area. Compressed indexes can be smaller compared with conventional indexes if the column has many repeating values. There is a minor increase in CPU usage during the processing of compressed indexes, which can be ignored safely.

The simplified syntax for the compressed index specification clause is as follows:

```
Create index <index name> on <schema.table_name>
 ( col1 [,col2... coln] )
Compress N Storage-parameter-clause
;
```

The number of leading columns to compress can be specified while creating a compressed index using the syntax compress N. For example, to compress two leading columns in a three-column index, the clause compress 2 can be specified. Repeating values in the first two columns are stored in the prefix area just once. You can only compress the leading columns; for example, you can't compress columns 1 and 3.

In Listing 12-12, a compressed index sales_fact_c1 is created on columns product, year, and week, with a compression clause compress 2 specified to compress the two leading columns. In this example, the repeating values of the product and year columns are stored once in the leaf blocks because the compress 2 clause is specified. Because there is higher amount of repetition in these two column values, the index size is reduced from 6MB (conventional index) to 2MB (compressed index) by compressing these two leading columns.

Listing 12-12. Compressed Indexes

```
select * from  (
  select product, year,week, sale from sales_fact
  order by product, year,week
) where rownum <21;


PRODUCT                             YEAR WEEK       SALE
---------------------------------- ---------- ----- ----------
1.44MB External 3.5" Diskette       1998   1       9.71
1.44MB External 3.5" Diskette       1998   1      38.84
1.44MB External 3.5" Diskette       1998   1       9.71
...


create index sales_fact_c1 on sales_fact ( product, year, week);

select 'Compressed index size (MB) :' ||trunc(bytes/1024/1024, 2)
from user_segments where segment_name='SALES_FACT_C1';


Compressed index size (MB) :6
...
create index sales_fact_c1 on sales_fact ( product, year, week) compress 2;

select 'Compressed index size (MB) :' ||trunc(bytes/1024/1024,2)
from user_segments where segment_name='SALES_FACT_C1';

Compressed index size (MB) :2
```

In Figure 12-4, a high-level overview of a compressed index leaf block is shown. This compressed index is a two-column index on the continent and country columns. Repeating values of continent columns are stored once in the prefix area of the index leaf blocks because the index is created with the clause compress 1. Pointers are used from the row area pointing to the prefix rows. For example, the continent column value ASIA occurs in three rows—(Asia, Hong Kong), (Asia, India), and (Asia, Indonesia)—but is stored once in the prefix area, and these three rows reuse the continent column value, avoiding explicit storage of the value three times. This reuse of column values reduces the size of the index.

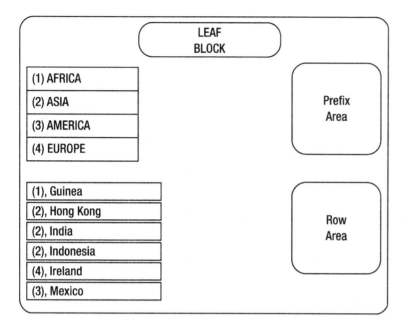

Figure 12-4. Compressed index

It is evident that data properties play a critical role in the compression ratio. If the repetition count of the column values is higher, then the compressed indexes provide greater benefit. If there is no repetition, then the compressed index might be bigger than the conventional index. So, compressed indexes are suitable for indexes with fewer distinct values in the leading columns. Columns compression and prefix_length in the dba_indexes/user_indexes view shows the compression attributes of the indexes.

The number of columns to choose for compression depends on the column value distribution. To identify the optimal number of columns to compress, the analyze index/validate structure statement can be used. In Listing 12-13, an uncompressed index sales_fact_c1 is analyzed with the validate structure clause. This analyze statement populates the index_stats view. The column index_stats.opt_cmpr_count displays the optimal compression count; for this index, it's 2. The column index_stats.cmpr_pctsave displays the index size savings compressing with the opt_cmpr_count columns. In this example, there is a savings of 67 percent in index space usage; so, the size of the compressed index with the compress 2 clause is 33 percent of the conventional uncompressed index size. This size estimate computes to 1.98MB and is close enough to actual index size.

Listing 12-13. Optimal Compression Count

```
analyze index sales_fact_c1 validate structure;

select opt_cmpr_count, opt_cmpr_pctsave from index_stats
where name ='SALES_FACT_C1';

OPT_CMPR_COUNT OPT_CMPR_PCTSAVE
-------------- ----------------
-------------2 --------------67
```

Beware that the analyze index validate structure statement acquires a share-level lock on the table and might induce application downtime.

There are a few restrictions on compressed indexes. For example, all columns can be compressed in the case of nonunique indexes, and all but the last column can be compressed in the case of unique indexes.

Function-Based Indexes

If a predicate applies a function on an indexed column, then the index on that column might not be chosen by the optimizer. For example, the index on the id column may not be chosen for the predicate to_char(id)= '1000' because the to_char function is applied on the indexed column. This restriction can be overcome by creating a function-based index on the expression to_char(id). Function-based indexes prestore the results of functions. Expressions specified in the predicate must match the expressions specified in the function-based index, though.

A function-based index can be created on user-defined functions, but those functions must be defined as deterministic functions—meaning, they must always return a consistent value for every execution of the function. User-defined functions that do not adhere to this rule can't be used to create the function-based indexes.

In Listing 12-14, a SELECT statement accesses the sales_fact_part table using the clause to_char(id)= '1000'. Without a function-based index, the optimizer chooses a full table scan access plan. A function-based index fact_part_fbi1 with the expression to_char(id) is added, and the optimizer chooses an index-based access path for the SELECT statement.

Listing 12-14. Function-Based Index

```
drop index sales_fact_part_fbi1;
select * from sales_fact_part where to_char(id)='1000';
```

```
---------------------------------------------------------------
| Id | Operation            | Name             | Pstart| Pstop |
---------------------------------------------------------------
|  0 | SELECT STATEMENT     |                  |       |       |
|  1 |  PARTITION HASH ALL|                    |     1 |    32 |
|* 2 |   TABLE ACCESS FULL| SALES_FACT_PART    |     1 |    32 |
---------------------------------------------------------------
```

```
create index sales_fact_part_fbi1 on sales_fact_part( to_char(id)) ;
@analyze_table_sfp
select * from sales_fact_part where to_char(id)='1000';
```

```
-----------------------------------------------------------------------
| Id | Operation             | Name                 | Pstart| Pstop |
-----------------------------------------------------------------------
|  0 | SELECT STATEMENT      |                      |       |       |
|  1 |  TABLE ACCESS BY GLOBAL | SALES_FACT_PART    | ROWID | ROWID |
|    |      INDEX ROWID BATCHED |                   | ROWID | ROWID |
|* 2 |    INDEX RANGE SCAN    | SALES_FACT_PART_FBI1 |       |       |
-----------------------------------------------------------------------
```

```
Predicate Information (identified by operation id):
---------------------------------------------------

   2 - access("SALES_FACT_PART"."SYS_NC00009$"='1000')
```

Note the access predicates printed at the end of Listing 12-14: "SYS_NC00009$"='1000'. A few implementation details of the function-based indexes are presented in Listing 12-15. Function-based indexes add a virtual column, with the specified expression as the default value, and then index that virtual column. This virtual column is visible in the dba_tab_cols view, and the dba_tab_cols.data_default column shows that expression used to populate the virtual column. Further viewing of dba_ind_columns shows that the virtual column is indexed.

Listing 12-15. Virtual Columns and Function-Based Index

```
select data_default, hidden_column, virtual_column from dba_tab_cols
where table_name='SALES_FACT_PART' and virtual_column='YES';

DATA_DEFAULT                      HID VIR
------------------------------    --- ---
TO_CHAR("ID")                     YES YES

select index_name,column_name from dba_ind_columns
where index_name='SALES_FACT_PART_FBI1';

INDEX_NAME                        COLUMN_NAME
------------------------------    -------------
SALES_FACT_PART_FBI1              SYS_NC00009$
```

It is important to collect statistics on the table after adding a function-based index. If not, that new virtual column does not have statistics, which might lead to performance anomalies. The script `analyze_table_sfp.sql` is used to collect statistics on the table with `cascade=>true`. Listing 12-16 shows the contents of the script `analyze_table_sfp.sql`.

Listing 12-16. `analyze_table_sfp.sql`

```
begin
   dbms_stats.gather_table_stats (
   ownname =>user,
   tabname=>'SALES_FACT_PART',
   cascade=>true);
end;
/
```

Function-based indexes can be implemented using virtual columns explicitly, too. An index can be added over that virtual column optionally. The added advantage with this method is that you can also use a partitioning scheme with a virtual column as the partitioning key. In Listing 12-17, a new virtual column, id_char, is added to the table using the VIRTUAL keyword. Then, a globally partitioned index on the id_char virtual column is created. The execution plan of the SELECT statement shows that table is accessed using the new index, and the predicate to_char(id)='1000' is rewritten to use the virtual column with the predicate id_char='1000'.

Listing 12-17. Virtual Columns and Function-Based Index

```
alter table sales_fact_part add
 ( id_char varchar2(40) generated always as (to_char(id) ) virtual );

create index sales_fact_part_c1 on sales_fact_part ( id_char)
global partition by hash (id_char)
partitions 32 ;

@analyze_table_sfp
select * from sales_fact_part where to_char(id)='1000' ;
```

```
-------------------------------------------------------------------------
| Id  | Operation                                    | Name              |
-------------------------------------------------------------------------
|   0 | SELECT STATEMENT                             |                   |
|   1 |  PARTITION HASH SINGLE                       |                   |
|   2 |   TABLE ACCESS BY GLOBAL INDEX ROWID BATCHED| SALES_FACT_PART    |
|*  3 |    INDEX RANGE SCAN                          | SALES_FACT_PART_C1 |
-------------------------------------------------------------------------

Predicate Information (identified by operation id):
---------------------------------------------------

   3 - access("SALES_FACT_PART"."ID_CHAR"='1000')
```

Reverse Key Indexes

Reverse key indexes were introduced by Oracle as another option to combat performance issues associated with right-hand growth indexes discussed in "Hash Partitioning vs. Range Partitioning." In reverse key indexes, column values are stored in reverse order, character by character. For example, column value 12345 is stored as 54321 in the index. Because the column values are stored in reverse order, consecutive column values are stored in different leaf blocks of the index, thereby avoiding the contention issues with right-hand growth indexes. In the table blocks, these column values are stored as 12345, though.

There are two issues with reverse key indexes:

- The range scan on reverse key indexes is not possible for range operators such as between, less than, greater than, and so on. This is understandable because the underlying assumption of an index range scan is that column values are stored in ascending or descending logical key order. Reverse key indexes break this assumption because the column values are stored in the reverse order, no logical key order is maintained, and so index range scans are not possible with reverse key indexes.

- Reverse key indexes can increase physical reads artificially because the column values are stored in numerous leaf blocks and those leaf blocks might need to be read into the buffer cache to modify the block. But, the cost of this increase in IO should be measured against the concurrency issues associated with right-hand growth indexes.

In Listing 12-18, a reverse key index Sales_fact_part_n1 is created with a REVERSE keyword. First, the SELECT statement with the predicate id=1000 uses the reverse key index, because equality predicates can use reverse key indexes. But, the next SELECT statement with the predicate id between 1000 and 1001 uses the full table scan access path because the index range scan access path is not possible with reverse key indexes.

Listing 12-18. Reverse Key Indexes

```
drop index sales_fact_part_n1;
create unique index sales_fact_part_n1 on sales_fact_part ( id ) global  reverse ;

select * from sales_fact_part where id=1000;
```

```
-------------------------------------------------------------------
| Id  | Operation              | Name               | Pstart| Pstop |
-------------------------------------------------------------------
|  0  | SELECT STATEMENT       |                    |       |       |
|  1  |  TABLE ACCESS BY GLOBAL| SALES_FACT_PART    |   25  |   25  |
|     |      INDEX ROWID       |                    |       |       |
|* 2  |    INDEX UNIQUE SCAN   | SALES_FACT_PART_N1 |       |       |
-------------------------------------------------------------------
```

```
select * from sales_fact_part where id between 1000 and 1001;
```

```
-------------------------------------------------------------
| Id  | Operation           | Name            | Pstart| Pstop |
-------------------------------------------------------------
|  0  | SELECT STATEMENT    |                 |       |       |
|  1  |  PARTITION HASH ALL|                  |   1  |   32  |
|* 2  |    TABLE ACCESS FULL| SALES_FACT_PART |   1  |   32  |
-------------------------------------------------------------
```

Especially in RAC, right-hand growth indexes can cause intolerable performance issues. Reverse key indexes were introduced to combat this performance problem, but you should probably consider hash partitioned indexes instead of reverse key indexes.

Descending Indexes

Indexes store column values in ascending order by default; this can be switched to descending order using descending indexes. If your application fetches the data in a specific order, then the rows need to be sorted before the rows are sent to the application. These sorts can be avoided using descending indexes. These indexes are useful if the application is fetching the data millions of times in a specific order—for example, customer data fetched from the customer transaction table in the reverse chronological order.

In Listing 12-19, an index Sales_fact_c1 together with the columns product desc, year desc, week desc specifies a descending order for these three columns. The SELECT statement accesses the table by specifying an ORDER BY clause with the sort order product desc, year desc, week desc matching the index sort order. The execution plan shows there is no sort step, even though there is an ORDER BY clause in the SELECT statement.

Listing 12-19. Descending Indexes

```
drop index sales_fact_c1;
create index sales_fact_c1 on sales_fact
( product desc, year desc, week desc ) ;

@analyze_sf.sql

select year, week from sales_fact s
where year in ( 1998,1999,2000) and week<5 and product='Xtend Memory'
order by product desc,year desc, week desc ;
```

```
---------------------------------------------------------------------------
| Id | Operation            | Name          | E-Rows | Cost (%CPU)|
---------------------------------------------------------------------------
|  0 | SELECT STATEMENT     |               |        |    5 (100)|
|  1 |  INLIST ITERATOR     |               |        |           |
|* 2 |   INDEX RANGE SCAN|  SALES_FACT_C1   |   109  |    5   (0)|
---------------------------------------------------------------------------
```

```
select index_name, index_type from dba_indexes
where index_name='SALES_FACT_C1';
```

```
INDEX_NAME                       INDEX_TYPE
-------------------------------  -----------------------------
SALES_FACT_C1                    FUNCTION-BASED NORMAL
```

Descending indexes are implemented as a function-based index as of Oracle Database release 11gR2.

Solutions to Management Problems

Indexes can be used to resolve operational problems faced in the real world. For example, to see the effects of a new index on a production application, you can use invisible indexes. You can also use invisible indexes to drop the indexes *safely* or, if working with Exadata, to test whether the indexes are still needed.

Invisible Indexes

In certain scenarios, you might want to add an index to tune the performance of a SQL statement, but you may not be sure about the negative impact of the index. Invisible indexes are useful to measure the impact of a new index with less risk. An index can be added to the database marked as invisible, and the optimizer does not choose that index. You can make an index invisible to ensure there is no negative consequence of the absence of the index.

After adding the index to the database, you can set a parameter optimizer_use_invisible_indexes to TRUE in your session without affecting the application performance, and then review the execution plan of the SQL statement. In Listing 12-20, the first SELECT statement uses the index sales_fact_c1 in the execution plan. The next SQL statement marks the sales_fact_c1 index as invisible, and the second execution plan of the same SELECT statement shows that the index is ignored by the optimizer.

Listing 12-20. Invisible Indexes

```
select * from (
 select * from sales_fact where product = 'Xtend Memory' and year=1998 and week=1
) where rownum <21 ;
```

```
-------------------------------------------------------------------------------------
| Id | Operation                              | Name          | Rows | Bytes|
-------------------------------------------------------------------------------------
|  0 | SELECT STATEMENT                       |               |    7 |   490|
|* 1 |  COUNT STOPKEY                         |               |      |      |
|  2 |   TABLE ACCESS BY INDEX ROWID BATCHED|  SALES_FACT    |    7 |   490|
|* 3 |    INDEX RANGE SCAN                    |  SALES_FACT_C1 |    9 |      |
-------------------------------------------------------------------------------------
```

```
alter index sales_fact_c1 invisible;
```

```
select * from  (
 select * from sales_fact where product = 'Xtend Memory' and year=1998 and week=1
) where rownum <21;
```

```
---------------------------------------------------------
| Id | Operation            | Name        | Rows | Bytes |
---------------------------------------------------------
|  0 | SELECT STATEMENT     |             |   7 |   490 |
|* 1 |  COUNT STOPKEY       |             |     |       |
|* 2 |   TABLE ACCESS FULL| SALES_FACT  |   7 |   490 |
---------------------------------------------------------
```

In Listing 12-20, the execution plan shows that the optimizer chooses the sales_fact_c1 index after setting the parameter to TRUE at the session level.

There is another use case for invisible indexes. These indexes are useful to reduce the risk while dropping unused indexes. It is not a pleasant experience to drop unused indexes from a production database, only to realize later that the dropped index is used in an important report. Even after performing extensive analysis, it is possible that the dropped index might be needed for a business process, and recreating indexes might lead to application downtime. From Oracle Database version 11g onward, you can mark the index as invisible, wait for few weeks, and then drop the index with less risk if no process is affected. If the index is needed after marking it as invisible, then that index can be reverted quickly to visible with just a SQL statement.

Listing 12-21. optimizer_use_invisible_indexes

```
alter session set optimizer_use_invisible_indexes = true;
select * from  (
 select * from sales_fact where product = 'Xtend Memory' and year=1998 and week=1
) where rownum <21 ;
```

```
-------------------------------------------------------------------------------
| Id | Operation                            | Name         | Rows | Bytes|
-------------------------------------------------------------------------------
|  0 | SELECT STATEMENT                     |              |   7 |   490|
|* 1 |  COUNT STOPKEY                       |              |     |      |
|  2 |   TABLE ACCESS BY INDEX ROWID BATCHED| SALES_FACT   |   7 |   490|
|* 3 |    INDEX RANGE SCAN                  | SALES_FACT_C1|   9 |      |
-------------------------------------------------------------------------------
```

Invisible indexes are maintained during DML activity similar to any other indexes. This operational feature is useful in reducing the risk associated with dropping indexes.

Virtual Indexes

Have you ever added an index only to realize later that the index is not chosen by the optimizer because of data distribution or some statistics issue? Virtual indexes are useful to review the effectiveness of an index. Virtual indexes do not have storage allocated and, so, can be created quickly. Virtual indexes are different from invisible indexes in that invisible indexes have storage associated with them, but the optimizer cannot choose them; virtual indexes do not have storage segments associated with them. For this reason, virtual indexes are also called *nosegment* indexes.

The session-modifiable underscore parameter _use_nosegment_indexes controls whether the optimizer can consider a virtual index. This parameter is FALSE by default, and the application does not choose virtual indexes.

You can test the virtual index using the following method without affecting other application functionality: create the index, enable the parameter to TRUE in your session, and verify the execution plan of the SQL statement. In Listing 12-22, a virtual index sales_virt was created with the nosegment clause. After modifying the parameter to TRUE in the current session, the execution plan of the SELECT statement is checked. The execution plan shows that this index is chosen by the optimizer for this SQL statement. After reviewing the plan, this index can be dropped and recreated as a conventional index.

Listing 12-22. Virtual Indexes

```
create index sales_virt on sales ( cust_id, promo_id) nosegment;

alter session set "_use_nosegment_indexes"=true;

explain plan for
select * from sh.sales
where cust_id=:b1 and promo_id=:b2;

select * from table(dbms_xplan.display) ;
```

```
--------------------------------------------------------------------------
| Id  | Operation                                | Name       | Cost(%CPU)|
--------------------------------------------------------------------------
|   0 | SELECT STATEMENT                         |            |    9  (0)|
|   1 |  TABLE ACCESS BY GLOBAL INDEX ROWID BATCHED| SALES    |    9  (0)|
|*  2 |   INDEX RANGE SCAN                       | SALES_VIRT |    1  (0)|
--------------------------------------------------------------------------
```

Virtual indexes do not have storage associated with them, so these indexes are not maintained. But, you can collect statistics on these indexes as if they are conventional indexes. Virtual indexes can be used to improve the cardinality estimates of predicates without incurring the storage overhead associated with conventional indexes.

Bitmap Join Indexes

Bitmap join indexes are useful in data warehouse applications to materialize the joins between fact and dimension tables. In data warehouse tables, fact tables are typically much larger than the dimension tables, and the dimension and fact tables are joined using a primary key, with a foreign key relationship between them. These joins are costlier because of the size of the fact tables, and performance can be improved for these queries if the join results can be prestored. Materialized views are one option to precalculate the join results; bitmap join indexes are another option.

In Listing 12-23, a typical data warehouse query and its execution plan is shown. The sales table is a fact table and the other tables are dimension tables in this query. The sales table is joined to other dimension tables by primary key columns on the dimension tables. The execution plan shows the sales table is the leading table in this join processing, and the other dimension tables are joined to derive the final result set. These are the four join operations in this execution plan. This execution plan can be very costly if the fact table is huge.

Listing 12-23. A Typical Data Warehouse Query

```
select sum(s.quantity_sold), sum(s.amount_sold)
  from sales s, products p, customers c, channels ch
where s.prod_id = p.prod_id and
      s.cust_id = c.cust_id and
      s.channel_id = ch.channel_id and
```

```
p.prod_name='Y box' and
c.cust_first_name='Abigail' and
ch.channel_desc = 'Direct_sales' ;
```

```
-------------------------------------------------------------------------------
| Id | Operation                          | Name              |Rows  |Bytes|
-------------------------------------------------------------------------------
|  0 | SELECT STATEMENT                   |                   |   1  |   75|
|  1 |  SORT AGGREGATE                    |                   |   1  |   75|
|* 2 |   HASH JOIN                        |                   |  10  |  750|
|* 3 |    TABLE ACCESS FULL               | CUSTOMERS         |  43  |  516|
|  4 |    NESTED LOOPS                    |                   |      |     |
|  5 |     NESTED LOOPS                   |                   | 1595 |   8K|
|  6 |      MERGE JOIN CARTESIAN          |                   |   1  |   43|
|* 7 |       TABLE ACCESS FULL            | PRODUCTS          |   1  |   30|
|  8 |       BUFFER SORT                  |                   |   1  |   13|
|* 9 |        TABLE ACCESS FULL           | CHANNELS          |   1  |   13|
| 10 |       PARTITION RANGE ALL          |                   |      |     |
| 11 |        BITMAP CONVERSION TO ROWIDS |                   |      |     |
| 12 |         BITMAP AND                 |                   |      |     |
|*13 |          BITMAP INDEX SINGLE VALUE | SALES_PROD_BIX    |      |     |
|*14 |          BITMAP INDEX SINGLE VALUE | SALES_CHANNEL_BIX |      |     |
| 15 |      TABLE ACCESS BY LOCAL INDEX ROWID| SALES          | 3190 |63800|
-------------------------------------------------------------------------------
```

In Listing 12-24, a bitmap join index Sales_bji1 is created to precalculate the join results. Notice the index creation statement joins the sales and dimension tables similar to the join predicates specified in the query. The SELECT statement is reexecuted after creating the index, and the execution plan of the SELECT statement shows access to the bitmap join index, followed by access to the sales table without any join processing. Internally, three new virtual columns are added to this table, and an index is created on these three virtual columns. In a nutshell, the bitmap join index materializes the result set with the indexes on the virtual columns, thereby avoiding costly join processing.

Listing 12-24. Bitmap Join Index

```
alter table products modify primary key validate;

alter table customers modify primary key validate;

alter table channels modify primary key validate;

create bitmap index sales_bji1 on sales ( p.prod_name, c.cust_first_name, ch.channel_desc)
from sales s, products p, customers c, channels ch
where s.prod_id = p.prod_id and
      s.cust_id = c.cust_id and
      s.channel_id = ch.channel_id
LOCAL ;

select sum(s.quantity_sold), sum(s.amount_sold)
  from sales s, products p, customers c, channels ch
where s.prod_id = p.prod_id and
      s.cust_id = c.cust_id and
      s.channel_id = ch.channel_id and
```

```
        p.prod_name='Y box' and
        c.cust_first_name='Abigail' and
        ch.channel_desc = 'Direct_sales';
```

```
---------------------------------------------------------------------
| Id  | Operation                          | Name       | Rows | Bytes |
---------------------------------------------------------------------
|   0 | SELECT STATEMENT                   |            |    1 |    20 |
|   1 |  SORT AGGREGATE                    |            |    1 |    20 |
|   2 |   PARTITION RANGE ALL              |            |   19 |   380 |
|   3 |    TABLE ACCESS BY LOCAL INDEX     | SALES      |   19 |   380 |
|     |        ROWID BATCHED               |            |      |       |
|   4 |     BITMAP CONVERSION TO ROWIDS    |            |      |       |
|*  5 |      BITMAP INDEX SINGLE VALUE     | SALES_BJI1 |      |       |
---------------------------------------------------------------------
```

There are a few restrictions on bitmap join indexes: all dimensions need to have validated primary or unique constraints defined, the index must be local, and so on. The first three statements in Listing 12-24 modify the constraint state to validated to enable creation of a bitmap join index.

Bitmap join indexes are useful in data warehouse environments, adhering to a good data model. These indexes are not useful in OLTP applications, though.

Summary

A good choice of index type and an optimal choice of indexed columns are essential to maintaining application performance. Armed with this new knowledge of various index types, you should focus on matching index types to application access paths. Because Oracle Database provides rich index functionality, it is best to use optimal index types to suit your application access patterns. It's also vitally important to add indexes only when necessary. Unnecessary indexes waste space, increase redo size and undo size, and waste valuable CPU cycles and memory.

■ ■ ■

Beyond the SELECT

This chapter is a collection of topics involving SQL statements that are not straight SELECTs. These statements are often referred to as *Data Manipulation Language* (or *DML*) *statements*. In this chapter, I provide some information on some of the less well-known options to the standard DML commands—namely, INSERT, UPDATE, DELETE, and MERGE. I also focus on alternate approaches, with an eye toward improving performance.

INSERT

INSERT is the primary command used in the SQL language to load data. If you are reading this book, you probably already have a pretty good handle on the INSERT command. In this section, I talk about some of the less often used options, some of which I rarely, if ever, see in the wild. I believe this is because of a lack of familiarity more than a lack of functionality.

There are two basic methods that Oracle uses for inserts. For simplicity, let's call them the *slow way* and the *fast way*. The slow way is usually called *conventional*. With this mechanism, the data go through the buffer cache, empty space in existing blocks is reused, undo is generated for all data and metadata changes, and redo is generated for all changes by default. This is a lot of work, which is why I call it the slow way. The fast way is also called *direct path*. This method does not look for space in existing blocks; it just starts inserting data above the high-water mark. The fast way protects the data dictionary with undo and redo for metadata changes, but it generates no undo for data changes. It can also avoid redo generation for data changes in some cases, such as nologging operations. Keep in mind that, by default, indexes on tables loaded with direct path inserts still generate both undo and redo.

Direct Path Inserts

Direct path inserts can be invoked by using the APPEND hint (parallel inserts do this by default, by the way). In Oracle Database 11g Release 2, the APPEND_VALUES hint was added and can be used for inserts that specify a VALUES clause as opposed to using SELECT to provide the values for inserting. Listing 13-1 shows a simple example of both forms.

Listing 13-1. Simple Insert APPEND and APPEND_VALUES

```
insert /*+ append */ into big_emp select * from hr.employees;

insert /*+ append_values */ into dual (dummy) values ('Y');
```

There are a few issues with the fast approach, however.

- Only one direct path write can occur on a table at any given time.

- Data are inserted above the high-water mark, so any available space in the blocks below the high-water mark are not used by the direct path inserts.

- The session that performs the INSERT APPEND can't do anything with the table (even select from it) after the INSERT until a commit or rollback is issued.

- Some of the less frequently used data structures (object types, IOTs, and so on) are not supported.

- Referential constraints are not supported (in other words, they cause the INSERT to be executed using the conventional method).

The first item in the list is the biggest issue. In an OLTP-type system with many small inserts occurring frequently, the direct path mechanism just does not work. The second bulleted item is also a big issue. It makes no sense for small inserts to be applied in empty blocks above the high-water mark. This results in a huge waste of space. In fact, in Oracle Database 11g, the behavior of the APPEND hint was modified to allow it to be used in INSERT statements using the VALUES clause (prior to 11g, it is ignored unless the insert statement has a SELECT clause). This behavior change resulted in a bug being logged because it was using so much space for small inserts. The eventual resolution was to return the APPEND hint to its original behavior and introduce the APPEND_VALUES hint in Oracle Database 11gR2. At any rate, note that the direct path inserts are designed for large, "bulk" inserts only.

Note also that, as with most hints, the APPEND hint is silently ignored if for any reason it is not possible for Oracle to obey the hint. When this occurs with the APPEND hint, the insert is done using the conventional mechanism. Listing 13-2 shows an example of the APPEND hint being ignored because of a foreign key constraint.

Listing 13-2. Disabled APPEND Hint

```
SQL> @constraints
Enter value for owner: KRM
Enter value for table_name: BIG_EMP
Enter value for constraint_type:

TABLE_NAME   CONSTRAINT_NAME      C SEARCH_CONDITION                        STATUS
-----------  -------------------  - -------------------------------------  -------
BIG_EMP      BIG_EMP_MANAGER_FK   R                                        ENABLED
BIG_EMP      SYS_C0026608         C "JOB_ID" IS NOT NULL                   ENABLED
BIG_EMP      SYS_C0026607         C "HIRE_DATE" IS NOT NULL                ENABLED
BIG_EMP      SYS_C0026606         C "EMAIL" IS NOT NULL                    ENABLED
BIG_EMP      SYS_C0026605         C "LAST_NAME" IS NOT NULL                ENABLED

SQL> @mystats
Enter value for name: write direct

NAME                                                    VALUE
------------------------------------------------------- -------
physical writes direct                                      0

SQL>
SQL>
SQL> insert /*+ append */ into big_emp select * from hr.employees;

107 rows created.

SQL> @mystats
Enter value for name: direct
```

```
NAME                                                    VALUE
------------------------------------------------------- -------
physical writes direct                                  0

SQL> select count(*) from big_emp;

COUNT(*)
--------
     107
```

The APPEND hint definitely does not do what it is intended to do in this case. The inserts are not done with direct path writes, as shown by the physical direct writes statistic and by the fact that you can select from the table after the insert. (If the insert had been done with direct path writes, you would have had to issue a commit or rollback before you could select from the table). Listing 13-3 shows the expected behavior if you disable the foreign key constraint responsible for disabling the APPEND hint.

Listing 13-3. Disabling Constraint Enables APPEND Hint

```
SQL> alter table big_emp disable constraint BIG_EMP_MANAGER_FK;

Table altered.

SQL> insert /*+ append */ into big_emp select * from hr.employees;

107 rows created.

SQL> @mystats
Enter value for name: direct

NAME                                                           VALUE
-------------------------------------------------------------- ----------------
physical writes direct                                         2

SQL> select count(*) from big_emp;
select count(*) from big_emp
                     *
ERROR at line 1:
ORA-12838: cannot read/modify an object after modifying it in parallel
```

The direct path method is clearly used in this example, as you can see from the statistics and from the fact that you cannot select from the table without issuing a commit first. By the way, the error message is a bit of a red herring. It says that the object was modified in parallel, which in this case is not true. This is a holdover from an earlier version in which a parallel insert was the only way to do an insert above the high-water mark. Next I discuss a couple of unusual variants on the INSERT statement.

Multitable Inserts

The multitable insert is rarely used, even though it has been around since at least version 9i. This construct can be useful for ETL-type processing when data are staged and then rearranged as they are loaded into permanent structures. In these cases, it is fairly common to stage data in a nonnormalized format that is later split into multiple tables or some other more normalized structure. The multitable insert is a convenient way to accomplish this type of work without having to write a bunch of procedural code. The syntax is very straightforward; just use INSERT ALL and then supply multiple INTO clauses.

These clauses can specify the same or different tables. Only one set of input values can be used (either via a VALUES clause or a subquery), but the individual values can be reused or not used at all. Listing 13-4 shows an example of the syntax inserting into a single table. (Note that the scripts are provided in the online code suite to create the people and denormalized_people tables).

Listing 13-4. Basic Multitable Insert into a Single Table

```
INSERT ALL
  INTO people (person_id, first_name, last_name) -- the parent
    VALUES (person_id, first_name, last_name)
  INTO people (first_name, last_name, parent_id) -- the child
    VALUES (child1, last_name, person_id)
  INTO people (first_name, last_name, parent_id) -- the child
    VALUES (child2, last_name, person_id)
  INTO people (first_name, last_name, parent_id) -- the child
    VALUES (child3, last_name, person_id)
  INTO people (first_name, last_name, parent_id) -- the child
    VALUES (child4, last_name, person_id)
  INTO people (first_name, last_name, parent_id) -- the child
    VALUES (child5, last_name, person_id)
  INTO people (first_name, last_name, parent_id) -- the child
    VALUES (child6, last_name, person_id)
  SELECT person_id, first_name, last_name,
         child1, child2, child3, child4, child5, child6
FROM denormalized_people;
```

This example shows that multiple INTO clauses can be used, although in this case all the INTO clauses referenced the same table. You can just as easily insert into multiple tables (hence the term *multitable insert*), as shown in Listing 13-5.

Listing 13-5. Basic Multitable Insert

```
INSERT ALL
  INTO parents (person_id, first_name, last_name)
    VALUES (person_id, first_name, last_name)
  INTO children (first_name, last_name, parent_id)
    VALUES (child1, last_name, person_id)
  INTO children (first_name, last_name, parent_id)
    VALUES (child1, last_name, person_id)
  INTO children (first_name, last_name, parent_id)
    VALUES (child1, last_name, person_id)
  INTO children (first_name, last_name, parent_id)
    VALUES (child1, last_name, person_id)
  INTO children (first_name, last_name, parent_id)
    VALUES (child1, last_name, person_id)
  INTO children (first_name, last_name, parent_id)
    VALUES (child1, last_name, person_id)
  SELECT person_id, first_name, last_name,
         child1, child2, child3, child4, child5, child6
FROM denormalized_people;
```

Conditional Insert

The INSERT command also has the ability to do conditional processing. It's like having a CASE statement embedded in the INSERT statement.

In the previous example, you inserted a record for every child, but most likely some of the child columns are null in this kind of a repeating column layout. So, it would be nice if we could avoid creating these records without having to write procedural code. This is exactly the situation a conditional insert was built for. By the way, this type of data layout is often seen when loading files from external systems. Creating external tables on files is an excellent way to load them, and it allows these less common insert options to be applied directly to the data-loading process, rather than after the files have been staged in an Oracle table. Listing 13-6 shows an example of the conditional insert in which the parent fields are always loaded but the child fields are loaded only if they have data in them.

Listing 13-6. Conditional Insert

```
INSERT ALL
WHEN 1=1 THEN -- always insert the parent
  INTO people (person_id, first_name, last_name)
    VALUES (person_id, first_name, last_name)
WHEN child1 is not null THEN -- only insert non-null children
  INTO people (first_name, last_name, parent_id)
    VALUES (child1, last_name, person_id)
WHEN child2 is not null THEN
  INTO people (first_name, last_name, parent_id)
    VALUES (child2, last_name, person_id)
WHEN child3 is not null THEN
  INTO people (first_name, last_name, parent_id)
    VALUES (child3, last_name, person_id)
WHEN child4 is not null THEN
  INTO people (first_name, last_name, parent_id)
    VALUES (child4, last_name, person_id)
WHEN child5 is not null THEN
  INTO people (first_name, last_name, parent_id)
    VALUES (child5, last_name, person_id)
WHEN child6 is not null THEN
  INTO people (first_name, last_name, parent_id)
    VALUES (child6, last_name, person_id)
SELECT person_id, first_name, last_name,
  child1, child2, child3, child4, child5, child6
FROM denormalized_people;
```

DML Error Logging

And now for something really cool: DML error logging. This feature provides a mechanism for preventing your one million-row insert from failing because a few rows had problems. This feature was introduced in 10gR2 and it's similar to the SQL*Loader error logging feature. DML error logging basically diverts any records that otherwise cause the statement to fail, placing them in an errors table. This is an extremely useful feature that is rarely used, which is a little surprising because it's very easy to implement. DML error logging also provides excellent performance and saves a lot of coding. Without this feature, we have to create a bad records table, write procedural code to handle any exceptions raised by any single record, insert the problem records into the bad records table, and preserve the integrity of the transaction by handling the error records in an autonomous transaction, which is a lot of work. By the way, the LOG ERRORS clause works with the other DML statements as well (UPDATE, DELETE, and MERGE).

Here is how to enable DML error logging:

1. Create the error log table using DBMS_ERRLOG.CREATE_ERROR_LOG.

2. Specify the LOG ERRORS clause on the INSERT.

That's it. Listing 13-7 shows how the CREATE_ERROR_LOG procedure works.

Listing 13-7. CREATE_ERROR_LOG

```
SQL> EXECUTE DBMS_ERRLOG.CREATE_ERROR_LOG('big_emp', 'big_emp_bad');
PL/SQL procedure successfully completed.
SQL> desc big_emp
Name                                             Null?    Type
------------------------------------------------ -------- ----------------
EMPLOYEE_ID                                               NUMBER(6)
FIRST_NAME                                                VARCHAR2(20)
LAST_NAME                                        NOT NULL VARCHAR2(25)
EMAIL                                            NOT NULL VARCHAR2(25)
PHONE_NUMBER                                              VARCHAR2(20)
HIRE_DATE                                        NOT NULL DATE
JOB_ID                                           NOT NULL VARCHAR2(10)
SALARY                                                    NUMBER(8,2)
COMMISSION_PCT                                            NUMBER(2,2)
MANAGER_ID                                                NUMBER(6)
DEPARTMENT_ID                                             NUMBER(4)

SQL> desc big_emp_bad
Name                                             Null?    Type
------------------------------------------------ -------- ----------------
ORA_ERR_NUMBER$                                          NUMBER
ORA_ERR_MESG$                                            VARCHAR2(2000)
ORA_ERR_ROWID$                                           ROWID
ORA_ERR_OPTYP$                                           VARCHAR2(2)
ORA_ERR_TAG$                                             VARCHAR2(2000)
EMPLOYEE_ID                                              VARCHAR2(4000)
FIRST_NAME                                               VARCHAR2(4000)
LAST_NAME                                                VARCHAR2(4000)
EMAIL                                                    VARCHAR2(4000)
PHONE_NUMBER                                             VARCHAR2(4000)
HIRE_DATE                                                VARCHAR2(4000)
JOB_ID                                                   VARCHAR2(4000)
SALARY                                                   VARCHAR2(4000)
COMMISSION_PCT                                           VARCHAR2(4000)
MANAGER_ID                                               VARCHAR2(4000)
DEPARTMENT_ID                                            VARCHAR2(4000)
```

As you can see, all the columns in the errors table are created as VARCHAR2(4000), which allows columns of most datatypes to be inserted into the errors table, even if records are failing as a result of data being too large to fit into a column or because of inconsistent datatype issues, such as number columns that contain nonnumeric data. There are also a few extra columns for the error number, the error message, and the rowid. Last, there is a column called ORA_ERR_TAG$ that allows user-defined data to be placed in the row for debugging purposes (such as the step the ETL process was on, or something of that nature).

The syntax is very straightforward. You simply add the keywords **LOG ERRORS INTO** and specify the name of your errors table. As another option, you can tell Oracle how many errors to allow before giving up and canceling the statement. This is done with the REJECT LIMIT clause. Note that, by default, REJECT LIMIT is set to zero, so if you hit one error, the statement aborts and rolls back (just the statement, not the transaction). The single error is preserved in the errors table, though. In most cases, you probably want to set REJECT LIMIT to UNLIMITED, which allows the INSERT statement to complete regardless of how many records are diverted to the errors table. It is somewhat surprising that UNLIMITED is not the default, because this is the most common usage. Listing 13-8 shows a simple example.

Listing 13-8. Insert Error Logging

```
SQL>
SQL> insert into big_emp
  2      (employee_id, first_name, last_name,
  3       hire_date, email, department_id)
  4    values (300,'Bob', 'Loblaw',
  5           '01-jan-10', 'bob@yourfavoritelawyer.com', 12345)
  6    log errors into big_emp_bad;
        '01-jan-10', 'bob@yourfavoritelawyer.com', 12345)
                                                  *
ERROR at line 5:
ORA-12899: value too large for column "KRM"."BIG_EMP"."EMAIL" (actual: 26, maximum: 25)

SQL> insert into big_emp
  2      (employee_id, first_name, last_name,
  3       hire_date, email, department_id)
  4    values (301,'Bob', 'Loblaw',
  5           '01-jan-10', 'bob@yflawyer.com', 12345)
  6    log errors into big_emp_bad;
        '01-jan-10', 'bob@yflawyer.com', 12345)
                                        *
ERROR at line 5:
ORA-01400: cannot insert NULL into ("KRM"."BIG_EMP"."JOB_ID")

SQL> insert into big_emp
  2      (employee_id, first_name, last_name,
  3       hire_date, email, department_id,job_id)
  4    values (302,'Bob', 'Loblaw',
  5           '01-jan-10', 'bob@yflawyer.com', 12345, 1)
  6    log errors into big_emp_bad;
        '01-jan-10', 'bob@yflawyer.com', 12345, 1)
                                           *
ERROR at line 5:
ORA-01438: value larger than specified precision allowed for this column

SQL> insert into big_emp
  2      (employee_id, first_name, last_name,
  3       hire_date, email, department_id,job_id)
  4    values (303,'Bob', 'Loblaw',
  5           '01-jan-10', 'bob@yflawyer.com', '2A45', 1)
```

```
  6     log errors into big_emp_bad;
              '01-jan-10', 'bob@yflawyer.com', '2A45', 1)
                                              *
ERROR at line 5:
ORA-01722: invalid number

SQL>
SQL> SELECT ORA_ERR_MESG$, ORA_ERR_TAG$, employee_id FROM big_emp_bad;

ORA_ERR_MESG$
------------------------------------------------------------------------
ORA_ERR_TAG$
------------------------------------------------------------------------
EMPLOYEE_ID
------------------------------------------------------------------------
ORA-01438: value larger than specified precision allowed for this column

302


ORA-01722: invalid number

303


ORA-12899: value too large for column "KRM"."BIG_EMP"."EMAIL" (actual: 26, maximum: 25)

300


ORA-01400: cannot insert NULL into ("KRM"."BIG_EMP"."JOB_ID")

301
```

Improving Insert Error Logging

The example in Listing 13-8 shows several insert statements, all of which fail. The records that fail to be inserted into the table, regardless of the error that caused the failure, are inserted automatically into the errors table. Because I didn't specify a value for REJECT LIMIT, all the statements are rolled back when they encounter the first error. Therefore, no records are actually inserted into the big_emp table. All the error records are preserved, though. I did this to demonstrate that a single errors table can be reused for multiple loads, preserving the records across multiple insert statements. Note that error logging is rarely used in this manner in real life. In real life, REJECT LIMIT is, in general, set to UNLIMITED. Listings 13-9 and 13-10 show better examples of using a multirow INSERT statement. Listing 13-9 shows what happens to an insert when a record fails without the error logging clause; Listing 13-10 shows how it works with the error logging clause.

Listing 13-9. Better Insert Error Logging

```
SQL> set echo on
SQL> create table test_big_insert as select * from dba_objects where 1=2;

Table created.

SQL>
SQL> desc test_big_insert
 Name                                      Null?    Type
 ----------------------------------------- -------- ----------------------
 OWNER                                              VARCHAR2(30)
 OBJECT_NAME                                        VARCHAR2(128)
 SUBOBJECT_NAME                                     VARCHAR2(30)
 OBJECT_ID                                          NUMBER
 DATA_OBJECT_ID                                     NUMBER
 OBJECT_TYPE                                        VARCHAR2(19)
 CREATED                                            DATE
 LAST_DDL_TIME                                      DATE
 TIMESTAMP                                          VARCHAR2(19)
 STATUS                                             VARCHAR2(7)
 TEMPORARY                                          VARCHAR2(1)
 GENERATED                                          VARCHAR2(1)
 SECONDARY                                          VARCHAR2(1)
 NAMESPACE                                          NUMBER
 EDITION_NAME                                       VARCHAR2(30)

SQL>
SQL> alter table test_big_insert modify object_id number(2);

Table altered.

SQL>
SQL> insert into test_big_insert
  2     select * from dba_objects
  3     where object_id is not null;
  select * from dba_objects
         *
ERROR at line 2:
ORA-01438: value larger than specified precision allowed for this column
```

Because I set up the situation, I have a pretty good idea which column is causing the problem. The object_id column is modified in the listing. But, in real life, the troublesome column is not usually so obvious. In fact, without the Error Logging clause, it can be quite difficult to determine which row is causing the problem.

The error message doesn't give me any information about which column or which record is causing the failure. I can determine which column is causing the problem by specifying the column names manually in the SELECT. However, there is no way to know which rows are causing the problem. The Error Logging clause in Listing 13-10 solves both problems. Remember that all the column's values are saved in the errors table, along with the error messages, making it easy to determine where the problem lies.

Listing 13-10. Better Insert Error Logging (continued)

```
SQL>
SQL> EXECUTE DBMS_ERRLOG.CREATE_ERROR_LOG('test_big_insert', 'tbi_errors');

PL/SQL procedure successfully completed.

SQL>
SQL> insert into test_big_insert
  2     select * from dba_objects
  3     where object_id is not null
  4     log errors into tbi_errors
  5     reject limit unlimited;

98 rows created.

SQL>
SQL> select count(*) from dba_objects
  2  where object_id is not null
  3  and length(object_id) < 3;

  COUNT(*)
----------
        98
SQL> select count(*) from test_big_insert;

  COUNT(*)
----------
        98

SQL>
SQL> select count(*) from dba_objects
  2  where object_id is not null
  3  and length(object_id) > 2;

  COUNT(*)
----------
     73276
SQL> select count(*) from tbi_errors;

  COUNT(*)
----------
     73276
SQL> rollback;

Rollback complete.

SQL> select count(*) from test_big_insert;

  COUNT(*)
----------
         0
SQL> select count(*) from tbi_errors;

  COUNT(*)
----------
     73282
```

This example shows the Error Logging clause with REJECT LIMIT at UNLIMITED, which allows the statement to complete despite the fact that most of the records fail to be inserted. In addition, you can see that, although a rollback removed the records from the base table, the error records remain.

DML Error Logging Restrictions

Although DML error logging is extremely robust, you should be aware of the following caveats:

- The LOG ERRORS clause does not cause implicit commits. The insert of error records is handled as an autonomous transaction—meaning, you can commit or rollback the entire set of records inserted into the base table (along with other pending changes), even if errors are returned and bad records are inserted into the errors table. The records loaded into the errors table are preserved even if the transaction is rolled back.

- The LOG ERRORS clause does not disable the APPEND hint. Inserts into the base table are done using the direct path write mechanism if the APPEND hint is used. However, any inserts into the errors table do not use direct path writes. In general, this is not a problem because you rarely expect to load a lot of data into an errors table.

- Direct path insert operations that violate a unique constraint or index cause the statement to fail and roll back.

- Any UPDATE operation that violates a unique constraint or index causes the statement to fail and rollback.

- Any operation that violates a deferred constraint causes the statement to fail and rollback.

- The LOG ERRORS clause does not track the values of LOBs, LONGs, or object-type columns. It can be used with tables that contain these unsupported types of columns, but the unsupported columns are not added to the errors table. To create the errors table for a table that contains unsupported column types, you must use the skip_unsupported parameter of the CREATE_ERROR_LOG procedure. The default for this parameter is FALSE, which causes the procedure to fail when attempting to create an errors table for a table with unsupported column types. Listing 13-11 shows the proper syntax for creating an errors table when there are unsupported column types in the base table.

Listing 13-11. DBMS_ERRLOG.CREATE_ERROR_LOG Parameters

```
exec DBMS_ERRLOG.CREATE_ERROR_LOG(err_log_table_owner => '&owner', -
                                  dml_table_name => '&table_name', -
                                  err_log_table_name => '&err_log_table_name', -
                                  err_log_table_space => NULL, -
                                  skip_unsupported => TRUE);
```

As you can see, the **INSERT** statement has several options that are rarely used. The most useful of these features, in my opinion, is DML error logging (which can also be used with the other DML commands). It allows very difficult problems, such as corruption issues, to be identified fairly easily, and it provides excellent performance compared with the row-by-row processing that is required without it. Note also the fairly extreme performance improvement provided by direct path inserts vs. conventional inserts; there are drawbacks with regard to recoverability and serialization, but for bulk loading of data, the positives generally far outweigh the negatives.

UPDATE

Massive updates are almost always a bad idea. I recently reviewed a system that updates a billion-plus rows in a single table every night—a full year forecast and every single value is recalculated every night. Aside from the observation that forecasting that far in the future is not necessary for items that have a 90-day turnaround time, it's much faster to load a billion records from scratch than to update a billion records.

Using CTAS vs. UPDATE

The traditional method when doing this type of processing is to do a truncate and then a reload. But, what if the truncate-and-reload method just won't work? One alternative is to use Create Table As Select (CTAS) to create a new table and then just replace the original table with the newly created one. It sounds easy if you say it fast. Of course, there are many details that must be addressed. Listing 13-12 shows a quick demonstration of the potential difference in performance between these two approaches.

Listing 13-12. Performance Delta between UPDATE and CTAS

```
SQL> set autotrace on
SQL> set timing on
SQL> update skew2 set col1 = col1*1;

32000004 rows updated.

Elapsed: 00:27:56.41

Execution Plan
----------------------------------------------------------
Plan hash value: 1837483169


-------------------------------------------------------------------------
| Id  | Operation          | Name  | Rows  | Bytes | Cost (%CPU)| Time     |
-------------------------------------------------------------------------
|   0 | UPDATE STATEMENT   |       |   32M |  793M | 28370   (1)| 00:05:41 |
|   1 |  UPDATE            | SKEW2 |       |       |            |          |
|   2 |   TABLE ACCESS FULL| SKEW2 |   32M |  793M | 28370   (1)| 00:05:41 |
-------------------------------------------------------------------------


Statistics
----------------------------------------------------------
      1908  recursive calls
  32743098  db block gets
    163363  consistent gets
    317366  physical reads
8187521328  redo size
      1373  bytes sent via SQL*Net to client
      1097  bytes received via SQL*Net from client
         5  SQL*Net roundtrips to/from client
         1  sorts (memory)
         0  sorts (disk)
  32000004  rows processed
```

```
SQL> create table skew_temp as
  2    select pk_col, col1*1 col1, col2, col3, col4 from skew2;

Table created.

Elapsed: 00:00:44.30

SQL> set timing off
SQL>
SQL> select count(*) from skew_temp;

  COUNT(*)
----------
  32000004

SQL> @find_sql_stats
Enter value for sql_text: %skew2%
Enter value for sql_id:

SQL_ID          ROWS_PROCESSED  AVG_ETIME  AVG_PIO     AVG_LIO SQL_TEXT
-------------   --------------  ---------  --------  ----------- --------------
2aqsvr3h3qrrg         32000004   1,676.78   928,124  65,409,243 update skew2
                                                                set col1 = col
4y4dquf0mkhup         32000004      44.30   162,296     492,575 create table
                                                                skew_temp as s
```

As you can see, the update took almost 30 minutes (1676.78 seconds) whereas the CTAS table took less than a minute (44.30 seconds). So it's clear that there are significant performance benefits to be had by recreating the table vs. updating all the records. And as you might already expect from the previous example, recreating a table can also be more efficient than updating a relatively small portion of the rows. Listing 13-13 shows a comparison of the two methods when updating approximately 10 percent of the rows.

Listing 13-13. Performance Delta between UPDATE and CTAS: 10 Percent

```
SQL> select count(*) from skew2 where col1 = 1;

  COUNT(*)
----------
   3199971

Elapsed: 00:00:10.90
SQL> select 3199971/32000004 from dual;

3199971/32000004
----------------
      .099999081

Elapsed: 00:00:00.01
SQL> -- about 10% of the rows col1=1
SQL>
SQL> update skew2 set col1=col1*1 where col1 = 1;

3199971 rows updated.
```

```
Elapsed: 00:03:11.63
SQL> drop table skew_temp;

Table dropped.

Elapsed: 00:00:00.56
SQL> create table skew_temp as
  2    select pk_col, case when col1 = 1 then col1*1 end col1,
  3    col2, col3, col4 from skew2;

Table created.

Elapsed: 00:01:23.62

SQL> alter table skew2 rename to skew_old;

Table altered.

Elapsed: 00:00:00.06
SQL> alter table skew_temp rename to skew2;

Table altered.

Elapsed: 00:00:00.05
```

In this example, I recreated a table using CTAS in less than half the time it took to update about 10 percent of the records. Obviously, there are many details that are ignored in the previous two examples. These examples had no constraints or indexes or grants to deal with, making them considerably less complicated than most real-life situations. Each of these complications can be dealt with in an automated fashion, however.

Using INSERT APPEND vs. UPDATE

Listing 13-14 shows a more realistic example of using an INSERT APPEND technique to replace an UPDATE statement. For this example, I use a script from the online code suite called recreate_table.sql. It uses the dbms_metadata package to generate a script with the necessary Data Definition Language (DDL) to recreate a table and its dependent objects. It then uses an INSERT APPEND in place of UPDATE to move the data. The last step is to use ALTER TABLE RENAME to swap the new table for the original one. After the script is generated, it should be edited to customize how the steps are performed. For example, you may want to comment out the swap of the tables via the RENAME at the end until you're sure everything works as expected. Note that the particulars of the INSERT APPEND also have to be built when editing the script. Note also that the script renames all existing indexes because you cannot have duplicate index names, even if they are on different tables.

Listing 13-14. INSERT APPEND Instead of a Mass UPDATE

```
SQL>
SQL> @recreate_table
Enter value for owner: KRM
Enter value for table_name: SKEW2
```

```
... Output supressed for readability

SQL> @recreate_SKEW2.sql
SQL> ALTER INDEX SYS_C0029558 RENAME TO SYS_C0029558_OLD;

Index altered.

Elapsed: 00:00:00.02
SQL> ALTER INDEX SKEW2_COL1 RENAME TO SKEW2_COL1_OLD;

Index altered.

Elapsed: 00:00:00.02
SQL> ALTER INDEX SKEW2_COL4 RENAME TO SKEW2_COL4_OLD;

Index altered.

Elapsed: 00:00:00.02
SQL>
SQL>    CREATE TABLE "KRM"."SKEW2_TEMP"
  2     (    "PK_COL" NUMBER,
  3          "COL1" NUMBER,
  4          "COL2" VARCHAR2(30),
  5          "COL3" DATE,
  6          "COL4" VARCHAR2(1)
  7     ) SEGMENT CREATION IMMEDIATE
  8     PCTFREE 10 PCTUSED 40 INITRANS 1 MAXTRANS 255 NOCOMPRESS LOGGING
  9     STORAGE(INITIAL 1483735040 NEXT 1048576
                MINEXTENTS 1 MAXEXTENTS 2147483645
 10     PCTINCREASE 0 FREELISTS 1 FREELIST GROUPS 1 BUFFER_POOL
 11     DEFAULT FLASH_CACHE DEFAULT CELL_FLASH_CACHE DEFAULT)
 12     TABLESPACE "USERS" ;

Table created.

Elapsed: 00:00:00.10
SQL>
SQL>    INSERT /*+APPEND*/ INTO SKEW2_TEMP SELECT /*+PARALLEL(a 4)*/
  2  PK_COL,
  3  COL1,
  4  case when COL1 = 2 then 'ABC' else COL2 end,
  5  COL3,
  6  COL4
  7  FROM SKEW2 a;

32000004 rows created.

Elapsed: 00:00:52.87
SQL>
SQL>    CREATE INDEX "KRM"."SKEW2_COL1" ON "KRM"."SKEW2_TEMP" ("COL1")
  2     PCTFREE 10 INITRANS 2 MAXTRANS 255 NOLOGGING COMPUTE STATISTICS
  3     STORAGE(INITIAL 595591168 NEXT 1048576 MINEXTENTS 1
```

```
  4     MAXEXTENTS 2147483645 PCTINCREASE 0 FREELISTS 1 FREELIST GROUPS 1
  5     BUFFER_POOL DEFAULT FLASH_CACHE DEFAULT CELL_FLASH_CACHE DEFAULT)
  6     TABLESPACE "USERS"
  7     PARALLEL 8 ;

Index created.

Elapsed: 00:01:40.16
SQL>
SQL>    CREATE INDEX "KRM"."SKEW2_COL4" ON "KRM"."SKEW2_TEMP" ("COL4")
  2     PCTFREE 10 INITRANS 2 MAXTRANS 255 COMPUTE STATISTICS
  3     STORAGE(INITIAL 65536 NEXT 1048576 MINEXTENTS 1 MAXEXTENTS 2147483645
  4     PCTINCREASE 0 FREELISTS 1 FREELIST GROUPS 1 BUFFER_POOL DEFAULT
  5     FLASH_CACHE DEFAULT CELL_FLASH_CACHE DEFAULT)
  6     TABLESPACE "USERS"
  7     PARALLEL 8 ;

Index created.

Elapsed: 00:01:11.05
SQL>
SQL>    CREATE UNIQUE INDEX "KRM"."SYS_C0029558"
  2             ON "KRM"."SKEW2_TEMP" ("PK_COL")
  3     PCTFREE 10 INITRANS 2 MAXTRANS 255 NOLOGGING COMPUTE STATISTICS
  4     STORAGE(INITIAL 865075200 NEXT 1048576
  5             MINEXTENTS 1 MAXEXTENTS 2147483645
  6     PCTINCREASE 0 FREELISTS 1 FREELIST GROUPS 1 BUFFER_POOL DEFAULT
  7     FLASH_CACHE DEFAULT CELL_FLASH_CACHE DEFAULT)
  8     TABLESPACE "USERS"
  9     PARALLEL 8 ;

Index created.

Elapsed: 00:01:34.26
SQL>
SQL> -- Note: No Grants found!
SQL> -- Note: No Triggers found!
SQL>
SQL>
SQL> ALTER TABLE "KRM"."SKEW2_TEMP" ADD PRIMARY KEY ("PK_COL")
  2     USING INDEX PCTFREE 10 INITRANS 2 MAXTRANS 255 NOLOGGING
  3     COMPUTE STATISTICS
  4     STORAGE(INITIAL 865075200 NEXT 1048576
  5             MINEXTENTS 1 MAXEXTENTS 2147483645
  6     PCTINCREASE 0 FREELISTS 1 FREELIST GROUPS 1 BUFFER_POOL DEFAULT
  7     FLASH_CACHE DEFAULT CELL_FLASH_CACHE DEFAULT)
  8     TABLESPACE "USERS"  ENABLE;

Table altered.
```

```
Elapsed: 00:00:15.16
SQL>
SQL>   ALTER TABLE SKEW2 RENAME TO SKEW2_ORIG;

Table altered.

Elapsed: 00:00:00.04
SQL>
SQL> ALTER TABLE SKEW2_TEMP RENAME TO SKEW2;

Table altered.

Elapsed: 00:00:00.03
```

The order of the steps is very important. In general, it is much faster to defer the creation of indexes and the enabling of constraints until after loading the data. Be aware that you need to drop the old table manually (maybe after a day or two, when everyone is quite sure the operation works correctly). By the way, I think it's a really bad idea to drop objects in a script. As a matter of fact, I recommend commenting out the last two statements that do the RENAME. It's safer to run them interactively after you make sure everything works as planned. For comparison, Listing 13-15 shows the timing of the same change made by using a standard UPDATE statement.

Listing 13-15. Mass UPDATE Timings for Comparison

```
SQL> select my_rows, total_rows,
  2  100*my_rows/total_rows row_percent from
  3  (select sum(decode(col1,1,1,0)) my_rows, count(*) total_rows
  4* from skew2)

   MY_ROWS TOTAL_ROWS ROW_PERCENT
---------- ---------- -----------
   8605185   32000004        26.9

1 row selected.

Elapsed: 00:00:01.29
SQL> update /*+ parallel 4 */ skew2 set col2 = 'ABC' where col1 = 2;

8605185 rows updated.

Elapsed: 00:12:37.53
```

To sum up this example, when modifying roughly 27 percent of the rows in the table, the straight UPDATE took about 12.5 minutes and the rebuild with INSERT APPEND took about 5.5 minutes. Keep in mind that there are many variables I have not covered in detail. Every situation has differences in the number of dependent objects and the percentage of rows affected by the update. These factors have a large effect on the outcome, so test thoroughly in your environment with your specific data.

In this section, you learned that it can be considerably faster to rebuild tables than to update a large percentage of the rows. Obviously, making use of the direct path write via the APPEND hint is an important part of that. The biggest negative to this approach is that the table must be offline for the entire time the rebuild is taking place—or at least protected in some manner from concurrent modifications. This does not usually present a major obstacle because these types of mass updates are rarely done while users are accessing the table. In cases when concurrent access is required, partitioning or materialized views can provide the necessary isolation.

DELETE

Just like massive UPDATEs, massive DELETEs are almost always a bad idea. In general, it is faster (if somewhat more complicated) to recreate a table or partition (without the rows you wish to eliminate) than it is to delete a large percentage of the rows. The biggest downside to the approach of recreating is that the object must be protected from other changes while it is being rebuilt. This is basically the same approach I used in the previous section with the UPDATE command, but DELETEs can be even more time-consuming.

The basic idea is pretty much the same as with the mass UPDATEs:

1. Create a temporary table.

2. Insert the records that are not to be deleted into the temporary table.

3. Recreate the dependent objects (indexes, constraints, grants, triggers).

4. Rename the tables.

Let's use the recreate_table.sql script again to create a script that I can edit, then I'll modify the INSERT statement to give me the records that are left behind after my DELETE. Listing 13-16 shows an example of how a DELETE statement compares with a rebuild using a reciprocal INSERT statement.

Listing 13-16. Mass DELETE

```
SQL > delete from skew2 where col1=1;

3199972 rows deleted.

Elapsed: 00:04:12.64

SQL> rollback;

Rollback complete.

Elapsed: 00:01:48.59

SQL> @recreate_SKEW3.sql
SQL> set timing on
SQL>
SQL> ALTER INDEX SYS_C0029558 RENAME TO SYS_C0029558_OLD;

Index altered.

Elapsed: 00:00:00.03
SQL> ALTER INDEX SKEW2_COL1 RENAME TO SKEW2_COL1_OLD;

Index altered.

Elapsed: 00:00:00.04
SQL> ALTER INDEX SKEW2_COL4 RENAME TO SKEW2_COL4_OLD;

Index altered.
```

```
Elapsed: 00:00:00.02
SQL>
SQL>    CREATE TABLE "KRM"."SKEW2_TEMP"
  2      (    "PK_COL" NUMBER,
  3           "COL1" NUMBER,
  4           "COL2" VARCHAR2(30),
  5           "COL3" DATE,
  6           "COL4" VARCHAR2(1)
  7      ) SEGMENT CREATION IMMEDIATE
  8      PCTFREE 10 PCTUSED 40 INITRANS 1 MAXTRANS 255 NOCOMPRESS LOGGING
  9      STORAGE(INITIAL 1483735040 NEXT 1048576
 10      MINEXTENTS 1 MAXEXTENTS 2147483645
 11      PCTINCREASE 0 FREELISTS 1 FREELIST GROUPS 1 BUFFER_POOL DEFAULT
 12      FLASH_CACHE DEFAULT CELL_FLASH_CACHE DEFAULT)
 13      TABLESPACE "USERS" ;

Table created.

Elapsed: 00:00:00.11
SQL>
SQL>    INSERT /*+APPEND*/ INTO SKEW2_TEMP SELECT /*+PARALLEL(a 4)*/
  2    PK_COL,
  3    COL1,
  4    COL2,
  5    COL3,
  6    COL4
  7    FROM SKEW2 a where col1 != 1;

28800032 rows created.

Elapsed: 00:00:42.30
SQL>
SQL>    CREATE INDEX "KRM"."SKEW2_COL1" ON "KRM"."SKEW2_TEMP" ("COL1")
  2      PCTFREE 10 INITRANS 2 MAXTRANS 255 NOLOGGING COMPUTE STATISTICS
  3      STORAGE(INITIAL 595591168 NEXT 1048576
  4           MINEXTENTS 1 MAXEXTENTS 2147483645
  5      PCTINCREASE 0 FREELISTS 1 FREELIST GROUPS 1 BUFFER_POOL DEFAULT
  6      FLASH_CACHE DEFAULT CELL_FLASH_CACHE DEFAULT)
  7      TABLESPACE "USERS"
  8      PARALLEL 8 ;

Index created.

Elapsed: 00:01:36.50
SQL>
SQL>    CREATE INDEX "KRM"."SKEW2_COL4" ON "KRM"."SKEW2_TEMP" ("COL4")
  2      PCTFREE 10 INITRANS 2 MAXTRANS 255 COMPUTE STATISTICS
  3      STORAGE(INITIAL 65536 NEXT 1048576 MINEXTENTS 1 MAXEXTENTS 2147483645
  4      PCTINCREASE 0 FREELISTS 1 FREELIST GROUPS 1 BUFFER_POOL DEFAULT
  5      FLASH_CACHE DEFAULT CELL_FLASH_CACHE DEFAULT)
  6      TABLESPACE "USERS"
  7      PARALLEL 8 ;
```

```
Index created.

Elapsed: 00:01:09.43
SQL>
SQL>    CREATE UNIQUE INDEX "KRM"."SYS_C0029558"
  2           ON "KRM"."SKEW2_TEMP" ("PK_COL")
  3    PCTFREE 10 INITRANS 2 MAXTRANS 255 NOLOGGING COMPUTE STATISTICS
  4    STORAGE(INITIAL 865075200 NEXT 1048576
  5           MINEXTENTS 1 MAXEXTENTS 2147483645
  6    PCTINCREASE 0 FREELISTS 1 FREELIST GROUPS 1 BUFFER_POOL DEFAULT
  7    FLASH_CACHE DEFAULT CELL_FLASH_CACHE DEFAULT)
  8    TABLESPACE "USERS"
  9    PARALLEL 8 ;

Index created.

Elapsed: 00:01:26.30
SQL>
SQL>    -- Note: No Grants found!
SQL>    -- Note: No Triggers found!
SQL>
SQL>    ALTER TABLE "KRM"."SKEW2_TEMP" ADD PRIMARY KEY ("PK_COL")
  2    USING INDEX PCTFREE 10 INITRANS 2 MAXTRANS 255
  3    NOLOGGING COMPUTE STATISTICS
  4    STORAGE(INITIAL 865075200 NEXT 1048576
  5           MINEXTENTS 1 MAXEXTENTS 2147483645
  6    PCTINCREASE 0 FREELISTS 1 FREELIST GROUPS 1 BUFFER_POOL DEFAULT
  7    FLASH_CACHE DEFAULT CELL_FLASH_CACHE DEFAULT)
  8    TABLESPACE "USERS"  ENABLE;

Table altered.

Elapsed: 00:00:20.42
```

Similar to the comparison with the UPDATE statement, the rebuild provides a viable alternative. In this example, I deleted roughly 10 percent of the records. The DELETE took about 4.25 minutes and the rebuild took about 5.25 minutes. In this case, the straight DELETE was actually faster. But, as the number of records increases, the time to rebuild remains basically the same whereas the time to run the DELETE increases. Eventually, there is a point when the rebuild becomes much cheaper than the DELETE.

TRUNCATE

I am sure you are aware of the TRUNCATE command, but I should mention it here anyway. If you need to delete all the rows from a table or a partition, the TRUNCATE command is the way to do it. Truncating a table moves the high-water mark rather than actually changing all the blocks that hold records. It is blazingly fast compared with using the DELETE command. There are only a few very minor negatives.

- TRUNCATE is a DDL command, so it issues an implicit commit; once a table is truncated, there is no going back.

- You cannot flash back to the state of the table prior to the truncate.

- TRUNCATE works on the whole table or nothing.

- In a RAC environment, all the nodes must be sent a message to invalidate the buffers of the table (which is not the case with a DELETE).

In addition to completing extremely quickly, the TRUNCATE command makes a big difference for future queries on the table. Because full table scans read every block to the high-water mark, and the DELETE command has no effect on the high-water mark, you may be giving up performance gains for future statements.

MERGE

The MERGE statement was introduced in Oracle Database 9i. It provides the classic UPSERT functionality. MERGE updates the record if one already exists, or inserts a new record if one doesn't already exist. (Oracle Database 10g enhanced the MERGE command to allow it to delete records as well.) The idea is to eliminate the extra code necessary to do error checking, and to eliminate the additional round-trips to the database when it's necessary to issue additional SQL statements (such as write a piece of code that attempts an update, check the status of the update, and, if the update fails, then issue the insert). The MERGE statement does all this at the database level without all the additional code. Obviously, it performs better than the procedural code version.

Syntax and Usage

The syntax of the typical MERGE statement is relatively easy to follow. The following is the basic syntax of a MERGE statement:

```
MERGE INTO table_name
USING (subquery) ON (subquery.column = table.column)
WHEN MATCHED THEN UPDATE ...
WHEN NOT MATCHED THEN INSERT ...
```

The first part of the MERGE statement looks just like an INSERT, specifying the table (or view) that is to be the target of the inserted, updated, or deleted data. The USING keyword specifies a data source (usually a subquery, although it could be a staging table as well) and a join condition that tells Oracle how to determine whether a record already exists in the target table. In addition, you must add an UPDATE clause or an INSERT clause or both. In most cases, you see both because there is little value in using the MERGE statement without both clauses. Now let's move on to the UPDATE and INSERT clauses (they probably should have called these the WHEN MATCHED and WHEN NOT MATCHED clauses instead).

The UPDATE clause tells Oracle what to do when a matching record is found. In most cases, finding a matching record results in an update to that record. There is also an optional WHERE clause that can be used to limit which records are updated, even if there is a match. Alternatively, you can delete matching records using yet another WHERE clause. Note that the records to be deleted must pass the criteria in the main WHERE clause *and* the criteria in the DELETE WHERE clause.

The DELETE clause is not actually used that often. It can be handy, though, for a job that needs to do more than just load data. For example, some ETL processes also perform cleanup tasks. For the DELETE portion of the UPDATE clause to kick in, a matching record must be found that passes the WHERE clause in the UPDATE clause as well as the WHERE clause associated with the DELETE. Listing 13-17 shows the MERGE command with an UPDATE clause that contains a DELETE.

Listing 13-17. MERGE with UPDATE Clause

```
MERGE INTO big_emp t
USING (select * from hr.employees) s
ON (t.employee_id = s.employee_id)
WHEN MATCHED THEN UPDATE SET
--  t.employee_id = s.employee_id, -- ON clause columns not allowed
  t.first_name = t.first_name,
  t.last_name = s.last_name ,
  t.email = s.email ,
  t.phone_number = s.phone_number ,
  t.hire_date = s.hire_date ,
  t.job_id = s.job_id ,
  t.salary = s.salary ,
  t.commission_pct = s.commission_pct ,
  t.manager_id = s.manager_id ,
  t.department_id = s.department_id
     WHERE (S.salary <= 3000)
DELETE WHERE (S.job_id = 'FIRED');
```

The INSERT clause tells Oracle what to do when a matching record is not found. In general, this means "do an insert." However, the INSERT clause can be left off altogether. There is also an optional WHERE clause that can be applied, so it is not always the case that an insert is done if a match is not found. Listing 13-18 shows two versions of a MERGE statement with an INSERT clause.

Listing 13-18. MERGE with INSERT Clause

```
MERGE INTO big_emp t
USING (select * from hr.employees) s
ON (t.employee_id = s.employee_id)
WHEN NOT MATCHED THEN INSERT
(t.employee_id ,
 t.first_name ,
 t.last_name ,
 t.email ,
 t.phone_number ,
 t.hire_date ,
 t.job_id ,
 t.salary ,
 t.commission_pct ,
 t.manager_id ,
 t.department_id)
VALUES
(s.employee_id ,
 s.first_name ,
 s.last_name ,
 s.email ,
 s.phone_number ,
 s.hire_date ,
 s.job_id ,
 s.salary ,
 s.commission_pct ,
```

```
    s.manager_id ,
    s.department_id)
        WHERE (S.job_id != 'FIRED');

MERGE INTO big_emp t
USING (select * from hr.employees where job_id != 'FIRED') s
ON (t.employee_id = s.employee_id)
WHEN NOT MATCHED THEN INSERT
(t.employee_id ,
 t.first_name ,
 t.last_name ,
 t.email ,
 t.phone_number ,
 t.hire_date ,
 t.job_id ,
 t.salary ,
 t.commission_pct ,
 t.manager_id ,
 t.department_id)
VALUES
(s.employee_id ,
 s.first_name ,
 s.last_name ,
 s.email ,
 s.phone_number ,
 s.hire_date ,
 s.job_id ,
 s.salary ,
 s.commission_pct ,
 s.manager_id ,
 s.department_id);
```

The statements accomplish the same thing but use a slightly different mechanism. One qualifies the set of records to be merged in the subquery in the USING clause; the other qualifies the statements to be merged in the WHERE clause inside the INSERT clause. Be aware that these two forms can have different performance characteristics and may even result in different plans. Listing 13-19 shows a more realistic example with both the INSERT clause and the UPDATE clause. Note that the UPDATE clause also contains a DELETE WHERE clause that cleans up records of employees who have been fired.

Listing 13-19. Full MERGE

```
SQL>
SQL> -- delete from big_emp where employee_id > 190;
SQL> -- insert into hr.jobs select 'FIRED', 'Fired', 0, 0 from dual;
SQL> -- update hr.employees set job_id = 'FIRED' where employee_id=197;
SQL> MERGE /*+ APPEND */ INTO big_emp t
  2    USING (select * from hr.employees) s
  3    ON (t.employee_id = s.employee_id)
  4    WHEN MATCHED THEN UPDATE SET
  5  --    t.employee_id = s.employee_id,
  6      t.first_name = t.first_name,
  7      t.last_name = s.last_name ,
```

```
 8      t.email = s.email ,
 9      t.phone_number = s.phone_number ,
10      t.hire_date = s.hire_date ,
11      t.job_id = s.job_id ,
12      t.salary = s.salary ,
13      t.commission_pct = s.commission_pct ,
14      t.manager_id = s.manager_id ,
15      t.department_id = s.department_id
16          WHERE (S.salary <= 3000)
17          DELETE WHERE (S.job_id = 'FIRED')
18   WHEN NOT MATCHED THEN INSERT
19   (t.employee_id ,
20    t.first_name ,
21    t.last_name ,
22    t.email ,
23    t.phone_number ,
24    t.hire_date ,
25    t.job_id ,
26    t.salary ,
27    t.commission_pct ,
28    t.manager_id ,
29    t.department_id)
30   VALUES
31   (s.employee_id ,
32    s.first_name ,
33    s.last_name ,
34    s.email ,
35    s.phone_number ,
36    s.hire_date ,
37    s.job_id ,
38    s.salary ,
39    s.commission_pct ,
40    s.manager_id ,
41    s.department_id)
42          WHERE (S.job_id != 'FIRED');
```

88140 rows merged.

Elapsed: 00:00:06.51

Performance Comparison

So how does the MERGE statement compare with a straight INSERT or CTAS operation? Obviously, there is some inherent overhead in the MERGE statement that makes such a comparison an unfair test, but MERGE is no slouch. Keep in mind that just like with the INSERT command, the fastest way to load a lot of data is to make sure it uses the direct path mechanism by using the APPEND hint. Listing 13-20 compares the performance of INSERT, MERGE, and CTAS. It also demonstrates that all are capable of doing direct path writes.

Listing 13-20. INSERT, MERGE, and CTAS Performance Comparison

```
SQL> @compare_insert_merge_ctas.sql

Table dropped.

Elapsed: 00:00:00.69
SQL> @flush_pool
SQL> alter system flush shared_pool;

System altered.

Elapsed: 00:00:00.46
SQL> select name, value from v$mystat s, v$statname n
  2  where n.statistic# = s.statistic# and name = 'physical writes direct';

NAME                                                             VALUE
---------------------------------------------------------------- ----------
physical writes direct                                               0

Elapsed: 00:00:00.03
SQL> create /* compare_insert_merge_ctas.sql */ table skew3
  2  as select * from skew;

Table created.

Elapsed: 00:00:32.92
SQL> select name, value from v$mystat s, v$statname n
  2  where n.statistic# = s.statistic# and name = 'physical writes direct';

NAME                                                             VALUE
---------------------------------------------------------------- ----------
physical writes direct                                          163031

Elapsed: 00:00:00.03
SQL>
SQL> truncate table skew3 drop storage;

Table truncated.

Elapsed: 00:00:01.01
SQL> INSERT /*+ APPEND */ /* compare_insert_merge_ctas.sql */
  2 INTO skew3 select * from skew;

32000004 rows created.

Elapsed: 00:00:31.23
SQL> select name, value from v$mystat s, v$statname n
  2  where n.statistic# = s.statistic# and name = 'physical writes direct';
```

```
NAME                                                               VALUE
---------------------------------------------------------------- ----------
physical writes direct                                             326062

Elapsed: 00:00:00.03
SQL>
SQL> truncate table skew3 drop storage;

Table truncated.

Elapsed: 00:00:00.84
SQL> MERGE /*+ APPEND */ /* compare_insert_merge_ctas.sql */
  2  INTO skew3 t
  3  USING (select * from skew) s
  4  ON (t.pk_col = s.pk_col)
  5  WHEN NOT MATCHED THEN INSERT
  6  (t.pk_col, t.col1, t.col2, t.col3, t.col4)
  7       VALUES (s.pk_col, s.col1, s.col2, s.col3, s.col4);

32000004 rows merged.

Elapsed: 00:00:49.07
SQL> select name, value from v$mystat s, v$statname n
  2  where n.statistic# = s.statistic# and name = 'physical writes direct';

NAME                                                               VALUE
---------------------------------------------------------------- ----------
physical writes direct                                             489093

Elapsed: 00:00:00.01

SQL> @fss2
Enter value for sql_text: %compare_insert%
Enter value for sql_id:

SQL_ID         AVG_ETIME AVG_CPU  AVG_PIO  AVG_LIO SQL_TEXT
------------- --------- -------  -------- -------- --------------------
6y6ms28kzzb5z     49.07   48.48  162,294  490,664 MERGE /*+ APPEND */
g1pf9b564j7yn     31.22   30.93  162,296  489,239 INSERT /*+ APPEND */
g909cagdbs1t5     32.91   31.25  162,294  494,480 create /* compare_in
```

In this very simple test, you can see that all three approaches are able to use the direct path writes, and that CTAS and INSERT are very similar in performance. The MERGE statement is considerably slower, as expected because of its additional capabilities and the necessary overhead associated with them. But, the MERGE statement provides the most flexibility, so don't overlook the fact that this single statement can perform multiple types of DML with a single execution.

Summary

There are four SQL commands for modifying data: INSERT, UPDATE, DELETE, and MERGE (and the latter is actually capable of performing all three functions). In this chapter I discussed these commands briefly and focused on one key performance concept: Direct path inserts are much, much faster than conventional inserts. There is a good reason for this difference in performance. Direct path inserts do a lot less work. There are a number of drawbacks when using the technique, however. The biggest drawback is that it is a serial operation; only one process can be engaging in a direct path insert on a table at any given time, and any other process that wishes to do the same simply has to wait. Another big drawback is that available space that's already allocated to the table is not used by direct path inserts. For these reasons, it's only applicable to large batch-type loading operations. Nevertheless, it is the fastest way to insert data into a table and, as such, should be considered whenever performance is among the most important decision-making criteria. Techniques have been developed for using direct path inserts in the place of updates and deletes. We explored a couple of these techniques in this chapter as well. Last, I explained several of the lesser known options of the DML commands, including the extremely powerful Error Logging clause, which can be applied to all four of the DML commands.

Transaction Processing

After you use Oracle Database for a while, you might have certain expectations of how it behaves. When you enter a query, you expect a consistent result set to be returned. If you enter a SQL statement to update several hundred records and the update of one of those rows fails, you expect the entire update to fail and all rows to be returned to their prior state. If your update succeeds and you commit your work to the database, you expect your changes to become visible to other users and remain in the database, at least until the data are updated again by someone else. You expect that when you are reading data, you never block a session from writing, and you also expect the reverse to be true. These are fundamental truths about how Oracle Database operates, and after you've become comfortable working with Oracle, you tend to take these truths for granted.

However, when you begin to write code for applications, you need to be keenly aware of how Oracle provides the consistency and concurrency you've learned to rely on. Relational databases are intended to process transactions, and in my opinion, Oracle Database is exceptional at keeping transaction data consistent, accurate, and available. However, you must design and implement transactions correctly if the protections you receive automatically at the statement level are to be extended to your transactions. How you design and code a transaction impacts the integrity and consistency of the application data, and if you do not define the transaction boundaries clearly, your application may behave in some unexpected ways. Transaction design also influences how well the system performs when multiple users are retrieving and altering the information within it. Scalability can be severely limited when transactions are designed poorly.

Although there are only a few transaction control statements, understanding how a transaction is processed requires an understanding of some of the more complex concepts and architectural components in Oracle Database. In the next few sections, I briefly cover a few transaction basics, the ACID properties (aka atomicity, consistency, isolation, and durability), ISO/ANSI SQL transaction isolation levels, and multiversion read consistency. For a more thorough treatment of these topics, please read the *Oracle Concepts Manual* (`http://www.oracle.com/technetwork/indexes/documentation/index.html`) and then follow up with Tom Kyte's *Expert Oracle Database Architecture Oracle Database 9i, 10g and 11g Programming Techniques and Solutions* (Apress 2010), Chapters 6, 7, and 8. The goal for this chapter is to acquire a basic understanding of how to design a sound transaction and how to ensure that Oracle processes your transactions exactly as you intend them to be processed.

What Is a Transaction?

Let's start by making sure we're all on the same page when it comes to the word *transaction*. The definition of a transaction is a *single, logical unit of work*. It is comprised of a specific set of SQL statements that *must succeed or fail as a whole*. Every transaction has a distinct beginning, with the first executable SQL statement, and a distinct ending, when the work of the transaction is either committed or rolled back. Transactions that have started but have not yet committed or rolled back their work are *active* transactions, and all changes within an active transaction are considered pending until they are committed. If the transaction fails or is rolled back, then those pending changes never existed in the database at all.

The most common example of a transaction is a banking transfer. For example, a customer wants to transfer $500 from a checking account to a savings account, which requires a two-step process: a $500 debit from checking and a $500 credit to savings. Both updates must complete successfully to guarantee the accuracy of the data. If both updates cannot be completed, then both updates must roll back. Transactions are an all-or-nothing proposition, because a partial transaction may corrupt the data's integrity. Consider the bank transfer. If the funds are removed from the checking account but the credit to the savings account fails, the data are no longer consistent and the bank's financial reporting is inaccurate. The bank also has a very unhappy customer on its hands because the customer's $500 has mysteriously disappeared.

It is also necessary to ensure that both updates are committed to the database as a single unit. Committing after each statement increases the possibility of one statement succeeding and the other statement failing; it also results in a point in time when the data are inconsistent. From the moment the first commit succeeds until the second commit completes, the bank records do not represent reality. If a bank manager happens to execute a report summarizing all account balances during that space of time between the two commits, the total in the deposited accounts would be short by $500. In this case, the customer is fine because the $500 does eventually end up in her savings account. Instead, there is a very frustrated accountant working late into the night to balance the books. By allowing the statements to process independently, the integrity of the data provided to the users becomes questionable.

A transaction should not include any extraneous work. Using the banking example again, it would be wrong to add the customer's order for new checks in the transfer transaction. Adding unrelated work violates the definition of a transaction. There is no logical reason why a check order should depend on the success of a transfer. Nor should the transfer depend on the check order. Maybe if a customer is opening a new account it would be appropriate to include the check order with the transaction. The bank doesn't want to issue checks on a nonexistent account. But then again, is the customer required to get checks for the account? Probably not. The most important element of coding a sound transaction is setting the transaction boundaries accurately around a logical unit of work and ensuring that all operations within the transaction are processed as a whole. To know where those boundaries should be, you need to understand the application requirements and the business process.

A transaction can be comprised of multiple DML statements, but it can contain only one DDL statement. This is because every DDL statement creates an implicit commit, which also commits any previously uncommitted work. Be very cautious when including DDL statements in a transaction. Because a transaction must encompass a complete logical unit of work, you must be certain that a DDL statement is either issued prior to the DML statements as a separate transaction or issued after all DML statements have processed successfully. If a DDL statement occurs in the middle of a transaction, then your "logical unit of work" ends up divided into two not-so-logical partial updates.

ACID Properties of a Transaction

Transaction processing is a defining characteristic of a data management system; it's what makes a database different from a file system. There are four required properties for all database transactions: *atomicity, consistency, isolation,* and *durability*. These four properties are known as *ACID properties*. The ACID properties have been used to define the key characteristics of database transactions across all brands of database systems since Jim Gray first wrote about them in 1976, and clearly he defined those characteristics very well because no one has done it better in the 37 years since then. Every transactional database must comply with ACID, but *how* they choose to implement their compliance has created some of the more interesting differences in database software products.

All Oracle transactions comply with the ACID properties, which are described in the *Oracle Concepts Manual* (http://www.oracle.com/technetwork/indexes/documentation/index.html) as follows:

> *Atomicity*: All tasks of a transaction are performed or none of them are. There are no partial transactions.

> *Consistency*: The transaction takes the database from one consistent state to another consistent state.

> *Isolation*: The effect of a transaction is not visible to other transactions until the transaction is committed.

> *Durability*: Changes made by committed transactions are permanent.

Think for a moment about the fundamental behaviors of the individual SQL statements you issue to the Oracle Database and compare them with the ACID properties just listed. These properties represent the behaviors you expect at the statement level, because Oracle provides atomicity, consistency, isolation, and durability for SQL statements automatically without you having to expend any additional effort. Essentially, when you design a transaction to be processed by the database, your goal is to communicate the entire set of changes as a single operation. As long as you use transaction control statements to convey the contents of an individual transaction correctly, and set your transactions to the appropriate isolation level when the default behavior is not what you need, Oracle Database provides the atomicity, consistency, isolation, and durability required to protect your data.

Transaction Isolation Levels

And now for a little more depth on one particular ACID property: isolation. The definition of isolation in the *Oracle Concepts Manual* referenced earlier states that the effects of your transaction cannot be visible until you have committed your changes. This also means that your changes should not influence the behavior of other active transactions in the database.

In the banking transaction, I discussed the importance of protecting (isolating) the financial report from your changes until the entire transaction is complete. If you commit the credit to checking before you commit the debit to savings, the total bank funds are overstated (briefly) by $500, which violates the isolation property, because any users or transactions can see that the checking account balance has been reduced before the funds were added to the savings account.

However, there are two sides to the requirement for transaction isolation. In addition to isolating other transactions from your updates, you need to be aware of how isolated your transaction needs to be from updates made by other transactions. To some extent, the way to deal with this issue depends on those business requirements, but it also depends on how sensitive your transaction is to changes made by other users, and how likely the data are to change while your transaction is processing. To appreciate the need for isolation, you need to understand how isolation, or the lack thereof, impacts transactions on a multiuser database.

The ANSI/ISO SQL standard defines four distinct levels of transaction isolation: read uncommitted, read committed, repeatable read, and serializable. Within these four levels, the standard defines three phenomena that are either permitted or not permitted at a specific isolation level: dirty reads, nonrepeatable reads, and phantom reads. Each of the three phenomena is a specific type of inconsistency that can occur in data that are read by one transaction while another transaction is processing updates. As the isolation level increases, there is a greater degree of separation between transactions, which results in increasingly consistent data.

The ANSI/ISO SQL standard does not tell you how a database should achieve these isolation levels, nor does it define which kinds of reads should or should not be permitted. The standard simply defines the impact one transaction may have on another at a given level of isolation. Table 14-1 lists the four isolation levels and notes whether a given phenomenon is permitted.

Table 14-1. *ANSI Isolation Levels*

Isolation Level	Dirty Read	Nonrepeatable Read	Phantom Read
Read uncommitted	Permitted	Permitted	Permitted
Read committed	X	Permitted	Permitted
Repeatable read	X	X	Permitted
Serializable	X	X	X

The definitions of each phenomenon are as follows:

- *Dirty read*: Reading uncommitted data is called a *dirty read*, and it's a very appropriate name. Dirty reads have not been committed, which means that data have not yet been verified against any constraints set in the database. Uncommitted data may never be committed, and if this happens, the data were never really part of the database at all. Result sets built from dirty reads should be considered highly suspect because they can represent a view of the information that never actually existed.

- *Nonrepeatable read*: A nonrepeatable read occurs when a transaction executes a query a second time and receives a different result because of committed updates by another transaction. In this case, the updates by the other transaction have been verified and made durable, so the data are valid; they've just been altered since the last time your transaction read it.

- *Phantom read*: If a query is executed a second time within a transaction, and additional records matching the filter criteria are returned, it is considered a phantom read. Phantom reads result when another transaction has inserted more data and committed its work.

By default, transactions in Oracle are permitted to read the committed work of other users immediately after the commit. This means that it is possible to get nonrepeatable and phantom reads unless you specifically set the isolation level for your transaction to either read only or serializable. The important question is "Will either phenomenon prevent my transaction from applying its changes correctly and taking the database from one consistent state to the next?" If your transaction does not issue the same query more than once in a single transaction or it does not need the underlying data to remain consistent for the duration of your transaction, then the answer is no and the transaction can be processed safely at the default read-committed isolation level.

Only a serializable transaction removes completely the possibility of all three phenomena while still allowing for updates, thus providing the most consistent view of the data even as they are changing. However, serializable transactions can reduce the level of concurrency in the database because there is a greater risk of transactions failing as a result of conflicts with other updates. If you require repeatable reads *and* you need to update data in the transaction, setting your transaction to execute in serializable mode is your only option. If your transaction requires repeatable reads but it does not update data, then you can set your transaction to read-only mode, which guarantees repeatable reads until your transaction completes or until the system exceeds its undo retention period. I talk about how to accomplish serializable and repeatable read transactions shortly.

Oracle does not support the read-uncommitted isolation level, nor is it possible to alter the database to do so. Reading uncommitted data is permitted in other databases to prevent writers from blocking readers and to prevent readers from blocking writers. Oracle prevents such blocks from occurring with multiversion read consistency, which provides each transaction with its own read-consistent view of the data. Thanks to multiversion read consistency, dirty reads are something Oracle users and developers never need to worry about.

Multiversion Read Consistency

As mentioned earlier, the ACID properties do not determine how the database should provide data consistency for transactions, nor do the ANSI/ISO SQL transaction isolation levels define how to achieve transaction isolation or even specify the levels of isolation a database product must provide. Each individual vendor determines how to comply with ACID and the levels of isolation it supports. If you develop applications that operate on multiple database platforms, it is crucial for you to understand the different implementations provided by each vendor and how those differences can impact the results of a given transaction.

Fortunately, you only have to worry about one approach in this chapter. Oracle provides data consistency and concurrency with the multiversion read consistency model. This can be a fairly complex concept to grasp, although it's transparent to users. Oracle is able to display simultaneously multiple versions of the data, based on the specific point in time a transaction requested the information and on the transaction's isolation level. The database accomplishes this amazing feat by retaining the before-and-after condition of altered data blocks so that the database can recreate a consistent view of the data for multiple sessions at a single point in time. If a transaction is running in the default read-committed mode, then a "consistent view of the data" means the results are based on the committed data as of when a query or update was initiated. When a transaction executes in serializable mode, the read-consistent view is based on the committed data as of when the transaction began. There is a limit to how far Oracle can reach into the past to create this consistent view of the data, and that limit depends on the allocation of undo space configured for the database. If Oracle cannot reach back far enough into the past to support a given statement, that statement fails with a "snapshot too old" error.

Undo blocks retain the before condition of the data whereas the redo information is stored in the online redo logs in the SGA. The redo logs contain both the change to the data block and the change to the undo block. The same structures that provide the means to roll back your changes also provide read-consistent views of the data to multiple users and multiple transactions. Because a transaction should always encompass a complete logical unit of work, the undo storage and retention level should be configured to support transactions at the required level of concurrency. If you are considering dividing your logical unit of work to prevent "snapshot too old" errors, you need to revisit your code or talk with your DBA. Or maybe do both.

The database buffers of the SGA are updated with changes for a committed transaction, but the changes are not necessarily written immediately to the data files. Oracle uses the system change number (SCN) to keep a sequential record of changes occurring throughout the instance and to connect changes to a particular point in time. Should the database fail, all pending transactions are rolled back so that when the database is restarted, the data are at a consistent state once again, reflecting only the committed work as of the time of failure. You get the exact same result if the DBA issues a command to flash the database back to a specific SCN. The database returns to the point in time marked by the SCN, and any transactions committed after that no longer exist in the database. This is necessary to prevent partial transactions from being stored in the database.

So how does multiversion read consistency impact individual transactions? If transaction B requests data that have been altered by transaction A, but transaction A has not committed its changes, Oracle reads the before condition of the data and returns that view to transaction B. If transaction C begins after transaction A commits its changes, the results returned to transaction C include the changes committed by transaction A, which means that transaction C receives a different result than transaction B, but the results are consistent with the point in time when each session requested the information.

Transaction Control Statements

There are only five transaction control statements: commit, savepoint, rollback, set transaction, and set constraints. There are relatively few variants of these statements, so learning the syntax and the options for controlling your transactions is not too difficult. The challenge of coding a transaction is understanding how and when to use the appropriate combination of statements to ensure your transaction complies with ACID and that it is processed by the database exactly as you expect.

Commit

Commit, or the SQL standard-compliant version commit work, ends your transaction by making your changes durable and visible to other users. With the commit write extensions now available, you have the option to change the default behavior of a commit. Changes can be committed asynchronously with the write nowait extension, and you can also choose to allow Oracle to write commits in batches. The default behavior processes a commit as commit write wait immediate, which is how commits were processed in earlier versions of Oracle. This is still the correct behavior for the majority of applications.

So when might you choose not to wait for Oracle to confirm your work has been written? By choosing an asynchronous commit, you are allowing the database to confirm that your changes have been received before those changes are made durable. If the database fails before the commit is written, your transaction is gone yet your application and your users expect it to be there. Although this behavior may be acceptable for applications that process highly transitive data, for most of us, ensuring the data have indeed been committed is essential. A nowait commit should be considered carefully before being implemented. You need to be certain that your application can function when committed transactions seem to disappear.

Savepoint

Savepoints allow you to mark specific points within your transaction and roll back your transaction to the specified savepoint. You then have the option to continue your transaction rather than starting a brand new one. Savepoints are sequential, so if you have five savepoints and you roll back to the second savepoint, all changes made for savepoints 3 through 5 are rolled back.

Rollback

Rollback is the other option for ending a transaction. If you choose to roll back, your changes are reversed and the data return to their previously consistent state. As noted earlier, you have the option to roll back to a specific savepoint, but rolling back to a savepoint does not end a transaction. Instead, the transaction remains active until either a complete rollback or a commit is issued.

Set Transaction

The set transaction command provides multiple options to alter default transaction behavior. Set transaction read only provides repeatable reads, but you cannot alter data. You also use the set transaction command to specify serializable isolation. Set transaction can be used to choose a specific rollback segment for a transaction, but this is no longer recommended by Oracle. In fact, if you are using automatic undo management, this command is ignored. You can also use set transaction to name your transaction, but the dbms.application_info package is a better option for labeling your transactions because it provides additional functionality.

Set Constraints

Constraints can be deferred during a transaction with the set constraint or set constraints commands. The default behavior is to check the constraints after each statement, but in some transactions it may be that the constraints are not met until all the updates within the transaction are complete. In these cases, you can defer constraint verification as long as the constraints are created as deferrable. This command can defer a single constraint or it can defer all constraints.

As far as the SQL language goes, transaction control statements may be some of the simplest and clearest language options you have. Commit, rollback, and rollback to savepoint will be the transaction control commands you use most often. You may need to set the isolation level with set transaction occasionally, whereas deferring constraints is likely to be a rare occurrence. If you want more information about the transaction control statements, referring to the SQL statement documentation is likely to give you enough information to execute the commands; but, before you use one of the less common commands, be sure to research and test it extensively so you know absolutely what effect the nondefault behavior will have on your data.

Grouping Operations into Transactions

By now, you should be well aware that understanding business requirements is central to designing a good transaction. However, what is considered a logical unit of work in one company may be very different at another. For example, when an order is placed, is the customer's credit card charged immediately or is the card charged when the order ships? If payment is required to place the order, then the procuring the funds should be part of the order transaction.

If payments are processed when the product is shipped, then payment may be authorized with the order, but processed just before shipment. Neither option is more correct than the other, it just depends on how the business has decided to manage its orders. If a company sells a very limited product, then expecting payment at the time of order is perfectly reasonable because the company makes that rare item unavailable to other customers. If the product is common, then customers generally don't expect to pay until the product ships, and choosing to process payments earlier may cost the company some business.

In addition to understanding the requirements of the business, there are some general rules for designing a sound transaction:

- Process each logical unit of work as an independent transaction. Do not include extraneous work.

- Ensure the data are consistent when your transaction begins and that they remain consistent when the transaction is complete.

- Get the resources you need to process your transaction and then release the resources for other transactions. Hold shared resources for as long as you need them, but no longer. By the same token, do not commit during your transaction just to release locks you still need. Adding commits breaks up the logical unit of work and does not benefit the database.

- Consider other transactions likely to be processing at the same time. Do they need to be isolated from your transaction? Does your transaction need to be isolated from other updates?

- Use savepoints to mark specific SQL statements that may be appropriate for midtransaction rollbacks.

- Transactions should always be committed or rolled back explicitly. Do not rely on the default behavior of the database or a development tool to commit or roll back. Default behavior can change.

- After you've designed a solid transaction, consider wrapping it in a procedure or package. As long as a procedure does not contain any commits or rollbacks within it, it is provided with the same default atomicity level Oracle provides to all statements. This means that the protections afforded automatically to statements also apply to your procedure and, therefore, to your transaction.

- Exception handling can have a significant impact on a transaction's integrity. Exceptions should be handled with relevant application errors, and any unhandled exceptions should always raise the database error. Using the WHEN OTHERS clause to bypass an error condition is a serious flaw in your code.

- Consider using the dbms_application_info package to label your transactions to help identify specific sections of code quickly and accurately when troubleshooting errors or tuning performance. I talk more about dbms_application_info and instrumentation in the next chapter.

The Order Entry Schema

Before I move on to talking about active transactions, let's talk about the sample schema we'll be using for our transaction examples. The order entry (OE) schema contains a product set that is available for orders, and it is associated with the human resources schema you may already be familiar with. In this case, some of the employees are sales representatives who take orders on behalf of customers. Listing 14-1 shows the names of the tables in the default OE schema.

Listing 14-1. OE Schema Tables

```
TABLE_NAME
------------------------------
CATEGORIES
CUSTOMERS
INVENTORIES
ORDERS
ORDER_ITEMS
PRODUCT_DESCRIPTIONS
PRODUCT_INFORMATION
WAREHOUSES
```

The OE schema may be missing a few critical components; there are no warehouses in the warehouses table and there is no inventory in the inventories table, so you are out of stock on everything and you have no place to store the stock if you did have any. It's hard to create orders without any inventory, so we need to add data to the existing tables first.

Start by adding a warehouse to the company's Southlake, Texas, location where there should be plenty of real estate, and then add lots of inventory to be sold. I used the dbms_random procedure to generate more than 700,000 items, so if you choose to follow along, your actual inventory may vary. But, you should end up with enough products in stock to experiment with a few transactions, and you can always add more. As you create your orders, notice the product_information table contains some very old computing equipment. If it helps, consider the equipment vintage and pretend you're selling collectibles.

The orders table contains an order_status column, but the status is represented by a numeric value. Create a lookup table for the order status values and, because the existing orders use a range of one through ten, your order_status table needs to contain ten records. Although this is not a PL/SQL book, I created a few functions and a procedure to provide some necessary functionality without having to show a lot of extra code that might detract from the primary purpose of the example. There are functions to get the list price from the product_information table, one to get a count of the number of line items added to an order, and another one to calculate the order total using the sum of the line items. The contents of the functions are not important to your transactions, but the code to create them is included in the download available at the Apress web site, along with the rest of the schema updates.

We also need to create a billing schema and a credit authorization procedure. The procedure accepts a customer ID number and order total, and then returns a randomly generated number to simulate the process of ensuring payment for the products. In the real world, billing likely represents an entire accounting system and possibly a distributed transaction, but for our purposes, we simply need to represent the customers' promise to pay for the items they wish to order. Remember, the most important rule for any transaction is that it should contain a complete logical unit of work. The credit authorization represents the exchange of funds for the product. We're not in business to give our products away, and customers aren't going to send us cash unless they receive something in return. It's this exchange that represents a transaction. Listing 14-2 shows the rest of the OE schema changes.

Listing 14-2. OE Schema Changes

```
-- create 'billing' user to own a credit authorization procedure

conn / as sysdba
create user billing identified by &passwd ;

grant create session to billing ;
grant create procedure to billing ;

--- add warehouses and inventory using a random number to populate inventory quantities
```

```
connect oe

insert into warehouses values (1, 'Finished Goods', 1400) ;

insert into inventories
select product_id, 1, round(dbms_random.value(2, 5000),0)
  from product_information;

commit;

--- check total quantity on hand

select sum(quantity_on_hand) from inventories;

--- create a sequence for the order id

create sequence order_id start with 5000;

--- create a table for order status

create table oe.order_status
 (
  order_status            number(2, 0) not null,
  order_status_name       varchar2(12) not null,
  constraint order_status_pk order_status)
 );

--- add values for order status 1 through 10 to match existing sample data

insert into order_status (order_status, order_status_name) values (0, 'Pending');
insert into order_status (order_status, order_status_name) values (1, 'New');
insert into order_status (order_status, order_status_name) values (2, 'Cancelled');
insert into order_status (order_status, order_status_name) values (3, 'Authorized');
insert into order_status (order_status, order_status_name) values (4, 'Processing');
insert into order_status (order_status, order_status_name) values (5, 'Shipped');
insert into order_status (order_status, order_status_name) values (6, 'Delivered');
insert into order_status (order_status, order_status_name) values (7, 'Returned');
insert into order_status (order_status, order_status_name) values (8, 'Damaged');
insert into order_status (order_status, order_status_name) values (9, 'Exchanged');
insert into order_status (order_status, order_status_name) values (10, 'Rejected');

--- create a function to get the list prices of order items

@get_listprice.fnc

--- create a function to get the order total

@get_ordertotal.fnc

--- create a function to get the order count
```

```
@get_orderitemcount.fnc

--- create order detail views

@order_detail_views.sql

--- Create credit_request procedure

connect billing

@credit_request.sql
```

Now that you know what we're selling and we have a `customers` table to tell us who we might be selling it to, let's take a look at an order transaction. Your longstanding customer Maximilian Henner of Davenport, Iowa, has contacted sales manager John Russell and placed an order for five 12GB hard drives, five 32GB RAM sticks, and 19 boxes of business cards containing 1000 cards per box. Mr. Henner has a credit authorization of $50,000, although our `customers` table does not tell us how much he may already owe for prior purchases. This information is stored in our imaginary billing system. John enters Mr. Henner's order in the order entry screen of our sales system and creates order number 2459 for customer 141. The order is a direct order entered into the system by our employee, ID number 145. When our sales manager sends a copy of this order to his customer, the order should look something like this:

Order no.:	**2459**	
Customer:	**Maximilian Henner**	
	2102 E Kimberly Rd	
	Davenport, IA 52807	
Sold by:	**John Russell**	

No.	Product	Description	Qty	Price	Sale Price	Total
1	2255	HD 12GB @7200 /SE	5	775.00	658.75	3293.75
2	2274	RAM, 32MB	5	161.00	136.85	684.25
3	2537	Business cards, box, 1000	19	200.00	170.00	3230.00

Mr. Henner wants to purchase multiple quantities of three different products, so we need to add three items to the `order_item` table. Each item needs a product ID, a quantity, and a list price. There is a discount percentage that is applied to the entire order, and it is used to calculate the discounted price. The discounted priced is multiplied by the item quantity to produce the line item total.

As we add the items to the order, we also must reduce the on-hand inventory for these items so that another sales person does not commit to delivering a product that is no longer available. Next, we need to calculate the order total as a sum of the line items and then call the credit authorization procedure to verify that Mr. Henner has the required amount available in his credit line. After we have the authorization, we set the order total to equal the amount charged, and the transaction is complete. All these steps are required for the order to exist and, therefore, these steps comprise our logical unit of work for an order.

Before we enter the order, check the inventory for the products the customer has requested, as shown in Listing 14-3.

Listing 14-3. Verify Available Inventory

```
SQL> select product_id, quantity_on_hand
       from inventories
     where product_id in (2255, 2274, 2537)
     order by product_id ;
```

```
PRODUCT_ID QUANTITY_ON_HAND
---------- ----------------
      2255              672
      2274              749
      2537             2759
```

When we look at the statements as they are received by the database to create this order, reduce the inventory, and obtain a credit authorization, they might look something like the transaction shown in Listing 14-4.

Listing 14-4. Order Transaction in a Procedure

```
SQL> begin

    savepoint create_order;

    insert into orders
           (order_id, order_date, order_mode,
            order_status, customer_id, sales_rep_id)
      values
           (2459, sysdate, 'direct', 1, 141, 145) ;

 --- Add first ordered item and reduce inventory

    savepoint detail_item1;

    insert into order_items
           (order_id, line_item_id, product_id,
            unit_price, discount_price, quantity)
      values
           (2459, 1, 2255, 775, 658.75, 5) ;

    update inventories set quantity_on_hand = quantity_on_hand - 5
     where product_id = 2255 and warehouse_id = 1 ;

 --- Add second ordered item and reduce inventory

    savepoint detail_item2;

    insert into order_items
           (order_id, line_item_id, product_id,
            unit_price, discount_price, quantity)
      values
           (2459, 2, 2274, 161, 136.85, 5) ;

    update inventories set quantity_on_hand = quantity_on_hand - 5
     where product_id = 2274 and warehouse_id = 1 ;

 --- Add third ordered item and reduce inventory
```

```
  savepoint detail_item3;
   insert into order_items
         (order_id, line_item_id, product_id,
          unit_price, discount_price, quantity)
   values
         (2459, 3, 2537, 200, 170, 19) ;

  update inventories set quantity_on_hand = quantity_on_hand - 19
   where product_id = 2537 and warehouse_id = 1 ;

  --- Request credit authorization

  savepoint credit_auth;

  begin billing.credit_request(141,7208); end;

  savepoint order_total;

  --- Update order total

  savepoint order_total;

  update orders set order_total = 7208 where order_id = 2459;

  exception
   when others then RAISE;
  end;
  /

Customer ID = 141
Amount = 7208
Authorization = 3452

PL/SQL procedure successfully completed.
```

We see the output from the credit authorization and get a confirmation that our procedure completed. We have not yet ended our transaction because we haven't issued a commit or a rollback. First, query the data to confirm our updates, including the update to reduce the on-hand inventory. The confirmation queries are shown in Listing 14-5.

Listing 14-5. Confirm Transaction Updates

```
SQL> select order_id, customer, mobile, status, order_total, order_date
       from order_detail_header
       where order_id = 2459 ;

  ORDER_ID  CUSTOMER           MOBILE           STATUS  ORDER_TOTAL  ORDER_DATE
---------- ---------------- --------------- ------- ------------ -----------
      2459 Maximilian Henner +1 319 123 4282 New        7,208.00 04 Jul 2010

1 row selected.
```

```
SQL> select line_item_id ITEM, product_name, unit_price,
            discount_price, quantity qty, line_item_total
       from order_detail_line_items
      where order_id = 2459
      order by line_item_id ;

 ITEM PRODUCT_NAME             UNIT_PRICE DISCOUNT_PRICE QTY LINE_ITEM_TOTAL
 ----- ------------------------ ---------- --------------- --- ---------------
     1 HD 12GB @7200 /SE            775.00         658.75   5        3,293.75
     2 RAM - 32 MB                  161.00         136.85   5          684.25
     3 Business Cards Box - 1000    200.00         170.00  19        3,230.00

3 rows selected.

SQL> select product_id, quantity_on_hand
       from inventories
      where product_id in (2255, 2274, 2537)
      order by product_id ;

PRODUCT_ID QUANTITY_ON_HAND
---------- ----------------
      2255              667
      2274              744
      2537             2740
```

All required operations within our transaction have been confirmed. The order is created, three products are added, the inventory is reduced, and our order total is updated to reflect the sum of the individual line items. Our transaction is complete, and we can commit the changes. Instead, however, we're going to roll them back and use this transaction again.

■ **Note**   The most important rule for transaction processing is to ensure the transaction is ACID compliant. The transaction in Listing 14-4 has been wrapped in a procedure with an exception clause to illustrate the atomicity principal. The remainder of the examples are shown as independently entered SQL statements and, in some cases, only a portion of the transaction is shown to keep the examples to a reasonable length. If there is one message you take away from this chapter, it is the importance of ensuring that the entire transaction succeeds as a whole or fails as a whole.

The Active Transaction

As soon as we issue the first SQL statement that alters data, the database recognizes an active transaction and creates a transaction ID. The transaction ID remains the same whether we have one DML statement in our transaction or 20, and the transaction ID exists only as long as our transaction is active and our changes are still pending. In the order example from the previous section, the transaction ID is responsible for tracking only one transaction: the new order for Mr. Henner. After we roll back the entire transaction, our transaction ends and the transaction ID is gone. We see the same result if we commit our work.

The SCN, on the other hand, continues to increment regardless of where we are in our transaction process. The SCN identifies a specific point in time for the database, and it can be used to return the database to a prior point in time while still ensuring the data are consistent. Committed transactions remain committed (durability), and any pending transactions are rolled back (atomicity).

If we check the transaction ID and SCN while executing the individual statements that comprised the order procedure shown earlier, we see something like the results in Listing 14-6.

Listing 14-6. Order Transaction with Transaction ID and SCN Shown

```
SQL> insert into orders
            (order_id, order_date, order_mode,
            order_status, customer_id, sales_rep_id)
      values
            (2459, sysdate, 'direct', 1, 141, 145) ;

1 row created.

SQL> select current_scn from v$database;

CURRENT_SCN
-----------
   83002007

SQL> select xid, status from v$transaction ;

XID              STATUS
---------------- ----------------
0A001800CE8D0000 ACTIVE
.......

SQL> --- Update order total

SQL> update orders set order_total = 7208 where order_id = 2459;
1 row updated.

SQL> select order_id, customer, mobile, status, order_total, order_date
      from order_detail_header
      where order_id = 2459;
  ORDER_ID CUSTOMER                     MOBILE          STATUS         ORDER_TOTAL ORDER_DATE
---------- -------------------------- --------------- ------------ --------------- -----------
      2459 Maximilian Henner            +1 319 123 4282 New             7,208.00 04 Jul 2010

SQL> select line_item_id, product_name, unit_price,
            discount_price, quantity, line_item_total
      from order_detail_line_items
      where order_id = 2459
      order by line_item_id ;

ITEM PRODUCT_NAME                       UNIT_PRICE DISCOUNT_PRICE  QUANTITY LINE_ITEM_TOTAL
---- -------------------------------- ---------- -------------- ---------- ---------------
   1 HD 12GB @7200 /SE                    775.00         658.75          5        3,293.75
   2 RAM - 32 MB                          161.00         136.85          5          684.25
   3 Business Cards Box - 1000            200.00         170.00         19        3,230.00

SQL> select current_scn from v$database;
```

```
CURRENT_SCN
-----------
   83002012

SQL> select xid, status from v$transaction ;

XID              STATUS
---------------- ----------------
0A001800CE8D0000 ACTIVE

SQL> rollback;

Rollback complete.

SQL> select current_scn from v$database;

CURRENT_SCN
-----------
   83002015

SQL> select xid, status from v$transaction ;

no rows selected
```

If the database flashed back to SCN 83002012, none of the operations in our order exist. Because any changes we made were pending at that point in time, the only way Oracle can guarantee data consistency is to roll back all noncommitted work. Whether we committed the transaction or rolled it back is immaterial. The updates were not committed at SCN 830020012, and pending changes are always reversed.

Using Savepoints

In the initial order transaction, we included savepoints but did not make use of them. Instead, we executed our transaction, confirmed the order information with two queries, and then rolled back the entire transaction. In the example shown in Listing 14-7, we roll back to savepoint item_detail1, which is recorded prior to adding any product to the order. Let's take a look at our data after returning to a savepoint.

Listing 14-7. Returning to a Savepoint

```
SQL> savepoint create_order;

Savepoint created.

SQL> insert into orders
          (order_id, order_date, order_mode,
           order_status, customer_id, sales_rep_id)
     values
          (2459, sysdate, 'direct', 1, 141, 145) ;

1 row created.
```

```
SQL> --- Add first ordered item and reduce inventory

SQL> savepoint detail_item1;

Savepoint created.

SQL> insert into order_items
            (order_id, line_item_id, product_id,
             unit_price, discount_price, quantity)
       values
            (2459, 1, 2255, 775, 658.75, 5) ;

1 row created.

SQL> update inventories set quantity_on_hand = quantity_on_hand - 5
       where product_id = 2255 and warehouse_id = 1 ;

1 row updated.

SQL> --- Add second ordered item and reduce inventory

SQL> savepoint detail_item2;

Savepoint created.

SQL> insert into order_items
            (order_id, line_item_id, product_id,
             unit_price, discount_price, quantity)
       values
            (2459, 2, 2274, 161, 136.85, 5) ;

1 row created.

SQL> update inventories set quantity_on_hand = quantity_on_hand - 5
       where product_id = 2274 and warehouse_id = 1 ;

1 row updated.

SQL> --- Add third ordered item and reduce inventory

SQL> savepoint detail_item3;

Savepoint created.

SQL> insert into order_items
            (order_id, line_item_id, product_id,
             unit_price, discount_price, quantity)
       values
            (2459, 3, 2537, 200, 170, 19) ;

1 row created.
```

```
SQL> update inventories set quantity_on_hand = quantity_on_hand - 19
        where product_id = 2537 and warehouse_id = 1 ;

1 row updated.

SQL> --- Request credit authorization

SQL> savepoint credit_auth;

Savepoint created.

SQL> exec billing.credit_request(141,7208) ;
Customer ID = 141
Amount = 7208
Authorization = 1789

PL/SQL procedure successfully completed.

SQL> savepoint order_total;

Savepoint created.

SQL> --- Update order total

SQL> savepoint order_total;

Savepoint created.

SQL> update orders set order_total = 7208 where order_id = 2459;

1 row updated.

SQL> select order_id, customer, mobile, status, order_total, order_date
        from order_detail_header
        where order_id = 2459;

  ORDER_ID CUSTOMER                    MOBILE           STATUS       ORDER_TOTAL ORDER_DATE
---------- ------------------------- ---------------- ------------ -------------- -----------
      2459 Maximilian Henner          +1 319 123 4282 New            7,208.00 04 Jul 2010

SQL> select line_item_id, product_name, unit_price, discount_price,
            quantity, line_item_total
        from order_detail_line_items
        where order_id = 2459
        order by line_item_id ;

ITEM PRODUCT_NAME               UNIT_PRICE DISCOUNT_PRICE   QUANTITY LINE_ITEM_TOTAL
---- ------------------------- ---------- -------------- ---------- ----------------
   1 HD 12GB @7200 /SE             775.00         658.75          5         3,293.75
   2 RAM - 32 MB                   161.00         136.85          5           684.25
   3 Business Cards Box - 1000     200.00         170.00         19         3,230.00

SQL> rollback to savepoint detail_item1;

Rollback complete.
```

When we reexecute the queries to check the order data, notice in Listing 14-8 that all changes occurring after the savepoint are reversed, yet the order itself still exists. Our sales rep has the option of continuing with Mr. Henner's order by adding new line items or rolling it back completely to end the transaction.

Listing 14-8. Verifying Data after Rollback to a Savepoint

```
SQL> select order_id, customer, mobile, status, order_total, order_date
        from order_detail_header
      where order_id = 2459;
```

ORDER_ID	CUSTOMER	MOBILE	STATUS	ORDER_TOTAL	ORDER_DATE
2459	Maximilian Henner	+1 319 123 4282	New		04 Jun 2010

```
SQL> select line_item_id, product_name, unit_price, discount_price,
            quantity, line_item_total
       from order_detail_line_items
      where order_id = 2459
      order by line_item_id ;

no rows selected

SQL> select product_id, quantity_on_hand
        from inventories
       where product_id in (2255, 2274, 2537)
       order by product_id ;
```

PRODUCT_ID	QUANTITY_ON_HAND
2255	672
2274	749
2537	2759

Notice how in the first set of query selects both the order and the three products are added to the order_items table. After we roll back to the item_detail1 savepoint, there are no products associated with the order, the inventory has returned to its previous level, and—although the order header still exists—the order total field is now null.

Serializing Transactions

When a transaction is executed in serializable mode, Oracle's multiversion read consistency model provides a view of the data as they existed at the start of the transaction. No matter how many other transactions may be processing updates at the same time, a serializable transaction only sees its own changes. This creates the illusion of a single-user database because changes committed by other users after the start of the transaction remain invisible. Serializable transactions are used when a transaction needs to update data and requires repeatable reads. Listings 14-9 and 14-10 demonstrate when a serialized transaction or repeatable read may be required.

Executing transactions in serializable mode does not mean that updates are processed sequentially. If a serializable transaction attempts to update a record that has been changed since the transaction began, the update is not permitted and Oracle returns error "ORA-08177: can't serialize access for this transaction."

At this point, the transaction could be rolled back and repeated. For a serializable transaction to be successful, there needs to be a strong possibility that no one else will update the same data while the transaction executes. We can increase the odds of success by completing any changes that may conflict with other updates early in our transaction, and by keeping the serialized transaction as short and as fast as possible.

This makes the need for serializable updates somewhat contrary to their use. If the data are unlikely to be updated by another user, then why do we need serializable isolation? Yet, if the data are changeable enough to require serializable isolation, this may be difficult to achieve.

For the next example, we open two sessions. Session A initiates a serializable transaction and adds an additional product to an existing order. After the item is added and before the order total is updated, we pause the transaction to make a change to the same order in another session. In session B, we update the status of the order to Processing and commit our changes. Then, we return to session A to update the order. This results in an ORA-08177 error, as shown in Listing 14-9.

Listing 14-9. Serialized Transaction and ORA-08177

```
Session A: Serialized transaction to add an additional item

SQL> set transaction isolation level serializable;

Transaction set.

SQL> variable o number
SQL> execute :o := &order_id
Enter value for order_id: 5006

PL/SQL procedure successfully completed.

SQL> variable d number
SQL> execute :d := &discount
Enter value for discount: .1

PL/SQL procedure successfully completed.

SQL> --- Add new ordered item and reduce on-hand inventory

SQL> variable i number
SQL> execute :i := &first_item
Enter value for first_item: 1791

PL/SQL procedure successfully completed.

SQL> variable q number
SQL> execute :q := &item_quantity
Enter value for item_quantity: 15

PL/SQL procedure successfully completed.

SQL> variable p number
SQL> execute :p := get_ListPrice(:i)

PL/SQL procedure successfully completed.
```

```
SQL> insert into order_items
            (order_id, line_item_id, product_id, unit_price, discount_price, quantity)
     values
            (:o, 1, :i, :p, :p-(:p*:d), :q) ;

1 row created.
SQL> update inventories set quantity_on_hand = quantity_on_hand - :q
     where product_id = :i and warehouse_id = 1 ;

1 row updated.

SQL> pause Pause  ...
Pause  ...

Session B: Order Status Update

SQL> variable o number
SQL> execute :o := &order_id
Enter value for order_id: 5006

PL/SQL procedure successfully completed.

SQL> variable s number
SQL> execute :s := &status
Enter value for status: 4

PL/SQL procedure successfully completed.

SQL> update orders
        set order_status = :s
     where order_id = :o ;

1 row updated.

SQL> select order_id, customer, mobile, status, order_total, order_date
        from order_detail_header
        where order_id = :o;

  ORDER_ID CUSTOMER                    MOBILE           STATUS          ORDER_TOTAL ORDER_DATE
---------- ------------------------- ---------------- ------------- --------------- -----------
      5006 Harry Mean Taylor          +1 416 012 4147 Processing         108.00    04 Jul 2010

SQL> select line_item_id, product_name, unit_price, discount_price,
     quantity, line_item_total
        from order_detail_line_item
        where order_id = :o
        order by line_item_id ;

ITEM PRODUCT_NAME               UNIT_PRICE DISCOUNT_PRICE   QUANTITY LINE_ITEM_TOTAL
---- ------------------------- ---------- --------------- ---------- ----------------
   1 Cable RS232 10/AM                  6            5.40         20           108.00
```

416

```
SQL> commit;
Session A: Return to the serializable transaction

SQL> --- Get New Order Total

SQL> variable t number
SQL> execute :t := get_OrderTotal(:o)

PL/SQL procedure successfully completed.

SQL> --- Update order total

SQL> update orders set order_total = :t where order_id = :o ;
update orders set order_total = :t where order_id = :o
*
ERROR at line 1:
ORA-08177: can't serialize access for this transaction
```

Because session B already committed changes to order 5006, session A is not permitted to update the order total. This is necessary to prevent a lost update. Session A cannot see the order status has changed; its serialized view of the data still considers the order to be New. If session A replaced the record in the order table with its version of the data, changes made by session B would be overwritten by the previous version of the data even though they were committed changes. In this case, the order total would have to be updated earlier during session A's transaction for this transaction to be successful. However, because the order total is a sum of the individual line items, that number is unknown until the new line item is added. This is also a case when serializable isolation might really be required. If two sessions are attempting to add line items to the same order at the same time, the calculated order total might end up inaccurate.

■ **Note** I switched from hard coded data values to user variables in the transactions, which makes it easier to execute the order transactions repeatedly for testing and to view the results at each step. The code to process orders with prompts, variables, and functions is available on the Apress web site.

Isolating Transactions

Using the same pair of transactions, let's take a quick look at what can happen when we don't isolate a transaction properly. In this case, session A commits the additional items to order 5007 before pausing, which means the product is added to the order and is made durable; but, the order total does not include the additional product. Listing 14-10 shows how permitting other sessions to see partial transactions can jeopardize data integrity.

Listing 14-10. Inappropriate Commits and Transaction Isolation Levels

```
Session A: Serializable transaction to add an additional item

SQL> set transaction isolation level serializable;
Transaction set.

SQL> variable o number
SQL> execute :o := &order_id
Enter value for order_id: 5007
```

```
PL/SQL procedure successfully completed.

SQL> variable d number
SQL> execute :d := &discount
Enter value for discount: .2

PL/SQL procedure successfully completed.

SQL> --- Add new ordered item and reduce on-hand inventory

SQL> variable i number
SQL> execute :i := &first_item
Enter value for first_item: 3127

PL/SQL procedure successfully completed.

SQL> variable q number
SQL> execute :q := &item_quantity
Enter value for item_quantity: 5

PL/SQL procedure successfully completed.

SQL> variable p number
SQL> execute :p := get_ListPrice(:i)

PL/SQL procedure successfully completed.

SQL> insert into order_items
        (order_id, line_item_id, product_id,
          unit_price, discount_price, quantity)
     values
        (:o, 1, :i, :p, :p-(:p*:d), :q) ;

1 row created.

SQL> update inventories set quantity_on_hand = quantity_on_hand - :q
        where product_id = :i and warehouse_id = 1 ;

1 row updated.

SQL> commit;

Commit complete.

SQL> pause Pause  ...
Pause  ...

Session B: Order Status Update
```

```
SQL> variable o number
SQL> execute :o := &order_id
Enter value for order_id: 5007

PL/SQL procedure successfully completed.

SQL> variable s number
SQL> execute :s := &status
Enter value for status: 4

PL/SQL procedure successfully completed.

SQL> update orders
        set order_status = :s
      where order_id = :o ;

1 row updated.

SQL> select order_id, customer, mobile, status, order_total, order_date
       from order_detail_header
      where order_id = :o;

  ORDER_ID CUSTOMER                 MOBILE           STATUS         ORDER_TOTAL ORDER_DATE
---------- ------------------------ ---------------- ------------ --------------- -----------
      5007 Alice Oates              +41 4 012 3563   Processing      16,432.00 04 Jul 2010

SQL> select line_item_id, product_name, unit_price, discount_price,
            quantity, line_item_total
       from order_detail_line_item
      where order_id = :o ;
      order by line_item_id ;

ITEM PRODUCT_NAME                       UNIT_PRICE DISCOUNT_PRICE  QUANTITY LINE_ITEM_TOTAL
---- --------------------------------- ---------- -------------- ---------- ---------------
   1 Monitor 21/HR/M                       889.00         711.20          5        3,556.00
   2 Laptop 128/12/56/v90/110            3,219.00       2,575.20          5       12,876.00
   3 LaserPro 600/6/BW                     498.00         398.40          5        1,992.00

SQL> commit;
```

Notice in the previous output that the LaserPro 600 printer is added to the order, but the order total does not reflect the additional $1992. The status update transaction is able to view changes made by the partial transaction. Because session A issued a commit, its serializable transaction ends. Either session is now able to record its view of the orders table, and the statement that is recorded last gets to determine the data in the order header. If session A completes first, session B alters the order status to Processing, but the order total remains wrong. If session B completes first, session A sets the correct order total, but the order is returned to an order status of New. Either option results in a lost update, which demonstrates why it's so critical to ensure that a transaction completes a single, logical unit of work. Because of session A's partial transaction, data consistency has been jeopardized.

What if session B is running a report instead of updating the order's status? Session A eventually results in a consistent update, but session B may end up reporting inaccurate data. This is a slightly less serious infraction because the data in the database are accurate. However, end users make decisions based on reports, and the impact of a poorly placed commit affects decisions to be made. The best solution to this issue is twofold. First, the code executed in session A should be corrected to removed the ill-placed commit and to ensure the entire transaction commits or fails as a single unit. Second, if data are changing quickly and the reports are not bound by date or time ranges, setting the report transaction to ensure a repeatable read may also be advisable.

Autonomous Transactions

Within our main transaction, we have the option of calling an autonomous transaction, which is an independent transaction that can be called from within another transaction. The autonomous transaction is able to commit or roll back its changes without impacting the calling, or main, transaction. Autonomous transactions are very useful if you have information you need to store, regardless of the final resolution of the main transaction. Error logging is possibly the best example of a good use of autonomous transactions, and in some cases auditing is an appropriate use as well, although overusing autonomous transactions is not a good idea. For most of us, there are better tools available in the database for auditing, and any attempts to circumvent normal database or transaction behavior is likely to create problems eventually.

So when would you want to use an autonomous transaction? I can think of a few examples in our ordering system, and—in both cases—the goal is to retain information to prevent lost sales opportunities. For example, we might want to record the customer ID and a timestamp in an `order_log` table in case the order fails. If the transaction is successful, the entry in `order_log` notes the order was created successfully. This allows us to provide our sales team with a report on any attempted orders that were not completed.

If you've done much shopping online, you may have received one of those e-mail reminders that you have left items in your shopping cart. Maybe you were shopping but something came up and you navigated away from the site, or perhaps you decided you didn't really need to purchase those items after all. Either way, the vendor knows you were interested enough in the items to think about buying them, and they don't want to miss an opportunity to sell products to an interested customer. I've been browsing Amazon lately for diving equipment, in part because I'm still learning about the gear and in part to do a little price comparison with my local dive shop. Within a day or two, Amazon sent me an e-mail to let me know about a special sale on one of the products I was browsing. I find this a little disconcerting, especially when I haven't even logged in while browsing, but I have to admit it can be awfully tempting when you receive the news that the shiny, expensive piece of equipment you really want now costs 20 percent less than before.

Another possibility for an autonomous transaction is to record customer information when new customers place their first order. Creating a new customer can be considered a separate logical unit of work, so we aren't breaking any of the transaction design rules by committing the customer information outside the order. If the order is interrupted for any reason, it is advantageous to retain the contact data so someone can follow up with the customer to make sure the order is placed correctly.

In Listing 14-11, we create an `order_log` table with four fields: `customer_id`, `order_id`, `order_date`, and `order_status`. Next, we create an autonomous transaction in a procedure. The `record_new_order` procedure logs the customer ID, the order ID, and the current date, committing the information immediately. We add a call to the procedure in the order transaction as soon as the order ID and customer ID are known.

Listing 14-11. Creating the Autonomous Order Logging Transaction

```
SQL> @autonomous_transaction
SQL> create table order_log
     (
        customer_id             number not null,
        order_id                number not null,
        order_date              date   not null,
        order_outcome           varchar2(10),
     constraint order_log_pk primary key (customer_id, order_id, order_date)
     );

Table created.
```

```
SQL> create or replace procedure record_new_order (p_customer_id  IN NUMBER,
                                                   p_order_id     IN NUMBER)
     as
     pragma autonomous_transaction;
     begin
       insert into order_log
        (customer_id, order_id, order_date)
      values
        (p_customer_id, p_order_id, sysdate);

     commit;
     end;
     /
Procedure created.
```

Listing 14-12 shows the execution of a new order transaction containing the autonomous transaction to log the customer information. The main transaction is rolled back, yet when we query the order_log table, the customer information is stored. This is because the write to the order_log table is an autonomous transaction and does not depend on the successful completion of the calling transaction.

Listing 14-12. Executing an Order Transaction with the Order Logging Autonomous Transaction

```
SQL> @order_transaction

SQL> WHENEVER SQLERROR EXIT SQL.SQLCODE ROLLBACK;
SQL> variable o number
SQL> execute :o := order_id.nextval

PL/SQL procedure successfully completed.

SQL> variable c number
SQL> execute :c := &customer_id
Enter value for customer_id: 264

PL/SQL procedure successfully completed.

SQL> execute oe.record_new_order(:c,:o);

PL/SQL procedure successfully completed.

SQL> variable s number
SQL> execute :s := &salesperson_id
Enter value for salesperson_id: 145

PL/SQL procedure successfully completed.

SQL> variable d number
SQL> execute :d := &discount
Enter value for discount: .1

PL/SQL procedure successfully completed.
```

```
SQL> savepoint create_order;

Savepoint created.

SQL> insert into orders
          (order_id, order_date, order_mode, order_status, customer_id, sales_rep_id)
       values
          (:o, sysdate, 'direct', 1, :c, :s) ;

1 row created.

SQL> --- Add first ordered item and reduce on-hand inventory

SQL> savepoint detail_item1;
Savepoint created.

SQL> variable i number
SQL> execute :i := &first_item
Enter value for first_item: 2335

PL/SQL procedure successfully completed.

SQL> variable q number
SQL> execute :q := &item_quantity
Enter value for item_quantity: 1

PL/SQL procedure successfully completed.

SQL> variable p number
SQL> execute :p := get_ListPrice(:i)

PL/SQL procedure successfully completed.

SQL> insert into order_items
          (order_id, line_item_id, product_id,
           unit_price, discount_price, quantity)
       values
          (:o, 1, :i, :p, :p-(:p*:d), :q) ;

1 row created.

SQL> update inventories set quantity_on_hand = quantity_on_hand - :q
       where product_id = :i and warehouse_id = 1 ;

1 row updated.

SQL> --- Get Order Total

SQL> variable t number
SQL> execute :t := get_OrderTotal(:o)
```

```
PL/SQL procedure successfully completed.

SQL> -- Request credit authorization

SQL> savepoint credit_auth;
Savepoint created.
SQL> execute billing.credit_request(:c,:t);
Customer ID = 264
Amount = 90
Authorization = 99

PL/SQL procedure successfully completed.

SQL> --- Update order total

SQL> savepoint order_total;

Savepoint created.

SQL> update orders set order_total = :t where order_id = :o ;

1 row updated.

SQL> select order_id, customer, mobile, status, order_total, order_date
       from order_detail_header
       where order_id = :o ;

  ORDER_ID  CUSTOMER                  MOBILE           STATUS        ORDER_TOTAL ORDER_DATE
---------- ------------------------- --------------- ------------ --------------- -----------
      5020 George Adjani             +1 215 123 4702 New                 90.00 05 Jul 2010

SQL> select line_item_id ITEM, product_name, unit_price, discount_price, quantity, line_item_total
       from order_detail_line_items
       where order_id = :o
       order by line_item_id ;

 ITEM PRODUCT_NAME             UNIT_PRICE DISCOUNT_PRICE   QUANTITY LINE_ITEM_TOTAL
----- ------------------------ ---------- -------------- ---------- ----------------
    1 Mobile phone                 100.00          90.00          1            90.00

SQL> rollback;

Rollback complete.

SQL> select * from order_log;

CUSTOMER_ID ORDER_ID ORDER_DATE          ORDER_STATUS
----------- -------- ------------------- ------------
        264     5020 2010-07-05 00:45:56
```

The order log retains a committed record of the attempted order. As for the order status, there are several ways we can handle this. We can create another procedure that sets the order status in the order_log table when the order is committed by the application. If the order status is not populated in order_log, we then know the order has not been committed. We could also schedule a process to compare the order_log table with the orders table. If no record is found in the orders table, we then update the order_log table to note the order failed.

When using autonomous transactions, be certain that you are not dividing a transaction or circumvent normal database behavior. Think carefully about the effect you create when you allow the autonomous transaction to commit while rolling back the main transaction. The work in the autonomous transaction should clearly be its own logical unit of work.

Summary

Transactions are the heart of a database. We create databases to store information and, if that information is going to be useful, the data must be protected and they must remain consistent. If we jeopardize the integrity of the data, we have devalued the system significantly. Data integrity is an all-or-nothing proposition; either we have it or we don't. Although I've heard people use percentage values to describe a database's level of accuracy, this seems to be a downward spiral into increasing uncertainty. When we know part of the data are wrong, how do we know any of the data are accurate? And how do we know which part of the data we can trust?

If our data are to remain trustworthy, we need to ensure that each transaction complies with the ACID properties. Transactions must be atomic, containing one logical unit of work that succeeds or fails as a whole. Transactions must be consistent; they need to ensure the data are consistent when they begin, and that the data remain consistent when the transaction ends. Transactions should occur in isolation; uncommitted changes should not be visible to users or other transactions, and some transactions require higher levels of isolation than others. Transactions must be durable; when the changes have been committed to the database and the database has responded that the changes exist, users should be able to count on the fact that there is a record of their changes.

Fortunately, Oracle makes it fairly easy for us to build ACID-compliant transactions as long as we define the boundaries of our transaction carefully and accurately. Oracle does not require us to specify that we are starting a new transaction; instead, the database knows which kinds of statements begin a transaction, and it creates a transaction ID to track the operations within it. Always commit or roll back your transactions specifically, because failing to do so can make those transaction boundaries a little fuzzy. Relying on the default behavior of software tools is risky because the behavior may change in a future release.

Building sound transactions requires both technical skills and functional knowledge, and having both of those is a rare and valuable commodity in the information technology (IT) industry. This book provides a solid foundation for the development of your technical skills—and you can develop these skills further by following up with the reference material mentioned earlier—but, learning to apply these skills requires practice. Start by downloading the changes I made to the OE schema and build a few transactions of your own. Deliberately introduce some bad choices just to see what happens. (But don't leave that code lying around; it can be dangerous!) Experimenting with isolation levels can be particularly interesting. Practice building a few more complex transactions, and make sure the transaction fails if any part of it fails. Then, add some custom exception handling and savepoints so that you don't have to lose the entire transaction if you need to revert part of it. When you've got something you're proud of, wrap it up in a procedure and be sure to share what you've learned with someone else.

■ ■ ■

Testing and Quality Assurance

As you've worked through the chapters of this book, you may have written some code to test the examples. And because you chose this particular book instead of a "Welcome to SQL"–style book, it's likely you have written quite a few SQL statements before you ever picked it up. As you've been reading this book, did some of the chapters remind you of your prior work? If so, how do you feel about the code you've written in the past?

If you're like most developers, there were times when you probably thought, "Hey, considering how little I knew about this functionality back then, I did pretty well." And there may have been a few times when you cringed a bit, realizing that something you were very proud of at the time wasn't such a great approach after all. Don't worry; we all have applications that we would write completely differently if we only knew then what we know now. Besides, it's always easier to write better code with hindsight or as an armchair code jockey.

If the code you write today is better than the code you wrote yesterday, you're continuing to evolve and learn, and that is commendable. Realizing our older work could have been done better is an inevitable part of the learning process. As long as we learn from our mistakes and do a little better with the next application or the next bit of code, we're moving in the right direction.

It's also true that we need to be able to measure the quality of our current code now, not five years from now when we've grown even wiser. We want to find the problems in our code before they affect our users. Most of us want to find all the errors or performance issues before anyone else even sees our work. However, although this kind of attitude may indicate an admirable work ethic, it's not an advisable or even an achievable goal. What we can achieve is a clear definition of what a specific piece of code needs to accomplish and how we can prove the code meets the defined requirements. Code should have measurable indicators of success that can prove or disprove the fact that we met our goal.

So what are these measurable factors? Although the target measurement varies depending on the application, there are several basic requirements for all application code. First and foremost, the code needs to return accurate results and we need to know that the results will continue to be accurate throughout the system's life cycle. If end users cannot count on the data returned by a database application, that's a pretty serious failure.

Performance is another measurable attribute of our code. The target runtimes are highly dependent on the application in question. A database used by a home owner's association to track who has paid their annual fees is not required to perform at the same level as a database containing the current stock quotes, but the methods used to compare execution plans and measure runtime can be the same. Code quality requires that we understand the application requirements, the function being performed, and the strengths and weaknesses of the specific system. Testing should focus on verifying functionality, pushing the weakest links to their breaking point, and recording all measurements along the way.

Test Cases

For the examples in this chapter, we work with the same OE sample schema that we used for the transaction processing examples in Chapter 14. We make more changes to our schema, adding new data and altering views and reports. We begin by defining the changes to be made and the tests to use to verify the success of those changes.

So here is the backstory: One of our suppliers, identified only as Supplier 103089 in the database, is changing its product numbers for the software we purchase from them to resell to our customers. The new identifiers are appended with a hyphen and a two-character value to identify the software package language. For example, the supplier's product identifier for all English software packages ends in -EN. The supplier requires its product identifier to be referenced for ordering, software updates, and warranty support. The new product identifiers have an effective date of October 10, 2010. This change presents the following challenges:

- The OE schema includes the supplier's identifier in the `product_information` table, but the supplier *product* identifier is not stored in the sample schema database at all. We must alter the OE schema to add this field and create a numeric value to serve as the current supplier product ID. These changes are a prerequisite to the changes instituted by our supplier.

- After we have added an initial supplier product identifier for all the products we sell, we need to determine how we will add the modified product identifiers for this one supplier. We also need to have a method of controlling the effective date of the new identifiers.

- The purchasing department uses an inventory report to determine which products are getting low on stock. This report needs to reflect the current supplier product identifier until October 10, 2010. After that date, the report should print the new supplier product identifier so purchasing agents can place and verify orders easily.

- The OE system will continue to use our internal product identifier when orders are received from our customers. Orders and invoices must show our product identifier and name, plus the supplier product identifier.

- We have inventory on hand that is packaged with the current supplier product identifier. We can continue to sell those products as is, but our customer invoices must show the actual supplier product ID found on the packaging. This means our inventory system must treat the items labeled with the new numbering scheme as a distinct product.

As we make these changes, there are several basic tests and quality issues to consider. The points that follow are not intended to be all inclusive, because every system has its own unique test requirements; however, there are some quality checks that can be applied to all systems. Let's use the following as a starting point:

- All objects that were valid before our changes should be valid when our changes are complete. Views, functions, procedures, and packages can be invalidated by a table change, depending on how the code for those objects was written originally. We need to check for invalid schema objects both before and after we make our changes. Objects that are invalidated as an indirect result of our planned modifications should recompile successfully without further changes.

- All data changes and results output must be accurate. Verifying data can be one of the more tedious tasks when developing or altering a database application, and the more data in the system, the more tedious the work. It's also the most critical test our code must pass. If the data are not accurate, it doesn't matter if the other requirements have been met or how fast the code executes. If the data being stored or returned cannot be trusted, our code is wrong and we've failed this most basic requirement. The simplest approach is to break down data verification into manageable components, beginning by verifying the core dataset, and then expand the test gradually to the more unique use cases (the "edge cases") until we are certain all data are correct.

- Query performance can be verified by comparing the before and after versions of the execution plan. If the execution plan indicates the process has to work harder after our modifications, we want to be sure that additional work is, in fact, required and is not the result of a mistake. Use of execution plans was addressed in detail in Chapter 6, so we can refer back to that chapter for more information on the topic plus tips on making the best use of the information found in the execution plan.

Later in this chapter, I discuss code instrumentation and the Instrumentation Library for Oracle (ILO). ILO uses Oracle's `dbms_application_info` procedures. Although it is possible to use the `dbms_application_info` procedures on their own, ILO makes it very easy and straightforward to add instrumentation to our code. I added some additional functionality to the ILO package; the updates are available for download at Apress. After the code is instrumented, these additional modules make it possible to build test systems that record processing times as iterative changes are made to the code or system configuration. These performance data make it very clear when changes have had a positive impact on processing times and when another approach should be considered.

Testing Methods

There are as many different approaches to software testing as there are software development—and there have quite possibly been an equal number of battles fought over both topics. Although it may be slightly controversial in a database environment, I advocate an approach known as *test-driven development* (TDD). TDD originated in the realm of extreme programming, so we need to make some modifications to the process to make it effective for database development, but it offers some very genuine benefits for both new development and modification efforts.

In TDD, developers begin by creating simple, repeatable tests that fail in the existing system but succeed after the change is implemented correctly. This approach has the following benefits:

- To write the test that fails, you have to understand thoroughly the requirements and the current implementation before you even begin to write application code.

- Building the unit test script first ensures that you start by working through the logic of the necessary changes, thereby decreasing the odds that your code has bugs or needs a major rewrite.

- By creating small, reusable unit tests to verify the successful implementation of a change, you build a library of test scripts that can be used both to test the initial implementation of the change and to confirm that the feature is still operating as expected as other system changes are made.

- These small-unit test scripts can be combined to create larger integration testing scripts or can become part of an automated test harness to simplify repetitive testing.

- TDD assists in breaking changes or new development into smaller, logical units of work. The subsets may be easier to understand and explain to other developers, which can be especially important when project members are not colocated.

- When test design is delayed until after development, testing frequently ends up being shortchanged, with incomplete or poorly written tests as a result of schedule constraints. Including test development efforts in the code development phases results in higher quality tests that are more accurate.

As acknowledged earlier, TDD needs some adjustments in a database environment or we run the risk of building yet another black box database application that is bound to fail performance and scalability testing. Whenever you develop or modify an application that stores or retrieves information from a database, as you prepare those first unit tests, you must consider the data model or work with the individuals responsible for that task. In my (sometimes) humble opinion, *the data model is the single most important indicator of a database application's potential to perform*. The schema design is crucial to the application's ability to scale for more users, more data, or both. This does not mean that development cannot begin until there is a flawless entity–relationship model, but it does mean that the core data elements must be understood and the application tables well designed for at least those core elements. And if the database model is not fully developed, then build the application using code that does not result in extensive changes as the data model is refactored.

So exactly what am I suggesting? To put it bluntly, if your application schema continues to be developed progressively, use procedures and packages for your application code. This allows the database to be refactored as data elements are moved or added, without requiring major front-end code rewrites.

■ **Note** This is far from being a complete explanation of TDD or database refactoring. I strongly recommend the book *Refactoring Databases: Evolutionary Database Design* by Scott W. Ambler and Pramodkumar J. Sadalage (Addison-Wesley 2006) for a look at database development using Agile methods.

But let's get back to our application changes, shall we? In the case of the changing supplier product identifier, let's begin by asking some questions. How will this new data element be used by our company and employees? How will this change impact our OE and inventory data? Will this change impact systems or processes beyond our OE system? At a minimum, our purchasing agents need the supplier's current product identifier to place an order for new products. Depending on how well recognized the component is, the supplier's product identifier could be used more widely than we might expect; a specific product or component may even be a selling point with our customers. A great example is CPUs. The make and the model of the processor in the laptop can be far more important than the brand name on the case. If this is true for the products we are reselling, the supplier's product ID may be represented throughout multiple systems beyond the ordering system, so it is necessary to extend our evaluation to include additional systems and processes.

Unit Tests

As noted in the previous section, our first goal is to write the unit tests we need to demonstrate that our application modifications are successful. However, because this is a database application, we need to determine where this data element belongs before we can even begin to write the first unit test. Although the Oracle–provided sample schemas are far from perfect, we cannot refactor the entire schema in this chapter, so there are many data design compromises in the examples. This can also be true in the real world; it is seldom possible to make all the corrections we know should be made, which is why correcting problems in the schema design can be a long, iterative process that requires very careful management.

■ **Note** Remember, the focus of this chapter is testing methods. I keep the examples as short as possible to avoid detracting from the core message. This means the examples do not represent production-ready code, nor do the sample schemas represent production-ready data models.

Considering the primary OE functions that make use of the supplier product identifier, let's store the supplier product ID in the `product_information` table. This table contains other descriptive attributes about the product and it is already used in the output reports that now need to include the newest data element. These are not the sole considerations when deciding where and how to store data, but for our purposes in this chapter, they will do. In the real world, the amount of data to be stored and accessed, the data values to be read most frequently, and how often specific data values are to be updated should all be considered prior to making decisions about where the data belong.

After we've decided where to keep the data, we can begin preparing the necessary unit tests for our change. So, what are the unit tests that fail before we add the supplier's product ID to our schema? Here's a list of the unit tests I cover in this chapter:

- Include the supplier's product ID on individual orders and invoices.

- Print the supplier's product ID on the open order summary report.

- Print a purchasing report that shows the current supplier's product ID.

If we use a TDD process throughout development, then there are likely to be several generic unit tests that are already written and may be appropriate to include in this round of tests. Typical verification tests may focus on the following tasks:

- Confirm that all objects are valid before and after changes are made.

- Confirm that an insert fails if required constraints are not met.

- Verify that default values are populated when new data records are added.

- Execute a new order transaction with and without products from this specific supplier.

If we are thorough in our initial evaluation and unit test development work, we will know which tests are expected to fail. Other operations, such as the new order transaction I covered in Chapter 14, we expect to succeed, because we did not note that any changes are required for a new order. Should the existing unit tests for creating a new order fail after our changes, this indicates we did not analyze the impact of this latest change as thoroughly as we should have.

Before we make any changes to the database objects, let's confirm the state of the existing objects. Preferably, all objects must be valid before we start making changes. This is important because it ensures we are aware of any objects that were invalid prior to our changes, and it helps us to recognize when we are responsible for invalidating the objects. Listing 15-1 shows a query to check for invalid objects and the result of the query.

Listing 15-1. Checking for Invalid Objects before Altering Database Objects

```
SQL> select object_name, object_type, last_ddl_time, status
       from user_objects where status != 'VALID';

no rows selected
```

Listing 15-2 shows our three unit test scripts. Each of these scripts represents a report that must include the correct supplier product identifier as related to our internal product number. The first test creates a report for a single order, which is essentially the customer's invoice. The second test is the purchasing report, which must print the correct supplier product identifier plus the inventory on hand. The third unit test is a complete listing of all open orders, and it is built using several views.

Listing 15-2. Unit Test Scripts

```
--- order_report.sql

set linesize 115
column order_id new_value v_order noprint
column order_date new_value v_o_date noprint
column line_no format 99
column order_total format 999,999,999.99

BREAK ON order_id SKIP 2 PAGE
BTITLE OFF

compute sum of line_item_total on order_id

ttitle left 'Order ID: ' v_order          -
       right 'Order Date: ' v_o_date       -
       skip 2

spool logs/order_report.txt
```

```
select h.order_id ORDER_ID, h.order_date, li.line_item_id LINE_NO,
       li.supplier_product_id SUPP_PROD_ID, li.product_name, li.unit_price,
       li.discount_price, li.quantity, li.line_item_total
  from order_detail_header h, order_detail_line_items li
 where h.order_id = li.order_id
   and h.order_id = '&Order_Number'
 order by h.order_id, line_item_id ;

spool off

--- purchasing_report.sql

break on supplier skip 1
column target_price format 999,999.99
set termout off

spool logs/purchasing_report.txt

select p.supplier_id SUPPLIER, p.supplier_product_id SUPP_PROD_ID,
       p.product_name PRODUCT_NAME, i.quantity_on_hand QTY_ON_HAND,
       (p.min_price * .5) TARGET_PRICE
  from product_information p, inventories i
 where p.product_id = i.product_id
   and p.product_status = 'orderable'
   and i.quantity_on_hand < 1000
 order by p.supplier_id, p.supplier_product_id ;

spool off

set termout on

--- order_reports_all.sql

set linesize 115
column order_id new_value v_order noprint
column order_date new_value v_o_date noprint
column line_no format 99
column order_total format 999,999,999.99

BREAK ON order_id SKIP 2 PAGE
BTITLE OFF

compute sum of line_item_total on order_id

ttitle left 'Order ID: ' v_order          -
       right 'Order Date: ' v_o_date       -
       skip 2

select h.order_id ORDER_ID, h.order_date,
       li.line_item_id line_no, li.product_name, li.supplier_product_id ITEM_NO,
       li.unit_price, li.discount_price, li.quantity, li.line_item_total
  from order_detail_header h, order_detail_line_item li
 where h.order_id = li.order_id
 order by h.order_id, li.line_item_id ;
```

Listing 15-3 shows the execution of our unit test scripts and the resulting (expected) failures.

Listing 15-3. Initial Unit Test Results

```
SQL> @ order_report.sql
       li.supplier_product_id,
       *
ERROR at line 2:
ORA-00904: "LI"."SUPPLIER_PRODUCT_ID": invalid identifier


SQL> @purchasing_report.sql
 order by p.supplier_id, p.supplier_product_id
                              *
ERROR at line 6:
ORA-00904: "P"."SUPPLIER_PRODUCT_ID": invalid identifier


SQL> @order_report_all.sql
 li.line_item_id line_no, li.product_name, li.supplier_product_id ITEM_NO,
                                              *
ERROR at line 2:
ORA-00904: "LI"."SUPPLIER_PRODUCT_ID": invalid identifier
```

Unit tests are typically created for and executed from the application interface, but it's extremely helpful to create database-only unit tests as well. Having a set of scripts that we can run independently of the application code outside of the database allows us to check database functionality before we hand new code over to the test team. And if the front-end application tests result in unexpected errors, we already have information about a successful database-level execution, which helps both teams troubleshoot problems more efficiently.

Regression Tests

The goal of regression testing is to confirm that all prior functionality continues to work as expected. We must be certain that we do not reintroduce old issues (bugs) into our code as we implement new functionality. Regression tests are most likely to fail when there has not been adequate source code control, so someone inadvertently uses an obsolete piece of code as a starting point.

If unit tests are written for the existing functionality as the first step when the functionality is developed, those unit tests become the regression tests to confirm that each component of the system is still working as expected. In our case, the tests used to verify the order transaction process can be used to verify that orders are still processed as expected. Although I'm cheating a bit, I skip the reexecution of the OE transactions because I spent many pages on this topic in Chapter 14.

Schema Changes

As a prerequisite to executing our examples, we need to make several changes to our schema to support storing a supplier product number at all. Let's add a new varchar2 column in the product_information table to store the supplier_product_id field for each item we sell. We then populate the new column with a value to represent the current supplier product IDs for all the products we sell, and we use the dbms_random package to generate these numbers. When these data exist, our basic unit tests referencing the supplier product identifier should succeed.

However, to support the concept of effective product IDs, we must add new records to the product_information table using our supplier's new identification values—a new internal product number with the same product description and pricing. Although we could update the existing records, this violates the requirement to reflect accurately the supplier's product identifier shown on the product packaging in our warehouse. It also results in changing historical data, because we've already sold copies of this software to other customers. Although the software in the package is unchanged, the fact that our supplier has relabeled it essentially creates a brand new product, which is why we need these new product records. Let's enter the new records with a product status of "planned," because the effective date is in the future. On October 10, 2010, the new parts will be marked as "orderable" and the current parts become "obsolete."

To manage the effective dates for the changing internal product identifiers, let's create a new table: product_id_effectivity. Let's also create a product_id sequence to generate our new internal identifiers, making certain that our sequence begins at a higher value that any of our existing product records. Although I don't cover it in this chapter, this table could be used by a scheduled process that updates the product_status field in the product_information table to reflect whether a product is planned, orderable, or obsolete. It is the change in product status that triggers which supplier's product ID is shown on the purchasing report, so purchasing agents can reference the correct number when placing new orders. Listing 15-4 shows the schema changes as they are processed.

Listing 15-4. Schema Changes and New Product Data

```
SQL> alter table product_information add supplier_product_id varchar2(15);

Table altered.

SQL> update product_information
        set supplier_product_id = round(dbms_random.value(100000, 80984),0) ;

288 rows updated.

SQL> commit;

Commit complete.

SQL> create sequence product_id start with 3525 ;

Sequence created.

SQL> create table product_id_effectivity (
        product_id            number,
        new_product_id        number,
        supplier_product_id   varchar(15),
        effective_date        date) ;

Table created.

SQL> insert into product_id_effectivity
    (select product_id, product_id.nextval,
            round(dbms_random.value(100000, 80984),0)||'-'||
           substr(product_name, instr(product_name,'/',-1,1)+1), '10-oct-10'
       from product_information, dual
      where supplier_id = 103089
        and product_name like '%/%') ;
9 rows created.
```

```
SQL> select * from product_id_effectivity ;
PRODUCT_ID NEW_PRODUCT_ID SUPPLIER_PRODUC EFFECTIVE_DATE
---------- -------------- --------------- -------------------
      3170           3525 93206-SP        0010-10-10 00:00:00
      3171           3526 84306-EN        0010-10-10 00:00:00
      3176           3527 89127-EN        0010-10-10 00:00:00
      3177           3528 81889-FR        0010-10-10 00:00:00
      3245           3529 96987-FR        0010-10-10 00:00:00
      3246           3530 96831-SP        0010-10-10 00:00:00
      3247           3531 85011-DE        0010-10-10 00:00:00
      3248           3532 88474-DE        0010-10-10 00:00:00
      3253           3533 82876-EN        0010-10-10 00:00:00

9 rows selected.
SQL> commit ;
Commit complete.
SQL>  insert into product_information (
            product_id, product_name, product_description, category_id,
            weight_class, supplier_id, product_status, list_price, min_price,
            catalog_url, supplier_product_id)
        (select e.new_product_id,
               p.product_name,
               p.product_description,
               p.category_id,
               p.weight_class,
               p.supplier_id,
                'planned',
               p.list_price,
               p.min_price,
               p.catalog_url,
               e.supplier_product_id
          from product_information p, product_id_effectivity e
        where p.product_id = e.product_id
          and p.supplier_id = 103089) ;

9 rows created.

SQL> select product_id, product_name, product_status, supplier_product_id
        from product_information
       where supplier_id = 103089
       order by product_id ;

PRODUCT_ID PRODUCT_NAME                    PRODUCT_STATUS       SUPPLIER_PRODUC
---------- ------------------------------- -------------------- ---------------
      3150 Card Holder - 25                orderable            3150
      3170 Smart Suite - V/SP              orderable            3170
      3171 Smart Suite - S3.3/EN           orderable            3171
      3175 Project Management - S4.0       orderable            3175
      3176 Smart Suite - V/EN              orderable            3176
      3177 Smart Suite - V/FR              orderable            3177
      3245 Smart Suite - S4.0/FR           orderable            3245
      3246 Smart Suite - S4.0/SP           orderable            3246
      3247 Smart Suite - V/DE              orderable            3247
      3248 Smart Suite - S4.0/DE           orderable            3248
```

```
3253 Smart Suite - S4.0/EN          orderable          3253
3525 Smart Suite - V/SP             planned            93206-SP
3526 Smart Suite - S3.3/EN          planned            84306-EN
3527 Smart Suite - V/EN             planned            89127-EN
3528 Smart Suite - V/FR             planned            81889-FR
3529 Smart Suite - S4.0/FR          planned            96987-FR
3530 Smart Suite - S4.0/SP          planned            96831-SP
3531 Smart Suite - V/DE             planned            85011-DE
3532 Smart Suite - S4.0/DE          planned            88474-DE
3533 Smart Suite - S4.0/EN          planned            82876-EN

20 rows selected.
```

After we've completed the necessary schema updates, our next step is to check for invalid objects again. All objects were valid when we ran our initial check, but now we altered a table that is likely to be referenced by several other code objects in our schema. If those objects are coded properly, we can recompile them as is and they become valid again. If the code is sloppy (perhaps we used a select * from product_information clause to populate an object that does not have the new field), then the recompile fails and we need to plan for more application modifications. The unit test to look for invalid objects, plus the two recompiles that are required after our changes, are shown in Listing 15-5.

Listing 15-5. Invalid Objects Unit Test and Object Recompile

```
SQL> select object_name, object_type, last_ddl_time, status
        from user_objects
      where status != 'VALID';

OBJECT_NAME                          OBJECT_TYPE          LAST_DDL_ STATUS
-----------------------------------  -------------------  --------- -------
GET_ORDER_TOTAL                      PROCEDURE            04-jul-10 INVALID
GET_LISTPRICE                        FUNCTION             04-jul-10 INVALID

SQL> alter function GET_LISTPRICE compile ;

Function altered.

SQL> alter procedure GET_ORDER_TOTAL compile ;

Procedure altered.

SQL> select object_name, object_type, last_ddl_time, status
        from user_objects
      where status != 'VALID';

no rows selected
```

Repeating the Unit Tests

After we've confirmed that our planned schema changes have implemented successfully and all objects are valid, it's time to repeat the remaining unit tests. This time, each of the tests should execute and we should be able to verify that the supplier's product ID is represented accurately in the data results. Results from the second execution of the unit test are shown in Listing 15-6. To minimize the number of trees required to print this book, output from the reports is abbreviated.

Listing 15-6. Second Execution of Unit Tests

```
SQL> @order_report
```

Order ID:5041 Order Date: 13 Jul 2010

NO	SUP_PROD_ID	PRODUCT_NAME	UNIT_PRICE	DISC_PRICE	QTY	ITEM_TOTAL
1	98811	Smart Suite - S4.0/DE	222.00	199.80	5	999.00

```
SQL> @purchasing_report
```

SUPPLIER	S_PRODUCT	PRODUCT_NAME	QTY_ON_HAND	TARGET_PRICE
103086	96102	IC Browser Doc - S	623	50.00
103088	83069	OSI 1-4/IL	76	36.00
103089	86151	Smart Suite - S4.0/EN	784	94.00
	89514	Smart Suite - V/DE	290	48.00
	92539	Smart Suite - V/EN	414	51.50
	93275	Smart Suite - V/FR	637	51.00
	95024	Smart Suite - S4.0/SP	271	96.50
	95857	Smart Suite - V/SP	621	66.00
	98796	Smart Suite - S3.3/EN	689	60.00
	98811	Smart Suite - S4.0/DE	114	96.50
	99603	Smart Suite - S4.0/FR	847	97.50

....

```
SQL> @order_report_all.sql
```

Order ID: 2354   Order Date: 14 Jul 2002

ID	PRODUCT_NAME	ITEM_NO	UNIT_PRICE	DISCOUNT_PRICE	QTY	LINE_ITEM_TOTAL
1	KB 101/EN	94979	48.00	45.00	61	2,745.00
1	KB 101/EN	98993	48.00	45.00	61	2,745.00
1	KB 101/EN	85501	48.00	45.00	61	2,745.00

....

Order ID: 5016   Order Date: 06 Jul 2010

ID	PRODUCT_NAME	ITEM_NO	UNIT_PRICE	DISCOUNT_PRICE	QTY	LINE_ITEM_TOTAL
1	Inkvisible Pens	86030	6.00	5.40	1000	5,400.00

Order ID: 5017   Order Date: 06 Jul 2010

ID	PRODUCT_NAME	ITEM_NO	UNIT_PRICE	DISCOUNT_PRICE	QTY	LINE_ITEM_TOTAL
1	Compact 400/DQ	87690	125.00	118.75	25	2,968.75

Order ID: 5041   Order Date: 13 Jul 2010

ID	PRODUCT_NAME	ITEM_NO	UNIT_PRICE	DISCOUNT_PRICE	QTY	LINE_ITEM_TOTAL
1	Smart Suite - S4.0/DE	98811	222.00	199.80	5	999.00

Take note that in each case when the product name shows a product that will be affected by our supplier's new identifiers, our reports still show the current supplier identifier. This is because these reports were prior to the October 10, 2010, effective date. What we have not yet addressed in our testing is a mechanism to set to "obsolete" products referencing the old supplier product identifiers and to make our new products referencing the new supplier product identifier "orderable." After the effective date passes, we need the purchasing report in particular to reference the new IDs. Order data should continue to represent the item ordered and shipped, which is not necessarily determined by the effective date for the part number change. Instead, we want our sales team to sell the older product first, so we only begin to see the new product identifiers on orders and invoices after the existing inventory is depleted. This thought process should trigger the development of a few more unit tests, such as testing the process to alter product status after a product change effective date had passed, and confirming that the OE system does not make the new product identifiers available for purchase until the old stock has been depleted.

Execution Plan Comparison

One of the best tools available for evaluating the impact of the changes you make to database objects and code is the execution plan. By recording the execution plan both before and after our changes, we have a detailed measurement of exactly how much work the database needs to complete to process requests for the data in the past, and how much work is required to process those same requests in the future. If the comparison of the before and after versions of the execution plan indicates that a significant amount of additional work is required, it may be necessary to reevaluate the code to determine whether it can be optimized. If the process is already as optimized as it can be, you can then use the information to explain, nicely, to the users that their report may take longer to run in the future because of the added functionality. When you express your findings in these terms, you will discover exactly how much the users value that new functionality, and it is up to them to decide whether the changes are important enough to move to production.

Comparing the execution plans can also make it very clear when there is something wrong with a query. If you find that a process is working much harder to get the data, but the new changes don't justify the additional work, there is a strong possibility there is an error in the code somewhere.

For the next example, let's review the execution plans of the complete order report from our unit testing. The execution plan recorded before we made any changes to the database is shown in Listing 15-7. The scripts to gather the execution plans are based on the approach demonstrated in Chapter 6.

Listing 15-7. Order Report Execution Plan (Before)

```
alter session set statistics_level = 'ALL';

set linesize 105
column order_id new_value v_order noprint
column order_date new_value v_o_date noprint
column ID format 99
column order_total format 999,999,999.99

BREAK ON order_id SKIP 2 PAGE
BTITLE OFF

compute sum of line_item_total on order_id

ttitle left 'Order ID: ' v_order        -
       right 'Order Date: ' v_o_date     -
       skip 2
```

```
spool logs/order_report_all_pre.txt
select /* OrdersPreChange */ h.order_id ORDER_ID, order_date,
       li.line_item_id ID, li.product_name, li.product_id ITEM_NO,
       li.unit_price, li.discount_price, li.quantity, li.line_item_total
  from order_detail_header h, order_detail_line_items li
 where h.order_id = li.order_id
 order by h.order_id, li.line_item_id ;

spool off

set lines 150
spool logs/OrdersPreChange.txt

@pln.sql OrdersPreChange

PLAN_TABLE_OUTPUT
--------------------------------------------------------------------------------
SQL_ID  ayucrh1mf6v4s, child number 0
-------------------------------------
select /* OrdersPreChange */ h.order_id ORDER_ID, order_date,
li.line_item_id ID, li.product_name, li.product_id ITEM_NO,
li.unit_price, li.discount_price, li.quantity, li.line_item_total
from order_detail_header h, order_detail_line_items li  where
h.order_id = li.order_id  order by h.order_id, li.line_item_id

Plan hash value: 3662678147
```

Id	Operation	Name	Starts	E-Rows	A-Rows	Buffers
0	SELECT STATEMENT		1		417	29
1	SORT ORDER BY		1	474	417	29
* 2	HASH JOIN		1	474	417	29
3	TABLE ACCESS FULL	PRODUCT_INFORMATION	1	297	297	16
4	NESTED LOOPS		1	474	417	13
5	MERGE JOIN		1	474	417	9
* 6	TABLE ACCESS BY INDEX ROW	ORDERS	1	79	79	2
7	INDEX FULL SCAN	ORDER_PK	1	114	114	1
* 8	SORT JOIN		79	678	417	7
9	TABLE ACCESS FULL	ORDER_ITEMS	1	678	678	7
* 10	INDEX UNIQUE SCAN	ORDER_STATUS_PK	417	1	417	4

```
Predicate Information (identified by operation id):
---------------------------------------------------

   2 - access("OI"."PRODUCT_ID"="PI"."PRODUCT_ID")
   6 - filter("O"."SALES_REP_ID" IS NOT NULL)
   8 - access("O"."ORDER_ID"="OI"."ORDER_ID")
       filter("O"."ORDER_ID"="OI"."ORDER_ID")
  10 - access("O"."ORDER_STATUS"="OS"."ORDER_STATUS")

35 rows selected.
```

The order report is generated by joining two views: the order header information and the order line item details. Let's assume the report is currently running fast enough to meet user requirements and that there are no indicators that the quantity of data in the underlying tables is expected to increase dramatically in the future. The report is deemed as meeting requirements, and the execution plan is saved for future reference.

This order report was executed as one of our first unit tests to verify that our unit tests work as expected. After we make the required database changes, we execute the order report again and confirm that it completes. The report also seems to complete in about the same amount of time as it did in the past, but let's take a look at the latest execution plan to determine how the report is really performing. The postchange execution plan is shown in Listing 15-8.

Lising 15-8. Order Report Execution Plan (After)

```
alter session set statistics_level = 'ALL';

set linesize 115
column order_id new_value v_order noprint
column order_date new_value v_o_date noprint
column ID format 99
column order_total format 999,999,999.99

BREAK ON order_id SKIP 2 PAGE
BTITLE OFF

compute sum of line_item_total on order_id

ttitle left 'Order ID: ' v_order        -
      right 'Order Date: ' v_o_date      -
      skip 2

spool logs/order_report_all_fail.txt

select /* OrdersChangeFail */ h.order_id ORDER_ID, order_date,
      li.line_item_id ID, li.product_name, p.supplier_product_id ITEM_NO,
      li.unit_price, li.discount_price, li.quantity, li.line_item_total
  from order_detail_header h, order_detail_line_items li,
      product_information p
 where h.order_id = li.order_id
   and li.product_id = p.product_id
 order by h.order_id, li.line_item_id ;

spool off

set lines 150
spool logs/OrdersChangeFail.log

@pln.sql OrdersChangeFail
```

PLAN_TABLE_OUTPUT

SQL_ID avhuxuj0d23kc, child number 0

```
select /* OrdersChangeFail */ h.order_id ORDER_ID, order_date,
li.line_item_id ID, li.product_name, p.supplier_product_id ITEM_NO,
   li.unit_price, li.discount_price, li.quantity, li.line_item_total
from order_detail_header h, order_detail_line_items li,
product_information p  where h.order_id = li.order_id    and
li.product_id = p.product_id  order by h.order_id, li.line_item_id
```

Plan hash value: 1984333101

Id	Operation	Name	Starts	E-Rows	A-Rows	Buffers
0	SELECT STATEMENT		1		417	45
1	SORT ORDER BY		1	474	417	45
* 2	HASH JOIN		1	474	417	45
3	TABLE ACCESS FULL	PRODUCT_INFORMATION	1	297	297	16
* 4	HASH JOIN		1	474	417	29
5	TABLE ACCESS FULL	PRODUCT_INFORMATION	1	297	297	16
6	NESTED LOOPS		1	474	417	13
7	MERGE JOIN		1	474	417	9
* 8	TABLE ACCESS BY INDEX RO	ORDERS	1	79	79	2
9	INDEX FULL SCAN	ORDER_PK	1	114	114	1
* 10	SORT JOIN		79	678	417	7
11	TABLE ACCESS FULL	ORDER_ITEMS	1	678	678	7
* 12	INDEX UNIQUE SCAN	ORDER_STATUS_PK	417	1	417	4

Predicate Information (identified by operation id):

```
   2 - access("PI"."PRODUCT_ID"="P"."PRODUCT_ID")
   4 - access("OI"."PRODUCT_ID"="PI"."PRODUCT_ID")
   8 - filter("O"."SALES_REP_ID" IS NOT NULL)
  10 - access("O"."ORDER_ID"="OI"."ORDER_ID")
       filter("O"."ORDER_ID"="OI"."ORDER_ID")
  12 - access("O"."ORDER_STATUS"="OS"."ORDER_STATUS")
```

39 rows selected.

Looking at this latest plan, the database is doing much more work after our changes, even though the report is not taking any appreciable amount of extra time to complete. There is no good reason for this to be so; we've only added one additional column to a table that was already the central component of the query. Furthermore, the table in question already required a full table scan, because most of the columns are needed for the report. But, the execution plan shows that our report is now doing two full table scans of the product_information table. Why?

In this case, I made a common error deliberately to illustrate how an execution plan can help find quality problems in changed code. Rather than simply add the new column to the existing order_detail_line_item view that is built on the product_information table, the product_information table has been joined to the order_detail_line_item view, resulting in a second full table scan of the central table.

This probably seems like a really foolish mistake to make, but it can be done easily. I've seen many developers add a new column to a query by adding a new join to a table or view that was already part of the existing report. This error has a clear and visible impact on an execution plan, especially if the query is complex (and it usually is when this type of error is made). Listing 15-9 shows the execution plan for the same query after the additional join is removed and the column is added to the existing order_detail_line_item view instead.

Listing 15-9. Order Report Execution Plan (Corrected)

```
alter session set statistics_level = 'ALL';

set linesize 115
column order_id new_value v_order noprint
column order_date new_value v_o_date noprint
column ID format 99
column order_total format 999,999,999.99

BREAK ON order_id SKIP 2 PAGE
BTITLE OFF

compute sum of line_item_total on order_id

ttitle left 'Order ID: ' v_order       -
       right 'Order Date: ' v_o_date    -
       skip 2

spool logs/order_report_all_corrected.txt

select /* OrdersCorrected */ h.order_id ORDER_ID, order_date,
       li.line_item_id ID, li.product_name, li.supplier_product_id ITEM_NO,
       li.unit_price, li.discount_price, li.quantity, li.line_item_total
  from order_detail_header h, order_detail_line_items li
 where h.order_id = li.order_id
 order by h.order_id, li.line_item_id ;

spool off

set lines 150
spool logs/OrdersCorrected_plan.txt

@pln.sql OrdersCorrected

PLAN_TABLE_OUTPUT
-------------------------------------------------------------------------------------------------
SQL_ID  901nkw7f6fg4r, child number 0
-------------------------------------
select /* OrdersCorrected */ h.order_id ORDER_ID, order_date,
li.line_item_id ID, li.product_name, li.supplier_product_id ITEM_NO,
    li.unit_price, li.discount_price, li.quantity, li.line_item_total
from order_detail_header h, order_detail_line_items li  where
h.order_id = li.order_id  order by h.order_id, li.line_item_id

Plan hash value: 3662678147
```

```
--------------------------------------------------------------------------------
| Id |Operation                    |Name                |Starts |E-Rows |A-Rows |Buffers |
--------------------------------------------------------------------------------
|  0 |SELECT STATEMENT             |                    |     1 |       |   417 |    29 |
|  1 | SORT ORDER BY               |                    |     1 |   474 |   417 |    29 |
|* 2 |  HASH JOIN                  |                    |     1 |   474 |   417 |    29 |
|  3 |   TABLE ACCESS FULL         |PRODUCT_INFORMATION |     1 |   297 |   297 |    16 |
|  4 |   NESTED LOOPS              |                    |     1 |   474 |   417 |    13 |
|  5 |    MERGE JOIN               |                    |     1 |   474 |   417 |     9 |
|* 6 |     TABLE ACCESS BY INDEX ROW|ORDERS             |     1 |    79 |    79 |     2 |
|  7 |      INDEX FULL SCAN        |ORDER_PK            |     1 |   114 |   114 |     1 |
|* 8 |     SORT JOIN               |                    |    79 |   678 |   417 |     7 |
|  9 |      TABLE ACCESS FULL      |ORDER_ITEMS         |     1 |   678 |   678 |     7 |
|* 10|    INDEX UNIQUE SCAN        |ORDER_STATUS_PK     |   417 |     1 |   417 |     4 |
--------------------------------------------------------------------------------
```

Predicate Information (identified by operation id):

```
  2 - access("OI"."PRODUCT_ID"="PI"."PRODUCT_ID")
  6 - filter("O"."SALES_REP_ID" IS NOT NULL)
  8 - access("O"."ORDER_ID"="OI"."ORDER_ID")
      filter("O"."ORDER_ID"="OI"."ORDER_ID")
 10 - access("O"."ORDER_STATUS"="OS"."ORDER_STATUS")
```

35 rows selected.

As you can see by this latest execution plan, our report now performs as expected, with no additional impact to performance or use of system resources.

Instrumentation

One of my favorite Oracle features is instrumentation. The database itself is fully instrumented, which is why we can see exactly when the database is waiting and what it is waiting for. Without this instrumentation, a database is something like a black box, providing little information about where resources are spending, or not spending, their time.

Oracle also provides the dbms_application_info package, which we can use to instrument the code we write. This package allows us to label the actions and modules within the code so that we can identify more easily which processes in the application are active. We can also combine our instrumentation data with Oracle's Active Session History (ASH), Active Workload Repository (AWR), and other performance management tools to gain further insight into our application's performance while easily filtering out other unrelated processes.

The simplest method I know for adding instrumentation to application code is the ILO, which is available at http://sourceforge.net/projects/ilo/. ILO is open-source software written and supported by my friends at Method-R. Method-R also offers the option to purchase a license for ILO so that it can be used in commercial software products. I've been using ILO to instrument code for several years, and I've added functionality to the 2.3 version. The enhancements allow me to record the exact start and stop time of an instrumented process using the database's internal time references. These data can then be used to calculate statistical indicators on process execution times, which helps to highlight potential performance issues before they become major problems. I've also added code to enable extended SQL tracing (10046 event) for a specific process by setting an on/off switch in a table. So, if I determine that I need trace data for a specific application process, I can set tracing to ON for that process by its instrumented process name and it is traced every time it executes until tracing is set to OFF again. The configuration module can also be used to set the elapsed time collection ON or OFF, but I usually prefer to leave elapsed time recording on and purge older data when they are no longer useful.

If you'd like to test the ILO instrumentation software as you go through the next few sections, start by downloading ILO 2.3 from SourceForge.net and install it per the instructions. You can then download the code to store elapsed time and set the trace and timing configuration from the Apress download site. Instructions to add the updates are included in the ZIP file.

Adding Instrumentation to Code

After you've installed the ILO schema, adding instrumentation to your application is done easily. There are several ways to accomplish this. Of course, you need to determine the best method and the appropriate configuration based on your environment and requirements, but here are a few general guidelines:

- Within your own session, you can turn timing and tracing on or off at any time. You can also instrument any of your SQL statements (1) by executing the ILO call to begin a task before you execute your SQL statement and (2) by executing the call to end the task after the statement. This approach is shown in Listing 15-10.

  Listing 15-10. ILO Execution in a Single Session

  ```
  SQL> exec ilo_timer.set_mark_all_tasks_interesting(TRUE,TRUE);

  PL/SQL procedure successfully completed.

  SQL> exec ilo_task.begin_task('Month-end','Purchasing');

  PL/SQL procedure successfully completed.

  SQL> @purchasing_report

  SQL> exec ilo_task.end_task;

  PL/SQL procedure successfully completed.

      Selected from ILO_ELAPSED_TIME table:

      INSTANCE: TEST
      SPID: 21509
      ILO_MODULE: Month-end
      ILO_ACTION: Purchasing
      START_TIME: 22-SEP-13 06.08.19.000000 AM
      END_TIME: 22-SEP-13 06.09.06.072642 AM
      ELAPSED_TIME: 46.42
      ELAPSED_CPUTIME: .01
      ERROR_NUM: 0
  ```

- You can encapsulate your code within a procedure and include the calls to ILO within the procedure itself. This has the added advantage of ensuring that every call to the procedure is instrumented and that the ILO action and module are labeled consistently. Consistent labeling is very important if you want to aggregate your timing data in a meaningful way or to track trends in performance. We look at the billing.credit_request procedure from Chapter 14 with added calls to ILO in Listing 15-11.

Listing 15-11. Incorporating ILO into a Procedure

```
create or replace procedure credit_request(p_customer_id      IN   NUMBER,
                                           p_amount           IN   NUMBER,
                                           p_authorization    OUT  NUMBER,
                                           p_status_code      OUT  NUMBER,
                                           p_status_message   OUT  VARCHAR2)
  IS

    /***********************************************************************
        status_code values
          status_code status_message
          =========== =====================================================
                    0  Success
              -20105   Customer ID must have a non-null value.
              -20110   Requested amount must have a non-null value.
              -20500   Credit Request Declined.
    ***********************************************************************/
    v_authorization NUMBER;
BEGIN
  ilo_task.begin_task('New Order', 'Credit Request');

  SAVEPOINT RequestCredit;

  IF ( (p_customer_id) IS NULL ) THEN
    RAISE_APPLICATION_ERROR(-20105, 'Customer ID must have a non-null value.', TRUE);
  END IF;

  IF ( (p_amount) IS NULL ) THEN
    RAISE_APPLICATION_ERROR(-20110, 'Requested amount must have a non-null value.', TRUE);
  END IF;

   v_authorization := round(dbms_random.value(p_customer_id, p_amount), 0);

  IF ( v_authorization between 324 and 342 ) THEN
    RAISE_APPLICATION_ERROR(-20500, 'Credit Request Declined.', TRUE);
  END IF;

  p_authorization:= v_authorization;
  p_status_code:= 0;
  p_status_message:= NULL;

  ilo_task.end_task;

EXCEPTION
  WHEN OTHERS THEN
    p_status_code:= SQLCODE;
    p_status_message:= SQLERRM;
```

```
    BEGIN
      ROLLBACK TO SAVEPOINT RequestCredit;
    EXCEPTION WHEN OTHERS THEN NULL;
    END;

    ilo_task.end_task(error_num => p_status_code);

END credit_request;
/
```

Execution Script:

```
set serveroutput on

DECLARE
  P_CUSTOMER_ID      NUMBER;
  P_AMOUNT           NUMBER;
  P_AUTHORIZATION    NUMBER;
  P_STATUS_CODE      NUMBER;
  P_STATUS_MESSAGE   VARCHAR2(200);

BEGIN
  P_CUSTOMER_ID := '&customer';
  P_AMOUNT := '&amount';

  billing.credit_request(
    P_CUSTOMER_ID => P_CUSTOMER_ID,
    P_AMOUNT => P_AMOUNT,
    P_AUTHORIZATION => P_AUTHORIZATION,
    P_STATUS_CODE => P_STATUS_CODE,
    P_STATUS_MESSAGE => P_STATUS_MESSAGE
  );
commit;

  DBMS_OUTPUT.PUT_LINE('P_CUSTOMER_ID = ' || P_CUSTOMER_ID);
  DBMS_OUTPUT.PUT_LINE('P_AMOUNT = ' || P_AMOUNT);
  DBMS_OUTPUT.PUT_LINE('P_AUTHORIZATION = ' || P_AUTHORIZATION);
  DBMS_OUTPUT.PUT_LINE('P_STATUS_CODE = ' || P_STATUS_CODE);
  DBMS_OUTPUT.PUT_LINE('P_STATUS_MESSAGE = ' || P_STATUS_MESSAGE);

END;
/
```

Execution:

```
SQL> @exec_CreditRequest
Enter value for customer: 237
Enter value for amount: 10000
```

```
P_CUSTOMER_ID = 237
P_AMOUNT = 10000
P_AUTHORIZATION = 8302
P_STATUS_CODE = 0
P_STATUS_MESSAGE =

PL/SQL procedure successfully completed.

SQL> @exec_CreditRequest
Enter value for customer: 334
Enter value for amount: 500

P_CUSTOMER_ID = 237
P_AMOUNT = 500
P_AUTHORIZATION =
P_STATUS_CODE = -20500
P_STATUS_MESSAGE = ORA-20500: Credit Request Declined.

PL/SQL procedure successfully completed.

    Selected from ILO_ELAPSED_TIME table:

    INSTANCE: TEST
    SPID: 3896
    ILO_MODULE: New Order
    ILO_ACTION: Request Credit
    START_TIME: 22-SEP-13 01.43.41.000000 AM
    END_TIME: 22-SEP-13 01.43.41.587155 AM
    ELAPSED_TIME: .01
    ELAPSED_CPUTIME: 0
    ERROR_NUM: 0
```

- You can create an application-specific wrapper to call the ILO procedures. One benefit of using a wrapper is that you can make sure a failure in ILO does not result in a failure for the application process. Although you do want good performance data, you don't want to prevent the application from running because ILO isn't working. A simple wrapper is included with the ILO update download at Apress.

The level of granularity you decide to implement with your instrumentation depends on your goals. For some tasks, it is perfectly acceptable to include multiple processes in a single ILO module or action. For critical code, I recommend that you instrument the individual processes with their own action and module values, which gives more visibility into complex procedures. If you are supporting an application that is not instrumented and it seems like too big a task to go back and instrument all the existing code, consider adding the instrumentation just to the key processes.

Again, how you decide to implement depends on your needs. Instrumentation is exceptionally useful for testing code and configuration changes during development and performance testing. After the calls to ILO have been built into the code, you can turn timing/tracing on or off in production to provide definitive performance data. Overhead is exceedingly low, and being able to enable tracing easily helps you find the problems much more quickly.

Using the ilo_elapsed_time table to store performance data typically allows you to retain critical performance data for longer periods of time. Although it is possible to set longer retention values for AWR data, some sites may not have the resources available to keep as much data as they would like. Because the ILO data are not part of the Oracle product itself, you have the option to customize the retention levels to your needs without endangering any Oracle-delivered capabilities.

> ■ **Note** Keep the ILO code in its own schema and allow other schemas to use the same code base. This keeps the instrumentation code and data consistent, which allows you to roll up performance data to the server level or across other multiple servers when appropriate.

Testing for Performance

When you add instrumentation to your code, you open the door to all kinds of potential uses for the instrumentation and the data you collect. Earlier in this chapter I talked about building test harnesses by automating many small-unit test scripts and then replaying those tasks to confirm that new and old functionalities are working as expected, and that old bugs have not been reintroduced. If your code is instrumented, you can record the timing for each execution of the test harness and you then have complete information on the exact amount of elapsed time and CPU time required for each labeled module and action.

The ILO package includes an `ilo_comment` field in addition to the `ILO_MODULE` and `ILO_ACTION` labels. In some cases, this field can be used to record some identifying piece of information about a specific process execution. For example, if you add instrumentation to the order transaction from Chapter 14, you can record the order number in the `ilo_comment` field. Then, if you find an exceptionally long execution in your `ilo_elapsed_time` table, you can connect that execution time with an order number, which then connects you to a specific customer and a list of ordered items. Combining this information with the very specific timestamp recorded in your table can help you troubleshoot the problem, ensure the transaction did process correctly, and determine the cause of the unusually long execution time.

In other cases, you may want to use the `comment` field to label a specific set of test results for future reference. When testing changes to an application or instance configuration, it's always better to make one change and measure the results before making additional adjustments. Otherwise, how will you know which change was responsible for the results you obtained? This can be very difficult to do, unless you've created a test harness and measurement tool that can be reexecuted easily and consistently multiple times. By making a single change, reexecuting the complete test package while recording timing data, and labeling the result set of that test execution, you create a series of datasets, each of which shows the impact of a specific change, test dataset, or stress factor. Over time, this information can be used to evaluate the application's ability to perform under a wide range of conditions.

A sample of data retained from one such test harness is shown in Table 15-1 (time is measured in seconds).

Table 15-1. *Repetitive Test Results*

ILO ACTION	COUNT	MIN	AVG	MAX	VAR	CPU MIN	CPU AVG	CPU MAX	CPU VAR
process 1	46	0	.01	.09	0	0	.008	.03	0
process 2	2	.12	.125	.13	0	.12	.125	.13	0
process 3	2772526	0	.382	4.44	.078	0	.379	2.6	.074
child 3a	2545208	.01	.335	2.26	.058	.01	.332	1.77	.055
child 3b	2752208	0	.065	2.24	.011	0	.065	1.39	.01
child 3c	2153988	0	0	.21	0	0	0	.02	0
child 3d	2153988	0	0	.36	0	0	0	.07	0
child 3e	2153988	0	0	.16	0	0	0	.02	0
child 3f	2153988	0	0	.42	0	0	0	.02	0

(continued)

Table 15-1. (*continued*)

ILO ACTION	COUNT	MIN	AVG	MAX	VAR	CPU MIN	CPU AVG	CPU MAX	CPU VAR
process 4	1564247	0	.001	.18	0	0	.001	.02	0
process 5	2873236	0	.043	6.2	.013	0	.041	.49	.006
process 6	149589	0	.018	5.53	.002	0	.013	.11	0
process 7	2395999	0	.001	6	0	0	.001	.03	0

Although the numbers shown in the table aren't particularly meaningful on their own, if you have this set of numbers representing code executions prior to a change and you have another set of numbers from the same server with the same dataset representing code execution after the code has been changed, you have definitive information regarding the impact of your code changes on the database. Imagine being able to repeat this test quickly and painlessly for subsequent code changes and configuration adjustments, and you just might begin to appreciate the potential of code instrumentation combined with repeatable, automated test processes.

Testing to Destruction

Testing a system to its breaking point can be one of the more entertaining aspects of software testing, and meetings to brainstorm all the possible ways to break the database are seldom dull. Early in my career, I developed and managed an Oracle Database application built using client/server technology. (Yes, this was long ago and far away.) The application itself was a problem tracking tool that allowed manufacturing workers to record issues they found and to send those problems to Engineering for review and correction. The initial report landed in Quality Engineering, where it was investigated and assigned to the appropriate Engineering group. As each Engineering department signed off on its work, the request moved on to the next group. The application was reasonably successful, so it ended up on many workstations throughout a very large facility.

If you ever want to see "testing to destruction" in action, try supporting a database application installed on the workstations of hundreds of electrical, hydraulic, and structural engineers. In a fairly short period of time, I learned that engineers do everything in their power to learn about the computers on their desks, and they considered breaking those computers and the applications on them to be an educational experience. I can't say that I disagree with them; sometimes, taking something apart just so you can build it again really is the best way to understand the guts of the tool.

However, after several months of trying to support this very inquisitive group of people, I developed a new approach to discourage excessive tampering. By keeping a library of ghosted drives containing the standard workstation configuration with all the approved applications, I could replace the hard drive on a malfunctioning computer in less than ten minutes, and the engineer and I could both get back to work. Because everyone was expected to store their work on the server, no one could really object to my repair method. However, most engineers did not like losing their customized desktops, so they soon quit trying quite so hard to break things.

Although I loved to grumble at those engineers, I really owe them a very big thank you, for now whenever I need to think about how to test a server or application to destruction, all I need to do is think about those engineers and wonder what they would do. And never discount even the craziest ideas; if you can think of it, someone is likely to try it. As you work to identify your system's weak links, consider everything on the following list, and then think of some more items:

- *Data entry*: What happens when a user or program interface sends the wrong kind of data or too much data?

- *Task sequences*: What happens when a user skips a step or performs the tasks out of order?

- *Repeating/simultaneous executions*: Can the user run the same process simultaneously? Will that action corrupt data or will it just slow down the process?

- *Unbounded data ranges*: Can the user request an unreasonable amount of data? What happens if the user enters an end range that is prior to the start range (such as requesting a report on sales from July 1, 2010, to June 30, 2010)?

- *Resource usage*: Excessive use of CPU, memory, temporary storage, and undo space can impact many users at the same time. Your DBA should limit usage with resource caps appropriately, but you still need to identify all the potential ways users and processes can grab more than their fair share.

I bet some of you could add some very interesting options for other ways to break systems. Can you also identify the ways to prevent those problems? Although finding the best correction is a bit harder and not as entertaining, every time you can make it difficult for a user to break your code, you create a more robust system—one that needs less support and less maintenance over the long run.

Every system has its own weakest links. When you've identified those weaknesses, assemble your unit tests into a test harness that pushes that resource beyond its limits so you can see how the system responds. In general, it seems that memory and IO usage are the primary stressors for a database system. However, lately I've been working on an Oracle 11g database with spatial functionality and, in this case, CPU processing is the system's bottleneck. When we designed the system capacity tests, we made certain that the spatial processes would be tested to the extreme, and we measured internal database performance using the ILO data as shown in the last section. We also had external measurements of the total application and system performance, but having the ILO elapsed time data provided some unique advantages over other test projects in which I've participated.

First and foremost, the ILO data provide specific measurements of the time spent in the database. This makes it easier to troubleshoot performance issue that do show up, because you can tell quickly when the process is slow in the database and when it is not. A second advantage is that the recorded timestamps give a very specific indicator of exactly when a problem occurred, what other processes were running at the same time, and the specific sequencing of the application processes. With this information, you can easily identify the point when the system hits the knee in its performance curve. And because the elapsed time module in ILO uses `dbms_utility.get_time` and `dbms_utility.get_cpu_time`, you can record exactly how much time your process was active in the database and what portion of that time was spent on CPU.

These detailed performance data are also useful for troubleshooting, because the low-level timestamps assist in narrowing down the time frame for the problem. When you know the specific time frame you need to research, you can review a much smaller quantity of AWR or StatsPack data to determine what happened and find the answers quickly. When the window is small enough, any problem is visible almost immediately. We look at a specific case in the next section.

Troubleshooting through Instrumentation

Sometimes it can be difficult to identify the cause of small problems. When you don't know the source of the problem, you also don't know the potential impact the problem can have on your application. In one such case, developers had noticed timeouts from the database at random intervals, yet the process they suspected of causing the issue showed no sign of the errors and the database appeared to be working well below its potential.

About a week after a new test server was installed, a review of the `ilo_elapsed_time` table showed that most tasks were performing well, except there were two processes that had overrun the 30-second timeout clock on the application. The error numbers recorded on the tasks showed the front-end application had ended the connection; this message was consistent with a possible timeout, but it was not very helpful. The captured ILO data are shown in Table 15-2.

Table 15-2. *Timeout Errors*

ILO ACTION	COUNT	MIN	AVG	MAX	VAR	CPU MIN	CPU AVG	CPU MAX	CPU VAR
process 1	4	0.01	0.015	0.03	0	0	0.01	0.03	0
process 2	2	0	0	0	0	0	0	0	0
process 3	56	0.01	0.112	0.8	0.015	0.01	0.109	0.62	0.011
child 3a	36	0.04	0.078	0.15	0	0.03	0.078	0.15	0.001
child 3b	56	0	0.01	0.09	0	0	0.009	0.07	0
child 3c	36	0	0	0.01	0	0	0.001	0.01	0
child 3d	36	0	0.001	0.01	0	0	0	0.01	0
child 3e	36	0	0.001	0.01	0	0	0.001	0.01	0
child 3f	36	0	0.001	0.01	0	0	0.001	0.01	0
process 4	8	0	0.01	0.02	0	0	0.008	0.02	0
process 5	1	0.01	0.01	0.01	0	0.01	0.01	0.01	0
process 6	152	0	0.002	0.1	0	0	0.002	0.09	0
process 7	90	0	**0.681**	**30.57**	**20.449**	0	0.002	0.02	0
process 8	1	0	0	0	0	0.01	0.01	0.01	0
process 9	77	0	0.001	0.01	0	0	0.001	0.01	0
process 10	8	0	0.008	0.01	0	0	0.008	0.01	0

Take a look at process 7. Note that the maximum completion time does exceed 30 seconds, and the variance in processing times is relatively high when compared with other processes in the application. The process spends almost no time on CPU, so this is a problem worth investigating. Where is this time going? It's also interesting to note that this was not a process that anyone would have expected to have a performance issue. Process 3 had been the target of previous timeout investigations; it has to perform considerably more work than process 7.

Next, let's take a look at Table 15-3, which contains the results of a query looking for all cases when process 7 exceeded 30 seconds.

Table 15-3. *Processes Exceeding 30 Seconds*

SPID	ILO ACTION	START TIME	END TIME	ELAPSED TIME	ERROR
28959	process 7	22-JUL-10 05.40.00.000000 PM	22-JUL-10 09.40.31.234635 PM	30.45	–1013
29221	process 7	22-JUL-10 05.55.30.000000 PM	22-JUL-10 09.56.00.619850 PM	30.57	–1013

The start and stop times shown in Table 15-3 reflect the connection pool start and stop times, which is a much wider window than you need to troubleshoot this problem. Internal database and CPU clock times are also recorded in the ilo_elapsed_time table, and these are the values that are used to calculate the elapsed times as shown in Table 15-4. Table 15-4 also shows the sequential execution of the processes. Notice that process 7 was executed repeatedly within intervals of just a few seconds.

Table 15-4. Sequential Listing of Processes with Internal Clock Times

SPID	ILO ACTION	GO TIME	STOP TIME	ELAPSED TIME	CPU TIME	ERROR
29221	process 7	498854690	498854690	0	0	0
28959	**process 7**	**498856045**	**498859090**	**30.45**	**0**	**-1013**
29047	process 7	498862109	498862109	0	0	0
29309	process 3	498862111	498862121	0.1	0.11	0
29309	child 3a	498862113	498862121	0.08	0.07	0
29309	child 3b	498862113	498862113	0	0	0
29309	child 3c	498862121	498862121	0	0	0
29309	child 3d	498862121	498862121	0	0	0
29309	child 3e	498862121	498862121	0	0	0
29309	child 3f	498862121	498862121	0	0	0
28959	process 7	498947571	498947571	0	0	0
29221	**process 7**	**498948957**	**498952014**	**30.57**	**0**	**-1013**
29047	process 7	498957717	498957717	0	0	0
29309	process 3	498957718	498957728	0.1	0.1	0
29309	assign_child1	498957720	498957728	0.08	0.07	0
29309	assign_child2	498957720	498957720	0	0	0
29309	assign_child3	498957728	498957728	0	0	0
29309	assign_child4	498957728	498957728	0	0.01	0
29309	assign_child5	498957728	498957728	0	0	0
29309	assign_child6	498957728	498957728	0	0	0

Looking at the two processes that exceeded 30 seconds, we can note a very small time frame when both errors occurred. The next step is to check the AWR for that particular time frame. On review of the AWR data shown in Listing 15-12, the problem is immediately clear.

Listing 15-12. AWR Output for One-Hour Time Frame

```
Top 5 Timed Foreground Events
~~~~~~~~~~~~~~~~~~~~~~~~~~~~~~~

                                              Avg
                                             wait  % DB
Event                        Waits Time(s)   (ms)  time Wait Class
---------------------------- ------ ------- ------ ----- ----------
enq: TX - row lock contention     2      61  30511  78.6 Application
DB CPU                                    12         15.0
SQL*Net break/reset to client 21,382      5      0   6.6 Application
log file sync                    32       0      1    .1 Commit
SQL*Net message to client    10,836       0      0    .0 Network
```

Between the series of events shown in Table 15-2 and the AWR output shown in Listing 15-12, the cause of the timeouts becomes clear. Process 7 was called two or even three times, when only one execution was necessary. If those calls came in fast enough, the second process attempted to update the same row, creating a lock and preventing the first process from committing. When process 1 could not commit in 30 seconds, the process terminated and the second (or third) process could save its changes successfully. Because the application has a built-in timeout, this problem is a minor one, and a self-correcting one at that.

Tables 15-1 to 15-4 show data from a newly installed server with only a few executions. I selected this particular dataset because it is easy to use as an example, but it does make it appear as if it would have been possible to spot this problem with almost any other troubleshooting tool. However, consider this: When these same data are reviewed on more active test servers over longer periods of time, timeouts for this process may occur on one day in any given month, and there are likely to be no more the four to six processes that exceed 30 seconds on that day. This process may execute hundreds of thousands of times over two or three months on a busy test server. And then there are test results like those shown in Table 15-1. In that case, the process is executed millions of times without a single timeout. Trying to spot this problem from an AWR report and then identifying the process that caused the application lock would take a bit more time with that many executions. And although this problem is not significant right now, it has the potential to cause the application to miss required performance targets. As a result of the data recorded by the instrumentation, the problem can be monitored and addressed before this happens.

Although this is a simple example, identifying these kinds of problems can be difficult, especially during typical development test cycles. Early in unit testing, tests are not usually executed in rapid succession, so some problems may not appear until later. And when testing has moved on to load testing, an occasionally longer running process or two may not be noticed among millions of executions. Yet, by using the ILO execution times to abbreviate the amount of AWR performance data that must be reviewed, problems like this can be identified and diagnosed in just a few moments. And although access to AWR and ASH data may not be available to you in all development environments, the instrumentation data you create are available.

Summary

I covered a wide range of information in this chapter, including execution plans and instrumentation, performance and failures, testing theory and practical application. Each of these topics could have been a chapter or even an entire book in its own right, which is why there are already many, many books out there that address these topics.

What I hope you take away from this chapter is the recognition that each system has its own strengths and limitations, so any testing and measurement approach should be customized to some extent for specific system needs and performance requirements. No single testing method can be completely effective for all systems, but the basic approach is fairly straightforward. Break down the work into measurable test modules, then measure, adjust, and measure again. Whenever possible, minimize the changes between test iterations, but keep the test realistic. You can test the functionality of your code with unit tests on a subset of the data, but testing performance requires a comparable amount of data on a comparably configured system. Verifying that a report runs exceptionally fast on a development server with little data and no other users doesn't prove anything if that report is to be run on a multiuser data warehouse. Understanding what you need to measure and confirm is crucial to preparing an appropriate test plan. Be sure to consider testing and performance early during the code development process. This does not necessarily mean that you need to write a perfectly optimized piece of code right out of the gate, but you should be aware of the limitations your code is likely to face in production, then write the code accordingly. It also doesn't hurt to have a few alternatives in your back pocket so you are prepared to optimize the code and measure it once again.

■ ■ ■

Plan Stability

One of the most frustrating things about Oracle's Cost-Based Optimizer (CBO) is its tendency to change plans for statements at seemingly random intervals. Of course, these changes are not random at all. But, because the optimizer code is so complex, it's often difficult to determine why a plan changes. Oracle recognized this issue years ago and has been working to improve the situation for at least a decade. It has provided many tools for identifying when plans change and why they change. Oracle has also provided numerous tools that allow you to exert varying degrees of control over the execution plans the optimizer chooses, but let's save that discussion for the next chapter.

This chapter's focus is plan instability, and it is concerned with issues that cause you not to experience the stability you expect. You'll discover how to identify when and why plans changed, and how to locate plan changes that create a significant performance impact, and gain some insight into common causes of plan instability issues. I use a number of scripts in this chapter, but for readability purposes, in most cases, I do not show the source of these scripts in the listings. The scripts can be found in the example download for this book.

Plan Instability: Understanding the Problem

Oracle's CBO is an extremely complex piece of software. Basically, its job is to work out the fastest way to retrieve a given set of data as specified by a SQL statement. Generally speaking, it must do this in an extremely short period of time using precalculated statistical information about the objects involved (tables, indexes, partitions, and so forth). The optimizer usually doesn't have the time to verify any of the information. The tight time constraints are imposed because parsing is a serialized operation. Therefore, the database needs to retrieve the data as quickly as possible and as infrequently as possible; otherwise, parsing becomes a severe bottleneck to scalability. I should note here that my comments are aimed at what I would typically call an OLTP-type environment—an environment with many users executing lots of relatively quick SQL statements. Of course, in environments with relatively few but long-running statements, it's much more important to get the correct plan than to get a decent plan quickly. These types of systems, though, don't suffer from plan stability issues nearly as often (in part because they tend to use literals as opposed to bind variables, but I talk about that more later).

So why do plans change? Well there are three main inputs to the CBO:

1. *Statistics*: associated with the objects that are referenced by the SQL statement

2. *Environment*: optimizer-related parameter settings, for example

3. *SQL*: the statement itself (including bind variable usage)

So, unless one of these three things changes, the plan should not change. Period. I believe frustration with plan instability arises primarily from the belief that "nothing has changed," when in fact something *has* changed. I can't even count the number of times I have heard that phrase. The story usually goes something like this:

> *Them*: Everything was working fine and then, all of a sudden, the system just started crawling.
>
> *Me*: When did this happen?
>
> *Them*: 12:00 noon on Thursday
>
> *Me*: What changed around that time?
>
> *Them*: Nothing changed!

Of course, they are not intentionally lying to me. What they really mean is, "Nothing has changed that I think could have anything to do with this particular issue." But, regardless of whether someone thinks an event is relevant, or if he or she even knows about it, there was a change that precipitated the issue.

So, the first thing I want you to get out of this chapter is that performance doesn't just magically get worse (or better). If a SQL statement gets a new plan, there is a reason. Something changed!

Let's take a brief look at the possibilities for why a plan can change.

Changes to Statistics

Changes to statistics is a rather obvious place to look for changes that can cause new plans to be generated. Object-level statistics are gathered frequently on most systems. By default, Oracle versions 10g and above have a job that runs on a nightly basis to calculate new statistics. If these jobs are running on your system, it means that, every day, you have an opportunity to get a new plan. Although a thorough discussion of statistics gathering is outside the scope of this chapter, be aware of the mechanisms in play in your environment. Also know that you can check quickly to determine when stats were last gathered on an object, and you can restore a previous version of an object's statistics in a matter of seconds. Last, be aware that, by default, the standard stats-gathering jobs in 10g and above allow statements to stay in the shared pool for some period of time after new stats have been gathered. This feature is called *rolling invalidation*. By default, the dbms_stats procedures set the no_invalidate parameter to dbms_stats.auto_invalidate. This means that cursors are not invalidated automatically when statistics are gathered. Existing cursors are invalidated at some random time during the next five hours. This is a feature designed to prevent parsing storms, which can occur if all statements referencing a specific object are invalidated at the same time. In general, this feature is a good thing, but be aware that a plan change can be the result of a statistics change, even though the statistics change occurred several hours before the new plan showed up. Listing 16-1 presents an example of checking the last statistics-gathering event for a table and for restoring a previous version (all scripts are in the example download for the book).

Listing 16-1. Table Statistics Setting and Restoring

```
SQL> exec dbms_stats.set_table_stats( -
 ownname => user, tabname => 'SKEW', -
 numrows => 1234, numblks => 12, -
 avgrlen => 123, no_invalidate => false);

PL/SQL procedure successfully completed.

SQL> @set_col_stats
Enter value for owner: KRM
Enter value for table_name: SKEW
Enter value for col_name: PK_COL
```

```
Enter value for ndv: 1234
Enter value for density: 1/1234
Enter value for nullcnt: 0

PL/SQL procedure successfully completed.

SQL> @dba_tables
Enter value for owner: KRM
Enter value for table_name: SKEW
```

OWNER	TABLE_NAME	STATUS	LAST_ANAL	NUM_ROWS	BLOCKS
KRM	SKEW	VALID	12-AUG-13	1234	12

```
SQL> @col_stats
Enter value for owner: KRM
Enter value for table_name: SKEW
Enter value for column_name:
```

COLUMN_NM	DATA_TYPE	DENSITY	NDV	HISTOGRAM	BKTS	LAST_ANAL
PK_COL	NUMBER	.000810373	1,234	NONE	1	12-AUG-13
COL1	NUMBER	.000002568	902,848	HEIGHT BAL	75	02-AUG-13
COL2	VARCHAR2	.500000000	2	NONE	1	03-AUG-13
COL3	DATE	.000002581	1,000,512	HEIGHT BAL	75	02-AUG-13
COL4	VARCHAR2	.000000016	3	FREQUENCY	2	02-AUG-13

```
SQL> @tab_stats_history
Enter value for owner: KRM
Enter value for table_name: SKEW
```

OWNER	TABLE_NAME	STATS_UPDATE_TIME
KRM	SKEW	31-JUL-13 09.06.42.785067 PM -05:00
KRM	SKEW	02-AUG-13 07.14.04.486871 PM -05:00
KRM	SKEW	02-AUG-13 09.29.48.761056 PM -05:00
KRM	SKEW	02-AUG-13 09.31.11.788522 PM -05:00
KRM	SKEW	02-AUG-13 09.38.00.524266 PM -05:00
KRM	SKEW	12-AUG-13 08.27.17.497396 PM -05:00

```
6 rows selected.

SQL> @restore_table_stats.sql

Note: No_Invalidate=false - means invalidate all cursors now (stupid triple negatives)

Enter value for owner: KRM
Enter value for table_name: SKEW
Enter value for as_of_date: 03-aug-13
Enter value for no_invalidate: false

PL/SQL procedure successfully completed.
```

```
SQL> @dba_tables
Enter value for owner: KRM
Enter value for table_name: SKEW

OWNER       TABLE_NAME                STATUS   LAST_ANAL   NUM_ROWS     BLOCKS
----------  ------------------------  -------  ----------  ----------  ----------
KRM         SKEW                      VALID    02-AUG-13   32000004     162294

SQL> @col_stats
Enter value for owner: KRM
Enter value for table_name: SKEW
Enter value for column_name:

COLUMN_NM  DATA_TYPE    DENSITY          NDV HISTOGRAM   BKTS LAST_ANAL
---------  ----------  -----------  ----------- ----------  ---- ---------
PK_COL     NUMBER      .000000032   32,000,004 HEIGHT BAL    75 02-AUG-13
COL1       NUMBER      .000002568      902,848 HEIGHT BAL    75 02-AUG-13
COL2       VARCHAR2    .000000016            2 FREQUENCY      1 02-AUG-13
COL3       DATE        .000002581    1,000,512 HEIGHT BAL    75 02-AUG-13
COL4       VARCHAR2    .000000016            3 FREQUENCY      2 02-AUG-13
```

Changes to the Environment

There are many parameters that affect the optimizer's calculations. Some of the optimizer parameters have values that are calculated automatically based on the values of other parameters or the physical characteristics of the machine on which the database is running, such as the number of CPUs. If any of these environmental values change, the optimizer may come up with a new plan. This is also one of the reasons that it is sometimes difficult to get the plans in development and test environments to match the plans that are generated in production.

The settings in effect when a statement is parsed can be obtained by enabling a 10053 (CBO) trace. Oracle also keeps track of the settings for each of the optimizer-related parameters in an X$ table called X$KQLFSQCE. This is the structure that underlies the V$SQL_OPTIMIZER_ENV view, which (much like V$PARAMETER) doesn't display the hidden parameters (unless they have been altered). The optim_parms.sql script shows all the parameters, including the so-called hidden parameters that start with an underscore (this is the complete list of parameters that affect the optimizer's calculations and the same ones that are dumped in a 10053 trace file). Listing 16-2 contains the optimizer parameter values for SQL statement 9du01uy8z1k04 in a 12.1.0.1 instance. Note that these are the values that were set when the statement was parsed.

Listing 16-2. Optimizer Parameter Values

```
SQL> @optim_parms
Enter value for sql_id: 9du01uy8z1k04
Enter value for isdefault:

NAME                                      VALUE               DFLT?
----------------------------------------  ------------------  -----
...
cpu_count                                 24                  YES
cursor_sharing                            exact               YES
db_file_multiblock_read_count             128                 YES
...
optimizer_adaptive_features               true                YES
```

```
optimizer_adaptive_reporting_only          false            YES
optimizer_capture_sql_plan_baselines       false            YES
optimizer_dynamic_sampling                 2                YES
optimizer_features_enable                  12.1.0.1         YES
optimizer_features_hinted                  0.0.0            YES
optimizer_index_caching                    0                YES
optimizer_index_cost_adj                   100              YES
optimizer_mode                             all_rows         YES
optimizer_mode_hinted                      false            YES
optimizer_secure_view_merging              true             YES
optimizer_use_invisible_indexes            true             NO
optimizer_use_pending_statistics           false            YES
optimizer_use_sql_plan_baselines           true             YES
parallel_autodop                           0                YES
...
parallel_degree_limit                      65535            YES
parallel_degree_policy                     manual           YES
parallel_dml_forced_dop                    0                YES
...
sqlstat_enabled                            true             NO
star_transformation_enabled                false            YES
statistics_level                           all              NO
total_cpu_count                            24               YES
total_processor_group_count                1                YES
transaction_isolation_level                read_commited    YES
workarea_size_policy                       auto             YES
...
_always_anti_join                          choose           YES
_always_semi_join                          choose           YES
_always_star_transformation                false            YES
...
_complex_view_merging                      true             YES
_connect_by_use_union_all                  true             YES
_convert_set_to_join                       false            YES
_cost_equality_semi_join                   true             YES
_cpu_to_io                                 0                YES
...
_db_file_optimizer_read_count              8                YES
_optim_adjust_for_part_skews               true             YES
_optim_enhance_nnull_detection             true             YES
_optimizer_adaptive_cursor_sharing         true             YES
_optimizer_adaptive_plans                  true             YES
_optimizer_adjust_for_nulls                true             YES
...
_use_column_stats_for_function             true             YES
_use_hidden_partitions                     false            YES
_virtual_column_overload_allowed           true             YES
_with_subquery                             OPTIMIZER        YES
_zonemap_control                           0                YES
_zonemap_use_enabled                       true             YES

415 rows selected.
```

Changes to the SQL

Changes to the SQL may not make much sense at first glance. How can the SQL statement change? When I talk about plan instability, I am talking about the optimizer coming up with different plans for a single statement (in other words, the same SQL text and therefore the same `sql_id`). However, there are a few reasons that the text of a statement (and its `sql_id` or `hash_value`) remains fixed, but the actual SQL statement that the optimizer evaluates may change. These reasons are as follows:

- If a statement references views and then an underlying view changes, the statement has changed.

- If a statement uses bind variables and then the values passed via the variables change, the statement has changed.

- If the optimizer uses statistics feedback (known as *cardinality feedback* prior to 12c), the statement has changed.

The first situation is easy to understand and is rarely a point of confusion. The third situation is a way the optimizer attempts to adjust the plan automatically to improve it to produce a better performing plan. It is intended to work for good by supplementing missing or stale information with better, updated information. The second situation, though, can be confusing. We have been trained over the years to use variables in our SQL statements so that Oracle can reuse the statements without having to reparse them. So instead of writing a statement like this:

```
select avg(col1) from skew where col1 > 1;
```

We typically write it like this:

```
select avg(col1) from skew where col1 > :X;
```

In this way, we can pass any value we want to our program via variable X, and Oracle does not have to reparse the statement. This is a very good thing when it comes to scalability, particularly for systems in which many users execute many statements concurrently. However, unless the bind variables always contain the same data, the optimizer is basically evaluating a different SQL statement every time it undergoes a hard parse. This is because Oracle introduced a feature in 9i that allows the optimizer to "peek" at the values of bind variables during the part of the parsing process where the execution plan is determined. This is the infamous *bind variable peeking* that you've probably already heard about, and it is one of the major contributors to plan stability issues.

Bind Variable Peeking

When Oracle introduced histograms in 8i, they provided a mechanism for the optimizer to recognize that the values in a column were not distributed evenly. That is, in a table with 100 rows and ten distinct values, the default assumption the optimizer makes, in the absence of a histogram, is that no matter which value you pick, you always get $100 \div 10$, or ten rows back. Histograms let the optimizer know whether this isn't the case. A classic example is 100 records with two distinct values, where value Y occurs 99 times and value N occurs only once. Without a histogram, the optimizer always assumes that, regardless of whether you request records with a Y or an N, you get half the records back $(100 \div 2 = 50)$. Therefore, always do a full table scan as opposed to using an index on the column. A histogram, assuming it is accurate (and I come back this topic later), lets the optimizer know the distribution is not normal—in other words, not spread out evenly (also commonly called *skewed*), and that a Y basically gets the whole table, whereas an N gets only 1 percent. This allows the optimizer to pick an appropriate plan regardless of which value is specified in the Where clause.

So let's consider the implications of this. Would this improve the response time for the query when the value is Y? The answer is no. In this simple case, the default costing algorithm is close enough and produces the same plan that the histogram produces. The full table scan takes just as long regardless of whether the optimizer thinks it's getting 50 rows or 99 rows. But, what about the case when you specify the value N? In this case, with a histogram, you pick up the index on that column and presumably get a much better response time than the plan with the full table scan. This is an important point. In general, it is only for the outliers—the exceptional cases, if you will—that the histogram really makes a difference.

So, at first glance, the histogram looks like a pretty good idea; but, there is a fly in the ointment. You have to use literals in your SQL statements for the optimizer to be able use the histograms. So you have to write your statements like this:

```
SELECT XYZ FROM TABLE1 WHERE COLUMN1 = 'Y';
SELECT XYZ FROM TABLE1 WHERE COLUMN1 = 'N';
```

This is not a problem in this simple example because there are only two possibilities. But, consider a statement with two or three skewed columns, each with a couple hundred distinct values. The possible combinations could grow quickly into the millions—not a good thing for the shared pool or scalability of your system.

Enter the star: *bind variable peeking*. This feature was introduced in 9i to allow the optimizer to peek at the value of bind variables and then use a histogram to pick an appropriate plan, just like it does with literals. The problem with this feature is that it only looks at the variables once, when the statement is parsed. So let's make our simple example a little more realistic by assuming you have a table with 10 million rows in which 99 percent have a value of Y and 1 percent has a value of N. In this example, if the first time the statement is executed it passes a Y, the full table scan plan is locked in and used until the statement has to be reparsed, even if the value N is passed to it in subsequent executions.

Let's consider the implication of this. When you get the full table scan plan (because you passed a Y the first time), it behaves the same way no matter which value you pass subsequently. Oracle always performs a full table scan, always does the same amount of work, and usually results in the same basic elapsed time. From a user standpoint, this seems reasonable. The performance is consistent. (This is the way it works without a histogram, by the way.) On the other hand, if the index plan gets picked because the first execution that caused the parse occurs with a value of N, the executions where the value is N are almost certainly faster than they were before (and maybe considerably faster), but the execution with a value of Y is incredibly slow. This is because using an index to read virtually every row in a table is incredibly slow, which is not at all what the users expect. They expect the response time to be about the same every time they execute a piece of code. And this is the problem with bind variable peeking. It's basically just Russian roulette. It depends on which value you happen to pass the statement when it's parsed (which could be any execution, by the way).

So is bind variable peeking a feature or a bug? Figure 16-1 illustrates how that can sometimes be a tricky question to answer.

Bug   **Feature**

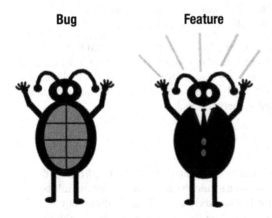

Figure 16-1. *Feature or bug? (Figure by Noah Osborne)*

Well, technically, it's not a bug because it works the way it's designed to work. I just happen to believe that it is not a good decision to implement it in this way, but what other choices did the optimizer development group members have?

- They could have evaluated the bind variables and reparsed for every execution of every statement using bind variables. This would eliminate the advantage of having bind variables in the first place and would never work for high-transaction systems. So, this is not an option.

- They could have just said no, and made us use literals to get the benefit of histograms. This is probably not a bad option, in retrospect. The fact that they added _optim_peek_user_binds, which allows us to turn off bind variable peeking altogether, probably means they decided later to give us this option via setting this hidden parameter.

- They could have implemented a system in which they could identify statements that might benefit from different plans based on the values of bind variables, and *then* peek at those variables for every execution of those "bind-sensitive" statements (Sound familiar? This is what they finally did in 11g with Adaptive Cursor Sharing).

So why is this such a pervasive problem? (And I do believe it is a pervasive problem, with 10g in particular.)

1. We've been taught always to use bind variables. It's a "best practice," which allows SQL statements to be shared, thus eliminating a great deal of work/contention. Using bind variables is an absolute necessity when building scalable high-transaction rate systems. Of course, just because it's a best practice doesn't mean you have to follow it blindly. There are situations when literals work better.

2. In 10g, the default stats-gathering method was changed to gather histograms automatically. So in a typical 10g database, there are a huge number of histograms, many of them inappropriate (in other words, on columns that don't have significantly skewed distributions) and many of them are created with very small sample sizes, which causes the histograms to be less than accurate. Note that 11g does a better job on both counts. That is to say, 11g seems to create fewer inappropriate histograms and appears to create many more accurate histograms, even with relatively small sample sizes. And in 12c, we now have two new types of histograms that help the accuracy of the histograms that do get created: top-frequency and hybrid histograms.

3. In my humble opinion, bind variable peeking is not that well understood. When I talk to people about it, they usually have heard of it and have a basic idea what the problem is, but their behavior (in terms of the code they write and how they manage their databases) indicates bind variable peeking is something they don't really have a good handle on.

So, what's the best way to deal with this issue? Well, recognizing that you have a problem is the first step to recovery. In other words, being able to identify that you have a problem with plan stability is an appropriate first step. Direct queries against the Statspack or AWR tables are probably the best way to identify the issue. You're looking for statements that flip-flop back and forth between two or more plans. Note that there are other reasons for statements to change plans, but bind variable peeking is high on the list of usual suspects.

Adaptive Cursor Sharing

Adaptive cursor sharing was a new feature added in 11g that aimed to fix performance issues resulting from bind variable peeking. The basic idea is to try to recognize automatically when a statement might benefit from multiple plans. If a statement is found that the optimizer thinks is a candidate, it is marked as bind aware. Subsequent executions peek at the bind variables, and new cursors with new plans may result. The feature does work, although it has a few quirks. The two biggest drawbacks are that it must execute a statement badly before it notices that an additional plan is needed, and that the information regarding bind sensitivity is not persistent (in other words, if the statement gets flushed from the shared pool, all information about bind sensitivity is lost). As a result, bind variable peeking issues continue in 11g.

The example in Listing 16-3 walks through how adaptive cursor sharing works.

Listing 16-3. Adaptive Cursor Sharing

```
SQL>@desc bigemp
 Name       Null?    Type
 ---------  -------- -------------
 EMPNO               NUMBER
 ENAME               VARCHAR2(20)
 PHONE               VARCHAR2(20)
 DEPTNO              NUMBER

SQL>select column_name, histogram from user_tab_cols
  2  where table_name = 'BIGEMP';

COLUMN_NAME                    HISTOGRAM
------------------------------ ----------------
EMPNO                          NONE
ENAME                          NONE
PHONE                          NONE
DEPTNO                         FREQUENCY

SQL>select deptno, count(*) ct from bigemp
  2  group by deptno ;

          DEPTNO              CT
--------------- ---------------
              1              10
              6              10
              2              10
              4              10
              5              10
              8              10
              3              10
              7              10
             10           99900
              9              10
              0              10
```

As you can see, the deptno column has skew such that when the value of deptno is 10, the query returns 99.9999 percent of that table's rows, and the execution plan choice that is likely the best is a full table scan. However, any other nonpopular value is best served by using an index scan. Listing 16-4 shows the execution plan choice for a query against a nonpopular value.

Listing 16-4. Execution Plan with a Nonpopular Value

```
SQL>variable v_dept number
SQL>exec :v_dept := 1
SQL>
SQL>select /* acs-ex-01 */ count(*), max(empno)
  2  from bigemp
  3  where deptno = :v_dept ;

     COUNT(*)      MAX(EMPNO)
--------------- ---------------
          10              91


SQL>@dcplan
Enter value for sql_id: 6xpk12dpa41ga
Enter value for child_no: 0

PLAN_TABLE_OUTPUT
----------------------------------------------------
SQL_ID  6xpk12dpa41ga, child number 0
--------------------------------------
select /* acs-ex-01 */ count(*), max(empno)
from bigemp where deptno = :v_dept

Plan hash value: 2854685483


--------------------------------------------------
| Id  | Operation                     | Name      |
--------------------------------------------------
|   0 | SELECT STATEMENT              |           |
|   1 |  SORT AGGREGATE               |           |
|   2 |   TABLE ACCESS BY INDEX ROWID | BIGEMP    |
|   3 |    INDEX RANGE SCAN           | BIGEMP_I1 |
--------------------------------------------------
```

As expected, the index scan was chosen. Now take a look at the information associated with this query.

```
SQL>col is_bind_aware for a10 heading "BIND_AWARE"
SQL>col is_bind_sensitive for a15 heading "BIND_SENSITIVE"
SQL>
SQL>select executions, buffer_gets, is_bind_sensitive, is_bind_aware
  2  from v$sql
  3  where sql_id = '6xpk12dpa41ga' ;

   EXECUTIONS     BUFFER_GETS BIND_SENSITIVE BIND_AWARE
--------------- --------------- --------------- ----------
            1              53 Y               N
```

Note that the statement is marked as bind sensitive. This is an indication that the optimizer thinks the best plan choice depends on the value of the bind variable, and it is marked this way because the deptno column has a histogram that is used to compute the predicate selectivity. Because a histogram is present, this means that the column contains skewed data and therefore different bind variable values may need to have different plans to execute optimally.

Listing 16-5 shows what happens if we change the bind variable to 10 (our popular value).

Listing 16-5. Execution Plan with a Popular Value

```
SQL>exec :v_dept := 10
SQL>
SQL>select /* acs-ex-01 */ count(*), max(empno)
  2  from bigemp
  3  where deptno = :v_dept ;

     COUNT(*)      MAX(EMPNO)
--------------- ---------------
        99900          100000

SQL>@dcplan
Enter value for sql_id: 6xpk12dpa41ga
Enter value for child_no: 0

PLAN_TABLE_OUTPUT
-------------------------------------------------------
SQL_ID  6xpk12dpa41ga, child number 0
-------------------------------------
select /* acs-ex-01 */ count(*), max(empno)
from bigemp where deptno = :v_dept

Plan hash value: 2854685483

-----------------------------------------------------
| Id  | Operation                    | Name      |
-----------------------------------------------------
|   0 | SELECT STATEMENT             |           |
|   1 |  SORT AGGREGATE              |           |
|   2 |   TABLE ACCESS BY INDEX ROWID| BIGEMP    |
|   3 |    INDEX RANGE SCAN          | BIGEMP_I1 |
-----------------------------------------------------

SQL>select executions, buffer_gets, is_bind_sensitive, is_bind_aware
  2  from v$sql where sql_id = '6xpk12dpa41ga' ;

   EXECUTIONS      BUFFER_GETS BIND_SENSITIVE BIND_AWARE
--------------- --------------- --------------- ----------
             2             957 Y               N
```

The plan still uses an index range scan, but (as you can see by the execution statistics) there is a big jump in the number of buffer gets, which increase from 53 to 957. Also note that the plan is still marked only as bind sensitive. Listing 16-6 shows what happens if we execute the query a third time and keep the bind variable value at 10.

Listing 16-6. Execution Plan for Second Execution with a Popular Value

```
SQL>select /* acs-ex-01 */ count(*), max(empno)
  2  from bigemp
  3  where deptno = :v_dept ;
```

```
      COUNT(*)      MAX(EMPNO)
--------------- ---------------
         99900          100000
```

```
SQL>select child_number, executions, buffer_gets, is_bind_sensitive, is_bind_aware
  2  from v$sql where sql_id = '6xpk12dpa41ga' ;
```

```
  CHILD_NUMBER      EXECUTIONS     BUFFER_GETS BIND_SENSITIVE BIND_AWARE
--------------- --------------- --------------- --------------- ----------
             0               2             957 Y               N
             1               1             818 Y               Y
```

```
SQL>@dcplan
Enter value for sql_id: 6xpk12dpa41ga
Enter value for child_no: 1
```

```
PLAN_TABLE_OUTPUT
-------------------------------------------------------
SQL_ID  6xpk12dpa41ga, child number 1
-------------------------------------
select /* acs-ex-01 */ count(*), max(empno)
from bigemp where deptno = :v_dept
```

```
Plan hash value: 870989070
```

```
-----------------------------------------------
| Id  | Operation                  | Name   |
-----------------------------------------------
|   0 | SELECT STATEMENT           |        |
|   1 |   SORT AGGREGATE           |        |
|   2 |    TABLE ACCESS STORAGE FULL| BIGEMP |
-----------------------------------------------
```

Finally, we have the proper plan—a full table scan—and a new child cursor has been created. So, we have two plans now: one for the nonpopular bind variable values and one for the popular values. Notice that our new cursor is marked as both bind sensitive and bind aware. From now on, the proper plan should be chosen based on the bind variable value. But, why doesn't the first cursor show that it is bind aware? Let's take a look at Listing 16-7.

Listing 16-7. Bind Aware Cursor Identification

```
SQL>exec :v_dept := 3
SQL>
SQL>select /* acs-ex-01 */ count(*), max(empno)
  2  from bigemp
  3  where deptno = :v_dept ;
```

```
      COUNT(*)      MAX(EMPNO)
--------------- ---------------
            10              93
```

```
SQL>col is_shareable for a9 heading "SHAREABLE"
SQL>select child_number, executions, buffer_gets,
```

```
2  is_bind_sensitive, is_bind_aware, is_shareable
3  from v$sql where sql_id = '6xpk12dpa41ga' ;
```

CHILD_NUMBER	EXECUTIONS	BUFFER_GETS	BIND_SENSITIVE	BIND_AWARE	SHAREABLE
0	2	957	Y	N	N
1	1	818	Y	Y	Y
2	1	3	Y	Y	Y

```
SQL>@dcplan
Enter value for sql_id: 6xpk12dpa41ga
Enter value for child_no: 2

PLAN_TABLE_OUTPUT
-------------------------------------------------------
SQL_ID  6xpk12dpa41ga, child number 2
-------------------------------------------------------
select /* acs-ex-01 */ count(*), max(empno)
from bigemp where deptno = :v_dept

Plan hash value: 2854685483

-----------------------------------------------------
| Id  | Operation                    | Name      |
-----------------------------------------------------
|   0 | SELECT STATEMENT             |           |
|   1 |  SORT AGGREGATE              |           |
|   2 |   TABLE ACCESS BY INDEX ROWID| BIGEMP    |
|   3 |    INDEX RANGE SCAN          | BIGEMP_I1 |
-----------------------------------------------------
```

Ah! Did you see what happened? A new child cursor was created (child_number 2). Note the additional column called is_shareable included in the query against v$sql. The first cursor (child_number 0), in which a nonpopular bind value is used, is marked as not shareable, but the new child cursor is shareable. What happened was that the original cursor was discarded when the cursor switched to bind aware. The original cursor is now basically marked to be aged out of the cursor cache because it is no longer shareable, and the two remaining cursors (1 and 2), which are shareable and bind aware, can be used for future executions of the statement.

Note that it is possible for additional cursors to get created. If the bind variable value's selectivity matches one of the aware and shareable plans, it is used. But, if it doesn't, then a new plan is created (just like we saw in this example) and the process repeats.

Statistics Feedback

Statistics feedback, known as *cardinality feedback* prior to Oracle 12c, is a mechanism used by the optimizer to improve automatically plans' repeated query executions that have cardinality misestimates. The first time a SQL statement executes, the optimizer determines the execution plan and marks the plan to enable statistics feedback monitoring if.

- Any of the tables in the statement have missing statistics

- There are ANDed or ORed filter predicates on a table

- Any predicates contain complex operators for which the optimizer cannot compute cardinality estimates accurately

After a completed statement execution, the optimizer then compares the original cardinality estimates with the actual cardinalities. If there are any significant differences, it stores the correct estimates to use during the next execution of that statement to reoptimize (reparse) it. Prior to Oracle 12c, this is as far as things went. But, in 12c, the optimizer also stores a SQL plan directive. A SQL plan directive contains additional information and instructions the optimizer can use to generate a better plan the next time the statement is executed; but, it isn't pertinent just to a single cursor. It is pertinent to any cursor that uses similar expressions.

About SQL Plan Directives

SQL plan directives are not tied to a specific SQL statement, but instead are defined on query expressions. By defining them on query expressions, the optimizer is able to use them on numerous SQL statements that use similar patterns. These directives are stored in the shared pool and are written periodically to the SYSAUX table space every 15 minutes. This is what makes the Oracle 12c statistics feedback different (and better) than its predecessor, cardinality feedback.

The presence of SQL plan directives alerts the optimizer that there may be missing or inadequate statistics such as histograms or extended statistics. The is_reoptimizable column in v$sql is marked with a Y to indicate that a hard parse should be performed on the next execution. Because these bits of information are recorded, not only can the optimizer use them to reparse statements to achieve better plans, but also even subsequent statistics collections using DBMS_STATS are alerted to create the proper statistics as well. Listing 16-8 shows an example of how SQL plan directives are used.

Listing 16-8. SQL Plan Directives

```
SQL>select /* sql-plan-dir */ * from sh.customers
  2 where cust_state_province = 'FL' and country_id = 52790 ;

2438 rows selected.

SQL>@dcplan
Enter value for sql_id: 94ykht2aac5xg
Enter value for child_no: 0
Enter value for format: ALLSTATS LAST

PLAN_TABLE_OUTPUT
---------------------------------------------------------------------------
SQL_ID  94ykht2aac5xg, child number 0
-------------------------------------
select /* sql-plan-dir */ * from sh.customers where cust_state_province
= 'FL' and country_id = 52790

Plan hash value: 2008213504
```

```
-----------------------------------------------------------------------
| Id  | Operation          | Name      | Starts | E-Rows | A-Rows | Buffers |
-----------------------------------------------------------------------
|   0 | SELECT STATEMENT   |           |    1   |        |  2438  |  1677   |
|*  1 |   TABLE ACCESS FULL| CUSTOMERS |    1   |   128  |  2438  |  1677   |
-----------------------------------------------------------------------

Predicate Information (identified by operation id):
---------------------------------------------------

   1 - filter(("CUST_STATE_PROVINCE"='FL' AND "COUNTRY_ID"=52790))

SQL>select is_reoptimizable
  2  from    v$sql
  3  where   sql_id = '94ykht2aac5xg' ;

IS_REOPTIMIZABLE
----------------
Y
```

The execution of the query reveals what appears to be a problem with the statistics. Note how the estimated rows estimate (E-Rows) of 128 is several orders of magnitude underestimated compared with the actual cardinality (A-Rows). The optimizer recognizes the issue and marks the cursor for reoptimization on the next execution. To see the SQL plan directives that are created, we can query the DBA_SQL_PLAN_DIRECTIVES view as shown in Listing 16-9.

Listing 16-9. Using the DBA_SQL_PLAN_DIRECTIVES View

```
SQL>exec dbms_spd.flush_sql_plan_directive;

SQL>select o.subobject_name col_name,
  2         o.object_type, d.type, d.state, d.reason
  3  from   dba_sql_plan_directives d, dba_sql_plan_dir_objects o
  4  where d.directive_id=o.directive_id
  5  and    o.owner = 'SH'
  6  and    o.object_name = 'CUSTOMERS'
  7  order by 1,2,3,4,5;

COL_NAME    TYPE    DIRECTIVE TYPE    STATE  REASON
----------  ------- ----------------- ------ -------------------------
COUNTRY_ID  COLUMN  DYNAMIC_SAMPLING  NEW    SINGLE TABLE CARDINALITY
                                             MISESTIMATE
CUST_STATE  COLUMN  DYNAMIC_SAMPLING  NEW    SINGLE TABLE CARDINALITY
                                             MISESTIMATE
PROVINCE    TABLE   DYNAMIC_SAMPLING  NEW    SINGLE TABLE CARDINALITY
                                             MISESTIMATE
```

Note there are three directives stored. The columns referenced are the two columns used in our example query predicate. The underestimation is noted and directives are now in place to make adjustments during the next execution of the query. As shown in Listing 16-10, we run the query again, check the plan, and see that it has changed (note that new child cursor number). Also note statistics feedback used for this statement, and the fact that the new child cursor is now marked as not reoptimizable, which indicates it will be used for all future executions of this cursor.

Listing 16-10. Statistics Feedback in Use

```
SQL>@dcplan
Enter value for sql_id: 94ykht2aac5xg
Enter value for child_no: 1
Enter value for format: ALLSTATS LAST


PLAN_TABLE_OUTPUT
-------------------------------------------------------------------------
SQL_ID  94ykht2aac5xg, child number 1
-------------------------------------
select /* sql-plan-dir */ * from sh.customers where cust_state_province
= 'FL' and country_id = 52790

Plan hash value: 2008213504
```

Id	Operation	Name	Starts	E-Rows	A-Rows	Buffers
0	SELECT STATEMENT		1		2438	1677
* 1	TABLE ACCESS FULL	CUSTOMERS	1	2438	2438	1677

```
Predicate Information (identified by operation id):
---------------------------------------------------

   1 - filter(("CUST_STATE_PROVINCE"='FL' AND "COUNTRY_ID"=52790))

Note
-----
   - statistics feedback used for this statement

SQL>select child_number, is_reoptimizable
  2    from   v$sql
  3    where  sql_id = '94ykht2aac5xg' ;

CHILD_NUMBER IS_REOPTIMIZABLE
------------ ----------------
           0 Y
           1 N
```

We can now collect statistics to determine whether the SQL plan directives will be used to update the statistics to avoid this problem in the future as shown in Listing 16-11.

Listing 16-11. SQL Plan Directives Utilized During Statistics Collection

```
SQL>exec dbms_stats.gather_table_stats('SH','CUSTOMERS')

SQL>select table_name, extension_name, extension
  2    from   dba_stat_extensions
  3    where  owner='SH'
  4    and    table_name='CUSTOMERS';
```

```
TABLE_NM   EXTENSION_NAME                      EXTENSION
---------  ----------------------------------- -------------------------------------
CUSTOMERS  SYS_STS#S#WF25Z#QAHIHE#MOFFMM_       ("CUST_STATE_PROVINCE","COUNTRY_ID")
```

Yes! They were! We now have an extended statistic for the column group of cust_state_province and country_id. This means that the optimizer now has the correct information to produce the proper cardinality estimates for any query using this column group in the future. Let's verify as shown in Listing 16-12.

Listing 16-12. Verifying Cardinality Estimates after Creation of Extended Statistics

```
SQL>select /* sql-plan-dirs */ distinct cust_postal_code from sh.customers
  2  where cust_state_province = 'LA' and country_id = 52790 ;


SQL>@dcplan
Enter value for sql_id: 789cx77mh8ftm
Enter value for child_no: 0
Enter value for format: ALLSTATS LAST


PLAN_TABLE_OUTPUT
-----------------------------------------------------------------------------
SQL_ID  789cx77mh8ftm, child number 0
-------------------------------------
select /* sql-plan-dirs */ distinct cust_postal_code from sh.customers
where cust_state_province = 'LA' and country_id = 52790


Plan hash value: 2048334152


-------------------------------------------------------------------------
| Id  | Operation          | Name      | Starts | E-Rows | A-Rows | Buffers |
-------------------------------------------------------------------------
|   0 | SELECT STATEMENT   |           |      1 |        |      2 |    1522 |
|   1 |  HASH UNIQUE       |           |      1 |     52 |      2 |    1522 |
|*  2 |   TABLE ACCESS FULL| CUSTOMERS |      1 |     54 |     54 |    1522 |
-------------------------------------------------------------------------


Predicate Information (identified by operation id):
---------------------------------------------------

   2 - filter(("CUST_STATE_PROVINCE"='LA' AND "COUNTRY_ID"=52790))
```

As you can see, statistics feedback and SQL plan directives can accomplish some pretty great things. So, even though they may cause plans to change, it's very likely they'll change for the better. But, like any "automatic" feature, always be aware of what it might and might not do. Don't get lazy and fail to identify issues and fix them on your own when possible.

Identifying Plan Instability

Sometimes it's painfully obvious when a plan has changed for the worse. A quick look at Enterprise Manager or a query against gv$session can show dozens of sessions executing the same statement. Other times, the problem is not as obvious. One of the best ways to identify the problem is to look for statements with multiple plans that have very different performance characteristics depending on which plan they use. AWR is extremely handy for this because it keeps copies of execution statistics as well as plans used for the most "important" statements. Note that not all statements are captured by AWR. Those that rank high in number of executions, logical IO, physical IO, elapsed time, CPU time, or parses are there, but if you have a statement that is very efficient that later becomes very inefficient, the very efficient version may not be captured by AWR. Regardless of the fact that AWR does not represent a complete record of every statement executed, it does provide data on most statements that are of interest.

Capturing Data on Currently Running Queries

One of my most used diagnostic scripts queries ¥ for all sessions that have a status of Active. This can be used to see what is actually running at any given point in time. It is not perfect, because really fast statements may not show up very often, even if they are dominating the workload. So, I often use Tanel Poder's snapper script for this same purpose. His script has many advantages, but one of the most useful is that it runs many times in a tight loop and aggregates the data so that very fast statements still show up in the output. Listing 16-13 shows both scripts in action.

Listing 16-13. Two Diagnostic Scripts: `as.sql` and Session Snapper

```
SQL> @as

SID PROG        SQL_ID          CHILD PLAN_HASH_VALUE EXECS AVG_ETIME
---- --------- ------------- ----- --------------- ----- ---------
  24 sqlplus@h gf5nnx0pyfqq2      0      4072605661    55     86.18
  42 sqlplus@h gf5nnx0pyfqq2      0      4072605661    55     86.18
 100 sqlplus@h gf5nnx0pyfqq2      0      4072605661    55     86.18
  83 sqlplus@h gf5nnx0pyfqq2      0      4072605661    55     86.18
  61 sqlplus@h gf5nnx0pyfqq2      0      4072605661    55     86.18

SQL> @snapper ash=sid+event+wait_class,ash1=sql_id 5 1 all
Sampling with interval 5 seconds, 1 times...

-- Session Snapper v3.11 by Tanel Poder @ E2SN ( http://tech.e2sn.com )


------------------------------------------------------------------
Active% |   SID | EVENT                     | WAIT_CLASS
------------------------------------------------------------------
   100% |    83 | ON CPU                    | ON CPU
    98% |    42 | ON CPU                    | ON CPU
    98% |    61 | ON CPU                    | ON CPU
    93% |    24 | ON CPU                    | ON CPU
    88% |   100 | ON CPU                    | ON CPU
    12% |   100 | direct path read temp     | User I/O
     7% |    24 | direct path read temp     | User I/O
     5% |   248 | control file parallel wri | System I/O
     2% |    42 | direct path read temp     | User I/O
     2% |    61 | direct path read temp     | User I/O


-------------------------
Active% | SQL_ID
-------------------------
   500% | gf5nnx0pyfqq2
     5% |

--  End of ASH snap 1, end=2013-08-12 22:23:17, seconds=5, samples_taken=42
```

The scripts have very different output formats. My as.sql script has one line per session and shows the sql_id being executed by the session, along with the average elapsed time for that statement. Keep in mind that this represents a single instant in time. So, you should run it several times in succession to get a feel for what is actually happening. Tanel's snapper, on the other hand, doesn't require repeated running. Just give it a length of time to run and it automatically samples repeatedly for that length of time. It is also considerably more flexible than my simple script. The format is quite different, too. The top section shows the activity percentage by session ID, or SID, and Event. Notice that the same SID may have multiple entries if it spends significant time on more than one thing during the sample period. The second section shows a breakdown of the work by SQL statement.

In the case shown, both snapper and my as.sql scripts show different views of the same situation. There are five sessions all running the same statement. Any time you are asked to look at a system and you see that many sessions are all running the same long-running SQL statement, you have a pretty good idea where to start your investigation into the plan stability problem.

Reviewing the History of a Statement's Performance

When a problem is obvious (as in the previous example, in which several sessions were all running the same long-running query), it is often instructive to view the performance of the statement of interest over time. This can be done easily by querying the AWR or Statspack tables directly. Listing 16-14 shows an example.

Listing 16-14. The awr_plan_change.sql Script

```
SQL> @awr_plan_change
Enter value for sql_id: 3dhwvfmkjzwtv
```

SNAP_ID	NODE	BEGIN_INTERVAL_TIME	PHV	EXECS	AVG_ETIME	AVG_LIO
1785	3	24-APR-13 05.00 PM	1093407144	6	1.102	2,872.7
1786	2	24-APR-13 06.00 PM		158	0.024	2,873.0
1786	3	24-APR-13 06.00 PM		223	0.023	2,873.0
1787	2	24-APR-13 07.00 PM		749	0.020	2,873.0
1787	3	24-APR-13 07.00 PM		873	0.019	2,873.0
1788	2	24-APR-13 08.00 PM		726	0.020	2,873.9
1788	3	24-APR-13 08.00 PM		871	0.020	2,873.9
1789	2	24-APR-13 09.00 PM		373	0.016	2,874.0
1789	3	24-APR-13 09.00 PM		566	0.016	2,874.0
1892	2	29-APR-13 04.00 AM		1	2.613	3,811.0
1897	2	29-APR-13 09.00 AM		2	8.179	8,529.0
1918	3	30-APR-13 06.00 AM		2	0.421	485.5
1919	2	30-APR-13 07.00 AM		1	1.152	1,242.0
1920	2	30-APR-13 08.00 AM		4	3.273	3,200.3
1920	3	30-APR-13 08.00 AM		12	2.491	3,314.2
1921	2	30-APR-13 09.00 AM		5	3.947	3,333.4
1921	3	30-APR-13 09.00 AM		2	2.416	1,769.5
1922	3	30-APR-13 10.00 AM	4076066623	2	54.237	2,291,432.5
1923	2	30-APR-13 11.00 AM	1093407144	2	0.812	975.0
1923	3	30-APR-13 11.00 AM	4076066623	3	134.031	933,124.3
1924	3	30-APR-13 12.00 PM		3	227.009	6,987,169.3
1926	2	30-APR-13 02.00 PM	1093407144	8	0.818	1,574.5
1926	3	30-APR-13 02.00 PM	4076066623	2	175.709	8,963,417.0
1927	2	30-APR-13 03.00 PM	1093407144	4	1.344	1,068.8
1927	3	30-APR-13 03.00 PM	4076066623	5	156.378	10,059,992.0

1928	2	30-APR-13 04.00 PM	1093407144	6	0.923	1,225.8
1928	3	30-APR-13 04.00 PM	4076066623	1	180.488	2,150,190.0
1930	3	30-APR-13 06.00 PM		2	180.371	8,255,881.5
1934	3	30-APR-13 10.00 PM		1	180.491	3,002,577.0
1939	2	01-MAY-13 03.00 AM	1093407144	21	0.825	1,041.8
1939	3	01-MAY-13 03.00 AM		4	0.575	1,211.8
1944	3	01-MAY-13 08.00 AM		6	1.328	1,788.3
1946	2	01-MAY-13 10.00 AM		1	1.170	2,411.0
1946	3	01-MAY-13 10.00 AM		4	2.041	2,414.3
1947	3	01-MAY-13 11.00 AM		10	1.725	2,937.1
1948	3	01-MAY-13 12.00 PM		3	2.232	3,415.7
1987	2	03-MAY-13 03.00 AM		7	1.029	901.0
1990	3	03-MAY-13 06.00 AM		3	1.225	1,465.7
1991	3	03-MAY-13 07.00 AM		26	0.370	710.5
1992	2	03-MAY-13 08.00 AM		6	0.213	685.7
1992	3	03-MAY-13 08.00 AM		3	0.658	883.0
1993	2	03-MAY-13 09.00 AM		8	0.769	950.9
1996	2	03-MAY-13 12.00 PM		2	0.101	861.5
2015	3	04-MAY-13 07.00 AM		4	0.376	854.5
2016	3	04-MAY-13 08.00 AM		6	0.143	571.0
2019	2	04-MAY-13 11.00 AM		12	0.937	1,352.1
2019	3	04-MAY-13 11.00 AM		10	1.612	1,341.9
2019	3	04-MAY-13 11.00 AM	4076066623	1	41.592	3,942,672.0
2020	2	04-MAY-13 12.00 PM	1093407144	15	1.037	1,734.6
2020	3	04-MAY-13 12.00 PM	4076066623	1	181.044	1,764,007.0
2022	2	04-MAY-13 02.00 PM	1093407144	2	2.214	2,780.5

The awr_plan_change.sql script simply queries DBA_HIST_SQLSTAT for a list of snapshots that contains information about the statement in question (based on its sql_id), and then prints out the relevant statistical information. In this output, I show the plan_hash_value, the average logical IO, and the average elapsed time. (This sort of a report can also be generated from data collected by Statspack, by the way.) One of the most interesting features of this kind of a historical view of a statement is the history of the plan or plans being used. The output in the example shows a classic case of plan instability. As you can see, the plan changes fairly often (note that the script uses the SQL*Plus break feature on the plan_hash_value column, so if the value does not change from row to row, the value is not printed). This is not a situation in which something changed in the environment that caused a plan to change; rather, the plans are in a constant state of flux. This is classic plan instability. If you note a single plan being used for many days and then an abrupt change to another plan, you should look for a change to statistics or some other environmental change, such as an optimizer setting.

You can also see clearly that the performance characteristics are wildly different between the two plans. In the sample output, you can see that plan 1093407144 does only a couple of thousand logical IOs, whereas plan 4076066623 does a few million. Consequently, the average elapsed time is several minutes for the "bad" plan and a couple of seconds for the "good" plan. This is another characteristic of classic plan instability. There is often a single plan that, although not the absolute best performance you can get for any combination of bind variables, is good enough to be acceptable and provides the desired stability.

Aggregating Statistics by Plan

In general, we don't care much about the optimizer changing its mind and picking a different plan unless the execution times vary widely from one plan to the other. When there are a lot of snapshots or a lot of plans, it's often helpful to aggregate the statistics by plan. The awr_plan_stats.sql script shown in Listing 16-15 does just that (note that I've cut some of the rows from the previous output so the averages don't match exactly, but they are close enough to get the point across):

Listing 16-15. The `awr_plan_stats.sql` Script

```
SQL> @awr_plan_stats
Enter value for sql_id: 3dhwvfmkjzwtv

SQL_ID        PHV          EXECS   ETIME  AVG_ETIME    AVG_LIO
------------- ----------   -----  ------- ---------  -----------
3dhwvfmkjzwtv 1093407144    207   100.0      .935      2,512.5
3dhwvfmkjzwtv 4076066623     22 1,236.5   154.559  4,072,416.3
```

The output from the `awr_plan_stats.sql` script clearly shows that, in this example, there are two plans with very different performance characteristics. This is a fairly normal situation (although there are often more than two plans). However, it is, nevertheless, a common occurrence that one plan is often consistent with a reasonable amount of work and a reasonable average elapsed time, but be aware that averages can hide a lot of important details (such as a few very fast executions with the plan that has the horrible averages). But again, the goal is to get stability at a reasonable performance level. So, finding a plan that you can stick with is often all you're after. (I talk about how you get the optimizer to stick with a single plan in a bit.)

■ **Note**   The default retention period for both AWR and Statspack is woefully inadequate for this type of diagnosis. The default is seven days for AWR. I've been involved in many cases when the necessary data have scrolled out of the retention window and been purged before a proper diagnosis was done. AWR (and Statspack) data do not take up that much space, so I routinely set the retention to several months (and I know of sites that retain multiple years of AWR data). There is even a supplied script that allows you to estimate the storage requirements for AWR based on the workload in your system: `$ORACLE_HOME/rdbms/admin/utlsyxsz.sql`.

Looking for Statistical Variance by Plan

When a problem is not obvious, but you suspect plan instability is an issue, it's often helpful to look for statements that have run with more than one plan that have a large statistical variance in their execution times or the amount of work they do (logical IOs, for example). Listing 16-16 shows the execution of a script (`unstable_plans.sql`) that can help identify statements that are suffering from plan instability.

Listing 16-16. The `unstable_plans.sql` Script

```
SQL> @unstable_plans
Enter value for min_stddev:
Enter value for min_etime:

SQL_ID        SUM(EXECS)   MIN_ETIME   MAX_ETIME   NORM_STDDEV
------------- ----------  -----------  -----------  -------------
4fc7tprp1x3uj      43212          .18          .84        2.0222
47s01ypztkmn6          6        54.46       210.28        2.0230
3rx5cnvua3myj       8126          .03          .12        2.0728
80tb4vmrsag5j      29544          .78         3.16        2.1433
cahnk07yj55st         17        26.35       113.09        2.3272
```

2azfw6wnqn01s	388	1.39	6.20	2.4522
a31u2rn7zup46	4	30.38	183.82	2.5271
607twnwf0ym10	30	146.50	728.15	2.8075
7y3w2mnqnp8jn	65	.56	3.05	3.1227
82rq0xvp6u1t2	34	12.34	119.20	3.4625
9cp3tujh0z4mt	42455	.02	.15	3.5998
6ykn5wq4jmu91	58584	.01	.21	3.7001
cvfj7g4fub5kn	116	.43	3.76	5.4863
26nrsfgurpgpm	427450	.07	1.08	5.5286
brntkgfqa9u1u	2	261.26	2,376.86	5.7258
d9ddsn04krw9d	99	.43	5.66	5.9018
fnwxd5kmnp6x9	2227	.47	4.46	6.0031
96567x1dqvzw1	23	27.02	311.04	7.4330
5wwnfumndntbq	10	98.58	1,481.40	7.7765
dm4hyyyxyay5t	1368	.03	.36	7.8945
5ub7xd1pn57by	1118281	.04	1.23	10.8031
870uasttnradg	441864	.12	2.07	11.3099
2p86vc476bvht	34	14.66	297.76	13.6548
2gz0c5c3vw59b	30	53.45	1,197.24	15.1320
4g22whjx1ycnu	818	.55	22.02	15.3194
48k8mu4mt68pw	1578	13.58	2,002.27	81.6759
1ct9u20mx6nnf	25782	.00	.93	287.5165

27 rows selected.

The output in Listing 16-16 shows there are several SQL statements in this system that are most likely suffering from plan instability issues. The script pulls the information from the AWR tables and displays the total executions, the average elapsed time for the fastest plan, the average elapsed time for the slowest plan, and a calculated normalized standard deviation. As you can see, statement 1ct9u20mx6nnf is the worst offender. However, it may not be all that noticeable to the users because the delta between the slowest plan and the fastest plan is still less than a second. If it is executed many times in succession, the users almost certainly suffer; otherwise, they may not notice. On the other hand, sql_id 48k8mu4mt68pw varies from 14 seconds to more than 30 minutes. Anyone that runs this statement will certainly notice the difference. And seeing that the statement is executed more than 1500 times makes this one appear to be a significant contributor to perceived inconsistency.

Last, after identifying the suspects, use awr_plan_stats.sql and awr_plan_change.sql to get a better idea of what's going with specific statements.

Checking for Variations around a Point in Time

The other thing I do occasionally to check for plan instability is to look for variations around a point in time. The whats_changed.sql script computes a normalized variance for elapsed time around a specific point in time. In fact, it computes the average elapsed time before a reference time and the average elapsed time after the reference time for every statement in the AWR tables. It then displays all statements with average elapsed times that are significantly different (two times, by default). It's similar to the unstable_plans.sql script, but it looks for variance around a point in time as opposed to variance among plans. It is most useful when new code is rolled out or a new index is created or, basically, whenever you want to see which statements have been affected either for better or for worse. Listing 16-17 shows an example of its use.

Listing 16-17. The whats_changed.sql Script

```
SQL> @whats_changed
Enter Days ago: 30
Enter value for min_stddev:
Enter value for min_etime:
Enter value for faster_slower:
```

SQL_ID	EXECS	AVG_ETIME_BEFORE	AVG_ETIME_AFTER	NORM_STDDEV	RESULT
5ub7xd1pn57by	1,118,281	0.18	0.05	2.0827	Faster
03rhvyrhjxgg9	3,838	0.10	0.38	2.0925	Slower
cahnk07yj55st	17	113.09	26.35	2.3272	Faster
4bf2kzg2h1sd0	148	0.60	0.13	2.6403	Faster
9cp3tujh0z4mt	42,455	0.12	0.02	2.7272	Faster
fnwxd5kmnp6x9	2,227	0.92	4.47	2.7283	Slower
607twnwf0ym10	30	146.50	728.15	2.8075	Slower
akm80a52q4qs9	649	6.16	1.21	2.9014	Faster
4g22whjx1ycnu	818	0.48	2.44	2.9272	Slower
14mxyzzjzjvpq	1,537	33.08	191.20	3.3800	Slower
6zncujjc43gsm	1,554	22.53	168.79	4.5894	Slower
6zt6cu6upnm8y	3,340	0.62	0.08	4.8153	Faster
870uasttnradg	441,864	0.98	0.12	4.9936	Faster
d9ddsn04krw9d	99	5.66	0.68	5.1708	Faster
cvfj7g4fub5kn	116	3.76	0.43	5.4863	Faster
2p86vc476bvht	34	14.66	297.76	13.6548	Slower
2gz0c5c3vw59b	30	53.45	1,197.24	15.1320	Slower

```
17 rows selected.
```

Summary

There are several things that contribute to plan instability. If you get one thing out of this chapter, I hope it is that you realize that plans do not change without a reason. Plans remain static unless something else changes in the system. Bind variable peeking and changes in statistics are the most likely causes of plan instability. Oddly enough, failure of statistics to keep up with changing data is another common cause of instability. Of these three issues, though, bind variable peeking is probably the most prevalent and the most frustrating to deal with. Although most shops are understandably reluctant to turn off the bind variable peeking "feature," turning it off altogether is a viable option. There are many production systems that have taken this approach. Part of the standard configuration of SAP, for example, is to set the _optim_peek_user_binds parameter to FALSE. This can prevent the optimizer from choosing the absolute best plan available for a certain set of queries, but the tradeoff is a more consistent environment. Short of turning off bind variable peeking altogether, using literals appropriately with columns that need histograms to deal with skewed data distributions is really the only effective way to deal with the issue while still providing the optimizer the ability to choose the absolute best execution plans. However, if circumstances prevent this approach, there are other techniques that can be applied. In the next chapter, we look at how to improve the situation.

■ ■ ■

Plan Control

As discussed in Chapter 16 on plan stability, Oracle's CBO can seem to change plans at random intervals, causing a great deal of frustration. However, these changes are not random at all, and we reviewed the reasons behind plan changes and examined how you can identify when plans change and why they change. This chapter's focus, as you can probably guess, covers various techniques for controlling execution plans. I probably should say "influencing" instead of "controlling," because there is really no foolproof method of locking in an execution plan. The tools we have at our disposal to help provide plan stability have evolved quite significantly in the more recent versions of Oracle. In this chapter, we take a walk through time and look at when plan control started and where it stands today in Oracle 12c.

Plan Control: Solving the Problem

When you have access to the code (and the change control requirements are not too stringent), you can make changes to get the plan you want. Mechanisms such as hints, changing the structure of the query itself, or using literals in key locations to avoid bind variable peeking issues are all viable options.

■ **Note** See a later section in this chapter, "Plan Control: Without Access to the Code," for help in exerting control over execution plans when you do not have the luxury of being able to modify the code that is being executed.

Discussions about controlling execution plans can turn into a religious debate. Questions concerning the degree and mechanism of control can all degenerate from spirited debate to questioning our rival's ancestry. There is a strong argument for letting the optimizer do what it was written to do. After all, it's one of the most complex pieces of software in existence, with countless man-hours invested in its programming. In many (I dare say, most) situations, the optimizer is capable of coming up with very serviceable execution plans. However, this assumes that the database is configured correctly, that the statistics are accurate, that the data model is reasonable, that the SQL is written correctly, and so on. This is a lot of assumptions, and rarely are they all true.

So, one camp says fix the configuration, the stats, the data model, or whatever else is leading the optimizer astray. On the surface, this seems like a perfectly reasonable position that is hard to argue. If the statistics are not accurate, there most likely will be numerous issues, even if they aren't readily apparent. So, fixing inaccurate statistics can improve things in many areas at the same time.

The flip side is that fixing some things is almost an insurmountable task. Changing the data model, for example, presents a substantial challenge even in a small application, and it is certainly not something that can be done with any degree of expediency. Likewise, changing configuration parameters can have sweeping effects that often require other adjustments. Because of these issues, there is a group that says, "Let's just focus on fixing the slow-running process." People in this camp tend to want to zero in on a SQL statement and fix it. This argument is also hard to argue with because we are often under the gun to provide relief to the users of the system.

The key, in my mind, is to weigh the costs—time to implement and risk—against the potential benefits. I tend to be a pragmatist and therefore rarely get into debates about which approach is "right." I am quite comfortable with making a decision to implement a solution that provides quick relief, even if there is a long-term solution that needs to be implemented at some point in the future. I consider myself akin to an emergency room doctor. When a patient's heart stops, I expect the doctor to break out the defibrillator and get the patient stabilized, not lecture him on proper lifestyle and put him on a diet and new exercise regime. There's plenty of time for that later. On the other hand, after the guy has had a triple bypass, it would be foolish for his cardiologist to tell him that he should keep doing what he's always been doing, just because the technology exists to give him another chance at life.

The bottom line is that, even when we have a system that is configured well with accurate statistics, we still occasionally run across plan stability issues. So, let's put the philosophical issues aside and talk about the basic tools we have at our disposal for controlling execution plans.

Modifying Query Structure

Prior to version 8, changing the structure of a query was basically the only tool available for influencing execution plans (other than making physical changes to the database objects, such as adding or dropping indexes). Modifying SQL structure is still a valid technique, but because the optimizer has become so adept at transforming queries, it is not nearly as useful as it once was. Nevertheless, being aware of alternative forms that return the same set of rows gives us an advantage when we are trying to get the optimizer to pick a certain plan. Alternative forms can open up or close off options from which the optimizer has to choose.

Making Appropriate Use of Literals

Although it's been drummed into our head for years that we should use bind variables, they are not appropriate in every situation. In fact, anywhere we have skewed data distributions and need histograms to get the best plans, we should use literals as opposed to bind variables, at least for the special cases (such as the values you want to make sure the optimizer is aware of). It is not necessary to choose one approach or the other for each statement, either. It is perfectly reasonable to code conditional logic that branches to a SQL construct that uses literals when the values are highly selective (or highly unselective). All the other values can be covered by a single version of the statement that uses a bind variable. Of course, if the number of very popular (or very nonpopular) values is high, we have to weigh the cost of the coding effort, the impact on the shared pool, and the additional impediment to scalability caused by the additional parsing for all these unique SQL statements. As my granddad used to say, "There's no such thing as a free puppy."

Giving the Optimizer Some Hints

One of the oldest and most basic methods of controlling execution plans is embedding optimizer instructions directly into the statement. Unfortunately, the name of this feature, *Hint*, is somewhat misleading. The word *hint* makes it sound like it is a mild suggestion that the optimizer can consider or ignore as it pleases. Nothing is further from the truth. Hints are actually directives to the optimizer. As long as the hint is valid, the optimizer obeys it. In general, hints are not well understood. One reason is that they are not particularly well documented. Worse than this, however, is that they return no error or warning message when an invalid hint is specified. In cases when there is a syntax error or object names are mistyped or the combination of hints cannot be applied together, they are simply silently ignored. So, it is difficult to know if a hint is even recognized as valid, much less whether it is doing what it is supposed to do. This lack of error or warning messages is probably the biggest reason for confusion about what they do.

There is a way to determine whether an error has occurred that prevents a hint from being used. By generating an optimizer trace (event 10053), you can review a section, labeled Dumping Hints, of the trace file that is emitted. To capture an optimizer trace, set event 10053 as follows:

```
alter session set events '10053 trace name context forever, level 1':
```

After the event is set, you simply execute the statement with the hint in it you wish to evaluate. However, even the collection information doesn't provide much help regarding why the hint is invalid. Listing 17-1 shows an excerpt from an optimizer trace file for a query that is attempting to apply FULL hints to the dept and emp tables.

Listing 17-1. Optimizer Trace (10053) File Excerpt

```
...
Dumping Hints
-------------------------------------------------------------
atom_hint=(@=0x31211124 err=0 resol=1 used=0 token=448 org=1 lvl=3 txt=FULL ("DEPT") )
atom_hint=(@=0x3120e100 err=0 resol=1 used=1 token=448 org=1 lvl=3 txt=FULL ("EMP") )
...
```

The err value shows a 1 if an error is noted in the hint or, as in this example, a 0 if no error is present. The other bit of information that can be useful is the used indicator. Using the same 0/1 indicator, a value of 1 indicates that the hint is used during the evaluation of the plan. However, just because the optimizer uses the hint during plan evaluation doesn't mean the chosen plan operations include one specified by the hint. So, there's no real way to know why a hint is or isn't used.

Hints can be used to tell Oracle to do a full table scan instead of using an index, or to do a nested loops join, or to use a specific index, or all the above. Each of these access path-oriented hints effectively reduces the universe of possible options the optimizer can consider when coming up with an execution plan for a statement. Hints can also be used to alter optimizer settings, object statistics, and even internal optimizer calculations. These kinds of hints alter the way the optimizer does its work or the calculations that it makes, but they do not limit directly the choices the optimizer has in terms of access paths. By the way, you can get a list of valid hints along with the version in which they were introduced via the V$SQL_HINT view. Listing 17-2 shows the valid_hints.sql script.

Listing 17-2. The valid_hints.sql Script

```
SQL> @valid_hints
Enter value for hint: pq
Enter value for version:
NAME                                               VERSION
-------------------------------------------------- --------
PQ_DISTRIBUTE                                      8.1.5
PQ_MAP                                             9.0.0
PQ_NOMAP                                           9.0.0
PQ_CONCURRENT_UNION                                12.1.0.1
NO_PQ_CONCURRENT_UNION                             12.1.0.1
PQ_REPLICATE                                       12.1.0.1
NO_PQ_REPLICATE                                    12.1.0.1
PQ_FILTER                                          12.1.0.1
PQ_SKEW                                            12.1.0.1
NO_PQ_SKEW                                         12.1.0.1
PQ_DISTRIBUTE_WINDOW                               12.1.0.1

11 rows selected.
```

Hints can be applied to individual statements by embedding them inside comments that begin with a plus sign (+) Any comment immediately following a SELECT, UPDATE, INSERT, or DELETE keyword that begins with + is evaluated by the optimizer. The comment can contain multiple hints (separated by spaces). The documentation also states that comment text can be interspersed with hints. I don't recommend this technique, however, because not all hints are documented and you may inadvertently put in a word that that has significance to the optimizer. There can only be one hint–comment per query block. Subsequent comments that start with + are not evaluated by the optimizer. If you use an alias for an object name in your SQL statement, all hints must refer to the object by its alias. Also note that if you specify an owner name in your statement, the hint should not include the owner name (use an alias; it makes it easier). Listing 17-3 shows a couple examples.

Listing 17-3. Examples of Hints

--Valid:
```
select /* real comment */ /*+ gather_plan_statistics full (a) */ avg(sal)
from emp a where deptno = 10;
select /*+ gather_plan_statistics full (a) */ /* real comment */ avg(sal)
from emp a where deptno = 10;
select /*+ gather_plan_statistics full (emp) */ /* real comment */ avg(sal)
from emp where deptno = 10;
```

--Invalid
```
-- don't use owner in hint
select /*+ gather_plan_statistics full (scott.emp) */ /* real comment */ avg(sal)
from scott.emp where deptno = 10;
-- if you use a table alias it must be used in the hint
select /*+ gather_plan_statistics full (emp) */ /* real comment */ avg(sal)
from emp a where deptno = 10;
-- apparently the word comment has a special meaning - disabling the hints
select /*+ real comment gather_plan_statistics more comment full (a) */ avg(sal)
from emp a where deptno = 10;
-- the 2nd hint will not be evaluated as a hint
select /*+ gather_plan_statistics */ /*+ full (a) */ /* real comment */ avg(sal) from emp a where
deptno = 10;
```

The format of hints is actually more complicated than the abbreviated version we usually see. The simplified format we normally see is used to specify tables in which the hints are embedded directly in the query blocks where the table occurs. This is not always desirable or even possible, so Oracle has a way of declaring hints that specify where the table is located in the SQL structure. This becomes important when specifying hints that affect objects inside of views, for example, and, as we see later on, for the hint-based mechanisms that Oracle uses to try to improve plan stability. The documentation refers to a "global hint format," which basically means the query block in which an object resides is specified within the hint. Any hint that applies to one or more tables can make use of this global format. The query block names can be specified manually with a hint (QB_NAME) or can be assigned automatically by the system. The system-generated names are not always intuitive. In simple statements, they often take the form of SEL$1, SEL$2, and so forth (or UPD$1 or DEL$1 for update and delete statements, respectively). Listing 17-4 shows some examples of query block naming using the FULL hint.

Listing 17-4. Examples of Hints Using Query Block Naming

```
select /*+ full (a) */ avg(sal)
from emp a where deptno = 10;

select /*+ full (@SEL$1 a@SEL$1) */ avg(sal)
from emp a where deptno = 10;

select /*+ full (a@SEL$1) */ avg(sal)
from emp a where deptno = 10;

select /*+ full (@SEL$1 a) */ avg(sal)
from emp a where deptno = 10;

select /*+ qb_name (MYQB) full (a@MYQB) */ avg(sal)
from emp a where deptno = 10;
```

All five of the previous statements are equivalent. The first @SEL$1 is the query block where the hint should be applied. The term @SEL$1 is the fully qualified table alias. In this case, the whole query block name is redundant. There is only one table and one query block. In general, even when there are multiple query blocks, specifying the query block and then fully qualifying the alias is not necessary. There are situations, though, when you may need both.

There are a couple of ways to determine the correct query block name when system-assigned query block names are in play. One is to use DBMS_XPLAN with the ALIAS parameter. The other is to look at the data in the other_xml column of v$sql that contains all the hints Oracle thinks are necessary to recreate the plan. These hints are fully qualified. Listing 17-5 shows examples of both techniques.

Listing 17-5. Examples of Determining the Correct Query Block Name

```
SQL> @sql_hints
SQL> select
  2   extractvalue(value(d), '/hint') as outline_hints
  3   from
  4   xmltable('/*/outline_data/hint'
  5   passing (
  6   select
  7   xmltype(other_xml) as xmlval
  8   from
  9   v$sql_plan
 10   where
 11   sql_id like nvl('&sql_id',sql_id)
 12   and child_number = &child_no
 13   and other_xml is not null
 14   )
 15   ) d;
Enter value for sql_id: f30tq1uck3171
Enter value for child_no: 0

OUTLINE_HINTS
----------------------------------------------------------------
IGNORE_OPTIM_EMBEDDED_HINTS
OPTIMIZER_FEATURES_ENABLE('12.1.0.1')
DB_VERSION('12.1.0.1')
ALL_ROWS
```

```
OUTLINE_LEAF(@"SEL$5DA710D3")
UNNEST(@"SEL$2")
OUTLINE(@"SEL$1")
OUTLINE(@"SEL$2")
INDEX(@"SEL$5DA710D3" "DEPARTMENTS"@"SEL$1" ("DEPARTMENTS"."DEPARTMENT_ID"))
BATCH_TABLE_ACCESS_BY_ROWID(@"SEL$5DA710D3" "DEPARTMENTS"@"SEL$1")
INDEX(@"SEL$5DA710D3" "EMPLOYEES"@"SEL$2" ("EMPLOYEES"."DEPARTMENT_ID" "EMPLOYEES"."JOB_ID"))
LEADING(@"SEL$5DA710D3" "DEPARTMENTS"@"SEL$1" "EMPLOYEES"@"SEL$2")
USE_MERGE(@"SEL$5DA710D3" "EMPLOYEES"@"SEL$2")
13 rows selected.
SQL>@dcplan
Enter value for sql_id: f30tq1uck3171
Enter value for child_no: 0
Enter value for format: TYPICAL -BYTES +ALIAS

PLAN_TABLE_OUTPUT
-------------------------------------------------------------
SQL_ID  f30tq1uck3171, child number 0
-------------------------------------------------------------
select /* not-in */ department_name from hr.departments where
department_id not in (select department_id from hr.employees)
Plan hash value: 3403053048
```

```
---------------------------------------------------------------
| Id  | Operation                 | Name          | Rows  | Cost (%CPU)|
---------------------------------------------------------------
|   0 | SELECT STATEMENT          |               |       |  1 (100)|
|   1 |  MERGE JOIN ANTI NA       |               |    17 |  1   (0)|
|   2 |   SORT JOIN               |               |    27 |  0   (0)|
|   3 |    TABLE ACCESS BY INDEX  | DEPARTMENTS   |    27 |  0   (0)|
|     |      ROWID BATCHED        |               |       |         |
|   4 |     INDEX FULL SCAN       | DEPT_ID_PK    |    27 |  0   (0)|
|*  5 |   SORT UNIQUE             |               |   107 |  1   (0)|
|   6 |    INDEX FULL SCAN        | EMP_JOB_DEPT_IX|  107 |  1   (0)|
---------------------------------------------------------------
```

Query Block Name / Object Alias (identified by operation id):

```
   1 - SEL$5DA710D3
   3 - SEL$5DA710D3 / DEPARTMENTS@SEL$1
   4 - SEL$5DA710D3 / DEPARTMENTS@SEL$1
   6 - SEL$5DA710D3 / EMPLOYEES@SEL$2
```

Predicate Information (identified by operation id):

```
   5 - access("DEPARTMENT_ID"="DEPARTMENT_ID")
       filter("DEPARTMENT_ID"="DEPARTMENT_ID")
```

Notice that the query block names in this example are more complex than the simple SEL$1, although the aliases still use the SEL$1 format to reference their original position in the statement. The complex query block names are the result of transformations done by the optimizer. Listing 17-6 shows what happens when you run the same query with query transformation turned off.

Listing 17-6. The Same Query with Query Transformation Turned Off

```
SQL>@dcplan
Enter value for sql_id: 79ps58yga4hfr
Enter value for child_no: 0
Enter value for format: TYPICAL -BYTES +ALIAS

PLAN_TABLE_OUTPUT
-------------------------------------------------------------
SQL_ID  79ps58yga4hfr, child number 0
-------------------------------------------------------------
select /* not-in */ /*+ no_query_transformation */ department_name from
hr.departments where department_id not in (select department_id from
hr.employees)
Plan hash value: 89172749

-----------------------------------------------------------------
| Id  | Operation          | Name          | Rows | Cost (%CPU)|
-----------------------------------------------------------------
|   0 | SELECT STATEMENT   |               |      |  17 (100)|
|*  1 |  FILTER            |               |      |          |
|   2 |   TABLE ACCESS FULL| DEPARTMENTS   |   27 |   3   (0)|
|*  3 |   INDEX FULL SCAN  | EMP_JOB_DEPT_IX |  2 |   1   (0)|
-----------------------------------------------------------------

Query Block Name / Object Alias (identified by operation id):
-------------------------------------------------------------

   1 - SEL$1
   2 - SEL$1 / DEPARTMENTS@SEL$1
   3 - SEL$2 / EMPLOYEES@SEL$2

Predicate Information (identified by operation id):
-------------------------------------------------------------

   1 - filter( IS NULL)
   3 - filter(LNNVL("DEPARTMENT_ID"<>:B1))
```

Notice that the more complicated query block names have disappeared. Furthermore, when you specify your own query block names, you still get a generated name if a transformation takes place. This makes sense if you think about it. Transformations can completely change the structure of the query, turning a statement with a subquery (such as this example) into a join, for example. This combines two query blocks into a single new block. It is for this reason that I prefer to use the fully qualified alias rather than the hint format that includes a query block name as the first element of the hint. For comparison, Listing 17-7 shows another plan dump in which transformations are allowed and the query blocks are named explicitly.

Listing 17-7. Explicitly Named Query Blocks

```
SQL>@dcplan
Enter value for sql_id: g0pu554n4z3cq
Enter value for child_no: 0
Enter value for format: TYPICAL -BYTES +ALIAS


PLAN_TABLE_OUTPUT
-------------------------------------------------------------
SQL_ID  g0pu554n4z3cq, child number 0
-------------------------------------------------------------
select /* not-in2 */ /*+ qb_name(outer) */ department_name from
hr.departments dept where department_id not in (select /*+
qb_name(inner) */ department_id from hr.employees emp)
Plan hash value: 3403053048
```

```
-------------------------------------------------------------------------
| Id | Operation                | Name          | Rows | Cost (%CPU)|
-------------------------------------------------------------------------
|  0 | SELECT STATEMENT         |               |      |   1 (100)|
|  1 |  MERGE JOIN ANTI NA      |               |   17 |   1   (0)|
|  2 |   SORT JOIN              |               |   27 |   0   (0)|
|  3 |    TABLE ACCESS BY INDEX | DEPARTMENTS   |   27 |   0   (0)|
|    |     ROWID BATCHED        |               |      |          |
|  4 |     INDEX FULL SCAN      | DEPT_ID_PK    |   27 |   0   (0)|
|* 5 |   SORT UNIQUE            |               |  107 |   1   (0)|
|  6 |    INDEX FULL SCAN       | EMP_JOB_DEPT_IX |  107 |   1   (0)|
-------------------------------------------------------------------------
```

```
Query Block Name / Object Alias (identified by operation id):
-------------------------------------------------------------


   1 - SEL$F38A2936
   3 - SEL$F38A2936 / DEPT@OUTER   ⇐== The alias remains intact even though
   4 - SEL$F38A2936 / DEPT@OUTER       a query block name has been generated
   6 - SEL$F38A2936 / EMP@INNER        due to transformation.

Predicate Information (identified by operation id):
-------------------------------------------------------------


   5 - access("DEPARTMENT_ID"="DEPARTMENT_ID")
       filter("DEPARTMENT_ID"="DEPARTMENT_ID")
```

Notice that the aliases retained their original names even though the query block was renamed as result of the transformation. The transformation can be verified by a 10053 trace, which details the decision-making process that the optimizer goes through when determining an execution plan. Listing 17-8 shows an excerpt from the trace file for the previous statement.

Listing 17-8. An Excerpt from the Trace File

```
Registered qb: OUTER Oxf64c3e34 (HINT OUTER)
QUERY BLOCK SIGNATURE
  signature (): qb_name=OUTER nbfros=1 flg=0
    fro(0): flg=4 objn=73928 hint_alias="DEPT"@"OUTER"

Registered qb: INNER Oxf64c1df0 (HINT INNER)
QUERY BLOCK SIGNATURE
  signature (): qb_name=INNER nbfros=1 flg=0
    fro(0): flg=4 objn=73933 hint_alias="EMP"@"INNER"

. . .

JPPD: Applying transformation directives
query block OUTER transformed to SEL$F38A2936 (#1)

. . .

Final query after transformations:******* UNPARSED QUERY IS *******
SELECT /*+ QB_NAME ("OUTER") */ "DEPT"."DEPARTMENT_NAME" "DEPARTMENT_NAME" FROM
"HR"."EMPLOYEES" "EMP","HR"."DEPARTMENTS" "DEPT" WHERE
"DEPT"."DEPARTMENT_ID"="EMP"."DEPARTMENT_ID" AND  NOT EXISTS (SELECT /*+ QB_NAME ("INNER") */
0 FROM "HR"."EMPLOYEES" "EMP" WHERE "EMP"."DEPARTMENT_ID" IS NULL)

. . .

Dumping Hints
-------------------------------------------------------------
atom_hint=(@=Oxf6473d1c err=0 resol=1 used=1 token=1003 org=1 lvl=2 txt=QB_NAME ("OUTER") )
====================== END SQL Statement Dump ======================
```

The trace file shows the original query blocks along with the objects in them. It shows that the first query block (named OUTER) was transformed into SEL$F38A2936. And it shows the final version of the statement that was executed. Notice that, in the final version, the original subquery is gone. It has been merged (unnested) into the OUTER query as a join, and a new subquery has been introduced that checks to see if department_id is null. Finally, there is the Dumping Hints section (as shown in Listing 17-1) that shows hints that have been evaluated.

Plan Control: Without Access to the Code

One of the most frustrating problems we face is not being able to fix bad code. Our inability to change the code occurs for many reasons. In some cases, we are dealing with packaged applications in which the code is just not available. In other cases, the politics of an organization can dictate lengthy delays in making changes to code. Regardless of the reasons, Oracle specialists often find themselves in the unenviable position of being asked to make things better without touching the code. Fortunately, Oracle provides many options for doing just that.

Both changing statistics and modifying database parameters come to mind as effective techniques for effecting execution plan changes. These techniques can cause sweeping changes that affect many SQL statements. Obviously, the statistics need to be as accurate as possible. It is very difficult to get reasonable performance if the statistics are not correct. The database also needs to be configured correctly, although from a stability standpoint, it is not imperative that every parameter be set to an "optimal" value. In fact, there are often tradeoffs that must be made. But, the good news is that stability can usually be accomplished regardless of the configuration, as long as it stays consistent.

Changing access paths (in other words, adding or removing indexes) can also be an effective tool. Of course, this is also a sweeping change that can affect many SQL statements (maybe for the better, maybe not). Certainly, adding an index imposes additional overhead to DML operations. This approach generally requires a fair amount of testing to ensure that statements other than the one you are attempting to fix are not impacted negatively.

Among the most effective approaches, though, are techniques that focus on modifying execution plans of individual statements. Oracle has provided various mechanisms for accomplishing this throughout the years, such as Stored Outlines, SQL Profiles, SQL Plan Baselines, SQL Patches, and, now with Oracle 12c, automatic generation of SQL Plan Directives (discussed in Chapter 16). These techniques provide laserlike specificity by limiting their effect to a single statement (or in some cases, a set of statements). Although these constructs are extremely powerful, they are not particularly well understood. They also suffer from some quirkiness. For example, despite what the documentation implies regarding Outlines locking execution plans, there are situations when creating an Outline on an existing statement, instead of locking in the current plan, actually causes the plan to change.

This quirk is not limited to the older Outline construct. It has been carried forward to the newer SQL Profiles and SQL Baselines as well. And if you think about it, the basic mechanism of these constructs (applying hints) is somewhat suspect. The more complicated a SQL statement is, the more options the optimizer has and the more difficult it becomes too narrow down the choices to a single plan. Nevertheless, it is a widely used technique and probably the best tool at our disposal for controlling the plan of a single statement. So let's discuss each of these options in a little more detail.

Option 1: Change the Statistics

If statistics are inaccurate, they should be fixed. For the optimizer to do its job, we must give it the information it needs to make good decisions. In terms of plan stability, just changing the stats is not sufficient. In general, it's the method of gathering them that needs to be addressed. Although a complete discussion of statistics gathering is out of the scope of this chapter, there are a few things that are important to know now:

- The default stats-gathering job in 10g generates histograms on most columns. This is usually not a good thing. Versions 11g and 12c do a much better job of gathering histograms where they are appropriate.

- Histograms generated in 10g with small sample sizes are often not very accurate (DBMS_STATS.AUTO_SAMPLE_SIZE often chooses very small sample sizes that result in inaccurate histograms). However, in 11g and above, using DBMS_STATS.AUTO_SAMPLE_SIZE is improved so that we can achieve a near-100 percent sample size quality estimate while taking only as much time as a 10 percent or less sample would take to complete.

- Histograms are most useful for columns in which the values are not distributed evenly.

- Bind variables and histograms do not work well together if the data distribution is uneven.

- Extended statistics, also known as *column-group statistics*, should be created as needed to let the optimizer know how to characterize related columns properly that are used frequently in query predicates together. In 12c, Oracle has automated the creation of column-group statistics but you still need to create your own in prior versions.

- Statistics should be gathered (or set) often enough to make sure that column max and min values are close to reality. This is especially important with large tables for which it takes a while for the default stats job to determine it's time to regather (more than 10 percent of the rows have been modified). Plans can change radically (and unexpectedly) when the values specified in WHERE clauses are above or below the range the optimizer thinks is there.

- Partitions should be prepopulated with representative stats if they are to be queried before the normal statistics-gathering job has had a chance to run; otherwise, you may get the dreaded "Why do my jobs always run slow on Mondays?" syndrome.

- Most important, be intimately familiar with how statistics are generated on your systems.

The bottom line is that object statistics need to be accurate. If they are way out of whack, there may be little choice but to address the issue before attempting any other measures. Of course, as in all triage situations, we may have to take some expedient actions to save the patient.

One last thing on stats: Oracle provides the ability to set the values manually for the object statistics that the optimizer uses. Setting statistics manually for an object is a perfectly valid technique in some situations. For example, setting a maximum value manually for a frequently queried column that is increasing constantly and running ahead of standard statistics gathering might be a perfectly reasonable thing to do. Building your own histogram with the values that are important to your application is also possible and may be a reasonable approach if you can't get the normal stats-gathering procedures to do what you want. Listing 17-9 shows a couple scripts that set column statistics manually.

Listing 17-9. Scripts That Set Column Statistics Manually

```
SQL> @col_stats
Enter value for owner: KRM
Enter value for table_name: LITTLE_SKEW
Enter value for column_name:
COLUMN_NM DATA_TYPE AVGLEN    NDV ... LAST_ANAL LOW_VALUE   HIGH_VALUE
--------- --------- ------ ------ ... --------- ----------- -----------
PK_COL    NUMBER         5 99,999 ... 03-AUG-13 1           1000002
COL1      NUMBER         4      2 ... 03-AUG-13 1           999999
COL2      VARCHAR2       8      1 ... 03-AUG-13 TESTING     TESTING
COL3      DATE           8      1 ... 03-AUG-13 08-nov-2008 08-nov-2008
COL4      VARCHAR2       2      2 ... 03-AUG-13 N           Y

SQL> @set_col_stats_max
Enter value for owner: KRM
Enter value for table_name: LITTLE_SKEW
Enter value for column_name: COL2
Enter value for minimum:
Enter value for maximum: XXXXXXX
PL/SQL procedure successfully completed.
SQL> @col_stats
Enter value for owner: KRM
Enter value for table_name: LITTLE_SKEW
Enter value for column_name:
COLUMN_NM DATA_TYPE AVGLEN     NDV ... LAST_ANAL LOW_VALUE    HIGH_VALUE
--------- --------- ------ -------- ... --------- ------------ -----------
PK_COL    NUMBER         5  99,999 ... 03-AUG-13 1            1000002
COL1      NUMBER         4       2 ... 03-AUG-13 1            999999
COL2      VARCHAR2       8       1 ... 13-AUG-13 TESTING      XXXXXXX
COL3      DATE           8       1 ... 03-AUG-13 08-nov-2008  08-nov-2008
COL4      VARCHAR2       2       2 ... 03-AUG-13 N            Y

SQL> @set_col_stats
Enter value for owner: KRM
Enter value for table_name: LITTLE_SKEW
Enter value for col_name: COL1
Enter value for ndv: 10
Enter value for density: 1/10
Enter value for nullcnt: 0
```

```
PL/SQL procedure successfully completed.
SQL> @col_stats
Enter value for owner: KRM
Enter value for table_name: LITTLE_SKEW
Enter value for column_name:
COLUMN_NM DATA_TYPE AVGLEN DENSITY    NDV...LAST_ANAL LOW_VALUE   HIGH_VALUE
--------- --------- ------ -------  ------...--------- ----------- -----------
PK_COL    NUMBER        5 .000010 99,999...03-AUG-13 1           1000002
COL1      NUMBER        4 .100000     10...13-AUG-13 1           999999
COL2      VARCHAR2      8 .000005      1...13-AUG-13 TESTING     XXXXXXX
COL3      DATE          8 .000005      1...03-AUG-13 08-nov-2008 08-nov-2008
COL4      VARCHAR2      2 .000005      2...03-AUG-13 N           Y
```

These scripts make use of the DBMS_STATS.SET_COLUMN_STATS procedure to set the column-level statistics manually . The set_col_stats_max.sql script is probably the more useful of the two. Notice, also, that the call to the procedure modifies the last_analyzed field.

Don't be afraid of this technique. Remember, you know your data and how your applications use it (often better than Oracle does). Oracle provides you the tools to set the statistics as you see fit. Keep in mind, though, that if you do decide to make manual changes to statistics, you have to decide how to integrate those changes into the normal statistics-gathering routine in place on your systems. Don't make the mistake of fixing some statistics issue manually and then have the standard stats-gathering job come along and wipe out your work a week later.

Option 2: Change Database Parameters

This is a SQL book, so I won't discuss this technique in depth. In general, I am very hesitant to attempt to modify plans by manipulating database parameters at the system level except in situations when something is completely misconfigured and I have a reasonable amount of time to test. There are a few parameters that show up on the frequent offenders list such as optimizer_index_cost_adj, optimizer_index_caching, optimizer_mode, cursor_sharing, and db_file_multiblock_read_count. Basically, anything with a nondefault value is suspect in my mind, particularly if there is not a well-defined reason why it's set to a nondefault value. The biggest problem with changing parameters is that they affect the optimizer's calculations for every single statement in the system, which means that every single statement is reevaluated and the optimizer may come up with a new plan. Maybe this is what you want, but changing parameters certainly provides the opportunity for many plans to change, which is, by definition, the opposite of increasing stability.

Option 3: Add or Remove Access Paths

There are definitely times when a new index improves performance of a query significantly, and occasionally the statement is important enough to create one in a production system. But, the problem with adding an index is that a single index can change the execution plans of a number of statements. Assuming the statistics are in good shape, adding an index rarely has a significant negative effect on a query. Nevertheless, indexes should be tested with a representative workload prior to introduction into production. Also, don't forget that adding an index most definitely adds overhead to DML that affects the columns you index.

And while I'm on the subject, removing unneeded indexes can improve DML statements significantly. It's actually more common to see tables that are overindexed than ones that are underindexed. That's because it's scarier to remove an index than to create one. As a result, it usually takes an Act of Congress to get one removed from a production system. One of the main reasons for this is that it can take a lot of time to recreate an index on a large table. Beginning in 11g, there is a feature that makes this process more palatable, by the way. Indexes can be marked as invisible, which means the optimizer doesn't consider them when determining execution plans. So you can see how your application behaves in production less the index you intend to drop, without actually dropping it. Invisible indexes continue to be maintained so you won't see any improvement in DML speed as a result of making an index invisible, but you can make it visible again simply by issuing an alter index statement, if dropping the index turns out to have been a bad idea. Refer back to Chapter 12 for a more detailed review of invisible indexes.

So, adding (or removing) an index is a technique that can be used to modify execution plans, but it is not a particularly useful one when it comes to plan stability issues. If plans change, you need to solve the issue that is causing them to change or prevent them from changing. So, although I hate to say *never*, adding or removing an index is unlikely to prevent a plan from changing.

Option 4: Apply Hint-Based Plan Control Mechanisms

Oracle Database 11g and above implements several plan control mechanisms that rely on optimizer hints. The hint-based mechanisms supported in Oracle Database 11g and above are as follows:

- Outlines (deprecated in 11g)
- SQL Profiles
- SQL Baselines
- SQL Patches

These mechanisms are each designed with slightly different goals in mind, but they use the same basic approach of giving the application a set of hints that is named and associated with a SQL statement. The hints are then applied behind the scenes to any matching statement that is executed.

Outlines

Outlines, or Stored Outlines as they are sometimes called, were introduced shortly after the CBO. They are the oldest of the hint-based mechanisms and should not be used in 11g and above. The documentation and marketing material when they were introduced also referred to the new feature as "Plan Stability." The design goal was to "lock" a specific plan for a statement. This was done by using the CREATE OUTLINE statement to parse a SQL statement (including coming up with an execution plan), determine a set of hints that should be sufficient to force the optimizer to pick that plan, and then store the hints. The next time a matching SQL statement was processed by the database, the hints were applied behind the scenes before the execution plan was determined. The intention was that the set of hints would be sufficient to allow one and only one plan for the given statement, regardless of the optimizer settings, statistics, and so on.

By the way, *matching* basically means that the text of the statement matches. Originally, Outlines had to match character for character, just like the normal rules for sharing SQL statements; but, for some reason, Oracle later decided that the matching algorithm should be somewhat relaxed. What this means is that in any version you're likely to run into today, whitespace is collapsed and differences in case are ignored. So (at least as far as Outlines are concerned), "select * from dual" is the same as "SELECT * FROM DuAl". You still get two different statements in the shared pool, but they use the same Outline, if one exists.

With 9i, Oracle started to enhance this feature by adding the ability to edit the Outlines themselves, but they never really completed the job. In fact, they pretty much quit doing anything with the feature after 10gR1. The script that creates the DBMS_OUTLN package ($ORACLE_HOME/rdbms/admin/dbmsol.sql), for example, has not been updated since early in 2004 (with the exception of a tweak to keep it working in 11g). At any rate, the feature has worked pretty well over the years; in fact, it still works in 12c, although the documentation has been warning us for the last several years that the feature has been deprecated and is no longer being maintained.

The first version of the feature required you to create an Outline by specifying the statement inline in a `CREATE OUTLINE` statement. Here's an example:

```
SQL> create or replace outline junk for category test on
  2  select avg(pk_col) from skew a where col1 > 0;
Outline created.
```

This syntax was a bit unwieldy because of having to specify the complete SQL statement as part of the command. Fortunately, a way to create an Outline was introduced later that allowed an Outline to be created on a statement that already existed in the shared pool. The `CREATE_OUTLINE` procedure was added to the `DBMS_OUTLN` package to do this. In general, it was a better approach because it was much easier to identify a cursor (with a hash value) than to cut and paste a long SQL statement to the command line. It also allowed you to see the plan arrived at by the optimizer prior to creating the Outline. Listing 17-10 shows the definition of the procedure and an example of its use.

Listing 17-10. `CREATE_OUTLINE`

```
PROCEDURE CREATE_OUTLINE
 Argument Name                 Type                     In/Out Default?
 ----------------------------  -----------------------  ------ --------
 HASH_VALUE                    NUMBER                   IN
 CHILD_NUMBER                  NUMBER                   IN
 CATEGORY                      VARCHAR2                 IN     DEFAULT

SQL> select sql_id, hash_value, child_number from v$sql
  2  where sql_text like 'select avg(pk_col) from skew where col1 = 136133'
  3  /
SQL_ID        HASH_VALUE CHILD_NUMBER
------------- ---------- ------------
fh70fkqr78zz3 2926870499            0

SQL> exec dbms_outln.create_outline(2926870499,0,'DEFAULT');
PL/SQL procedure successfully completed.
SQL> select category, ol_name, hintcount hints, sql_text from outln.ol$;
CATEGORY OL_NAME                          HINTS SQL_TEXT
-------- -------------------------------- ------------------------------------
DEFAULT  OUTLINE_11.2.0.3                      6 select /*+ index(a SKEW_COL2_COL1)
DEFAULT  SYS_OUTLINE_10081416353513714         6 select avg(pk_col) from skew where
TEST     JUNK                                  6 select avg(pk_col) from skew a wher
```

So you can see that the Outline was created in the `DEFAULT` category with a very ugly name and that it has 6 hints assigned to it. Let's have a quick look at the hints:

```
SQL> @outline_hints
Enter value for name: SYS_OUTLINE_10081416353513714
Enter value for hint:
NAME                          HINT
----------------------------- --------------------------------------
SYS_OUTLINE_10081416353513714 IGNORE_OPTIM_EMBEDDED_HINTS
SYS_OUTLINE_10081416353513714 OPTIMIZER_FEATURES_ENABLE('11.2.0.3')
SYS_OUTLINE_10081416353513714 DB_VERSION('11.2.0.3')
SYS_OUTLINE_10081416353513714 ALL_ROWS
```

```
SYS_OUTLINE_10081416353513714 OUTLINE_LEAF(@"SEL$1")
SYS_OUTLINE_10081416353513714 INDEX_RS_ASC(@"SEL$1"
                                "SKEW"@"SEL$1"("SKEW"."COL1"))
6 rows selected.
```

In 10g and above, v$sql_plan has a column called other_xml. This column is a clob, and all the rows are null except the top record in the plan, which contains a mishmash of stuff, including the database version, the parsing schema name, the plan hash value, and so on. But, the most interesting bit is that the complete set of hints that is to be assigned to an Outline, if one is created using the DBMS_OUTLN.CREATE_OUTLINE procedure, is also contained in that column. Of course, it's all in XML format, so you have to do an XML-type query to get it to come out nicely (or you can just use the sql_hints.sql script):

```
SQL> @sql_hints
Enter value for sql_id: fh7Ofkqr78zz3
Enter value for child_no: 0

OUTLINE_HINTS
---------------------------------------------------------------
OPTIMIZER_FEATURES_ENABLE('11.2.0.3')
DB_VERSION('11.2.0.3')
ALL_ROWS
OUTLINE_LEAF(@"SEL$1")
INDEX_SS(@"SEL$1" "SKEW"@"SEL$1" ("SKEW"."COL2" "SKEW"."COL1"))
6 rows selected.
```

Outlines definitely suffer from some quirkiness. In fact, I have described them previously as "half baked." Here are a few of things you should be aware of:

- Outlines aren't used unless you set the USE_STORED_OUTLINES pseudoparameter, which can be set at the session level or the system level. Setting this at the session level only makes sense to me for testing purposes. The value can be TRUE, FALSE, or a category name. (More about categories in a minute.) The default value is FALSE. This means that even if an Outline is created, it won't be used. The really irritating thing about USE_STORED_OUTLINES is that it is not a full-fledged parameter, so you can't see what it's set to by selecting from the v$parameter view or its underlying X$ views (where the hidden parameters are exposed). More important, this quirk means that the USE_STORED_OUTLINES setting does not persist across instance bounces. This issue prompted an official bug and enhancement request (see Oracle Support Note 560331.1). The official response was to suggest a database trigger to set the value when an instance is started (see outline_startup_trigger.sql in the example download for the recommended trigger).

- The DBMS_OUTLN.CREATE_OUTLINE procedure uses the old hash_value identifier as opposed to the newer sql_id that was introduced in 10g. Although most of the internal structures were updated to use sql_id, Outlines never were. This is just a slight irritation because it means you have to find the hash value to use the DBMS_OUTLN.CREATE_OUTLINE procedure. (See the create_outline.sql script in the example download for a way to get around this.)

- The DBMS_OUTLN.CREATE_OUTLINE procedure is a bit buggy. It often results in error 1330, which disconnects your session from Oracle. There is an Oracle Support Note describing this issue (Note 463288.1) that references a bug (Bug 5454975) that was supposed to be fixed in 10.2.0.4. Anyway, the bottom line is that you should execute the command to enable stored Outlines at the session level (ALTER SESSION SET USE_STORED_OUTLINES=TRUE) before attempting to create an Outline with the DBMS_OUTLN.CREATE_OUTLINE procedure (again, see the create_outline.sql script).

- The DBMS_OUTLN.CREATE_OUTLINE procedure does not allow a name to be specified for an Outline. Instead, it creates a system-generated name. This is another minor irritation because Outlines can be renamed easily enough with the ALTER OUTLINE command (see the create_outline.sql script yet again for a way to do this when creating an outline).

- Outlines are grouped together into categories. Each Outline is assigned to a single category. The default category is DEFAULT. If USE_STORED_OUTLINES is set to TRUE, Outlines in the DEFAULT category are used. If USE_STORED_OUTLINES is set to some other text string, only Outlines in the category that matches the value of USE_STORED_OUTLINES are used.

- As with all hints, Outline hints are directives that are obeyed unless they are invalid. Invalid hints are silently ignored. An invalid hint does not necessarily cause other hints in the Outline to be ignored or disabled, however.

Despite their minor flaws, Outlines have been a standard method for influencing execution plans for the past decade and, prior to 10g, they were the only option available. They also work with RAC, so if you create an Outline (or Profile or Baseline, for that matter), it is picked up across all the nodes in the cluster. If you find yourself working on a 9i database, don't discount their usefulness. If you're working on 10g and above, read on, because there are other options available.

▪ **Note** I find it useful to include the sql_id and the plan_hash_value of a statement in the name of Outlines (and SQL Profiles and Baselines). For Outlines, I have used a convention of OL_sqlid_planhash, which makes it very easy to track the object back to a SQL statement and see what the original plan was that I was trying to "lock in." See the create_outline.sql script for an example.

SQL Profiles

SQL Profiles were introduced in 10g. They are the second iteration of Oracle's hint-based mechanisms for influencing execution plans. SQL Profiles are only documented as a part of the SQL Tuning Advisor (STA), so the only documented way to create a SQL Profile is to run an STA job. In some cases, STA offers to create a SQL Profile for you. The task of STA is to analyze a SQL statement and determine whether there is a better plan. Because it is allowed as much time as it needs, the advisor can sometimes find better execution plans than the optimizer, because it actually validates the optimizer's original estimates by running various steps in a plan and comparing the actual results with the estimates. When it's all done, if STA has found a better plan, it offers to implement a SQL Profile that hopefully causes the optimizer to generate a new and better plan.

Those offered SQL Profiles are simply a collection of hints (much like Outlines), and they almost always contain a lightly documented hint (OPT_ESTIMATE) that allows the optimizer to scale its estimates for various operations. Essentially, it's a fudge factor. The problem with this hint is that, far from locking a plan in place, it locks an empirically derived fudge factor in place, which still leaves the optimizer with a lot of flexibility when it comes to choosing a plan. It also sets up a commonly occurring situation in which the fudge factors stop making sense because things change over time. It is common for SQL Profiles generated by STA to work well for a while and then lose their effectiveness, thus the observation that SQL Profiles tend to sour over time.

Regardless of their intended purpose, the fact remains that SQL Profiles provide a mechanism for applying hints to SQL statements behind the scenes in the same basic manner as Outlines. In fact, it appears that the code is actually based on the earlier Outline code. Of course, SQL Profiles have some additional features that provide some distinct advantages, such as the following:

- SQL Profiles are turned on by default in 10g and above. They can be disabled by setting SQLTUNE_CATEGORY to FALSE. This parameter behaves in much the same way as the USE_STORED_OUTLINE parameter; however, it is a real parameter that is exposed via v$parameter and it retains its value across bounces. The value can be TRUE, FALSE, or a category name.

- SQL Profiles are assigned to categories just like Outlines. Each SQL Profile is assigned to a single category. The default category is DEFAULT. If SQLTUNE_CATEGORY is set to TRUE, outlines in the DEFAULT category are used. If SQLTUNE_CATEGORY is set to some other text string, only SQL Profiles in the category that matches the value of SQLTUNE_CATEGORY are used. As with Outlines, this parameter can be changed with an ALTER SESSION statement that allows SQL Profiles to be tested without enabling them for the whole database (more on this later).

- The DBMS_SQLTUNE.IMPORT_SQL_PROFILE procedure creates a SQL Profile for a given SQL statement. Any set of hints may be passed to the procedure. Although this procedure is not mentioned in the documentation (at least as of 12.1.0.1), it is used by STA and migration procedures. It is also referenced by at least one Oracle Support document (Note 215187.1) as a way of creating what I call a manual SQL Profile. This is a giant leap forward from Outlines. With the IMPORT_SQL_PROFILE procedure, you can create any hints you want and apply them to any statement you want.

- SQL Profiles have the ability to ignore literals when it comes to matching SQL statements. Think of this as being similar to the cursor_sharing parameter. This means you can have a SQL Profile that matches multiple statements that differ only in their use of literals—without having to set the cursor_sharing parameter for the whole instance. This attribute of a SQL Profile is called FORCE_MATCHING. When you create a SQL Profile, you tell it whether you want to set this attribute. If the attribute is set to TRUE, the Profile applies to all statements that have the same signature, regardless of the literals used in the statement.

- There is a view (DBA_SQL_PROFILES) that exposes the SQL profiles that have been created.

- As with all hints, SQL Profile hints are directives that are obeyed unless they are invalid. Invalid hints are silently ignored. An invalid hint does not necessarily cause other hints in the SQL Profile to be ignored or disabled, however.

- SQL Profiles appear to be able to apply most, if not all, valid hints.

SQL TUNING ADVISOR

STA is not the answer to plan stability issues. However, occasionally it is capable of finding a better plan than the one the optimizer comes up with for the reasons I already discussed. Sometimes I create a tuning task for a problem statement to see what suggestions STA might have. The example download for this book contains a number of scripts to help with this task (look for create_tuning_task.sql and accept_sql_profile.sql).

If STA recommends a SQL Profile, do yourself a favor and create it in an alternate category (TEST, for example). This allows you to review the hints and test the performance before making your users the guinea pigs in your experiment.

The hints can provide valuable information regarding where the optimizer is having problems. Remember that the OPT_ESTIMATE hint applies a scaling factor to various calculations based on its more thorough analysis.

Anywhere STA comes up with a very large or very small scaling factor is a direct pointer to a place in the plan where the optimizer is having trouble. Such a scaling factor can often point out a problem with statistics or, in some cases, a shortcoming of the optimizer itself. If it is an optimizer shortcoming and if the optimizer is going to keep making the same error no matter how the data change, then leaving an STA SQL Profile in place may be perfectly reasonable.

If, on the other hand, you're looking for a way to lock in a specific plan, then you may want to consider creating another hint-based object (Profile, Baseline, or Patch) that contains directive hints instead of the OPT_ESTIMATE hint. This is fairly easy to accomplish, because all of these mechanisms can exist on the same statement. For example, you could accept the STA SQL Profile and then create a Baseline on the same statement. You could also use the lock_STA_profile.sql script from the example download to do away with the OPT_ESTIMATE-based profile and replace it with a SQL Profile using directive-type hints.

Listing 17-11 shows an example of a couple of scripts for finding SQL Profiles and statements that are using them.

Listing 17-11. Scripts for Finding SQL Profiles

```
SQL> @sql_profiles.sql
Enter value for sql_text:
Enter value for name:
NAME                              CATEGORY   STATUS    FORCE SQL_TEXT
--------------------------------- ---------- --------- ----- ----------------
PROFILE_fgn6qzrvrjgnz             DEFAULT    DISABLED  NO    select /*+ index(
PROFILE_8hjn3vxrykmpf             DEFAULT    DISABLED  NO    select /*+ invali
PROFILE_69k5bhm12sz98             DEFAULT    DISABLED  NO    SELECT dbin.insta
PROFILE_8js5bhfc668rp             DEFAULT    DISABLED  NO    select /*+ index(
PROFILE_bxd77v75nynd8             DEFAULT    DISABLED  NO    select /*+ parall
PROFILE_7ng34ruy5awxq             DEFAULT    DISABLED  NO    select i.obj#,i.t
SYS_SQLPROF_0126f1743c7d0005      SAVED      ENABLED   NO    select avg(pk_col
PROF_6kymwy3guu5uq_1388734953     DEFAULT    ENABLED   YES   select 1
PROFILE_cnpx9s9na938m_MANUAL      DEFAULT    ENABLED   NO    select /*+ opt_pa
PROF_79m8gs9wz3ndj_3723858078     DEFAULT    ENABLED   NO    /* SQL Analyze(25
PROFILE_9ywuaagwscbj7_GPS         DEFAULT    ENABLED   NO    select avg(pk_col
PROF_arcvrg5na75sw_3723858078     DEFAULT    ENABLED   NO    select /*+ index(
SYS_SQLPROF_01274114fc2b0006      DEFAULT    ENABLED   NO    select i.table_ow

18 rows selected.
SQL> @find_sql_using_profile.sql
Enter value for sql_text:
Enter value for sql_id:
Enter value for sql_profile_name:
SQL_ID          PLAN_HASH SQL_PROFILE
------------- ---------- -------------------------------
bqfx5q2jas08u 3755463150 SYS_SQLPROF_01281e513ace0000
SQL_TEXT
--------------------------------------------------------------
SELECT TASK_LIST.TASK_ID FROM (SELECT /*+ NO_MERGE(T) --
ORDERED */ T.TASK_ID FROM (SELECT * FROM DBA_ADVISOR_
TASKS ORDER BY TASK_ID DESC) T, DBA_ADVISOR_PARAMETERS_
PROJ P1, DBA_ADVISOR_PARAMETERS_PROJ P2 WHERE T.
ADVISOR_NAME='ADDM' AND T.STATUS = 'COMPLETED' AND
```

```
T.EXECUTION_START >= (SYSDATE - 1) AND T.HOW_CREATED
= 'AUTO' AND T.TASK_ID = P1.TASK_ID AND P1.PARAMETER_
NAME = 'INSTANCE' AND P1.PARAMETER_VALUE = SYS_CONTEXT
('USERENV','INSTANCE') AND T.TASK_ID = P2.TASK_ID AND
P2.PARAMETER_NAME = 'DB_ID' AND P2.PARAMETER_VALUE
= TO_CHAR(:B1 ) ORDER BY T.TASK_ID DESC) TASK_LIST
WHERE ROWNUM = 1
```

The sql_profiles.sql script queries DBA_SQL_PROFILES; the find_sql_using_profile.sql queries v$sql. The SQL Profiles with names that begin with SYS_SQLPROF are generated by STA; the others are created manually using the DBMS_SQLTUNE.IMPORT_SQL_PROFILE procedure.

Creating SQL Profiles

Now that we've reviewed the basics of SQL Profiles, let's create one. To do this, we use a script called create_1_hint_profile.sql that simply prompts for a sql_id and a hint, and then creates a SQL tProfile for the statement containing the hint. As you review the example in Listing 17-12, note how we have a SQL that uses an INDEX SKIP SCAN operation in the plan and we use a Profile to change the plan to use a FULL scan operation.

Listing 17-12. The create_1_hint_profile.sql Script

```
SQL> select /* test 1 hint */ avg(pk_col) from skew a where col1 = 222222;
AVG(PK_COL)
---------------------------------
   15722222
1 row selected.

SQL> @find_sql
Enter value for sql_text: select /* test 1 hint */ avg(pk_col) from skew % 222222
Enter value for sql_id:
SQL_ID        CHILD  PLAN_HASH EXECS AVG_ETIME  AVG_LIO
------------- ----- ---------- ----- --------- --------
0pvj94afp6faw     0 2650913906     1       .10 876
SQL_TEXT
------------------------------------------------------------
select /* test 1 hint */ avg(pk_col)
 from skew a where col1 = 222222

1 row selected.

SQL> @dcplan
Enter value for sql_id: 0pvj94afp6faw
Enter value for child_no:
Enter value for format: BASIC +ROWS +COST +PREDICATE
PLAN_TABLE_OUTPUT
------------------------------------------------------------
SQL_ID  0pvj94afp6faw, child number 0
------------------------------------------------------------
select /* test 1 hint */ avg(pk_col) from skew a where col1 = 222222
Plan hash value: 2650913906
```

```
-------------------------------------------------------------------
| Id  | Operation                    | Name          | Rows  | Cost (%CPU)|
-------------------------------------------------------------------
|   0 | SELECT STATEMENT             |               |       | 34  (100)|
|   1 |  SORT AGGREGATE              |               |   1   |          |
|   2 |   TABLE ACCESS BY INDEX ROWID| SKEW          |  32   | 34   (0)|
|*  3 |    INDEX SKIP SCAN           | SKEW_COL2_COL1|  32   |  5   (0)|
-------------------------------------------------------------------

Predicate Information (identified by operation id):
-------------------------------------------------------

   3 - access("COL1"=222222)
       filter("COL1"=222222)

21 rows selected.

SQL> -- So it's using an index skip scan
SQL>
SQL> -- Now lets create a SQL Profile with a FULL hint
SQL>
SQL> @create_1_hint_sql_profile
Enter value for sql_id: 0pvj94afp6faw
Enter value for profile_name (PROFILE_sqlid_MANUAL): PROF_0pvj94afp6faw_FULL
Enter value for category (DEFAULT):
Enter value for force_matching (false):
Enter value for hint: FULL( A@SEL$1 )
Profile PROF_0pvj94afp6faw_FULL created.

SQL> select /* test 1 hint */ avg(pk_col) from skew a where col1 = 222222;
AVG(PK_COL)
---------------------------------
   15722222
1 row selected.

SQL> @find_sql
Enter value for sql_text: select /* test 1 hint */ avg(pk_col) from skew a where col1 %
Enter value for sql_id:
SQL_ID        CHILD PLAN_HASH EXECS AVG_ETIME AVG_LIO SQL_TEXT
------------- ----- --------- ----- --------- ------- -----------------------
0pvj94afp6faw     0 568322376     1      6.34 162,309 select /* test 1 hint */
                                                      avg(pk_col) from skew a
                                                      where col1 = 222222

1 row selected.

SQL> -- Well it has a different plan hash value and it took a lot longer
SQL>
SQL> @dcplan
Enter value for sql_id: 0pvj94afp6faw
Enter value for child_no:
Enter value for format: BASIC +ROWS +COST +PREDICATE
PLAN_TABLE_OUTPUT
```

```
-----------------------------------------------------
SQL_ID  Opvj94afp6faw, child number 0
-----------------------------------------------------
select /* test 1 hint */ avg(pk_col) from skew a where col1 = 222222
Plan hash value: 568322376


-----------------------------------------------------
| Id  | Operation          | Name | Rows  | Cost (%CPU)|
-----------------------------------------------------
|   0 | SELECT STATEMENT   |      |       | 28360 (100)|
|   1 |  SORT AGGREGATE    |      |     1 |            |
|*  2 |   TABLE ACCESS FULL| SKEW |    32 | 28360   (1)|
-----------------------------------------------------

Predicate Information (identified by operation id):
-----------------------------------------------------
   2 - filter("COL1"=222222)

Note
-----------------------------------------------------
   - SQL profile PROF_Opvj94afp6faw_FULL used for this statement

23 rows selected.

SQL> -- So it is using the SQL Profile and it did change to a FULL SCAN
SQL>
SQL> -- Let's check the hints in the SQL Profile
SQL>
SQL> @sql_profile_hints
Enter value for profile_name: PROF_Opvj94afp6faw_FULL

HINT
-----------------------------------------------------
FULL( A@SEL$1 )
1 rows selected.

SQL> -- Let's check the hints in the OTHER_XML field of V$SQL_PLAN
SQL>
SQL> @sql_hints
Enter value for sql_id: Opvj94afp6faw
Enter value for child_no: 0

OUTLINE_HINTS
-----------------------------------------------------
IGNORE_OPTIM_EMBEDDED_HINTS
OPTIMIZER_FEATURES_ENABLE('12.1.0.1')
DB_VERSION('12.1.0.1')
ALL_ROWS
OUTLINE_LEAF(@"SEL$1")
FULL(@"SEL$1" "A"@"SEL$1")

6 rows selected.
```

Notice that the hint was specified using the fully qualified alias for the skew table, FULL (A@SEL$1). This was done on purpose because Profiles and Baselines are more picky about object identification than those normal hints that are embedded in the SQL statement text. For example, it would be perfectly acceptable to use FULL (A) in the text of the SQL statement; but, if you put that into a SQL Profile, the optimizer does not know what to do with it (and so it silently ignores it). Notice also that the complete syntax for the FULL hint would also include the query block name as shown in the output from the sql_hints.sql script. Remember that this is the set of hints that Oracle thinks is necessary to recreate the plan, and thus is the set of hints that is used if you create an Outline on the statement. You may wonder how I knew that SEL$1 was the correct query block name to use. The answer is: Experience. And you know how I got the experience? By making lots of mistakes! Actually, because I know that the default query block names are SEL$1, UPD$1, and DEL$1, and this is a very simple query with only one query block and very little (if any) way that the optimizer could transform it to something else, it was a pretty good guess. But why guess when you can know? If you use DBMS_XPLAN.DISPLAY_CURSOR with the alias option, you can see exactly what the query block name and fully qualified aliases are (see Listing 17-13).

Listing 17-13. DBMS_XPLAN.DISPLAY_CURSOR with the Alias Option

```
SQL> @dcplan
Enter value for sql_id: 0pvj94afp6faw
Enter value for child_no:
Enter value for format: BASIC +ROWS +COST +PREDICATE +ALIAS


PLAN_TABLE_OUTPUT
-----------------------------------------------------------------------
SQL_ID  0pvj94afp6faw, child number 0
-------------------------------------------------------------
select /* test 1 hint */ avg(pk_col) from skew a where col1 = 222222
Plan hash value: 568322376


---------------------------------------------------------
| Id  | Operation          | Name | Rows  | Cost (%CPU)|
---------------------------------------------------------
|   0 | SELECT STATEMENT   |      |       | 28360 (100)|
|   1 |  SORT AGGREGATE    |      |     1 |            |
|*  2 |   TABLE ACCESS FULL| SKEW |    32 | 28360   (1)|
---------------------------------------------------------

Query Block Name / Object Alias (identified by operation id):
-------------------------------------------------------------
   1 - SEL$1
   2 - SEL$1 / A@SEL$1

Predicate Information (identified by operation id):
-------------------------------------------------------------
   2 - filter("COL1"=222222)

Note
-------------------------------------------------------------
   - SQL profile PROF_0pvj94afp6faw_FULL used for this statement

29 rows selected.
```

Creating a SQL Profile to "Lock in" a Plan

SQL Profiles can also duplicate the functionality of Outlines, but without all the quirks, so you can create a SQL Profile using the same hints that an Outline uses (in other words, the ones in the other_xml column). The goal is to have all the hints necessary to "lock in" the plan. There is no way to guarantee the plan will never be able to change, but the technique works fairly well. It is actually quite easy to create a SQL Profile using the hints that an Outline would use, and of course there is a script in the example download to help you out (create_sql_profile.sql). Listing 17-14 shows an example.

Listing 17-14. The create_sql_profile.sql Script

```
SQL> select /* NOT IN */ department_name
  2       from hr.departments dept
  3       where department_id not in (select department_id from hr.employees emp);
no rows selected

SQL> @find_sql
Enter value for sql_text: select /* NOT IN */ department_name%
Enter value for sql_id:
SQL_ID          CHILD   PLAN_HASH EXECS  AVG_ETIME  AVG_LIO SQL_TEXT
------------- ----- ---------- ----- --------- ------- -------------------

875qbqc2gw2qz       0 4201340344     3       .00        9 select /* NOT IN */
                                                          department_name


1 row selected.


SQL> @dcplan
Enter value for sql_id: 875qbqc2gw2qz
Enter value for child_no:
Enter value for format: BASIC +ROWS +COST +PREDICATE


PLAN_TABLE_OUTPUT
-------------------------------------------------------------------------
SQL_ID  875qbqc2gw2qz, child number 0
-------------------------------------------------------------------------
select /* NOT IN */ department_name    from hr.departments dept
where department_id not in (select department_id from hr.employees emp)
Plan hash value: 4201340344
```

Id	Operation	Name	Rows	Cost (%CPU)
0	SELECT STATEMENT			1 (100)
1	MERGE JOIN ANTI NA		17	1 (0)
2	SORT JOIN		27	0 (0)
3	TABLE ACCESS BY INDEX ROWID BATCHED	DEPARTMENTS	27	0 (0)
4	INDEX FULL SCAN	DEPT_ID_PK	27	0 (0)
* 5	SORT UNIQUE		107	1 (0)
6	TABLE ACCESS FULL	EMPLOYEES	107	1 (0)

Predicate Information (identified by operation id):
----

   5 - access("DEPARTMENT_ID"="DEPARTMENT_ID")
       filter("DEPARTMENT_ID"="DEPARTMENT_ID")

25 rows selected.

SQL> @create_sql_profile
Enter value for sql_id: 875qbqc2gw2qz
Enter value for child_no (0):
Enter value for profile_name (PROF_sqlid_planhash):
Enter value for category (DEFAULT):
Enter value for force_matching (FALSE):

SQL Profile PROF_875qbqc2gw2qz_4201340344 created.

SQL> select /* NOT IN */ department_name
  2   from hr.departments dept
  3   where department_id not in
  4   (select department_id from hr.employees emp);

no rows selected

SQL> @find_sql
Enter value for sql_text: select /* NOT IN */ department_name%
Enter value for sql_id:
SQL_ID   CHILD PLAN_HASH EXECS AVG_ETIME AVG_LIO SQL_TEXT
------------- ----- ---------- ----- --------- ------- ------------------
875qbqc2gw2qz   1 4201340344   1   .01   17 select /* NOT IN */
                                                     department_name

1 row selected.

SQL> @dcplan
Enter value for sql_id: 875qbqc2gw2qz
Enter value for child_no:
Enter value for format: BASIC +ROWS +COST +PREDICATE

PLAN_TABLE_OUTPUT

SQL_ID 875qbqc2gw2qz, child number 1
----
select /* NOT IN */ department_name   from hr.departments dept
where department_id not in (select department_id from hr.employees emp)
Plan hash value: 4201340344

```
-----------------------------------------------------------------
| Id  | Operation                    | Name        | Rows | Cost (%CPU)|
-----------------------------------------------------------------
|   0 | SELECT STATEMENT             |             |      |   1 (100)|
|   1 |  MERGE JOIN ANTI NA          |             |   17 |   1   (0)|
|   2 |   SORT JOIN                  |             |   27 |   0   (0)|
|   3 |    TABLE ACCESS BY INDEX     | DEPARTMENTS |   27 |   0   (0)|
|     |      ROWID BATCHED           |             |      |          |
|   4 |     INDEX FULL SCAN          | DEPT_ID_PK  |   27 |   0   (0)|
|*  5 |   SORT UNIQUE                |             |  107 |   1   (0)|
|   6 |    TABLE ACCESS FULL         | EMPLOYEES   |  107 |   1   (0)|
-----------------------------------------------------------------

Predicate Information (identified by operation id):
-------------------------------------------------

   5 - access("DEPARTMENT_ID"="DEPARTMENT_ID")
       filter("DEPARTMENT_ID"="DEPARTMENT_ID")

Note
-----
   - SQL profile PROF_875qbqc2gw2qz_4201340344 used for this statement

29 rows selected.
SQL> @sql_profile_hints
Enter value for profile_name: PROF_875qbqc2gw2qz_4201340344

HINT
-----------------------------------------------------------------
IGNORE_OPTIM_EMBEDDED_HINTS
OPTIMIZER_FEATURES_ENABLE('12.1.0.1')
DB_VERSION('12.1.0.1')
ALL_ROWS
OUTLINE_LEAF(@"SEL$5DA710D3")
UNNEST(@"SEL$2")
OUTLINE(@"SEL$1")
OUTLINE(@"SEL$2")
INDEX(@"SEL$5DA710D3" "DEPT"@"SEL$1" ("DEPARTMENTS"."DEPARTMENT_ID"))
FULL(@"SEL$5DA710D3" "EMP"@"SEL$2")
LEADING(@"SEL$5DA710D3" "DEPT"@"SEL$1" "EMP"@"SEL$2")
USE_MERGE(@"SEL$5DA710D3" "EMP"@"SEL$2")
12 rows selected.
```

So, this is handy if you have a SQL statement in the shared pool with a plan that you like.

Creating a SQL Profile Using AWR

But, what if you have a statement that goes bad and there is no longer a copy of the good plan in the shared pool? No problem, as long as your AWR retention allows you to get back to a previous execution that used a plan you like, because all the hints are stored in the other_xml column of the dba_hist_sql_plan table along with the rest of the plan data. So, it is a relatively simple matter to create a SQL Profile using those hints to restore your previous plan (while you go looking for the reason it went south in the first place). Of course there is a script for that one as well (create_sql_profile_awr.sql). Listing 17-15 shows an example of its use (note that this example was run in 10g because it's easier to get the optimizer to behave badly in 10g than in 11g or 12c).

Listing 17-15. The create_sql_profile_awr.sql Script

```
SYS@LAB1024> @awr_plan_change
Enter value for sql_id: 05cq2hb1r37tr

SNAP_ID NODE BEGIN_INTERVAL_TIME    PLN_HSH_VAL EXECS AVG_ETIME   AVG_LIO
------- ---- -------------------- ----------- ----- --------- ---------
9532    1    12-AUG-13 15.00.09.212  68322376     1    90.339   162,298
9534    1    12-AUG-13 10.00.08.716               1    51.715   162,298
9535    1    13-AUG-13 18.00.10.280               4    23.348   162,298
9536    1    15-AUG-13 16.00.05.439 3723858078     1   622.170 9,218,284

SYS@LAB1024>
SYS@LAB1024> -- statement 05cq2hb1r37tr has taken a turn for the worse
SYS@LAB1024> -- let's get it back to plan 568322376
SYS@LAB1024>
SYS@LAB1024> @create_sql_profile_awr
Enter value for sql_id: 05cq2hb1r37tr
Enter value for plan_hash_value: 568322376
Enter value for profile_name (PROF_sqlid_planhash):
Enter value for category (DEFAULT):
Enter value for force_matching (FALSE):
SQL Profile PROF_05cq2hb1r37tr_568322376 created.
SYS@LAB1024> @sql_profile_hints
Enter value for profile_name: PROF_05cq2hb1r37tr_568322376

HINT
---------------------------------------------------------------
IGNORE_OPTIM_EMBEDDED_HINTS
OPTIMIZER_FEATURES_ENABLE('10.2.0.4')
ALL_ROWS
OUTLINE_LEAF(@"SEL$1")
FULL(@"SEL$1" "A"@"SEL$1")
5 rows selected.
```

This approach is very handy if you have a statement that ran well at some point and AWR captured it.

Creating a SQL Profile by Using Another SQL Plan

What if you need to tune a statement from scratch, but you don't have access to the code? Well, SQL Profiles have one more trick up their sleeve. Because we have already demonstrated that we can build SQL Profiles with any set of hints and associate them with any SQL statement, and because we have shown we can use other_xml as a source of hints, why not move a set of hints from one statement to another? This allows you to take a statement and manipulate it to get the plan you want (via hints, alter session statements, and so forth) and then create a SQL Profile on your unmanipulated statement using the hints from your manipulated statement. And, of course, there is a script in the example download to do this (move_sql_profile.sql). There are several steps to this process. First, we need to identify the statement and get its sql_id, then we need to make a copy of it to manipulate, then we need to create a SQL Profile on the new manipulated version, and, last, we need to move the hints to the original statement. Listing 17-16 shows an example.

Listing 17-16. The move_sql_profile.sql Script

```
SQL> select count(*) from skew where col3 = '01-jan-10';
  COUNT(*)
---------------------------------------------------------------
        0
1 row selected.

SQL> @find_sql
Enter value for sql_text: select count(*) from skew where col3 = %
Enter value for sql_id:
SQL_ID        CHILD  PLAN_HASH EXECS AVG_ETIME AVG_LIO SQL_TEXT
------------- ----- ---------- ----- --------- ------- ----------------
4cp821ufcwvgc     0 3438766830     1       .39     675 select count(*)
                                                        from skew where
                                                        col3 = '01-jan-10'

1 row selected.
SQL> @dcplan
Enter value for sql_id: 4cp821ufcwvgc
Enter value for child_no:
Enter value for format: BASIC +ROWS +COST +PREDICATE
PLAN_TABLE_OUTPUT
---------------------------------------------------------------
SQL_ID  4cp821ufcwvgc, child number 0
---------------------------------------------------------------
select count(*) from skew where col3 = '01-jan-10'
Plan hash value: 3438766830


---------------------------------------------------------------
| Id  | Operation        | Name       | Rows  | Cost (%CPU)|
---------------------------------------------------------------
|   0 | SELECT STATEMENT |            |       |    3 (100)|
|   1 |  SORT AGGREGATE  |            |     1 |            |
|*  2 |   INDEX RANGE SCAN| COL3_INDEX |     1 |    3   (0)|
---------------------------------------------------------------


Predicate Information (identified by operation id):
---------------------------------------------------------------

   2 - access("COL3"='01-jan-10')

19 rows selected.
```

So we have identified our statement and found the sql_id. Now let's create another version of the statement and force it to use a different index. We do this by adding a hint to the select statement text (Listing 17-17).

Listing 17-17. Adding an Inline Hint to the Select Statement Text

```
SQL> -- let's create a statement that does the same
SQL> -- thing but uses a different index
SQL>
```

```
SQL> select /*+ index (skew skew_col3_col2_col1) */ count(*)
  2 from skew where col3 = '01-jan-10';
  COUNT(*)
------------------------------------------------------------
         0
1 row selected.

SQL> @find_sql
Enter value for sql_text: select /*+ index (skew skew_col3_col2_col1) */ count(*)%
Enter value for sql_id:
SQL_ID        CHILD  PLAN_HASH EXECS AVG_ETIME AVG_LIO SQL_TEXT
------------- ----- ---------- ----- --------- ------- --------------------
09gdkwq1bs48h     0  167097056     1       .06       8 select /*+ index(skew
                                                       skew_col3_col2_col1)
                                                       */ count(*) from skew
                                                       where '01- jan-10'

1 row selected.

SQL> @dcplan
Enter value for sql_id: 09gdkwq1bs48h
Enter value for child_no:
Enter value for format: BASIC +ROWS +COST +PREDICATE

PLAN_TABLE_OUTPUT
------------------------------------------------------------------
SQL_ID  09gdkwq1bs48h, child number 0
------------------------------------------------------------------
select /*+ index (skew skew_col3_col2_col1) */ count(*) from skew
where col3 = '01-jan-10'
Plan hash value: 167097056


------------------------------------------------------------------
| Id | Operation          | Name               | Rows  | Cost (%CPU)|
------------------------------------------------------------------
|  0 | SELECT STATEMENT   |                    |       |   4 (100)|
|  1 |  SORT AGGREGATE    |                    |     1 |          |
|* 2 |   INDEX RANGE SCAN | SKEW_COL3_COL2_COL1 |    1 |   4   (0)|
------------------------------------------------------------------

Predicate Information (identified by operation id):
------------------------------------------------------------------
   2 - access("COL3"='01-jan-10')

20 rows selected.
```

In Listing 17-17, you created a new statement (SQL_ID: 09gdkwq1bs48h) that has the same structure but uses a different execution plan (because of the hint). The next step is to create a SQL Profile on the new statement. We do this with the create_sql_profile.sql script, as shown in Listing 17-18.

Listing 17-18. The create_sql_profile.sql Script

```
SQL> -- now let's create a profile on our new statement
SQL>
SQL> @create_sql_profile
Enter value for sql_id: 09gdkwq1bs48h
Enter value for child_no (0):
Enter value for profile_name (PROF_sqlid_planhash):
Enter value for category (DEFAULT):
Enter value for force_matching (FALSE):
SQL Profile PROF_09gdkwq1bs48h_167097056 created.
SQL> select /*+ index (skew skew_col3_col2_col1) */ count(*)
  2 from skew where col3 = '01-jan-10';
  COUNT(*)
------------------------------------------------------------
         0
1 row selected.

SQL> @find_sql
Enter value for sql_text: select /*+ index (skew skew_col3_col2_col1) */ count(*)%
Enter value for sql_id:
SQL_ID        CHILD  PLAN_HASH EXECS AVG_ETIME AVG_LIO SQL_TEXT
------------- ----- ---------- ----- --------- ------- --------------------
09gdkwq1bs48h     0  167097056     1       .01      16 select /*+ index(skew
                                                        skew_col3_col2_col1)
                                                        */ count(*) from skew
                                                        where '01- jan-10'

1 row selected.
SQL> @dcplan
Enter value for sql_id: 09gdkwq1bs48h
Enter value for child_no:
Enter value for format: BASIC +ROWS +COST +PREDICATE

PLAN_TABLE_OUTPUT
------------------------------------------------------------------
SQL_ID  09gdkwq1bs48h, child number 0
------------------------------------------------------------------
select /*+ index (skew skew_col3_col2_col1) */ count(*) from skew
where col3 = '01-jan-10'
Plan hash value: 167097056


--------------------------------------------------------------------
| Id | Operation          | Name               | Rows | Cost (%CPU)|
--------------------------------------------------------------------
|  0 | SELECT STATEMENT   |                    |      |   4 (100)|
|  1 |  SORT AGGREGATE    |                    |    1 |          |
|* 2 |   INDEX RANGE SCAN | SKEW_COL3_COL2_COL1 |   1 |   4  (0)|
--------------------------------------------------------------------
```

```
Predicate Information (identified by operation id):
-----------------------------------------------------------------------
   2 - access("COL3"='01-jan-10')

Note
-----------------------------------------------------------------------
   - SQL profile PROF_09gdkwq1bs48h_167097056 used for this statement

24 rows selected.
```

The last step is to move the newly created SQL Profile to the original statement. We do this with the move_sql_profile.sql script in Listing 17-19. Then, we verify that the SQL Profile is being used and has the desired effect.

Listing 17-19. The move_sql_profile.sql Script

```
SQL> -- let's attach that same SQL Profile on to our original statement
SQL>
SQL> @move_sql_profile
Enter value for profile_name: PROF_09gdkwq1bs48h_167097056
Enter value for sql_id: 4cp821ufcwvgc
Enter value for category (DEFAULT):
Enter value for force_matching (false):
PL/SQL procedure successfully completed.
SQL> select count(*) from kso.skew where col3 = '01-jan-10';
  COUNT(*)
-------------------------------------------------------------
         0
1 row selected.

SQL> @find_sql
Enter value for sql_text: select count(*) from kso.skew where col3 = %
Enter value for sql_id:
SQL_ID        CHILD  PLAN_HASH EXECS AVG_ETIME AVG_LIO SQL_TEXT
------------- ----- ---------- ----- --------- ------- ----------------
4cp821ufcwvgc     0 167097056      1       .12      16 select count(*)
                                                       from skew where
                                                       col3 = '01-jan-10'
1 row selected.

SQL> @dcplan
Enter value for sql_id: 4cp821ufcwvgc
Enter value for child_no:
Enter value for format: BASIC +ROWS +COST +PREDICATE

PLAN_TABLE_OUTPUT
-----------------------------------------------------------------------
SQL_ID  4cp821ufcwvgc, child number 0
-----------------------------------------------------------------------
select count(*) from skew where col3 = '01-jan-10'
Plan hash value: 167097056
```

```
-----------------------------------------------------------------------
| Id  | Operation           | Name                | Rows | Cost (%CPU)|
-----------------------------------------------------------------------
|   0 | SELECT STATEMENT    |                     |      |    4 (100)|
|   1 |  SORT AGGREGATE     |                     |   1  |           |
|*  2 |    INDEX RANGE SCAN | SKEW_COL3_COL2_COL1 |   1  |    4   (0)|
-----------------------------------------------------------------------

Predicate Information (identified by operation id):
-----------------------------------------------------------------------
   2 - access("COL3"='01-jan-10')

Note
-----------------------------------------------------------------------
   - SQL profile PROFILE_4cp821ufcwvgc_moved used for this statement


23 rows selected.
```

As you can see, the move worked and the new plan is in effect for the original statement. Moving SQL Profiles from one statement to another is a very useful technique and very easy to do. It basically allows you to manipulate a SQL statement until you get the plan you want and then attach the plan to a statement you can't touch. There are a few restrictions you should be aware of, however:

- You cannot change the structure of the statement. Remember that SQL Profile hints are very specific when it comes to query block names. Anything that changes the query blocks does not work.

- You cannot change any object aliases. Remember that all hints must reference objects by alias names (if aliases exist in the statement). Adding, removing, or changing an alias name in your manipulated statement creates hints that won't match the original, and so they are silently ignored.

Using FORCE_MATCHING with SQL Profiles

As mentioned earlier, SQL Profiles have a FORCE_MATCHING attribute that allows you to create a Profile with the ability to ignore literals, similar to how the cursor_sharing parameter works—converting literals to bind variables. Therefore, if you have a SQL Profile that matches multiple statements that differ only in their use of literals, setting the FORCE_MATCHING attribute of the Profile to TRUE allows the Profile to be used for all the statements, not just the one SQL that matches exactly the SQL text used originally to create the Profile. This is a fantastic option in the case when you either can't or don't want to change the cursor_sharing parameter at the instance level. And, it is a feature unique to SQL Profiles in that Baselines don't use such an attribute.

There is one "gotcha" with the use of FORCE_MATCHING, however. This option works great if you're working with SQL that has been generated from a tool and is formulated with all literals. But, if the SQL you wish to create a FORCE_MATCHING Profile for includes both literal strings and bind variables, you'll run in to a bit of a problem, as shown in Listing 17-20. First, let's test two queries that differ only by the literal string used. Notice that the FORCE_MATCHING_SIGNATURE (from v$sql) for each query is the same.

Listing 17-20. SQL Profile Using the FORCE_MATCHING Restriction

```
SQL>
SQL>variable v1 varchar2(10)
SQL>exec :v1 := 'Sunday';

PL/SQL procedure successfully completed.
SQL>
SQL>select /* kmfmtst00 */ count(*) ct from km1 where mcal_year = 2011 ;
    CT
-------
    365


SQL>select /* kmfmtst00 */ count(*) ct from km1 where mcal_year = 2012 ;
    CT
-------
    366
SQL>
SQL>select /* getfm */ sql_id, plan_hash_value, force_matching_signature,
  2  substr(sql_text,1,200) sql_text
  3  from v$sql
  4  where upper(sql_text) like '%KMFMTST00%'
  5  and sql_text not like '%/* getfm */%' ;

SQL_ID        PLAN_HV    FORCE_MATCHING_SIGNATURE SQL_TEXT
------------- ---------- ------------------------ ------------------------
6sz5sqg1yu2u7 3996576519      9139782190997132164 select /* kmfmtst00 */
                                                   count(*) ct from km1
                                                   where mcal_year = 2011
88bgq57sjbtkt 3996576519      9139782190997132164 select /* kmfmtst00 */
                                                   count(*) ct from km1
                                                   where mcal_year = 2012
```

Now, let's make a change to the SQL to add a bind variable in addition to the literal. Notice what happens to the FORCE_MATCHING_SIGNATURE:

```
SQL>select /* kmfmtst00 */ count(*) ct from km1 where mcal_year = 2011
  2  and mcal_day_name = :v1 ;
    CT
-------
    52
SQL>select /* kmfmtst00 */ count(*) ct from km1 where mcal_year = 2012
  2  and mcal_day_name = :v1 ;
    CT
-------
    53
SQL>
SQL>select /* getfm */ sql_id, plan_hash_value, force_matching_signature,
  2  substr(sql_text,1,200) sql_text
  3  from v$sql
  4  where upper(sql_text) like '%KMFMTST00%'
  5  and sql_text not like '%/* getfm */%' ;
```

SQL_ID	PLAN_HV	FORCE_MATCHING_SIGNATURE	SQL_TEXT
6sz5sqg1yu2u7	3996576519	9139782190997132164	select /* kmfmtst00 */ count(*) ct from km1 where mcal_year = 2011
88bgq57sjbtkt	3996576519	9139782190997132164	select /* kmfmtst00 */ count(*) ct from km1 where mcal_year = 2012
48rxh2r545xqy	3996576519	5839486434578375421	select /* kmfmtst00 */ count(*) ct from km1 where mcal_year = 2011 and mcal_day_name = :v1
6q610fykrr4d3	3996576519	8791659410855071518	select /* kmfmtst00 */ count(*) ct from km1 where mcal_year = 2012 and mcal_day_name = :v1

As you can see, when we add a bind variable to the SQL, it causes FORCE_MATCHING_SIGNATURE to become unique, which means that if we were to create a SQL Profile and set the FORCE_MATCHING attribute to TRUE on the statement that uses both a bind variable and a literal, the Profile does not work. Well, actually, it does work, but only on the one specific statement we used to create the Profile. Just make sure to keep this in mind when creating a Profile with FORCE_MATCHING_SIGNATURE set.

SQL Profiles Wrap-up

So, to wrap up the section on SQL Profiles, let me state that I believe they provide a very powerful tool for controlling execution plans. The ability to match multiple statements via the FORCE_MATCHING attribute and the ability to attach any set of hints to a statement via the IMPORT_SQL_PROFILE procedure sets SQL Profiles apart as one of the most useful tools in our tool belt. But remember, they are a tool and should be used carefully and consciously. If you use a Profile to remedy a problem situation but you don't take time to go back and evaluate why there was a problem in the first place, you'll end up with a lot of patches over a leak that may continue to get worse and worse. Always try to find and fix the root cause of the problem so that you can disable or drop Profiles after the problem is corrected. In this way, you can be assured the leak has been fixed, not just patched.

SQL Plan Baselines

Oracle Database 11g provided a new method of dealing with plan instability. The third iteration of Oracle's hint-based mechanisms for influencing execution plans is called a SQL Plan Baseline (Baseline, for short). With Baselines, the design goal has morphed into eliminating backward movement ("performance regressions," as the Oracle documentation calls them)—in other words, not allowing a statement to switch to a plan that is significantly slower than the one it has already been executing. This new mechanism depends on Baselines, which look very much like SQL Profiles; in fact, they are actually stored in the same structure in the data dictionary.

Baselines are, at their core, a set of hints given a name and attached to a specific SQL statement. They are associated with a SQL statement using the same "normalized" text matching as Outlines and SQL Profiles. Here are some key features of Baselines:

- Baselines are used by default if they exist. There is a parameter to control whether they are used (OPTIMIZER_USE_SQL_PLAN_BASELINE). It is set to TRUE by default.

- Baselines are not created by default. So, like the older Outlines or SQL Profiles, you must do something to create them.

- The concept of categories has disappeared from Baselines.

- Unlike Outlines and Profiles, you can have multiple plans within a Baseline for each SQL statement. In an even more confusing twist, there's a concept of a preferred set of Baselines called the *fixed set*.

- One of the key features of Baselines is that they are the first hint-based mechanism to have knowledge of the plan that was used to create them. That is to say, they store a plan_hash_value along with the hints. So, if a Baseline is applied to a statement and the optimizer doesn't come up with the same plan_hash_value that it had when the Baseline was created, all the hints are thrown out and the optimization is redone without any of the hints.

■ **Note** It doesn't actually happen in this order, but the point is that this mechanism is very different from Outlines and Profiles, in which the optimizer has no idea what plan the hints were trying generate. With Baselines, it does.

- There is a view called dba_sql_plan_baselines that exposes the Baselines that have been created.

- Just like Outlines and SQL Profiles, Baselines apply to all instances in a RAC environment. They are not localized to a specific instance.

SQL PLAN MANAGEMENT INFRASTRUCTURE

Baselines are a part of the SQL Plan Management (SPM) infrastructure introduced in 11g. The concept of SPM is to have a Baseline associated with every statement that runs through the database. The optimizer then uses the Baselines to attempt to recreate the original plans from which they were created.

Every time a statement is parsed, the optimizer goes through its normal process, including coming up with an execution plan. It then checks to see whether the plan it just came up with is already stored in a Baseline. If it is, the optimizer uses that plan. If it's not, the optimizer uses the Baseline plan and stores the alternate plan in the history for later evaluation with the DBMS_SPM.EVOLVE_SQL_PLAN_BASELINE function (assuming that the database is configured to do this).

The approach of saving plans for later evaluation sounds like a great idea to limit instability resulting from unexpected plan changes. The only real downside to this approach is that seeding the Baselines can be a difficult task, and it is not done by default. Although the result is that many shops have not fully embraced this feature yet, I see it being used more and more, at least for key SQL statements.

You can do pretty much the same things with Baselines that you can do with Outlines and SQL Profiles. For example, you can find a list of them, see what hints are contained by them, see what their status is, see which SQL statements are using them, and so on. Listing 17-21 shows a quick example using a few scripts from the example download.

Listing 17-21. Using Baselines

```
SQL> @find_sql_using_baseline
Enter value for sql_text:
Enter value for sql_id:
Enter value for plan_hash_value:
SQL_ID         PLAN_HASH SQL_PLAN_BASELINE                 AVG_ETIME SQL_TEXT
------------- ---------- ------------------------------- --------- -------------------------------
04s94zftphcgb 2650913906 SQL_PLAN_3mmrpt1hutfzs7456d135        .00 select sum(pk_col) from
12417fbdsfaxt 2333976600 SQL_PLAN_0j493a65j2bamc0e39d1a        .01 SELECT SQL_HANDLE FROM DB
2us663zxp440c  329476029 SQL_PLAN_6dny19g5cvmaj059cc611        .04 /* OracleOEM */ select at
3972rvxu3knn3 3007952250 SQL_PLAN_05a32329hrft07347ab53        .00 delete from sdo_geor_ddl_
              3007952250 SQL_PLAN_05a32329hrft07347ab53        .00 delete from sdo_geor_ddl_
62m44bym1fdhs 3137838658 SQL_PLAN_2jvcuyb2j5t1g4d67c3d9        .00 SELECT ID FROM WWV_FLOW_M
              3137838658 SQL_PLAN_2jvcuyb2j5t1g4d67c3d9        .00 SELECT ID FROM WWV_FLOW_M
6abthk1u14yb7 2848324471 SQL_PLAN_5y7pbdmj87bz3ea394c8e        .00 SELECT VERSION FROM V$INS
              2848324471 SQL_PLAN_5y7pbdmj87bz3ea394c8e        .00 SELECT VERSION FROM V$INS
9xw644rurr1nk 2848324471 SQL_PLAN_ba7pvw56m6m1cea394c8e        .00 SELECT REGEXP_REPLACE(VER
aukfj0ur6962z 2366097979 SQL_PLAN_adx60prqvaaqhf8e55c8a        .00 SELECT VALUE V FROM WWV_F
              2366097979 SQL_PLAN_adx60prqvaaqhf8e55c8a        .00 SELECT VALUE V FROM WWV_F
b1um9gxnf22a3 1475283301 SQL_PLAN_1kj53db9w5gzga4a6b425        .00 select count(*) from sqll
d56r760yr1tgt 2650913906 SQL_PLAN_dn32tuq14sj5q7456d135        .01 select sum(pk_col) from
f1b04310fhv7a 2650913906 SQLID_AR5DZ1STDPFC6_2650913906        .00  select sum(pk_col) from
fg5u3ydzcqzvw 3291240065 SQL_PLAN_3ndjuqr0f58a716c3d523        .03 select spb.sql_handle, sp
              3291240065 SQL_PLAN_3ndjuqr0f58a716c3d523        .03 select spb.sql_handle, sp

17 rows selected.

SQL> @baselines
Enter value for sql_text: %skew%
Enter value for name:
Enter value for plan_name:
SQL_HANDLE        PLAN_NAME          SQL_TEXT             ENABLED ACC FI
----------------- ------------------ -------------------- ------- --- --
SYS_SQL_17fbdf94 SQL_PLAN_1gyyzkj90 select avg(pk_col)   YES     NO  NO
                 SQL_PLAN_1gyyzkj90 select avg(pk_col)   YES     NO  NO
SYS_SQL_36bf1c88 SQL_PLAN_3dgswj3vr select avg(pk_col)   YES     NO  NO
                 SQL_PLAN_3dgswj3vr select avg(pk_col)   NO      YES NO
SYS_SQL_39cef5c8 SQL_PLAN_3mmrpt1hu select sum(pk_col)   YES     YES NO
SYS_SQL_3a363ab5 SQL_PLAN_3ndjuqr0f select spb.sql_hand  YES     YES NO
SYS_SQL_3c55382b SQL_PLAN_3sp9s5cpk select sum(pk_col)   YES     YES NO
SYS_SQL_94dc89c0 SQL_PLAN_99r49s08j select avg(pk_col)   YES     NO  NO
                 SQL_PLAN_99r49s08j select avg(pk_col)   YES     NO  NO
SYS_SQL_d0686c14 SQL_PLAN_d0u3c2kat select avg(pk_col)   YES     YES NO
SYS_SQL_da0c59d5 SQL_PLAN_dn32tuq14 select sum(pk_col)   YES     YES NO
SYS_SQL_f1140cdd DODA               select sql_id, chil  YES     YES NO
SYS_SQL_f5cd6b7b SQLID_F1B04310FHV7 select sum(pk_col)   YES     YES NO

13 rows selected.
```

```
SQL> @baseline_hints
Enter value for baseline_plan_name: SQLID_F1B04310FHV7A_2650913906
OUTLINE_HINTS
----------------------------------------------------------------------IGNORE_OPTIM_EMBEDDED_HINTS
OPTIMIZER_FEATURES_ENABLE('12.1.0.1')
DB_VERSION('12.1.0.1')
ALL_ROWS
OUTLINE_LEAF(@"SEL$1")
INDEX_SS(@"SEL$1" "SKEW"@"SEL$1" ("SKEW"."COL2" "SKEW"."COL1"))

6 rows selected.
```

The naming of Baselines is not particularly friendly. The sql_handle is a unique identifier for a SQL statement whereas the sql_plan_name is a unique identifier for a plan. By the way, the sql_plan_name is also called sql_plan_baseline in the v$sql view.

Creating SQL Baselines

There are many ways to create Baselines. They can be created automatically for every statement that is executed by setting the OPTIMIZER_CAPTURE_SQL_PLAN_BASELINES parameter to TRUE. They can also be created for statements in a SQL Tuning Set using the LOAD_PLANS_FROM_SQLSET function, or they can be migrated from Outlines using the MIGRATE_STORED_OUTLINE function. These mechanisms are primarily designed for seeding Baselines when doing migrations.

Creating a Baseline for an individual statement that is already in the cursor cache can be accomplished via the DBMS_SPM.LOAD_PLANS_FROM_CURSOR_CACHE function. All the function needs is a sql_id and a plan_hash_value. Optionally, a parameter can be used to define the baseline as FIXED. If it's FIXED then it gets priority over any other Baselines for that statement, except other FIXED Baselines. Confused? Well, it's not exactly the most straightforward setup. Keeping it simple, I'd think one FIXED Baseline is plenty. After all, you're looking to minimize plan changes. So, with that said, let's look at an example of creating a Baseline for a single statement in Listing 17-22.

Listing 17-22. Creating a Baseline for a Single Statement

```
SQL> select sum(pk_col) from skew where col1=666666;

SUM(PK_COL)
-----------
  517333312


SQL> @find_sql
Enter value for sql_text: %66666%
Enter value for sql_id:
SQL_ID         CHILD  PLAN_HASH EXECS AVG_ETIME AVG_LIO SQL_TEXT
-------------  -----  ---------- ----- --------- ------- ------------------
dv1qm9crkf281      0 2650913906     1       .08      45 select sum(pk_col)
                                                        from skew
                                                        col1=666666

SQL> @create_baseline
Enter value for sql_id: dv1qm9crkf281
Enter value for plan_hash_value: 2650913906
```

```
Enter value for fixed (NO):
Enter value for enabled (YES):
Enter value for plan_name (ID_sqlid_planhashvalue):
Baseline SQLID_DV1QM9CRKF281_2650913906 created.

SQL> select sql_handle, plan_name, sql_text
  2  from dba_sql_plan_baselines where sql_text like '%66666%';
SQL_HANDLE               PLAN_NAME                        SQL_TEXT
------------------------ -------------------------------- --------------------
SYS_SQL_8a22ceb091365064 SQLID_DV1QM9CRKF281_2650913906 select sum(pk_col)
                                                                      from skew

1 row selected.

SQL> select sum(pk_col) from skew where col1=666666;
SUM(PK_COL)
-----------
  517333312

1 row selected.

SQL> /
SUM(PK_COL)
-----------
  517333312

1 row selected.

SQL> @dcplan
Enter value for sql_id: dv1qm9crkf281
Enter value for child_no:
Enter value for format: BASIC +ROWS +COST +PREDICATE

PLAN_TABLE_OUTPUT
----------------------------------------------------------------------------
SQL_ID  dv1qm9crkf281, child number 1
----------------------------------------------------------------------------
select sum(pk_col) from skew where col1=666666
Plan hash value: 2650913906
```

Id	Operation	Name	Rows	Cost (%CPU)
0	SELECT STATEMENT			34 (100)
1	SORT AGGREGATE		1	
2	TABLE ACCESS BY INDEX ROWID	SKEW	32	34 (0)
* 3	INDEX SKIP SCAN	SKEW_COL2_COL1	32	5 (0)

```
Predicate Information (identified by operation id):
---------------------------------------------------------------------------
   3 - access("COL1"=666666)
       filter("COL1"=666666)
Note
---------------------------------------------------------------------------
   - SQL plan baseline SQLID_DV1QM9CRKF281_2650913906 used for this statement

46 rows selected.
```

Listing 17-22 shows the use of the create_baseline.sql script that creates a Baseline on an existing statement in the shared pool. The script also renames the Baseline to something more meaningful (SQLID_sqlid_planhash by default). This renaming works only in 11gR2 and above, by the way; 11gR1 allows you to rename a Baseline, but there is a bug that causes a statement that uses a renamed Baseline to fail. Consequently, the create_baseline.sql script does not rename Baselines if the version is not 11.2 or higher.

Creating SQL Baselines from AWR

Baselines can also be used to retrieve a plan from the AWR history, although it's not quite as straightforward as getting the plan from the cursor cache. Listing 17-23 shows an of example of doing this with the create_baseline_awr.sql script.

Listing 17-23. The create_baseline_awr.sql Script

```
SQL> @find_sql_awr
Enter value for sql_text: %cursor%skew%
Enter value for sql_id:

SQL_ID        SQL_TEXT
------------- -------------------------------------------------------------
3ggjbbd2varq2 select /*+ cursor_sharing_exact */ avg(pk_col) from skew
                            where col1 = 1
48up9g2j8dkct select /*+ cursor_sharing_exact */ avg(pk_col) from skew
                            where col1 = 136135
2z6s4zb5pxp9k select /*+ opt_param('cursor_sharing' 'exact') */ avg(pk_col)
                            from skew where
13krz9pwd6a88 select /*+ opt_param('cursor_sharing=force') */ avg(pk_col)
                            from skew

4 rows selected.

SQL> @dplan_awr
Enter value for sql_id: 3ggjbbd2varq2
Enter value for plan_hash_value:
PLAN_TABLE_OUTPUT
---------------------------------------------------------------------------
SQL_ID 3ggjbbd2varq2
---------------------------------------------------------------------------
select /*+ cursor_sharing_exact */ avg(pk_col) from skew where col1 = 1
Plan hash value: 568322376
```

```
-----------------------------------------------------------------------
| Id  | Operation          | Name | Rows  | Bytes | Cost (%CPU)| Time     |
-----------------------------------------------------------------------
|   0 | SELECT STATEMENT   |      |       |       | 28366 (100)|          |
|   1 |  SORT AGGREGATE    |      |     1 |    24 |            |          |
|   2 |   TABLE ACCESS FULL| SKEW | 3149K |   72M | 28366  (1) | 00:05:41 |
-----------------------------------------------------------------------

15 rows selected.

SQL> @find_sql
Enter value for sql_text:
Enter value for sql_id: 3ggjbbd2varq2

no rows selected

SQL> -- so it's not in the cursor cache
SQL>
SQL> @create_baseline_awr
Enter value for SQL_ID: 48up9g2j8dkct
Enter value for PLAN_HASH_VALUE: 568322376
Enter value for fixed (NO):
Enter value for enabled (YES):
Enter value for plan_name (ID_sqlid_planhashvalue):

Baseline SQLID_48UP9G2J8DKCT_568322376 created.

SQL>
SQL> select sql_handle, plan_name, sql_text
  2  from dba_sql_plan_baselines where plan_name like 'SQLID_48UP9G2J8DKCT_568322376';

SQL_HANDLE                   PLAN_NAME
---------------------------  -------------------------------
SYS_SQL_d52c57087080269e     SQLID_48UP9G2J8DKCT_568322376

SQL_TEXT
-----------------------------------------------------------
select /*+ cursor_sharing_exact */ avg(pk_col)

1 row selected.
```

Evolving SQL Baselines

Whether you've set the OPTIMIZER_CAPTURE_SQL_PLAN_BASELINES parameter to TRUE to create Baselines for every statement automatically or you are creating them manually, what happens when Baselines need to be updated? Because Baselines are accepted and put into use, the plan "locked in" by a Baseline may, over time, have different plans generated for it. Those plans may be better or they may be worse, but they are simply added to the statement's plan history until they can be verified and not used. This is the whole idea behind plan stability; plans won't change, but sometimes better plans are developed and must be evaluated, verified, and evolved to be used.

Plans that have been generated and stored in a statement's plan history but not yet accepted for use can be verified using the DBMS_SPM.EVOLVE_SQL_PLAN_BASELINE function. Each unaccepted plan is executed, and its performance is compared with that of the existing accepted plan. To make it a fair comparison, the conditions in effect at the time the unaccepted plan was added are used (things like instance parameters, bind variables, and so forth). If the new plan's performance exceeds the current one, it is accepted and added to the Baseline. Listing 17-24 shows an example of an Evolve SQL Plan Baseline Report.

Listing 17-24. An Evolve SQL Plan Baseline Report

```
SQL> -- Check the status of plans in plan history.
SQL> select plan_name, enabled, accepted from dba_sql_plan_baselines;

PLAN_NAME                       ENABLED ACCEPTED
------------------------------- ------- --------
SYS_SQL_PLAN_d52c57084a620f25   YES     YES
SYS_SQL_PLAN_d52c57087080269e   YES     NO

SQL> var report clob;
SQL> exec :report := dbms_spm.evolve_sql_plan_baseline();

PL/SQL procedure successfully completed.
SQL> print :report

REPORT
-------------------------------------------------------------------------
                        Evolve SQL Plan Baseline Report
-------------------------------------------------------------------------

Inputs:
-------------------------------------------------------------------------
  SQL_HANDLE =
  PLAN_NAME  =
  TIME_LIMIT = DBMS_SPM.AUTO_LIMIT
  VERIFY     = YES
  COMMIT     = YES

Plan: SYS_SQL_PLAN_d52c57087080269e
-------------------------------------------------------------------------
  Plan was verified: Time used .1 seconds.
  Passed performance criterion: Compound improvement ratio >= 10.13
  Plan was changed to an accepted plan.
                        Baseline Plan    Test Plan      Improv. Ratio
                        -------------    ---------      -------------
  Execution Status:       COMPLETE        COMPLETE
  Rows Processed:              960             960
  Elapsed Time(ms):             19              15                1.27
  CPU Time(ms):                 18              15                 1.2
  Buffer Gets:                1188             116               10.24
  Disk Reads:                    0               0
  Direct Writes:                 0               0
  Fetches:                       0               0
  Executions:                    1               1
```

```
--------------------------------------------------------------------
                            Report Summary
--------------------------------------------------------------------
Number of SQL plan baselines verified: 1.

SQL> -- Check the status of plans in plan history to verify acceptance.

SQL> select plan_name, enabled, accepted from dba_sql_plan_baselines;

PLAN_NAME                        ENABLED ACCEPTED
------------------------------   ------- --------
SYS_SQL_PLAN_d52c57084a620f25    YES     YES
SYS_SQL_PLAN_d52c57087080269e    YES     YES
```

You can also evolve an unaccepted plan from plan history by using STA. If you have access to Enterprise Manager, using STA from that tool is likely the quickest and easiest way to do this. But, if you don't have access to Enterprise Manager or if you just like having a bit more control over the process, here are the basic steps to do it from the command line (in other words, SQL*Plus):

1. Create a tuning task for a single SQL statement or for multiple statements. See create_tuning_task.sql.

   - There are actually three parts to this: creating the tuning task, executing it, and then reporting on it.

     - DBMS_SQLTUNE.CREATE_TUNING_TASK

     - DBMS_SQLTUNE.EXECUTE_TUNING_TASK

     - DBMS_SQLTUNE.REPORT_TUNING_TASK

   - Note the default time limit for the execute part is 30 minutes, so you may want to reduce that (the create_tuning_task.sql script prompts you for a value in seconds). By the way, the reason it can take so long is that the advisor can actually execute parts of the statement to get better estimates of the number of rows returned by a particular step.

   - Primary recommendations are often to accept a SQL Profile, but there may be other recommendations such as creating indexes and so forth.

   - The report output shows the old plan and the proposed new plan.

2. Review recommendations.

   - Never, ever, ever (I really mean it) blindly accept a recommendation.

   - Look at the new plan as proposed by REPORT_TUNING_TASK.

   - Specifically, evaluate the proposed plan and, if possible and if time permits, test it further.

3. Prepare a script to disable the SQL Profile to be created. See disable_sql_profile.sql.

   - You do have a back-out plan right?

   - It is very easy to disable a profile. However, once a plan is selected, it is not changed. The execution continues to use that plan until it finishes.

4. Accept the SQL Profile. See `accept_tuning_task.sql` (or `accept_sql_profile.sql`).

   - `DBMS_SQLTUNE.ACCEPT_TUNING_TASK`

5. Confirm the performance improvement. See `find_sql.sql`, `find_sql_stats.sql`, `dcplan.sql`.

   - Existing active cursors continue processing.

   - A new child cursor is created using the Profile, and subsequent executions use it.

   - You can compare the performance of the old plan and the new one.

6. Remember, SQL Profiles do not lock the execution plan.

7. Figure out why the plan went crazy in the first place.

Plan evolution can be done manually or it can be automated by scheduling it to run during a maintenance window. But, allowing automatic evolution of plans can be a bit risky in that you forgo any oversight on your part. I'm not that trusting, but if you're comfortable, go for it.

Automatic Plan Evolution in 12c

Beginning in 12c, automatic plan evolution has been enhanced to be done by the SQL Plan Management Evolve Advisor. This advisor is an AutoTask named `SYS_AUTO_SPM_EVOLVE_TASK` and it operates during the nightly maintenance window to evolve unaccepted plans automatically. Because the maintenance window is time limited by default, the unaccepted plans are ranked from oldest to newest, then the process attempts to evolve as many plans as possible before the end of the maintenance window.

Any unaccepted plans that are evaluated to perform better than any existing accepted plans in their SQL plan Baseline are accepted automatically—without any intervention from you. But, if an unaccepted plan doesn't measure up to current performance measurements, it remains unaccepted and is held for at least another 30 days before the AutoTask job tries to evolve it again (but only if the `LAST_EXECUTED` date has been updated to indicate the statement was run within that 30-day period).

You can still evolve unaccepted plans manually or through Enterprise Manager, but using the `DBMS_SPM.EVOLVE_SQL_PLAN_BASELINE` method as described in Listing 17-24 should be changed to use the evolve advisor, because this procedure has been deprecated. Instead, the steps to evolve plans manually include the following:

1. Use `DBMS_SPM.CREATE_EVOLVE_TASK` to create the evolve task for the plan you want to evolve.

2. Use `DBMS_SPM.EXECUTE_EVOLVE_TASK` with the task name from the create evolve task step.

3. Use `DBMS_SPM.REPORT_EVOLVE_TASK` to report how the evolve task turned out.

4. If you agree with the report findings and wish to accept the plan, use `DBMS_SPM.ACCEPT_SQL_PLAN_BASELINE` to accept it manually.

Furthermore, 12c has changed things such that not only does the SQL Plan Baseline contain the complete set of hints needed to reproduce a specific plan, but also the actual execution plan itself is recorded when the plan is evolved and added to the Baseline. For any plans that had Baselines present from 11g, the actual execution plan is captured and added to the baseline the first time it is executed in 12c. Keep in mind that having the actual execution plan and being able to review it isn't the same as being able to reproduce the plan, the hints are still needed for that, but it does provide a guide so that if the plan can't be reproduced, you can see what it "should" be.

So Baselines are obviously the wave of the future, but they still lack some of the flexibility of SQL Profiles when it comes to applying custom controls to statements. They can attempt to lock in plans from the cursor cache or from AWR history, but they cannot import arbitrary hints or apply to many statements at a time like SQL Profiles can via the FORCE_MATCHING attribute. However, they can collect alternate plans for later evaluation and they are designed to store a large set of plans in an attempt to keep any plan from changing without warning.

SQL Patches

One final option you have to help exert a bit of influence over SQL execution plans is to use a SQL Patch. Using a SQL Patch, you can inject a hint (or set of hints) into a SQL statement that you otherwise cannot touch. This could be in the case of vendor-supplied code or even for your own SQL when it is embedded in an application that can't be modified as quickly as you may need. The documented use of a SQL Patch is that it is a SQL manageability object intended to be generated by the SQL Repair Advisor to work around a plan that causes a failure. Generally speaking, the SQL Patch tells the optimizer to adjust the plan in some way or to avoid a particular optimization so that the failure no longer occurs.

But, even though the documentation doesn't mention it, you can create SQL Patches yourself. Any SQL Patch you create can provide a set of hints that you want the optimizer to use during parse time for a particular query. The end result is that you can inject hints into code that you otherwise couldn't touch. To create a SQL Patch manually, use DBMS_SQLDIAG_INTERNAL.I_CREATE_PATCH. Using the function, specify the query text you wish to patch as well as a set of hints to apply to that query. Listing 17-25 shows a very simple example of using a SQL Patch to add a GATHER_PLAN_STATISTICS hint to a SQL statement that is performing poorly. We want to inject the hint to be able to get more detailed row-source execution statistics when it executes to help our problem diagnosis efforts.

Listing 17-25. Using a SQL Patch to Add a GATHER_PLAN_STATISTICS Hint

```
SQL>-- The setting of the statistics_level = TYPICAL.
SQL>-- No rowsource execution statistics will be captured.
SQL>
SQL>show parameter statistics_level
NAME_COL_PLUS_SHOW_PARAM        TYPE         VALUE_COL_PLUS_SHOW_PARAM
------------------------------ ----------- -------------------------------
statistics_level               string       TYPICAL
SQL>
SQL>select count(*) from class_sales ;

  COUNT(*)
----------
  90000000

SQL>select * from table(dbms_xplan.display_cursor(null,null,'ALLSTATS LAST')) ;
PLAN_TABLE_OUTPUT
-----------------------------------------------------------
SQL_ID  6fpdvs2gy4vu3, child number 0
-----------------------------------------------------------
select count(*) from class_sales
Plan hash value: 3145879882
```

```
-----------------------------------------------------------
| Id  | Operation                   | Name        | E-Rows |
-----------------------------------------------------------
|   0 | SELECT STATEMENT            |             |        |
|   1 |  SORT AGGREGATE             |             |     1  |
|   2 |   TABLE ACCESS STORAGE FULL | CLASS_SALES |   90M  |
-----------------------------------------------------------
```

Note

    - Warning: basic plan statistics not available. These are only collected when:
       * hint 'gather_plan_statistics' is used for the statement or
       * parameter 'statistics_level' is set to 'ALL', at session or system level

```
SQL> -- Create a SQL Patch to inject the hint
SQL> begin
  2  dbms_sqldiag_internal.i_create_patch(
  3  sql_text => 'select count(*) from class_sales',
  4  hint_text => 'gather_plan_statistics',
  5  name => 'PATCH_KMTEST1',
  6  category => 'DEFAULT');
  7  end;
  8  /

PL/SQL procedure successfully completed.
SQL> -- Run the SQL again and try to display the plan statistics.
SQL>select count(*) from class_sales ;

  COUNT(*)
----------
  90000000

Elapsed: 00:00:04.46
SQL>select * from table(dbms_xplan.display_cursor(null,null,'ALLSTATS LAST')) ;

PLAN_TABLE_OUTPUT
-----------------------------------------------------------
SQL_ID  6fpdvs2gy4vu3, child number 1
-----------------------------------------------------------
select count(*) from class_sales
Plan hash value: 3145879882
```

```
--------------------------------------------------------------------------
| Id  | Operation                   | Name        | E-Rows | A-Rows | Buffers|
--------------------------------------------------------------------------
|   0 | SELECT STATEMENT            |             |        |     1  |   18K  |
|   1 |  SORT AGGREGATE             |             |     1  |     1  |   18K  |
|   2 |   TABLE ACCESS STORAGE FULL | CLASS_SALES |   90M  |   90M  |   18K  |
--------------------------------------------------------------------------
```

Note

    - SQL patch "PATCH_KMTEST1" used for this statement

As you can see by the Note and by the fact that the ALLSTATS LAST format parameter didn't generate an error, the Patch we applied to add the GATHER_PLAN_STATISTICS hint was used. After we get the information we want, we can drop the Patch (using DBMS_SQLDIAG.DROP_SQL_PATCH) or we can disable it (DBMS_SQLDIAG.ALTER_SQL_PATCH).

SQL Patches give you the ability to inject a hint, or set of hints, quickly into a SQL statement with relative ease. They are tied to a specific SQL text, so they are like Baselines in that aspect and not as flexible as SQL Profiles. However, if you need a quick way to hint a SQL statement you can't otherwise touch, they can be a great option.

Hint-Based Plan Control Mechanisms Wrap-up

Of the options available, I believe that SQL Profiles are the most straightforward and functional. They have the advantage of force matching, which allows a single SQL Profile to apply to multiple SQL statements by ignoring literals (much like cursor_sharing=force; in other words, the "force" matching). They also have a built-in procedure (DBMS_SQLTUNE.IMPORT_SQL_PROFILE) that allows any set of hints to be attached to any SQL statement. You can similarly attach a set of hints using SQL Patches, but because they must be attached to a specific SQL text, they are not as flexible as Profiles. Both Profiles and Patches are extremely powerful tools that basically allow you to apply any hint to any statement, even if you don't have access to the code. Baselines don't allow you to apply hints in the same manner and are thus a disadvantage in that way over Profiles or Patches. Baselines do store the original plan_hash_value, which means they can determine whether the hints are still generating the original plan. But, until 12c, they have no way of getting back to the original plan in cases when the hints fail to do their job. Their only option at that point is to throw away the hints all together and try again. In 12c, the actual execution plan is stored in the Baseline, too, so instead of just having a set of hints that "should" get you back to the same plan, you have the actual plan itself to refer to.

Summary

There are several things that contribute to plan instability and several techniques that can be applied to correct and stabilize plan performance. SQL Profiles and SQL Patches provide an extremely valuable tool in situations when the need is urgent and the ability to change the code is nonexistent. They also have the advantage of being very specific in their scope (they can be targeted at a single statement without the possibility of having negative effects on other statements). Baselines can also be very useful if you are using 11g and above. Although they are not as flexible as Profiles or Patches, they do have the advantage of knowing what plan they are trying to recreate. They also have the capability of keeping a list of alternate plans that can be evaluated later. STA Profiles can be useful for identifying better plans and pointing out problem areas, but I am not a fan of implementing them in most cases. In general, I would rather have a mechanism that applies directive hints that lists specific objects and join methods rather than fudge factors. All these types of hint-based control mechanisms, though, should be considered temporary fixes. Although they may work well for an extended period of time while a more permenant solution is contemplated, they really should be considered a temporary fix while appropriate statistics-gathering methodology is implemented or code is changed to make appropriate use of literals or while any other long-term solution is put in place.

From a philosophical standpoint, I strongly believe that consistency is more important than absolute speed. So when a choice must be made, I always favor slightly reduced but consistent performance over anything that doesn't provide that consistency.

Miscellaneous SQL Constructs

The SQL language offers a wide variety of constructs—from the very simple to the extremely complex. In this book, we looked at many examples that demonstrate the core topics. This chapter is devoted to a review of several use cases for constructs that should help round out your knowledge.

Conditional Logic Constructs

Oracle supports many different ways to implement conditional IF–THEN–ELSE logic in SQL statements. Sometimes you need to determine conditionally which column data are emitted in the column list. Sometimes you need to determine which rows are returned by having a more complex condition in the predicate. Wherever you need to apply conditional logic, you have several constructs from which to choose that I describe in this section:

- DECODE
- CASE
- NVL, NVL2
- COALESCE
- NULLIF

Using DECODE

DECODE is a proprietary Oracle function that provides a simple conditional construct. Prior to Oracle version 8.1.6, when the CASE statement was introduced, DECODE was the only way to implement conditional logic. DECODE is limited to use with equality operators, so a CASE statement is certainly more flexible. But, DECODE can be useful for writing short, simple logical comparisons, as shown in Listing 18-1.

Listing 18-1. Using a Simple DECODE Construct

```
SQL> select ename, decode (deptno, 10, 'Accounting',
  2  20, 'Research',
  3  30, 'Sales',
  4  'Unknown') as dept
  5  from scott.emp
  6  where rownum < 6 ;
```

```
ENAME      DEPT
---------- ----------
SMITH      Research
ALLEN      Sales
WARD       Sales
JONES      Research
MARTIN     Sales
```

One difference between DECODE and CASE is that DECODE does not expect datatype consistency in the conditions and resulting statements, as shown in Listing 18-2.

Listing 18-2. DECODE Using Different Datatype Comparisons

```
SQL>select decode(42,42,1,
  2                  '42','2',
  3                  3) tst
  4  from dual ;

       TST
----------
         1

1 row selected.

SQL>select case 42 when 42   then 1
  2                 when '42' then '2'
  3                 else 3    end tst
  4  from dual ;
            when '42' then '2'
                   *
ERROR at line 2:
ORA-00932: inconsistent datatypes: expected NUMBER got CHAR
```

Although this isn't a big factor most of the time, it is something to keep in mind. Also note that this datatype mismatch oversight on the part of DECODE is only applicable for number and string datatypes. If we try to use a date datatype with a number or string, we get the same error as CASE.

Another thing to keep in mind about DECODE is how it handles null values. If you use DECODE(null,null,'NULL','NOT NULL'), the answer is 'NULL'. This is different from most null comparisons in that null usually does not equal null (in other words, null = null does not match). In reality, using DECODE for null checks isn't really the proper function to use because NVL, NVL2, or CASE is actually better. Generally speaking, CASE is a better, more flexible, easier to read alternative, but DECODE remains an old standby for simple logic.

Using CASE

A CASE statement is used to choose from a set of conditions to execute a corresponding statement when a condition is matched. There are two types of CASE statements: simple and searched. For simple CASE statements, a single expression is evaluated and compared with several possible values, as shown in Listing 18-3.

Listing 18-3. A Simple CASE Statement

```
SQL>create table grades (
  2   student_id number,
  3   subject_id number,
  4   grade      char(1));

Table created.

SQL>insert into grades values (1,1,'A');

SQL>insert into grades values (2,1,'C');

SQL>insert into grades values (3,1,'A');

SQL>insert into grades values (4,1,'D');

SQL>insert into grades values (5,1,'F');

SQL>insert into grades values (6,1,'B');

SQL>insert into grades values (7,1,'C');

SQL>insert into grades values (8,1,'C');

SQL>select student_id,
  2   case grade
  3   when 'A' then 'Very Good'
  4   when 'B' then 'Good'
  5   when 'C' then 'Fair'
  6   when 'D' then 'Poor'
  7   when 'F' then 'Failure'
  8   else 'Withdrawn' end as grade
  9   from grades;

STUDENT_ID GRADE
---------- ---------
         1 Very Good
         2 Fair
         3 Very Good
         4 Poor
         5 Failure
         6 Good
         7 Fair
         8 Fair

8 rows selected.
```

A searched CASE statement differs from the simple type in that it allows for more complex conditions to be evaluated. With a searched CASE statement, multiple—possibly differing—Boolean expressions are evaluated, and the first one with a value of TRUE is chosen, as shown in Listing 18-4.

Listing 18-4. A Searched CASE **Statement**

```
SQL>select student_id,
  2   case when grade <= 'B' then 'Honor Roll'
  3        when grade = 'F' then 'Needs Tutoring'
  4        else 'Satisfactory' end grade_category
  5  from grades ;

STUDENT_ID GRADE_CATEGORY
---------- --------------
         1 Honor Roll
         2 Satisfactory
         3 Honor Roll
         4 Satisfactory
         5 Needs Tutoring
         6 Honor Roll
         7 Satisfactory
         8 Satisfactory

8 rows selected.
```

In both the simple and searched CASE constructs, the conditions are evaluated sequentially from top to bottom and execution halts after the first match is found. This means if more than one condition is TRUE, only the first result action is taken.

CASE statements can be used throughout a SQL statement and not just in the SELECT column list, as shown in the previous two listings. One way to use a CASE statement is to eliminate repeating accesses on the same table (or tables), as shown in Listing 18-5.

Listing 18-5. Using CASE to Eliminate Repeated Table Accesses

```
-- Original SQL using UNION
select customer_id, order_total, 0 as disc_rate
from
(select c.customer_id,  nvl(sum(o.order_total),0) as order_total
   from oe.customers c, oe.orders o
 where c.customer_id = o.customer_id(+)
 group by c.customer_id ) t2
where order_total = 0
union
select customer_id, order_total, .1 as disc_rate
from
(select c.customer_id,  nvl(sum(o.order_total),0) as order_total
   from oe.customers c, oe.orders o
 where c.customer_id = o.customer_id
 group by c.customer_id ) t2
where order_total > 0 and order_total < 100000
union
select customer_id, order_total, .15 as disc_rate
from
(select c.customer_id,  nvl(sum(o.order_total),0) as order_total
   from oe.customers c, oe.orders o
 where c.customer_id = o.customer_id
```

```
 group by c.customer_id ) t2
where order_total >= 100000 and order_total <= 500000
union
select customer_id, order_total, .2 as disc_rate
from
(select c.customer_id,  nvl(sum(o.order_total),0) as order_total
  from oe.customers c, oe.orders o
 where c.customer_id = o.customer_id
 group by c.customer_id ) t2
where order_total > 500000
;

SQL>@dcplan
Enter value for sql_id: c7ngvkwthdaak
Enter value for child_no:
Enter value for format: BASIC +PREDICATE +ROWS

PLAN_TABLE_OUTPUT
-----------------------------------------------------------------
Plan hash value: 729697565


-----------------------------------------------------------------
| Id  | Operation                     | Name           | Rows  |
-----------------------------------------------------------------
|   0 | SELECT STATEMENT              |                |       |
|   1 |  SORT UNIQUE                  |                |    10 |
|   2 |   UNION-ALL                   |                |       |
|*  3 |    FILTER                     |                |       |
|   4 |     SORT GROUP BY NOSORT      |                |     1 |
|   5 |      MERGE JOIN OUTER         |                |   377 |
|   6 |       INDEX FULL SCAN         | CUSTOMERS_PK   |   319 |
|*  7 |       SORT JOIN               |                |   105 |
|   8 |        TABLE ACCESS BY INDEX ROWID| ORDERS     |   105 |
|*  9 |         INDEX RANGE SCAN      | ORD_CUSTOMER_IX|   105 |
|* 10 |    FILTER                     |                |       |
|  11 |     SORT GROUP BY NOSORT      |                |     3 |
|  12 |      TABLE ACCESS BY INDEX ROWID| ORDERS       |   105 |
|  13 |       INDEX FULL SCAN         | ORD_CUSTOMER_IX|   105 |
|* 14 |    FILTER                     |                |       |
|  15 |     SORT GROUP BY NOSORT      |                |     3 |
|  16 |      TABLE ACCESS BY INDEX ROWID| ORDERS       |   105 |
|  17 |       INDEX FULL SCAN         | ORD_CUSTOMER_IX|   105 |
|* 18 |    FILTER                     |                |       |
|  19 |     SORT GROUP BY NOSORT      |                |     3 |
|  20 |      TABLE ACCESS BY INDEX ROWID| ORDERS       |   105 |
|  21 |       INDEX FULL SCAN         | ORD_CUSTOMER_IX|   105 |
-----------------------------------------------------------------
```

527

Predicate Information (identified by operation id):

```
   3 - filter(NVL(SUM("O"."ORDER_TOTAL"),0)=0)
   7 - access("C"."CUSTOMER_ID"="O"."CUSTOMER_ID")
       filter("C"."CUSTOMER_ID"="O"."CUSTOMER_ID")
   9 - access("O"."CUSTOMER_ID">0)
  10 - filter((NVL(SUM("O"."ORDER_TOTAL"),0)>0 AND
              NVL(SUM("O"."ORDER_TOTAL"),0)<100000))
  14 - filter((NVL(SUM("O"."ORDER_TOTAL"),0)>=100000 AND
              NVL(SUM("O"."ORDER_TOTAL"),0)<=500000))
  18 - filter(NVL(SUM("O"."ORDER_TOTAL"),0)>500000)
```

```
-- Rewritten SQL using CASE
select c.customer_id, nvl(sum(o.order_total),0) as order_total,
case when nvl(sum(o.order_total),0) = 0 then 0
    when nvl(sum(o.order_total),0) < 100000 then .1
    when nvl(sum(o.order_total),0) between 100000 and 500000 then .15
    when nvl(sum(o.order_total),0) > 500000 then .2
    else 0 end
as disc_rate
from oe.customers c, oe.orders o
where c.customer_id = o.customer_id(+)
group by c.customer_id
;
```

PLAN_TABLE_OUTPUT

Plan hash value: 3685486572

```
----------------------------------------------------------------
| Id  | Operation                     | Name           | Rows  |
----------------------------------------------------------------
|   0 | SELECT STATEMENT              |                |       |
|   1 |  SORT GROUP BY NOSORT         |                |    47 |
|   2 |   MERGE JOIN OUTER            |                |   377 |
|   3 |    INDEX FULL SCAN            | CUSTOMERS_PK   |   319 |
|*  4 |    SORT JOIN                  |                |   105 |
|   5 |     TABLE ACCESS BY INDEX ROWID| ORDERS        |   105 |
|*  6 |      INDEX RANGE SCAN         | ORD_CUSTOMER_IX|   105 |
----------------------------------------------------------------
```

Predicate Information (identified by operation id):

```
   4 - access("C"."CUSTOMER_ID"="O"."CUSTOMER_ID")
       filter("C"."CUSTOMER_ID"="O"."CUSTOMER_ID")
   6 - access("O"."CUSTOMER_ID">0)
```

Notice how much simpler the SQL becomes when using CASE. Not only is it simpler, but also it is more efficient. The two tables, orders and customers, only have to be accessed once instead of once per condition. Keep in mind that CASE is a great alternative when you need different sets of data from the same tables.

Using NVL, NVL2, and COALESCE

The functions NVL, NVL2, and COALESCE all deal specifically with nulls. Although you could use DECODE or CASE to formulate null comparison logic, these functions are specifically available to provide special, simple treatment for nulls. Consider the syntax for each:

```
NVL(expr1, expr2)
If expr1 is null, then NVL returns expr2.
If expr1 is not null, then NVL returns expr1.

NVL2(expr1, expr2, expr3)
If expr1 is null, then NVL2 returns expr3.
If expr2 is not null, then NVL2 returns expr2.

COALESCE(expr[,expr]...)
Returns the first non-null expr in the expression list.
```

Now take a look at the examples of their use in Listing 18-6.

Listing 18-6. *NVL, NVL2, COALESCE, CASE, and DECODE Examples*

```
SQL>select nvl(comm,0)
  2  from scott.emp
  3  where comm is null
  4  and rownum = 1;

NVL(COMM,0)
-----------
          0

1 row selected.

SQL>select nvl2(comm,comm,0)
  2  from scott.emp
  3  where comm is null
  4  and rownum = 1 ;

NVL2(COMM,COMM,0)
-----------------
                0

1 row selected.

SQL>select coalesce(comm,0)
  2  from scott.emp
  3  where comm is null
  4  and rownum = 1 ;
```

```
COALESCE(COMM,0)
----------------
               0

1 row selected.

SQL>select case when comm is null then 0
  2                    else comm end comm
  3  from scott.emp
  4  where comm is null
  5  and rownum = 1 ;

      COMM
----------
         0

1 row selected.

SQL>select decode(comm,null,0,comm) comm
  2  from scott.emp
  3  where comm is null
  4  and rownum = 1 ;

      COMM
----------
         0

1 row selected.
```

In each of the examples, the answer is the same. The decision regarding which one to use is really just a matter of personal preference. When the comparison is truly intended to work with nulls, I prefer to avoid CASE and DECODE just because they require a bit more typing. Plus, by using NVL, NVL2, or COALESCE, the intent to deal specifically with nulls is clear. Listing 18-7 shows one of my favorite ways to use NVL in scripts when I want to have a dynamic WHERE clause.

Listing 18-7. Using NVL for a Dynamic WHERE Clause

```
SQL>select sql_id, child_number, plan_hash_value plan_hash, executions execs,
  2  (elapsed_time/1000000)/decode(nvl(executions,0),0,1,executions) avg_etime,
  3  buffer_gets/decode(nvl(executions,0),0,1,executions) avg_lio,
  4  sql_text
  5  from v$sql s
  6  where upper(sql_text) like upper(nvl('&sql_text',sql_text))
  7  and sql_id like nvl('&sql_id',sql_id)
  8  order by 1, 2, 3
  9  /
Enter value for sql_text: %karen%
Enter value for sql_id:

no rows selected
```

The very simple technique shown here allows me to enter either value as input. Or, I can leave the values both empty and the null value causes the comparison to be made against the same column value, resulting in all rows being matched. I discussed similar techniques in Chapter 5, if you want to refer back for more detail. As I said, this is a quick way to be able to write a single SQL statement to cover several inputs. However, I caution you about using this technique in SQL when you're concerned about performance. The technique can make it hard for the optimizer to produce the very best plan that covers all scenarios given different inputs. Be careful and test thoroughly!

Using NULLIF

If you've ever had to write a SQL statement that needed to include expressions that could result in a "divide by zero" error, NULLIF should be your friend. The syntax for NULLIF is as follows:

```
NULLIF(expr1,expr2)
If expr1 = expr2, NULLIF returns null.
If expr1 <> expr2, NULLIF returns expr1.
```

Typically, this function is to be used for numeric comparisons. You may use nonnumeric datatypes as well, as long as both expressions have the same datatype. As I mentioned, one of the reasons I love NULLIF is that it makes it easy to avoid the "divide by zero" error, as shown in Listing 18-8.

Listing 18-8. Using NULLIF to Avoid the "Divide by Zero" Error

```
SQL> select sql_id, child_number, plan_hash_value plan_hash, executions execs,
  2  (elapsed_time/1000000)/nullif(executions,0) avg_etime,
  3  buffer_gets/nullif(executions,0) avg_lio,
  4  sql_text
  5  from v$sql s
  6  where upper(sql_text) like upper(nvl('&sql_text',sql_text))
  7  and sql_id like nvl('&sql_id',sql_id)
  8  order by 1, 2, 3
  9  /
Enter value for sql_text:
Enter value for sql_id: c7ngvkwthdaak
```

SQL_ID	CHILD_NUMBER	PLAN_HASH	EXECS	AVG_ETIME	AVG_LIO	SQL_TEXT
c7ngvkwthdaak	0	729697565	1	.012356	13	select cust

```
1 row selected.
```

Did you notice that the SQL statement I used here is the same one I used in Listing 18-7 with a combination of DECODE and NVL? This syntax yields the same result but is much simpler and easier to read.

Conditional logic constructs provide a level of flexibility similar to what you'd find in PL/SQL or other programming languages. However, the ability to include conditional processing directly in a SQL statement allows us to exploit fully the power of set-based data access. There are several options that can be used interchangeably and your choice of which to use is mainly a personal preference. However, I encourage you to review options you've never used before to see if they help you write simple, easy-to-understand code.

PIVOT/UNPIVOT Queries

Pivoting is a common technique that allows you to write cross-tabulation (also called *crosstab, matrix,* or *transposed*) queries that rotate rows of data into aggregated columns of data. Data may also be "unpivoted" (in other words, rotated from columns into rows) using similar techniques, but unpivoting is not the reverse of pivoting. Pivoting data creates aggregates; unpivoting cannot undo aggregations made by pivoting, so it's not truly an opposite function.

Using PIVOT

Prior to Oracle 11g, pivoting data required some bulky and tedious manipulation to formulate a SQL statement to pivot. However, beginning with Oracle 11g, the PIVOT SQL function was introduced to provide a much more elegant solution. Listing 18-9 shows a simple example of how a pivot query was written prior to 11g and after using the PIVOT function.

Listing 18-9. Comparing Old Pivot Query Formulation with the PIVOT Function

```
-- Old way

SQL>select *
  2  from (select job, sum(decode(deptno,10,sal)) dept10,
  3                     sum(decode(deptno,20,sal)) dept20,
  4                     sum(decode(deptno,30,sal)) dept30,
  5                     sum(decode(deptno,40,sal)) dept40
  6            from scott.emp
  7          group by job)
  8  order by job ;
```

JOB	DEPT10	DEPT20	DEPT30	DEPT40
ANALYST		6000		
CLERK	1300	1900	950	
MANAGER	2450	2975	2850	
PRESIDENT	5000			
SALESMAN			5600	

```
5 rows selected.

-- New way using PIVOT function

SQL>select * from
  2   (select job, deptno, sum(sal) sal from scott.emp group by job, deptno)
  3     PIVOT ( sum(sal) FOR deptno IN (10, 20, 30, 40) )
  4  order by job;
```

JOB	10	20	30	40
ANALYST		6000		
CLERK	1300	1900	950	
MANAGER	2450	2975	2850	
PRESIDENT	5000			
SALESMAN			5600	

```
5 rows selected.
```

As shown in the listing, pivoting data is the process of taking multiple rows, aggregating them, and transposing them into columns, with each column representing a different range of aggregate data. And, as you can see, using the PIVOT function is much simpler than the old way. The syntax of a PIVOT statement is as follows:

```
SELECT ...
FROM    ...
PIVOT [XML]              ← Note the placement between the FROM and WHERE clauses
        ( pivot_clause
          pivot_for_clause
          pivot_in_clause )
WHERE   ...
```

The three clauses used with the PIVOT keyword are the following:

1. pivot_clause: defines the columns to be aggregated

2. pivot_for_clause: defines the columns to be grouped and pivoted

3. pivot_in_clause: defines the range of values to which to limit the results; the resulting aggregations for each value are transposed into a separate column

Using the PIVOT query from Listing 18-9 as an example, the clauses are as follows:

```
select * from
  (select job, deptno, sum(sal) sal
     from scott.emp group by job, deptno)
            PIVOT ( sum(sal)             ← pivot_clause
              FOR deptno                 ← pivot_for_clause
        IN (10, 20, 30, 40) )            ← pivot_in_clause
order by job;
```

In this query, the aggregate salary totals by department have been transposed into columns. Our example used a single aggregation on the sal column, but you can specify multiple columns if desired. Another thing to keep in mind is that pivot operations perform an implicit GROUP BY using any columns not in the pivot_clause. In our example, we used an inline view to group by the data first, but this actually was not necessary because of the implicit GROUP BY, as shown in Listing 18-10.

Listing 18-10. Impliciting GROUP BY When Using the PIVOT Function

```
SQL>select * from
  2  (select job, deptno, sal from scott.emp)
  3   pivot (sum(sal) for deptno in (10,20,30,40)) ;
```

JOB	10	20	30	40
CLERK	1300	1900	950	
SALESMAN			5600	
PRESIDENT	5000			
MANAGER	2450	2975	2850	
ANALYST		6000		

5 rows selected.

The data are pivoted on the deptno aggregations only, and the range of values is limited to the hard coded pivot_in_clause list. As you can see, the column names are the same as the pivot_in_clause. This is the default behavior and it can be changed by using column aliases if desired, as shown in Listing 18-11.

Listing 18-11. Using Aliases with the PIVOT Function

```
SQL>select * from
  2  (select job, deptno, sal from scott.emp)
  3  pivot (sum(sal) as sum_sal
  4  for deptno
  5  in (10 as dept10,
  6      20 as dept20,
  7      30 as dept30,
  8      40 as dept40)) ;

JOB        DEPT10_SUM_SAL DEPT20_SUM_SAL DEPT30_SUM_SAL DEPT40_SUM_SAL
---------  -------------- -------------- -------------- --------------
CLERK               1300           1900            950
SALESMAN                                          5600
PRESIDENT           5000
MANAGER             2450           2975           2850
ANALYST                            6000

5 rows selected.
```

Notice how Oracle concatenates the aliases to form the column names. This means if we don't alias the values in the pivot_in_clause, the column names are a concatenation of the list of values and our aggregated column alias (for example, 10_SUM_SAL).

You can also pivot multiple columns, but be careful because each additional column means doubling the number of aggregates. Listing 18-12 shows the addition of one new aggregate and a limiting WHERE clause as well.

Listing 18-12. Using Multiple Aggregates for the PIVOT Function

```
SQL> select * from
  2  (select job, deptno, sal from scott.emp)
  3  pivot (sum(sal) as sum, count(sal) as ct
  4  for deptno
  5  in (10 as dept10,
  6      20 as dept20,
  7      30 as dept30))
  8  where job = 'MANAGER';

JOB        DEPT10_SUM  DEPT10_CT DEPT20_SUM  DEPT20_CT DEPT30_SUM  DEPT30_CT
---------  ----------  --------- ----------  --------- ----------  ---------
MANAGER          2450          1       2975          1       2850          1

1 row selected.
```

There are a few things to be aware of when using PIVOT:

- Any columns referenced only in the pivot_clause cannot be used in the SELECT column list.

- Any columns referenced only in the pivot_for_clause cannot be used in the SELECT column list.

- All columns in the pivot_clause must be aggregate functions.

Last, whenever you use a PIVOT function, it is typically reflected in the execution plan, as shown in Listing 18-13.

Listing 18-13. Execution Plan for the PIVOT Function

```
-----------------------------------------------------
| Id  | Operation                 | Name  | Rows  |
-----------------------------------------------------
|   0 | SELECT STATEMENT          |       |       |
|   1 |  SORT GROUP BY NOSORT PIVOT|      |     1 |
|*  2 |   TABLE ACCESS FULL       | EMP   |     3 |
-----------------------------------------------------

Predicate Information (identified by operation id):
-----------------------------------------------------

   2 - filter("JOB"='MANAGER')
```

Depending on how we limit our pivot data, it is possible for the optimizer not to use the PIVOT operation. When this happens, the optimizer determines that it is more effective to do a normal AGGREGATE operation instead. However, most of the time, the PIVOT operation is chosen as the most effective.

One thing you may have noticed is that the examples have used a known list of values for the pivot_in_clause. Unfortunately, there isn't support for dynamic lists of values. Listing 18-14 shows the resulting error message if you try to use a subquery to provide a list of values.

Listing 18-14. Dynamic pivot_in_clause Is Not Allowed

```
SQL>select * from scott.emp
  2  pivot (sum(sal)
  3  for deptno in (select deptno from scott.dept));
for deptno in (select deptno from scott.dept))
               *
ERROR at line 3:
ORA-00936: missing expression
```

But never fear! There is a remedy! When I listed the PIVOT syntax earlier in this section, did you notice the optional XML keyword? If you add the XML keyword, the generated pivot set provides the results in XML format. The root element is <PivotSet>, and each value is identified by a name–value pair, as shown in Listing 18-15.

Listing 18-15. Using the XML Option

```
SQL>select *
  2  from (select job, deptno, sal from scott.emp)
  3  pivot XML
  4  (sum(sal)
  5  for deptno in (ANY));
```

```
JOB       DEPTNO_XML
--------- -------------------------------------------------------
ANALYST   <PivotSet><item><column name =
          "DEPTNO">20</column><column name =
          "SUM(SAL)">6000</column></item></PivotSet>

CLERK     <PivotSet><item><column name =
          "DEPTNO">10</column><column name =
          "SUM(SAL)">1300</column></item><item><column name
          = "DEPTNO">20</column><column name =
          "SUM(SAL)">1900</column></item><item><column name
          = "DEPTNO">30</column><column name =
          "SUM(SAL)">950</column></item></PivotSet>

MANAGER   <PivotSet><item><column name =
          "DEPTNO">10</column><column name =
          "SUM(SAL)">2450</column></item><item><column name
          = "DEPTNO">20</column><column name =
          "SUM(SAL)">2975</column></item><item><column name
          = "DEPTNO">30</column><column name =
          "SUM(SAL)">2850</column></item></PivotSet>

PRESIDENT <PivotSet><item><column name =
          "DEPTNO">10</column><column name =
          "SUM(SAL)">5000</column></item></PivotSet>

SALESMAN  <PivotSet><item><column name =
          "DEPTNO">30</column><column name =
          "SUM(SAL)">5600</column></item></PivotSet>

5 rows selected.
```

The resulting data can now be manipulated with XPath or XQuery expressions. You can also use any subquery you desire in place of the ANY keyword. If you use a subquery, make sure the result set is unique; otherwise, an error occurs. Another thing to keep in mind about generating XML elements is that quite a bit of data above and beyond the results themselves are generated. Consider your requirements carefully and weigh the overheads of this method with how you'll process the XML results to make sure your performance doesn't suffer adversely.

Using UNPIVOT

The UNPIVOT function also appeared with PIVOT in Oracle 11g. To unpivot data means to rotate data from columns back to rows. As mentioned earlier, if you PIVOT data, you can't simply UNPIVOT the pivoted dataset and expect it to return the output as it was prior to pivoting. UNPIVOT has no capability to convert aggregates back to their raw data elements. The syntax of an UNPIVOT statement is as follows:

```
SELECT ...
FROM   ...
PIVOT [INCLUDE|EXCLUDE NULLS]
       ( unpivot_clause
         unpivot_for_clause
         unpivot_in_clause )
WHERE  ...
```

The three clauses used with the UNPIVOT keyword are the following:

1. unpivot_clause: defines the name for a column to represent the unpivoted values

2. unpivot_for_clause: defines the name for the column that results from the unpivot query

3. unpivot_in_clause: defines the list of pivoted columns (not values) to be unpivoted

To demonstrate how UNPIVOT works, let's start by creating a PIVOTed set of data using our example query, as shown in Listing 18-16.

Listing 18-16. Creating a Table with PIVOTed Data

```
SQL>create table pivot_tab as
  2  select * from
  3  (select job, deptno, sal from scott.emp)
  4  pivot (sum(sal) as sum_sal
  5  for deptno
  6  in (10 as dept10,
  7      20 as dept20,
  8      30 as dept30,
  9      40 as dept40)) ;

Table created.

SQL>select * from pivot_tab ;
```

JOB	DEPT10_SUM_SAL	DEPT20_SUM_SAL	DEPT30_SUM_SAL	DEPT40_SUM_SAL
CLERK	1300	1900	950	
SALESMAN			5600	
PRESIDENT	5000			
MANAGER	2450	2975	2850	
ANALYST		6000		

```
5 rows selected.
```

Now, let's unpivot our dataset, as shown in Listing 18-17.

Listing 18-17. Using UNPIVOT

```
SQL>select * from pivot_tab
  2  unpivot ( sal_amt
  3  for deptsal_desc
  4  in (dept10_sum_sal, dept20_sum_sal, dept30_sum_sal, dept40_sum_sal)) ;
```

JOB	DEPTSAL_DESC	SAL_AMT
CLERK	DEPT10_SUM_SAL	1300
CLERK	DEPT20_SUM_SAL	1900
CLERK	DEPT30_SUM_SAL	950
SALESMAN	DEPT30_SUM_SAL	5600
PRESIDENT	DEPT10_SUM_SAL	5000
MANAGER	DEPT10_SUM_SAL	2450

```
MANAGER    DEPT20_SUM_SAL       2975
MANAGER    DEPT30_SUM_SAL       2850
ANALYST    DEPT20_SUM_SAL       6000
```

9 rows selected.

Note that the list of column names from our pivoted table data provides the column value for the unpivot_for_ clause column named deptsal_desc. The values themselves are used to populate the sal_amt column values, as indicated in unpivot_clause. Although we used our example table of pivoted data, we can unpivot the columns of any table or view.

It is useful to alias the columns in the unpivot_in_clause because it allows us to change the descriptive data to something different from the original column name. Unlike the PIVOT function, the column or columns referred to in the unpivot_in_clause are the only ones that can be aliased. This makes sense, because the unpivot_clause (sal_amt) is the name we wish to use and it doesn't need further aliasing. Listing 18-18 shows an example of using an alias with a bit of creativity to reverse engineer back to deptno.

Listing 18-18. Using Aliases with UNPIVOT

```
SQL> select * from pivot_tab
  2  unpivot ( sal_amt
  3  for deptno
  4  in (dept10_sum_sal as '10',
  5      dept20_sum_sal as '20',
  6      dept30_sum_sal as '30',
  7      dept40_sum_sal as '40')) ;

JOB        DEPTNO    SAL_AMT
---------  ------  ----------
CLERK      10          1300
CLERK      20          1900
CLERK      30           950
SALESMAN   30          5600
PRESIDENT  10          5000
MANAGER    10          2450
MANAGER    20          2975
MANAGER    30          2850
ANALYST    20          6000
```

9 rows selected.

Similar to the PIVOT function, the optimizer identifies the presence of the UNPIVOT function in the execution plan using an UNPIVOT operation, as shown in Listing 18-19.

Listing 18-19. Execution Plan for the UNPIVOT Function

```
---------------------------------------------------
| Id | Operation          | Name      | Rows |
---------------------------------------------------
|  0 | SELECT STATEMENT   |           |      |
|* 1 |  VIEW              |           |   20 |
|  2 |   UNPIVOT          |           |      |
|  3 |    TABLE ACCESS FULL| PIVOT_TAB |    5 |
---------------------------------------------------
```

```
Predicate Information (identified by operation id):
--------------------------------------------------

   1 - filter("unpivot_view_007"."SAL_AMT" IS NOT NULL)
```

Note the presence of the VIEW operation that uses a filter predicate to remove the null values for sal_amt. This is the default behavior resulting from the EXCLUDING NULLS clause. If we use INCLUDING NULLS instead, the filter is removed and rows with null values are displayed.

A really nifty use of UNPIVOT that is related to unpivoting a previously pivoted dataset is simply using it to pivot particularly wide output to read down the page instead of across, as shown in Listing 18-20.

Listing 18-20. Using the UNPIVOT Function

```
SQL>select column_name, column_value from
  2  (select to_char(empno) as empno, ename, job, to_char(mgr) mgr,
  3   to_char(hiredate,'mm/dd/yyyy') hiredate, to_char(sal) sal,
  4   to_char(comm) comm, to_char(deptno) deptno
  5   from scott.emp where rownum = 1)
  6  unpivot (column_value
  7  for column_name
  8  in (empno, ename, job, mgr, hiredate, sal, comm, deptno));


COLUMN_N COLUMN_VALUE
-------- ----------------------------------------
EMPNO    7369
ENAME    SMITH
JOB      CLERK
MGR      7902
HIREDATE 12/17/1980
SAL      800
DEPTNO   20

7 rows selected.
```

In this example, note how the results are now displayed down the page instead of across. Also note that all the columns have converted to string datatypes in the inline view. This is because of a restriction on how an UNPIVOT query is processed. Unless all the columns have the same datatype, the query fails with "ORA-01790: expression must have same datatype as corresponding expression." This restriction certainly makes things a bit tedious but, given a bit of effort, we could write a dynamic SQL wrapper for this type of query and use it to unpivot data from any table. I leave that exercise to you for additional practice.

SQL to Generate Test Data

There are times when you may find it difficult to performance test your SQL because of the lack of appropriate test data. This could be a result of the fact that your application is new and lacks real data that can be copied for development use, or it could be that your development environment only loads partial datasets and not a full copy ofproduction. Or, maybe you just want to test how a particular bit of SQL works and only need dummy data. Using some very simple SQL constructs, you can generate random test data quite easily.

What to Watch out For

Before you start generating any data, make sure you know what to watch out for. The main thing to keep in mind is to try and keep to a minimum the overhead required to create your data. One of the most frequently used techniques can be a real resource hog if you're not careful. This technique involves using an actual "big" table as a driver to create your test data, as shown in Listing 18-21.

Listing 18-21. Generating Rows Using a "Big" Table

```
SQL>create table from_big as
  2  select * from dba_source ;

Table created.

Elapsed: 00:00:10.40

SQL>select count(*) from from_big ;

  COUNT(*)
----------
    403941

1 row selected.
```

In this case, we get a good-size set of data, but it took more than ten seconds and it had to read from a system view. This isn't too bad if you only plan on generating a single copy of the data. But, what happens when you want to create ten times the data? There are several other techniques to consider to produce more random data without requiring you to query preexisting tables:

- CONNECT BY clause
- MODEL clause
- WITH clause

Using CONNECT BY

You can use CONNECT BY to generate data using FAST DUAL as the source. Listing 18-22 shows how to use this method most efficiently.

Listing 18-22. Generating Rows Using CONNECT BY

```
SQL>create table conn_by as
  2  select count(*) ct from
  3  (select rownum rn from
  4  (select rownum rn from dual connect by rownum <= 1000) t1,
  5  (select rownum rn from dual connect by rownum <= 1000) t2,
  6  (select rownum rn from dual connect by rownum <= 1000) t3
  7  where rownum <= 1000000);

Table created.

Elapsed: 00:00:03.15
```

```
SQL> @dcplan
Enter value for sql_id: 84s1cjrn9sumf
Enter value for child_no: 0
Enter value for format: BASIC


PLAN_TABLE_OUTPUT
----------------------------------------------------------------------------
EXPLAINED SQL STATEMENT:
------------------------
create table conn_by


Plan hash value: 2015107946


-----------------------------------------------------------
| Id  | Operation                        | Name |
-----------------------------------------------------------
|   0 | CREATE TABLE STATEMENT           |      |      |
|   1 |  LOAD AS SELECT                  |      |      |
|   2 |   OPTIMIZER STATISTICS GATHERING |      |      |
|   3 |    SORT AGGREGATE                |      |      |
|   4 |     VIEW                         |      |      |
|   5 |      COUNT STOPKEY               |      |      |
|   6 |       MERGE JOIN CARTESIAN       |      |      |
|   7 |        MERGE JOIN CARTESIAN      |      |      |
|   8 |         VIEW                     |      |      |
|   9 |          COUNT                   |      |      |
|  10 |           CONNECT BY WITHOUT FILTERING |  |      |
|  11 |            FAST DUAL             |      |      |
|  12 |         BUFFER SORT              |      |      |
|  13 |          VIEW                    |      |      |
|  14 |           COUNT                  |      |      |
|  15 |            CONNECT BY WITHOUT FILTERING|  |      |
|  16 |             FAST DUAL            |      |      |
|  17 |        BUFFER SORT               |      |      |
|  18 |         VIEW                     |      |      |
|  19 |          COUNT                   |      |      |
|  20 |           CONNECT BY WITHOUT FILTERING |  |      |
|  21 |            FAST DUAL             |      |      |
-----------------------------------------------------------
```

In this example, it took just more than three seconds to generate a one million-row table. You may be wondering why there are three inline views being cartesian joined to create the data instead of just using a single CONNECT BY ROWNUM < 1000000. This method is used to prevent the process from running out of private memory, as shown in Listing 18-23.

Listing 18-23. Memory Error When Using CONNECT BY

```
SQL>select count(*) from
  2 (select rownum rn from dual connect by rownum <= 10000000) ;
    (select rownum rn from dual connect by rownum <= 10000000)
                       *
ERROR at line 2:
ORA-30009: Not enough memory for CONNECT BY operation
```

As shown, I used a large number of rows (ten million instead of one million), but this simple statement can consume enough UGA/PGA to error out as a result of a lack of memory. CONNECT BY is recursive in nature and therefore consumes more memory as you increase the number of rows you want in a single shot. So, to create large amounts of data, you simply have to use CONNECT BY with lower recursion. Writing the statement to use MERGE JOIN CARTESIAN does the trick!

Personally, I prefer a combination method of using the CONNECT BY method and WITH clause, but it doesn't use a recursive WITH (discussed later). Instead, it simply uses the WITH clause to avoid repeating the inline query, as shown in Listing 18-22. Listing 18-24 demonstrates how to combine the WITH and CONNECT BY clauses to formulate an easy-to-read, understandable, and efficient data generator.

Listing 18-24. Using WITH and CONNECT BY

```
SQL>create table with_conn_by as
  2  with data_gen as
  3  (
  4  select /*+ materialize */ rownum rid
  5  from dual
  6  connect by level < 1000
  7  )
  8  select mod(rownum-1, 1000) as num_mod1,
  9    trunc(dbms_random.value(0,1000)) rand_val1,
 10    trunc(dbms_random.value(0,1000)) rand_val2,
 11    rpad('z',100) pad_data
 12  from data_gen t1, data_gen t2, data_gen t3
 13  where rownum <= 1000000 ;

Table created.

Elapsed: 00:00:32.97
```

Notice how in this example I also demonstrated how to populate additional columns with various types of data. Using variations of this example, you can create any quantity and type of data you wish.

Using the MODEL Clause

We discussed the MODEL clause in great detail in Chapter 9. Although it may seem a bit intimidating at first, using the MODEL clause is quite powerful and particularly useful—and simple—when generating dummy data, as shown in Listing 18-25.

Listing 18-25. Generating Rows Using the `MODEL` Clause

```
SQL>create table model_tab as (
  2    select *
  3    from dual
  4    model
  5      dimension by (0 d)
  6      measures (0 rnum)
  7      rules iterate (1000000)
  8      (rnum[ITERATION_NUMBER] = ITERATION_NUMBER+1)
  9    ) ;

Table created.

Elapsed: 00:05:09.26
```

The `MODEL` clause method took significantly longer than the `CONNECT BY` method to produce the same one million-row dataset (more than five minutes vs. a few seconds!). This time difference results from the way the two constructs use memory. Memory usage reported by `CONNECT BY` doesn't use work-area memory, so normal PGA size restrictions such as `PGA_AGGREGATE_TARGET` don't apply to it. But, the `MODEL` clause does use work-area memory traditionally, and if there is too much information to be retained in the private memory allocation, it spills over to disk (`TEMP`). For this reason, using the `MODEL` clause is more limiting in terms of time and resources required. I have only used this method a handful of times and I find it most useful when I want to create a limited amount of data with numerous columns using spreadsheetlike formulas to populate them.

Using the Recursive WITH Clause

Subfactored queries were discussed in Chapter 10. Listing 18-26 shows an example of using a recursive `WITH` clause to generate test data.

Listing 18-26 Generating Rows Using the Recursive `WITH` Clause

```
SQL>create table with_tab as
  2    with data_gen(rn)
  3    as
  4    (select 1 rn from dual
  5     union all
  6     select rn+1 from data_gen
  7     where rn < 1000000 )
  8    select * from data_gen;

Table created.

Elapsed: 00:00:26.43
```

Once again, the time it takes to use a recursive `WITH` clause is significantly greater than the `CONNECT BY` construct, but it is also significantly less than the `MODEL` clause. Always keep in mind that the more rows you wish to create—particularly if you are creating random data (similar to what I showed in Listing 18-24) and not just a one-column table—as shown in most of the examples, the longer it takes and the more resources (particularly CPU) it uses.

Data Generator Wrap-up

In this section, I showed you a few of the more common ways to generate data. There are others, including a pipelined PL/SQL function, that can be used as well. The construct you choose certainly makes a difference with regard to the time it takes to generate the amount and type of data you want as, well as the database resources used. Always keep in mind that both your time and your database's resources are valuable. Don't waste either one!

Summary

The SQL language offers many constructs to help you build and extract data from your database. Many constructs have similar functionality and serve the same purpose, such as NVL, NVL2, and COALESCE. Others, such as PIVOT and UNPIVOT, help you manipulate data to report it more understandably. Using the examples in this chapter as a guide, I urge you to continue to explore out-of-the-box uses for the SQL language that help you do your job more proficiently.

Index

V

■ W, X, Y, Z

Get the eBook for only $10!

Now you can take the weightless companion with you anywhere, anytime. Your purchase of this book entitles you to 3 electronic versions for only $10.

This Apress title will prove so indispensible that you'll want to carry it with you everywhere, which is why we are offering the eBook in **3 formats** for only $10 if you have already purchased the print book.

Convenient and fully searchable, the PDF version enables you to easily find and copy code—or perform examples by quickly toggling between instructions and applications. The MOBI format is ideal for your Kindle, while the ePUB can be utilized on a variety of mobile devices.

Go to www.apress.com/promo/tendollars to purchase your companion eBook.